Workers and Unions in Wisconsin

A Labor History
ANTHOLOGY

Workers and Unions in Wisconsin

A Labor History *ANTHOLOGY*

BY DARRYL HOLTER

STATE HISTORICAL SOCIETY OF WISCONSIN

MADISON, 1999

To Rachael and Julia,
"Badger Girls" of the '80s

Book design and production by PJBF Design, Madison, Wisconsin.

Printed and bound by Inland Press, Menomonee Falls, Wisconsin.

Library of Congress Cataloging-in-Publication Data

Holter, Darryl.
Workers and Unions in Wisconsin: A Labor History Anthology.
Darryl Holter, editor.
Includes index.

1. Trade-unions—Wisconsin—History.
2. Labor movement—Wisconsin—History.
I. Title.

ISBN: 0-87020-315-0 (clothbound)
ISBN: 0-87020-314-2 (paperbound)

HD6517.W5h65 1999
331.88'09775—dc21
99-20817 CIP

Preface

THE idea for this anthology emerged out of my work with labor unions and historians in Wisconsin in the 1980s. As Educational Director for the State AFL-CIO, I spent a great deal of time discussing labor-related issues with unionists, college and high school students, and members of the general public. I began to compile various articles and clippings to distribute to the audiences I addressed. I collected some very interesting material, both published (in books, scholarly articles, journals, and newspapers) and unpublished (in dissertations and MA theses, memoirs, or speeches by union leaders or political activists). The Wisconsin "vein" of labor history, I found, was quite rich. After a while, however, the task of making copies and collating a constantly growing body of materials became time-consuming and costly and I began to consider putting some of these materials together in a single volume.

Wisconsin State AFL-CIO

Packinghouse workers at the Patrick Cudahy plant in Cudahy rally during strike by Local P-40, 1951.

It seemed to me that what was needed was a book that was usable and accessible to a broad audience. I wanted to bring together a wide range of scholarly material as well as excerpts or fragments from unpublished pieces. And I thought the book should feature arresting photos that would highlight the people who made this history and entice viewers to read the text. Fortunately, H. Nicholas Muller III, former director of the State Historical Society of Wisconsin, was very supportive of this approach to the project. We had worked together when the Society brought the Smithsonian traveling exhibit, "Badges of Pride: Images and Symbols of Labor," to Madison in 1990. Nick saw the value of the project in the popular response the exhibit received from the public and he supported the anthology from the very beginning.

Union leaders who helped in countless ways include John W. Schmitt, Jack B. Reihl, David Newby, Ken Clark, Charles Heymanns (deceased), Bob Blessington, Tom Parker, Earl Lepp, Carole Casamento, Joe Robison, Jim Cavanaugh, David Poklinkoski, Neal Gleason and many, many more. Officers of the Wisconsin Labor History Society also played a role in the anthology, including the society's founding president, Joanne Ricca, Ralph Jirikowic (deceased), Nellie Wilson, Darina Rasmussen (deceased), Kelly Sparks, Arvo Mattson, George Daitsman (deceased), Ken Germanson, and Harvey Kaye. I benefited from

discussions with some great labor and social historians including Harvey Goldberg (deceased), James Cronin, Stephen Meyer, Robert Zieger, Dexter Arnold, Rebecca Mead, Robert Ozanne, James Lorence, and Alan Ruff. Production of the book was assisted by Brikti Abraha, Ann Ben-Porat, and Sommay Simasingh. Bob Blessington and Joanne Ricca helped locate photos. Patrick Flynn created the book design and lay-out.

Many institutions and their staff members helped in a wide variety of ways, especially the Wisconsin State AFL-CIO, the University of Wisconsin, and the University of California, Los Angeles. Thanks also to a number of archivists and librarians across the state who helped gather material and photos for the anthology. A special thanks is due the State Historical Society of Wisconsin, not only for agreeing to publish the anthology but for the assistance of its professional staff: Jim Danky, R. David Myers, Harry Miller, and, especially, Paul Hass, Senior Editor of the State Historical Society of Wisconsin.

The book is dedicated to my daughters, Rachael and Julia, both of whom grew up in Wisconsin and have warm memories of our years in the Badger State. Thanks to Carole Shammas for never asking me when the book would be finished.

—DARRYL HOLTER
Los Angeles, California, January 1999

Contents

Preface   v

Abbreviations   1

Introduction   3

SECTION 1: EARLY TRADE UNIONISM

Early Unions in Milwaukee, 1850–1884   13
  Thomas W. Gavett

Lead Mining in La Fayette County   16
  Daniel M. Parkinson

Work on a Farm, 1848   20
  John Muir

Lumber Industry Strikes: Eau Claire, Marinette, Ashland, La Crosse   22
  Robert W. Ozanne

The Knights of Labor in Milwaukee   26
  Leon Fink

Frank Weber: Labor's "General Organizer"   28
  Robert W. Ozanne

Early Labor Legislation   30
  Gordon M. Haferbecker

Unemployment: The "Tramp Problem" in Beloit   32
  Robert C. Nesbit

The Bay View Tragedy   34
  Robert C. Nesbit

Employer Rights   38
  Robert C. Nesbit

The Founding of the Wisconsin State Federation of Labor, 1893   40
  Darryl Holter

The Very First Kohler Strike, 1897   42
  Walter H. Uphoff

Problems in Workplace Health and Safety   43
  Robert C. Nesbit

A Strike for Cash Pay in Two Rivers, 1895   45
  Paul J. Cigler, Jr.

Women and the Oshkosh Woodworkers Strike, 1898   46
  Lee Baxandall

Unions in Kenosha   47
  John W. Bailey

From Union Town to Open Shop: Beloit 1903–1904   50
  Robert W. Ozanne

Labor in Racine 52
Joseph M. Kelly

SECTION 2: UNIONISM IN AN INDUSTRIAL SOCIETY

The Paperworkers' Fight for Saturday Night 57
Robert W. Ozanne

War Hysteria and the Wobblies 61
John D. Stevens

Vocational Education 64
Paul W. Glad

Labor's Daily Newspaper: *The Milwaukee Leader* 69
Elmer Axel Beck

Labor Spies and Union–Busting 71
Darryl Holter

Organizing the Unorganized in Milwaukee, 1900–1903 75
Darryl Holter

The Law to Limit Injunctions 76
Gordon M. Haferbecker

The Machinists Battle the Injunction 79
Robert W. Ozanne

Organized Labor and Socialism: Two Views 80
Frederick I. Olson and Elmer A. Beck

A Lock-Out: The Hosiery Workers in Kenosha, 1928–1929 82
Leon Applebaum

The Labor Forward Movement 88
Thomas W. Gavett

The Wisconsin School For Workers: Two Views 89
Barbara Wertheimer and Darina Rasmussen

The Wisconsin Labor Code of 1931 90
Gordon M. Haferbecker

Workers' Compensation 92
Robert W. Ozanne

African American Workers and the Labor Movement in Milwaukee, 1870–1930 93
Joe W. Trotter, Jr.

"Fighting Bob" La Follette 96
Debra E. Bernhardt

Why I Unionized My Plant 97
George W. Mead

SECTION 3: THE PROMISE OF INDUSTRIAL UNIONISM

Industrial Unions: The Organizers' Views 103
Charles Heymanns, Victor Cooks, Kenneth Clark, and Carl Griepentrog

Building the Union at Ray-O-Vac in Madison 107
Robert H. Zieger

African American Workers and the Labor Movement in Milwaukee, 1930–1945 110
Joe W. Trotter, Jr.

The Farmer-Labor Progressive Federation   115
    Robert W. Ozanne

The Wisconsin Milk Strike of 1933   118
    Roman Piech

Sources of CIO Success: The New Deal Years in Milwaukee   120
    Darryl Holter

The Wisconsin Plan for Labor Unity, 1936   122
    Elmer A. Beck

The Nation's First Unemployment Compensation Law   124
    Irving Bernstein

Maud McCreery: Unionist and Suffragist   130
    Milwaukee Leader

Unionism at Oscar Mayer in Madison   135
    Robert H. Schultz, Jr.

Industrial Unionism: A Communist Perspective   138
    Peggy Dennis

Madison Labor in the 1930s   140
    Dexter Arnold

The Riot at Kohler, 1934   143
    Walter H. Uphoff

Organizing Garment Workers   147
    Rose Pesotta

A Radio Talk by Jacob F. Friedrick   149
    Jacob F. Friedrick

Gerald Boileau and the Politics of Unemployment   151
    James J. Lorence

The United Auto Workers at Nash Motors in Kenosha   155
    John Drew

The Founding of AFSCME   161
    American Federation of State, County and Municipal Employees

Organizing the Unemployed: The Case Strike of 1936   163
    Joseph M. Kelly

SECTION 4: FROM WORLD WAR TO COLD WAR

Battery Workers at War   169
    Robert H. Zieger

Rosella Wartner: The Making of a Wausau Unionist   175
    Rosella Wartner and Joanne Ricca

Organizing Clerical Workers   178
    Alice Holz

Women and the War Effort at Allis-Chalmers   180
    Stephen Meyer

Nellie Wilson: A Black Woman Meets the Union   184
    Nellie Wilson

Labor Law: Wisconsin's "Little Wagner Act" and the Road to Taft-Hartley   186
    Darryl Holter

Erik Bjurman: Kenosha Unionist   191
    Elmer A. Beck

Cold War Politics at Allis-Chalmers   192
    Stephen Meyer

Anatomy of a Strike in Marinette   206
    Bernard Karsh

Jacob F. Friedrick in 1954   214
    John D. Pomfret

SECTION 5: LABOR AND CONTEMPORARY SOCIETY

Madison Labor in the 1960s and 1970s   221
    Dexter Arnold

An Isolated Survivor: *Racine Labor*   223
    Richard W. Olson

John W. Schmitt: A Profile   228
    Harold "Red" Newton

Wisconsin: Teaching Assistants Strike Ends in Contract Signing   229
    Andrew Hamilton

Catherine Conroy: Unionist and Feminist   232
    Tony Carideo

A Female Machinist in Milwaukee   235
    Sue Doro and Karen Matthews

Blue-Collar Aristocrats: The View From a Working-Class Tavern   236
    E. E. LeMasters

The Hortonville Teachers' Strike of 1974   240
    Wisconsin Education Association Council

The Union Comes to Wisconsin Physicians Service   244
    Cynthia B. Costello

The Formation of the State AFL-CIO Women's Committee   248
    Helen Hensler

An Agenda for Working Families   252
    Jack B. Reihl

Labor Cartoons: Drawing on Work Culture   256
    Mike Konopacki and Gary Huck

New Union Strategies: Electrical Workers in Wausau   261
    Dale Kurschner

Labor Meets History   265
    Robert W. Ozanne, Darryl Holter, and David Newby

Notes   267
Credits   277
Index   279

Abbreviations

AFL	American Federation of Labor
AFSCME	American Federation of State, County and Municipal Employees
CIO	Congress of Industrial Organizations
CP	Communist Party–USA
FDR	Franklin Delano Roosevelt
FLPF	Farmer Labor Progressive Federation
FLU	Federal Labor Union
IAM	International Association of Machinists
IBPM	International Brotherhood of Paper Makers
ILGWU	International Ladies Garment Workers Union
IWW	Industrial Workers of the World
KWA	Kohler Workers Association
LRL	Legislative Reference Library
LRB	Legislative Reference Bureau
MCHS	Milwaukee County Historical Society
MCIUC	Milwaukee County Industrial Union Council
MFL	Madison Federation of Labor
MFTC (or FTC)	Milwaukee Federated Trades Council
MJ	Milwaukee Journal
ML	Milwaukee Leader
MS	Milwaukee Sentinel
MUL	Milwaukee Urban League
NIRA	National Industrial Recovery Act (1933)
NLRA	National Labor Relations Act (1935)
NLRB	National Labor Relations Board
NWLB	National War Labor Board
OPEIU	Office and Professional Employees International Union
RTLC	Racine Trades and Labor Council
SHSW	State Historical Society of Wisconsin
SP	Socialist Party–USA
SWOC	Steel Workers Organizing Committee
TAA	Teaching Assistant Association
UAW	United Automobile Workers
UBPM	United Brotherhood of Paper Maker
UFCW	United Food and Commercial Workers Union
ULP	Unfair Labor Practice
WEAC	Wisconsin Education Action Council
WEPA	Wisconsin Employment Peace Act
WERB	Wisconsin Employment Relations Board
WSIUC	Wisconsin State Industrial Union Council
WLHS	Wisconsin Labor History Society
WLRA	Wisconsin Labor Relations Act
WLRB	Wisconsin Labor Relations Board
WMH	Wisconsin Magazine of History
WPS	Wisconsin Physicians Service
WSFL	Wisconsin State Federation of Labor

Introduction

DARRYL HOLTER, EDITOR

WISCONSIN accounts for about two per cent of the nation's total population. Yet its contribution to the history of working people and social reform extends far beyond these numbers. The working men and women of Wisconsin wrote many important chapters in American history, and their stories add a crucial dimension to our knowledge of our past. On May 4, 1886, for example, in the midst of a nationwide labor campaign for an eight-hour workday, the world was shocked by the bombing and riot at Haymarket Square in Chicago, which killed seven and wounded many others. But the following day, an equally deadly confrontation occurred in the industrial suburb of Bay View, Wisconsin, where state militia fired into a crowd of striking workers. Five persons were killed outright in the Bay View tragedy—and the eight-hour movement died as well. In 1889, the famous defense attorney Clarence Darrow came to Oshkosh to defend striking woodworkers charged with conspiracy. In a dramatic trial, Darrow pled their case, and the strikers were acquitted. One afternoon in 1932, a group of state employees met in a room at the state capitol in Madison to express concern about efforts to replace Wisconsin's civil service system with a system of political patronage. They decided to form a union and asked for a charter from the Wisconsin State Federation of Labor. Their efforts resulted in the creation of the American Federation of State, County and Municipal Employees (AFSCME), which evolved into one of the largest unions in the nation, with a million members. During the Progressive and the New Deal eras—from about 1905 to 1935—Wisconsin became a veritable laboratory for reform and social experimentation. The labor and social legislation enacted in the Badger state, including workers' compensation, unemployment insurance, and other progressive measures, served as models for similar laws in other states.

The study of the history of labor itself began in Wisconsin around the turn of the century, when University of Wisconsin economist John R. Commons and a group of associates set out to document the history of work and labor in America. Their undertaking, which became known as the "Wisconsin school of labor history," dominated the field for decades. In addition, the Commons group teamed up with Wisconsin labor leaders, with the business community, and with state lawmakers to enact groundbreaking social policies.

While most labor history tends to focus on urban and industrial settings, Wisconsin also provides a wide variety of rural backdrops for labor struggles. In 1902, for example, papermill workers along the Fox and Wisconsin rivers went on strike to protest mandatory work on Saturday nights. A generation later, the well-tended and attractive "company town" of Kohler, just southwest of Sheboygan, was the setting for two famous strikes (1934-1941 and 1954-1960) that rank among the longest and most bitter in American history. In 1974, the small Outagamie County town of Hortonville was rocked by controversy when public school teachers walked off the job in protest against a local school board that was hostile and militantly anti-union. The strike lasted for months and produced many nasty confrontations on the picket line. The Hortonville strike so horrified state lawmakers that they passed legislation that established procedures for mediating and arbitrating such disputes between labor and management.

Wisconsin labor generally pursued a somewhat independent path within the national union movement. Breaking with national leaders Samuel Gompers and William Green and their policy of "voluntarism," Wisconsin unionists instead pushed aggressively for state legislation to improve the situation for workers. This included child labor laws, unemployment insurance and worker's compensation, limits on employers' use of injunctions during labor disputes, prohibitions against labor spies to disrupt unions, and collective bargaining rights for public employees. Eventually, the national American Federation of Labor (AFL) and the Congress of Industrial Organizations (CIO) incorporated all these issues into their legislative agenda. The Wisconsin movement also differed from the national unions in its approach to organizational questions. Most national unions practiced "craft unionism," in which skilled trades workers grouped together by craft, leaving less skilled production workers outside the union. But many unions and labor leaders in Wisconsin pursued a strategy of "industrial unionism," organizing workers in a given industry "wall-to-wall" without regard to their particular craft or skills. This approach resulted in the unusually large number of federal labor unions (meaning local unions affiliated directly with the AFL and not with any particular national union) established in Wisconsin, especially in the early 1930's. The backlog of experience with industrial unionism and the institutional support for vigorous organizing across craft lines contributed to the rapid growth of the CIO in Wisconsin in the late 1930's and 1940's.

Wisconsin labor also carved out a distinctive political strategy. The national AFL counseled "nonpartisanship" in an effort to gain the best possible from Republicans or Democrats and to "elect our friends and punish our enemies." On the other hand, a large portion of the labor leadership in Wisconsin (especially in Milwaukee and other smaller cities like Manitowoc) went its own way in politics, forming a close alliance with the Socialist party. While many unions established newspapers, Milwaukee was the only city in America that could boast of having its own daily labor newspaper: *The Milwaukee Leader*, founded by the German-born socialist Victor Berger in 1911 and published for three decades.

In 1935, while most of the labor movement coalesced behind Franklin D. Roosevelt and a revived Democratic party, the Wisconsin State Federation of Labor played a pivotal role in forming an independent coalition party, the Farmer-Labor Progressive Federation, for state races. In November, 1936, the Federation's candidate for governor, Philip La Follette, swept to victory, and the new coalition fell just one seat short of obtaining a majority in both houses of the state legislature.

Wisconsin contributed to labor history in another way by sending many local union leaders to top positions at the national level. Among them were Al Hayes of the International Association of Machinists and Aerospace Workers, Arnold Zander of AFSCME, William Cooper of the Service Employees International Union, Walter Burke of the United Steelworkers of America, Peter Schoemann and Marvin Boede of the International Association of Plumbers and Steamfitters, William Connors from the Bricklayers, Masons and Plasterers International Union, Harvey Brown of the International Brotherhood of Electrical Workers, Raymond Majerus, Ed Hall, and George Addes of the United Auto Workers, Carl Greipentrog, Anthony Doria, and William Salamone of the Allied Industrial Workers, Milan Stone of the United Rubber Workers, and Robert Clark of the United Electrical, Radio and Machine Workers of America. In addition, Joseph Padway, attorney for the Wisconsin State Federation of Labor, went on to represent the American Federation of Labor under William Green, and Andrew Biemiller rose to become the top lobbyist for the AFL-CIO from 1953 to 1978.

THE STORY of Wisconsin's workers and unions is best understood by reference to three basic elements: the evolution of the economy and the work force; experimentation with different forms of labor organization; and the role of unions in providing a voice for working people. Because these factors recur throughout the anthology, it is worthwhile discussing them at the outset.

Economy and Workforce

The nature of work in Wisconsin closely reflects the evolution of the state's economy and its work force since the nineteenth century. In the mid-eighteenth century, French explorers ventured onto the the upper Great Lakes in search of water routes to the west, visiting the shores of Lake Michigan and Lake Superior. Wisconsin became a connecting point between the Great Lakes and the Mississippi. The French were interested in furs, in precious metals, and in lead for bullets. For several decades thereafter, the lead mines of Wisconsin and Illinois were worked by both the Indians and the French. The fur trade also expanded rapidly as rival French and British merchants established trade relations with the Indians, setting up trading posts at strategic points and exchanging various types of goods for furs.

The fur trade, like lead mining, was an important but a transitory component of the regional economy. By about 1832, at the close of the Black Hawk War and four years before Wisconsin attained territorial status, an influx of new settlers rapidly transformed the fertile prairies of southern Wisconsin into some of the nation's most productive farmland. By 1848, when Wisconsin became the thirtieth state of the Union, agriculture was the state's major industry. By the midpoint of the century, Wisconsin was a major exporter of wheat and other grains, and numerous milling centers had emerged, especially in towns with ports on Lake Michigan.

Then came the Civil War (1861-1865), which stimulated the growth of manufacturing and industry in Wisconsin just as it did elsewhere. After the war, wheat farming declined as cheaper lands became available farther west. Wisconsin farmers began to shift to other grain crops as well as to commercial dairying. Even more importantly, the Wisconsin economy was stimulated by the building of railroad systems, which occurred in two big spurts (1867-1873 and 1875-1890), and by the rise of the lumber industry.[1] The state's abundant forests provided lumber for westward expansion and jobs for many thousands of workers, mostly men, in the lumber camps that flourished after the Civil War. By 1880, logging and lumbering had displaced flour milling as the state's largest industry. But in the southeastern quadrant of the state, especially along the Lake Michigan shore and in the Fox River valley, manufacturing and industry were on the rise.

Despite the importance of agriculture and the lumber industries, the last two decades of the nineteenth century saw a remarkable growth in new manufacturing industries. The number of factory workers in Wisconsin more than doubled between 1880 and 1890, from 57,000 to 132,000. Foundries and machine shops became the third-largest industry in the state by 1900. Greater demand for work-related durable goods created large markets for machine shop products, agricultural implements, carriages and wagons, plane-milled wood products, and paper. Manufacturing expanded dramatically in Milwaukee, Racine, and Kenosha, as well as in the Fox valley and in cities elsewhere in the state. This rapid economic growth spurred more demand for labor, both skilled and unskilled, and served as a magnet for struggling farmers in rural counties and for immigrants from Europe.

In the burgeoning mass-production industries, the nature of work changed dramatically after the turn of the century. Workers were the first to feel the impact of the introduction of new labor-saving machinery, increased division of labor, piece-rate payment systems, and tighter control by management. The

The signing of Wisconsin's pioneer unemployment compensation law, 1932. From left: Henry Ohl, Jr., president of Wisconsin State Federation of Labor; Elizabeth Brandeis; Paul A. Raushenbush; John R. Commons, economics professor; Governor Philip F. La Follette; Henry A. Huber, lieutenant governor; Harold M. Groves, assemblyman, economist; Robert A. Nixon, assemblyman.

State Historical Society of Wisconsin WHi (X3) 33375

very makeup of the industrial work force changed with the influx of immigrants from Germany, the United Kingdom, and the Scandinavian countries, and later from Poland, Italy, Hungary, Greece, and Russia. During World War I, and especially after World War II, increasing numbers of black Americans moved northward from the rural South as the employers' need for labor overcame long-standing patterns of discriminatory hiring.

Wisconsin's immigrants spoke many languages, and most came in search of employment. Their entry into the work place did not occur without friction; it was not black workers alone who felt the sting of bigotry and exclusion. Moreover, the integration of these newcomers into the broader society was even more problematic. The availability of jobs and the inequities of hiring frequently created tensions among the various working-class communities. Within the labor market and the work place, a sort of ethnic pecking order emerged among the immigrants. Germans and Britons tended to get the skilled jobs in machine shops and tool-and-die factories; Poles, Irishmen, Italians and, later, black Americans, were assigned to lower-paid, less-skilled jobs. The unspoken rule of "last hired, first fired" frequently applied to the relatively unskilled immigrant workers.

Nothing affected the lives of wage earners and their families more than the state of the economy and the job market. Many jobs in Wisconsin were highly seasonal. Most wage earners were threatened by the ups and downs of the largely unregulated economy. The infamous "long depression" which lasted from 1873 to 1878 took a terrible toll on Wisconsin workers. Half a century later, the Great Depression (1929-1935) created a small army of unemployed in the state's urban areas. Another fifty years later, in 1980, yet another economic recession cut deeply into Wisconsin's powerful manufacturing sector, throwing tens of thousands of workers, from Kenosha to Superior, out of well-paying, family-supporting jobs.

In general, periods of prosperity and growth have been better times for workers and unions. Thus, union membership in Wisconsin grew in the period from 1900 to 1905. When the labor market tightened, workers were in a better position to try to improve their wages and increase their job security. But when depressions and recessions struck, workers lost ground. Many unions were seriously weakened or eliminated altogether in the early 1930's and during the Reagan era of the 1980's.

Wisconsin's work force was substantially altered by another factor: the steady influx of women into the labor market during and after the two world wars. Most significantly, in wartime women were able to move into the better-paying industrial jobs traditionally held only by males. And the movement of women into the work force continued long after 1945 as more and more women chose to work outside the home—partly to gain more financial independence, partly to keep up with inflation. The "traditional" single-earner family of the 1950's soon became a distinct minority. By the 1980's, as Wisconsin AFL-CIO president (1986-1994) Jack Reihl tells us, the old "Ozzie and Harriet" family where Dad worked and Mom stayed home comprised only about 4 per cent of American households. At the end of the 20th century, the composition of Wisconsin's working class, like the economy itself, remains in a state of unceasing change.

Forms of Labor Organization

Wisconsin history provides a unique laboratory for exploring how workers experimented with various forms of labor organization. Faced with an ever-changing economy, wage earners were very limited in their ability to improve their economic situation. Landlords, merchants, and manufacturers, for example, could adjust to economic trends by raising or lowering their rents or prices. Similarly, employers, including master craftsmen and contractors, could respond to changes in the economy by altering their pay to employees or increasing the rates they charged merchants or landlords for labor. By contrast, wage earners received a specified payment for a specific act of physical exertion, and few had the ability to adjust to economic change. Of course, workers had the "right" to reduce the amount of wages they were willing to work for, thus "protecting" their jobs against other wage earners. But they found it nearly impossible to move wage levels upward because their employers owed most of their profit to their ability to reduce what they paid their workers.

As a result, by the end of the century a large percentage of wage earners lived on the edge of poverty. While most workers responded to their situation by engaging in a desperate struggle for individual survival, others began to join with competing wage earners in a common defense of wage levels or job standards. The emergence and decline of various forms of labor organization—among them mutual-aid societies, craft unions, industrial unions, and social unions—was determined not only by the changes taking place in the economy, in industry, and in the work force, but also by the degree to which those forms of organization succeeded or failed to enhance the power of wage earners in the labor market. When they succeeded, they were embraced by wage earners. When they failed, they were discarded. Furthermore, union success in organizing usually triggered a response by management—meaning an effort to curb further union expansion. This forced unions to adopt alternative tactics which, if effective, led employers to create new barriers to union growth. Gradually, step by step, skirmishes between labor organizers and the managers of business and industry escalated into virtual warfare.

Wisconsin history provides a laboratory to study the development of labor organizations. In the nineteenth century, construction tradesworkers, printers, and other skilled workers were sometimes able to achieve limited control of local labor markets and enforce premium wages. Brewery workers were quick to organize in Wisconsin's larger cities, but the paperworkers struggled unsuccessfully year after year with few victories. It was not until the 1930's that unions had gathered sufficient strength and numbers to represent more than a fraction of the non-agricultural work force. Most employers opposed labor organization and often used sophisticated strategies to contain and weaken unionism. Particularly important were court injunctions that prohibited strikes, the use of labor spies to disrupt organizing activities, and the notorious "yellow dog" contracts which pledged workers not to join a union. The first few years of the Great Depression of the 1930's nearly destroyed unionism in the state; but the situation changed beginning in 1933, thanks to the advent of the Roosevelt administration in Washington, an upsurge of worker militancy, and important changes in the laws governing labor relations.

The dynamic movement for industrial unionism swept rapidly through Wisconsin's large manufacturing sector. One by one, the large industries fell under union influence: the automobile plants in Kenosha, Janesville, Milwaukee, and La Crosse; the metal-fabricating plants of Milwaukee County; the cookware factories in Washington County; and eventually the large paper mills of the Fox River Valley. The rise of the Congress of Industrial Organizations (CIO), with its call for "industrial unionism" posed a challenge to the American Federation of Labor, whose membership was based primarily upon the construction trades and skilled workers. In Wisconsin, the split between the AFL and the CIO actually resulted in many more union members because the two federations competed for the allegiance of workers in shop after shop statewide. Union membership in Wisconsin grew exponentially in the late 1930's and during the years of World War II, and union membership in private-sector industries continued to rise in the 1950s.

The emergence of public employee unionism was advanced by the enactment of several collective bargaining laws for city, county, and state workers between 1959 and 1972. The union ranks were greatly strengthened as large numbers of public-sector workers and teachers joined the union movement. In the 1970's and 1980s new efforts were made to organize the large numbers of mostly female office and clerical workers as well as nurses and other health-care workers.

A Voice for Working People

While unions proved useful in helping workers win better wages and working conditions, they also served as a legitimate voice for working people. Churches, ethnic organizations, and immigrant societies gave many workers a sense of community, but they had less impact within the controlled regime of the shop or factory, where workers spent more than half their waking lives. In this sense, unions were unique in American society, for no other institution could match the labor movement in expressing the concerns of working-class America and in providing representation for employees in the workplace and the wider world.

The emergence of unions reflected the fact that, toward the latter part of the nineteenth century, wage earners had begun to view themselves as a distinct group within society. But while unions were used by workers to increase their power in the labor market, they also served as vehicles for working people to

State Historical Society of Wisconsin WHi (X3) 32192

The United Brotherhood of Carpenters and Joiners of America, Local 1074, photographed in Eau Claire about 1910.

express themselves, to participate in political and social activities, and to become more tightly integrated within the larger community. This duality—looking inward and looking outward—was reflected in the way unions approached their members and the encompassing society.

In Racine, Milwaukee, Superior, La Crosse, and other cities, the labor movement established newspapers that were aimed not solely at dues-paying union members but rather at working people in general—and often at anyone else who would support them. From one end of the state to the other, local unionists initiated Labor Day marches and parades without ever deciding whether the goal was to draw attention to the power that workers could win through mass organization or to celebrate the important role played by labor in the economy and in the life of the nation.

Unions in Wisconsin offered workers a path to involvement in political activity that transcended ethnic voting patterns and spoke to larger, societal needs. Unionists established legislative programs, ran labor candidates for public office, and lobbied in city halls and the state capitol. In Milwaukee and elsewhere, representatives from organized labor exercised a good deal of power at the local level. Wisconsin labor's close association with Socialist and Progressive politics underscored this broader, humanitarian perspective. Also, labor's legislative agenda in Wisconsin extended well beyond the specific concerns of its affiliated unions. All employees, not just union members, benefited from workers' compensation when they were injured on the job; similarly, all workers, union and non-union alike,

received jobless benefits during economic downturns. Within the structures where public and civic decisions are made, organized labor sought to represent working people. In Wisconsin, for example, union representatives held positions on local vocational and technical education boards and on the University of Wisconsin's board of regents, on the governing boards of the United Way and other charities, and on school boards and municipal boards and committees.

Like the constantly changing economy and work force, the goal of providing voice and citizenship for working people continues to be an important objective for unions in Wisconsin. America has never fully accepted unionism as an institution or ideology. Labor's emphasis on class-based collective action goes against the stubborn grain of the individualism and belief in social mobility that loom so large in American ideology. In the nineteenth century, worker combinations were viewed as conspiracies against free trade. At the turn of the century, the labor movement was blamed for industrial conflict and violence. After the Russian revolution in 1917, unions were attacked as agents of international communism. More recently, unions have been accused of being yet another "special interest." But despite their critics, within and without, unions continue to play a significant part on the American stage. Labor's unique role in providing a voice for working people seems likely to continue so long as the capitalist economy endures.

ANOTHER important connection between Wisconsin and labor is the fact that the field of labor history originated in the Badger state. The first labor historians were not historians at all, but rather a group of economists from the University of Wisconsin in Madison. They were led by John R.

Commons, who taught at the University from 1904 to 1932. Commons and a group of scholars which included Selig Perlman, Philip Taft, Elizabeth Brandeis, David Saposs, Helen Sumner, and Don Lescohier, among others, dominated the field of labor history for half a century.

Commons and his associates were the first scholars to explore the new industrial system and the role of workers and unions within it. The most important achievement of this "Wisconsin school of labor history" was to provide intellectual legitimacy for collective action and labor unions in a nation where unions were widely viewed as controversial organizations or obstacles to business development. Their achievements took place at a time when most historians took little interest in such everyday topics as work or labor unions.

The Commons group began by gathering the records of workers—a big task that resulted in a ten-volume *Documentary History of American Industrial Society* (1910-1912). Next they undertook the first scholarly history of workers in America. The four volumes of their *History of Labour in the United States* (1918-1935) covered the long period from the Colonial period to the 1930's and became the standard treatment of labor history for decades. Encouraged and stimulated by the Wisconsin model, economists, sociologists, and historians elsewhere in the nation began producing a large number of monographic studies of unions, labor leaders, and strikes. The institutional tradition of Commons and his associates continued into the 1950's and 1960's in the University of Wisconsin's department of economics, where Jack Barbash and Robert Ozanne wrote about organized labor for many years.

The dominance of the Commons tradition began to weaken in the 1960's and 1970's as a new group of historians began to focus on workers rather than on organized labor. The new social historians raised questions that required looking beyond the older institutional framework. David Brody's *Steelworkers in America: The Non-Union Era* (1960) broke new ground by focusing on steelworkers rather than their unions. Herbert Gutman, who completed his Ph.D. dissertation in history at the University of Wisconsin in 1959 (and who had studied with Selig Perlman), criticized Commons' exclusive focus on unions as being too narrow. Gutman and other social historians wanted to know how modern capitalism and industrialization had affected working-class communities and culture.

In the 1970s, the old institutional school of labor history came under attack from new directions. During this period a number of historians at the University of Wisconsin in Madison developed a new "corporate liberal" interpretation of recent American history. From this perspective, Big Business and Big Labor (meaning the established unions and the AFL-CIO leadership) were often seen as collaborators in a strategy aimed at preventing popular movements from achieving radical reform. During the years of the Vietnam War (c. 1965-1975), the AFL-CIO's hawkish stance often served to reinforce this perspective. In addition to the corporate liberal interpretations, another group of young historians was going beyond the old Commons school, often in search of working class protest and militancy that had been neglected or even denied by earlier historians. The new labor historians produced a number of "history from

below" studies of grassroots radicalism in which rank-and-file activists were pitted against conservative unions and tunnel-visioned labor leaders. David Montgomery's *Workers' Control in America* (1979) described how skilled workers used union work rules and labor solidarity to restrict production and maintain a certain degree of autonomy on the job. Other historians, using historical documentation not utilized by the older institutionalists, also began to consider the relationships between work and family, how unions affected women and minority workers, the role of Communists and anti-communism in the labor movement, and the response of immigrant workers to industrialization.[2]

The Wisconsin Labor History Society

In 1981, a new link between history and labor was created with the founding of the Wisconsin Labor History Society (WLHS). The WLHS began with a meeting of thirty historians, labor leaders, and union activists in the Sellery Room of the State Historical Society of Wisconsin; it held its first conference on May 1, 1982, at Turner Hall in Milwaukee. The program highlighted the years of World War II. The meeting ended at the offices of the Wisconsin State AFL-CIO with an unveiling of a marker commemorating the history of the Wisconsin labor movement. The Wisconsin Labor History Society developed and expanded its activities to include a newsletter and an annual essay contest for high school students. Historians and unionists came together at annual conferences around themes that reflected both the older institutional history as well as the new social history. Conference themes included the role of the labor press, women workers and labor in Wisconsin, unions and black workers, industrial unionism in the 1930's, the history of public employee unionism, labor culture, the Kohler strike, and organizing the packinghouse. This new interaction between unionists and historians in Wisconsin gave rise to a number of unique efforts to document labor's past. In some cases unionists combed through their organizational records in order to tell the story of their local union, resulting in the production of various pamphlets and books. Taking advantage of the new technology, several videos were produced which brought labor's story to a wider audience. Statewide, the acquisition and preservation of historical records increased, adding to the already plentiful collections held by the State Historical Society of Wisconsin and its Area Research Centers.

THE selections in this anthology draw upon both the old and the new labor history. Some of the pieces originated as papers at annual meetings of the Wisconsin Labor History Society. Many of them reflect the older, institutional history: how unions were organized, the use of strikes to win contracts, and the role of specific labor leaders. Several articles which deal with progressive social and labor policies reflect the precepts of John R. Commons and others whose research was rooted in policy issues. But the anthology also features material that is more representative of the new social history being produced by contemporary historians. For example, Leon Fink connects the Bay View tragedy of 1886 to the ethnic pecking order of immigrant workers and the sharp divisions between skilled and

Wisconsin loggers standing atop a day's labor.

less skilled workers. Joe Trotter, Jr., offers a new interpretation of the relations between black workers and organized labor in Milwaukee. Maude McCreery, Alice Holz, Catherine Conroy, Sue Doro, and others show how female unionists survived in a male-dominated work environment across four decades. Stephen Meyer uncovers the connections between the culture of the workplace and the role of radical labor unions at the huge Allis-Chalmers plant in West Allis. The older history is more prevalent in the earlier chapters of the anthology; the newer issues, especially the growing importance of women in the work force, appear more often in the final two chapters. This reflects reality. While much of the old manufacturing sector, which mainly employed men, had been organized by the mid-1950's, labor's future rests upon efforts to organize the growing number of workers in the service sector, especially females.

Too often, today's historians write history almost exclusively for other historians, rather than attempting to reach a broader audience. This seems unfortunate, for ultimately, the value of this anthology will be determined by those readers who make use of it in examining our common heritage. *Workers and Unions in Wisconsin* is designed to be useful for professional historians, but it is also aimed at the general public. For the first time, historical material on Wisconsin labor, drawn from a wide variety of published and unpublished sources, has been compiled in a single volume. All the original footnotes have been retained to allow readers to delve more deeply into Wisconsin history. The detailed index will enable researchers and family members to identify the large cast of characters that have left their mark on Wisconsin's labor history. High school and college teachers should find this anthology useful in teaching history and social studies courses.

Every citizen of the state with an interest in the past should take pride in the working people who helped turn Wisconsin's prairies into farms, and its forests into lumber. It was they who built and staffed the great factories and forges of Milwaukee, Racine, and Kenosha and the sawmills and papermills of Wausau, Green Bay, and Appleton. They dredged the canals, paved the streets and dug the sewers, erected the girders, laid the bricks and railroad tracks, and transported all manner of industrial and agricultural goods by road, rail, and water. Few of these workers became famous, and fewer yet became wealthy; indeed, most workers remain nameless and faceless, even in a volume such as this. But we owe them a large debt. For it was their sweat and toil, combined with their courage and willingness to engage in collective action, that made Wisconsin both a great economic power and a pioneer of social reform.■

SECTION

1

Early Trade Unionism

Allis-Chalmers plant. Front view showing Allis Chalmers No. 27, double discharge Gates Gyratory Breaker during erection. Built for the Utah Copper Company, Utah.

Early Unions in Milwaukee, 1840-1884

THOMAS W. GAVETT

The development of industry in cities like Milwaukee attracted larger numbers of skilled and less skilled wage earners. In this section, Thomas Gavett reveals the tenuous nature of early efforts to form unions in steel mills, on the waterfront and railroad yards. Workers made news when there were labor disputes and strikes, but most of the strikes failed. Note how the printers' union responded to "the problem of female labor" and how their position changed in 1884.

THE 1840's and 1850's were years of relative inactivity for unions in America. The aggressive union movement of the 1830's had all but perished in the long depression beginning in 1837. Nevertheless, on the local level unionism survived, however sporadically. In Milwaukee the first evidence of unionism appeared in August, 1847. At that time forty masons and bricklayers struck for an increase in their daily wage from $1.50 to $1.75. In April, 1848, the journeymen coopers held a protest meeting against a reduction in the rate for flour barrels, apparently unsuccessful.[1]

In July, 1848, a strike of journeymen shoemakers at a shop owned by Benjamin Bosworth displayed the problems and tactics of the very early labor organizations and the attitude of management. Bosworth had brought a number of journeymen shoemakers from Boston and paid their expenses with the understanding that they would work for him until their passage had been repaid. He had promised to pay them 20 per cent more than they had received in Boston, but to retain the increase to pay for their transportation debts. According to Bosworth, as quoted in the Milwaukee *Sentinel* of August 1, 1848, he had actually paid them 50 per cent more than they had been receiving in Boston. "They were perfectly satisfied," he claimed, "till some meddlesome pile drivers, that knew no more about making Ladies fine work than an ass (as they themselves expressed it about the one that drew up their list of wages) . . . first enticed them to join their society, then brought their list of prices to me to sign."

Bosworth refused to sign the list, claiming that some operations in the production of shoes had been omitted and some were priced too high. However, he finally did sign the list on the promise that the union would submit a new list at its next meeting. But when the next meeting was held, the union refused to submit a new list since other manufacturers had refused to sign. Therefore, Bosworth claimed the right to manufacture any kind

of shoe he wished and to set his own prices. Evidently Bosworth continued to use the former list of prices as a guide, but a strike was precipitated when he refused to pay nineteen cents more to put the bottoms on "Goat bootees" which the "Captain of the Lodge" claimed were "Gaiter bootees" since they laced up. The strikers voted to continue the protest until Bosworth agreed to abide by a price list that had recently been developed. Bosworth refused, terming it a "bungling list, that they all admit is wrong." The strikers put a letter in the newspaper claiming that Bosworth ran a scab shop. According to Bosworth, the strikers also gave five dollars to two men owing him money so they could leave town, "thinking thereby to punish me . . . ." Bosworth charged that the strikers had been humbugged and intimidated by foreigners and that their blustering was the result of alcohol. He ignored the strikers, and evidently their demands failed.

First Successful Strike

The first successful strike in Milwaukee was called in September, 1848, by a Ship Carpenters and Caulkers Association at the shipbuilding company of George Barber. The skilled workers demanded improvements in hours and wages, and a restriction on the number of unskilled workers— "barndoor joiners" as the strikers dubbed them—employed. With a number of contracts to fill, the employers conceded the demands after one month. The strikers won a reduction in hours from twelve to ten, an increase in wages for all skilled workers, and a restriction in the number of apprentices.

In the fall of 1848 a Cabinetmakers and Joiners Union with sixty-one members made an agreement with employers for an increase in wages and a restriction of the number of apprentices. When the agreement was broken, the union members, for the first time in Milwaukee, decided to start a cooperative store and warehouse with $1,200. The union members purchased supplies from the cooperative and displayed their finished work in the cooperative salesroom. However, internal dissension soon arose, and the enterprise was closed.[2]

The first time a labor dispute in the area was brought into the courts was in August, 1851. The schooner *Bristol* of Montreal had come to Milwaukee from Burlington, Vermont. On August 27, 1851, the schooner left Milwaukee for Chicago, but when it was off Racine, the crew refused to obey orders unless their wages were increased to the rates paid on Lake Michigan. The captain refused their demand and, with the mate and the cook, brought the vessel back to the Milwaukee port and appealed to the law for assistance. The sailors were brought to court but discharged by Justice Walworth on the grounds that he did not have jurisdiction.

On August 30 of the same year there was another strike of sailors—some unemployed and others employed on the brigs *Mechanic* and the *David Smart*—for higher wages. Since some of the employed sailors refused to strike, a fight started. Because of threats of further violence, three or four of the leaders were arrested and brought before Justice Walworth, who sent them to jail to await examination.[3]

The problem of female labor as a "competitive menace" came to Milwaukee in the spring of 1852. At that time, Madame Mathilde Franziska Anneke founded the first woman suffrage paper of the state, *Die Frauen Zeitung*. Madame Anneke had been offered the use of Moritz Schoeffler's printshop where the first German daily of the state, the *Wisconsin Banner,* was published. However, the printers at Schoeffler's establishment refused to set the type, perhaps because of their opposition to a woman-suffrage paper, but more likely because of Madame Anneke's advocacy of female compositors. The printers organized a Typographical Union and set forth a number of demands, including restriction of apprentices. Schoeffler gave in to their demands, and Madame Anneke was forced to transfer her paper to the *Volksfreund* shop owned by Frederick Fratney. After publishing only six more issues, Madame Anneke moved her newspaper back East.[4] The Typographical Union continued sporadically for a number of years, but like many unions of the era, was more social than economic in character. In 1859 the Typographical Union achieved permanent status and became the first Milwaukee union to have national affiliation when it joined the International Typographical Union as Local 23, becoming the oldest union still in existence in Milwaukee.[5]

Railway Workers
Demand Back Wages

On July 11, 1853, between 300 and 400 Germans who had been working on the La Crosse and Milwaukee Railroad came to Milwaukee to demand their pay. Their action was caused by the lack of adequate laws to assure collection of back wages. They claimed that the contractor, a Mr. Schultz, had promised to pay them but did not. The men gathered about the entrance of the office of the company on the southeast corner of West Water and Spring streets. The mayor, several aldermen, and a number of policemen went to talk to the men and told them that they must look primarily to the contractor for payment, but that the company would attempt to protect them against fraud by

the contractor. The men were also warned against using violence. In the afternoon boys in the crowd broke into a barrel of sugar in the dry goods and grocery store below the company office. The owner called a deputy sheriff to arrest a man who took some of the sugar. When his companions, misunderstanding the cause of his arrest, attempted to rescue him from the officer, two were arrested. The entire group, led by a man displaying a tricolor flag, hurried to the jail to rescue the prisoners. Sheriff Page met them and warned that any violence on their part would be met by force. The fire department was called out to direct water on the rioters and act as additional police, if necessary. Mayor Walker again appeared and attempted to remove the flag, which was the rallying point of the rioters. When the mayor was hit on the side of the head with the blade of a shovel carried by one of the demonstrators, a riot started. The firemen turned water on the rioters who in turn threw brickbats at the firemen. Firemen and police charged the mob and drove them away; a number of persons were wounded. After the struggle the firemen and police were disbanded, but they and the military companies in the area were told to be ready for action. That night the mayor issued a proclamation, in German, that the company would pay the laborers out of money due the contractor. Eight men who had been arrested during the incident were released. The proclamation and the release of the prisoners sparked a parade by a large number of the men.[6]

The absence of adequate legal protection for collection of back wages inspired another incident in October, 1856, as reported in the *Daily Sentinel* of October 7. Four men, employed by the Cochrane and Hubbard Brick Company, were arrested after they tried to prevent teamsters from hauling bricks from the yard. They had also struck one of the owners of the yard because he failed to pay their wages on schedule. The men were brought to court on charges of disorderly conduct; two were fined $5 and the other two, $3. A similar incident occurred on September 15, 1858, when workmen in the lumber yard of Stronach and Company on Erie Street took direct action when they were not paid for their work. The company had gone into receivership after the death of one of the partners, and no one had paid the workers. The men assaulted the office, smashed the furniture, seized one of the partners, Nathan Engleman, and threatened violence if they were not paid. The men were soon arrested, but released when no one appeared to file charges, according to the *Sentinel's* account on September 17.

The first case of multi-employer bargaining was during the strike of journeymen tailors in 1853. On August 18, 1853, the journeymen tailors met at Military Hall to formulate a bill of prices. The employers, according to the *Sentinel* of September 3, agreed to increases of 25 to 30 per cent on many articles of clothing, but would not accept the entire bill of prices drawn up by the tailors. The tailors, therefore, went out on strike, and on September 2 about 120 tailors marched through the streets of the city, preceded by banners and music, to demonstrate their opposition to the position of the employers. A few days later the tailors appointed a "Committee of 18" to meet with the employers to seek a compromise. At the meeting the major point of difference was the demand of the strikers that those who worked by the week should receive a minimum of $7.50, claiming it was impossible to live on less. The employers contended that those who were hired during the busy season were often worth no more than $5 a week. The Committee of 18 reported back to the strikers at the City Hotel. The Committee maintained that the employers often took advantage of the foreign-born who could not speak English and consequently were hired for less than their worth. The tailors passed a resolution refusing to work until "two-thirds from Wisconsin Street to Walker's Point had signed the bill of prices." However, the employers refused to sign the bill, and the strike failed.[7]

The journeymen shoemakers were the first unionists in Milwaukee to strike over the issue of the closed shop. The shoemakers called a strike at Bradley and Metcalf's in January, 1855, because, although the company had reduced wages as agreed to by the union, it had not asked for proof of union membership when employing workers.[8]

Aside from the few strikes mentioned above, the efforts of the laborers in Milwaukee were sporadic. When the Association of Tailors was founded in 1850, they attempted to start a cooperative. Apparently nothing came of this, however, or of their attempts to regulate wages, hours, apprentices, and female labor. The Cigar Makers Union, organized in 1852, failed to obtain higher wages, abolition of the piece-work system, or restriction of the number of women workers. Like many other unions of this period, the German Custom Tailors Union, organized in 1860, was largely a social organization.[9]

There were also a few attempts to establish, rather prematurely, a labor press. The *Workingman's Advocate,* founded in 1842, and the *Arbeiter,* founded in 1854, came to a Milwaukee unprepared for labor papers; each died within a year. The weekly *Workingman,* started in 1856, maintained its tenuous existence for two years. After that labor received only incidental support in Freethinker and Turner Bund publications.[10]

Labor During the Civil War

The Milwaukee labor movement had been dormant between the years 1855 and 1860, but with the advent of the Civil War and the ensuing inflation, trade-union activity revived. During the early years of the Civil War, prices rose from 50 to 75 per cent although wages rose by less than half that amount. On August 15, 1862, the *Daily Sentinel* reported a shortage of labor among brewers and publishers as a result of enlistments in the Civil War. The inflation received new impetus in 1863 with the issuance of greenback currency by the federal government. For the first time in the history of Milwaukee, skilled labor began to organize into trade unions. Bricklayers and masons, custom tailors, and sailors were organized. Those unions organized before the Civil War discarded their benevolent role and assumed a more militant character. In 1864 and 1865 strikes became a common method of gaining wage increases. A fair number of these strikes, which usually involved only one enterprise, were successful. By the end of the war, labor had secured wage increases of 60 to 75 per cent to compensate partially for the enormous price increases.[11]

An early manifestation of this new militancy was the strike of the journeymen tailors in July, 1860. Approximately 250 tailors demonstrated in the streets for an increase in wages. The

An early banner of the Building Trades Council of Milwaukee.

State Historical Society of Wisconsin WHi (X3) 35445

journeymen designed their own price list and paraded the streets to induce the employers to sign the list. Fifteen did. In 1864 the custom tailors gained an increase of $2 a week without a strike.

The printers, organized before the Civil War, first reasserted themselves in a brief strike at the *Evening Wisconsin* and the *Daily Sentinel* offices, gaining a wage increase. But the shortage of male printers caused by the war again brought the problem of female labor to the sharp attention of the Typographical Union. Jermain and Brightman, the owners of the *Daily Sentinel,* had been considering the possibility of introducing female labor since 1861. Finally in January, 1863, the proprietors of the paper decided to employ a few female compositors. Local 23 of the Typographical Union held a special meeting on January 11 and adopted a resolution informing the owners that "the principles of our Union and the honor and integrity of its members, do not tolerate such help under any circumstances whatever." The owners denied that they intended to supplant the men with females, although they admitted that one man had been discharged as the result of the employment of females. The *Daily Sentinel* maintained that there was a shortage of printers and that many of the women employed were dependents of men now in the army. The paper also claimed that it had had letters from women all over the state anxious to learn typesetting. Further, the female compositors worked in a separate building from the males.

The union again pointed out that there had been no provision in its constitution for admitting females and that the quota for apprentices in the office was full. The union was determined not to concede; fourteen union compositors walked out. Mr. Jermain had evidently been prepared for the emergency. For several months prior to the strike he had had ten or twelve girls training in rooms outside the building. With the aid of these girls and a few "stray" compositors, the paper was able to continue publication.

The press of the state and of Chicago had a field day in denouncing the strikers. The Racine *Journal* exclaimed, "Such dictation as that of the Printer's Union, in this case is unreasonable and tyrannical." The Sparta *Herald* chided the union say-

LEAD MINING IN LA FAYETTE COUNTY

■ REMOVED my family to the mines in the fall of 1827, and settled at New Diggings, now in La Fayette county. So intent were the new-comers on making money by mining, that they could not take time to erect for themselves and families even a comfortable dwelling place. Instead of houses, they usually living in dens or caves; a large hole or excavation being made in the side of a hill or bluff, the top being covered with poles, grass and sods. A level way from the edge of the hole at the bottom was dug out, some ten or twelve feet; and this gang-way being closed up on either side, was covered over on top, thus forming a sheltered entrance to the "*dug-out*," as such places were usually called. In these holes or dug-outs, families lived in apparent comfort and the most perfect satisfaction for years, buoyed up the constant expectation of soon striking a *big lead*. To these miserable places of abode, men were compelled to carry upon their backs every thing they and their families required for food and fuel. The miners all lived in similar or worse places, or encamped upon the open ground.

What was then called *prospecting*, was the general business of the country. This consisted in digging "*succor holes*," in all imaginable shapes and depths, and in all manner of places. When a lead was struck, then all would flock to that vicinity to mine; and hence, in the course of a few years, mining was concentrated, in some considerable degree, in certain localities, such as New Diggings, Hard Scrabble, Coon Branch, Fair Play, Platteville, Mineral Point, Dodgeville, Blue Mounds, etc., places still of considerable note. During these few early years, the mines were worked chiefly by men from the Southern and Western states, who possessed and practiced many of the noblest traits of our race. As an illustration of their innate integrity of character, it is perhaps only necessary to state, that locks and keys were unknown in the country; and all places of abode were always left unfastened, and open to the reception of all, who received a cordial welcome, and a free invitation to partake of every hospitality the dug-

out or shanty afforded. Upon the return of the lone miner to his "hole in the ground," after a hard day's work, we would frequently be cheered with the sight of some weary prospector, who had, in his absence, there taken up his lodgings for the night. Having passed a pleasant night, they would separate in the morning, perhaps never to meet again. Mining tools, and every thing of this description, were left out, and nothing ever stolen or disturbed.

Debts were contracted without reserve, at the first interview with a new-comer, and he seldom ever failed to meet his promises of payment. The mode of doing business was something like this: A young man would enter a store, or go to a smelter, who usually kept miners' supplies, and would say: "Sir, I have just arrived in the mines, am out of money, and wish to go to mining; it you will let me have some tools and provisions, I will pay you as soon as I strike mineral, which I hope will be in a few days, or weeks at the most." The prompt [and] friendly reply would be — "Yes, Sir, you can have them;" and the pay, sooner or later, was almost sure to come. This custom was so universally prevalent, and men were so prompt to pay their debts, that I have often heard business men of that day declare, that they never knew debts so promptly paid, even in States where they had stringent laws to enforce their collection.

After this apparent prosperity, business very much declined, and in the fall and winter ensuing, the inhabitants experienced the severest times that they ever had in the country. Lead and mineral fell in value from a good price, to almost nothing — lead depreciating to one dollar or one dollar and a quarter per hundred, and mineral only brought no more than four dollars per thousand, and often but three. And not only was our great and exclusive product so depressed, but provisions rose to a very high price. Flour commanded from fifteen to eighteen dollars per barrel, pork thirty dollars per barrel, coffee fifty cents and sugar twenty-

ing, "It is both ungentlemanly and unjust to attempt to curb Woman's sphere of usefulness in this arbitrary manner," and the Chicago *Post* cleverly chimed in, "The proprietors have certainly shown themselves more gallant than 'the boys,' who ought to be ashamed of themselves thus to strike women."

To replenish its labor force, the *Sentinel* advertised for compositors who would work with women, offering union wages. Some aid was given to the Milwaukee printers by union printers in Chicago in the form of an advertisement in the Chicago *Tribune* warning all printers not to work at the *Sentinel,* or to be prepared to bear the label of "rats."[12]

A Failed Cooperative

The striking printers were soon conscious that some new course of action was needed to be taken. Ferdinand Shurr, writing in 1886, gives this amusing account of their action:

"The fourteen 'prints,' after walking out, met at the old rendezvous, 'The Old Menominee Beer Hall,' to discuss the situation. All went well for the first day; but on assembling on the second day they were politely informed by Peter Enders, proprietor [of the hall], that the 'slate is broke.'

"Having an eye to business, he could tell for a certainty that as the point was not gained on the first day, the strike was lost. The expression of the "slate being broke" opened our eyes to the fact that we were beaten as far as the strike was concerned, and being the aggrieved parties, we proposed to start a co-operative daily wherein we could mix our grievances with the news and at the same time bury the *Sentinel*.

"After holding three or four meetings and counting what little money there was in the crowd, we made arrangements with Mr. Miller, the type founder, for an outfit, and actually succeeded in getting it. As a matter of course the types were not new, and by paying

Dover Publications, New York

five cents per pound. At these ruinous prices for lead and mineral, and high prices for provisions, it required a desperate effort on the part of the miner to secure even a scanty living. It took from four to five thousand pounds of mineral to pay for one barrel of flour; I gave four thousand pounds for a barrel. In consequence of the great depression of the times, many persons became discouraged and left the country, many more gave up business, and the country at that period, and during the years 1830 and 1831, presented a most gloomy and unpromising appearance, and was, in fact, any thing but flattering to inhabitants or strangers.

During all this time, the people were compelled to pursue the uncertain and precarious fortune of mining as a means of livelihood, the cultivation of the soil being expressly prohibited by the laws and regulations governing the mines. But in the spring of 1832, however, the Superintendent of the mining country, seeing the absolute necessity of the thing, signified to the inhabitants, that he would not take any measures to prevent them from cultivating the soil; but could not, under his instructions from the General Government, give them any special permission to

do so. Up to this time, it was necessary, under the mining regulations, to procure a permit even to mine. The regulations governing the mines, were of the most rigid character, and they were sometimes rigidly enforced, sending officers with instructions to remove persons from certain localities. An instance of this kind, I believe, occurred in which Gen. Dodge was the person sought to be removed. He was then mining at Dodgeville, a region to which the Indian title had not been fully extinguished. This was in the year 1828; but these instances were, however, quite rare.

In consequence of the inhabitants being partially permitted to cultivate the soil, there as an evident appearance of increasing improvement and prosperity throughout the country, and the settlers everywhere were looking forward to a season of plenty and comfort. The country now began once more to hold out inducements to immigration, and the population was evidently on the increase from this source.

—DANIEL M. PARKINSON

From "Pioneer Life in Wisconsin,"
Wisconsin Historical Collections, II (Madison, 1856).
Footnotes in the original omitted.

a little down we got six months time on the balance.

"There never was a prouder set of men than those fourteen when the first number of the *Daily Union* appeared on the street—every one his own boss, every one a proprietor. Not having any advertisements we worked day and night to fill the columns of the paper with the choicest and spiciest of reading matter, paying special rates for our telegrams—having the reports made up in Chicago and sent to us as specials—which made great inroads in our last assets.

"Matters run on in this way for seventeen days and we had the *Sentinel* all but laid on the shelf, when the coal gave out. As printers are never known to set type in a cold room, we had no other alternative than to call a meeting and devise some means to replenish the fire. As we had a circulation of over 900, and there had been no collecting done, we formed ourselves into a committee on collections.

"Through some oversight there was no time set for the commit-

tee to report, and so I have been waiting all these years to find out whether our co-operation scheme really had 'millions in it.'

"Mr. Miller was not slow in taking back his material and calling it square, and as we had to pay in advance for paper and presswork, the company, whenever it shall see fit to resume business, can do so with the assurance that there are no outstanding liabilities. . . .

"Some of the boys drifted to Chicago, St. Louis and other places—some into the army, myself included, and some into that other world where strikes and co-operative newspapers are unknown. When the remnant returned in 1865, T. P. Germain *[sic]* and Horace Brightman were amongst the first men to open their doors for work to the surviving co-operatives . . . if we could have had $2,000, or $1,000, the venture would have been a success and might have been alive and prosperous to day."[13]

Because of the large number of their members who had enlisted in the army, Typographical 23 temporarily disbanded in 1864 but reorganized in 1865 or 1866, this time with women included as members. In 1866 the printers on the *Evening Wisconsin* successfully struck for a higher wage.[14]

Women workers were probably the group worst off during the Civil War era. In 1864 women tailors in Milwaukee received an average of only $3 a week, but had to work 11 hours a day and provide their own sewing machines. By 1867 the average wage for all women workers was $5 a week compared to the average wage for men of $13 to $14 a week. But it was to be a long time before the concept of equal wages for equal work would take hold.[15]

A Revival of Unions

The return of prosperity in 1878 brought a revival of unionism throughout the nation. After unemployment and wage reductions in the mid-1870's, workers were now passionately interested in a return to union activity which would recoup their losses and raise wages to new heights. This change in attitude, made possible by a more favorable economic climate, was signaled in Milwaukee by the strike of the flour millers in 1878.

The flour-mill workers had been forced to accept a reduction in wages in June, 1878. In July the employers resolved to reduce wages another 24 per cent because wages were allegedly lower in Minneapolis and St. Louis. The workers, while at first reluctant to strike or to form a union, successfully resisted the reduction and went back to work at the old rates.

The activity of the unions increased slowly, but in 1879 took a more aggressive turn. The coal heavers throughout the city struck for a 25 per cent increase in wages in June, 1879. Despite the presence of the police (a not too unusual occurrence during the times) the employers were unable to get the workers to return to work or to find replacements. A strike of the tanners in July for an increase of 10 per cent was similarly successful. An unusual feature of this strike was the charge of Milwaukee firms that Chicago tannery owners had sent a delegation to Milwaukee to organize a union, hoping to raise Milwaukee wages to the Chicago level and eliminate a "competitive disadvantage."[16]

Iron and Steel Workers

Probably the strongest union in Milwaukee during the period of the revival was the Amalgamated Association of Iron and Steel Workers founded in 1876. The union had two lodges with 800 members located in Bay View. In 1880 the union gained a daily wage ranging from two to eight dollars a day, rejecting a company counter offer of a 25 per cent increase. But not all workers at the Bay View plant of the North Chicago Rolling Mills were content with merely the increased wages. In 1881 the 450 puddlers working at the mill were angered by the long hours they often labored because the previous shifts were unable to complete their work on time. The day shift started at three-thirty in the morning. By one o'clock in the afternoon, they usually had completed four of the five required "heats." However, a break would often occur or the machinery would be out of order, and it would be impossible to complete the five heats within twelve hours. Consequently the first shift, often working fifteen and sixteen hours before the furnaces, would still be on the job when the next shift came to work. The puddlers therefore demanded that each shift be restricted to eleven or twelve hours. These workers gained some changes in working hours the following June when the Iron and Steel Workers won another wage increase during the course of a nation-wide strike involving 35,000 men in six states.[17]

The Waterfront

Another important scene of renewed union activity during the economic revival of 1878-82 was the waterfront—with a notable lack of success. The dock laborers had been angered by the employers' practice of deducting wages for time lost while making repairs during the unloading of the vessels. The laborers hopefully appealed to the courts. In April, 1880, seventy-five dock workers struck when the agent of the Anchor Line, D. M. Brigham, refused a demanded increase from 20 to 25 cents an hour. The strikers attempted to keep replacements from working, but were dispersed by the police. Another strike in August to gain a wage increase to compensate for their irregular employment also failed. Despite the organization of the Milwaukee Dock Laborers Union that followed, two strikes in 1881 for wage increases—one of them including 300 men—also failed.[18]

More successful was the Milwaukee Branch of the Chicago Seamen's Union, founded in 1880 or 1881. This union soon grew to include 250 men. The primary incentive for its organization was the competition of unskilled laborers, including skilled workers of other trades who frequently came to the lake for employment during their slack seasons. Though beset with frequent, and sometimes violent, strikes between the owners and workers and frequent encounters between the seamen and non-union workers, the union was able to minimize the competition of the unskilled and established benefits for its sick and disabled members.[19]

Railroad Workers

One of the most publicized disputes of the time occurred among railway-yard employees. In 1878 workers in the yards of the Chicago, Milwaukee and St. Paul Railroad quit work for three days in protest against a rumored (*Sentinel,* August 12) reduction of working hours and wages. In the *Sentinel* of August 14 the rumor was denied by the company manager, Sherburns Merrill. In the summer of 1880 the machinists and blacksmiths employed in the St. Paul railway shops presented a list of grievances to the management. The workers demanded immediate full wage payment upon termination of employment, a revision of prices in the "tool list" so a worker was charged no more than the replacement cost of a lost tool, and a 10 per cent increase in wages. The company agreed to the first two demands and granted a wage increase putting wages at the St. Paul yards on a par with others in the West. On August 26 the management called workers into the office and presented statistics purporting to show that their wages were higher than in any other company in the West. However, the management indicated they would be willing to grant a small increase to a few skilled mechanics.

The workers claimed the cost of living was higher in Milwaukee and pointed out that they had previously accepted a

A hydraulic forge press employed at Allis-Chalmers in Milwaukee.

State Historical Society of Wisconsin WHi (X3) 50226

5 per cent reduction when business was poor. Further irritated by the removal of the company's shops to the Menomonee Valley, making it necessary to carry cold dinners and ride in unheated boxcars to get to work, and by the "tyrannical spirit" of Superintendent William C. Van Horne, the workers refused the offer of the management and voted to strike. The company posted notice that the 260 strikers must return to work by August 27 or be peremptorily discharged. The company also demanded that the workers turn in their keys and checks. The workers refused to comply. Superintendent Van Horne then reported that the company would not compromise with the strikers and had made arrangements to hire men from out of the city to replace the strikers. When the strikebreakers came to the city, they were met by committees of the strikers and induced to leave. The committees were sometimes misled by the claims of tramps. Under the pretense that they were strikebreakers hired by the company, the tramps took three dollars apiece from the strikers to pay their transportation out of the city, using the money to buy liquor. Between 100 and 200 workers remained on the job, claiming the strike vote had been pushed by a few younger members and denying there were arbitrary or obnoxious rules in force in the shop. The strikers denied the allegation, charging they had been forbidden to talk to coworkers while on the job and accusing those who remained on the job of being the original strike agitators. As the strike dragged on, the men received financial support from the employees of E. P. Allis and from the Mechanical Engineers Union. There were threats to spread the strike over the entire line.

Finally on September 7 the men decided to go to the shop in a body, demanding their wages due and severing all connections with the company. However, the general manager and the superintendent appeared before the meeting of the strikers, asked them to return to work, and promised that wages would be raised to the level in Chicago. The strikers countered with a proposal to return, provided wages were immediately increased 10 per cent. The issue was finally compromised by appointing a committee of two strikers and one manager to go to Chicago to report on wage levels. After the report of the committee, the strikers returned to work, accepting a scale similar to that paid in three leading railway shops of Chicago.[20]

The gains made during the two-week strike of late 1880 did not long satisfy the desires of the men, who were conscious of the increased business of the railroads. By April, 1881, the painters at the shops of the Chicago, Milwaukee and St. Paul Railroad were demanding increases in pay, and the following month a strike broke out that involved most of the employees of both the St. Paul and the Chicago and Northwestern railroads. On May 2, 42 of the 54 employees in the freight sheds of the Chicago and Northwestern sent a petition to the local freight agent, C. E. Moody, asking for an increase from $1.20 to $1.50 a day and one hour's call-in pay. The petition denied, the men struck on May 5, refusing a company offer of $1.35. Because two of the strikers returned to work, the men decided to accept the company's offer the following day, but one of the leaders in the strike was not rehired.

On the same day the freight-house employees, the switchmen, yardmen, and brakemen struck at both railway companies. The brakemen, who had to pay for their own food and lodging while on the road, demanded an increase of $5 a month. The yardmen demanded a $10 increase. While the brakemen and yardmen soon won part of their demands, the switchmen fared much worse. Encouraged by the strike and subsequent wage increases of the railroad workers in Chicago, the switchmen had sought an increase averaging 57 cents a day. The St. Paul Road notified the strikers to collect any wages due and refused to listen to their demands. Both the St. Paul and the Northwestern roads required brakemen and conductors to replace the switchmen, though six brakemen were fired for their refusal to scab. The switchmen had added to their claims a demand for double time on Sundays, asserting that during the winter they had worked seven days a week but were allowed only one-half day's wages for Sunday and were often compelled to work nights for nothing. The switchmen induced the night shift to join the strike. When the employers began to hire green hands on a per-

WORK ON A FARM, 1848

BUT those first days and weeks of unmixed enjoyment and freedom, reveling in the wonderful wildness about us, were soon to be mingled with the hard work of making a farm. I was first put to burning brush in clearing land for the plough. Those magnificent brush fires with great white hearts and red flames, the first big, wild outdoor fires I had ever seen, were wonderful sights for young eyes. Again and again, when they were burning fiercest so that we could hardly approach near enough to throw on another branch, father put them to awfully practical use as warning lessons, comparing their heat with that of hell, and the branches with bad boys. "Now, John," he would say, — "now, John, just think what an awful thing it would be to be thrown into that fire: — and then think of hellfire, that is so many times hotter. Into that fire all bad boys, with sinners of every sort who disobey God, will be cast as we are casting branches into this brush fire, and although suffering so much, their sufferings will never end, because neither the fire nor the sinners can die." But those terrible fire lessons quickly faded away in the blithe wilderness air; for no fire can be hotter than the heavenly fire of faith and hope that burns in every healthy boy's heart.

At first, wheat, corn, and potatoes were the principal crops we raised; wheat especially. But in four or five years the soil was so exhausted that only five or six bushels an acre, even in the better fields, was obtained, although when first ploughed twenty and twenty-five bushels was about the ordinary yield. More attention was then paid to corn, but without fertilizers the corn-crop also became very meager. At last it was discovered that English clover would grow on even the exhausted fields, and that when ploughed under and planted with corn, or even wheat, wonderful crops were raised. This caused a complete change in farming methods; the farmers raised fertilizing clover, planted corn, and fed the crop to cattle and hogs.

But no crop raised in our wilderness was so surprisingly rich and sweet and purely generous to us boys and, indeed, to everybody as the watermelons and muskmelons. We planted a large patch on a sunny hill-slope the very first spring, and it seemed miraculous that a few handfuls of little flat seeds should in a few months send up a hundred wagonloads of crisp, sumptuous, red-hearted and yellow-hearted fruits covering all the hill. We soon learned to know when they were in their prime, and when over-ripe and mealy. Also that if a second crop was taken from the same ground without fertilizing it, the melons would be small and what we called soapy; that is, soft and smooth, utterly uncrisp, and without a trace of the lively freshness and sweetness of those raised on virgin soil. Coming in from the farm work at noon, the half-dozen or so of melons we had placed in our cold spring were a glorious luxury that only weary barefooted farm boys can ever know.

Spring was not very trying as to temperature, and refreshing rains fell at short intervals. The work of ploughing

Dover Publications, New York

commenced as soon as the frost was out of the ground. Corn- and potato-planting and the sowing of spring wheat was comparatively light work, while the nesting birds sang cheerily, grass and flowers covered the marshes and meadows and all the wild, uncleared parts of the farm, and the trees put forth their new leaves, those of the oaks forming beautiful purple masses as if every leaf were a petal; and with all this we enjoyed the mild soothing winds, the humming of innumerable small insects and hylas, and the freshness and fragrance of everything. Then, too, came the wonderful passenger pigeons streaming from the south, and flocks of geese and cranes, filling all the sky with whistling wings.

The summer work, on the contrary, was deadly heavy, especially harvesting and corn-hoeing. All the ground had to be hoed over for the first few years, before father bought cultivators or small weed-covering ploughs, and we were not allowed a moment's rest. The hoes had to be kept working up and down as steadily as if they were moved by machinery. Ploughing for winter wheat was comparatively easy, when we walked barefooted in the furrows, while the fine autumn tints kindled in the woods, and the hillsides covered with golden pumpkins.

In summer the chores were grinding scythes, feeding the animals, chopping stove-wood, and carrying water up the hill from the spring on the edge of the meadow, etc. Then breakfast, and to the harvest or hay-field. I was foolishly ambitious to be first in mowing and cradling, and by the time I was sixteen led all the hired men. An hour was allowed at noon for dinner and more chores. We stayed in the field until dark, then supper, and still more chores, family workshop, and to bed; making altogether a hard, sweaty day of about sixteen or seventeen hours. Think of that, ye blessed eight-hour-day laborers!

In winter father came to the foot of the stairs and called us at six o'clock to feed the horses and cattle, grind axes, bring in wood, and do any other chores required, then breakfast, and out to work in the mealy, frosty snow by daybreak, chopping, fencing, etc. So in general our winter work was about as restless and trying as that of the long-day summer. No matter what the weather, there was always something to do. During heavy rains or snow-storms we worked in the barn, shelling corn, fanning wheat, thrashing with the flail, making axe handles or ox-yokes, mending things, or sprouting and sorting potatoes in the cellar.

—JOHN MUIR

From *The Story of My Boyhood and Youth*
(Houghton Mifflin, New York, 1913).

manent basis, the switchmen attempted to gain the support of other workers in the area.

The strike of the switchmen took a new turn at midnight on May 9 when a bomb, loaded with glass and metal slugs, was thrown at Michael Kaiser, a foreman who had been riding a switch engine. Fortunately he was not hurt. Later it was contended that the bomb had been intended for H. L. Teal, a foreman the strikers loathed. The St. Paul Company immediately hired detectives and placed guards on the bridges leading out of the Menomonee Valley. Despite a resolution of the Switchmen's Mutual Aid Association that "we have not so far and do not [now] sanction any such acts or proceedings," the incident served to reinforce the position of the company. It adamantly refused to discuss the issues further. By May 16 the strike was near an end, with many of the older workers willing to return at former wage levels.[21]

The Printers

Even more noteworthy were the strikes and boycotts of the printers in 1882 and 1884. During the depression following the Panic of 1873, wages of printers in the city were reduced several times. At the time no union in the city included a majority of printers, and the only existing body of printers agreed to the reductions. With the return of prosperity in 1878-79, wages were not restored, although prices rose. In April, 1881, a meeting was held to reorganize the union. Before the union, which hoped "to protect just and honorable employers from the unfair competition of greedy cheap-labor huckstering rivals,"[22] had become a full-fledged branch of the International Typographical Union, a strike started. The Cream City Typographical Union, as the local was called, demanded an increase from 33 to 38 cents per thousand ems (a measurement of type). The strike involved the *Sentinel, Republican and News,* and the *Evening Wisconsin.* The *Evening Wisconsin* acceded to the demands of the printers prior to the strike, contingent upon the acceptance of the new rates by the *Sentinel* and the *Republican and News.*

Despite efforts by the newspapers to run the papers without the aid of the compositors, and later to bring recruits from Chicago and New York (who joined the strikers upon reaching the city), the strike continued successfully. The union was encouraged when it was able to get nine women employed by the *News* to join the strike. At about the beginning of May the strike was settled, the union winning a compromise of 36 cents per thousand ems. However, conflict continued with the *Republican and News.* At the end of the strike the *Sentinel* had recognized the union, but the *News* announced its hostility to the union and refused to recognize it. Some of the *News* printers belonged to the union, but a considerable number did not. Since the paper was not organized, the union could not establish a grievance committee to take complaints to the owners. One of the principal problems at the *News* was the attitude of the foreman, Andrew C. Macrorie, who had been brought from Chicago during the strike. The foreman was an avowed and bitter enemy of the union and asked the remaining union compositors to renounce the Typographical Union if they wanted to keep their jobs. The paper also formed a Printers Protective

Association to defend the interests of the non-union employees. Because of the unsure position of the unionists, they appealed to the Cream City Typographical Union for help, "and the Union made their cause its own."

Wisconsin's First Boycott

In the beginning of August a strike was launched against the *Republican and News,* the principal demand being the replacement of Macrorie by a union foreman. The union forbade its members to work at the paper and, with the aid of its newspaper, the *Printers Bulletin,* brought out at the beginning of the April strikes, launched the first boycott in Wisconsin's history. The boycott received the wholehearted support of the Milwaukee trade-union movement. Within a few weeks the *News* lost over 700 subscribers and was forced to offer former subscribers free issues for one month if they would again take the paper. In its eagerness to make the boycott successful, the union extended it to cover the Quiet House, a gathering place of printers. Because the owner, Adam Roth, had refused to drop his subscription to the *News,* the union resolved to fine any member five dollars if he patronized Roth's place.

The boycott against the *Republican and News* continued until May, 1882, when the *News* purchased the *Sentinel,* forming the *Republican-Sentinel.* The *Sentinel* had been unionized, but the new owners decided to take their old non-union employees into the new office. The owners offered to operate an open shop, but the union insisted upon a completely unionized shop. The strike and boycott continued, now in opposition to the policies of the *Republican-Sentinel.* When, about two months later, the Buffalo (New York) *Courier* had a strike and offered free transportation to non-union workers who would move to Buffalo and replace the strikers, several of the employees of the *Republican-Sentinel* left and union printers were hired to replace them. Later, the printers marched into the office in a group, took possession of the type cases, and demanded 38 cents per thousand ems, the rate received by non-union employees. The employers conceded and the boycott was ended, eleven months after it began.

Two years later, on February 2, 1884, a second major strike and boycott by the Typographical Union began, now against the *Evening Wisconsin.* The union demanded that women compositors on the paper receive the same wages as men. The owners claimed there was no discrimination against women other than during the apprenticeship period. The union conceded the point but wanted the office reorganized and the strikebreakers replaced. To make the strike more effective, the printers reissued their *Printers Bulletin* and asked organized labor to boycott anyone who subscribed to or advertised in the *Evening Wisconsin.* Boycott resolutions were adopted by the Machinery and Stove Molders, Bricklayers and Masons, Cigar Makers, Seamen's, Blacksmiths and Machinists, Plasterers, Boilermakers, Upholsterers, and Broommakers Unions and the Milwaukee Trades Assembly. The boycott was formally lifted in April, 1886, when all men employed by the *Evening Wisconsin* joined the union.[23] ■

From *Development of the Labor Movement in Milwaukee* (University of Wisconsin, Madison, 1965).

Lumber Industry Strikes:
Eau Claire, Marinette, Ashland, La Crosse

ROBERT W. OZANNE

*The early labor movement is usually associated with the larger cities.
But in the 1880s, about one in every four workers in Wisconsin was employed in
the lumbering industry. Robert Ozanne describes the somewhat haphazard
attempts by sawmill workers to organize unions. He explains why the workers
hated the "scrip" system of wage payment and uncovers the role played by the state
militia in quelling a labor dispute in Eau Claire in 1881. What does the
testimony of the Wisconsin commissioner of labor statistics reveal about his
assumptions regarding the workers' efforts to organize?*

UNDER the slogan "Ten Hours or No Sawdust," Jerry Sullivan, an employee at the steam mill of the Eau Claire Lumber Company, led 2,000 sawmill workers out on strike in the summer of 1881, five years before the great Milwaukee eight-hour strikes. Directed by Sullivan and a union committee of twenty-four men representing nine Eau Claire area mills, the strike began on Monday morning, July 18, 1881. Three hundred eighty men walked out en masse after reporting for work. They formed a procession and marched to each of the other mills, triggering new walkouts at each. That afternoon, a crowd of 1,200 workers gathered to listen to speeches by union leaders given in both English and "Scandinavian."[1]

Grievances were many. Topping the list was the twelve-hour day; also prominent was the contract system of hiring. In the spring, workers were hired for the season, which lasted into the fall, on the basis of a contract drawn up by the employer. Besides the twelve-hour day, the contract's terms included a holdback on wages of as much as 20 per cent, to be forfeited if the worker did not finish out the season. Wages at Eau Claire in 1881 ranged from $1.00 to $1.25 for the twelve-hour day. Setting up a company store, as well as paying wages in "due bills" or scrip instead of cash, were techniques frequently used to exploit workers. The existence of "due bills" meant that wages were payable only at the close of the logging or sawmilling season. In the meantime, workers had to make all their essential purchases at the company store, which extended them credit. For workers who needed cash, the employer would discount due bills by 10 per cent or more. At the company store, prices were high and quality often low. In 1890 the Wisconsin legislature made due bills negotiable; workers could cash them with parties other than their employers. Even so, the worker might have to take a discount of up to 20 per cent.[2]

The first week of the strike was, from the standpoint of the union, remarkably successful. Strikers prevented "scabs" from working. The mayor ordered all saloons closed. There was no violence. The Wisconsin Bureau of Labor Statistics reported that the city was in the possession of the strikers. Growing nervous, the mayor wired Governor William E. Smith for troops to aid in keeping the peace. The governor, vacationing on Lake Superior, appeared personally in Eau Claire on Friday, July 29. He immediately wired the adjutant-general to send state troops. The next day eight companies, 376 men in all, reported for duty, each with twenty rounds of ammunition.[3]

Despite the absence of violence, after the arrival of the troops the sheriff arrested five union leaders, including Sullivan. Other leaders fled the town, effectively destroying the strike's leadership. Saturday afternoon Governor Smith gave a public speech in which he said he had not called up the troops to force sawmill workers to work twelve hours a day, but only to allow those who wished to work such hours to do so. Ignoring the unilateral aspect of the so-called contract, he stated that the men should abide by their contractual obligations and that in calling out the troops he was doing his duty to uphold the laws and constitution of the state.[4] With the strike leaders in jail or having fled, the mills reopened on Monday, operating with limited crews and under the protection of the state troops. Each day through Thursday, more replacements and returnees manned the mills. At this point the strike was called off. Many strikers already had left to find work elsewhere.

This was the first occasion in Wisconsin in which state troops had been called out on strike duty, and it raised a considerable controversy. The Oshkosh *Northwestern* called it "a sad day for the people when it becomes necessary to thrust the bayonet into the faces of the citizens, and especially of the laboring

Loggers posing with railroad velocipede, Jackson County, Wisconsin, 1889.

State Historical Society of Wisconsin WHi (V24) 1804

class. It looks as though the governor had been governed more by fear than discretion, and more by the representations of a few interested employers than by a free consultation with the employed."[5]

According to the *Madison Daily Democrat,* Governor Smith's action in calling out the militia to deal with Eau Claire strikers brought widespread state and even national press criticism from the Green Bay *Gazette,* the La Crosse *Chronicle,* the Jefferson *Banner,* the Beloit *Free Press,* the New York *Sun,* and the New York *Herald.*[6]

Supporting Governor Smith's use of troops were the Eau Claire *Free Press* and the Commissioner of the Wisconsin Bureau of Labor Statistics, Frank A. Flower, whose report, published three years after the event, described it as follows:[7]

At Eau Claire they [the state troops] met two thousand men armed with guns, clubs, pistols, crow-bars and mill tools—large, horny handed and resolute fellows, accustomed to hard work and hard usage, and fearless of danger.

Demagogues, who had never worked a stroke, incited the men to attack the militia, declaring that it was an insult to Eau Claire to send soldiers there to keep the peace, an insult to free citizens and a menace to workingmen. One well-known local politician mounted a box and advised the mill men to attack the militia at the moment

when Col. C. P. Chapman, in charge of the third battalion, was picketing the public park. The men in Col. Chapman's command had service belts from each of which plainly protruded twenty rounds of fixed ammunition. This seemed to have greater influence on the half-frenzied mob, the most turbulent of whom were not strikers or workingmen, but bummers—than the appeals of the politicians, and no collision took place....

The lesson taught by this strike to the lawless classes, who are never union men or workingmen, was salutary. It demonstrated that after crowds of rioters have defied civil authority and overridden the sheriff, they have not yet secured control of the country nor subjugated a community of peaceable citizens; and that those who have grievances, or wrongs to redress, must resort to courts and peaceful methods, not to riotings and destruction of property and life. The state possesses abundant power to protect both, which responds quickly to the command of the governor.

There had been nothing in the newspaper accounts of the strike to support Flower's inflammatory accusations against the Eau Claire lumber mill strikers. One Eau Claire paper, the *Daily Leader,* denied that there was any destruction of property whatsoever.[8]

Although the 1881 sawmill strike was unsuccessful, in the sense that the short-lived union was defeated, in 1882 the Eau Claire area mills reduced the workday from twelve to eleven hours. Many future strikes were to occur over the same issue— reduction of hours.

Strike Actions in Subsequent Years

In this era lumber strikes affected a substantial portion of the state's workers, for lumbering was by far the largest industry in Wisconsin. As late as 1889, it employed over one-fourth of all industrial workers in the state. The nearest industry in size comprised the various railroads, which employed only 6 per cent of the industrial labor force.

Several distinct occupations were involved in lumbering. The first was logging, primarily a winter trade. Because logging camps were remote and frequently shifted location, their labor force was individualistic and migrant. Consequently, unionism never developed in the camps. "Booming"—floating the logs to the mill—required considerable skill, but it, too, never became unionized except occasionally, as part of related sawmill strikes. Union growth occurred primarily in the cities, where there were sawmills, sash and door plants, and a variety of woodworking industries such as coopering, butter pails manufacturing, and, of course, the construction trades.

The next large wave of lumbering industry strikes occurred in 1885 and 1886 in the mills of the Menominee River Valley, on both the Michigan and Wisconsin sides. The strike actions were triggered by a ten-hour-day law, passed by the Michigan legislature, which took effect September 23, 1885. As was true of other such laws, it was not valid if individual workers agreed by contract with the employer to waive the ten-hour provision. The result was that employers simply presented their workers with a statement waiving the provision, and required them to sign the statement as a condition of employment. The workers immediately went out on a strike that lasted until October 5, when the employers indicated that they would agree to a ten-hour day for the 1886 season, but would continue the eleven-

hour day for the remainder of 1885. The strike was resumed ten days later, when Michigan employers tried to get their men to sign a waiver agreeing to an eleven-hour day for as long as they were employed.

Although the strike only began when the Michigan law became effective in September, union organizing had been going on since July at Marinette and Peshtigo in Wisconsin, and Menominee in Michigan. Union goals were the reduction of working hours, payment of wages in cash, and adequate time for dinner. The Menominee River Laboring Men's Protective and Benevolent Union was affiliated directly with the Knights of Labor. Its president was an able man, J. H. Fitzgibbons, who established a union newspaper, the *Menominee River Laborer*. Robert Schilling, whom we have met before as a leader of the Knights of Labor in Milwaukee, visited Marinette twice in September 1885, setting up four Knights lodges in Marinette and three in Peshtigo. According to the Marinette *Eagle*, on September 9, "The Hon. Robert Schilling addressed the union at a gala evening complete with procession and band," and on September 24, Schilling and A. G. von Schaick, manager of the L.W. and V.S. Lumber Company, addressed a gathering of 3,000 people at Turner Hall.[9]

In the Marinette-Menominee strike, 2,500 men left their jobs. On October 15, millowners locked out all workers in an effort to force acceptance of the eleven-hour day. The lockout failed to achieve its purpose; many workers left the area rather than agree to eleven hours. The employers then negotiated with the unions, and the ten-hour day, plus cash payment of wages, were secured for the Menominee River Valley. Schilling personally participated in the final negotiations at Marinette. According to the Wisconsin Bureau of Labor Statistics, ninety

State Historical Society of Wisconsin/WHi (X3) 30340

A logging operation on a Wisconsin river. In the 1880s the lumber industry employed one-fourth of the state's industrial workers.

Mill workers of the Paine Lumber Company at Oshkosh, circa 1895.

Oshkosh Public Museum (no.2672)

other Wisconsin sawmills throughout the state adopted the ten-hour day, but another 120 mills retained the long hours.[10]

A third strike wave hit the lumber mills of Ashland and Washburn in 1890, when 1,400 men went on strike under the leadership of the North Wisconsin Millmen's Union, an affiliate of the American Federation of Labor. The strike leader was William O'Keefe, an AFL organizer who was also the publisher of the Ashland *Daily News*. The settlement that ended the strike established a workday of ten and a half hours.

In 1892, strikes broke out among mills on the Wisconsin River. They began on July 25 at the Gilkey-Anson Company sawmill at Merrill, where twenty-four men asked for a raise from $1.60 per day to $1.75. The request was granted to nineteen of the men, who nevertheless struck on behalf of the other five workers. Two days later a thousand men were out on strike against seven of the town's eight mills.[11] Robert Schilling arrived and negotiated the strikers' demands. The final settlement granted the ten-hour day and pay on a weekly basis.[12]

Following the Merrill settlement, strikes for reduction of hours broke out at Stevens Point, Wausau, and Schofield. At the end of August, six mills at Rhinelander struck and received the ten-hour day. By the end of September, mills in every town on the Wisconsin River, with the exception of Tomahawk, had succeeded in establishing the ten-hour workday. William O'Keefe, who had led the Ashland strikes, also led the Rhinelander strikes.[13]

Not all lumber strikes were successful. In late April, 1892, a strike began in La Crosse when the John Paul Lumber Company discharged three union leaders. In 1873 La Crosse had been the site of the first recorded lumber strike for the ten-hour day. That action had been unsuccessful; the union leaders were blacklisted and replaced. By 1892, however, La Crosse mills were operating at ten hours, and it was union leaders' dismissal that incited the strike. Mr. Collins of the "grand labor council" negotiated for the

union in an effort to gain reinstatement for the three men,[14] but the union soon gave in to company pressure. The first left town; the second left the union. When the third agreed that he would not neglect his work to circulate and talk to the men about the union, John Paul consented to take him back. The union nevertheless persisted in its demand that no man could be discharged without good cause, and on May 1 asked for a wage increase. The employers, all members of the Lumbermen's Exchange, stood together. Two thousand men were out for almost two weeks, but then went back to work under the previous conditions. The Knights of Labor was active in the La Crosse action. Terence Powderly, national Grand Master of the Knights, was expected to appear in support of the workers, but the strike collapsed before he could reach the city.[15]

Except for the northwest section of the state, Wisconsin lumber workers had won the ten-hour day by 1892. Labor's next struggle would be for the nine-hour day, generally, and in the building trades for the eight-hour day. At Marinette, where workers first had won the ten-hour day, they struggled for the eight-hour day in 1892, but were unsuccessful.

The sawmill strikes in general had a great impact on shortening the working day, but they had less effect on other grievances, such as the complaints against pay in scrip, the company store, and the withholding of pay until the end of the season. A list of cities and towns with the dates of their strikes shows the widespread character of the workers' protest against long hours in the sawmills: La Crosse, 1873; Eau Claire, 1881; Marinette, 1885; Porterville, 1886; Ashland, 1890; La Crosse, 1892; Wisconsin River, 1892; Merrill, 1892; Stevens Point, 1892; Wausau, 1892; Schofield, 1892; Flanner, 1892; Manawa, 1892; Rhinelander, 1892; Eagle River, 1892; Woodboro, 1892; Eau Claire, 1892; Marinette, 1892; Chippewa Falls, 1898; Rice Lake, 1899; Marinette, 1899; Sheboygan, 1899-1900; Marinette, 1903 and 1904.■

From *The Labor Movement in Wisconsin: A History* (State Historical Society of Wisconsin, Madison, 1984).

The Knights of Labor
in Milwaukee

LEON FINK

The first group of labor historians, mostly the economists associated with John R. Commons and the "Wisconsin school," focused their attention on the leaders and institutions of the union movement. More recent historians have shifted their focus into the workers themselves—what they did in their workplaces and communities, the role of ethnic and gender factors, and how rank-and-file workers participated in public and political life. Leon Fink's analysis of the rise of the Knights of Labor in Milwaukee in the 1880s is a fine example of contemporary labor history. Note the important role of immigrant workers in the economy, and the difficulties faced by the Knights as they tried to square union organizational strategies with political objectives in a city defined by ethnic diversity.

MILWAUKEE provides the exceptional example of a successful third-party tradition stretching from the labor politics of the Knights of Labor era through the Great Depression of the 1930s. As the only major city in the country to be governed by a Socialist mayor for much of the twentieth century, Milwaukee, one might quickly surmise, must have been affected by a most particular and even peculiar set of local circumstances. Of course, one focus for such an analysis is offered in the immigrant German-American political culture of this most foreign of large American cities. The city, which as early as the 1850s became known as the "Deutsche Athens," by 1890 contained a population in which nearly four out of every ten citizens were immigrants and nearly nine out of ten were of foreign parentage. Among the immigrants themselves, 70 percent came from Germany. From the vantage point of other Gilded Age communities, however, political developments in Milwaukee do not look so alien. The evolution of a third-party Socialist presence, in fact, appears to be a distinct form of a political process rooted in the social upheaval of the 1880s.[1]

The principal dilemma facing Gilded Age political radicals in Milwaukee as elsewhere in America was the organization and mobilization of a heterogenous and divided working class. The degree of success or failure on this score, while not dictating the exact contents of labor's political message, did at any given moment generally define the electoral options available to working-class political leaders. In Milwaukee this primary task was accomplished less as a function of the peculiar local political culture than as a consequence of the activity of the Knights of Labor as well as the public responses that their activity evoked. In subsequent years Socialist electoral advances coincided with

the organizational consolidation of one part of the working-class community; at the same time the fragility of local Socialist rule may be traced to the fragmentation of a coalition first built in the 1880s. Throughout, the electoral fortunes of the party of the workers were intimately bound up with changing dimensions of workplace and community life in the city....

From Agriculture to Manufacturing

While Milwaukee could not really challenge Chicago's claim as "Queen City" of the Old Northwest in the 1870s, that decade nevertheless witnessed a critical expansion in the economic life of Wisconsin's urban center. Until the mid-1870s, Milwaukee acted as dispenser to the world's largest primary wheat market. But the combined influence of the 1873 price crash, poor harvests, and increased competition caused Wisconsin wheat production to slacken. Farmers turned to coarse grains (for malting and brewing) and to the production of dairy goods. Within the city flour-milling assumed a more modest position as one industry among several including meat-packing, tanning, brewing, and men's clothing. As an important early terminus for Minnesota ore and Pennsylvania soft coal, Milwaukee also developed into a center for the iron industry.[2] The shift in investment from agriculture and railroads to diverse manufacturing marked Milwaukee's emergence as a modern industrial metropolis. Increase in the number of establishments between 1870 and 1880 was negligible, but a 147 percent jump in the number of wage earners over the same period indicated a growing concentration of industry. Population rose from 71,000 to 116,000 between 1870 and 1880 and reached 204,000 ten years later, making Milwaukee the nation's sixteenth city.[3]

Interior of the International Harvester factory, Milwaukee, circa 1880.

State Historical Society of Wisconsin WHi (X3) 26721

Two key ingredients—metal and beer—paced the city's expansion through the century's last two decades. Milwaukee's metal and iron products rose in value from $402,000 in 1870 to $3.5 million in 1880 and to more than $14 million by 1900. When Edward Allis died in 1889, his Reliance Iron Works, purchased in 1857 for $31,000, returned $3 million annually. Although iron represented only half the value of beer as a product in 1885, the iron industry employed one and one-half as many workers as the city's breweries. Three thousand employees of the Milwaukee Iron Company and the North Chicago Rolling Mill made the South Side Milwaukee suburb of Bay View practically synonymous with iron-making.[4]

Not until the 1890s did such breweries as Schlitz, Pabst, and Blatz exploit the mass-marketing techniques that made them and their city nationally famous. But by the 1880s brewing had already matured from a household industry into a big business. Geoffrey Best (bought out by his son-in-law Captain Fred Papst in 1889), the biggest of the early brewers, had eight employees in 1860, 100 in 1870, and nearly 500 by 1886.[5]

Foreign Accents

In the 1880s the city's productive life was conducted primarily in foreign accents. Immigrants and their children comprised 90 percent of the work force in 1890 and only in the highest rungs of the occupational ladder did native-born Americans make up more than a quarter of the population. The working class of the city was not simply ethnic but overwhelmingly (65 percent) foreign-born; in general, the less skilled the position, the more like-ly it was to be filled by an immigrant. Three-quarters of Milwaukee general laborers, for example, were foreign-born (Table 1).

Since the 1840s only the Germans among the incoming groups had kept pace with the city's general expansion. By 1860, as Kathleen Neils Conzen has carefully documented, the Germans "were an occupationally stratified group fitting in, to a greater or lesser degree, at all levels of the city's economy." The relatively even occupational dispersion of the Germans was maintained through the following three decades, with new recruits continually resupplying the industrial sector even as others of their countrymen supplied the necessary internal services to the sprawling ethnic community. The German-born alone thus accounted for almost half of the city's wage-earning population. A typical advertisement in a local English-language newspaper ran, "Maidchen verlangt [Girls wanted] in der paper box factory." Certain industries, including brewing, carpentry and joining, cigarmaking, and tailoring, were essentially "German trades," with two-thirds to three-quarters of the work force of German origin. In 1890 only a few of the skilled trades (e.g., English iron workers, Irish railroad workers) still witnessed the concentrated presence of older, non-German immigrant groups.[6]

By the mid-1880s German-American workers had already exercised considerable influence over the institutional life of the city. As early as 1850, when the printers and typesetters of the radical *Banner und Volksfreund* brought Milwaukee its first legitimate theater, workers' organizations had formed an important cultural as well as political counterpoint to the roles of the Lutheran Synod and Catholic church among German-Americans. For years the councils of the carpenters, brewers,

FRANK WEBER: LABOR'S "GENERAL ORGANIZER"

A major role in the building of the labor movement in Wisconsin was played by Frank J. Weber. Beginning in the 1880s, Weber led efforts to organize unions, win strikes, and use state government to defend unions. Widely regarded as "the father of labor in Wisconsin," Weber disdained the title of "president" of the Wisconsin State Federation of Labor and prefered to be known as the "general organizer." He continued to be active until he was 84 years old.

Frank J. Weber, "general organizer."

State Historical Society of Wisconsin WHi (X3) 49765

THE most influential leader of the new Wisconsin State Federation of Labor was Frank Weber. As president of the Milwaukee Federated Trades Council he took the lead in getting the FTC to invite all Wisconsin unions to come to Milwaukee on June 5, 1893, for the purpose of founding the Wisconsin State Federation of Labor. At that time, forty-three-year-old Weber was already a veteran unionist. At eighteen he had become a sailor on the Great Lakes and within five years had risen to the post of captain; later he sailed around the world on clipper ships. Quitting the sea, he became a ships's carpenter in Milwaukee shipyards and joined the Knights of Labor. He then moved to the Carpenters Union and was active in the eight-hour-day movement of 1886.

During his twenty-three years as state organizer (president) of the WSFL, he furnished inspiration and knowledge for workers who wanted to unionize. The advice and evcouragement he gave to first-time unionists in such towns as Oshkosh in 1898, Marinette in 1916, and Nekoosa in 1919 was invaluable. He was an inspirational speaker at strike rallies, in Labor Day ceremonies, and at annual conventions of the WSFL.

Fortunately, he was a consummate politician, holding together diverse factions within the labor movement. These groups included: (1) the Milwaukee building trades, which were frequently open enemies of the Socialists in the FTC and the WSFL; (2) the Socialist faction that was centered in Milwaukee, especially among the Brewery Workers, Cigar Makers, and skilled metal trades; and (3) the unions outside

of Milwaukee, usually anti-Socialists, with the exceptions of Sheboygan and Manitowoc. The Socialists were Weber's solid supporters, but often did not constitute a majority of the WSFL. He found it necessary on occasion to avoid issues on which the unions were divided.

From 1900 to 1917, Weber held the principal post in both the WSFL and the FTC. With the rapid growth of the State Federation after 1914, he turned the leadership of that organization over to Henry J. Ohl, Jr., whom he and the Milwaukee Socialists had been preparing for leadership for several years. Weber continued to hold the post of organizer for the FTC until 1934, when he resigned at age eighty-four.

Weber was always a fighter for groups outside of the unions who were too weak to help themselves: children, the unemployed, and exploited women. He realized early the need for protective legislation, such as restrictions on child labor and provision for workers' compensation. He served regularly as legislative representative for the WSFL and the Milwaukee FTC. From 1886 to the mid-1890's, he was a Populist, but turned to the socialists after becoming head of the State Federation of Labor. Running as a Socialist, he served twelve years in the Wisconsin State Assembly, where he introduced key labor and other progressive legislation ten years ahead of its time.

—ROBERT W. OZANNE

From *The Labor Movement in Wisconsin: A History* (State Historical Society of Wisconsin, Madison, 1984).

---

cigar-makers, and printers in the city's original "Germantown" district constituted a Socialist nucleus within which Lassalleans, Marxists, and anarcho-syndicalists vied for supremacy. Milwaukee was surely one of the few places in America, for example, where Lassallean Social Democrats in 1877 not only outpolled their Greenback-Labor rivals but also elected several men to local office. In the late 1870s and early 1880s a citywide trades assembly loosely coordinated the interests of some fourteen craft unions, including both German and

English language printers, coopers, brewers, iron molders, railroad shopmen, building trades workers, cigar makers, and a section of the Amalgamated Association of Iron and Steel Workers. When a fourteen-week lockout practically destroyed the cigarmakers' organization in 1881, the trades assembly with Democratic and Greenback-Labor backing carried its protest into the political arena and elected a sympathetic iron manufacturer as mayor on a labor slate.[7]

Neither the ideological third party nor the coalition of

trades, however, proved a very durable political option. The trades assembly was, from the beginning, susceptible to down-swings of the business cycle and only barely survived the recession of 1884-85; politically, it had no means to attract an electoral majority except by merger with one of the major parties. The labor-based third parties, for their part, similarly struggled against strong counter currents. In the early 1880s, for example, much of their constituency was swallowed up by a swelling tide of German nationalism expressed in the mayoral campaigns of Emil Wallber. For despite their numbers Milwaukee Germans had long remained underrepresented in political affairs. With the state's dominant Republican party in the hands of pietistic temperance reformers and Americanizers inimical to both German-Lutheran and Catholic sentiments, the Germans had generally made the Democratic party their home. Yet even here the Germans served for years as troops behind a persistent old Irish general staff. Not until 1878, for example, did the editor of the Democratic Catholic *Seebote* become the city's first German-American Congressman. Of twenty-two state assembly positions chosen in Milwaukee County between 1879 and 1881, only four were filled by Germans or German-Americans. Thus, by 1883, pressure from the newly formed German Society spurred nomination by Republicans of Wallber, a Berlin-born lawyer, businessman, and president of the Turnverein for mayor. Narrowly defeated in his first attempt, this political moderate won the following year in a flush of cross-class ethnic feeling.[8]

TABLE 1
Male Occupational Structure in Milwaukee by Ethnic Group, 1890

Occupations	Native-Born, Native-Parents	Native-Born, Foreign-Parents	Foreign-Born	German-Born	Polish-Born[a]
Non-Wage Earners					
(N= 14,830)	18	40	42	28	6
Capitalists-professionals					
(N = 2,021)	28	34	38	26	4
Merchants					
(N = 6,312)	15	33	52	37	8
Salaried positions					
(N = 6,497)	17	50	33	21	3
Working class					
(N= 38,608)	6	29	65	45	12
Skilled workers (carpenters, printers, etc.)					
(N = 15,455)	5	36	59	45	8.5
Industrial workers (machinists, iron and steel, brewers, railroad workers)					
(N = 10,333)	8	30	62	42	10
Unskilled workers (laborers, teamsters)					
(N = 12,820)	11	19	75	47	19
Total	(9%)	(33%)	(58%)	(40%)	(10%)
(N= 59,578[b])	5,667[c]	19,342	34,569	23,760	6,084

Source: U.S. Eleventh Census, 1890, *Population*, Pt. 2 (Washington, D.C., 1896), 692-93.
Note: All data are given as percentages, and are based on males, age ten and older.
[a]"Polish" is substituted here for the category "Other Countries" used in the 1890 census to describe immigrants other than those born in Germany, Ireland, Great Britain, Canada, Sweden, Norway, and Denmark. As such it undoubtedly includes some scattered non-Poles but is the closest approximation possible for 1890. [b]Includes 6,140 individuals of unspecified occupation. [c]Includes 206 persons of color (blacks, orientals).

TABLE 2
A Comparison between Crime and Nativity in Milwaukee, 1884-90

Place of Birth	Number of Arrests	Percentage of Arrests	Percentage of Population [a]	Arrest Index [b]
United States (white)	11,049	51	61	0.84
Germany	6,171	28	27	1.04
Ireland	1,825	8	8	4.00
Poland	831	4	4	1.00
Other	1,870	9	6	1.50
Total	21,746	100	100	1.00

Source: Annual Reports of Chief of Police, Milwaukee, 1884-85, 1886-87, 1887-88, 1888-89, 1889-90, New York Public Library.
[a] Based on figures from the U.S. Eleventh Census, 1890. As explained in the text, the census estimate of Polish population is probably low; correspondingly, the number of Poles arrested is probably underestimated. This table assumes that the key relationship—i.e., the comparison of percentage arrested to percentage in the population—should therefore remain constant.
[b] Arrest index computed as: percentage arrested/percentage of population.

Polish Immigrants

The labor movement in Milwaukee was restricted not only by ready absorption into ethnic politics but also by the fact that the organized skilled trades ignored the increasing role that ethnic Poles played within the city's economic life. While their exact number remains difficult to fix (without a nation of their own the Poles were improperly enumerated in the state and federal census until after World War I), Polish laborers represented a significant minority presence within the manual working class by the 1880s. A few Polish settlers had arrived as early as the 1840s. The community that established a Polish parish on the South Side in 1866 grew to an estimated 1,000 members by 1880. During the ensuing decade, however, a mass emigration from the German Partition, spawned both by a crumbling agrarian order and Otto von Bismarck's *Kulturkampf*, had an immediate impact on Milwaukee. Milwaukee Poles likely exaggerated when they claimed 25,000 kinsmen (or nearly half the number of German-born) in the city in 1886 and 30,000 in 1890, but the 1890 federal census just as surely misidentified many poles as Germans when it listed only 9,222 Polish residents. Scanty immigration data suggest that while most of the arriving Polish immigrants may have been of peasant origin, many undoubtedly had had first-hand experience with the industrial revolution in Germany. In Milwaukee the Polish immigrants overwhelmingly occupied the lowest rungs of manual labor. As late as 1895 the South Side Polish community included only nineteen contractors, two attorneys, and two physicians; similarly, there were twice as many Poles in unskilled jobs as in the skilled trades. Hundreds of Polish immigrants reportedly took the lowest-paid jobs in the Bay View iron mills.[9]

Despite the poverty and roughness of employment that they experienced in Milwaukee, the Poles quickly formed a tight, self-regulating community. According to Milwaukee police records, for example, the percentage of Poles arrested on all counts between 1884 and 1890 corresponded exactly to their proportion within the city's population, a remarkable fact given the Poles' low socioeconomic position (Table 2). A roster of male House of Correction inhabitants confirms the impression of internal community discipline; of 1,500 inmates in 1885, only ten were of Polish birth.[10]

This is not to say, however, that the new Polish immigrants generally found life to their liking, even as compared to the Old Country. A recent survey of letters written back to Europe in this period stresses the ambivalence of reactions to new conditions, including a sense of bitter disappointment that there was "no freedom in America." Such feelings, no doubt, contributed to a little-studied wave of industrial rebellion from 1882 to 1887 in the form of Polish mobs or crowd action in Detroit, Cleveland, South Bend, and Michigan's Saginaw Valley as well as in Milwaukee.[11]

Initial neglect of the exploding Polish laboring community by the established German radical and trade union organizations was quite predictable. A history of national enmities combined with conflicting cultural and immediate economic interests tended to keep the two groups apart. Milwaukee's secular-minded German trade unionists and Socialists, for example, contrasted with a Polish laboring community that in its struggle for survival had remained closely tied to the Catholic church. Aside from ideology, the rules and regulations of the trades assembly themselves intrinsically operated to exclude the lesser-skilled newcomers.

A craft union like the Amalgamated Association of Iron and Steel Workers, locked as it was in a far-flung battle for control of the new industrial technology, tended to view the immigrants as willing tools of the employers. When in 1876 some Milwaukee Poles were recruited to break a coal-handlers' strike, the incident reinforced suspicions on both sides. The labor movement, therefore, had little to do with the Poles' first assertive steps into the city's political affairs. When August Rudzinski took office as city supervisor in 1878, he became the city's first elected Pole. An emigré from Russia in 1859, Rudzinski had set up a tailoring shop and made army uniforms during the Civil War. By 1880 Rudzinski's Hall, doubling as saloon and meeting room, was a center of political life in what would become the Polish Fourteenth Ward. Rudzinski had also played a leading role in establishing the city's first of three Polish parishes and in organizing the Kosciusko Guards, a company of the state militia, to which prominent members of the Polish-American community might be honored with an appointment as captain. Attorney Francis Borchardt, chief officer of the guard, was elected as the state's first Polish assemblyman in 1882. The following year Rudzinski's twenty-six-year-old son Theodore, who ran a travel agency featuring trips to Hamburg, was elected Milwaukee's first Polish alderman. Both Borchardt and Rudzinski's successes came in the face of the trades assembly tickets that had failed to include any Polish candidates.[12]

EARLY LABOR LEGISLATION

The enactment of new labor laws in the late 19th century—putting limits on picketing and boycotts—reflected the tactics that union leaders and activists were utilizing. Why were the procedures for enforcing the laws so important?

THE revised statutes of 1849 included provisions for the suppression of unlawful assembly and riot. These are still in effect and have on occasion been applied to union activity. The first specific legislation relative to union and employer conflict came in 1887, when three laws were passed concerning blacklisting, boycotting, and picketing. The latter two were part of a general movement to restrain union activities. The 1880's, both nationally and in Wisconsin, were a period of rapid union growth, of strikes, and of interunion conflict. The Wisconsin Commissioner of Labor listed eighty strikes between January, 1885, and September, 1886, half of them occurring in Milwaukee. The first recorded boycott in Wisconsin occurred in 1880 when the printers' union of Milwaukee boycotted an eating house which refused to stop its subscription to a newspaper whose compositors were on strike. Boycotts became very common in the years that followed.

In the anti-boycott law the legislature stated:

Any two or more persons who shall combine, associate, agree, mutually undertake or concert together for the purpose of wilfully or maliciously injuring another in his reputation, trade, business or profession by any means whatsoever, or for the purpose of maliciously compelling another to do or perform any act against his will, or preventing or hindering another from doing or performing any lawful act shall be punished by imprisonment in the county jail for not more than one year or by fine not exceeding five hundred dollars.

The anti-picketing law forbade the use of threats, force, or coercion to prevent any person from working . . . Organized labor made unsuccessful attempts to have these laws repealed. . . .

The third of the 1887 laws was favorable to organized labor. It forbade employers to circulate blacklists or to cooperate in other ways to discriminate against the future employment of workers who were discharged or who voluntarily quit. Employers were also forbidden to require a prospective employe to sign a yellow-dog contract (an agreement not to join a labor organization). The anti-blacklist law was weakened in 1895 by an amendment which stated, "Nothing in this section shall prohibit any employer of labor from giving any other such employer, to whom a discharged employe has applied for employment . . . a truthful statement of the reasons for discharge." Anti-blacklist laws are of doubtful value because of the difficulty of enforcing them.

—GORDON M. HAFERBECKER

From *Wisconsin Labor Laws*
(University of Wisconsin, Madison, 1958).

The Knights of Labor

The growth of the Knights of Labor in Milwaukee accentuated many tendencies evident in the Order nationwide. After a slow beginning the Knights grew in exponential fashion. From early spring 1885 to late spring a year later, a single mixed assembly composed mostly of German printers who had affiliated in 1878 exploded into forty-two assemblies representing some 12,000 members. Initially the Knights' strength and numbers rested squarely on those sections of Milwaukee's working class with a history of labor organization. The universalism of the Knights' message, however, combined with the self activity of the formerly unorganized, quickly intensified the scope of the campaign. The resulting movement within a movement touched off a polarizing confrontation with local industrialists and state authorities. The rise of a sturdy third-party tradition in Milwaukee, ultimately under Socialist direction, may be traced directly to the tumult of the Knights' era. The very strength of the Milwaukee Knights as a social movement, in short, carried a lasting structural impact on local political affairs.

There is no underestimating the Knights' reliance on craft organization in the initial months of their expansion in Milwaukee. Of twenty-six assemblies formed by March 1886, seventeen officially represented specific trades. In addition, some of the other mixed assemblies were, in fact, aggregations of craftsmen like the feeders, heaters, rollers, molders, and nailers who formed a mixed metal trades assembly. Some of the sudden surge to the Knights may be attributed to skilled workplace groups who reorganized at a propitious moment.

The cigar-makers' union, for example, had dwindled to forty members by January 1886. In mid-March Knights' initiatives had so revitalized their movement that the Progressive Cigarmakers' secured an eight-hour day with increased pay, plus a prohibition on lower-paid female and child employment as long as unionized men were out of work. The predominant ethnic make-up of the Order also suggests its strong ties to the city's skilled work force; an Irish Knight of Labor complained that at least eleven assemblies conducted business only in German.[13]

Like the Order's advance elsewhere, the Knights' growth in Milwaukee was experienced as a spiraling momentum, wherein a victory for one group of workers seemed to carry ramifications for all. By October 1885, for example, the Knights were reportedly "whooping things up," alternating weekly enrollment ceremonies with "amusements—readings, recitations, songs, jigs and clog dancing," and discussions of the relations between "capital and labor." When a jeweler marketed nonunion, officially boycotted watches in December, he experienced the Order's power. "Mystic marks were made on the sidewalk and street. His store was full of people that night [with] hundreds standing outside. But not a sale did he make. No one spoke to him or his clerks. Next morning he decamped." In February 1886 a week-long boot-and-shoe strike secured Knights' workers their requested new scale. During the same month the popular German *Herold* caved in to Knights' demands for a union shop. The collective power of the Order was such that the *Herold's* capitulation was due not so much to demands of its own printers but to pressure from striking carpenters upset at its editorial policy. Economic influence also translated into

Labor reformer Robert S. Schilling emerged as a leader of the Knights of Labor in the 1880s.

political currency. Seeking to head off the possibility of another independent labor challenge, Mayor Wallber met with Knights' leaders in February 1886 and endorsed their demands for an eight-hour day for city workers. A month later the demand passed the common council with only one dissenting vote. A few days before the April balloting, the mayor helped assure his reelection by his conspicuous appearance at a comic opera benefit performance for the Knights' Agitation Fund.[14]

Robert Schilling and Henry Smith: Labor Reformers

The political portraits of two key figures in the Milwaukee Knights, state organizer Robert Schilling and future political representative Henry Smith, suggest that one key to a movement that would combine native-Americans with Irish, German, and ultimately also Polish immigrants was an ideological common-denominational Americanism. Robert S. Schilling, brought to the United States from Germany as a young boy, had already established himself as one of America's most influential labor reformers when he became state organizer for the Knights in 1881. He grew up in St. Louis, served an enlistment in the wartime Union Army, trained as an apprentice cooper, and joined the Coopers' Union in 1863. In 1871 the Coopers' International (CIU) elected him its first vice-president, and he moved to Cleveland to edit the union's German-language paper. The coopers' involvement in the late 1860s with the cooperative movement and the National Labor Union (NLU) acquainted Schilling with the world of labor reform. When a few leaders of suffering national trade unions came together in 1874 to create a successor to the NLU, Schilling succeeded to the presidency of the new Industrial Brotherhood. The preamble of this short-lived organization, as drafted by Schilling, became a tenet of faith for both the Knights of Labor and the Populists in later years. It was in the brotherhood that Schilling first met Terence Powderly, five years before Powderly became the Knights' grand master workman. Schilling reportedly joined the Knights himself in 1875, the same year he was elected president of the CIU.

Like other early leaders of the Knights, Schilling jumped enthusiastically into Greenback-Labor politics, serving as Ohio state chairman of the new party until his 1880 move to Milwaukee, where he launched two German-language papers, *Der Reformer* and *Volksblatt*. While attempting to dislodge the national Greenback party from its agrarian and entrepreneurial moorings, Schilling showed more interest in results than in consistent political doctrine. The *Volksblatt*, for example, was friendly to both Karl Marx and Henry George.[15]

Henry Smith likewise established links between an older reform tradition of democratic-minded artisans and manufacturers and the new movement of industrial workers. Smith, as his son would write in 1916, was "pre-eminently a self-made man." Born in Baltimore, Maryland, in 1838, Henry moved with his German-born parents first to Stark County, Ohio, and then to Milwaukee in 1844. By age ten he had already worked summers

UNEMPLOYMENT: THE "TRAMP PROBLEM" IN BELOIT

When wage earners were out of work, they often took to the road in search of employment. But crowds of jobless men sometimes made local communities nervous, as Robert Nesbit found in the case of Beloit.

PUBLIC attitudes in times of stress illustrate the response to the new economic order. In the summer of 1878, Beloit discovered that it had a "tramp problem." Job seekers who commonly sought harvest work, railroad construction jobs, and work in the lumber industry by riding freight trains found themselves in oversupply and meeting hostile responses wherever they congregated. The governor of Iowa had forcibly ejected some, and many gathered in Beloit where they could retreat across the Illinois state line in the event of trouble. Trouble came, in the form of armed guards hired by the C&NW to protect its "private property." An aroused citizenry, which just a few years before had applauded Chief Justice Ryan's decision that railroads where public highways operated by dangerous monopolies meriting regulation, now applauded the railroad's use of employees armed with revolvers and clubs to repel the unemployed. A Madison minister attracted favorable notice in the press with an address on "What Can We Do For The Tramp?" These "scum of the earth" and "robbers of the industrious," he said, were clearly outside the pale of civilized society. "Now, what is our Christian duty to the tramp? *He must be treated with the utmost severity of the law*."[1]

—ROBERT C. NESBIT

From *The History of Wisconsin, Volume III*
(State Historical Society of Wisconsin, Madison, 1985).

as a cattle guard and helper in a tobacco factory. Although his "scholastic training" ended in 1850 after four years in the public schools, Smith loved to read and "ofttimes would pick up scraps of newspapers from the street." In later years he became a student of the Bible ("but no believer"), world history, political economy, and scientific subjects. Smith began his apprenticeship as a bookbinder in 1851 but turned for health reasons to the trade of millwright. By the early 1860s the firm of Smith Brothers, Millwrights, was constructing most of the state's flour mills and many of its tanneries, grain elevators, and malt houses. Together, Henry and his three brothers added numerous improvements to agricultural and industrial machinery, including the roller flour-mill system, pneumatic malting, and the installation of the state's first turbine water wheel.[16]

Smith also applied his mechanical ingenuity to local government. From his election to the city council in 1868, he took the greatest interest in the details of a city waterworks and sewerage system and even invented a special metal cover for sewerage catch-basins. In 1871 he convinced the council to build the city's first iron bridge and thus avoid the continuing repair bills incident to wooden construction. He also expedited the preparation of the Milwaukee River for docking by persuading his father to turn over to the city land use rights around the family flour mill. Elected state assemblyman in 1877 with the support of the Social Democrats (he later claimed he was an independent, not a Socialist), Smith took a leading role in securing Milwaukee's municipal library. A few years later he cooperated with Edward Allis in getting municipal title to a dam for river flushing and port development. By the mid-1880s Henry Smith (elected alderman in 1880, city comptroller in 1882, and re-elected alderman in 1884) was one of the city's most experienced municipal architects. During his term as city comptroller, Smith so advanced the system of municipal bookkeeping that even financier and railroad owner Alexander Mitchell begged the trades' assembly representative to seek reelection.[17]

Smith's guiding star from the late 1860s onward was the philosophy of radical Greenbackism. To the disbelieving eyes of this young Douglas Democrat, the "demonetization act" first proposed in 1869 inflicted "more misery" on "the farmer and laboring man and small businessman . . . than the civil war." Together with the centralizing 1863 National Banking Act, demonetization constituted "the most stupendous piece of class legislation ever perpetrated upon the people"; "it made me a bitter enemy of both the Republican and Democratic parties and I cannot get over that feeling." Starting in the 1870s, Smith always ran on an independent or third-party ticket. He dutifully supported the national candidacies of Peter Cooper, James Weaver, and Ben Butler. In 1885 the radical manufacturer joined a mixed assembly of the Knights of Labor because "its Declaration of Principles coincided with my views as a greenbacker." With their appeal to significant numbers of their fellow German-Americans, the political philosophies of both Schilling and Smith may offer a particular labor variant of Conzen's thesis that "ethnicity for Milwaukee's Germans . . . accompanied rather than precluded Americanization.[18]

As with other social movements the development of the Milwaukee Knights of Labor depended both upon an internal

Interior of the Boone Tire Factory at Chippewa Falls, 1919.

dynamic and the intervention of outside circumstances. By the beginning of 1886 the organization that Schilling led and Smith joined had substantially consolidated and revitalized the traditional roots of trade union strength within the city. Moreover, it was also making gains in places previously ignored by every labor organization. As early as July 1885, Milwaukee District Master Workman and iron molder Timothy Cruise had pointed to "the great army of unskilled labor" as the Order's next target. Formation of two women's assemblies (including one of tailoresses) provided one indication of the important change. Another was evident in the Reliance assembly's admission of predominantly unskilled Polish workers; 618 men joined the Order in a single day. By mid-March 1886 the Reliance's 1,600 workers formed the country's largest Knights' assembly, part of a 3,000-man Milwaukee contingent of organized metal trades workers. In addition, 1,000 Polish workers, drawn mostly from Bay View plants, had joined the Polonia assembly. The crucial opening for the less skilled iron workers seems to have been stimulated by the stalemated end of a nine-month strike and lockout of Bay View nailers in February, a struggle that graphically demonstrated the weaknesses of skilled Amalgamated iron workers acting alone. Labor's 1885-86 expansion thus ultimately depended on lowering the tailgate to the Knights' bandwagon.[19]

Polish Workers and the Knights

Acceptance of the Knights by Polish workers, in particular, was aided by the efforts of a group of liberal Polish nationalists asso-

ciated with the weekly *Krytyka*. The newspaper was an early manifestation of what would become by the early 1900s a bitter dispute within the Polish-American middle class over the hegemony of the Catholic church hierarchy in the affairs of Polonia.

The activities of *Krytyka* publisher Michael Kruszka and editor Anton Parysso suggest the degree to which American domestic issues shaped the positions of lay leaders, whose efforts have usually been defined in relation to the struggle for restoration of the European homeland or to resentment against Irish (and in Milwaukee, German) control of the American Catholic church. Kruszka had emigrated to New Jersey in 1880 at age twenty from an uncommonly well-educated family of landholding peasants. Already something of a rebel in German Posen, he had been disciplined in school for insisting on speaking Polish. After working in a sewing machine factory in Elizabeth, New Jersey, and trying his luck as an insurance agent in Bayonne, Kruszka moved to Milwaukee in 1883 to set type in a small print shop. Parysso was a man of middle-class family and considerable education. With a background as a revolutionary "nihilist," he appeared, even to friends, as "occasionally indiscreet in his utterances respecting the Church and labor organization." It was no accident that *Krytyka* spread to 3,500 Polish readers in the same period that the Knights of Labor were themselves attracting Polish workers. From the beginning, Parysso served as a paid Knights' organizer. Kruszka, too, soon became an officer of the Polonia assembly. As early as 1886 *Krytyka* was known as the official "organ of the Polish Knights of Labor."[20] ∎

From *Workingmen's Democracy: The Knights of Labor*
(University of Illinois, Urbana, 1985).

The Bay View Tragedy

ROBERT C. NESBIT

One of the saddest episodes in Wisconsin labor history occurred when several workers and others were shot by militia during a labor disturbance in Bay View, an industrial area on Milwaukee's south side. In this section, Robert Nesbit provides a setting for the Bay View tragedy. He describes why workers began to view themselves as "a separate class," how the "ethnic pecking order" among workers functioned in the local labor market, and how disagreements over political strategies often fragmented labor's power.

THE growing body of industrial workers in the 1880's came to a heightened consciousness of itself as a separate class. This consciousness had much to do with the sense of insecurity in dealing with employers, who hired toilers by scores and hundreds in factories and workshops where a minority of skilled workers directed the labors of those who provided mostly muscle or simply a pair of hands. Employers were equally insecure in a fiercely competitive economy subject to rapid technological changes and expansion of the marketing areas of the lowest-cost producers. It was a deflationary period which, in turn, hit the rural debtor particularly hard—moderating sympathy for the urban wage earner, who lived in a different world. Wisconsin industries were vulnerable to the frequent sinking spells experienced by the general economy, as well as more specific slow times that were often the lot of such major employers or customers as lumbering, railroad building, iron mining, milling, or grain farming.

The general society seemed more sympathetic to the insecurity of the entrepreneur-employer than to the worker who had only his daily labor to sell. Certainly the notion of the sanctity of private property and the right of the employer to control absolutely the terms of employment—as an extension of his private property—was widely accepted. This is scarcely surprising in a population that was mostly rural, property-owning, and subject to the vagaries of weather and markets.

Governor Jeremiah Rusk, probably the most effective politician to hold the office before Robert La Follette, understood the limits of respectable opinion in this regard. An immediate test came during his first weeks in office, when the failure of the latest recipient of the St. Croix land grant, the Air Line Railroad, left 1,700 construction workers stranded in the wilderness of northwestern Wisconsin. To pleas from the contractors for militia to control the desperate men, Rusk replied that these men needed bread, not bayonets. He dispatched relief and managed the eventual restitution of the state's costs and the men's wages from the solvent successor to the eternally

troublesome grant. Rusk's biographer editorially concluded that his " timely action was of more practical benefit . . . than all the demagoguery and buncombe of the professional agitators who live off the workingmen . . . ," thus putting in bold relief the prevailing opinion.[1]

But Governor Rusk was also the one who on May 5, 1886, directed the militia during the culmination of the Eight Hour Day agitation in Bay View—the day after the Haymarket bombing in Chicago. When the officer in command at the Bay View Iron Works reported that the "mob" was approaching, Rusk reportedly ordered him by telephone: "Very well, sir. Fire on them." This the militia did, with devastating effect.[2]

Obstacles to Collective Action

The history of Wisconsin's industrial workers' efforts to achieve collective action, whether by individual shop organizations, trade and industrial unions, broad federations of all such organizations, or united political action, paralleled the general fate of labor movements at the time. They sometimes enjoyed limited success in prosperous times, only to lose ground and generally disappear in the frequent depressions and recessions which characterized the period 1873-1893. The Knights of Labor, a national organization that flourished in the 1880's, enjoyed broad but shallow popular support. The vicissitudes of the economy, judges who automatically equated unions with conspiracy, and a public that found the words "strike," "boycott," and "riot" interchangeable, only begin the litany of obstacles to collective action. Industrial workers were a part of the general public and many shared these attitudes. However, at the peak of its strength as a popular movement, the Knights of Labor claimed a Wisconsin membership of 30,000. The enthusiasm generated during the months before that May Day "riot" to challenge the status quo with strikes, boycotts, and mass demonstrations was certainly unique.[3]

There appears not to have been any appreciable shortage of workers—even of those with particular skills—in Wisconsin

Bridge under construction in Milwaukee, 1905.

J. Robert Taylor/State Historical Society of Wisconsin WHi (X3)45312

industry at this time. The cities continued to attract many immigrants, who were joined by a flow of young people from rural areas. A common refrain in news stories about strikes—which were usually spontaneous actions in individual shops—was that the employer immediately filled their places with no difficulty.[4]

The ethnic pecking order which characterized most large plants in Milwaukee and elsewhere made common action difficult. German, British, and Scandinavian skilled workers, who were more union-conscious than Americans, assumed that Poles, Italians, and other latecomers were incapable of sustained union activity, and thus were readily available to employers as strikebreakers. Women and children in industry bore much the same reputation.[5]

As was illustrated in the Eau Claire "Sawdust War" of 1881, strike actions by other than established, disciplined unions of skilled workers were usually spontaneous in character, lacked competent leadership, had little chance of success without the cooperation of the skilled workers, readily attracted outsiders eager to fill the jobs, and commonly ended in ugly confrontations. Unless the employer capitulated immediately, the strikers usually faced a choice between either overt action (which would bring the police and courts and even the militia to the employer's aid) or a rapid melting away of their supporters (and the loss of their jobs to others). Picketing and boycotts were considered illegal activities. As Judge James A. Mallory

put the case to striking cigar makers when their employer readily recruited replacements: " . . . [T]hey had an undoubted right to strike, if the conditions . . . did not suit them, but they had no right to hang around the shop they had left and intimidate those who wanted to work." Associations of employers to implement lockouts, import strikebreakers, or establish blacklists were looked upon with equanimity. The legal system did not offer much leverage to workers.[6]

The Sons of Vulcan, the skilled ironworkers' union at the Milwaukee Iron Works in Bay View, was one of the strongest unions in its ability to sustain discipline and win concessions. Iron reduction, unlike steelmaking, involved operations dependent upon highly skilled labor. The Sons of Vulcan were mostly of British origin and had little in common with the numerous unskilled workers who shared the unpleasant conditions of the seventy-two-hour week and the heat, noise, and hazards of the workplace for about one-fifth the wages. It was unskilled Poles who met the militia's gunfire on May 5, 1886, as they crossed over the boundary of Bay View Village from their enclave on Milwaukee's South Side. The Sons of Vulcan were inside the plant, taking no part in the Eight Hour Day agitation and unwilling to join the general work stoppage.[7]

Not the least of the troubles of Wisconsin's industrial workers was their lack of common agreement on means and goals. This was the proper function of leadership. Competence and a practical approach to the problems at hand did not necessarily accompany the attributes of bilingualism and commanding pres-

Paul Grottkau organized the Central Labor Union to recruit unskilled workers in Milwaukee.

State Historical Society of Wisconsin WHi (X3) 24593

ence. By 1893, Victor Berger and Frank Weber, the architects of Milwaukee socialism and of the Wisconsin Federation of Labor (AF of L), provided the competence and practical sense in these roles. But earlier, leaders vied for center stage in the noisy struggles leading to the Eight Hour Day riots in Milwaukee, the climactic Bay View incident, and its aftermath.[8]

Robert Schilling

The career of Robert Schilling, who was the principal leader of the Wisconsin Knights of Labor through the eighties, may well stand as a metaphor for the trials of industrial labor in those tumultuous years. His was the most persuasive voice arguing for a community of purpose and action. He considered race, nationality, and religion irrelevant bars to participation in a common cause. His bluff honesty, general good nature, and readiness to seek sensible compromise gave him a central role wherever such a solution was possible. But he was essentially an orator and publicist, not much interested in organizational details, who readily mistook the word for the deed. Schilling started as a trade unionist, but soon found third-party politics more congenial; he always welcomed an opportunity to turn a labor union into a base for political action. No radical, he was a pragmatist whose talents were not disturbed by the tenets of any coherent philosophy. Schilling achieved nationwide prominence as the national secretary of the People's (Populist) party at its 1892 convention in Omaha. The Milwaukee *Sentinel* wryly noted prior to the Omaha convention: "Robert Schilling has held his usual state convention and has decided to call his party the People's party this year. It continues to be the old Greenback and free coinage party, however, and smells just as sweet with one name as another."

Schilling is a neglected figure in Wisconsin history, usually given only passing mention as one of the leaders of the Eight Hour Day agitation in 1886 and for his role in Milwaukee third party politics immediately before and after. While the Wisconsin Knights of Labor centered in the metropolis, where it had fully half of its membership at its peak, Schilling became a familiar figure in Wisconsin lumber centers and other industrial cities as the state organizer for the Knights, as a union negotiator, and as an accomplished stump speaker. In a day when political oratory ranked high as public entertainment—and could be piped into the home only on paper—Schilling provided it in both forms. He normally edited a minimum of two weeklies, in German and/or English, and was fluent in both. He often boasted of the distances he traveled and the number of speeches he had given in a day. Many Wisconsinites, in the 1880's and 1890's, readily recognized references to "Old Bob," and they did not mean La Follette but "Old Bob" Schilling.[9]

Robert Schilling came to this country from Saxony at age three and left school to go to work at thirteen after his father died. He apprenticed as a cooper in St. Louis in a shop serving the brewing industry. It was a trade shortly threatened by machine-made barrel staves. As skilled workers requiring a relatively lengthy apprenticeship, the coopers had a national union of some consequence. Schilling—fluent in German and English, an avid reader, and a competent public speaker—rose within the Coopers' International Union, which had had problems recruiting German-speaking members. Martin Foran, head of the Coopers' International, brought Schilling to Cleveland. The two men were compatible, since both looked beyond their trade to the general problems of workingmen in an industrial society increasingly dominated by large employers. Cleveland was the home of the Standard Oil Company, which could afford the expensive machinery for fabricating barrel staves to be assembled by coopers who had only modest skills. Ohio was also a hotbed of greenbackism, a monetary theory and hopeful basis for agrarian and urban labor political co-operation. Foran and Schilling were leaders in various efforts to organize industrial unions that would recruit across the lines of trades, skills, and occupations. A problem was that these efforts usually attracted theoretical reformers rather than rank-and-file members. Schilling was certainly inclined to think in terms of third-party platforms.[10]

The times were ripe for an organization to reach beyond the existing trade unions. The far from inevitable instrument for change was the Knights of Labor. What made the Knights different was that during its first seven years (1869-1876) the order, centered in Philadelphia, was controlled by pure and simple unionists who sought closer ties among the various craft unions but did not reach out to the unskilled as well. They professed no aims to rebuild American society and made no provisions to take in other than craftsmen and industrial workers. Given the problems of the times for unions, the order adopted the trappings of secrecy and ritual common to the popular fraternal organizations of the day. By 1878 however, the professional reformers had moved in on the Knights . . . .[11]

In the summer of 1880, Schilling moved to Oshkosh to join the editorial staff of the *Standard,* a greenback paper backed by Edward P. Allis and other substantial greenbackers. The Oshkosh connection was a brief one. He shortly moved to Milwaukee to edit a German-language weekly, *Der Reformer,* for the local greenbackers. Milwaukee remained his home. He went to his first Wisconsin convention of the Greenback party about the time of his move to Milwaukee, where he took his accustomed place on the platform resolutions committee. The platform produced was pure Schilling, featuring quotations from Aristotle, Lincoln, Webster, Jefferson, President Grant, Edward P. Allis, and Republican and Democratic platforms that had wobbled on hard money.[12]

The 1881 gubernatorial campaign was the last hurrah for the Greenback party in Wisconsin. Over his own objections, Allis was given the nomination and received about 4 per cent of the vote. Casting about for a constituency to support *Der Reformer*, Schilling's eye fell upon the union movement. He wrote his old friend, Terence Powderly, now national president of the Knights of Labor, who renewed his commission as an organizer for the order. Schilling wasted no time in reviving the Milwaukee Knights Assembly and attempting to steer it towards political action.[13]

Milwaukee labor history becomes intricate at this point. Interest in union activity was renewing rapidly, but the potential leadership was more interested in political activity than in practical unionism. The political action virus was endemic among those who specialized in editing union newspapers, composing union constitutions, and writing resolutions for reviving unions and trades assemblies.[14]

In 1885 everything began to break at once for Schilling. That summer, the Knights temporarily won recognition in a strike against the southwestern railroads controlled by Jay Gould. This short-lived triumph was largely responsible for the tremendous growth of the Knights in 1885 and 1886. At the same time, Schilling was making important gains outside Milwaukee. Michigan had passed a ten-hour workday law for industry. Across the river in Marinette, an eleven-hour day was standard, and the workers organized, preparing to strike. Schilling, who agreed with Powderly's rejection of the strike as a useful weapon, hurried to offer his services as arbitrator. It was a mark of his conservatism, despite his oratory about heartless monopolists or the inequity of the national money system, that Schilling's services were so readily accepted by both sides. His mediation efforts resulted in a settlement of a ten-hour day for ten hours' pay and some wage concessions, but the mill owners were adamant against any real recognition of the workers' unions.[15]

Schilling's reputation was enhanced by the Marinette settlement, and calls came from around the state to organize new Knights assemblies. The Knights rapidly became the principal voice of labor in most Wisconsin cities and many lumber towns. Schilling's speeches had changed very little over the past ten years—sounding fiery when condemning monopoly and the "money power," but repeatedly counseling against violence and strikes. Unlike Powderly, he was prepared to use the boycott as a weapon, confident of his ability to sway public opinion. Conservatives feared him, but he was infinitely preferable to his immediate rivals.[16]

Schilling was also at odds with Powderly because of his enthusiastic acceptance of the growing eight-hour-day agitation. This was an old rallying cry that had excited occasional interest and support over the past quarter-century. In 1884 the Federation of Organized Trades and Labor Unions, from which emerged the American Federation of Labor two years later, had

Interest in union activity was renewing rapidly in 1885, but the potential leadership was more interested in political activity than in practical unionism.

declared that the eight-hour day would become a fact by united action on May 1, 1886. The Knights inherited this impractical pledge as the ascendant labor organization at the time. Powderly wanted no trouble from this dubious promise, and suggested that local members write essays on the eight-hour day to be published on Washington's birthday. Somehow, this seemed to fall short of the popular expectation. So popular was the eight-hour-day idea with the rapidly growing rank and file of the Knights in Milwaukee that Schilling could not resist promoting it. Early in 1886, he formally organized the Eight Hour League in Milwaukee.[17]

A problem that continually plagued Schilling was that his left flank was exposed. A German expatriate socialist, Paul Grottkau, with roots in European anarchism (though he broke with the anarchists before Haymarket), moved to Milwaukee in March, 1886, where he edited the German socialist paper *Arbeiter-Zeitung*. Grottkau positioned himself to the left of the majority of German socialists but to the right of those willing to espouse violent action. He organized the Central Labor Union, which recruited actively among unskilled workers, although it also included some local craft unions. In numbers, the Central Labor Union had less than half as many members as Schilling's Milwaukee assembly of the Knights of Labor. Both organizations had substantial Polish contingents. This would be of some significance in the light of later events.[18]

Grottkau spoke for the majority of the German socialists, but the active members had undergone the usual schisms. Frank Hirth, a cigar maker who had edited socialist newspapers in Detroit and Chicago, had adopted the anarchistic doctrines which Grottkau had earlier rejected. Most of the public did not distinguish between socialism and anarchism. Hirth was prominent in a small faction that advocated violence against the "bosses" and the system. They were noisy participants at Eight Hour League general meetings, particularly heckling Schilling for his lack of militancy.[19]

Schilling's part in the Eight Hour League was compromised by Master Workman Powderly's hostility towards the whole idea. Grottkau and Hirth successfully challenged Schilling's leadership, calling for a mass confrontation with employers on May 1, 1886. Schilling began looking for a way out. Late in February, the League held a hugely successful mass meeting at the West Side Turner Hall, with an estimated 3,000 in attendance. The purpose was to put pressure on the city common council to approve a resolution to adopt an eight-hour rule for all day laborers working for the city or on municipal projects. Schilling, who had become a friend of the Republican mayor, Emil Wallber, persuaded him to endorse the resolution. Shortly thereafter, the council adopted the resolution with only one dissenting vote, but it made no provision for enforcement.[20]

The action by the city council was advanced by Schilling as evidence that the triumph of the eight-hour day would be accomplished simply by the mobilization of public opinion and continued peaceful pressure. He predicted that this would come about by May first without the proposed general strike. This led to angry exchanges with the radicals, who scoffed at his timidity. Grottkau's new Central Labor Union had joined the Eight Hour League, and it now took over its direction as Schilling and the Knights' Milwaukee Central Committee, under pressure from Powderly, forced all but three of the thirty-seven local assemblies to abstain from participation in the proposed general strike action.[21] In Wisconsin, the strike threat in support of the eight-

EMPLOYER RIGHTS

In his description of the rights of employers, Robert Nesbit exposes the fundamentally unequal relationship between management and wage laborers before the formation of unions.

THE employer possessed all of the advantages in dealing with labor. There was no limit, other than the relative efficiency of his operations, upon his right to hire and fire at will. With the premises and necessary equipment centralized under his control, the employer defined all of the terms of employment: hours, wages, standards of production, work rules, conditions of the workplace, and so forth. He was free to discriminate in any way he might choose: to exclude on the basis of ethnic origin, religion, presumed attitudes, or suspected union activity; or to proscribe certain behavior ranging from conversation on the job to drinking on any occasion. This control extended beyond the limits of the plant, particularly in an isolated lumber town where the political and economic activities of the community were commonly assumed to be the principal employer's business. There he frequently owned much of the housing and the general store, and was free to pay in scrip, rent, or room and board. Proscription of "troublemakers" could extend beyond the community by means of the familiar blacklist. Even in the Milwaukee tanneries, for instance, it was accepted practice that a man needed a recommendation from his previous employer to transfer from one tannery to another.

—ROBERT C. NESBIT

*From The History of Wisconsin, Volume III
(State Historical Society of Wisconsin, Madison, 1985).*

hour agitation was almost entirely confined to Milwaukee. Most of the city's industries depended upon a corps of skilled operatives who exhibited some organization and militancy, but who usually dealt with individual employers rather than engaging in general strike actions. The rapid growth of the Knights in 1886, plus the eight hour-day agitation, added a new element—industrial unionism—to labor relations in the city.[22]

Schilling was an opportunist driven swiftly by events, which he tried to influence. The Knights grew so rapidly in the spring of 1886—not alone in Milwaukee—that his days and nights were filled with engagements to speak and organize new chapters. He had little time to contemplate strategies or concentrate upon particular situations. It must have been largely fortuitous that he played a personal role in two Milwaukee strikes that were industry-wide in character, and involved industries particularly vulnerable to working-class pressure.

The Milwaukee cigar makers had engaged in a protracted strike in 1881-1882 that had broken the union and left bitter factionalism behind. The local of the International Cigar Makers was reviving at the same time that Schilling was recruiting a Knights assembly among cigar makers. The competing unions were about evenly matched in membership. The largest cigar-manufacturing firm struck a bargain with the international, abandoning a settlement being negotiated with the Knights. Schilling invoked a boycott, on which the conventional judicial view was that this constituted an illegal conspiracy, and some of the cigar makers went out on strike.[23]

The breweries presented a different type of target. Their employees worked unconscionably long hours for straight wages—often as many as thirteen hours a day with some Sunday work expected. But much of this work, especially for those involved directly with the brewing process, was leisurely. There were also traditional privileges, such as free beer on the job. An old trade association existed among Milwaukee brewery workers—primarily a relief and benefit lodge, which was typical in the seventies. Schilling was especially effective in organizing brewery workers. Their standard language was German; coopers were involved both as employees and suppliers; and the nine Milwaukee breweries had a total payroll of "no less than 3,000 men."

Early in 1886 the brewery workers won substantial concessions from the brewers, who presented a united front. Working hours were reduced to ten and general raises totaling over 10 percent were offered, to become effective on May first. Stunned by their easy victory—the brewers recognized a popular movement and knew who consumed their product—the brewery workers decided to hold out for their original demands and a closed shop. These concessions were not made. The men walked out on May 1, the Saturday when the eight-hour-day excitement began, adding to the crowds. The brewers conceded again on the wage demands but not on the closed shop. The men went back to work on May 6, the day after the shootings at Bay View.[24]

The Allis Reliance Works was organized as one of the largest (1,600 members) Knights of Labor assemblies. A senior molder was the spokesman, who doubtless felt that he and his men could strike a bargain on wages and hours without advice

National Guard troops marshalled at the Allis Reliance Works in Milwaukee during the eight-hour-day movement strikes in May, 1886.

State Historical Society of Wisconsin WHi (X3) 49572

or assistance from others. In April, 1886, the negotiations with Edward P. Allis shortly came to an impasse. Allis agreed to an eight-hour day, but in a reasoned reply he also told his men that he could not compete on the basis of ten hours' pay for the eight-hour day. He agreed to some minor adjustments in pay for the common labor, but said he would simply shut down and await better times if the other workers insisted upon an eight-hour day at ten hours' wages.[25]

A committee of employees met with Allis and reported back that it was satisfied with his explanations. An initial meeting accepted these findings, but a subsequent meeting with a smaller attendance, which was evidently dominated by Grottkau's followers, repudiated the agreement. Bad blood developed between the two opposing factions. On May 1, there was a walkout of 150 men from the foundry, about 10 per cent of the work force. Allis said that he understood that these men were simply exhibiting solidarity with the eight-hour-day movement and would return on Monday. As May 1 was a Saturday, a general holiday atmosphere pervaded the city and many workers failed to report or left early.[26]

Schilling was concerned with the growing militancy of his abandoned creation, the Eight Hour League. There were

crowds in the streets on Saturday, May first, and a grand parade and general meeting planned for the following day at the Milwaukee Garden, a large beer garden in the old German quarter west of the Milwaukee River. Schilling arranged a meeting for Monday night, May third, inviting businessmen and labor representatives to the West Side Turner Hall. His speech offered no practical alternatives and was simply a plea for calm. It received no particular notice in the press. Events had moved beyond his power to influence them. And Monday had offered more excitement than another speech from Schilling. Protesters invaded the Chicago, Milwaukee & St. Paul Railway car shops, attempting to shut them down, and part of the work force at the Bay View iron works went out. Also, Governor Rusk arrived in town on Monday night in case he was needed.[27]

After the Sunday demonstration at the Milwaukee Garden, which was huge but orderly, the Milwaukee Journal acknowledged that the fears of many had not been realized, but deplored the leadership that had come to the fore since the withdrawal of the Knights from the Eight Hour League. The paper estimated that there were 10,000 men on strike by May 1, but aside from the brewery and cigar makers, most of the strikers were from less concentrated industries: tailors, carpenters, coal yard hands, German bakers, broommakers, brickyard employees, and slaughterhouse hands.[28]

A mob of several hundred men had appeared at the CM&StP car shops just before noon on Monday, the third. Late

arrivals kept coming until the number mounted from an estimated 300— identified as mostly Poles by the Milwaukee
Journal—to possibly 1,500, all milling about in the sprawling
shops. They jostled workmen at the machines, yelling and
threatening. Some carried sticks, and a few knives were in evidence. But the only violence occurred when a group tried to
reach the offices above the shop floor and a shop foreman
grabbed one of the interlopers and threw him down the stairs.
The group retreated.

The railroad shop men did not welcome their deliverers,
whom they clearly considered their social inferiors. Some wanted to attack the interlopers, but cooler heads prevailed. The
workmen were directed to lay down their tools and go home to
await a call. The sides were about evenly matched, because the
order to go home had released another 1,800 to become spectators. Some sheriff's deputies appeared but were helpless in the
face of the numbers involved and the extent of the shops. The
company brought in hired guards from outside, and their own
employees volunteered as "special police." Most employees
were back at work the following afternoon.[29]

The incident at the car shops was not an isolated one.
Euphoric with their assumed success there, some members of
the crowd moved on to the Allis Reliance Works where they
were repelled by fire hoses and strong words from the belliger-
ent skilled workers. Another gang of about 200 Bohemian lumber shovers was also roaming the Menomonee Valley, closing
down the lumber yards. Brewery workers from the West Side,
estimated at about 650, passed over the Sixth Street bridge and
marched down National Avenue to the Falk Brewery. The Falk
workers had not gone out with the general brewery strike. This
crowd was met by Sheriff George Paschen and deputies, plus
Major George Traeumer and Adjutant Otto Falk of the Fourth
Battalion. A committee was allowed to parley with the Falk
workers, who refused to strike on this occasion.[30]

Governor Rusk was to emerge as the hero of the riots. He
was a military man who had risen to the command of the
Twenty-Fifth Wisconsin Infantry during the Civil War and had
been mustered out with the rank of brevet brigadier general.
Rusk played the role of professional veteran to the hilt. He often
traveled to Grand Army of the Republic affairs with a "staff" of
"maimed heroes" which the press seldom failed to note. Rusk's
adjutant general, Chandler P. Chapman of Madison, aided by
Charles King of Milwaukee, had reorganized the national guard
into a force of some 2,400 officers and men.[31]

Charles King, like his father Rufus who had made the
Sentinel a power in Republican politics, was a West Point graduate, but had seen most of his service after the Civil War in
Indian campaigns in the Southwest. Invalided out in 1879, he
joined the Wisconsin National Guard as inspector and instructor. In this capacity, King took no pains to hide his ultra-nativist
views or his opinion that Milwaukee harbored a population
"from whose dregs can be swept up . . . a mob [on] whom it
might be a municipal blessing to fire . . . ." Strikes by laborers,
he held, could only be the work of "designing demagogues" or
"temporary insanity."[32]

Governor Rusk was watching the situation in Milwaukee.
He distrusted Wallber and Paschen, the German mayor and

THE FOUNDING OF THE WISCONSIN STATE FEDERATION OF LABOR, 1893

*While individual unions sought to organize
the local workplace, they often found that their
ability to have an impact at the state or federal
level was very limited. By banding together in
a statewide federation of labor organizations,
local unions hoped to make their voices heard
in the state capitol in Madison and in
Washington, D.C.*

IN June of 1893, thirty-five union activists met at Fraternity
Hall in Milwaukee for three days of debate and action. A
brief look at the groups sending delegates gives us a snap-
shot of the kind of jobs that existed near the turn of the century. Delegates included brewery workers, carpenters, cigar
makers, coal heavers, coopers, electrical workers, furniture
workers, horseshoers, iron molders, plasterers, tanners,
trunk makers, typographers and machine woodworkers.
Delegates from six central labor councils — Ashland,
Madison, Marinette, Milwaukee, Oshkosh and West
Superior — also attended.

Frank J. Weber, an AFL state organizer who also served
as president of the Milwaukee Federated Trades Council
(founded in 1887), was generally regarded as the driving
force behind the WSFL convention. At age 43, Weber had
worked as an organizer for more than 20 years in a variety of
occupations and locations. He had recently returned from a
successful assignment with striking mineworkers in West
Virginia and had also been a key figure in establishing several AFL central labor bodies in Wisconsin. A populist in the
1880s and early 1890s, Weber was moving toward the
socialist persuasion at the time of the founding convention.
Yet Weber always maintained an ability to communicate with
all the various factions within organized labor, thus helping
to preserve unity during the 23-year period in which he
served as the leader of the WSFL.

At the convention, speeches were the most important
form of communication. They were offered in English and
German, reflecting the strong German presence, especially
among brewery workers. Speakers at the founding convention
included Weber and Victor Berger, the socialist leader and
editor of the German newspaper, *Vorwaerts* ("Forward"). A
professor from the state college at Milwaukee, a couple of
lawyers, and a minister also addressed the delegates. Often
the speechmaking continued into the wee hours of the morning. The delegates set the per capita tax at 1 cent per month,
elected Frank Weber president, and allowed him $5 per day

Frank J. Weber, 1923, principal founder of the Wisconsin State Federation of Labor. Weber is seated at his desk in the Assembly chambers of the State Capitol where he served for years.

when he was acting as in this capacity. Frederick Brockhausen was elected secretary-treasurer.

The State Federation's Program

The 15-point program adopted by the delegates revealed an emphasis on traditional forms of solidarity as well as a new orientation toward independent political action. For the first time, organized labor had become an important player in Wisconsin politics. Reflecting divergent political opinions among the delegates, the platform combined elements of socialism, populism, and traditional union solidarity. Principle number one described the ballot as "labor's most effective weapon." Number two called for universal suffrage, including women. Compulsory public school attendance for children along with free books came next followed by the prohibition of child labor. Number five emphasized the need for health and safety inspection laws to curb occupational injuries and fatalities. The next principle called for the repeal of state laws prohibiting boycotts. Number eight called for the eight-hour day. Principle number nine advocated the abolishment of the banking system in favor of a government-run bank. Number ten called for the government to take over the railroads, telephones and telegraphs and run them for the people. Street railways, gas, electricity,

and water supplies would be properties of the municipalities. Number 12 advocated initiative and referenda for making state laws. Number 13 called for all immigrant workers who were union members to be able to become citizens and vote. Principles fourteen and fifteen criticized the use of Pinkerton spies against unions and called upon workers to avoid the militia and refuse to fire on fellow workers during labor disputes.

In retrospect, the platform could be described as being both visionary and practical. While all the socialistic proposals were not enacted, some of them were, such as municipal control of utilities. Universal suffrage, public education, child labor and health and safety laws, and the eight-hour-day were at least partially achieved over the course of the last century.

The WSFL platform also provides insight into the creative way the new federation's leaders approached the thorny question of how to sustain a day-to-day struggle for incremental reform without losing sight of an ultimately radical goal of changing the economic system. In a sense, the WSFL platform prefigured the rather unique political strategy that came to be known as "Milwaukee socialism." Across the country, unions were often sharply divided between those who sought radical political activity to overthrow the system and others who favored an evolutionary, bread-and-butter unionism. Leaders of the WSFL, however, struck a balance between the political and economic struggles and called upon unionists to participate in union and party activities and not to let one institution dominate the other.[2]

As the years passed, the sweeping goals envisioned by the first delegates never materialized, but the WSFL played a major role in winning pathbreaking reforms which benefitted all workers in the state. The Federation also took up the cause of women's suffrage (when it was still unpopular), led a campaign to organize industrial workers in the 1930s, and proposed a strategy for repairing the growing rift between the AFL and the CIO.

At a time when the national AFL generally opposed state intervention in labor relations, the WSFL conducted an active legislative and political program. The goal was to use state power to change the relationship between labor and management in ways that would enhance unionism, promote collective bargaining, and build industrial democracy.[3] One result of this strategy was the enactment of social and labor legislation that served as models for other states and the federal government. These reforms included workers compensation, unemployment insurance, and laws to prohibit "yellow dog" contracts, outlaw labor spies and limit the use of injunctions in labor disputes.

—DARRYL HOLTER

THE VERY FIRST KOHLER STRIKE, 1897

THE strikes of 1934 and 1954 at Kohler are relatively well known, but few are aware that there was an earlier strike at Kohler, Hayssen & Stehn Manufacturing Company. On March 13, 1897, about 75 molders who belonged to the Molders' Union No. 286, left their work, protesting a 50 percent cut in wages. . . The molders' strike of 1897 dragged on from March into the fall. . .

The men organized marches about the city and picketed the foundry by parading around it every evening and "escorting" home the men who continued to work at the plant. The paper admitted that there had been no "overt" acts by the strikers and one of them, arrested on charges of assault and battery during the summer, was acquitted of the charges. . .

". . . The strikers claim they can stay out for years because the union pays a married man $7.00 per week and a single man they pay $5.00 per week," *The Sheboygan Herald* had written on July 3, 1897, but by fall the strike was given up.

—WALTER H. UPHOFF

From *Kohler on Strike: Thirty Years of Conflict* (Beacon, Boston, 1967).

county sheriff, on whose appeal he had to depend for any official call for aid. He was in touch with presumably more reliable witnesses, such as Colonel King and other prominent Milwaukeeans. King warned the governor that the pawn shops were being emptied of guns as the Reds prepared to take over the city. But a more practical man had set things in motion for the governor. When Alexander Mitchell, president of the CM&StP, found that his car shops had been closed by the strikers, he summoned Governor Rusk to the scene on a special train placed at his disposal. Rusk arrived that evening, Monday, May 3, and established his headquarters at the Plankinton House.[33]

Early on Tuesday morning, the fourth, the action shifted to the rolling mills at Bay View. A largely Polish crowd had assembled at St. Stanislaus Church, about a mile and a half away, to march on the mills and close them down. They were ready to set off by 8:00 A.M. Not long after, Mayor Wallber appeared at Schilling's door to persuade him to intervene. Sheriff Paschen had also sent a message to the same effect. Having persuaded all but three of the thirty-seven Milwaukee assemblies of the Knights to officially withdraw from the Eight Hour League, Schilling had become the voice of reason by contrast with Paul Grottkau and others now vying for leadership of the popular movement. Schilling was memorialized by banners carried in the May Day parade: "Humbug, your name is Robert."[34]

Schilling arrived at Bay View to find a crowd surrounding the superintendent of the plant, who was not succeeding very well with his explanations of why the skilled laborers inside

were not particularly interested in the eight-hour-day proposal. There were some hard words. The size of the crowd, estimated at over 1,000 men, caused understandable concern. The *Sentinel* described the superintendent, John C. Parkes, as standing in their midst with a big Pole at one side, a burly Pole on the other, a stout Pole behind, and a Samson Pole in front. Fortunately, the master workman of the Polonia Assembly was on hand, as he had been the day before, trying to calm things down. He seemed to be a minority of one.[35]

The crowd, recognizing Schilling, turned more good-natured, and agreed that he should head a delegation to go inside the plant and parley with the Sons of Vulcan. This delegation was just returning, with Schilling earnestly advising Parkes to close down, when the first contingent of the National Guard arrived by train near the front gate. Schilling, always confident of his ability to sway a crowd, was furious. In Schilling's absence, Sheriff Paschen had gauged the mood of the strikers and observed among them some who had been at the car shops the day before. Some were armed with clubs. He ordered them to disperse, and they asked him to repeat it in German. When he did so, the strikers answered, "Wir wollen nicht." The sheriff, fearing worse trouble, went to the phone and formally requested Governor Rusk to send the militia. When the troops first arrived, as the sheriff later stated, "The effect was magical . . . the turbulent mob was turned into quite an orderly assemblage." Then the Kosciusko Guard arrived, and came in last—a mistake, said the sheriff.[36]

The scene that followed had much to do with the events of the next day. The guardsmen were forced to detrain and form ranks in the midst of the crowd. To make matters worse, the Kosciusko Guards were fellow Poles whose regular meeting place was in the parish school of St. Stanislaus. The strikers were more than threatening. Some grabbed for the soldiers' weapons, struck them from behind, and treated them to a shower of missiles. Captain Francis Borchardt was struck in the head by a stone. As the Kosciusko Guard reached the plant gate, five or six in the rear rank, without orders, turned and fired above the crowd. The strikers did not disperse, but the action brought some caution to the boldest, and they held their ground for some hours. The portentous Haymarket bomb exploded in Chicago that same evening.[37]

While the militia was moving in at the rolling mills, other events were unfolding in the city. Another mass meeting of strikers was taking place at the Milwaukee Garden on, the German West Side. Paul Grottkau advised them that they had the power to close down the city. A large group formed and marched to the Brand and Company stove works, about three-quarters of a mile east near the Milwaukee River, and forced the plant to shut down. They were then within a few blocks of the Plankinton House where Governor Rusk had his headquarters. This, plus the news from Bay View, moved Rusk to call up units of the First Regiment, consisting of companies from Madison, Janesville, Beloit, Monroe, Darlington, Delavan, Whitewater, and Racine, since the only units he had in reserve were the Milwaukee Light Horse Squadron and the local artillery battery. The First Regiment units were all in the city by 5:30 that afternoon.[38]

The men who had spent the previous day threatening the Bay View rolling mills reassembled the next morning (Wednesday, May fifth) at St. Stanislaus. They were better prepared, came in something resembling ranks, and had a standard bearer with a tricolor banner. On Monday, Schilling had held his poorly attended public meeting at Turner Hall and also met with the Milwaukee Knights of Labor executive committee, which called on all Knights to assist in maintaining order. The Knights Assembly at Bay View had met and offered its services as "special police" to protect the rolling mills, conditioned upon the removal of the militia. Instead, the four Milwaukee companies at Bay View were reinforced by two of the newly arrived companies from out of town. They spent an uncomfortable night, as it was cool and they had no blankets.[39]

As the strikers marching from St. Stanislaus came on, they presented an imposing array. Estimated at 1,500 men, they had a crowd of onlookers, including women and schoolchildren, tagging along. Major Traeumer had his command of six companies, numbering thirty-five to forty men each, drawn up in line just inside the plant fence.

Major Traeumer called the governor by phone when he was aware of the approach of the crowd. Rusk's orders were: "Should the rioters . . . attempt to seek an entrance, 'fight 'em.'" The approaching men were not visibly armed with anything other than sticks and stones. They apparently had no firearms and no shots were fired by them. Traeumer did not wait to learn their intent. He ordered them to halt when they were about a quarter of a mile away, but obviously he was not heard and his hand signals were ignored. Receiving no response to his repeated commands to halt, he ordered his troops to fire. By Traeumer's own account, the distance was two hundred yards—somewhat more by the *Journal's* account. Only the Sheridan Guard, posted where the fence dipped into a ravine, had a clear field of fire. Only two of the companies fired a full volley,

PROBLEMS IN WORKPLACE HEALTH AND SAFETY

Workers employed in factories faced unsafe working conditions. Nearly a century before the passage of the Occupational Safety and Health Act (in 1970), it was not unusual for workers to lose fingers, hands, or arms on the job. Can you imagine what had transpired when a factory worker was "killed, wound up on shaft"?

ANOTHER deficiency of the times was that the workplace was commonly a hazard to the health and safety of the workers. This grew out of the assumption that the surroundings of the job were simply dictated by the given conditions. Factory design was an art that arrived late on the Wisconsin scene. Makeshift sheds and adapting whatever buildings were available were the rule. Steam power was transmitted throughout the factory by means of leather belting and turning shafts which might be overhead or under the floor. Individual machines ran by belting which functioned like pulleys from the constantly turning shafts. Whether the work man's machine was engaged remotely or by physically shoving the turning belt from an idler to a fixed pulley, the power was always turning—and it did not respond to shouts or to a hand, arm, or body caught in a machine or belting or by the turning shafts. Inattention was a common denominator in such accidents, which also occurred while oiling or attempting to correct some malfunction. Sawmills and woodworking plants took the heaviest toll, but of the forty-four fatal accidents reported in 1893-1894, eight involved belting, gearing, and turning shafts in other types of plants. "Killed, wound up on shaft," was the laconic comment. Rush-hour traffic was less hazardous.

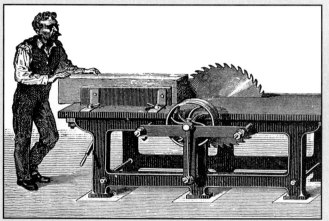

Dover Publications, New York

Despite the liability of the employer for injuries if the worker could establish that he had not been careless or was the victim of another's carelessness, sawmills were rarely equipped with elementary safeguards around saws, pulleys, and shafts. Although state factory inspectors were charged with responsibility for health and sanitary conditions as well as elementary safety under the legislation of 1883 and subsequent modifications of that law, most violations reported involved fire exits, unguarded machinery, or open elevator shafts. During 1893-1894 there were 1,075 individual inspectors' orders for changes involving worker safety, and only four orders for the installation of suction fans, presumably for the workers' comfort and health.

Workplaces were not expected to have plumbing when most city homes and schools did not. If the job was excessively hot, cold, dirty, or dangerous, it was accepted as common to the nature of the work or the circumstances of the employer.

—ROBERT C. NESBIT

From *The History of Wisconsin, Volume III* (State Historical Society of Wisconsin, Madison, 1985)

A sense of genuine community was the source of strength of the trades union movement.

despite prior orders that each man should pick his man and not fail to shoot. The *Journal* reported five killed and eight or ten wounded. The crowd fell flat, then withdrew with some of the wounded. Traeumer ordered a cease-fire when he saw the effect of his guardsmen's volley.[40]

The dramatic event at Bay View did not immediately end the agitation, but the shots fired and the presence of fresh troops made it clear that the momentum of the movement was gone. Colonel King took the Light Horse unit to deal with a crowd gathered for an early Wednesday morning meeting called at the Milwaukee Garden. Later action centered there throughout the day, with the cavalry and foot units exercising a restraining influence with horse, rifle butt, and occasional threats of sterner measures. King was sorely disappointed that Mayor Wallber not only refused him permission to clear the streets—the owner of the Garden having prudently locked up at the suggestion of Governor Rusk—but the Mayor also advised King to withdraw the military and leave affairs to the police. Wallber justified his action by mingling with the crowd, which was not hostile. He commented: "In the rear [of the crowd] on every street was a long line of buggies and wagons, containing men, women and children, who anticipated no danger, there simply 'to see the fun.'" With his usual temper, King reportedly gave his men orders "to shoot to kill, if the mayor is not obeyed." Wallber proved correct. The police earlier even made some arrests of men identified as known agitators, from among the crowd. Thursday was quiet.[41]

The majority of the state press was unreservedly favorable to Governor Rusk's prompt action, which was assumed to have saved Milwaukee from total anarchy. Few questioned the necessity for the shooting. The press reaction was colored by the nation's response to the Tuesday Haymarket bombing in Chicago. *Germania* contrasted Rusk's actions favorably with those of the vacillating governor of Illinois. Mayor Wallber was generally condemned for a want of resolution.[42]

The crisis passed quickly. The troops were discharged a few days later, despite anxious appeals from businessmen for Rusk to delay this action. The governor knew his business. The day after the shooting, he toured Bay View and the Polish section of the South Side by carriage, escorted by the Light Horse Squadron.[43]

The actions of Major Traeumer and his troops at Bay View were not seriously questioned. A coroner's jury pronounced the deaths and woundings justified. Major Traeumer was generally complimented for his humane action in ordering a cease-fire after a single volley. The *Journal* implied that the Sons of Vulcan could have handled the matter. They had irons heated and hoses hooked to the boilers with which to greet the crowd.[44]

The pride of the occasion may well have been dimmed by the list of the victims. Among the five killed outright was an elderly man feeding his chickens a half-mile away. Another was a school boy—he fell on his books—who was on the railroad embankment paralleling the road where the strikers were marching. The directed fire struck the man carrying the banner at the head of the column; he was hit in several places and had his lower jaw carried away. (There was much editorial talk about the risks of carrying red banners, although this one was a tricolor.) Colonel King was still exulting over the affair thirty-six years later: "The mob was still nearly two hundred yards off, and flattened out at the crash of the rifles as though a hundred were hit, but only six were really punctured."[45]

Aside from the wisdom of Major Traeumer's ordering his men to fire at a range of two hundred yards, there was the troubling matter of the Kosciusko Guard firing towards the crowd without orders the day before. The fact is that these were "Sunday soldiers" and they were understandably confused and apprehensive in a situation for which they had neither been trained nor otherwise prepared. The drillmaster of the Wisconsin National Guard was Colonel King. The guards' brief training sessions used the Regular Army manual, which presumably prepared them to refight the Civil War. King treated the officer corps at summer camp to a lecture on "social disorder"—meaning strikes, which he found uniformly insane—and recommended Napoleonic instructions to fire two well-aimed volleys by battalion. King's other contribution to the mayhem, beyond this basic lack of instruction, was to secure 31,000 rounds of ball cartridge that could kill at a distance. "We had no riot guns and cartridges in those days, deadly at less than two hundred yards, but warranted not to harm innocent spectators a block or two away. Such as it was, however, the death-dealing ammunition came only just in time." (So much for the man feeding his chickens half a mile away.)[46]

The coroner's jury found that troops had followed orders and returned a verdict: "We hold the troops executing the orders, as well as the commander-in-chief, entirely blameless in the matter." Those killed, including the boy, were "making an unlawful attempt to proceed to the rolling mills." Apparently Governor Rusk's order ("Should they attempt to enter . . .") had been liberally translated. The militiamen were showered with gifts, given public dinners, and inordinately praised. The *Journal* called for a halt to this: "The militia were in no danger; not a man of them that did not realize that the unorganized, unarmed mob of men and boys before them would scatter at the first shot. These facts are patent to everybody—to the greenest civilian as well as to the 'old veterans.'" This came perilously close to saying that the killings were unnecessary, but the *Journal* backed away from that. The inference seemed to be that the killings were justified by the results rather than by the immediate circumstances of Bay View.[47]

Twenty-five men were charged with "riot and unlawful assembly" as a result of the events of May 1-5, 1886. This was not necessarily an indication of their respective roles as leaders. Some were doubtless simply unlucky enough to be conspicuous at a given moment. The names of those charged are indicative: Bauer, Dampf, Hussfeldt, Gabrielski, Woicechowski,

A STRIKE FOR CASH PAY IN TWO RIVERS, 1895

Paul Cigler, Jr., shows how tub and pail turners in the sawmills of Two Rivers fought against the use of "scrip" or company-printed "money" that could be used only at the company-owned stores. How did the sawmill workers win their demands?

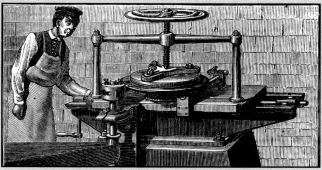

Dover Publications, New York

ON October 23, 1894, a branch of the International Machine Wood Workers of America was organized. Thirty-eight members joined, mostly tub and pail turners employed at the pail factory owned by the Mann Brothers. Officers elected were William Ahearn, President, John Wilkes, Vice-President, Fred Althen, Secretary, Peter Scherer, Financial Secretary, and William Boehringer, Treasurer.

The stated aim of the union was the establishment of the eight-hour work day, equalized wages, and an end to the jobbing out system at the factory. This was the first successful organization of a union in Two Rivers, but it took no immediate actions.

The depression that started in spring of 1893 only lasted through December of that year in Two Rivers. By January of 1894, the local newspaper reported that all the factories in the city were running full time again. The Two Rivers Manufacturing Company even expanded its plants and built new kilns in the spring of 1894. By summer of 1894, extra shifts were added to meet production demands. The only thing that did not change from 1893 was wages. The 10 percent wage cut remained and employees were paid once a month in scrip redeemable only at the Mann Company store, plus small cash amounts. The situation lasted until September of 1895 when the union struck for a cash only payday.

The union sent a letter to Henry Mann, President of the Two Rivers Manufacturing Company, requesting that a cash payday be established and the employees be granted the privilege of trading at the store of their choice. The letter stated that:

> Trusting that you will consider our just demand we have appointed a committee with whom you are to confer. Should this committee not hear from you by Sept.1 We will take it for granted that you refuse to negotiate with us.

Mann did not respond and on August 28, a telegram was sent by the union informing Mann of a walkout set for August 29.

The union had organized quietly over the past several months and put their strike plan into action. On the morning of the 29th, 300 workers at the pail factory walked off the job. They formed a line and marched through the city to the chair factory. There, the strikers called out for the workers to join them. Few did.

During the noon lunch break, the strikers returned to the chair factory and this time they were successful. Most of the workers marched away with them. Of over 300 workers, only 35 remained at the chair factory.

The 600 strikers formed a parade twice daily at 6:30 A.M. and at 5:00 P.M., and marched past the company property carrying banners for the union and a cash payday. A police committee was set up to keep the strikers out of the taverns. Mass meetings were held daily; speeches were given in English, Polish, German and Bohemian. A committee was formed to collect food from local merchants and area farms. A committee was also created to watch the incoming trains and harbor for strike breakers. On the second day of the strike, four men were turned out of town as strike breakers.

The daily meeting allowed the men to express their demands. The men stated they could not get their pay in cash only because to demand it was equal to discharge. One employee stated that if he had $25 in pay owed to him, he might get $5 in cash, the rest in company scrip. The men denied that "any agitator" had been in town to influence the strike. When told that the Mann Brothers claimed they were running the shops for the last three years at a loss to show their sympathy to the workers, one employee replied that "it seems unlikely that the Mann Brothers are working their mills for charity's sake."

The workers received support from outside the city. At one of the meetings a letter from Frank J. Weber, state organizer for the Wisconsin State Federation of Labor, was read. In part, it stated:

> . . . the capitalists and moneyed men fear nothing so much as the unity of the laboring masses and as long as they are not they will be robbed and wronged, but if they unite then will end the galling rule of moneyed lords, then we will be able to observe the sunrise of liberty . . . the good work must go on, organization must be printed on every human heart. Now is the time to organize . . .

The strike was settled on September 9, 1895, and the first all cash payday was set for December of 1895. The strike had been orderly and successful. The strike also gave the local Populists an issue to exploit and prestige in the community.

—PAUL J. CIGLER, JR.

From *A History of Populism and Socialism in Two Rivers, Wisconsin* (master's thesis, University of Wisconsin, Oshkosh, 1989).

Hofer, Strehlow, Gastell, Runge, Luppnow, Heiber, Piepenberg, Gertz, Datara, Kroeger, Rozga, Dolnig, Andrsezewski, Ady, Skrezipenzinski, Protzmann, Lampel, Gondek, Datka, and Boncel. Those charged with "riot and conspiracy" were marked as the real ringleaders, wherever they were when events took place: Frank Hirth, Carl Simon, Anton Palm, Paul Grottkau, and Albert Moessinger.[48] . . .

The drive for an eight-hour day died as a popular movement. Within two weeks the common council considered repeal of the eight-hour ordinance that had passed in March. Actual repeal came in July. Labor commissioner Frank A. Flower pronounced the epitaph of the movement in his biennial report: "Summing up all the facts, it may be safely stated that no benefits whatever have been derived from the agitation by any class of workingmen."[49] . . .

The rise of the American Federation of Labor led to a more fruitful political alliance between the AF of L in Milwaukee and Victor Berger's Socialists (Social-Democratischer Verein, or Social Democrats as they became known after 1896). Schilling was only intermittently concerned with the Knights of Labor, which was melting away rapidly. Powderly, with his enthusiasm

for temperance, drove out the brewery workers. In 1886 the American Federation of Labor was beginning to gather in the fragmented trade unions.[50]

With the emergence of the AF of L as the dominant labor organization in Milwaukee, something was gained in the way of a trades-oriented labor organization that could assert itself—often effectively—in the hostile environment that followed the Bay View riot. The AF of L was more successful than Schilling's Knights of Labor with its loose coalition, ill-defined aims, and politically oriented leadership.

The difference was well summed up by one old-time Milwaukee trade unionist: "After working for more than twelve years in the city, five years ago I hardly knew any craftsmen except those working with me in the same shop. Today I am personally acquainted with four-fifths of all the men engaged at my trade, and everybody seems to know me. This fact I appreciate more than almost anything connected with my social position." A sense of genuine community was the source of strength of the trades union movement.[51] ■

From *The History of Wisconsin, Volume III*
(State Historical Society of Wisconsin, 1985).

WOMEN AND THE OSHKOSH WOODWORKERS STRIKE, 1898

In the 1890s, Oshkosh became the world's capital of the door and sash industry—and the second largest city in Wisconsin. In the summer of 1898, 1,500 woodworkers formed a union and launched a carefully planned strike that lasted for 14 weeks and resulted in a dramatic conspiracy trial when famous attorney Clarence Darrow successfully defended the strikers. A less well known episode is the role of the wives of the strikers, here described by Lee Baxandall.

Dover Publications, New York

THE women who had to make do, often with large families, on the pay arbitrarily decided upon by Mr. Paine and his peers—they were the most fierce fighters and the hard core among the strikers. "A dozen infuriated women, wives of the strikers, constituted the most disorderly element in the crowd" at the Morgan plant, wrote the *Daily Northwestern.* "Urged on by the cheers of the men, the women, with pouches filled with eggs, sand and pepper hanging in front of them, and with great clubs in their hands, three and four feet long, swung up and down the street halting pedestrians and chasing every non-union man who appeared within a block of a mill." Their men mostly

hung back, available but slightly out of the action, perhaps fearing that to be recognized at such tasks would result in being blacklisted from a mill job forever. At McMillan "the mob seemed to center around a half dozen women who carried clubs in their hands, stones or eggs in their aprons, and packages of salt or pepper in their pockets. While a number of full grown men could be seen in the crowd, the major portion of it seemed to be boys between the ages of sixteen and twenty years of age. The women seemed to follow the lead of one who is said to be conspicuous in the riot at the Morgan plant in the morning"—probably Mrs. Hando or Mrs. Pommeraning, to guess from subsequent accounts.

The Milwaukee Sentinel typically commented that except "for this class of late born arrivals, the laboring people are much more inclined to peace than war. The women were the most vicious. They were largely Poles and Bohemians and perfect viragoes." The resentment against immigrants is explicit in the newspaper accounts—and yet these are the people Mr. Paine, Tommy Morgan, and the other millowners actively recruited to come to Oshkosh, in the belief they'd work cheaper.

—LEE BAXANDALL

From "The Oshkosh Woodworkers Strike of 1898,"
Green Mountain Quarterly (1976), pp. 22-23.

Unions in Kenosha

JOHN W. BAILEY

*Kenosha emerged as an important industrial town by the turn of the century.
John Bailey describes how the local unions formed a central labor council and
used Labor Day parades and other social activities to promote support for the
union movement. Labor disputes occurred frequently at the Allen Tannery.*

THE last two decades of the nineteenth century brought industrial expansion to Kenosha on a large scale. The city also enjoyed a large growth in population to accommodate the industrialization, and the quiet shipping port was now transformed into a community bustling with activity. Industry demanded cheap labor, and the streets of Kenosha were soon crowded with energetic but poor workers fresh off recently arrived boats from Europe or trains from other urban centers. By 1907, the state reported that 6,130 males and 1,021 females worked in Kenosha factories. In addition 316 boys and girls under sixteen years of age also plied their skills in the plants. Factory owners employed workers for $1.50 to $3.00 per day on the average.[1]

Despite long hours, low pay, discriminatory practices, and sometime hazardous working conditions, Kenosha workers in the early years of the twentieth century as yet lacked the perspective, leverage, and unity to create a strong labor movement. Before the newly arrived immigrant workers, for example, could develop any strong commitment to unionization they would need time to come to terms with American culture. Although many unions were formed during the early 1900's most were never chartered and disappeared quickly. The most important step taken by labor during this period was the organization of the Trades and Labor Council, chartered by the American Federation of Labor on February 25, 1902. Those locals that joined were the Metal Polishers and Buffers, Carpenters, Joiners, Machinists, Musicians, Retail Clerks and Cigar Makers. James Ferris and Andrew Stemsen of the Metal Polishers union at Simmons Company together with Dwight House of the Typographical union and Stanley Saunders of the Bakery and Confectionery workers were the key organizers of the Trades and Labor Council.

The operating philosophy of the council was that a union is an "organization of wage earners to do collectively what they cannot do as individuals." They maintained that capital and labor were essential in labor and each was dependent on the other. Since capital had organized many years ago, labor demanded the same right. The Council members further stated that in order to gain "human betterment" or the abundant life

all wage earners have a right in determining wages, hours, working conditions, safety, and health.[2]

Other groups were quick to join the Trades and Labor Council. In 1903 the barkeepers of Kenosha held an organizational meeting with the encouragement of an outside national organizer and decided to form a union and join the council. Their primary interest was a decrease of working hours, for some bartenders worked from twelve to eighteen hours a day. These "concocters of drinks" hoped in the future to serve only "the Union Highball" in saloons of Kenosha if they were successful in obtaining a solid union. Earlier closing hours and shorter working days were the solutions that the barkeepers sought through union membership.[3]

Aside from its basic concerns with salaries, working conditions, and hours, the Trades and Labor Council also was mindful of the significant social needs of the workers. On one occasion in 1903 it sponsored a three-day gala fair in the city. Combining philanthropy and good times, the council promised one-fourth of the receipts to be donated to a fund to build an emergency hospital.[4] Although the various unions sponsored dances and parties, Labor Day celebrations were usually the highlight of the working man's social season. All stores and factories were closed in honor of Labor Day and the people of Kenosha enjoyed parades, picnics, and speakers in the parks of the city.[5]

In 1904 ten thousand people attended the Labor Day celebration. A giant parade occupied the morning hours and included some five hundred members of unions, three bands, and numerous floats. The highlight, perhaps, was the Polisher's Union contingent of almost a hundred men dressed in white duck trousers and shirts who marched in straight lines down Market street and over to Anderson Park. In the afternoon there were races, baseball games, and sports of all kinds. Speakers and dances also took up the afternoon and evening hours. It was fortunate for a few that the police agreed that arrests on Labor Day would not count, because there were some who consumed the liquid refreshments over enthusiastically.[6] It was well that Kenoshans could frolic on occasion because most of their days were filled with the grim reality of hard work, long hours,

Allen Tannery in Kenosha, 1914–1918.

meager wages, and strikes. The first decade of the 1900's had its share of labor strife. The first serious strike of the century came in late May, 1901, when the machinists in several Kenosha factories left their jobs. They demanded a reduction in hours from ten to nine over the six day work week. Several factory managers were willing to accept this proposal but only with a proportionate drop in salary. For the one hundred striking machinists who worked at A.D. Meiselbach, Simmons, Jefferies, Chicago-Rockford Hosiery, and Badger Brass this could hardly be considered an offer. Since no quick settlement could be reached, Simmons was forced to close the entire plant because it could not operate without the machinists. This put a large number of people out of work and labor discontent grew.

Before officials settled the strike, a soon-to-be familiar pattern emerged. A.D. Meiselbach threatened to move his factory to another location rather than put up with the local labor situation. Newspaper headlines related how Kenosha was gaining a "Black Eye in Industrial Circles," while few citizens seemed concerned about abuses that workers suffered. After two months of unemployment the machinists finally had to return to work. They had gained little by the strike other than the original terms laid down by management—a nine-hour work day with nine-hour wages. Thus they had suffered a reduction in pay and hours. Several factory managers predicted that labor would soon vote to return to the ten-hour work day at comparable wages.[7]

Other strikes followed in rapid succession in these forma-

tive days of Kenosha unions. In 1902 the ice handlers struck at Twin Lakes protesting their low wages which were 20 cents an hour for a ten-hour work day. They demanded an increase to 25 cents an hour and double pay for overtime and on Sunday. Since the ice companies of Kenosha County supplied Chicago, Kenosha, and Milwaukee as well as other cities, the situation was crucial. Ice handlers and wagon drivers in Chicago threatened a sympathy strike if the demands were not met. Soon workers made similar demands at other lakes. The ice handlers at Powers Lake made only 15 cents an hour and they demanded a raise to 25 cents in 1903. Since there was no uniform wage in the lake region, company managers always feared that the men would get organized and demand one. On one occasion Knickerbocker Company officials transported thirty men from Chicago to Twin Lakes to work. When these men realized the situation, they refused to work as scabs and walked back to Chicago. Although the picture remained chaotic in the ice fields, generally the ice company officials met the demands of labor because they had to move the ice before spring.[8]

Other strikes plagued Kenosha during the following years. There were labor troubles at Simmons in 1909 and 1917 which were of short duration, non-violent, and settled with little change for the economic betterment of labor.[9] In 1907 strike action took place at Badger Brass and there was a minimum of violence. Factory owners expressed concern that damage might be done at the plant when company-hired detectives uncovered a plot to blow up the factory. Authorities did not suspect union men but rather anarchists from out of town. While searching the room of suspected agitators detectives uncovered details of the plot including maps of Badger Brass and explosive materials. The men were not present in the room, but they were identified as having connections with anarchists in Chicago and at one time were thought to be associates of Emma Goldman, "the high priestess of anarchy." While the suspected men were in Chicago, several prominent Kenosha industrialists received letters which threatened their lives. Nothing came of the plot, however, and local union men were not charged or suspected in the plot.[10]

The most dramatic labor strike in Kenosha during the first twenty-five years of the century was that at the Allen Tannery in 1906. With the intense feelings on both sides and the violence and reactionary efforts that followed, this strike serves as an example of where labor and management were in the early twentieth century. The strike started on April 25, when 150 men employed in the lower yards walked out demanding 50 cents per week increase in wages, which would bring their weekly income to $10. Foremen notified the main office and a rush call to the police department brought numerous patrolmen to the factory to curtail the spread of the strike. They were too late. The yardsmen had marched to the upper yards, overpowered the foreman at the gate and successfully called out the remainder of the yardsmen. No other departments at the tannery, however, cooperated at this time with the strikers.

Charles W. Allen, one of the local directors of the company, talked with the strikers, who had no union. He announced that the Kenosha yardmen already received 50 cents more than those in Milwaukee and that he was powerless to raise the Kenosha wages. He related that the Allen Tannery was one of many that the Central Leather Company controlled and that the trust could easily close down the Kenosha plant and still fill outstanding orders from its other tanneries. Allen claimed he had difficulty in dealing with the men because most were foreign born and few spoke English. He concluded that although there was little violence, there was a great deal of excitement among the other men employed at the plant.

Events took a turn for the worse when Allen was not able to satisfy the yardmen's demands. Some of the strikers began patrolling the streets while others relaxed in nearby saloons. About three o'clock in the afternoon a group of strikers suddenly began rushing about the plant "shouting like madmen," in an effort to persuade other workers to join them. The entire Kenosha police force was called to the factory and somehow managed to restore order. City officials quickly swore-in additional deputy sheriffs and police officers to meet the violence that they expected that night. Around five o'clock a new scuffle broke out and two men were arrested. A great crowd gathered at the jail and only quick action by Mayor James Gorman restored the peace. He ordered the release of the prisoners and persuaded the crowd to return home and wait until he had set up a conference the next morning.

The crowd dispersed from the jail but an hour later 250 strikers moved to the tannery and a melee followed. Armed with clubs and stones the strikers forced their way into the plant, broke windows, and dragged the few men still working in the factory out in the street. Several people were slightly injured as a result of this fracas. Mayor Gorman returned to the factory and again restored peace. Later that night the strikers moved their headquarters to Congress Hall. While discussing future action, word arrived that a Slovonic worker, I. Michelas, had been shot in the chest and hospitalized. Now the strikers wanted blood. It took all the mayor's considerable persuasive powers to convince the men to go to their homes and await the outcome of the next morning's conference.

Tension at the tannery seemed to be mounting as fast as the sun, as workers awaited the outcome of the conference. Law enforcement officers were again present in strength and all but a score of workers had walked out in support of the yardmen.

State Historical Society of Wisconsin 41514

First annual turnout of Local Boilermakers and Helpers, Madison, 1914.

FROM UNION TOWN TO OPEN SHOP: BELOIT 1903-1904

The fragile nature of early unionism is aptly described in this passage. Robert Ozanne describes the rise and fall of organized labor in Beloit.

IN the spring of 1903 Beloit, with a population of 14,000, was proportionately perhaps the best union-organized city in the state. With the help of two organizers, George Mulberry, fifth vice-president of the International Association of Machinists, and Robert Hogan, organizer for the American Federation of Labor, union membership rose from 200 in three unions in June, 1901, to 2,000 members in twenty-one unions two years later. Not only were the building trades and the industrial plants unionized, but such service trades as bartending, tailoring, and retailing were well organized. Union cards were displayed in store windows. Customers bought union goods from union clerks. In accordance with their Retail Clerks' Union contract, the leading grocery stores in the city closed at 6:00 P.M. and the leading meat markets closed at 6:30 P.M. The Retail Clerks had over a hundred members.

The Iron Molders Union was especially strong. In 1902 the Molders successfully struck the Fairbanks-Morse Company to protest what they considered the unfair discharge of a molder. After three weeks the company reinstated the man and the strike was called off. In March, 1903, a Molders walkout at the N. B. Gaston Sons' Scale Works

forced the firm to comply with the union's demand for a minimum of $3 a day, which was already in force at other plants.

The banner union in Beloit, however, was the International Association of Machinists, with 525 members in 1903. At its national convention in Milwaukee on May 6-9, 1903, the International voted full support, including strike benefits, to the demands that Beloit machinists had put forth earlier at the Berlin Machine Works: a nine-hour day, a minimum of 26.5 cents per hour, and no more than one apprentice for every five machinists. The company ignored the demands, and on May 9 the union men went out at the Berlin Works, closing down operations.

Week after week the company made no concessions. On July 6, the State Board of Arbitration proposed a compromise. The minimum wage demand was to be cut to 25 cents; for every nine hours of work the company would pay the equivalent of nine and a half hours; and there would be no change in the number of apprentices. The company's president replied to the compromise proposal:

> Please accept my thanks for your suggestion as I appreciate your efforts. We shall have to refuse to accept the proposition, however, as the time has gone by for treating with the unions. Their treatment with us during the strike does not warrant our wishing to be connected in any way with the union or to treat with them as a body. If we ever start again, it shall be on the line of individual contract and no other.

The strike was called off after sixteen weeks. The men returned on an individual basis, with no union contract.

What happened to the Machinists happened to all Beloit unions. Within a year the powerful Beloit union movement had been destroyed. Union cards were removed from

The new demands that a committee of fifteen strikers presented to company officials included a $1.00 per week increase for all employees and a three-year contract. While negotiations droned on many strikers were consuming large amounts of beer in local taverns. Finally, A.E. Buckmaster, a labor representative, emerged with a counter-proposal from the company which he subsequently explained to the strikers at Congress Hall. A thousand men listed intently as Buckmaster revealed that management would only grant a 50 cent raise to the yardmen. Spontaneous shouts and catcalls from the assemblage left no doubt how the vote would go.

Although there were minor skirmishes near the plant on April 27, a compromise settlement was hammered out later in the day. Company officials offered the yardmen, setters, finishers, washers, machine setters, and buffers a 50 cent per week increase in wages, but they placed no time limits on the agreement. The workers initially voted to accept the agreement but after further consideration decided to reject the offer. Factory officials concluded that men of a "revolutionary nature" controlled the strikers and were now prepared for a continuation of the violence. Plant officials turned the factory over to police protection and Mayor Gorman was reportedly considering an

appeal to the governor for state troops. In the end he decided against this course of action and continued his efforts to reopen serious negotiations. On April 28, there were several incidents of brick throwing and shots being fired into the plant. Police arrested a few suspects and more serious disturbances would surely have occurred had a final settlement not been reached that evening. According to the terms of the agreement all workers received a 50 cent wage increase and the buffers secured a $1.00 raise per week. It further agreed that the two days of wages lost during the strike would be paid by the company.

Thus, in the end labor won a partial victory without benefit of a formal union organization. Further strikes would soon prove that such victories were rare. The calming influence of Mayor Gorman may actually have been the strikers' biggest asset, for had serious disturbances broken out management would have doubtless gained the upper hand.[11]

Despite this settlement, labor troubles at the Allen Tannery resurfaced again in 1907 and 1909. The pattern was about the same in both cases. In the 1907 strike nearly 1,100 men walked out. Within a few days scabs and strikebreakers were brought in by the company from Milwaukee. At first the striking workers seemed peaceful enough and the neighborhood Polish and

all stores. Union labels were removed from both city newspapers. Union after union gave up its charter. The trade union paper, the Beloit *Labor Journal,* collapsed. Its editor, AFL organizer Robert Hogan, left town. Working hours of some establishments were lengthened to include Saturday afternoons. The word "union" was seldom heard.

The "Open Shop" Offensive

What had happened? What was the source of the anti-union campaign? On June 16, 1903, the secretary of the Chicago Employers' Association had visited Beloit and organized an association of employers, whose chief purpose was the elimination of unions. Such associations nationally were making a crusade of the open-shop movement. Technically, the term "open shop" meant that the employer would hire workers regardless of whether they were or were not affiliated with a union. In practice, "open shops" usually discriminated against union members and adamantly refused to recognize unions.

The Beloit Employers' Association became part of the rapidly growing national open-shop movement which would dominate American labor relations until passage of the National Labor Relations Act in 1935. To increase its effectiveness in 1903, the Beloit Employers' Association converted the organization into one called the Citizens' Alliance. The new group accepted small employers and even persuaded non-union workers to join. Its membership soon reached a thousand. The devastating effect it exerted upon the union movement is demonstrated by the declining membership rolls of several typical unions in the city. The Chicago Employers' Association representative compared the membership figures when he wrote up the Beloit story:

Beloit Union Membership, 1903—1904

	Spring, 1903	Winter, 1903-4
Federal Labor Union	400	0
Machinists	525	106
Clerks	84	0
Teamsters	99	0
Garment Workers	90	0
Painters and Decorators	46	0
Electrical Workers	51	11
Shoe Workers	46	0
TOTAL	1,341	117

Employers all over the country joined in the movement. It attracted not only employers but also members of the professions-clergymen, academic professors, and lawyers whose support lent respectability to an otherwise partisan activity. The president of Harvard University, Charles Eliot, praised the strikebreaker as an American hero, preserving individual liberty.[6] A Milwaukee attorney, Joseph V. Quarles, who as a federal judge was to play a strong role in the Milwaukee Molders' strike of 1906, wrote a widely distributed pamphlet extolling the open shop.

The union movement nationally, which had seen such rapid growth from 1898 through 1903, was stopped in its tracks by the employers' offensive. In Beloit the effects were especially long-lived. Several unions managed a rather feeble organization during World War I, but soon faded. Beloit remained an open-shop town until the great upsurge of unionism in the mid-1930's.

—ROBERT W. OZANNE

From *The Labor Movement in Wisconsin: A History* (State Historical Society of Wisconsin, Madison, 1984)

Austrian bars gradually filled to capacity. Soon Charles Allen was busy negotiating with labor leaders and Mayor Gorman was again doing his best to insure peace. Although his efforts were successful on the first day, the second day of the strike produced serious trouble. When Matt Zibulker, a striker, attempted at gunpoint to prevent several workers from saving some leather in vats, he was arrested. In protest strikers began to throw stones and bricks through the factory windows and the call was sent to Milwaukee for more detectives. Mayor Gorman immediately banned the sale of firearms in the city. Although feelings ran high, local officers managed to keep the violence in check and after passing an uneasy week a settlement was reached. The strikers had won a salary of $11.00 a week and such additional benefits as fifteen minutes to clean up at the end of the day.[12]

The strike of 1909 followed a similar pattern. The workers demanded more pay, violence followed, arrests were made, and with the help of state arbitrators a settlement was finally reached. Only superficial concessions were won in this strike, however, and some workers began to realize the advantages that a union might offer.[13]

Organized labor in Kenosha stood behind the efforts of the workers who fought for higher wages. The strikes at Allen Tannery, Badger Brass, and Simmons between 1906 and 1909 also generated state interest in Kenosha's labor problems. The State Federation of Labor and the Kenosha Trades and Labor Council brought speakers to Kenosha who lectured on matters of interest to all workers. As many as a thousand people filled the Rhode Opera House for these programs. On one occasion, William Kaufman, a former Kenosha alderman and the city representative on the executive board of the Wisconsin Federation of Labor, warned the people about the newly formed Citizen's Alliance and Manufacturer's Association. According to Kaufman, the only purpose of this organization was to "destroy the labor unions and replace well paid mechanics and union men with cheap and degraded labor."[14] At a subsequent meeting he spelled out the Federation's stance on a number of issues including an eight-hour day for industrial labor, industrial insurance, compulsory arbitration, prohibition of the leasing of convict labor to private contractors, one day of rest per week for every wage earner, and prohibition of persons under eighteen to be employed in breweries.[15] ■

From "Labor's Fight for Security and Dignity," in John A. Neuenschwander, *Kenosha County in the Twentieth Century* (Kenosha County, Kenosha, 1976).

Labor in Racine

JOSEPH M. KELLY

Racine became an important industrial center in the last two decades of the nineteenth century. The growth of diverse industries, including manufacturing, stimulated employment opportunities and attracted large numbers of workers, specially immigrants from Germany and Scandinavia, to the Racine area. The Knights of Labor were active in the 1880s. On July 4, 1886 an estimated 10,000 people rallied in Racine to support the political candidates endorsed by the Knights. Joseph M. Kelly describes how craft unionism flourished in the early years of the twentieth century with the founding of the Racine Trade and Labor Council.

MOST of the early trade unions in Racine were organized along craft lines affiliated with the new and pragmatic American Federation of Labor, which effectively began in 1886. A typical trade union was that of the plumbers, who had a closed shop. This meant simply that an employer hiring a plumber had to employ one who belonged to the union. A union member had to pay an initiation fee and serve in an apprenticeship training program before becoming a full-fledged journeyman plumber. Between the early 1890s and World War I the plumbers union was concerned primarily with increasing wages, reducing hours, and strictly enforcing union regulations.

The union felt so strongly about the last point that it might levy a one-hundred-dollar fine on any member who worked for less than the required scale or might arrange a visit by a union committee to any contractor who employed a "stranger."[1]

Racine's oldest continuous union is probably that of the building laborers, Local 108, chartered in 1888, which had originally been part of the Knights of Labor. One of the largest Racine unions was that of the moulders, Local 310. It had reorganized in 1897, although it had been in existence since the early 1880s, and had more than four hundred members by 1912. The moulders, then regarded as skilled workers, had gone on

State Historical Society of Wisconsin WHi (X3) 49772

The United Association of Journeymen and Apprentices of the Plumbing and Pipe Fitting Industry, Local 118, Racine, 1910.

The J.I. Case Threshing Machine Company in Racine was the site of a strike by molders in 1902 and 1904.

strike at various hardware shops in 1899 and had struck the J.I. Case Company in 1902 and 1904.

The most organizationally active of the early unions was the now-defunct cigar makers, Local 304, which had received its charter on July 3, 1891. Union records from the period credit Local 304 with organizing the first Labor Day celebration in Racine in 1892 and with being the major force in organizing the Racine Trade and Labor Council (RTLC) in September, 1894, as well as other unions.

The seven original member unions of the Racine Trade and Labor Council (RTLC) were those of the cigar makers, bricklayers, masons, plumbers, brewery workers, barbers, and typographers. By 1901 fifteen more unions had joined, and the RTLC had a combined membership list of 2,200 persons. From its beginning, the RTLC considered the promotion of the union label one of its most important functions. Throughout the minutes of the RTLC there are lists of places to buy union-made clothes. There was even a proposed resolution, rejected upon reconsideration, requiring that all delegates have at least four union labels on their clothing at any given time. The RTLC fined members twenty-five dollars for buying non-union brooms and protested non-union construction projects, such as the building of a Bohemian Catholic Church, using non-union labor. Printers, bakers, and especially cigar makers urged union members to buy or order their goods in Racine. Western

Printing and Lithographing Company, for example, began selling union-labeled stationery.[2]

The most extreme case of union support was that which the RTLC gave the bartenders union after it reorganized in March, 1914. Union sentiment was so strong that the RTLC advocated a boycott of Welch's grape juice because the company had donated $50,000 to the prohibition campaign and "every dollar spent means a vote against the bartenders union." It was not surprising, then, that all union members would be urged to look for the bartenders union button, which changed monthly, and that a representative would even lose his seat on the RTLC if he patronized a non-union bar.[3]

The early unions, of course, did more than simply promote the union label. From its commencement, the RTLC realized the necessity of building a Union Hall, control of which was to be in the hands of a non-stock, non-dividend corporation, totally separate from the RTLC. Thus, the Union Hall association was formed in August, 1899. After it held fund-raising picnics, ran an amusement park, received the donation of a day's pay from certain locals, and finally completed a complicated land sale with the County Board, the association had enough money to construct a two-story building, dedicated on October 27, 1912. The unions also worked to pass legislation such as the eight-hour bill on the national, state, and municipal levels. They tried to elect progressive politicians, usually socialists, though the RTLC did not officially support candidates. The unions lobbied for free textbooks in schools, an elective school board, non-entry of America into World War I, a county hospital

Harbor at Racine on Lake Michigan, 1919.

instead of Memorial Hall as a monument to the World War I dead, increased vocational education, and an end to alleged police third-degree practices.[4]

The Council also tried to minimize inter-union jurisdictional disputes and other conflicts. The carpenters, for example, refused to have anything to do with activities that involved the masons and announced their intention to withdraw from the Council when masons were included in the annual Labor Day parade. When the dispute over musicians' instruments between the metal polishers and musicians became bitter, the RTLC cancelled the entire parade.[5]

The RTLC also tried to keep member unions in line. When the barbers quit the RTLC, the Council sent a notice of this fact to the barbers international union headquarters. The Council sent a similar report if a union's attendance at RTLC meetings was especially poor.[6] Undoubtedly, one of the Council's most important functions was its support of the organization of new unions. It was only with great difficulty that the unions in the RTLC were persuaded in October, 1913, to support the employment of a full-time organizer.

The Council had allowed impoverished and beginning unions to use its meeting rooms free of charge and occasionally had even paid their dues for them. Nonetheless, many of these early unions failed after a short time. The woodworkers union lasted only from 1902 to 1904; the metal and machine workers union lasted less than a year in 1903 and 1904; the leather and novelty workers union lasted from 1904 to 1908; the engineers union failed after two months in 1911; the stage employees union lasted from July, 1911, to December, 1919. Nevertheless, organizational attempts continued, often with the realization that certain satisfied groups, such as laundry workers, had no

desire for a union and that other groups, such as teachers, worked under conditions which did not predispose them to union organization.[7]

Labor historians have sometimes charged that craft guilds were indifferent or even hostile to industrial unionism, but if so, Racine's were an exception. The most important union leader in Racine labor history, William Sommers, believed the new industries should be unionized "more along industrial lines" than along the traditional craft line. He did, however, admit that once a company was unionized, the old established craft unions, such as those of the moulders, machinists, and carpenters, should be allowed to dominate their craftsmen within that company. Sommers believed, moreover, that certain places, such as J.I. Case or Western Printing, would be impossible to organize.[8]

William Sommers (1869-1946) was the son of pioneer parents and a moulder by trade. Because Racine industries blackballed him for his participation in strikes, he had to rely on the money he received in 1919 as a business agent for the RTLC and later as the janitor for Union Hall, a position which he held for twenty-three years, often working without pay. Sommers was also a member of the executive board of the Wisconsin Federation of Labor for twenty-two years.[9]

As early as October, 1912, the RTLC had supported industrial unionism. A short time thereafter, it assisted a Chicago organizer from the Garment Workers Union in establishing a union at the Chicago Rubber Clothing Company (now Rainfair) in Racine. In August, 1915, the RTLC asked the national offices of both the automobile and the machinists unions to send organizers for their respective industries, and they quickly complied.[10] ■

From "Growth of Organized Labor," in Nicholas C. Burckel, *Racine: Growth and Change in a Wisconsin County* (Racine County, Racine, 1977).

SECTION

2

Unionism In An Industrial Society

Machinery operation on naval gun slides at the Allis-Chalmers Manufacturing Company, 1920.

The Paperworkers' Fight
for Saturday Night

ROBERT W. OZANNE

*After 1900, the papermaking industry began its emergence as
one of Wisconsin's major industries, as large factories were constructed
along the Fox, Wisconsin, Eau Claire, Marinette and Peshtigo rivers.
Robert Ozanne uncovers a revealing episode in which papermakers struck in
order to abolish work on Saturday night. But while they were able to achieve
their demands on the Fox River, the paperworkers faced tough employer opposition
in other parts of the state. Compare the two distinctly different interpretations of
the same meeting called by management in Eau Claire in 1902. The use of the
Wisconsin State Board of Arbitration as a means of resolving disruptive
industrial conflict is characteristic of the period.*

AFTER 1900 Wisconsin's paper workers took up the struggle for the reduction of working hours. The men who worked the sawmills had been as restless and as mobile as the mills themselves, which moved on when the white pines had been devoured. But the paper mills, with their huge factories and highly-skilled work force, were permanent residents. Here the struggle between workers and managers was to be long and hard fought.

1902: Victory on the Fox River

Men and women have been making paper in the Fox River Valley since the water of the river first washed through the beater and powered the machine at the C. P. R. Richmond Brothers mill in Appleton in 1853.[1] In October of 1872, about forty people began work at the new Globe mill, which the Kimberly-Clark Paper Company had built on a gristmill site in Neenah. As the wheat fields moved westward during the 1870's, the flour mills often were replaced by paper mills. By the end of the decade there were twenty paper mills along the Fox. In the Wisconsin River Valley, paper mills replaced sawmills as the timber was depleted, and by the early 1900's it, too, was an important paper-producing valley. In 1910, 6,000 people were working in paper mills throughout Wisconsin, along not only the Fox and Wisconsin rivers, but also along the Menominee, Wolf, Oconto, Peshtigo, and Flambeau rivers.[2]

Before 1901 there were no unions in the paper mills, but there was dissatisfaction. The work was dangerous: "willingness to take risks [was] one of the requisites for a good paper-mill man."[3] Many had fingers cut off, arms burned, and bodies mangled by the open machinery and the hot rolls and felts that dried and supported the fragile paper as it made its long journey from the beater to the spindles which wound the finished paper. Sometimes the huge boilers exploded. Charity was the only source available to help pay the medical bills, to make up for the loss of wages, and even to compensate for loss of life.

There was a hierarchy among the workers on a paper machine: first came the machine tender, followed by the back-tender, third hand, fourth hand, and fifth hand. The highly skilled machine tenders and backtenders were generally the core of the unions. On a Monday afternoon in May, 1892, nine "boys"—backtenders and third hands—walked out of the Thilmany Pulp and Paper Company in Kaukauna. The backtenders demanded that their daily wage of $1.25 be increased to $1.50; the third hands wanted their $1.00 a day to be increased to $1.25. "The boys miscalculated their power, however," reported the Kaukauna *Times*, "and instead of the mill shutting down, everything ran as of yore and their places were soon filled."[4] If wages were low, the hours were long. Because the water which powered the mills flowed twenty-four hours a day, the machinery was operated day and night, six days a week, by an eleven-hour day shift working sixty-six hours a week, and a thirteen-hour night shift working seventy-eight hours a week. The workers alternated shifts on a weekly basis.

The paperworkers especially loathed the Saturday night shift. It was that shift, rather than the physical hazards or wages, which goaded them to organize their first union in Wisconsin. They had a precedent, for at the paper mills in Holyoke, Massachusetts, the Saturday night shift had been the chief irritant that had driven the machine tenders and beater engineers (who supervised the mixing and cooking of the raw pulp) to transform their social club into a labor union, which was chartered by the American Federation of Labor (AFL) in 1893.[5] In 1901 this union, by then a part of the United Brotherhood of Paper Makers (UBPM), AFL, struck successfully to abolish the Saturday night shift and to set a minimum wage of $2.00 per day.

To protect these gains from the competition of the unorganized mills in the Midwest, the UBPM sent their general organizer, William Hamilton, to the Fox River Valley in March, 1901.[6] The Fox Valley workers, hoping to end the Saturday night shift, responded enthusiastically and established lodges in Neenah-Menasha (named the Hamilton Lodge), Appleton, and Kaukauna. By fall they were well enough organized to issue the following demands to all paper manufacturers in the valley:[7]

> Gentlemen:
>
> At a meeting of the United Brotherhood of Paper Makers of America, it was voted unanimously to submit the following propositions to the paper manufacturers of the Fox River Valley, viz:
>
> 1. To grant tour [shift] workers off from 6 o'clock Saturday night till 7 o'clock Monday morning without any reduction in week's pay for said time off.
> 2. To grant finishing room help off at Saturday noon without any deduction in week's pay for said time off.
> 3. To grant time and a half for all Sunday repair work.

The manufacturers were asked to respond on or before December 1. It was understood that "if the request is not granted, a general strike will be instituted."

The manufacturers did not join together in a uniform response. When the president of the Appleton lodge called on Kimberly-Clark, he was told that although the company considered the union demands reasonable, it could not afford to close Saturday night unless all other mills did so.[8] The Gilbert Paper Company at Menasha sent an offer to the Hamilton Lodge:[9]

> . . . tour workers in our machine, engine and calender rooms [to be] off from 6 o'clock Saturday night to 7 o'clock Monday morning without deduction of pay...we grant the above January 1st, experimentally...we will continue on this basis until the shorter schedule becomes generally adopted or we demonstrate that its working is detrimental to our company, when we haven't the least doubt. . . . you will willingly return to the old schedule.

Two days later, Kimberly-Clark, which had mills in Neenah, Appleton, Kimberly, and Niagara, changed its mind and offered to close on Saturday night, with a specific qualifier: "If the mills competing for the same business that we sell to have by April 1st [1902], granted like favors . . . then this agreement . . . to remain indefinitely. But if . . . not . . ., then the men employed by Kimberly & Clark Company agree to resume work on old basis of working hours and pay." In a fatherly manner President John A. Kimberly added: "We should never cease regretting, if these extra hours were used in dissipation that would lead to a lowering of the morals of our men . . . extra time for rest making you better husbands, fathers, citizens and Christians, . . . appeals to us very forcibly."[10] The Fox River Paper Company in Appleton and the Neenah Paper Company, a mill controlled by Kimberly-Clark, made the same offer.[11]

The Hamilton Lodge voted to accept the Gilbert and Kimberly-Clark offers, but the Appleton lodge held back at first,

Huge piles of pulp wood at the Riverside Paper Company. The Telulah Mill looms in the background, circa 1900.

then accepted the April 1 qualifier and assured Kimberly-Clark that the shorter hours would not only benefit "home and family life," but would result in "more and . . . better work" since "air, sunshine, love, home, recreation and rest make muscles as well as beefsteak."[12] During the next three years the Appleton lodge had cause to wonder if its initial rejection had, in fact, been the right move.

A union committee called on the other paper companies, with dismal results. At 6:00 P.M. on the first Saturday in January of 1902, the mills which had agreed to the request for "Saturday night off" closed down. On Sunday afternoon the Appleton and Neenah-Menasha lodges met to celebrate, but the workers employed at the other Neenah and Menasha mills had worked as usual that Saturday night. Not for long, however; the next Saturday, workers at the Strange, Whiting, Menasha, and Winnebago mills did not report for the night shift. The mills closed, and the strike was on.[13]

The Wisconsin State Board of Arbitration called on the owners of the struck mills and found them not only opposed to the shorter hours, but unalterably opposed to dealing with a union: each owner agreed to meet with his own employees, but only on condition that no union representatives would be allowed to attend. The result of the meetings was that the Strange Company proposed to close Saturday night, but with a comparable reduction in pay; the Menasha Paper Company offered double wages for Saturday night; the Whiting and Winnebago companies warned their employees to return to

work before they were replaced.

Ignoring the threats and counteroffers, the Appleton and Neenah-Menasha lodges voted to continue the strike and to present their hourly demands to every paper manufacturer in Wisconsin; any company which did not meet these demands within two weeks would be struck. The lodges called their members to a big "Saturday night off" rally, where they spurred them on with the question, "Why do all [paper] mill owners require their help to work seventy-eight hours per week, when all other industrial enterprises require only sixty-six hours of labor?"

The millowners stiffened in their resolve. George Whiting, in Menasha, warned that the next thing manufacturers could expect would be demands for a three-shift, eight-hour schedule. John Strange, also in Menasha, placed guards around his mill.[14] In Appleton, the Patten Company workers announced that they would not return to work on Monday morning.[15] John McNaughton, secretary-treasurer of the company, stated that "it is to the best interests of our men to work Saturday nights. Most of them would visit the saloons.... They are much better off in the mill. Then, too, Saturday night is our most productive time, because of the water power." He warned that if the papermakers did strike, he would operate the plant by any means possible.

Nevertheless, the workers struck on Monday morning. After a meeting with McNaughton, William Hamilton, who was there on behalf of the UBPM to help the Fox Valley strikers, announced that "the men have extreme obstinacy to overcome." The UBPM considered the Fox Valley fight so difficult that it levied on every member an assessment of ten cents a week for a defense fund.[16]

For the next three and a half months the Fox Valley strikers tried to keep the mills from operating, with limited success. By mid-January each of the struck mills was managing to run at least one machine with the help of management and backtenders. When the owners began to import workers, the strikers met the newcomers at the railroad station and told them of the strike. Some were willing to return home, especially when the UBPM offered them a return ticket.[17] The townspeople seemed to side with the strikers. The Neenah *Daily Times* reported that the demand for Saturday night off was "regarded with a great deal of favor by the general public." The Oshkosh *Northwestern* editorialized: "To all appearances the workmen seem to have the elements of right and justice on their side."[18] Feelings against the strikebreakers became stronger. In Menasha, boarding house owners who rented to strikebreakers received threatening letters and felt compelled to buy their groceries outside the city.

As the termination date for the trial period, April 1, approached, the continuing strikes put the "Saturday night off" contracts in increasing jeopardy. The United Brotherhood of Paper Makers had achieved Saturday night closings in only four more companies: the Northern Tissue Company and Hoberg Toilet Paper Company in Green Bay, the Combined Locks Paper Company at Combined Locks, and the Wisconsin Tissue Paper Company of Appleton. Consequently, at the end of March, the Neenah-Menasha and Appleton lodges prepared to admit defeat and arranged a meeting with Kimberly-Clark. They were not prepared for the reception which Kimberly himself described:[19]

We were waited upon Monday by representatives of the

Appleton and Neenah lodges.... They offered to have the Brotherhood men go back to work in our mills on the long hour plan according to the agreement made last December, but we told them that we would extend our short hour system indefinitely in our mills now operating under it and also in the Neenah Paper Company's mill.

Kimberly also announced that the company would extend the shorter schedule to its Niagara mill as well, even though the employees there had not asked for it. Niagara Lodge No. 43 had been organized earlier in the year by a member of the Neenah lodge. The Gilbert Paper Company and the Fox River Company let it be known that they would continue the shorter-hour schedule "no matter what happened at the other mills."[20]

In April there finally was a break for the strikers at the Winnebago Paper Company in Neenah, who had been out for fourteen weeks. When the United Brotherhood of Paper Makers called on all Wisconsin paper mill workers who were still working on Saturday nights to strike on Saturday, April 5, workers at the Thilmany Pulp and Paper Company in Kaukauna "walked out to a man" and management could keep only one of the company's five paper machines running. Most of the people of Kaukauna sided with the strikers. Thilmany announced that after April 21, the strikers' jobs would be "filled by others."

The truth of that statement was never tested, because on Saturday, April 19, a new figure came into the Fox River Valley, bringing with him a breath of outside air. Monroe A. Wertheimer, from Los Angeles, succeeded Oscar Thilmany as president. On Monday and Tuesday mornings he met with a committee of the UBPM lodge. An agreement was reached, and at noon on Tuesday, April 22, the strikers returned to work.[21] On Thursday, April 24, the co-owner of the Winnebago Paper Company met the president of the Hamilton Lodge and agreed to settle the strike on the "Thilmany terms." The next day, twenty-five of the fifty workers who had been striking the Winnebago mill for almost four months returned to work. The remaining twenty-five had found other jobs.

In mid-June, when all back orders had been completed, the Thilmany and Winnebago mills abolished the Saturday night shift. The Neenah *Times* proclaimed that "the situation among the paper mill circles of Neenah is now as calm as a mid-summer night's dream."[22] It was no dream, however, for the workers who still worked the Saturday night shift at the George A. Whiting Paper Company and the Menasha Paper Company mills.

1902: Defeat on the Wisconsin River

The United Brotherhood of Paper Makers realized that eventually the competition from non-union mills, especially those along the Wisconsin River, would destroy the Fox River Valley gains. As soon as he had arrived, William Hamilton had visited paper mill workers along the Wisconsin River. Workers at Grand Rapids (now Wisconsin Rapids) staged rallies for fellow workers from Rhinelander and Nekoosa, but almost no one came. Finally, late in 1901, the United Brotherhood was able to organize a lodge in Brokaw.[23]

The problem was that the Wisconsin River millowners were more determined opponents than many of those on the Fox River. For example, the Wausau Paper Mill Company in Brokaw soon reined in the Brokaw lodge by calling in the men for a talk, which resulted in each individual signing a contract that granted a 10 per cent wage increase coupled with a "no strike" pledge, and stipulated that any signer quitting the mill would give sixty days notice or forfeit ten days' pay.[24] Other Wisconsin River Valley manufacturers used the same tactic, and paper mill workers in the Stevens Point area signed similar agreements.[25]

The Wisconsin River manufacturers also formed an association to counter the union. George Whiting, who had mills in both the Wisconsin and the Fox River valleys, called a meeting in Appleton that was attended by employer representatives from Nekoosa, Grand Rapids, Centralia, Marinette, Menominee, Eau Claire, Wausau, Stevens Point, and seven mills on the Fox River. They established the Northwestern Manufacturers Association,

State Historical Society of Wisconsin WHi (X3) 30345

A double-header freight train pulls cars of malt away from a warehouse fire in Manitowoc, March 24, 1898.

WAR HYSTERIA AND THE WOBBLIES

While the Industrial Workers of the World was strongest in the West and in a few industrial centers of the Northeast, the radical labor organization also struck terror in Wisconsin and in Milwaukee. The Wobblies were involved in strikes in the state as early as 1911, and during World War I they took the blame for almost every fire, labor dispute and commotion in the state. They wrote much of their Wisconsin chapter in the cutover pine lands of the north, but they also held sway in Milwaukee.

IN 1914, the only local listed in Wisconsin was in Milwaukee; however, there was considerable I.W.W. activity in the lumber camps, shipping docks and mining camps throughout the state. Often an organizer would show up, sign up some men, and then flee for his life ahead of the company's guards or local deputies—as often as not, the same men. Although that "local" disappeared, the men left behind might be sympathetic to the next organizer they met.

The Wobblies struck the docks at Superior in 1911 and at Allouez in 1913. They were involved in the strike of quarry workers at Red Granite in 1916 and struck the Superior docks again in 1916. During 1916, the I.W.W. conducted a vigorous recruiting campaign among the lumberjacks of the upper midwest, an effort ending with the bitter strike in the Minnesota forests which the National Guard helped break.

Not all the Wisconsin strikes were confined to the north. In February, 1917—about two months before the United States entered the war—an I.W.W. organizer and six assistants were arrested and fined $5.00 each in Milwaukee city court for disturbing the peace during a strike against a construction company. In that case, when the assistant city attorney asked for a dismissal, the judge instead dismissed the attorney. After passing sentence on the defendants, the judge gave the attorney a tongue-lashing for "casting aspersions" on the arresting policemen.

With the coming of war, the cost of living soared. From August, 1915, to June, 1918, it was up 58 per cent; by the end of the war, the cost of living had climbed another 16 per cent. Wages did not keep pace with prices, and this explains why there were more strikes during World War I than in any previous 20-month period in American history. This was in spite of a no-strike agreement on the part of the American Federation of Labor, an agreement which the I.W.W. haughtily refused to consider. In Milwaukee, as elsewhere, there were many strikes, but most of them were brief.

War hysteria prodded citizens from all over the state to pour reports of I.W.W. activity—by their definition but not by any legal definition disloyal—to state and federal officials.

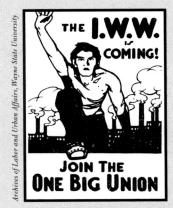

THE I.W.W. is COMING!

JOIN THE ONE BIG UNION

Archives of Labor and Urban Affairs, Wayne State University

The state Council of Defense was besieged with such reports, most of which it referred to federal agents. Police and sheriffs often acted on their own to jail men suspected of I.W.W. work, and apparently many policemen considered any out-of-town troublemaker a Wobbly.

During July, 1917, an Industrial Workers organizer was jailed at Milwaukee for inciting strikes, for insulting the president and for lying to obtain his naturalization papers. He had a German name. There was no record of any indictment. During the same month, a thirty-four-year-old man was arrested near the armory at Whitefish Bay. When his pockets revealed an I.W.W. dues book, he was charged with vagrancy.

Two incidents in September, 1917, indicate the fear that the I.W.W. evoked in Wisconsin. Police thought it worth an investigation when a Civil War veteran at Portage said he saw a stranger with an I.W.W. button on his vest inquiring about a hotel room; the police found no trace of the man. The other incident involved Albert Wolfe, federal attorney for the Western District of Wisconsin. While working in his Madison office one morning, Wolfe pinned on a red-and-black button confiscated from an I.W.W. member. It was an office joke, but he forgot to remove it before going to lunch. When he returned, there were reports on his desk about the Wobbly seen in that restaurant. There was no local, state or federal law against belonging to or working for the I.W.W.

On September 5, 1918, federal agents raided Wobbly offices in 33 cities, including three branches in Milwaukee. The agents expressed disappointment that no members were present, but a national officer of the Industrial Workers wrote that all locals knew in advance of the impending "secret" raids. Without warrants, the agents ransacked drawers and safes, hauling off great piles of records and literature. They also swooped down on homes of individual union leaders, in one case seizing a bundle of old love letters. On September 13, they made a second pass at one I.W.W. office in Milwaukee, arresting two local officials and again filling their sacks with records—records which never were returned, incidentally.

Unlike most states with Wobbly activity, Wisconsin did not enact an anti-syndicalist law. Such laws punish membership in any group which seeks to use force to bring about industrial and/or political reforms. The laws were aimed directly at the Industrial Workers. Each house of the Wisconsin legislature adopted a version of such a bill in 1919, but they could not agree on a compromise version.

—JOHN D. STEVENS

From "War Hysteria and the Wobblies," in *The Badger State: A Documentary History of Wisconsin*, Barbara and Justus Paul, eds. (Eerdmans, 1979).

designed to "resist the demands of the union." Whiting was elected president.[26]

Despite the employers' intransigence, some workers continued to meet with Hamilton, and in February and March they formed lodges in Nekoosa, Grand Rapids, and Stevens Point. Nevertheless, even Hamilton acknowledged that there was more bravado than substance behind the ultimatum which he had sent to the Wisconsin millowners in February:[27]

If the men are permitted to resume work at 7 a.m. Monday, April 7, 1902 it will be taken as . . . your acceptance of . . . the shorter-hour schedule.... You are hereby notified that if workmen or women in your employ are discriminated against because of their sympathy with or . . . are members of the United Brotherhood of Papermakers of America . . . it shall be sufficient cause for immediate and concerted action on the part of the United Brotherhood.

The replies from the mill managers in the Grand Rapids and Stevens Point areas had differed only in their degree of disdain. The manager of the Nekoosa Paper Company had responded that "no . . . bloodsucker representing . . . an alleged union will ever be permitted to inject his . . . vile slandering lies between us." The response from George Whiting's Plover mill was to discharge a shipping clerk who had worked at the mill for five years and was trying to organize the plant. "He was discharged for reasons sufficient for the management," declared the mill manager.[28]

The paperworkers held a protest rally at which they formed a new lodge, elected officers whose names they refused to divulge, and demanded that the company reinstate the clerk. When nothing happened, about twenty-five union men shut down the plant and walked out, followed by "some 15 or 20 of the young ladies employed in the finishing room."[29] (A UBPM spokesman noted in April that about one-third of the workers striking the paper mills throughout Wisconsin were "girls employed in the finishing rooms."[30]) At Whiting's mill at Stevens Point, union members also walked out, making about seventy strikers in both mills. According to management, a dozen strikers returned to work within a week and, with some additional replacements, both mills were able to operate fully.[31]

Nevertheless, the struggle continued. Whiting stated that the mills would run if it meant that every man in the plant had to be imported from the East. An organizer from the UBPM national headquarters in Massachusetts came to Stevens Point. AFL President Samuel Gompers sent an organizer from Springfield, Illinois, to explain the strikers' case to the public and to organize Stevens Point workers who were not employed in the paper mills. Frank Weber, head of the Wisconsin State Federation of Labor, came from Milwaukee to organize the paper mill women. The strikes in the Whiting mills led the manager of the Grand Rapids Pulp and Paper Company in Biron to expect a strike "at any moment." He dismissed six of his men, replaced them with a non-union crew, and announced that he would dismiss all union men and make the entire mill non-union.[32]

The union's ultimatum date of April 1 drew nearer. The *Wood County Reporter* warned the workers that if they struck they would "never have an opportunity to return to work" and might "force the paper mills on the Wisconsin River to employ only non-union help."[33] On April 5 the workers made their own decision. Fifty-five at the Nekoosa Paper Company and twenty at the company in Biron did not report for the Saturday night shift, stopping all but one machine in each of these mills. The members of the Brokaw lodge shut down the papermaking division of the Wausau Paper Mills. The Stevens Point and Plover strikers, who had been out since February, appealed to the strikebreakers still working inside these mills to honor the April 5 deadline and join the strike. The AFL organizer and William Hamilton tried to win their support with a special public meeting in Stevens Point, but no one came out of the mills to join the strikers.[34]

By the end of April, 1902, the strikers in the Wisconsin River Valley were defeated. Those strikers who had been living in company houses in Brokaw moved away. A large number of the Biron and Nekoosa strikers now were shoveling sand for the Chicago and North Western Railroad Company at $1.75 per day—"not in [competition] with the $3.75 a day workers inside a paper mill." The Brokaw, Nekoosa, Stevens Point, and Grand Rapids lodges died.[35]

1902: Defeat on the Eau Claire River

In the course of this drive to extend the shorter-hour contract to all mills, two Neenah paper mill workers took the train to Eau Claire in March, 1902, and talked with the workers employed by the Dells Paper and Pulp Company. They were followed by Hamilton, who established a UBPM lodge and held several meetings with the Dells management. This was done despite of the fact that the Dells management, in recognition of the "condition of affairs in the Fox River Valley," had followed the Wisconsin River tactics and had called its employees together in an early December meeting at which an anti-union agreement was reached. The Dells superintendent described how he later, in April, maneuvered against the union and into a strike:[36]

One of the men came and told me that two or three of the men wanted to meet me. I told them that I . . . could not meet with them that evening. The men replied that the following day would be perfectly satisfactory. That evening I made a canvass throughout the plant, asking every man and boy to meet me in conference next morning, I agreeing to pay each a half-day's wages in addition for their time at the conference. Next morning I ordered the mill closed down so that night and day forces might attend the conference. All but one man attended—some 250 or more hands.

At the conference, the superintendent asked the workers to await the outcome of a meeting of Eastern paper manufacturers and their employees, scheduled for May 15, at which the shorter-hour schedule was to be discussed. He asked the men to vote on his proposal by moving to the right (for) or left (against) side of the room. All but five moved to the right. Those five then submitted their resignations. The superintendent's narrative continued:

We supposed everything O.K. until this morning when one machine tender and about fifteen helpers refused to work under existing conditions and were paid off. We shut the mill down, made some much needed repairs, and expected to start our two large machines in the morning. Our beater engineers and helpers to a man, we are proud to say ... were all at their posts ready for duty ....

The Marathon Paper Company in Rothschild, circa 1900.

State Historical Society of Wisconsin WHi (X3) 49769

There was no dissatisfaction whatever in our mill until the advent of the organizers.

Hamilton's report of this episode was entirely different:[37] Mr. O'Brien [the superintendent] . . . especially abused the officers and influential members of the unions. His language is said to have been so vile and abusive that five of his machine tenders, helpers and engineers quit on the spot. This action was the cause of a sympathetic strike, a day or two following, which involved almost the entire mill, all except two machine tenders, . . . [another man] and his brother.

According to Hamilton, the Eau Claire police force joined the company against the strikers,

> . . . with the chief at the head riding around to the homes of the men and boys, using all kinds of arguments either to persuade or compel them to return to work. These tactics were very effectual . . . and succeeded in driving a few back to work. By this time several scabs had been imported from other points.

When Hamilton returned to Eau Claire, the police went after him. On the afternoon of April 30, Hamilton was writing a letter in the writing room of the Eau Claire House while the chief of police was in the hotel office. Hamilton was called to the phone, and when he returned, the letter was gone. Using this letter as evidence, the municipal judge issued a warrant for Hamilton's arrest. Hamilton was taken to jail for the night. The complaint, read in court the next morning, charged that Hamilton and several others, who were named but never arrested, conspired to close the mill and conspired to cause the employees to go out on strike.

Trial was scheduled for May 6 and bail was set at $400. Hamilton reported that although the strikers took up a collec-tion for the bail, it actually was paid for by Mayor David Hammel of Appleton. At the trial, a witness who earlier had admitted to being a detective now admitted that he had taken the letter. After two days of argument the judge discharged Hamilton. The company lost the case, but the UBPM lost the strike and the Eau Claire lodge died.[38]

Annihilation of the Unions, 1903-1904

The losses in Eau Claire, Menasha, and the Wisconsin River Valley made the gains in the rest of the Fox River Valley untenable. Whistling in the dark, organizer David Sullivan from the International Brotherhood of Papermakers (formed in 1902 when a second union of machine tenders, the International Paper Machine Tenders, merged with the UBPM) stated that "a determined effort will be made to bring everyone of the Fox River paper mills into the short hour agreement, though methods different from those in the past will be adopted."[39] As an omen of success he cited the Nicolet Lodge, which he had just organized in De Pere among workers at the American Writing Paper Company. Sullivan expressed faith in the power of the new IBPM union label and in the International Typographical Union's promise to work only on paper bearing that label.

A letter from Kimberly-Clark, however, to the first lodge meetings at Neenah-Menasha and Appleton in the new year, 1903, confronted the paper mill workers with their true situation. The letter, pointing out that Kimberly-Clark's competitors were getting twelve hours more work for the same weekly pay, was a signal that Kimberly-Clark was planning to resume the Saturday night shift.

The Fox Valley lodges joined forces to fight, and throughout January, 1903, presented petitions and counterproposals to Kimberly-Clark, all to no avail. Even their own International president declared that, under the terms of their contract, it was the "duty" of the Fox Valley lodges to return to the Saturday night shift.[40] The papermakers, however, had the support of George Gilbert, President of the Gilbert Paper Company in Menasha, who "assert[ed] the justice of their demand" and continued the shorter hours in his mill.[41] It should be noted that Gilbert's competitors were in the East and consequently were on the shorter schedule. Shorter hours were continued also by the Combined Locks Paper Company, the Union Bag and Paper Company, the Thilmany Pulp and Paper Company, and Shattuck and Babcock, a subsidiary of the American Writing Paper Company in De Pere. The remainder of the Fox Valley paperworkers returned to the Saturday night shift in early 1903.

This was an intolerable reverse for the paperworkers, who, in February, issued an ultimatum demanding reinstatement of the shorter schedule by March 1.[42] The issue was not joined fully until mid-April, when Kimberly-Clark agreed to operate its Neenah mill and the Neenah Paper Company mill on the short schedule without a pay reduction because other mills making that particular type of paper were on short schedules. Kimberly-Clark's Globe mill and its Badger mill, however, would continue to work Saturday nights until mills making their type of paper stopped the Saturday night shift. The lodges replied that they would not consider the proposal, and demonstrated their indignation by agreeing to strike if their demands were not met.[43] But even with new contracts from the Strange, Winnebago, and Neenah Paper companies in hand, the union could not move Kimberly-Clark. A strike against the former champion of the shorter schedule appeared certain.

About forty-eight hours before the scheduled strike time, the State Board of Arbitration stepped in. As the deadline approached, the board came up with a proposal for extending negotiations: if the union would stay out on Saturday night, April 18, the Board would convince Kimberly-Clark to pay for that one night not worked. With its credibility thus saved, the union could postpone its full strike for one more week.[44]

Kimberly-Clark agreed, but when 600 paper mill workers walked out in Neenah, Menasha, and Appleton on Saturday night, not even they knew if it was a strike or a gesture.[45] Not until Sunday did the union decide to postpone the strike for one week. This was a compromise that paid off, for after several days of sparring with the union at meetings held by the State Board, Kimberly-Clark capitulated and signed a contract granting the "short hour term with full pay for one year from May 1, 1903 to May 1, 1904 with all conditions of wages, hours, etc. to be the same as enjoyed during 1902."[46]

The Hamilton Lodge hosted a victory celebration for 200 paperworkers from Appleton, Little Chute, Combined Locks, and Kaukauna. A "bountiful supper" was served and local delegates gave a report on the Paper Makers' national convention. Euphorically, the Menasha newspaper concluded that it was only a question of time until the men would be granted the eight-hour shift. No one had the ability to foresee that this would be the last celebration for a long time to come.

The victorious workers knew their shorter-hour schedule could not continue if non-union mills across the state continued to operate long hours. So, once more an IBPM organizer, John

Malin, traveled up and down the paper mill rivers of Wisconsin, and once more he found the mill owners on the offensive. Along the Wisconsin River, for example, after Malin had established a local in Stevens Point, one of its twenty-three members was called to the mill office and given an ultimatum by a principal stockholder in the company: "You must either quit the mill or quit the union." The worker quit the mill. The organizer dashed back to Stevens Point in panic, because "a strike would retard us all over the West [Wisconsin]." It took two weeks of negotiation to get this "brother" back to work, but the new local remained intact with twenty members.[47]

In the entire Wisconsin River Valley, however, Malin had only one success. In Port Edwards, "after spending . . . four

Dover Publications, New York

VOCATIONAL EDUCATION

A MORE promising avenue towards an alternative education, however, was one to which Wisconsin had already made a commitment. The legislature of 1911, after considering the report of a blue ribbon committee appointed to study the problem of keeping young people in school, had passed the first of a series of laws creating a state system of vocational education. By 1921, every city with a population of 5,000 or more was compelled to establish a vocational school. Children not attending a full-time school were required to attend a vocational school half-time until they had reached sixteen years of age, and then they were required to spend eight hours a week in classes until they were eighteen. Vocational education received support in matching grants from the federal government after passage of the Smith-Hughes Act of 1917, and by the school year 1925-1926 the State Board of Vocational Education could report a daytime student enrollment of more than 34,000 in the vocational schools of some forty Wisconsin cities. In 1926-1927, the state spent nearly $3 million on vocational schools, or about 4 per cent of its total expenditures for education.

During the early years of its operation, and especially during the war, the Wisconsin system of vocational education met criticism from educators who believed that separating vocational education from the regular public schools came dangerously close to following a Prussian model. Charles H. Judd, head of the department of education at the University of Chicago, charged that the Wisconsin system was "un-American, undemocratic, unwise, and unheeding of a great deal of experience." He believed that "we are as a nation committed to utter and relentless opposition to the caste system fostered by any such scheme." To offset criti-

weeks . . . I formed a local. I had all of the men in Port Edwards and half of those in the Hurlytown mill.... The rest ... were working under a [company] contract," and joined when their contract expired on January 1, 1904.[48]

In Oconto Falls, on the Oconto River, it was Malin himself whom the mill workers feared: "They were under the impression that we or the executive board [of the IBPM] would order them on strike and I could not get it out of their heads." However, the backtenders and third hands wanted to organize and were granted an IBPM charter. They learned, unfortunately, that their lodge could not survive without the skilled papermakers. When required to quit the union or quit the mill, the backtenders and thirdhands chose the latter. The company kept

the mill running, and the union died. At Park Falls, on the Flambeau River, Malin "found a good crowd of boys" and organized the Flambeau-Park Falls Lodge. On the Menominee River he organized a new Marinette-Menominee Lodge to replace the one that had lost a strike for "Saturday night off" in April, 1902, but this one also died within a year.[49]

The International Brotherhood of Paper Makers lodges along the Fox River thus continued to stand alone and vulnerable. Furthermore, a significant change in the attitude of the Fox River millowners put not only the short hour schedules, but the very existence of the union in jeopardy. In the crises of 1902 and 1903, each Fox River paper mill owner had acted independently, but when their union contracts expired on May 1, 1904,

---

cisms such as Judd's, vocational schools in Wisconsin began offering more courses of a general and theoretical character rather than concentrating solely on courses typical of trade schools. Charles McCarthy, who had been a member of the committee that initiated the program in 1911, urged the state's manufacturers to get for their employees "that broad education which will lead to the efficiency which is needed . . . and which will open wide the doors of opportunity for the poorest boy and girl."

Wisconsin's system of vocational education managed to survive the war years, and during the New Era it continued to expand its program for part-time students. Local boards of industrial education received authorization to establish evening classes as well as day classes, and evening enrollments more than kept pace with daytime classes. By the end of the decade, nearly 50,000 Wisconsin people were attending school at night, while daytime enrollments numbered fewer than 37,000. For some of the night students, particularly for recent immigrants, evening classes took the place of elementary school. For others who wished to go on in mathematics, history, language, or literature, the evening classes served the same purposes as undergraduate college courses. For those who wished to develop special skills or a trade, the emphasis was more typically vocational.

A major reason for the success of the Wisconsin vocational schools during the New Era was the support they received from organized labor. Early in the decade, the Wisconsin State Federation of Labor backed the establishment of labor colleges to provide training in trade-union administration for the workers of several Wisconsin cities. The idea gained support, and by mid-decade labor leaders were urging the expansion of labor college programs. "The greatest enemy of the masses is ignorance," wrote Frank J. Weber in a letter to the Milwaukee *Leader*. "But the time is coming when the workers will realize ignorance is the pillar that upholds wage slavery." As if to fulfill Weber's prediction, the Wisconsin State Federation of Labor held a general conference on education in Milwaukee in 1926. The workers in attendance were quick to respond to the new theories of education then being applied in the public schools. In their

discussions they reached a consensus that "education is not a matter of formal instruction for merely a few years, but a process of a lifetime; that it is not enough to send children to school, but it matters much what is done with them while there; . . . that the old way had for its aim the storing of knowledge for future use, while the objective of the new school is the child as the starting point." In general agreement on educational purposes and approaches, the conferees turned to planning for the future education of workers. One conference suggestion was that a labor committee on education be formed in every Wisconsin community. Such a committee could then see to it that every city secured a special college for workers. Ultimately, the practice of according preferential treatment on the basis of social caste could be eliminated, equal opportunities for all could become an accepted rule in the realm of learning, and the new system could produce "a superior citizenry," well qualified to meet its responsibilities in a "permanent democracy."

The labor college idea made modest headway until arrival of the Great Depression and the subsequent expansion of the School for Workers at the University of Wisconsin. In the meantime, the state vocational system bore marks of the workers' demand for courses in liberal as well as technical subjects. When William John Cooper, United States commissioner of education, visited Milwaukee in the summer of 1929, he found the city's vocational school program "the best of its kind in the country." Touring the facility and visiting classes, he thought, led one "to realize that a human being is more than an adjunct to a machine, that to be a resourceful individual he needs music, art, literature as well as mechanical skill." He found the students earnest, and he thought them intent upon getting the most out of what the school had to offer. "In this age of change when you never can tell what moment your job will be wiped out," he concluded on the eve of the stock market crash, "the function of education must be to teach individuals how to adjust themselves to these sudden changes."

—PAUL W. GLAD

From *The History of Wisconsin, Volume V*
(State Historical Society of Wisconsin, Madison, 1990). Notes omitted.

The Northern Paper and Pulp Mills, Green Bay, circa 1900.

they united in a determinedly anti-union effort. Charles W. Howard, president of the Howard Paper Company, Menasha, expressed the change succinctly: "I am tired of unionism and will stand with the other manufacturers."[50]

The manufacturers took the offensive by polling their employees individually on whether they would work the longer schedule. In response, the IBPM delivered an ultimatum to the manufacturers on Monday, May 30: "You are hereby notified that in dealing with your employees you cannot deal with them individually but [only] through the International Brotherhood of Papermakers.[51] The ultimatum brought the manufacturers together in a meeting the next day at the Howard Paper Company office. The strength of their anti-union feeling was demonstrated when the superintendent of the Combined Locks Paper Company went directly from the meeting to the mill and ordered all employees to quit the union or call at the office for their pay. Sixty of the workers replied by going out on strike.[52]

Saturday, June 4, was the day when the Saturday-night shift was to be reinstated. Both sides prepared for confrontation. The manufacturers polled employees on whether they would walk out, and offered extra pay to leading union men if they would work during the strike and teach non-union men to operate the machines. Merchants warned that they would not extend credit to strikers. IBPM president George W. Mackey came to Neenah to prepare for a strike. As the 6:00 P.M. deadline neared, the mill owners admitted that the "effort to secure union men to run a few machines has been so unsuccessful that no effort will be made to keep them running, until replacements can be slowly secured." The manufacturers threatened to blacklist: "The men who go out tonight will be considered members of the union by the manufacturers. As such, they cannot be again employed in the mills of any of the manufacturers interest-

ed in the controversy. This has been agreed upon by the manufacturers who are determined to break up the union."[53]

Undeterred, the workers struck at the Atlas, Vulcan, Tioga, Telulah, Riverside Fibre and Paper, and Wisconsin Tissue mills in Appleton; the Combined Locks Paper Company in Combined Locks; the C. W. Howard Paper Company and the John Strange Paper Company in Menasha; and the Kimberly-Clark and Neenah Paper companies in Neenah. In total, these mills employed about 900 workers. The Gilbert Paper Company in Menasha and the Fox River Paper Company in Appleton continued their shorter-hour schedule; in both cases their Eastern competitors were also on shorter hours. The Winnebago Paper Company in Neenah continued the shorter schedule, instituted after its long strike in 1902.[54]

The State Board of Arbitration found the millowners adamant in their refusal to deal with the union, but willing to pay for the hours added by reinstituting the Saturday night shift; the union rejected this offer. Despite this militant spirit, the first ten days of the strike were peaceful, and none of the struck mills tried to open. President Mackey felt confident enough to leave the Fox Valley and go to Stevens Point to muster support.

But on June 14 the picnic ended: forty men, half of them experienced papermakers brought in from the East and the remainder made up of former Kimberly-Clark employees, reported for work at the Badger mill "amid the jeers of striking papermakers and other union men." The strikers who had planned to camp out for the duration of the strike were called back to town to picket the mill. Probably they had no premonition of the total disaster that awaited them.[55]

While the State Board of Arbitration and a special union committee were searching for a compromise, the strikers were taking direct action. Three hundred gathered at the Russell House in Neenah, where the imported strikebreakers were

State Historical Society of Wisconsin WHi (X3) 49767

The influx of strikebreakers diminished the strikers' strategic position and, consequently, their spirit.

housed. A band played; the crowd threw eggs. James Kimberly and Frank J. Sensenbrenner, an official of Kimberly-Clark, went to Mayor Charles Schultz's office to ask for protection. The Neenah Common Council debated hiring special police, but the issue so divided the council that it referred the question to the mayor. In Appleton none of the struck mills were able to open. In Menasha, the Howard mill tried to open on Monday, June 20, but only four of the hundred men who had agreed to come to work reported at the mill.[56]

The next day there was shooting in Neenah. About 150 angry strikers followed a group of strikebreakers who were being escorted to the Russell House by a Kimberly-Clark Company guard, Fred Potter, who was either knocked down and kicked or simply fell down amid the surging crowd. He got up and fired his pistol three times from the Russell House steps. He told the police, who promptly seized him: "I am from Chicago and was employed by the millmen to carry supplies to the men at work. I am not a papermaker and know nothing about the business." The police took Potter to Oshkosh immediately "to avoid a lynching."[57]

Violence continued to erupt sporadically in Neenah over the next ten days. Strikers and strikebreakers chased each other, beat each other with shovels, and on one occasion, one fired a gun at another. When a worker from the Kimberly-Clark Niagara mill was seen with a union officer in Neenah, he was called to the central office and fired for being in collusion with the union. In Menasha, union members helped to keep the peace, and in Appleton the strikers avoided confrontation by staying off the streets and away from the mills.[58]

In July, Fred Potter, the Kimberly-Clark guard, went on trial at the Winnebago County Courthouse in Oshkosh. He testified that he worked for the B. H. Holmes agency in Chicago, doing "secret service work," often in the guise of a plant fireman, and that Holmes had put him to work for various midwest compa-

nies during strikes and lockouts. Holmes had sent him to do this "secret work" for Kimberly-Clark. The judge dismissed Potter on the second day of the trial.[59]

The Neenah-Menasha millowners continued to import non-union workers. It was rumored that these imports, many of them unskilled, were being paid considerably higher wages than had been paid to the skilled papermakers on strike. The strikers received a weekly stipend from the IBPM, beginning on the first Saturday in July, of five dollars a week for those with families, three dollars for those without. Since there was a labor shortage in Neenah-Menasha, some strikers found other jobs.[60]

The influx of strikebreakers diminished the strikers' strategic position and, consequently, their spirit. When Kimberly-Clark's Badger mill reopened in mid-June, the strikers picketed and demonstrated, but when the Howard and Strange mills opened a month later, they made no move. On the last Saturday in July, twenty-five strikers asked to return to work at the Howard mill. They were accepted, began work at noon, and worked on into the night. Company president Charles Howard said he was working a double crew so that "all the men might be together." The remaining strikers rallied, and during the evening about a hundred of them gathered outside the mill to call out the deserters. Finally, about 4:30 A.M. Sunday morning, the twenty-five walked out of the mill. A union meeting was held then and there, and the strikers decided to continue the strike.[61]

In Appleton the strikers continued to have the sympathy of the community and overwhelmingly had endorsed the strike at every union meeting through early August. But, like their fellow strikers in Neenah-Menasha, they had been unable to keep the Appleton mills from operating. During the first week in August, Kimberly-Clark brought new workers, guarded by five members of the police force and six Pinkerton detectives, into its Atlas mill to operate the last idle machine in that mill. Its Tioga mill was being operated under the protection of Pinkerton guards, and its Vulcan plant was due to open as soon as more outside workers arrived. The apparently limitless supply of outside labor, together with some defections from their own ranks, finally forced the Appleton strikers to surrender. On Saturday, August 13, exactly ten weeks after the start of the strike, they met and voted to accept the Saturday night shift.[62]

The next day, IBPM President Mackey advised all of the Fox Valley strikers to return to work, which most of them did on Monday morning. Kimberly-Clark announced that it would

A march by labor groups in Rhinelander, 1919.

South Central Federation of Labor

"take back as many as we have places for. Some of the positions are already filled by outside help and these we will retain." By Monday afternoon a majority of the strikers were back at work, and the millowners notified their Eastern agents to stop sending strikebreakers. When some of the local union officials and strike leaders reported for work, they were turned away, and it was rumored that at least five of them never would be hired by a Wisconsin paper mill again. The president of the Appleton lodge, James Tolan, sold his house for $1,015 two days before the vote to surrender. The day after the vote, he left to take a job as machine tender in Fitchburg, Massachusetts.[63]

When the vice-president of the IBPM visited the Appleton and Kaukauna lodges at the end of 1904, he found the meetings were attended chiefly by "brothers placed on the blacklist by the manufacturers of the Fox River Valley."[64] By July, 1905, these two lodges no longer existed. Also dead by this time was the Niagara lodge, to which "every skilled man" in the Kimberly-Clark plant had belonged just the year before.[65]

The Hamilton Lodge of Neenah-Menasha died more slowly. In 1905 it still had enough strength to elect a delegate to the IBPM national convention and to help the Trades Council plan a Labor Day parade and picnic, to which the merchants and businessmen had promised to contribute "quite generously."[66]

The next year it sent to the *Paper Makers' Journal* a vigorous declaration of its continuing existence:[67]

> Certain papermakers have been parading around the country claiming to be good union men giving as the reason for being behind in their dues the following stuff and nonsense: They were members of Hamilton No. 18 and went out on strike and Hamilton No. 18 busted up, and the union owed them money, and it will be a long time before they have another local there. . . . Now, Mr. Editor, in justice to our local . . . Hamilton No. 18 has never been out of existence since it was organized over four years ago, and we stand to pay any claim of a member in good standing . . . we reinstated seven members last meeting and we have three applications for next meeting. Who says Hamilton No. 18 busted up?

Despite this bravado, by February of 1907 the Hamilton Lodge was dead, as was the Nicolet Lodge in De Pere. There were no more IBPM lodges in Wisconsin.[68]

The last attempt to obtain Saturday night off came in 1905, when a bill to reduce the weekly hours of the night shift from seventy-eight to sixty-five was introduced and subsequently killed in the Wisconsin legislature. The desire for shorter hours was not expunged, however, and some years later the Wisconsin paper mill workers reorganized and fought again, this time for the eight-hour day. ■

From *The Labor Movement in Wisconsin: A History* (State Historical Society of Wisconsin, Madison, 1984).

Labor's Daily Newspaper:
The Milwaukee Leader

ELMER AXEL BECK

The most successful Socialist daily newspaper in America, The Milwaukee Leader, *was launched in 1911. It also was the longest-lived Socialist daily, continuing to publish, despite government restrictions during World War I and unending fiscal problems, until 1939. In this piece, Elmer A. Beck describes how* The Leader *defined itself as both a labor paper and a political paper.*

THE *Milwaukee Leader* was Victor Berger's paper. As much as any institution can be said to be the creation of one man, *The Leader* was that. Berger founded it and kept it going for the eighteen years that were left of his life. Assuming all other circumstances were the same, it would be difficult to imagine *The Leader* coming into being and fulfilling the destiny it did without Berger.

Victor Berger was one of the founders and leaders of the Socialist movement in America; in Milwaukee and Wisconsin he was the leader. He was the complete political leader: boss, strategist, organizer, fund-raiser, propagandist, speaker. He was respected, admired, liked, and he was a vote-getter. He had his fault-finders and enemies too. What Berger and the Milwaukee Socialists created was more than a political machine; it was a political-economic movement, although of local scope.

To work with the movement in Milwaukee, Berger built a Socialist press. He started it in 1893 when he became editor of the *Arbeiter-Zeitung*, a triweekly German newspaper, and changed it to the daily *Wisconsin Vorwaerts*. For ten confident years between 1901 and 1911, Berger expounded on Socialism in editorials in the weekly *Social-Democratic Herald*. The mounting success of the party led to the founding of the daily *Milwaukee Leader* and the building and equipping of a newspaper plant in Brisbane Hall in 1911. Plans for the financing of the daily were announced in "Progress Edition" of *The Herald* on February 11, 1911. A goal of $100,000 was deemed necessary to assure success. Bonds were sold in $10 denominations, paying 4 percent interest. The funds were needed to pay for new presses and other equipment.

A winter publication date for the daily was decided in August when almost half of the bond issue had been subscribed. A wire service contract was negotiated with United Press in October. When the first edition of *The Leader* was published, $85,000 had been raised. But in the next eight months, less than $5,000 in bonds were sold, and the campaign ended—

more than $10,000 short of the original goal. Nearly $15,000 of bonds were bought by twenty-seven local unions in Milwaukee and by unions in twenty-one states. Socialist branches in Milwaukee and in 37 states bought a total of $7,750.

On September 21, 1911, under the headline, "Brisbane Hall Now Great Labor and Socialist Center," *The Social-Democratic Herald* reported: "The new home of the Socialist press and labor unions is now finished and practically all rented to first-class tenants."

The Milwaukee Leader was born December 7, 1911. The essence of *The Leader* as a Socialist paper was exemplified by the first issue, which carried on its front page a three-column cartoon of a ship labeled "Milwaukee Leader,' flying the flag "Socialism," full sails billowing, shooting down a sinking ship identified as "Capitalism and the Old Parties."

The lead story, under the banner head "Gas Records Reveal Extortion for Benefit of Wall Street," started a crusade against the gas monopoly and its high rates. It reported that Congressman Berger had introduced a bill to nationalize industrial combinations that were more than 40 percent monopoly; the story also noted Berger's bills to nationalize the railroads, express companies, coal mines and telegraph and telephone companies, and his bill to provide for old-age pensions. There was a column on page ten, "Work and Workers," by Carl Sandburg. The women's page carried a column of women's suffrage news. The well-known boxing promoter, T.S. Andrews, edited the sports page. A copy of the newspaper cost 1 cent.

While *The Leader*'s regular run would be eight pages, the first was sixteen with a normal variety of advertising including three large ads from the department stores, Schuster's, Gimbel's and the Boston Store.

The new Socialist daily would find the capitalist competitive world very palpable from the beginning. The competition would be ceaseless and comprehensive, overt and covert, throughout the paper's existence. In its first week *The Leader* found it necessary to send out "flying squads" to protect its newsboys from being beaten up.

Before the spring election in 1912, *The Milwaukee Sentinel* printed American and red flags in color on its front page and called on voters to choose between them. Seidel was defeated, and the Socialists were set back by a so-called fusion of the Democrats and the Republicans. And Berger was defeated for re-election in the fall of that year. After the 1912 spring election, the going became difficult. Many advertisers boycotted *The Leader*, deficits mounted, and on May 7, 1912 the price of the paper was raised to 2 cents although the other papers were still a penny.

State Historical Society of Wisconsin

Victor L. Berger's credentials to the convention of the International Typographical Union, 1904.

imposed upon each a sentence of twenty years in Leavenworth. On January 31, 1921 the supreme court reversed the decision of Judge Landis, and all proceedings against the defendants were dropped.

Beginning in August 1918 delivery of mail to *The Leader* was stopped; these were stamped "Undeliverable under Espionage Act" and returned to the senders. A Leader editorial of October 19, 1918, stated:

> The following cannot reach us by mail: money due on subscriptions; money for new subscriptions; money for advertising; mail from our paid correspondents; mail and feature service; change of address . . . Since October 3, 1917, when the mailing right of *The Leader* was revoked, we have lost $70,000 in subscription money and $50,000 in local and national advertising.
>
> Now, mind you, no court has found us guilty of any crime. The tremendous loss of $120,000 was the result of the act of one man, the Postmaster General of the United States. Plutocracy is safe, but democracy is being murdered."

In many ways *The Leader*'s first year, with its ups and downs, foretold what the following years would be; each would be marked by struggle and crisis and transient triumph.

In 1916, on the paper's fifth anniversary, Berger wrote in an editorial:

> The Leader has lived through the hardest years of its existence. . . . *The Milwaukee Leader* is convinced that when the time comes to decide whether the people of the United States shall own our country, or a few men shall own it, the verdict of the American people will be for themselves. The verdict will be for Socialism and to lead in that fight is the mission of The Milwaukee Leader.

Even rougher days lay directly ahead; these resulted from the Socialists' opposition to America's entrance into the war in Europe in 1917. *The Milwaukee Leader* was barred from the second-class mailing privilege. Berger explained that the "authorities object to the general tendency of the paper as being against war. In case *The Leader* should be suppressed it will keep its plant and even the organization intact—as far as possible—and start *The Leader* again the day after peace is declared."

Some of the local department stores withdrew their advertising. The readers numbered 25,000. Lost by the denial of second-class mail rights were 15,650 out-of-town readers. *The Milwaukee Journal*, in a front-page editorial, fired a violent attack on *The Leader* on December 11, 1917, which charge that persons who subscribed to *The Leader* and those who advertised in it were directly encouraging disloyalty. *The Leader* reacted the next day. Berger said *The Journal* was guilty of printing misrepresentations and falsehoods.

Three months later *The Leader* reported that Berger and four other Socialists had been indicted under the Espionage Act of 1917 because of their opposition to the World War. The trial in Chicago began December 9, 1918. Five weeks later the defendants were found guilty. Judge Kenesaw M. Landis

The Leader's tribulations with the government had no apparent adverse effect on the political fortunes of the Socialists. In the spring election of 1918, Mayor Hoan was re-elected and the Socialist representation in the common council increased from 12 to 13. In the fall election that year, Berger was returned to congress and the Socialists carried the entire county ticket and elected eleven state legislators in Milwaukee County.

One year later, after the House of Representatives had refused to seat Berger, he won again in a special election. Again Berger was denied admission to Congress and again he was elected. He was finally seated on December 5, 1923, after the supreme court's reversal of his conviction. Berger was returned to Congress in 1924 and 1926. In 1928, Berger received the largest vote of his career, but he trailed the Republican William H. Stafford by 729 votes.

Berger died on August 7, 1929, twenty-two days after he had been struck by a streetcar at Third and Clarke streets. He was sixty-nine.

Any account of *The Milwaukee Leader* from its beginnings until August 1919 must also be an account of Victor L. Berger. The lives of this Socialist daily and this remarkable man for the years of their coexistence were inextricable. But *The Leader* as an institution was not subject to the abrupt mortality of a man; its death would take longer. ∎

From *The Sewer Socialists: A History of the Socialist Party of Wisconsin, 1897–1940* (Westburg, Fennimore, Wisconsin, 1982).

Labor Spies
and Union-Busting

DARRYL HOLTER

As unions became better organized, the employers' movement responded by improving its own efforts to thwart union organization. A big part of the new "open shop" strategy involved the use of undercover spies and detectives. Wisconsin enacted landmark laws that put some restrictions on detective work in industrial settings.

BULLETS fired by steelworkers and Pinkerton guards in 1892 at the Carnegie steel works in Homestead, Pennsylvania, ricocheted across America even to Wisconsin, where early trade unionists clearly perceived the threat posed by the Pinkertons. If employers could legally hire armed guards and detectives to repress strikers, then unionism had no future. Thus the small but growing labor movement in America began a half-century battle against professional union-busting and anti-labor espionage.[1]

Labor's fight for laws limiting espionage and strikebreaking went hand in hand with its efforts to win collective bargaining rights. But while a mountain of material on collective bargaining has appeared over the years, very little is known about the practice—or the practitioners—of labor espionage. The Wisconsin record, however, contains an unusually rich store of information about labor spies, and it reveals how organized labor confronted this threat. During the twenty years following the Homestead Strike, leaders in Wisconsin waged a campaign to pass a law prohibiting labor espionage. In 1925 they succeeded in securing passage of a new law inhibiting union-busting which served as a model for similar legislation in other states. A few years later, controversy over the use of professional strikebreakers in Kenosha focused more attention on union-busting, prompting yet more political and legislative action to limit professional strikebreaking. In the paper mills of northern Wisconsin especially, union organizers confronted a powerful network of employer-backed espionage. During the height of the CIO organizing drives of the 1930's, Wisconsin Senator Robert M. La Follette, Jr., chaired the dramatic congressional hearings that unmasked the labor spy racket and ultimately compelled the Pinkerton company to abandon its lucrative industrial operations.

Tracing this illegal and often invisible side of industrial relations demonstrates how management and union strategies changed over time, becoming more sophisticated and more costly, evolving in response to economic trends, political events, and changes in federal and state laws governing labor relations. The Wisconsin experience confirms the value of laws designed to curb such activities, but it also shows that laws alone could not eliminate union-busting.

The Pinkerton problem was very much in the minds of the thirty-five trade unionists who met in 1893 at Fraternity Hall in Milwaukee to found the Wisconsin State Federation of Labor. These were ideological men, mostly of socialist or populist persuasions. They were also practical unionists who believed that political action might be used to compel the state to intervene on their behalf against professional strikebreaking. These two trends were evident in the "Declaration of Principles" that emerged from a nine-hour debate at the end of the convention. While criticizing the Pinkertons in the rhetoric of the time as "the private standing army of the plutocrats," these delegates to Wisconsin's first significant organizing convention called also for laws to abolish anti-labor detective agencies.[2] Within a year, the Wisconsin legislature passed legislation that prohibited the use of armed guards for the suppression of strikes or protection of property unless authorized to do so by the state.[3] The weakness of the new law, however, became apparent in 1896 when strikebreakers were simply deputized to crush a strike of street-railway workers.[4] Nevertheless, the passage of similar bills across the country signalled a growing public concern with strikebreaking and forced the detective agencies to shift tactics on the labor front. As it became more difficult to stop unions by cruder forms of repression, the agencies moved their operations underground. A more sophisticated labor spy system soon developed in the shops and factories of industrial America.

Who were the labor spies? What did they do? And what motivated them to engage in this occupation? Because of its clandestine nature, little is known for certain about anti-labor espionage. However, information from various studies and investigations allows us to describe how labor spies operated.

Because of his position in the shop, where he worked alongside other employees, the labor spy could perform a number of valuable tasks. With his help, union organizers could be easily identified and quickly fired. Their names were added to a blacklist maintained by the agency. If a union already existed in the shop, the spy reported who was in the union and the names of sympathizers. Spies also reported on strike related activities, which often resulted in conspiracy charges being leveled at pro-union workers. A spy might even join the union drive in order to obtain a list of the members. A round of selective firings, intimidation, and anti-union rumors often did the trick. A spy might also join the union in order to lead it to its demise. In strike situations, an agent provocateur could adopt a super-militant posture, perhaps even inducing other strikers to promote a violent act that would require police intervention. Or the labor spy could rise to leadership in the union in order to discredit the union and encourage the members to disband it. In a promotional letter to the Cutler Hammer Manufacturing Company of Milwaukee, a major detective agency, Corporations Auxiliary, indicated that where their services had been employed, union membership often fell and that "in many cases local union charters have been returned without publicity and a number of local unions have disbanded."[5] The agency's claim to be able to defeat the union "without publicity" appealed to the employer. Likewise, the spy required secrecy in order to continue his work.

Historians and others who have investigated the issue have disagreed over the role played by labor spies in industrial relations. Supporters of trade unions have viewed Pinkertonism in an entirely negative light. Morris Friedman, who worked as a stenographer for the Pinkerton's Denver office, left the group in 1905 to write an exposé entitled *The Pinkerton's Labor Spy.*[6] He related how the spies often promoted violence and fabricated reports in order to frighten the mine operators and stimulate a need for their services. Edward Levinson portrayed "Pearl" Bergoff, the notorious "King of the Strikebreakers," as a thoroughly despicable character.[7] Trade-union leaders reserved a special hatred for industrial detectives, viewing them as cruel and heartless men who sought to profit from the misery of others. Frank J. Weber, the first president of the Wisconsin State Federation of Labor, stated that "the labor spy is the most degraded human specimen of society."[8] Socialists saw anti-labor spies as mercenaries of capitalism.[9] Leo Huberman, in his book *The Labor Spy Racket,* showed how some workers' lack of class consciousness and desire for easy money had led them to become pliant tools of industrial repression.[10]

Besides simply collecting information for management, some spies were clever and energetic enough to be able to confuse fellow workers, frustrate a union organizing drive, or undermine an existing union.[11] It was widely assumed that only desperate persons, criminals, eccentrics, or persons of low moral character would embark on a career of strikebreaking or labor espionage. As businessmen increasingly sought to keep their distance from these controversial figures, agencies like Pinkerton emerged to fill the new demand for halting unionization.

Not everyone saw the Pinkertons in such a negative light, however. J. Bernard Hogg, who studied the Homestead Strike,

viewed the rise of industrial detective agencies as a byproduct and a logical outgrowth of industrialization itself. Before the industrial age, the sheriff maintained law and order because virtually all elements of society favored the protection of private property.[12] But when thousands of workers struck as one and demonstrated their willingness to defy authority, the Pinkertons and other similar agencies intervened because local police could not defend private property. In effect, they represented the will of the community in preserving order. A more recent article by R. Jeffreys-Jones offers an even more sympathetic interpretation of labor spies.[13] Jeffreys-Jones contends that industrial detectives were a group of specially qualified professionals who skillfully exploited fears of impending revolution and class war in order to make profits. Far from being rootless men of low moral character, these former military men, ex-policemen, and one-time union leaders supplied a necessary force for law and order. Disputing the old claim that labor spies were tools of the bosses, the author expressed the view that they opposed neither unionism nor the workers, but merely saw an opportunity to make money out of conflict.

If labor spies could have stepped forward to make their case, they no doubt would have followed this line of defense. Indeed, this view is promoted in the two published labor spy memoirs. In 1906 a writer using the pseudonym Thomas Beet revealed how a skilled detective could fan worker discontent and cultivate employer fears in order to create a continuing need for his services.[14] Beet, who claimed to be "just an honest private detective," saw himself as standing apart from both labor and capital. In 1937 a writer calling himself GT-99 authored a book called *Labor Spy* which chronicled the rise of a twentieth century industrial spy. Recruited to help a machine shop employer to quell a union drive, GT-99 worked his way through various shops and cities to become a top state labor official in the 1930's.[15] Like his predecessor Beet, GT-99 did not see himself as either for or against labor or management. Rather, he saw himself as an entrepreneur who worked behind the scenes to maintain order and to smooth out the rough edges of labor-management conflict.

When considering the value of these accounts written by former labor spies, it is hard to know where self-serving ends and the truth begins. Since the agents were paid by management, it is difficult to see them as a neutral force in industrial conflict. Then, too, if spies played such a beneficial role, it is surprising that only two such memoirs have appeared.

Most labor spies did not provide much information on who they were and why they chose such a strange occupation. Ex-spies purposely left their personal matters and details about their backgrounds cloaked in obscurity. Here the Wisconsin experience is instructive. One result of the 1925 detective law was that a surprisingly large amount of information provided by labor spies was recorded with Wisconsin's secretary of state. These records offer the only known profile of industrial detectives. The best example is the group of twenty-four operatives registered by the state's largest industrial detective firm, the Russell Agency, in 1928.[16]

Like other occupations related to industry in 1928, labor espionage was sex-segregated work. Only one woman was

The Union Labor Hall in Milwaukee, 1915.
The Federated Trades Council met here in 1900.

Milwaukee County Historical Society

civil service training or experience in the office or shipping room. By their education and training, the Russell detectives resemble the type of spy described by Jeffreys Jones: "specially qualified" agents who brought their experience and contacts in the military and police to the side of business in its fight to curb labor.[17] Besides knowing how to handle a weapon, wrote GT-99, many labor spies also knew how to use typewriters—a fairly unusual combination of skills in the 1920's.

While such training may have enhanced their effectiveness as spies, it hardly proves Jeffreys-Jones' contention that they were independent from their employers or the clients they served. Indeed, most of the Russell spies soon lost their jobs in 1929 when the agency began to abandon its industrial work. A Russell spokesman explained that the death of a man who headed up the agency's industrial work caused the change, but labor leaders claimed that the new Wisconsin law had made the difference.[18]

The Pinkertons and other national detective agencies also closed their doors in Wisconsin after 1928, actions that symbolized labor's temporary victory over the agencies. The new law greatly hindered anti-labor espionage, but the labor movement had to fight for twenty years in order to win it. A close look at that long legislative battle shows how business and union strategies clashed over the issues of labor espionage.

The tactics used by employers, business associations, and detective agencies evolved in response to labor's combativeness and degree of organization as well as to changes in the laws governing labor relations. Near the turn of the century, Milwaukee socialists and trade-unionists joined in a plan to strengthen the labor movement with more political action and bolder organizing efforts. By 1904 the movement had grown considerably, and the Milwaukee Federated Trades Council included more than 100 locals with 23,000 members. Historian Thomas Gavett notes that employers regarded the growing labor movement with attitudes ranging from grudging tolerance to outright hostility.[19] Each union victory fed their fears and led them to organize against unionization. A new employers' association called the Metal Trades and Founders' Bureau brought together most of the city's leading industrial figures and soon became a rallying point for the open shop crusade. The bureau collected information from member companies on each employee's work

found in the group of twenty-four. Most of the Russell spies were relatively young, with the largest group in their late twenties and early thirties. The notion that labor spies were nomadic or homeless itinerants is contradicted by the Russell sleuths. For one thing, most were home- grown: seventeen were born in Wisconsin, including nine from Milwaukee. Five more were born in neighboring states. Nor were they mysterious loners: about two-thirds were married and living with their spouses. Six were former policemen, and ten had worked in detective or intelligence work before coming to Russell. Several came to spy work through a railroad job, moving from the ranks of the workers to the rail company's private police and detective crews. Six had served in the military. The Russell detectives were relatively well-educated. All but two had completed at least eight years of school and seven more had graduated from or nearly completed high school. Five detectives had attended college. Others had

habits, attitudes, and union affiliation. It also sought to acquire membership lists from local labor organizations in order to make a more comprehensive blacklist of pro-union workers.

Speaking before the Milwaukee Federated Trades Council in March, 1903, Frank J. Weber, Wisconsin State Federation of Labor founder, claimed that for the first time, several Milwaukee employers had begun to use detective agencies to spy on workers.[20] National agencies that specialized in labor espionage, including the Burns Agency, Corporations Auxiliary, Gordon and Ferris, and Pinkerton, started operations in Wisconsin.[21] The dimensions of the spy problem emerged more clearly when 1,200 Milwaukee molders struck in 1906 for a wage hike and shorter hours. Most of the struck companies belonged to the bureau, which helped them by importing strikebreakers from the East Coast. One company hired the Burr-Herr detective agency, paying out more than $21,000 in less than a year. In the city council the Socialists introduced a resolution condemning the strikebreakers and supporting the strikers. With a large group of angry workers packing the common council hall, the motion passed. Allis Chalmers successfully asked for an injunction against the striking molders. The Wisconsin State Federation of Labor fought the injunction in the courts and, although it took two years, obtained a ruling that allowed limited picketing and boycotting of companies that used strikebreakers. The Molders Union also confronted the detectives with a counter espionage strategy when William O'Connor joined the detectives in order to learn their plans and later to testify against the agencies. Fifty-three strikebreakers were indicted on various charges and all but two were convicted. But the strike failed and the spy problem continued.[22]

At the Wisconsin State Federation of Labor convention in 1907, Friedman's new book, *The Pinkerton's Labor Spy,* was discussed and the group ordered the purchase of 100 copies to distribute to the workers.[23] Reporting to the convention, Secretary-Treasurer Fred Brockhausen ventured that "if the public became familiar with the underhanded and treacherous methods of the private detectives, there would be legislation in Wisconsin to put an end to this evil."[24] Based on the idea that public exposure could thwart the work of anti-labor spy agencies, the delegates demanded a law to make detective agencies register and obtain licenses from the secretary of state. But a bill introduced by Weber and Brockhausen was defeated in 1907. Two years later they tried a different approach with a bill to prohibit the hiring of detectives who had not lived in the state for more than a year. They hoped that wide spread antipathy to the transporting of strikebreakers across state lines would help to pass a measure that would be the first step in fighting the labor spy racket. But that bill also failed to pass.

As the trade-union movement grew, the spy problem grew as well. In 1911 the personal union between the Socialists and organized labor bore fruit as eleven Milwaukee Socialists were elected to the state legislature. Membership in the Wisconsin State Federation of Labor increased from 5,000 members near the turn of the century to 15,000 in 1914. The movement also attracted many young intellectuals such as the young labor news reporter, Carl Sandburg. At the federation's 1912 convention, Sandburg chaired the resolutions committee. He drafted a reso-

lution that linked the need to combat "strikebreakers, finks, and working class traitors" with the task of organizing the industrial workers.[25] As the convention ended, Weber took the floor to claim that the use of labor spies had increased and that the unions had uncovered a larger number of suspects than in previous years. The former seaman and carpenter, who had worked as a union organizer among miners in West Virginia, exclaimed that private detectives were committing: "One of the foulest stains upon the pages of American history. In no other civilized country would such practices be tolerated. We need legislation to curb these activities and this matter should receive our utmost attention."[26] However, bills introduced in 1909 and 1911 that had aimed at curbing private detectives were easily defeated and labor leaders were left uncertain as to the best means of curbing the spy business. Henry J. Ohl, a Milwaukee printer and Socialist who had succeeded Weber, tended to agree with those critics who felt that prohibiting spies from employment on the basis of how long they had resided in the state would not prove constitutional.[27] Reflecting this quandary, labor did not introduce a detective bill for the next session.

In 1912 Congress established the Commission on Industrial Relations to study labor management issues. Its research staff, directed by Charles McCarthy, chief of Wisconsin's Legislative Reference Library, made some initial inquiries into the labor spy business. The commission's preliminary report noted the use of industrial detectives and supported further study. But employer representatives on the commission balked, and this information was not included in the commission's final report. In 1915 funding for the commission's staff was cut and its research ended.[28]

In 1917 the Wisconsin State Federation of Labor again addressed the issue of labor spies through legislation when Ohl joined with Jack Handley, a machinist who had been elected secretary-treasurer of the organization in 1912. When the Socialists swept to power in 1910 in Milwaukee, Handley was named to direct the city's bureau of street cleaning and sanitation, while Ohl became the deputy city clerk and led a successful and cost-effective reorganization of the city clerk's department.[29] In 1914 Ohl was elected to the state assembly. In shaping their new legislation, Ohl and Handley returned to the earlier approach of licensing and regulation. However, they added two elements that seemed eminently reasonable but which, if implemented, would impose heavy hardships upon the spy agencies. The first provided that licenses would be issued to detective agencies only after application had been approved by the local police and fire commissions. A few other states had similar laws on the books, usually in order to protect the public from unreliable detectives. However, Milwaukee's police and fire commission differed from that of most cities because it was well represented by unionists and Socialists who had been appointed by Socialist mayors. This meant that labor spy agencies would have great difficulty winning approval for licensing. Labor's hidden agenda—to put the agencies out of business in Milwaukee, where most of the labor movement was concentrated—was not missed by the detective agencies and employer organizations. They bitterly fought this provision of the bill.[30]

A second, and in some ways more important, feature of labor's 1917 bill was the licensing of individual operatives employed by a detective agency. Experience with espionage had taught labor that spies, like vampires and bats, could not exist in the light of day. Exposure meant their undoing. The careers of several spies had come to an abrupt halt when union organizers circulated photos of undercover finks to fellow unionists in other cities. Thus Ohl and Handley drew up a bill requiring all operatives to register their name, address, age, former occupations, and other information with the secretary of state.

Their bill succeeded where previous detective bills had failed. It passed the senate, although the individual licensing feature was removed. In the assembly, an amendment for individual licensing was introduced but it failed. That same afternoon Henry Ohl introduced a bill that omitted the police and fire commission's role but included individual licensing. With Socialists gaining support from progressive Republicans, Ohl's bill passed the assembly and advanced to the senate. There the individual licensing provision met strong opposition. Labor representatives considered this provision vital and made it their bottom line. The bill was defeated in the senate.

Two years later the legislative battle followed a similar pattern, but resulted in a partial victory for labor. A bill requiring individual licensing passed the assembly but failed in the senate. Then a senate bill calling for police and fire commission approval passed in that house. When the bill came to the floor in the assembly, an amendment for individual licensing was introduced, but it failed.[31] This time Wisconsin's labor leaders were willing to take half a loaf and the senate bill became law in 1919.[32]

Labor's success in passing the detective bill reflected the movement's new strength in Wisconsin in the first few years following the First World War. Milwaukee labor leaders claimed that union membership increased from 20,000 in 1913 to 35,000 in 1920.[33] In June, 1917, the Milwaukee Federated Trades Council opened discussions on organizing the unorga-

ORGANIZING THE UNORGANIZED IN MILWAUKEE, 1900-1903

WE learn something about the manner in which the FTC organized workers with an examination of the weekly minutes of the FTC meeting for the years from 1900-1903. A report from the organizing committee occurred early in almost every meeting. Unfortunately details in the recorded minutes are often scanty. Nels Anderson was named first organizer in 1891. He wasted little time organizing a group of south side garment workers, some metal workers, a marine section, a teamsters' local, bartenders, milk wagon drivers, a blacksmiths' union. Anderson worked among diverse groups: bottling employees, tanners, capmakers, grocery drivers, glass workers, chandelier hangers and steamfitters. He resigned in 1902 and the FTC turned the job over to Frank J. Weber. Weber was a real dynamo. After two days on the job, he organized the commercial telegraphers and applied for the AFL charter for them. He uncovered a sweatshop garment factory and began organizing efforts there.

By December 1902, after only five months, Weber reported eleven new unions had been formed and two had been reorganized. Eight agreements had been reached and four strikes had taken place. In the next two months, eight more unions were formed. It was an impressive campaign for Weber and the other FTC leaders. When the Socialists gained a majority in the FTC in 1899, there were seventy locals affiliated with 20,000 total members. But in the next four years, thirty-five more locals affiliated with the Council, adding 3,000 more members. . . .

—DARRYL HOLTER

From "Organizing the Unorganized in Milwaukee, 1900-1903," *Milwaukee Labor Press* (April 25, 1985).

Dover Publications, New York

nized, and in 1918 provided $500 to launch the Labor Forward Movement. The organizing drive sponsored rallies, distributed leaflets at plant gates, and sent union representatives to speak to unorganized workers. By October, 1918, 21,000 workers had joined the union ranks and nine new unions had been organized.[34] Legislative efforts by the Wisconsin State Federation of Labor helped in 1919 when a law limiting the use of injunctions passed. That same year, the federation, the Milwaukee Federated Trades Council, and the Socialist party established a committee to provide strike support for organizing drives. The federation's legal advisor, Joseph Padway (who later served as chief counsel for the American Federation of Labor in Washington), provided legal assistance for strikers. In December, 1919, Frank Weber claimed that twenty-eight new unions had been formed in the past year.[35]

The employers responded by stepping up their own efforts to stop unionization. For many years the Milwaukee Merchants and Manufacturers Association had pooled information on local labor organizations and leaders through an agency called the Inspection Bureau. In 1920 the association turned over its bureau to the Russell (Detective) Agency which specialized in labor espionage. Similarly, a number of Milwaukee businessmen formed an open shop movement in answer to labor's call for union shops. The open shop movement culminated in the creation, in 1919, of the Milwaukee Employers' Council. The council provided anti-labor legal assistance to its members and published a monthly bulletin called *Freedom in Employment*. In 1921 the council claimed to have recruited twenty eight industrial groups, representing over 600 plants in the Milwaukee area.[36]

No one was satisfied with the 1919 detective law.[37] Delegates to the 1920 Wisconsin State Federation of Labor

THE LAW TO LIMIT INJUNCTIONS

FROM about 1900 to 1930 much of the legislative effort of organized labor was directed toward the restriction of the use of the injunction in labor cases by state and federal courts. An injunction is an order issued by a court commanding an individual or a group of individuals to do or not to do certain acts. Injunctions are emergency measures to prevent possible damage to property . . .

Labor particularly objected to the use of temporary restraining orders which were sometimes issued upon insufficient evidence. Many strikes were lost before the union's objections to the restraining order could be presented at a preliminary hearing. Unions objected to the absence of a jury trial in contempt cases. They criticized the sweeping nature of many restraining orders and injunctions, which often forbade normally legal union activities such as peaceful picketing, public assembly, and persuasion to join a union. Injunctions hurt the strikers' morale and damaged their cause in the eyes of the police and the public. Exact statistics on the number of injunctions issued by state and federal courts in Wisconsin are not available, but we know that they were used rather frequently after 1900 . . .

No specific bill was introduced to restrict the use of the injunction by Wisconsin courts until 1913. From then until 1931, such legislation was a major goal of the Wisconsin State Federation of Labor. Principal opposition came from manufacturers and in the 1920's from the Employers' Council, a Milwaukee open shop organization formed in 1922.

Wisconsin's first anti-injunction law was passed in 1919. It provided that injunctions or restraining orders could not be used by Wisconsin courts in labor disputes to prohibit persuasion, peaceful picketing, or the payment of strike benefits. The legislation was narrowly interpreted by the courts which held that it did not apply in strikes for a closed shop.[1]

State Historical Society of Wisconsin WHi (X3) 49771
Rolling sheets of aluminum for the manufacture of household utensils at the Allis-Chalmers company.

To remedy this defect the State Federation of Labor sponsored an amendment in 1923 which provided that temporary restraining orders could not be issued without forty-eight hours' notice to the party or parties whom the injunction sought to restrain. This gave strikers a chance to state their case and to protest specific parts of the order. Wisconsin led the states and the federal government in this new method of regulating the injunction by modifying injunction procedure. This legislative restriction tended to discourage the use of the injunction in Wisconsin courts.

—GORDON M. HAFERBECKER

From *Wisconsin Labor Laws* (University of Wisconsin, Madison, 1958).

convention resolved to ask all candidates who were running for the legislature whether or not they would support a bill to abolish labor spy activities. While labor planned to strengthen the act in the next session, the agencies sought to weaken it. First they refused to testify in Milwaukee police and fire commission hearings in September,1919, contending that the sheriff, the deputy, and several commission members who were Socialists would scuttle their applications. Three of the eight agencies summoned—Pinkerton, Ferris, and Russell— refused to appear and were denied licenses in 1919. But they won a temporary injunction restraining the city from issuing warrants against them. A lower court ruling, however, overturned the injunction. The matter went to the state supreme court, which ruled against the agencies. Next the agencies filed suit to stop the police and fire commission from holding hearings to obtain evidence, arguing that the commission's decision should be based strictly upon information provided to the secretary of state. Again the supreme court ruled against the agencies, upholding the commission's right to hold hearings.[38]

This set the stage for another legislative battle in 1921 when the agencies and the business community pushed a bill removing the police and fire commission's power to issue detective licenses. The lobbying effort was so strong that the bill quickly passed both houses. But Senator Walter Polakowski, a Socialist from Milwaukee's south side, brought the bill to Governor John Blaine with a special request to kill the bill, and the progressive Republican vetoed the measure.[39]

In 1923 Ohl and Handley again introduced a bill adding individual licensing provisions, but the bill failed, by one vote, in the senate. A companion bill was then introduced in the assembly. It passed, but was again defeated when it reached the senate.[40]

In 1923, when the Russell Agency applied for legal status as an "employment service," the Wisconsin State Federation of Labor protested to the Wisconsin Industrial Commission. For more than a year, in the course of several hearings, the federation fought the agency. In November, 1924, the commission found that: "The conduct of a private detective agency specializing in industrial work renders the character of the applicant unfit to engage in the business of an employment agent. It is essential that an employment agency be impartial, serving alike the interests of employer and employee. An agency frankly aligned with the employer whenever industrial strife occurs cannot render this impartial service."[41]

Joseph Padway introduced a bill for individual licensing in 1925. This time the agencies were particularly active. Besides the Wisconsin employer groups and detective agencies, national agencies such as Burns, Corporations Auxiliary, and Pinkerton sent lobbyists to Madison. In both houses several attempts were made to amend the bill in order to remove individual licensing and police and fire commission power. Handley's legislative report noted that: "The agency representatives were constantly lobbying from the opening of the session. Every method known to the manipulators of the legislature was used to defeat this measure."[42] Although it was buffeted from committee to committee, the bill gained wider support. The more the public knew about the issue, the more the legislators were inclined to

support it. Governor Blaine's support was also particularly important.[43] Many opponents, seeing that the bill was gaining strength, switched their votes in favor of the bill. When Senate Bill 79 passed in May, 1925, on a nineteen to fourteen vote, labor's twenty year legislative battle came to a close.

The new law required that licenses be obtained by all inside-shop operatives. These were defined as persons not employed directly by an owner of a place of employment but engaged by an independent agency to render reports of the activities in the place of employment.[44] Both the agency and the individual operative were required to pay fees and bonds. As the *Monthly Labor Review* noted in December,1925, the Wisconsin law, with its licensing of individual operatives, went much farther than other laws regulating detective agencies. Convinced that the new law would put them out of business, Corporations Auxiliary and Pinkerton asked for an injunction from a federal court but their request was denied. They appealed to the U.S. Supreme Court, but the court supported the previous ruling.[45] The Russell Agency, unlike the national detective agencies, did all its business in Wisconsin. Denied a license from the Milwaukee police and fire commission, Russell applied for a license in Whitefish Bay, a north shore suburb. Because Whitefish Bay had no police and fire commission, all that was required was approval by the chief of police and five citizens. This being easily obtained, Russell's application was forwarded to the secretary of state. In this way the agency obtained a license. Padway protested that since the agency operated chiefly in Milwaukee, the Milwaukee commission should decide on the application. When the secretary of state agreed to ask the attorney general for an opinion on the issue, the Russell Agency decided to abandon its Milwaukee office and locate permanently in Whitefish Bay.[46]

The law had an immediate effect. Before the 1925 law was passed twenty-one agencies had obtained licenses from the secretary of state. One year later the number had dropped to three. In Milwaukee the police and fire commission continued to deny applications from agencies involved in labor espionage. Several national agencies abandoned Milwaukee or pledged to avoid industrial work. Ohl, Padway, and Handley, when interviewed by Gertrude Schmidt in 1931, claimed that the law had proved very effective. The veteran labor reporter and former editor of *Kenosha Labor* Elmer Beck wrote: "The exposure of the espionage agencies was tantamount to their destruction. This was the intent of the law. It worked."[47]

Perhaps the best assessment of the effectiveness of Wisconsin's detective law came from the detective agencies themselves. An exchange between U.S. Senator Robert La Follette, Jr., and Asher Rossetter, vice-president and general manager of Pinkerton, before the Senate Committee on Education and Labor in 1938 is revealing:

La Follette: In view of the nation-wide scope of your business, you have informants in most of the states of the Union, don't you?

Rossetter: Yes. sir.

La Follette: Do you purchase from any informants in the state of Wisconsin?

Rossetter: To my knowledge, we don't.

La Follette: Why not?

NEWSPAPER MAILERS UNION No. 23
JUNE 20TH 1915

MAYER PHOTO

The Newspaper Mailers Union, Milwaukee, 1915.

State Historical Society of Wisconsin

Rossetter: I don't know, sir.

La Follette: You haven't the slightest idea?

Rossetter: Well, I don't think we have any clients of any magnitude in Milwaukee. We closed our office in Milwaukee here a few years ago, you know.

La Follette: Why?

Rossetter: What?

La Follette: Why?

Rossetter: Because of a state law that you were responsible for putting through.

La Follette: And what does that law provide?

Rossetter: It provides—it does not say that we can't do industrial work.

La Follette: No. But it says you have to register your operatives, doesn't it?

Rossetter: Register the operatives, yes sir.

La Follette: You can't do this kind of business if you do that, can you?

Rossetter: Not very long, because the men would be exposed.[48]

The new law confronted the labor spy business with two options. It could try to adapt its practices to the newer, more restrictive circumstances or it could attempt to function illegally either within the state or by trying to conduct its operations from outside the state. The first option was attempted by

Corporations Auxiliary, which tried to circumvent the Wisconsin law by claiming, in a circuit court, that it was not employing inside-shop operatives but workers who sought to "harmonize industrial conditions: welfare workers, efficiency experts, and educational experts."[49] The judge dismissed the agency's appeal. Although Corporations Auxiliary was unsuccessful in attempting to turn its spies into educational experts, its approach prefigured the current practice by anti-labor agencies and consulting firms to serve as "missionaries of industrial harmony" or guarantors of a union-free environment. But some agencies chose the second option.

In 1926 four unlicensed agencies and five investigating bureaus were listed in the Milwaukee telephone directory. And some detectives were sent into Wisconsin at the request of employers whose fear of unionization outweighed their fear of breaking the law. But operating outside the law made the agencies more shadowy, less reliable, and more expensive than ever. Business leaders in Milwaukee, mindful of their public image, began to distance themselves from the agencies after 1925. Two years later the Milwaukee Employers' Council publicly criticized the same detective agencies that it had funded for many years.[50] Thus, even if the law did not eliminate the agencies altogether, it made it more difficult for them to operate, and it drove a wedge between them and most of the Milwaukee employers. ■

From "Labor Spies and Union-Busting in Wisconsin, 1890–1940," *Wisconsin Magazine of History* (Summer, 1985).

THE MACHINISTS BATTLE THE INJUNCTION

IN 1897 the AFL decided to renew its nationwide drive for shorter hours. This time the International Association of Machinists was selected to lead the movement. In realistic fashion, the Machinists set as their first goal the nine-hour day, since a direct reduction from ten to eight hours was unlikely. In self-defense, the employers formed the National Metal Trades Association and entered into negotiations with the Machinists over reduction of hours. In 1900 they reached what was known as the Murray Hill Agreement, which provided for the nine-hour day to begin on May 20, 1901, in those factories across the country which were members of the National Metal Trades Association and which were represented by the Machinists.

State Historical Society of Wisconsin WHi (X3) 49773
Men working on turbines at the Allis-Chalmers plant.

The Murray Hill Agreement appeared to be a milestone in peaceful labor-management relations. But as the agreed date for introducing the nine-hour day approached, local unions like Lodge 66 of Milwaukee found that the employers intended to cut weekly pay commensurate with the 10 per cent reduction in hours. The International Association of Machinists considered this a repudiation of the agreement and ordered a nationwide strike. In Milwaukee the members of the three lodges, 66, 300, and 301, all heeded the strike call. The minutes of Lodge 66 for the meeting of May 20, 1901, reported that all Machinists had walked off the job at Filer and Stowell; Kempsmiths; Pawling and Harnischfeger; Browning, Pfeiffer and Smith; and Milwaukee Harvester. Almost all workers, 99 per cent, were out at Lutter and Giess; 90 per cent were out at E. P. Allis and at Milwaukee Electric; 75 per cent were out at Nordberg Manufacturing Company and at Kearney and Trecker. In the suburb of Cudahy, ninety out of 101 machinists walked out at the Bucyrus Steam Shovel and Dredge Company.

On a national basis, the strike effort was a long one. The resistance of employers in Milwaukee and elsewhere was strengthened by the leadership of the National Metal Trades Association, which made no concessions. The International Association of Machinists spent $154,000 on strike benefits, but after seven months was forced to call off the strike. Its struggle with the national employers' association was to continue for another thirty years.

In Milwaukee the strike lasted only eight weeks and ended in defeat for the workers, largely because both there and in Cudahy the employers tried a strikebreaking tactic new to Wisconsin: the injunction. Because injunctions were court orders and because the workers had no experience either with them or with asserting their legal rights, they

obeyed the orders without protest. (Later, they learned to resist.) The injunction was a restraining order, issued by a judge, forbidding workers and union officers from carrying out particular activities in connection with a strike.

For example, in Cudahy the injunction prohibited picketing. One of the injunctions issued in Milwaukee was even more restrictive. The language of the court concerning strike action at the Vilter Manufacturing Company was specific:

It is ordered, That until the further order of this court, the above named defendants and the International Association of Machinists, and each and every of its members, and subordinate lodges Nos. 66, 300 and 301 of the Grand Lodge of the International Association Of Machinists, and each and every member of the said lodges or associations ...be and they are hereby enjoined and restrained from congregating or being upon or about the sidewalks or streets or alleys or places adjoining or adjacent to the premises of said plaintiff hereinafter described, or upon or about said premises. . . .

And from compelling anyone in the employ of or seeking employment from said plaintiff, to listen to any arguments of the said defendants or their coconspirators or pickets, or any of them, against his will.

And from persuading or inducing, in any manner, any person to join in the organization or furtherance of any conspiracy to compel this plaintiff to give up or abate in any way, its control of its factory and business. . . . —Dated Milwaukee, June 22, 1901. Hugh Ryan, Court Commissioner, Milwaukee County, Wis.

The Machinists' experience in 1901 demonstrated the stiffening attitude of employers in the face of workers' demands for better conditions.

—ROBERT W. OZANNE

From *The Labor Movement in Wisconsin: A History* (State Historical Society of Wisconsin, Madison, 1984).

Organized Labor
and Socialism: Two Views

FREDERICK I. OLSON AND ELMER A. BECK

A key feature that distinguished the Wisconsin labor movement from its counterparts in other states was its close connection with a grass-roots socialist movement. But the relationship between unionism and socialism has remained a subject of debate. Frederick I. Olson saw "an interlocking directorate" between the unions and the socialist party leaders. Elmer Beck bristles at Olson's characterization and contends that a "personal union" was created between the unions and their political allies.

"An Interlocking Directorate"

FROM 1893 until his death in 1929, Victor Berger dominated the Milwaukee Socialist movement, setting forth its philosophy, defining its objectives, and determining the means it would employ. Its trade union policy, in particular, was largely of his making....

In Berger's view, the economic activity of the trade union was complementary to the political activity of the Socialist party. ... Basically, [the Socialists'] aim was to preserve a single trade-union movement as the economic arm of the working class, while developing the Socialist party as the political arm....

In the first five years of their party activity, Berger's Milwaukee Socialists sought a close and often formal relationship between party and unions, a relationship which came the more readily because of Berger's close ties with the unions prior to the party's formation in 1897. Not only had he participated in the affairs of local unions and the Federated Trades Council (FTC) and the Wisconsin State Federation of Labor (WSFL), but he had also gained their endorsements for his daily, *Wisconsin Vorwarts*, founded in 1893. After 1897, in his dual role as party leader and publisher he extended this connection by obtaining designation, as the official FTC organ, for the weekly *Social Democratic Herald*...

After 1902 the Milwaukee Socialists pursued a more restrained trade-union policy. Although continuing to receive FTC and WSFL endorsements for their platform, their candidates, and their principles, they no longer encouraged union delegates to participate in their party councils. Berger's papers continued as official organs; the FTC remained Socialist in its orientation and voted funds for party activities.[1] But the relationship now established was largely maintained by an interlocking directorate, by the placing of party officials in union offices, the proselytizing of union officials for party membership, and by the nomination of trade-union Socialists for public office....

Moreover, Socialist strength in the unions as represented by the interlocking directorate and a fairly broad common membership provided the party with more than endorsements and campaign donations. It also yielded funds needed for private projects basic to the party's growth in Milwaukee.... The *Milwaukee Leader*, launched on December 7, 1911, while the Socialists were enjoying their first and broadest local victory, was made possible by still further drafts on the capital of the party and trade-union members and on the trade unions themselves....

In their local union views, Milwaukee's Socialists were intensely practical, to the point that their membership blanks even inquired about one's union affiliation. In resolutions, statements of party principles, and campaign platforms they endorsed union membership and the observance of the union label. Furthermore, anti-union activity was a serious charge against a party member, sufficient to deny him nomination for public office if uncovered by the Vigilance Committee or to deprive him of an official position within the party or even of membership itself. As individuals and party members, Berger and Socialist leadership in Milwaukee endorsed strikes, boycotts, and other union weapons, and actively aided in their use....

As a disciplined membership party, the Socialists treated nominations for office, election campaigns, and public service quite differently than did the Democrats or the Republicans. The party machinery determined through referendum the selection of Socialist nominees, always making allowance for the special influence exerted by Berger and a few other party leaders. Each nominee had to be screened for party purity, including a test of trade-union attitudes; he had to pledge support of the party platform and acceptance of party discipline if elected; and he reportedly had to sign an undated resignation from the office he aspired to, for party use in the event he should defy party discipline....

From left,
Frederick Brockhausen,
Frank J. Weber,
Edmund J. Bernes,
and Winfield R. Gaylord
—Socialist legislators
of Wisconsin, 1904–1906.

Milwaukee Country Historical Society

On the national scene the Socialist party had passed its peak by 1912. But in Milwaukee, because of Socialist support, the trade union movement had gained new stableness and structure; one might even say respectability. In fact, no sharp break between Milwaukee Socialists and their union allied occurred until the CIO episode of the 1930's. On the surface, the Berger concept of the two arms of the labor movement and the reality of an interlocking directorate served reasonably well. ∎

—FREDERICK I. OLSON

From "The Socialist Party and the Union in Milwaukee, 1900-1912," *Wisconsin Magazine of History* (Winter, 1960-1961).

"The Personal Union"

THE relationship between the Socialist Party and the unions—the association, the connection, the partnership, the coalition, the alliance, the friendship—have been noted . . . by several Wisconsin historians. Marvin Wachman . . . found that in the period of his study the memberships of the trade unions and the party "overlapped to a large degree, and by 1910, the result for which the Socialists had been striving—to make their party the political arm of the trade-union movement—had surely been reached . . . It is noteworthy that most of the same men who guided the affairs of the unions also guided the affairs of the Social Democratic party of Milwaukee and Wisconsin . . . A kind of 'interlocking directorate' existed between the two movements."[2] The simile, in the *modus operandi* of some research and writing, was later adopted as a metaphor, and then, after some repetition, has almost become generally accepted as descriptive of the relationship. Frederick I. Olson . . . wrote, "Socialist strength in the unions . . . represented by the interlocking directorate and a fairly broad common membership provided the party with endorsements and campaign donations. . . . "

The term, "interlocking directorate," is of the capitalist glossary. It is defined, "a corporate directorate one or more of whose members serve simultaneously in the directorate of another corporation or other corporations." To use a big business denotative phrase in a connotative description of working class organizations is certainly more than just somewhat *malapropos*. . . .

A contemporary and more accurate delineation and academic understanding of the relationship between the Socialist party and the unions is that of "symbiosis" as expressed in two books published by the State Historical Society of Wisconsin. Herbert Margulies wrote, "Under the leadership of the forceful immigrant intellectual, Victor Berger, a close, symbiotic relationship had been established between the Social Democrats and the trade unionists of Milwaukee."[3] Robert Nesbit wrote, "The local success of Victor Berger's Socialist party, in a symbiotic relationship with organized labor, created a strong labor influence."[4]

Symbiosis . . . is a borrowing from biology and has this one definition: "the living together of two dissimilar organisms, especially when this association is mutually beneficial." History deals with people. People made up the Socialist party and the unions—the organizations. Victor Berger [wrote in 1905]: "We say that we must have a two-armed labor movement—a labor movement with a political arm and with an economic arm. Each arm has its own work to do, and one arm ought not to interfere with the other, although they are parts of the same body. That is the 'Milwaukee idea.' In the personal union of the workers of both, that is, in having the same persons take an active interest in both the trade unions and the political labor movement, we find the strongest connecting link between the Social-Democratic party and the trade union organization."[5] ∎

—ELMER A. BECK

From *The Sewer Socialists: A History of the Socialist Party of Wisconsin, 1897-1940* (Westburg, Fennimore, Wisconsin, 1982).

A Lock-Out:
The Hosiery Workers
in Kenosha, 1928-1929

LEON APPLEBAUM

Kenosha had grown from a small town of 6,000 in 1890 to a burgeoning manufacturing center of 40,000 in the 1920s. Thousands of workers were employed making automobiles, auto equipment, beds, machine tools, and hosiery. Leon Applebaum describes a "lock-out" at the Allen-A hosiery company that rocked the city of Kenosha in 1928. While the strike is often a tactic used by the unions, the lock-out tactic was often utilized by employers. In Kenosha, Allen-A management called together all the hosiery workers and announced that all would be discharged. Then, they proclaimed their willingness to rehire only workers who agreed to turn in their union cards and desert the union. The strike began the next day, but Allen-A brought in strikebreakers and refused to negotiate. The lock-out lasted for two years, marked by violence and controversy.

IT was against this background that the struggle in the hosiery industry was played out. Inevitably, conflict arose between management and labor over the impact of changes in production techniques on the skill levels, status, and employment opportunities of skilled knitters. During the recession of 1921 the two sides locked horns in a life-and-death struggle in Philadelphia, the center of the hosiery industry in the United States. The eight-year-old Full Fashioned Hosiery Workers Union engaged in a bitter, nine-month battle over a proposed 15 per cent reduction in wages and a plan to implement more extensive use of the two-machine system of production.

In opposing the extension of the two-machine system, the union argued that, over time, the single-machine system was more profitable for firms which were primarily concerned with production and quality because the two-machine system increased the number of "seconds" and the imperfect goods raised the labor cost per stocking in two-machine plants above the labor cost in single-machine plants. Union leaders claimed that the use of less-skilled helpers shortened the life of sensitive machines and increased the wastage of expensive materials. Naturally they also feared that the two-machine system would create a surplus of workers in the industry, reducing employment opportunities for their members and leading to the "abolition of the knitters" union.[1]

When the settlement came in September, there was a compromise on the wage reduction, but the two-machine system continued in segments of the industry. The trend was against the union. In its early days, the federation was dominated by the knitters, who were primarily male, and who had little interest in the problems of the toppers, who were primarily female, or the seamless hosiery workers, who were less skilled. According to one industry expert, not until 1918 did a woman delegate attend the federation's national contention.[2] The rapid expansion of the hosiery industry during the 1920's led to organizational drives by the knitters' union among the toppers as union leaders attempted to move from a strict craft union to one that was more industrial in nature; but the historian of the national union has estimated that "while the full-fashioned industry had been ninety per cent organized in 1919, by 1929 the union controlled but fifty per cent of the machines, and because of the age of the machines and the union limitation on hours, these did not control even fifty per cent of the total production."[3]

In a unique and innovative approach for its time, the union attempted in 1929 to negotiate a multi-employer, industry-wide agreement—to bring stability to the industry and to reduce the increasing competitive threat of non-union firms. The union and fifty-two firms approved an agreement which required that all employees in the knitting and topping departments would become union members, that departments already organized would remain organized, and that grievance procedures would be backed up by binding arbitration.[4]

The agreement established an employment office to be

Knitters and toppers locked out of Allen-A Hosiery, Kenosha, 1928.

State Historical Society of Wisconsin WHi (X3) 43479

jointly administered through which employers were to hire their help. This provision attempted to provide an element of job security for union members and, thus, an element of security for the union itself.

Many in the union must have been surprised that the agreement permitted the doubling up of machines under certain conditions. Up to 25 per cent of the thirty-nine and forty-two gauge machines—the older machines—could be operated on a two machine basis by the end of the first year of the agreement, at which time employers and the union would jointly decide what the percent age would be in the second year.[5] Newer and speedier machines could not be doubled up. Under the terms of the agreement, each knitter operating two machines was provided one helper. Once a helper had served a four-year apprenticeship, the employers had to provide a job operating either a thirty-nine or a forty-two gauge machine. At the end of a six-year period the helper-apprentice would become a full-fledged knitter. Thus, while there was limited approval of the two-machine system, conditions were established which sought to control the number of helper-apprentices by controlling the type and number of machines that could be doubled up while, at the same time, providing conditions that required employers to provide employment for helper- apprentices as their skills increased.[6]

Finally, the contract provided for a national pay scale, thus "taking wages out of competition" for the signatory firms, and for a general understanding for the application of time study methods. Commenting on the agreement, *Knit Goods Weekly*, a hosiery industry publication, suggested that "a note-worthy industrial development has been accomplished by peaceful negotiation between employer and employee instead of by forceful—which means wasteful—methods. Nothing to compare with it has ever been seen in the entire textile industry...."[7]

The agreement did not extend to Kenosha, and in 1928, the local of the Full Fashioned Hosiery Workers found itself locked in combat with the Allen-A Hosiery Company, one of the major employers in the community.

The Allen in the company name came from a family that traced its roots to the founding of Kenosha in the 1830's. Nathan R. Allen, Sr., had walked most of the way from New York state to Wisconsin Territory and participated in establishing Southport, which later became Kenosha. The tannery which he helped start was, at its peak, "the largest tannery in the world," employing over 1,000 men and utilizing over 1,000,000 hides a year. After N. R., Sr., died in 1890, his sons, Charles and N. R., Jr., controlled the tannery until 1905, when they sold it to Central Leather Company, a New Jersey corporation that produced approximately one-third of the sole leather in the United States. The brothers' relationship with the tannery continued until 1912 when they entered the hosiery business by acquiring control of the Chicago-Rockford Hosiery Company, which had opened a plant in Kenosha in 1892. The company name was subsequently changed to Chicago-Kenosha Hosiery in 1903, Black Cat Textiles in 1916, and to Allen-A in 1920.[8]

In January, 1927, Charles Allen resigned as president of Allen-A and Robert W. Allen, N. R. Sr.'s grandson, succeeded him. Day-to day operations were under the control of Roger N. Kimball, the vice-president and general manager, and John H. Brine, the superintendent of the mill. Kimball, a Kenosha native, had worked for the Milwaukee Gas Company and the Kenosha Gas and Electric Company before he purchased a large amount of stock of the Chicago-Rockford Hosiery Company in 1916 and assumed his managerial duties. Brine had risen from needle boy to general superintendent over a twenty-year period.

Along with the expansion of the national hosiery industry,

Striking toppers modeling Allen-A's line of full-fashioned hosiery at the anniversary dance, February 16, 1929.

Allen-A had grown rapidly in the early 1920's. A new building had been erected by 1924, and additional floors were added in 1925. An exact replica of the existing mill was erected in 1926. Employment had grown also, from 800 workers at Black Cat Textiles, Allen-A's predecessor, in 1920, to 2,300 in 1928, with 1,300 at the plant in Kenosha.[9] The weekly payroll was $40,000.

Allen-A's product line included women's, men's, and children's hosiery, swimsuits, and underwear. Women and men's hosiery were produced in Kenosha, while the other lines were manufactured in Bennington, Vermont, and Sheboygan. In its women's line, Allen-A produced full-fashioned and seamless hosiery, with full-fashioned being the firm's top of-the-line. Seamless hosiery, a cheaper type of stocking, did not require the detailed work or the complex machines which were necessary for making full-fashioned hosiery.

Of the 1,300 Kenosha Allen-A employees in 1928, approximately 700 were employed in the full-fashioned-department. Skilled knitters accounted for about 250 of the workers; the remaining 450 were toppers. It was among the knitters that the Federation of Full Fashioned Hosiery Workers had established a local union, Branch No. 6, during World War I. During the 1920's there had been considerable employee turnover as the company expanded production and employment, and Branch No. 6 encountered organizing problems.[10]

The company boasted that "the workers of the Allen-A Company were well paid for their efforts: and "full fashioned workers as an average are the highest paid factory workers in the City of Kenosha." A sample of eighty men who were full-fashioned knitters at the company, culled from the 1927 city directory and the Kenosha County individual income tax roll for

1928, reveals an average annual income of $2,572, or $51.44 per week. Some knitters earned $80 to $90 a week, an excellent wage in the 1920's. In the words of a relative of one of the strike leaders, "the knitters were the envy of all the workers." A similar sampling of fifty toppers reveals an average weekly wage of slightly better than $21 in 1927. Almost all of the knitters and toppers were American born, descendants of immigrants primarily from northern and western Europe and the British Isles who had arrived in Kenosha prior to 1900. Most of the skilled knitters had high school diplomas. The toppers were closely allied with the knitters, not only in their daily work but in many of their social relationships as well.[11]

Approximately 650 to 700 Allen-A employees worked outside the full-fashioned department, in the seamless, dyeing, and shipping departments. They were unorganized and not directly involved in the labor dispute. They continued to work and the union does not appear to have seriously attempted to seek the support of these employees.[12]

Kenosha County, where the company was located, had grown rapidly in the early twentieth century, from 32,929 residents in 1910 to 63,277 in 1930. Not only did the numbers increase greatly; the pattern of immigration also changed radically. Kenosha County's population during the last seventy years of the nine tenth century was the product of migration from the northeastern United States and immigration from northern and western Europe and the British Isles. During the first thirty years of the twentieth century, the character of immigration to Kenosha changed, with an infusion of individuals from southern and eastern Europe. By 1930, the "new" immigrants comprised more than 60 per cent of the city's foreign-born population, and with their children, they made up almost 45 per cent of the total population.[13]

Rapid industrialization and urbanization which occurred in the late nineteenth and early twentieth centuries drew immi-

grants to Kenosha. While the county had been 25 per cent urban in 1850, it was over 70 per cent urban by 1900. By 1930, it was 84 per cent urban. (By contrast, the United States was 56 per cent urban.) Kenosha's industrial growth began in the nineteenth century in the textile, bedding, tanning, boxing, furniture, wagon-making, and metals industries. With the addition of automobile, tool, and wire rope industries after 1900, Kenosha became the most industrialized city in Wisconsin. By 1920, approximately 75 per cent of the city's work force was employed in manufacturing.[14]

By 1928, Allen-A's 1,300 employees approximated 10 per cent of the factory workers in Kenosha. Only Nash Motor Company, Simmons Manufacturing Company, and American Brass had more employees.[15] Production at Allen-A had been increasing rapidly, and the company had been operating two shifts for a number of years. By their earnings, educational levels, and ethnic background, Allen A's full-fashioned knitters were undoubtedly the company's elite and the community's most-envied workers. It would take only a year to change the situation.

The showdown between management and labor came in early 1928 when the company announced its decision to adopt the two-machine system of production by installing new knitting machines valued at $1 million. On February 10, the company called the knitters together to explain the changes. Company officials contended that the two-machine system would reduce the costs of production and increase knitters' "earnings from fifteen to twenty per cent with no additional physical effort." Operators "were also absolutely guaranteed that the institution of this system would not result in a single one of them losing his position."[16]

The unionized knitters met the following day and overwhelmingly approved a strike if the company carried out the new system. The knitters, all male and mostly between the ages

of eighteen and twenty-eight, argued that the two-machine system would result in physical and emotional strain, pose an employment threat, and reduce the quality of the product.

In response to a request for aid from Branch 6, Gustav Geiges, president of the Full Fashioned Hosiery Workers, dispatched Harold E. Steele and Louis F. Budenz to Kenosha. Steele was a national union vice president, the business representative for the middle west district, and president of Branch 16 in Milwaukee. Budenz, who was later to rise to national prominence, began his trade union career in 1913 when he took a position with the United Carpenters and Joiners shortly after his admission to the Indiana bar at age twenty-two. From 1921 to 1931 he was the editor of *Labor Age* and from 1927 to 1934 he also served as a troubleshooter and organizer for the Federation of Full Fashioned Hosiery Workers. By February 14 both men had met with local union leaders to formulate a statement which asked the company for a meeting at which "a peaceful and constructive program of cooperation guaranteed to produce greater financial return than the two machine system could possibly bring" could be presented. In effect, the union was asking for recognition by the company. At the meeting, Branch 6 also admitted a hundred toppers as new members.[17]

The company was not about to agree to the union proposal. It declared its willingness always to deal with its employees as individuals and its unwillingness to deal with outsiders. Management hinted darkly that there was more to the situation than the two-machine system. Company officials indicated that other issues would be aggravated if any other stand was taken.[18]

It did not take long for the full-fashioned department employees to learn about the other issues. Late in the day on February 15, management called on-duty full-fashioned knitters together and informed them that all knitters, both members and nonmembers of Branch 6, were being released. Only nonunion members could return to work. The night shift received the same message. Thus, the company revealed as its true objective its intention to operate as an open, nonunion shop. Company vice-president John Brine stated, "We have always operated on the open shop basis but with the growth of the union in the department we saw a showdown coming and decided to have it at this time." The company action amounted to a one-two punch: the knitters could return to work if they turned in their union cards, and they would be returning to a two-machine shop.[19]

Acting swiftly, the knitters and those toppers who supported them met that same evening to reject the company proposal, call for a strike, and plan for picketing beginning the next morning.[20]

As soon as the picketing began, the company declared that "the present unpleasantness at the Allen-A plant is the result of the work of outside agitators, who have made a determined effort to organize the workers.... The two-machine system is not the real issue in the particular case, as the only issue as far as the management is concerned is whether or not the plant is to be operated as a Union plant...." Company officials insisted that they did not have a strike on their hands and that the Kenosha mill would continue to operate regardless of the union position.[21]

From the beginning of the dispute, company and union estimates of the effectiveness of the strike differed. Of the 236 men affected, the union claimed that only twelve knitters returned; the company counted forty. In either case, by February 20 the company was accepting applications for a completely new work force, including 100 men who would begin training as knitters immediately. These men were to be carefully chosen from Kenosha workers, and young men with families would be given preference.[22] The company made it clear that striking workers were no longer considered employees and that 1,100 employees outside the full-fashioned department was unaffected by the dispute and continued to work.

It was inevitable that tensions would increase when the company attempted to operate the full-fashioned department with strikebreakers or "scabs." While the company no longer considered the strikers employees, the strikers had not quit. In a strike situation, strikers expect to return to work when the issues have been resolved through negotiations. In the Allen-A dispute, the company was adamant that it would not negotiate while at the same time accepting applications to hire and train new knitters to replace the strikers. This stand posed a direct threat to the strikers' jobs and, therefore, to their economic security. In such situations strikers often attempt to prevent strikebreakers from working and inevitably violence results.

In the Allen-A dispute the earliest violence was simple enough: the window in the home of a nonstriking knitter was shattered and some physical encounters took place between strikers and nonstrikers. Before the strike withered away in 1929—it was never formally called off—hundreds of incidents occurred, including fights, shootings, bombings, and destruction of property. Police statistics for 1927 through 1930 clearly show a marked increase in arrests during 1928 and 1929. (Tables 1 and 2.) The chief of police reported at the end of 1928 that his department had added four regular policemen

Table 1
Arrests in Kenosha

Year	Number
1927	3,060
1928	4,213
1929	3,397
1930	2,583

Source: Ninth Annual Report of the City of Kenosha.

and sixty-nine special policemen "on account of the labor disturbance." The cost of operating the department for the year—$183,578.94—had increased 37 per cent over the previous year, the same percentage increase as the total number of arrests. Out of 4,213 arrests, 3,230 were residents, 983 were nonresidents.[23]

The Kenosha police department was in an unenviable position. According to veterans of the dispute, some members supported the strikers and some supported the company. The chief's sympathies lay with the strikers, among whom he had many friends.[24] Inevitably, his attitude brought him into conflict with members of the city council, most of whom were local businessmen, and he was replaced.

Branch 6 prepared for a long battle by creating a number of committees to carry on strike activities. The national union announced that strike benefits raised by a national levy on all union members would be paid at a rate of $16 per week for married men, $12 for single men, and $8 for women. Members of the union's Milwaukee Branch 16 unanimously voted to assess themselves $2 per week for the duration of the dispute.[25] The Kenosha Trades and Labor Council announced its support with a number of affiliated unions pledging financial support to the strikers.

Branch 6 staged a number of activities to maintain striker morale and increase community support. On Saturday, March 3, over 300 automobiles paraded through Kenosha, and that evening 3,000 persons attended a dance, one of the largest ever held in the city. The following month the Kenosha Trades and Labor Council called for a show of support for the striking knitters and toppers and on the fourteenth, during a snowstorm, some 2,000 persons paraded through the business district. The march, which included the striking workers and supporters from Kenosha, Racine, and Milwaukee labor unions, was completed without incident. On May 12 a mass meeting of 4,000 listened to Milwaukee Mayor Daniel Hoan attack the company. A resolution was adopted protesting the company's importation of professional strikebreakers, gunmen, and thugs and demanding their immediate expulsion from the company.[26]

On March 2, six members of the Kenosha clergy offered to mediate the dispute. The clergymen—Reverend E. M. Muelder of the Immanuel Methodist Church, Rabbi Julius Rappaport of Temple Beth Hillel, Reverend E. Burns Martin of the First Methodist Church, Reverend George R. Cady of the First Congregational Church, Reverend Kenneth D. Martin of St. Matthews Episcopal Church, and Father Martin H. Buenger of the Roman Catholic Saint James Church—expressed their con-

Wisconsin State Historical Society

Louis F. Budenz, organizer for the Hosiery Workers Union, and Harry E. Steele, national union vice president, in Kenosha, 1928.

Table 2
Offenses Leading to Arrests

	1927	1928	1929	1930
Assault and battery	80	132	112	30
Disorderly conduct	168	551	297	218
Speeding	318	461	352	165
Traffic violations	568	958	529	393

Source: Ninth Annual Report of the City of Kenosha.

cern that the continuing dispute was detrimental to both sides and to the community. The union sent a letter of acceptance; the company sent a letter of rejection.[27] Through out the dispute the company consistently refused offers of mediation and arbitration.

On March 8, 1928, Judge Ferdinand A. Geiger of the federal district court in Milwaukee issued a "blanket" injunction which, if obeyed, would prevent any union activity in furtherance of the strike. His ruling came in response to a bill of complaint brought by Allen-A which cited instances of picketing, of the use of abusive language, and of personal violence including threats, telephone calls, and hurling bricks through windows of homes. It claimed that serious violence and damage to the plant would occur if picketers were permitted to congregate as a mob in front of and adjoining the company's property.[28]

Judge Geiger, in accepting the arguments of the company, issued a broad restraining order which forbade all members of Branch 6, its employees, and national representatives Harold Steele and Louis Budenz from interfering in any way with Allen-A employees and from damaging company property. Forty defendants were named specifically, based upon a court finding that "by reason of the combination, federation and conspiracy on the part of the defendants the plaintiff is threatened with immediate and irreparable damage to its property, property rights and business, unless the defendants and all members of Branch 6 ...are restrained forthwith...."[29]

The immediate union response was to mass an estimated 2,000 strikers and supporters at the plant gate at closing time the day the restraining order was issued. As employees exited the plant, they were greeted with catcalls and epithets, in violation of the court's restraining order. This was duly noted by a federal marshal.[30] The stakes in the strike had risen, for now the union found itself in a confrontation with the federal district court as well as with Allen-A.

On March 16, nineteen citations were served on members of Branch 6, Harold Steele, and Louis Budenz, ordering them to appear before the district court in Milwaukee "to show cause why they should not be punished for contempt of court" for violating the court restraining order. A number of the defendants were identified in affidavits as participants in incidents at the plant. At the request of Joseph Padway, the union's counsel, Judge Geiger granted a jury trial to determine whether a conspiracy to violate the court order existed. Newspapers reported that this was the first time in Wisconsin courts, state or federal, that a jury trial had been granted under such circumstances.[31] Before the trial began, police made additional picket line arrests and the federal court issued additional contempt citations.

At the trial, Paul Newcomb, the company's attorney, argued that the defendants had engaged in a conspiracy to violate the court's restraining order. Padway, in response, claimed that the defendants had not agreed to commit an unlawful act; that is, they had not engaged in a conspiracy. What had occurred, explained Padway, was the usual picketing that takes place in any labor dispute. It took the jury four hours to find the defendants innocent.

While union leaders applauded the jury's decision, Allen-A officials announced that company policy remained unchanged, that the federal injunction remained in force, and that the company intended to insist on prosecution of violations of the court order.[32] In October, 1928, when twenty-seven knitters were brought to trial on contempt of court charges, Judge Geiger refused to grant a jury trial, found them guilt and fined each of them $100, with the stipulation that the fine monies would go to Allen-A in compensation for damage to plant windows broken by the picketers. The knitters refused to pay and were sentenced to prison until the fines were paid.[33] Using the incident to enlist support for their cause, union leaders held a series of rallies around the county to raise funds, and, after the knitters had been in jail for a month, the fines were paid and they were released. ■

From "Turmoil in Kenosha: The Allen-A Hosiery Dispute of 1928–1929," *Wisconsin Magazine of History* (Summer, 1987).

THE LABOR FORWARD MOVEMENT

The entrance of the United States into the First World War drew tens of thousands of workers into the military. The war greatly altered the labor market and opened up new possibilities for union organizing. The Labor Forward Movement was an interesting experiment in organizing.

THE militancy of the years during and following the war also reflected itself in the field of union organization. As early as June, 1917, the FTC discussed the advisability of starting a movement to organize the unorganized workers in Milwaukee. However, it was not until early 1918 that the Labor Forward Movement, as it was called, got underway. In March the FTC appropriated $500 for the Movement, and organization began in earnest. The Movement distributed hundreds of thousands of flyers and had representatives of the various international unions speak to unorganized workers. Open meetings were held in every section of the city. The favorable labor market created by the war, the attitude of the federal government on labor policy, and the vigorous organizing work resulted in the unionization of 2,100 workers by October. The secretary of the Movement, Louis J. Green, was able to report in October that nine new unions had been organized: Meat Cutters and Butchers, Furriers, Tannery Workers, Flat Janitors, Auto Truck Drivers and Teamsters, Molders (in railway shops), Ship Carpenters, Street Railway Employees, and Maintenance of Way Employees. Many of the existing unions increased their membership.

A campaign was started in the steel mills just prior to the outbreak of the influenza epidemic which called a halt to all public meetings in the city. With the end of the war (and the epidemic) the work of organizing the steel workers began in earnest. In August a conference of twenty-four national iron and steel trade unions met in Chicago. The conference adopted a program of cooperative action and created a National Committee for the Organization of the Iron and Steel Industry. Louis Green was appointed local secretary for the organizational campaign in Milwaukee, and the FTC elected William Coleman as part-time assistant business manager to work with the Movement...

With the belief that the new labor legislation would in some measure curb the use of injunctions and private detectives, and capitalizing on the favorable economic conditions and the militancy of the era, the FTC and the County Central Committee of the Socialist Party formed a Strikers

State Historical Society of Wisconsin WHi (X3) 278 3

U.S. postal employees parade in 1919 demanding higher wages to keep pace with war-time increases in the cost of living.

Aid Committee to provide help to strikers, primarily in the Cudahy packing houses, the Wisconsin Motor Company, and the Illinois Steel Company. The original union representatives were Frank Weber, William Coleman and Maude McCreery, and the representatives of the Socialist Party were S. H. Franklin, George Hampel, Casimir Kowalski, and Emil Seidel.

The Committee took a census of the strike situation. Rations of staples were either given to the strikers or sold at low prices. Legal aid, handled primarily by Joseph Padway, was provided in all cases growing out of the strikes. The Committee also provided medical aid, headed by Dr. S. H. Franklin. A nurse, or "strike mother," was appointed to care for the wives and children of the strikers. If any striker was threatened with eviction because he was unable to pay his rent, the Committee asked the owner to donate the rent to the strike or to give the tenant additional time to pay the rent. If all else failed, the Committee paid the rent. A number of strikers had subscribed for war bonds but had paid for only part of them when the strike began. The company refused to pay the money back or allow the strikers to get the money or bonds until the pledge had been paid in full. Therefore, the treasurer of the Strikers Aid Committee arranged for a bank loan to purchase the bonds. All told, the Committee spent about $3,500 in aiding the strikers.

In December, 1919, Frank Weber reported that twenty-eight new unions had been organized during the past year and that there had been major gains in membership in existing unions. This was the greatest increase in the number of local unions and in membership in Milwaukee since 1903.

—THOMAS W. GAVETT

From *Development of the Labor Movement in Milwaukee* (University of Wisconsin, Madison, 1965).

The Wisconsin School
for Workers: Two Views

BARBARA WERTHEIMER AND DARINA RASMUSSEN

Although the general public probably knows very little about the University of Wisconsin's School for Workers, its role in labor education is well known to union leaders and labor activists across the country. However, most of them probably do not know that, as Barbara Wertheimer points out in this first selection, the origin of the School for Workers goes back to the 1920s when a summer school program for women workers was established. Darina Rasmussen tells us what it was like to attend the School for Workers summer school in 1935.

DURING this period, the movement of summer schools for women workers began to extend throughout the country. The Wisconsin School for Women Workers in Industry became the first resident program on the campus of a state-supported university. Impetus for the program emanated from the Industrial Department of the Madison YWCA. This active chapter had organized evening discussions on labor problems for college students and working women, and in 1924 had experimented unsuccessfully with sponsoring eight women workers to attend regular summer classes at the university. In 1925, forty women workers from nine midwestern states were recruited by YWCA industrial departments to take part in the first eight-week residential program planned for women workers by a committee of university faculty, YWCA staff, and university students connected with the Y's.

The school melded a progressive, "inspirational" ideology with a traditional, conservative approach. There were no labor members on the planning committee, and the program used no labor-problem orientation or workers' education techniques. The women workers lived in dorms and co-op houses alongside students enrolled in the university's regular summer session. Classes in literature, composition, and drama took on a feminine role perspective with extracurricular sessions in beauty culture, lectures on "what is a lady," and the proper way to set tables and serve food for sitdown dinners. Recruited largely by the Y's, the women came from non-unionized industries. There was little positive response or financial support from the labor movement in the state, which saw little reason to raise money to send non-union women to a university summer program. Much of the funding was raised by the Y's from members of women's business and professional clubs, who assumed, as a 1942 report stated, that the working girls would enjoy a pleasant vacation from the monotony of labor and would return to their work

breathing "sweetness and light." Their financial backing cooled when the club women found that the women workers returned to their jobs eager to turn "sweetness and light" into practical service in and for the labor movement.

In order to solicit organized labor's sanction and financial support, YWCA leaders, representatives of the Wisconsin Federation of Labor, and the staff of the Milwaukee Workers' College met to form a coeducational School for Workers at the University of Wisconsin. Alice Shoemaker, a YWCA Industrial Department secretary with teaching experience at the Bryn Mawr Summer School, was hired as the first executive secretary. The new school, financially supported almost entirely by the unions, emphasized steward training, collective bargaining, and union administration, along with courses in labor history, economics, and politics, conducting one- and two-week on-campus sessions. Courses on women in industry were eliminated. Nearly all of the students attending after 1928 were union members. Most of them were men. ■

—BARBARA MAYER WERTHEIMER

From *Labor Education for Women Workers*
(Temple University Press, Philadelphia, 1981).

ANOTHER day, another dollar" was an expression bandied about during the days when the economic structure of the country was tottering. The meaning came alive to me when I got my first job on an assembly line working for 16¢ an hour in 1930.

With 16 million people unemployed, one-third of the labor force, President Roosevelt during the famous 100 Days in 1933 rushed anti-depression legislation through Congress to encourage industrial recovery, promote purchasing power, and provide work and vocational training for single men. Thus the emergence of the National Recovery Act, the Agricultural

THE WISCONSIN LABOR CODE OF 1931

A COMPLETE labor code was passed in 1931 by the progressive Republican legislature. This was substantially the same as the Norris-La Guardia Anti-injunction Act passed by Congress a year later. The legislature declared that it was the public policy of the state to promote collective bargaining and to encourage workers to organize for mutual aid and protection. The code stated in more detail the previous ban against the enforcement of yellow-dog contracts. It specifically provided that certain acts were legal and not subject to court restraint. These acts included union membership, payment of strike benefits, publicizing the facts of a dispute, peaceful assembly, and peaceful picketing. The rights of a person charged with contempt of court were outlined in detail. Labor union officers were not to be held liable for the unlawful acts of individual members unless a preponderance of evidence indicated that the officers had authorized, participated in, or ratified such unlawful acts. Further limitations on the use of the injunction were provided. The employer was to be denied injunctive relief if he had failed to comply with any legal obligations involved in the dispute in question. Provision was made for prompt appeal to an appellate court after an injunction had been issued or denied by a lower court.

The Wisconsin Supreme Court in 1934 upheld the law and an injunction to prevent its violation. A corporation had been ordered not to interfere with its employees' right to organize and to choose representatives for collective bargaining. The company was also ordered not to require anyone, as a condition of employment, to join a company union or to refrain from joining a labor organization of his own choosing. In 1936 the Supreme Court also accepted the labor code's broad definition of a labor dispute and upheld the right of unions to picket to unionize a plant where no employees were on strike.

In 1937 the United States Supreme Court upheld the part of the Wisconsin labor code which declared peaceful picketing and patrolling lawful and prohibited the granting

Wisconsin State Historical Society WHi (X3) 30391
Registering for unemployment compensation at Milwaukee City Hall.

of an injunction against such conduct *(Senn v. Tile Layers' Protective Union,* 301 U.S. 468). Senn was a tile layer who often worked with his men on the job. His employees were union men, but the union objected to his working on his own jobs and picketed him as unfair. Senn was denied an injunction by the trial court and the Wisconsin Supreme Court. He appealed to the United States Supreme Court, claiming that he was denied equal protection of the law and due process. The federal court upheld the Wisconsin law and denied the injunction in a 5-4 decision.

—GORDON M. HAFERBECKER

From *Wisconsin Labor Laws*
(University of Wisconsin, Madison, 1958).

Adjustment Administration, and the Civilian Conservation Corps, known as the NRA, AAA, and CCC. (One of my brothers worked in the CCC.)

In 1935, with six notches in my work experience belt, I was back on the job market. This was the year the Works Progress Administration was established. There were critics. There were photos and snide remarks about workers "who leaned on their shovels." Yet, through its Building Project there were 116,000 buildings, 78,000 bridges and 651,000 miles of road constructed and 800 airports improved. Under its Federal Writers Project a valuable series of state and regional books were put together. Artists under the Federal Arts Project contributed nearly 10,000 drawings, paintings and sculptured works and decorated many public buildings with murals.

The Federal Theater Project gave 4,000 musical performances each month and provided a nationwide audience with inexpensive, high quality theatrical productions. I remember one in particular, the highly acclaimed "Pins and Needles" produced by the International Ladies Garment Workers Union, that toured the country and performed at the Pabst Theater in Milwaukee. An Educational Project was also a part of the WPA In the spring of 1935 I attended a night class on labor history that was offered through the project at the Cudahy Vocational School. At the end of the course, I was told that a scholarship was available for a woman for the Summer School for Workers at the University of Wisconsin. It was being offered by the Wisconsin State Federation of Labor. Would I apply for it?

Within a few weeks I found myself surrounded by a most

State Historical Society of Wisconsin WHi (X3) 40276

Delegates at the Wisconsin State Federation of Labor convention at Sheboygan, 1912.

interesting group of women and men, varying in age, background, skill and experience. There, in the flesh:

- a striker on leave from the Kohler picket line
- a "wobblie," a card carrying IWW member and seasoned traveler
- a scholarly, soft-spoken "blacklisted" college professor from South Carolina
- a member of the Farmer's Union, an organization very much in the news for dumping truck loads of milk to keep it off the market. (Milk was selling for less than the cost to produce it.)

There were knowledgeable, articulate, militant women—many unemployed—some active in unions and YWCAs. There, too, was the qualified, supportive staff and its fine director, Alice Shoemaker.

There were approximately fifty of us enrolled in the School —twenty women and thirty men. We met for meals in the dining room of the women's dorm, situated on Lake Mendota's shore. Dinner conversation was lively and not without controversy. The assorted "isms" of the times gave us much to talk about. News of the movement within the AFL of a strong minority faction that advocated organizing workers on an industry-wide basis became an exciting topic.

Ours was a singing group. There were sing-a-longs around the piano most every evening—songs of work and freedom. Lots of spirit and harmonizing. No amplifiers, nor electronic gear, but we were heard. What's more, we gathered a repertoire of songs that would carry us through a lifetime singing with family and friends at rallies and meetings.

In the classes there was:

- hands-on training in layout and print for posters and flyers
- compositions about work-related experiences
- discussions about work situations in the shops and the difficulty of organizing workers
- an opportunity to experience negotiating from both sides through mock collective bargaining sessions

- publishing a newspaper as a class project

And on the evening of the class farewell the drama group presented a play and mass recitation. Though I have but a precious few mementos, the memory of the Summer School for Workers experience is still alive.

Looking back over the past fifty-two years I tried to gather some of the bits and pieces that relate to my 1935 School for Workers background. We almost organized a small group of state employees in 1936, but almost wasn't good enough. In 1937 we organized a shop of sixty employees—100%—men who were cutters, printers, machinists; women who were power sewing machine operators. I was a member of the Milwaukee Joint Board of the Amalgamated Clothing Workers.

As a farm wife in the 1940's I saw the devastation of family farms due to the drought and Depression and came to know the value of price supports, subsidies, and the soil conservation program of the AAA—and the value of cooperation among the farmers. In 1941 when the People's Progressive Party was launched, I obtained the necessary signatures in Forest County so that its candidate for president, Henry Agard Wallace, would be placed on the ballot in the State of Wisconsin.

When I returned to Milwaukee in 1952, I worked in the office of Local 1111, United Electrical, Radio and Machine Workers, the Allen-Bradley workers' union. After 26 years of service, I retired in June 1978. I am also a retired member of Local 9, OPEIU.

I continue to think back on Ralph Chaplin's poem and its message that keeps me "on the move":

Mourn not the dead
But rather mourn the apathetic throng
The cowed—and meek
Who see the world's great anguish
And its wrong
And dare not speak. ∎

—DARINA RASMUSSEN

From "Remembering the Summer School for Workers in 1935,"
Wisconsin Labor History Newsletter (1988).

WORKERS' COMPENSATION

IN 1905, when WSFL Secretary-Treasurer Frederick Brockhausen, an Assembly member, introduced the first workers' compensation bill in the Wisconsin legislature, the need for such legislation was long overdue. Each year thousands of workers were killed or maimed on the job without compensation from the employer. common law recognized three principles that served to exonerate the employer. The first was that of "contributory negligence," under which, for example, an employee who had lost an arm would have to convince the court that he had not been negligent to any degree in order to recover such damages as medical and hospital care, lost wages, and financial damages for permanent injury or death. The second principle was "assumption of risks": if an injured employee had known that a piece of machinery was dangerous and in need of repair, he was denied damages—and if the worker had protested the unsafe condition to the foreman, this was evidence that he had knowledge of the unsafe condition and voluntarily had assumed the risks of the job. The third principle was the "fellow servant doctrine," which meant that an injured worker could not receive damages from the employer if the employer could blame any part of the accident on a fellow employee. For example, if a foundry worker's failure to properly plug a furnace containing molten metal resulted in the death of workers on the succeeding shift, the employer under common law was blameless.

Although the WSFL had advocated workers' compensation in its convention resolutions since 1894, the legislature took no notice until labor leaders were elected to the State Assembly and introduced their own bills. In 1904, workers' compensation was put at the top of the agenda at the WSFL state convention. In each biennium thereafter, 1905, 1907, and 1909, Brockhausen introduced the federation's bills to provide compensation. The legislation was expertly drafted by the eminent Charles McCarthy, head of the state's Legislative Reference Library.

By 1909 public sentiment regarding workers' compensation was catching up with the position of the State Federation. A great deal of the credit for selling workers' compensation to business and to the public must go to John R. Commons, a distinguished member of the Department of Economics at the University of Wisconsin. For several years he had worked closely with State Federation officers Weber and Brockhausen. Commons urged the members of the powerful Milwaukee Merchants and Manufacturers Association to support workers' compensation. Addressing their meeting in December, 1908, he told the packed house that a proper bill "would place the relations of capital and labor in this state on a more harmonious basis than any state in the Union can boast of."

There was as yet no agreement on the specific terms of

State Historical Society of Wisconsin WHi (X3) 40290
Interior of Milwaukee's Nordberg Manufacturing Company.

the bill. There was no functioning workers' compensation law anywhere in the country and hence no model to draw upon. The 1909 legislature, therefore, appointed a joint interim Committee on Industrial Insurance to study the components of such a bill and report back to the 1911 legislature. Repesentative of the WSFL and of the Wisconsin Manufacturers Association assisted the committee. Representative Wallace Ingalls from Racine, a member of the legislative committee, made a trip to Germany and England where workers' compensation had been in operation for many years. In Wisconsin, the employers generally wanted workers to contribute one-third or one-half of the cost of the insurance; the WSFL insisted that employers bear all the costs. The employers wanted a voluntary system, under which each employer could elect to offer workers' compensation or to remain under the old system. The WSFL fought for compulsory enrollment of all employers, but also wanted to permit an injured worker to choose between accepting the modest compensation payments specified in the law or suing in the courts for damages under the old system.

The Workmen's Compensation Act, passed in 1911, was a compromise. Labor gained in that the employers were obligated to pay full costs, but employers gained the voluntary provision, although, if they opted to remain in the old system, they had to give up the principle of "assumption of risks" and the "fellow servant doctrine." Labor agreed to a provision allowing the worker to choose, at the time of hiring, whether to be covered under workers' compensation insurance or to retain the right to sue the employer for damages. Most workers and large employers enrolled under the compensation act. In 1931, workers' compensation finally became compulsory for employers and employees.

—ROBERT OZANNE

From *The Labor Movement in Wisconsin: A History*
(State Historical Society of Wisconsin, Madison, 1984).

African American Workers
and the Labor Movement
in Milwaukee, 1870–1930

JOE W. TROTTER, JR.

In 1989 the Wisconsin Labor History Society featured Joe W. Trotter, Jr.
as a keynote speaker at its annual conference in Milwaukee. Trotter, the author
of Black Milwaukee: The Making of an Industrial Proletariat, 1915-1945
(University of Illinois, 1985), presented an insightful analysis of the complex
relationship between African American workers and labor organizations.

THE relationship between blacks and white unions is a key theme in the history of the state and nation. Because African Americans migrated to Milwaukee in larger numbers than they did to other areas of the state, race relations in the labor movement gained its most intense expressions in the Cream City. As elsewhere in urban industrial America, however, the history of blacks and organized labor was a complicated process—one that changed over time and was shaped by a variety of socioeconomic forces. Although certain continuities characterized the interaction between African Americans and the labor movement in Milwaukee between 1870 and 1945, exclusion marked the late nineteenth and early twentieth centuries; all-black unions emerged during World War I and the 1920s; and interracial black unions emerged during World War I and the 1920s; and interracial unions rose under the impact of the New Deal and World War II. During each period, the relationship between black workers and the labor movement was shaped by the attitudes and behavior of white employers, workers, and the state, as well as by the activities of African American workers themselves. In order to understand these developments in Wisconsin's labor history, it is necessary to turn briefly to the larger socioeconomic and political development of Milwaukee as a city.

Between 1870 and World War I, the city of Milwaukee witnessed a dynamic transition from commercial to industrial capitalism. New industries moved to the forefront of the city's economy. As early as 1870, flour milling, meatpacking, tanning, and brewing had become firmly established, but the future lay with iron and steel production. By 1901, the city's major iron and steel firm, the Bay View Works, was reorganized as the Illinois Steel Corporation and became part of the giant U.S. Steel Corporation. On the basis of its tremendous industrial growth, the city's population increased from 72,000 in 1870 to nearly 400,000 by World War I. Immigration played a key role in the city's growth. As elsewhere, immigrants from Poland, Russia, and Italy increasingly displaced the older German and Irish sources of immigrant labor.

As the new immigration accelerated, the city fragmented along class and ethnic lines. American-born whites of English background moved to the far west and upper east side; German factory workers moved to the northwest side; and the new immigrants settled around the central business district. Ethnic divisions soon gained expression in the political system. The Democratic party gained growing support among Irish and Polish Catholics, while the Republican party attracted the increasingly conservative German-American element of the population. Ethnic divisions also divided the Milwaukee working class. As one scholar of the Milwaukee labor movement has noted, for example, the Milwaukee Federated Trades Council (FTC, an affiliate of the American Federation of Labor) was largely an association of skilled German workers. It barred other ethnic groups and unskilled German labor as well because "craft unions were also social clubs."

It was within the context of this increasingly fragmented metropolis that the experiences of black workers unfolded. The African American population increased from less than 200 in 1870 to nearly 1,000 in 1910. Representing less than 1 percent of the total, it was one of the smallest African American communities among the top twenty-five American cities. As elsewhere during the pre-World War I years, however, blacks migrated to Milwaukee from the Upper South and border states. They came primarily from Virginia, North Carolina, and Tennessee. Despite their small numbers, black workers were almost totally excluded from the expanding industrial sector. Between 1870 and 1910, nearly 70 percent of African American men and women worked as domestic, personal service, and common laborers, as porters, waiters, servants, cooks, and as sanitation and construction workers. Reflecting the dearth of industrial opportunities for black men during the period, women slightly outnumbered men in the city's small stream of black migrants.

Although African Americans were fundamentally excluded from the industrial labor force, a few entered the industrial labor force as strikebreakers. When white workers struck the Illinois Steel Company in 1898, the leading black newspaper, the *Advocate*, advertised for "250 colored men to work in the rolling mills of Bay View." The strikebreaking efforts of the company were apparently successful. According to local historian Thomas Buchanan, blacks became "part of a heterogeneous labor force, whose diverse elements the union would find difficult to unite" and hard to rely upon in subsequent labor disputes. Unable to secure their jobs, African American steel workers gradually disappeared by 1904.

Although they faced exclusion from the industrial sector, African American common laborers fought class and racial inequality through both formal and informal means. In 1877, black construction workers struck in protest against the treatment that they received as blacks and as workers. They marched from Market Street to the corner of Strand and Twenty-Fourth streets and succeeded in getting another group of blacks to quit. Before long, African Americans working at Levine's Picklery, Stump's planing mill, and the freight depot, flour mills, and other establishments joined the demonstration. A large force of policemen was sent to control the strikers and the movement collapsed. In 1897, to cite another example, some bootblacks organized what they called a Shoe Artists Association. They protested the practice of stores giving free shines to purchasers of shoes. Bootblacks, they maintained, had "to live as well as the shoe dealers." These men aimed to secure their position in the shoeshine trade.

Organized white labor did little to encourage the integration of blacks into the labor movement before World War I. Although the Knights of Labor sought to unite black and white workers into one union, its efforts in Milwaukee were short-lived. After 1886, the skilled craft-oriented Milwaukee Federated Trades Council displaced the Knights. Although Socialists gained control of the executive board of the FTC in 1899, the organization continued to ignore unorganized and largely unskilled laborers, which included nearly all black workers. Thus, until World War I and its aftermath, black workers were largely excluded from the labor movement. Moreover, their own efforts to build all-black unions produced few results during the late nineteenth and early years of the twentieth century.

World War I transformed the racial dynamic of Milwaukee's labor movement. Under the impact of war production, the city's black population increased from less than 1,000 to over 2,000 in 1920 and to over 7,000 in 1930, though it still remained only a fraction of the total (1.1 percent). The sources and characteristics of black migration also changed. Blacks born in the Deep South states of Mississippi, Georgia, and Alabama entered the city in rising numbers. Moreover, whereas black

women outnumbered black men on the eve of World War I, the sex ratio shifted to a predominance of men over women. For the first time in the city's history, African Americans moved out of the domestic and personal service jobs into the industrial sector. The percentage of black men in skilled, semiskilled, and unskilled work increased from 19 percent in 1910 to over 70 percent in 1920 and 1930. The percentage of black women in such jobs also increased, but they remained largely in the domestic service sector.

Although African American men entered industrial jobs in increasing numbers, they were relegated to the bottom. Black men found employment in the most difficult, low paying, and disagreeable jobs. They were restricted to four major industrial groups: iron and steel; slaughtering and meatpacking; tanneries; and building and construction. During the war years, only 11 of the city's 2,000 manufacturing firms hired black workers. More importantly, six of the eleven hired over 75 percent of all black workers: Plankinton Packing, Albert Trostel Leather, Pfister-Vogel Tannery, Allis Chalmers, Falk Manufactory, and the Milwaukee Coke and Gas Company. The racial attitudes and practices of employers obstructed black access to better jobs. Milwaukee employers often perceived African Americans as unfit for factor employment: "They are slow and very hard to please. Not good on rapid moving machinery, have not had mechanical training. Slow. Not stable."

According to the oral testimonies of black men, they were "limited, they only did the dirty work . . . jobs that even Poles didn't want." African Americans worked in the hottest areas of the plant. They fed the black furnaces, and performed the most tedious operations in rolling mills that made rails for the railroads. In the packing houses, African Americans worked as muckers or slaughters. They unloaded trucks, slaughtered the animals, transported intestines, and cleaned the plant. Black tannery employees worked mainly in the beam house. They put animal hides in a pit filled with lime, in order to remove the hair. According to one tannery workers, this operation required rubber boots, rubber aprons, and rubber gloves, "everything rubber because that lime would eat you up."

White workers reinforced the lowly position of black workers by erecting their own barriers to black industrial employment. From the outset of World War I, the Milwaukee Federated Trades Council resisted black migration and employment in Milwaukee industries. According to Frank Weber, organizer of the FTC, "The Shortage of Labor Cry" was a "Propaganda for Low Wages." White workers also had a sympathetic mayor in Socialist Daniel W. Hoan. In 1922, for example, when the Milwaukee Railroad brought in black strikebreakers, Mayor Hoan informed the owners that he would not tolerate the use of black strikebreakers and permit racial strife to disrupt what he called "the most peaceful city in the entire world." Upon receiving Hoan's letter, William Finley, president of the Chicago, Milwaukee, and St. Paul Railway, announced that "no more colored labor [would] be sent to Milwaukee." Racism among white workers, their leaders, and supporters sometimes received clear verbal expression. According to the well-known Milwaukee Socialist Victor Berger, for example, blacks belonged to "a lower race." On one occasion, at a Socialist Party convention in the

Foundry workers at Fairbanks-Morse and Company, Beloit, 1925.

State Historical Society of Wisconsin

cushions against unexpected deaths, sickness, and unemployment. By 1930, however, blacks belonged to only four unions: Asphalt Workers Local 88, Musicians Local 587, a carpenter's local, and a common labor local. The asphalt and musicians locals were all-black, the common labor union was 50 percent black, and only two blacks belonged to the carpenters' union.

African Americans also used their locals to fight racial discrimination by organized white labor. In June 1925, for example, Asphalt Workers petitioned the Milwaukee FTC, the Wisconsin State Federation of Labor, and all Milwaukee trade unions to "lift the ban on colored workers [that] . . . exist in some of the organized trades." The petition also reminded white workers that they had a common enemy in the employers and should therefore unite with black workers across racial lines. "The prevailing attitude toward the Negro worker on the part of the organized labor," the resolution concluded, "is a potent weapon for the capitalist . . . and a tremendous drawback to the successful achievements of the workers in general."

Milwaukee auditorium, Mayor Hoan amused the gathering with a "darky story," although he later apologized when his black supporters protested. Most importantly, however, racism had its greatest impact when white workers barred—formally and informally—African Americans from membership in their unions. Hoan recognized the hostility of rank and file white workers when he accepted the formation of separate all black locals: "I don't like segregation in theory but colored locals are better than no locals."

As African Americans confronted restrictions on their participation in the labor movement, they promoted their own interests through a variety of labor organizations. These organizations provided African Americans with important instruments for increasing their demands for higher wages, better treatment, and better working conditions in general. Some blacks gained access to predominantly white carpenters and hod carriers locals, but most belonged to separate all-black unions. During the war years, blacks established the Colored Workingmen's Liberty Club. In 1918, they belonged to the 200-member butchers' union, an AFL local in which they were too numerous to exclude, but were increasingly segregated. By the mid-1920s, the butchers' union nearly disappeared under the impact of growing racial hostility, the postwar economic depression, and, especially, the Milwaukee Employers Council's growing counter offensive against the labor movement. Still, African Americans in Milwaukee continued to organize separate all-black labor organizations. In 1926, for example, they formed the Working Men's League; through burial funds and social welfare committees, the organizations offered

Organized white labor sometimes acknowledged the importance of black labor in the success of the labor movement. In 1925, the Milwaukee FTC endorsed the Communist-spearheaded American Negro Labor Congress (ANLC). Organized in Chicago in 1925, the ANLC aimed to unify black and white workers across racial and ethnic lines. In 1927, the organization pushed for a black alderman in the city's 6th ward, where blacks concentrated in growing numbers. According to the ANLC, "a colored worker" who worked "in a packing plant" was "just as capable to represent the interest of workers as anybody else, and because of his understanding of the objective conditions" even more so. Although the council failed to elect a black alderman, it gained the endorsement of white as well as black labor organizations and foreshadowed the rise of interracial unionism during the New Deal era. In other words, although a variety of forces—the persistence of racial discrimination among rank and file white workers, the antiunion activities of the Milwaukee Employers Council, and the very small size of Milwaukee's black population—helped to undermine the effectiveness of separate all-black unions, such organizations established the groundwork for the subsequent movement of black workers into the predominantly white labor movement. ∎

From *Wisconsin Labor History Newsletter* (1989).

"FIGHTING BOB" LA FOLLETTE

AMERICA at the end of the last century had strayed far from the democratic ideals of its founding fathers. The robber barons of big business built trusts which exploited natural resources, labor and consumers, alike. Big money bought political power. Between 1890 and World War I, a generation of legislative reformers challenged the power of the industrialists and bankers.

The Progressives, as they were called, struggled for regulatory laws intended to curb the rapacity of big business. They fought against corrupt machines by enacting devices—the initiative, referendum, and recall—to increase popular participation in politics. Prominent among them was the insurgent Republican from Wisconsin, Robert M. La Follette.

In a log cabin in rural Primrose Township, Dane County, Wisconsin on June 14, 1855, Robert La Follette was born. The fourth child of a poor pioneering farmer who died before he was a year old, La Follette struggled to get the education he coveted. His stepfather's illness forced him to quit high school at fourteen and take over management of the family farm. After his stepfather died, he rented the farm and took his mother and sister to Madison where he enrolled in the University of Wisconsin. He taught school, sold books, published the student newspaper and worked at odd jobs, nevertheless managing to take part in university dramatics, politics, and oratorical contests. Upon graduation, he chose a career in law and after studying for seven months, passed the bar examination.

La Follette wrote in his *Autobiography* that he ran for Dane County district attorney purely for the salary the post paid. But it was an independent-minded Progressive in-the-making, one who defied the Dane County Republican machine by running against its hand-picked candidate and narrowly won by taking his campaign on a run-down old horse to the people. He later served three terms in Congress during which he became increasingly aware of corporate power brokerage in the halls of Congress. His final break with the lumber and railroad-controlled machine occurred in 1891 when La Follette refused to accept a bribe from the State Republican boss who wanted him to "influence" the outcome of a court case. Shocked, outraged, and outcast by his party, "I determined," he wrote in his *Autobiography*, "that the power of this corrupt influence, which was undermining and destroying every semblance of representative government in Wisconsin, should be broken."

It took ten years of stump speeches at county fairs and Chautauqua tents with little money, no newspaper, and the support of few. After unsuccessfully fielding candidates against the machine, he embarked on a massive campaign of public education for the direct primary—removing nominations for political office out of backroom caucuses and into the voting booth.

Wisconsin State Historical Society WHi (X31) 6201
Senator Robert M. La Follette, AFL-backed candidate for President, delivering Labor Day address, 1924, on Washington D.C. radio station WCAP.

In 1900, La Follette was elected governor, causing reverberations throughout the country. He transformed the state into a vast laboratory for Progressive ideas. In his three terms as governor, he signed legislation to regulate railroads and public utilities, provide for primary elections, improve working conditions for labor and provide for injured workers through worker's compensation, strengthen civil service, reform the tax code, expand the state university system, curtail lobbying and banking abuses, and the wholesale slashing of the state's forests.

From 1906 until his death nineteen years later, La Follette served as an eloquent Senate spokesman for Progressivism and against bossism. He was courageous in his stands: his unpopular opposition to U.S. involvement in World War I; his resolution initiating the investigation of President Warren Harding's Teapot Dome scandal. Among his legislative contributions were passage of the 1915 Seamen's Act which ended the virtual peonage of sailors. He gave crucial support for the Adamson Act which established the eight-hour day for rail employees.

His labor record earned him the only third party endorsement ever made by the American Federation of Labor when he ran for President in 1924 on the Progressive Party ticket. "Fighting Bob" La Follette polled 12 million votes in that election, more than any other third party candidate before or since.

—DEBRA E. BERNHARDT

From *"Fighting Bob" La Follette*
(New York State Labor History Association, 1990).

Why I Unionized My Plant

GEORGE W. MEAD

In 1928 George W. Mead, president of Consolidated Water Power and Paper in Wisconsin Rapids, wrote a very unusual piece for an academic journal specializing in personnel issues. Mead explained how his views of the role of unions in the workplace had evolved over time. Mead's description sheds light on the possibilities for labor-management cooperation, an important aspect which is almost always overshadowed by the more visible and controversial activities such as strikes and lock-outs.

NINE years ago this spring a union-membership campaign gave the paper-maker's union a foothold in our Wisconsin Rapids plant. We were opposed to the union idea, "on principle," as many other manufacturers are. In fact we just about saw red at the thought of having our plant unionized.

Why, indeed, should our men want to join with outsiders in organizing against us? We had always treated them fairly; they themselves would be the first to admit it. We had paid good wages and had voluntarily given the men bonuses when war prices had increased our income. Our plant was pleasant to work in. Our hours were reasonable. We had given every proof of our desire to be square. Or so it seemed to us.

Why, then, this business of tying up with an outside union?

My first reaction was to tell the men that if they belonged to a union they could not work for me. We had got along without unions for 16 years; we could get along a while longer. We had always been fair; we would continue to be fair, and loyal men would stay with us and others fill the places of the disloyal. Other plants in Wisconsin were not unionized; if they could keep out the unions we could. So we had what union men would call a lockout.

Some of our men came to me in person and told me they wanted to stick with us while the union men were out. We could undoubtedly have continued to operate, especially if we had wanted to employ non-union men from other cities.

But we wanted to be fair to the men who were fair to us. Why brand them to their fellowmen, who would undoubtedly be back at work as soon as they had time to think over their unreasonableness? No use causing a permanent split in our ranks. And then, with the plant idle, I myself had time to cool off and do some thinking. I had reacted on an emotional basis. Now I acted on a basis of reason.

Men who had been with us for years were out of work, their families without income. Our mill was idle, our business hazarded if we kept it idle too long. Local merchants and the local community as a whole would suffer while this big slice of

its support was cut off. Wasn't there another way out? It seemed to me that there was. The whole affair—lockout or walkout, whatever you call it—was due to my own personal opposition to unions. Had I carried this opposition further than was necessary? The result of my three days' thinking was that I sent word to our men that they could come back if they wished, on these conditions: Any man who wanted to retain his union membership could do so, but they must not expect me or the company to recognize or deal with the union. And they all came back.

As I sat in my office that next morning and watched them come walking past my window with eager step and bright eye, talking, laughing, and with never a sign of bitterness or resentment, I gained a new sense of what a man's job means to him. Most of these men had been with us for years; the plant was in a real sense their home. They were just as glad to be back as I was to have them back. We had gained our real point, and lost nothing. So we started work with an "open shop."

But the incident had started our thinking in different lines. Or, rather, we had discovered the vital fact that our prejudices and emotions had at least as much to do with our actions as did calm, constructive reasoning.

We had been planning to raise wages in the spring—this was in 1919. But there were some problems connected with the increase which we in the office could not solve to best advantage by ourselves. For a proper solution we needed certain information that only the men themselves could give us.

Another thought ran somewhat along these lines. Now that we must have a union here in our plant, is there anything we can do to make it a good union rather than a troublesome one? And have unions good points that we can develop to advantage? If so, what are these points?

Deliberately and independently we began to investigate. We looked into union ideas and principles as we would have looked into a chemical problem in paper-making, or a problem in developing our supplies of pulp wood.

One of the steps we took was to call in some of the union

leaders in the plants, at various times, for questioning. We gave them no encouragement. But we went pretty thoroughly into all the doubts and fears and prejudices that every no-union employer has. And we sought to learn what were the actual aims and ideals of our union men and those of their outside associates and leaders.

The result was that a new view-point was presented to us, of which we had never before been conscious. We found that the union men, although they too were beset by fears and prejudices, had also an unexpected store of well-reasoned plans and aspirations. Above all they exhibited a striking candor and honesty. They talked very frankly about what seemed to them our shortcomings, and they were equally unreserved on points more favorable to us and less favorable to them.

We decided, when this stage of inquiry was passed, to keep on applying the scientific method to our union-labor relations. Inquiry first, then trial and error. We would see what would happen if we attempted negotiations with the union. And if something reasonably promising resulted, we might give it a year's trial. Our position could be made more difficult by so doing, but at least experience and information would be gained that would guide us in shaping our course in the future.

As a result, in May of 1919, we signed a one-year's contract, or "joint labor agreement," with representatives of three unions: The International Brotherhood of Paper Makers; The International Brotherhood of Pulp, Sulphite, and Paper Mill Workers; and the International Brotherhood of Electrical Workers.

The further result is that each of the eight springs since 1919 has seen a new contract based on the experience of the previous year and signed by both parties after fresh negotiations have cleared the atmosphere of any new aspirations or dissatisfaction on the one side or the other.

I do not have to wonder what the average employer who has never made year-to-year contracts with a union thinks of all this. I have been an anti-union employer myself. And I have talked with too many anti-union employers not to know, "If you encourage union labor, where is it going to stop in its demands?" is the first reaction of the employer to whom the word "union" connotes only "strikes" and "blacklists."

"You are putting in the hands of workmen authority that belongs only to the management," says another.

"I don't want outsiders telling me how to run my business," is the comment of the employer who has visions of a walking delegate coming into his plant and ordering the men to lay down their tools if demands of the delegate are not met.

Certainly, if our experiment had proved any of these forebodings true we would not have kept on through nine successive contracts. However, our experience has been quite the opposite of what the employer would expect who holds himself in a mood of opposition. Instead of our unions going on and on to bolder and bolder demands, they have progressed year by year to a more and more effective cooperation.

The other day I had a visitor who was very much interested in finding out all he could about our union experiences. I asked this visitor to go out into the mill and talk to one of the union leaders. The man he talked to is secretary of the central labor union of our city and carries a card as organizer for the state labor federation. His heart and soul are in the labor movement. After their talk in the mill, the union man brought to the other's hotel in the evening a printed copy of a speech made last Labor Day by John P. Burke, president of the International Brotherhood of Pulp, Sulphite, and Paper Mill Workers. And the corner that he turned down marked this passage:

"Workers Urged to Cooperate. Now let me say to you men who are employed by this company here at Wisconsin Rapids that our union mills may, in the years to come, be faced with quite severe competition from those non-union mills paying a low rate of wages.

". . . However, I have always contended that if the management in the union mills will give us somewhere near the same equipment we shall not have to fear the competition of non-union mills. Union mills can be run more efficiently because of the greater intelligence of union men and because of the greater team-work and cooperation with the management. Therefore, I say to you union men in this audience: Cooperate with the management of the Consolidated Water Power and Paper Company to the fullest extent. Cooperate so that we may be able to maintain our union scale of wages here and get a little more from year to year. Cooperate to guard the eight-hour day. Cooperate so that you may have full running time. Cooperate so that the union men may be employed."

We feel that this plea for cooperation, coming from the workmen's own representative, is more effective than anything an employer could say or urge.

We were fair with our workers before they were unionized, we thought. And we were generous. But we were not fair or generous in an arrangement to which they were voluntary parties; it was only in a way of our own choosing. In other words we were paternalistic. And paternalism may be generous, which is easy, but it often does not succeed in being just, which is hard.

In this connection it is interesting that in one of our five plants there is no union. At this plant the men voted on the question of setting up a union arrangement such as we have in Wisconsin Rapids, and the vote was 75–25 against it. Our men here asked us whether, since we found the union method so satisfactory, we would not help them unionize the other plant. To this our answer was that the other mill was in a district not yet unionized and that we would be unfair to other employers if we deliberately brought in a union. Besides, if the men there did not want a union the union method would not work as well as the plant committee now in effect. It would be unsuccessful for the same reason that our pre-union paternalism was only partly successful here.

One thing we do not do is to tell workmen that their interests and ours are common interests. They are not common. They are opposed. It is true that employers and men may have certain interests in common, as the quotation from John P. Burke's speech shows. Likewise a buyer and a seller have certain interests in common, but in themselves the interests of buyer and seller are opposed. But how does this philosophy work out in practice?

Said one of our union men to an inquiring visitor: "We've

South Central Federation of Labor

Construction workers and engineers building the Loraine Hotel in Madison, 1923.

had some sweet arguments. We don't always win, and we don't always lose. The big thing is that the management is always ready to 'listen in.' And just you let some one from the management pass the word to the boys that some job needs a special rush and see how they all jump onto it."

It is true that the union men do not always win their arguments. And this is the biggest part of the answer to the employer who fears that when the union comes in, his business will be "run by outsider."

Take the bugaboo of the seniority rule, for instance: Must the oldest man in point of service always get the plum when a desirable job is vacant?

Suppose we have a machine tender's job to fill. Our joint labor agreement authorizes us to hire an outsider, provided no man in the mill is as competent as the outsider we would get. But we prefer not to go outside.

The men expect that we will promote the man next in line. But perhaps it is our judgment that the man next in line is not sufficiently competent. Very likely the disappointed man's representative will ask why the senior man did not get the job. If he fails to get satisfaction the case will probably be brought up by the grievance committee at its next meeting with the mill manager.

It is quite possible that Bill himself will be sitting in the meeting while his case is before the committee. At first or representative felt a natural hesitation about telling, in the man's presence, that we had withheld promotion because of his own incapacity. But experience taught us that the men prefer honesty above everything else.

But perhaps the most interesting part of the working out of this seniority question is the effect it has had on or own policies of training and promotion. Suppose that when we refused Bill promotion for lack of ability, Bill has been 15 years at his present job.

"But why," ask the union representatives, "did it take 15 years to find this out? Wouldn't it have been better to have had Bill on some job to which he was more suited?"

Of course it would have been better. But nowadays we are not likely to have any 15-year Bills. For, stimulated in large part by this practical view-point of the men themselves, we study a man's aptitude for the highest job on a machine when we set him to work on the bottom-of-the-ladder job.

We try a man six months as a helper. And during these six months he is on trial for his ability to go up in the ranks of machine tenders just as much as for his qualities as a helper.

What this means to us in the development of a stable force of highly able operators, especially in this day when the quality of our paper is so important a factor, can readily be imagined.

Thus the seniority rule has in our case proved an asset rather than a liability. And it is the same with some of the other rules and agreements.

One of these is that no man can be discharged without having his case subject to review, at his complaint, by the grievance committee. There is no question that in the days before our union agreement, capable men were sometimes discharged by an irate foreman or superintendent for rather slight cause. Under the new arrangement we not only save good men for the company, but also have lost one or two superintendents who were, it now appears, good riddance.

But here again the rule has stimulated an improvement in our own procedures. Today we make no discharge without thorough study and thought. To our minds the discharge of a man is a serious reflection upon the employer himself. Time and careful thought in the selection of men; training foremen to take pride in the progress of their men; study and transfer of men who are not measuring up to what is expected of them; continuous effort to avoid injustice; with all these it should almost never be necessary to fire a man.

What this thorough respect for a man's right in the possession of his job means to us, is a thing no man can measure. Surely, any man who is free from the fear that something may happen to take his job from him can accomplish more in his daily work than can the man who is haunted by such a fear.

In the fixing of wages we do experience some interference by outsiders. But so far we are none the worse for it.

The wage schedule asked each year by our paper-makers is decided upon at a meeting of the international union, which at the same time sets wage scales to be considered by union mills throughout the United States and Canada. Two years ago the union advocated a scale of wages which seemed to us to be based upon a fallacy. It proposed that men working at the largest and most modern paper machines should receive a higher wage than men tending machines lower capacity.

So firm were we in our objection to this method that we refused to sign any contract embodying it. We told the union representatives that although we had been pleased with the results of our several years' dealing with them and should regret very much any termination of the experiment, still we could not see our way clear to signing such an agreement as they now proposed.

Apparently we had reached a deadlock.

But what one who has not dealt with the American Federation of Labor does not perhaps realize is the disposition of its leaders, in recent years, to be conciliatory. But in the end we reached a friendly and practical agreement.

In this instance the union men took a few days to talk and think about the problem. Then they came back to us. Their president admitted as frankly as I had done that they would regret any termination of our relationship. He also said, with surprising candor, that it would be impossible for him to call a strike in our plant. He was still convinced, however, that their position on the wage matter was sound and that we would come to their view-point.

It was proposed, therefore, that the disputed wage scale be left out of the annual contract and that we take further time to investigate it. A special agreement on the wage scale could be signed later.

And it happened that when we did take further time to consider the new wage proposal, in our own way and under no pressure of personality or of time, we completely changed our mind about the "fallacy" of paying more for work at the larger machines. We realized, for instance, that what our men are really paid for is to keep the machines going without interruption. The greater the output of a machine, the more serious is an interruption and therefore the heavier the responsibility of the operators.

We found, in short, another indication of a fact we had already observed, namely, that the union men of today pick unusually intelligent and forward-looking men as their leaders.

Recently the foresightedness of the union leaders has been evidenced in their attention to business conditions in the paper industry. The paper industry of America is at present overbuild. There is an excess capacity of at least 15%. This condition has called forth all the ability that we and other paper manufacturers have, to look ahead and safeguard our future. But I sometimes think the union leaders, who are close students of economics, saw what was coming before we did.

At any rate they recently asked us and our employees to "take our share" of lessened business. That is, instead of each mill fighting to keep 100% busy by cutting prices or sacrificing standards of quality, they would like to see each one running, let us say, 85% of its capacity, with normal prices and improved quality. Similarly they would like to have each man in the mill take his share of the slack instead of seeing part of the men continuously employed and part of them out of work. In line with this policy our men suggested, last fall, that we shut down on Thanksgiving Day, which is not one of the holidays agreed upon in our contract.

In the long run this may not be the best possible method of meeting the great problem of how to make men secure in their jobs at a time when the jobs of some are threatened by current business conditions. On the other hand, it is at least a method which is better than no method at all. And it has the advantage both of being cooperative and of inspiring further cooperation.

In other phases of our relations with the unions, results have been satisfactory. No subject is too large, none too small to come up in our grievance committee meetings or our annual negotiations. But no matter what the subject, the discussions are marked by the utmost truth and sincerity, and give-and-take on both sides.

We find the men very receptive to our undertakings toward economy, even when this means that fewer men will be employed; and very willing to modify their pet rules, such as not having non-union men come into the plant for construction work, when they see that a rule blocks the path of efficiency. The union organization, through its grievance committee, also helps us in management decisions because facts come out in our discussions that would otherwise be hidden.

For nine years now, our experiment with unions has been successful. It may not always be so. But as long as it is successful we shall, I imagine, continue to prefer dealing with unions to any alternative method.■

From "Why I Unionized My Plant," in *Factory and Industrial Management* (February, 1928).

SECTION

3

The Promise of Industrial Unionism

Milwaukee Mayor Daniel Hoan addresses a labor demonstration favoring a strike at the Seaman Body Corporation, March 20, 1934.

Industrial Unions:
The Organizers' Views

The success of industrial unionism depended ultimately upon the efforts of union leaders and labor activists at the local level. In 1986 the Wisconsin Labor History Society brought together several of the pioneers of industrial unionism in Wisconsin for its annual conference. The following section features excerpts from four speakers, all of whom began as rank-and-file activists and rose to positions of leadership in the local, state, and national labor movements.

CHARLES HEYMANNS

WHEN we think of the early days of industrial unionism, we often think of the CIO. In Wisconsin, however, the history of industrial unions began well before the advent of the CIO. When we organized the employees in the Kohler plant, the real start came at a mass meeting attended by more than 10,000 at lakefront in Sheboygan in 1933. Our speaker was Jake Friedrick, representing the Milwaukee Federated Trades Council and Wisconsin State Federation of Labor. That rally kicked off the organizing drive. Federal labor unions were formed, but also so-called craft unions, such as the Carpenters, organized on a industrial basis, especially the foundry workers and furniture workers.

We were helped by new laws such as the National Industrial Recovery Act with its famous "7(a)" provision, and the Wagner Act. We had always felt that we had the right to organize; now we had the protection in that right. But the employers had a great deal of power and we were new to unionism at the Kohler plant. In 1934 we were dragged out to a captive meeting during business hours. There we were addressed by the president of the Kohler company, Walter J. Kohler, Sr., the former governor of the state. On the platform with Kohler sat the hand-picked officers of the Kohler Workers Association, a company union. Kohler pointed to the KWA officers and announced, "Here is your union." Many times in later years I thought back and wished I had known better. If

only I had gotten up and spoken against the captive meeting and the formation of the company union, maybe the history of the Kohler union would have been different. We learn by history, but history is sometimes a hard teacher.

In 1934, I was elected to the WSFL convention in Racine, but I didn't attend because of the bloody turn of events that took place in Kohler. I was involved in leading our union on strike when a police riot occurred. Two of our members were shot in the back and killed. Some forty-seven others were also wounded by gunfire, mostly shot in the back.

After going to work as a representative for the national AFL in 1937, I was deeply involved with industrial organizing. At that time we already had many federal labor unions organized. The big Simmons plant was started in 1933. In Superior we had a public employees union for the city police department. In New London we organized a federal labor union and put everyone who was eligible to join a union into it, including the building trades, factory workers, plumbers, and all other types of workers. Later, they went into other unions. In Madison we organized the public employees in a federal labor union. Later they received a charter from the AFL and that was the beginning of the American Federation of State, County, and Municipal Employees, or AFSCME. In La Crosse, the workers at Trane were organized and in Eau Claire, the rubber workers were established as a federal labor union that later affiliated with the United Rubber Workers union. In Manitowoc, three unions of aluminum workers were formed.

I should point out that during these years we had to fight like hell all over to get any kind of union security. Also, in may cases we were assigned bargaining rights for three times as many more people than we had dues-paying members. Sometimes we would win the collective bargaining elections, but we couldn't win union security. Later those things were changed and unions gained more stability.

In those days there were not may organizers available.

This was true not only of the AFL, the WSFL, and local labor federations, but also of the international unions. They didn't have the manpower, the money, or the means to service the people that they needed. But I'd be surprised if the people today could do what they did back then.■

Elected President of Federal Labor Union 18545 at the Kohler Company in 1933, Charles Heymanns became a representative for the national AFL in 1937. In 1951 he was named Regional Director for the AFL in the Midwest.

VICTOR COOKS

WE got the movement for industrial unionism started in Racine in 1932 when about 50 percent of the workers were laid off and on relief. In those days there wasn't any unemployment insurance.

We organized a Workers Committee to improve the relief. We organized several committees all around town. We picketed the relief department and got into politics. We had a meeting every week. I give a lot of credit to the Socialist party which had a hall that we used. We brought in speakers and preached unionism and politics. We set up a relief committee to help workers and their families get what they needed. We got people active in politics and elected a Socialist mayor, two or three alderman, and a couple of supervisors. The relief got better.

Then the economy picked up and the shops started rehiring. There weren't really any craft unions in these plants and the AFL federal labor unions didn't really amount to much. In those days, they could start you out on any kind of wage. Some got 20 cents an hour; some got 25 cents an hour. But members of the Workers Committee who went back to the job still retained their membership status. We started to organize the shops around town using the Workers Committee. We didn't have much trouble organizing.

After we organized in these shops, we needed to be recognized. But in most cases, the companies refused and we had to strike. At J.I. Case there was a federal labor union, but it wasn't very large. When the AFL started a federal labor union, the company started a company union. That raised a problem in knowing which union would be recognized. We went on strike over this issue in 1934. We formed the Wisconsin Industrial Union Local 1, an independent union. We had 12 shops organized. We elected someone to head the outfit and charged 25 cents a month to pay for renting a hall for meetings. We won partial recognition. They would look at us and talk with us.

In 1937 the CIO was formed and we all went into the CIO and the UAW. The management at J.I. Case fired all the union stewards, about 37 or 40 members. We went on strike. The strike lasted about 4 months.

During all this time, it was the rank and file workers in the shop that we counted on. We educated them. We made them militant. I give a lot of credit to the Socialist party for the help it gave us during this important period.■

Organizer for the Racine County Workers Council in 1932, Victor Cooks was a founder of the Wisconsin Industrial Union Local 1 in 1934.

KENNETH CLARK

THE great depression hit the farms in the late 1920s. My father lost his farm in 1928 and we first moved to Mauston. Then in 1929 we moved to Milwaukee. My dad worked in the foundry at Allis Chalmers, but he was soon laid off. He could not find another job until 1941. I was the oldest child in the house. I had a paper route for the *Milwaukee Sentinel* and I caddied at the Woodmount Country Club. There I had my first taste of a labor dispute. We caddies had to wait after nine holes for the golfers until they were ready to play again. Most of the younger guys went into the bar room to meet some gals and we had to sit for two or three hours and we didn't get paid for waiting. Finally we couldn't take it any longer and demanded 25 cents for waiting time. At first the golfers did not budge. Then one night some greens alongside 124th street were damaged and some of the old guys at the club got together to change the rules and so we won.

During those days I had a sweater that said "NEW DEAL-NEW DEAL" in big letters. I used to caddy for some guys who were pretty liberal. They gave me a buck to wear the sweater when they played with one guy who was a right-wing lawyer for Allis-Chalmers company. One day when I was parading in front of him, he turned to the others and said, "You dirty SOBs! I bet you're paying the kid to do this!"

Then I got a job working at Tesch's farm where I was paid 10 cents an hour for ten hours a day. We decided to go on strike, but the strike was quickly defeated when the sheriff came in and really took care of us. After that he was known as "Baseball Bat Shinners."

In high school I got involved in strike support efforts in the Milwaukee area, such as the Lindemann-Hoverson strike that lasted eighteen months and the Milwaukee Electric Railway and Transport strike in which a striker was killed. After high school I did volunteer organizing with the steel workers union. I worked with Meyer Adelman, the first director of District 32. This was when all the metal fabricating plants in Milwaukee were first organized. I went to a lot of meetings and rallies for the steel workers and was once arrested with Meyer Adelman. He was the top organizer for the steel workers and became the first Regional Director in this area. He was about 5 feet tall—and 5 feet wide! On the picket line a guy taunted Adelman and ended up flat on his back. But Adelman and I ended up in jail.

I got a job with Davidson and Thompson in West Allis in 1937 for 35 cents an hour with no fringe benefits. We worked ten hours a day and five hours on Saturdays. The company president vowed that the plant would close down if the workers formed a union. But there was interest and we soon started a union. That was the case in most companies in those days. The employers did not want unions, period. We had 220 workers in the plant and in the course of the organizing drive I was beaten up. The guy who did it, I found out later, was an ex-golden glove boxer. Then they fired me. After an NLRB hearing, the company was forced to reinstate me. I was given a job in the engineering department. They figured I would screw up and they could fire me, but it didn't work. Actually, it changed my life.

While working in the office, I continued to be secretary of the steel workers union. After the owner saw the union was going to organize, he sold out to another company. The workers then called a strike for recognition and won after one day, doubling the hourly rate for every worker in the shop. I was kept out of the bargaining unit, but remained active with the SWOC at the Falk corporation, Grede foundries, Waukesha Motors, and other places where there was an organizing drive. My brother worked in the foundry in Grede. He was the organizing force and the president of the local. I was going to night school and during a strike I met my brother after class. We parked a car on the railroad tracks to keep the trains from hauling sand into the foundry. But we lost the strike. My brother got another job as crane operator but was killed on the job in 1944 at the age of thirty-eight.

In 1942 I went to work at International Harvester as a time-study expert. After I had been on the job a few weeks, a group of workers came to me and said that they had heard I had been an organizer. They wanted me to help them organize the office workers. I agreed and advised them to come out openly in favor of a union. That way when they got fired, they could show that they had been fired for union activity. They agreed. The group included myself, and a representative of Local 9 of the Office Workers, led by Harold Beck. We held an NLRB election. We had only thirty-two paid up members of the union at the time of the election. When the ballots were being counted, I would have sworn that the stack of no votes were a lot taller than the yes votes. But in the end we won on a vote of 235-228. I think this was the first industrial office in Milwaukee organized into a genuine union. I served in this union until 1961.

We all thought during those years that we were going to create a great new world for workers. It sure saddens me to see what we have got now.■

A volunteer for the Steel Workers Organizing Committee in 1937, Ken Clark served as president of the Office and Professional Employees union and as a staff representative for the Wisconsin State AFL-CIO.

CARL GRIEPENTROG

■ WAS born in North Dakota, but spent much of my childhood in Wisconsin. When I was 11 the dust storms came. My dad moved to a farm near West Bend, and after 8th grade, I went to work, spending summers working on farms in the area. In the winters I worked in a sawmill nailing cheese boxes together. When I was nineteen I went on as an apprentice electrician for the West Bend Heating and Lighting Company. Four years later, I went to work at the Line Material Company plant in Barton as chief electrician. I worked there about fourteen years.

With a bunch of friends, we organized the union in that plant in 1937. We just decided to have a union and we chose the UAW-CIO. As far as I can tell, it was the first union in Washington County. In those days everybody in the country was joining unions, and it seemed the right thing to do. There were only thirty-seven people working there at the time. We had no trouble negotiating with Mr. Kyle, the owner of Line Material. They had even given us a raise with the intent, I suppose, of getting us to drop the union, but we still negotiated more. We just took it for granted that they were trying to buy us.

Then we decided we wanted more unions in Washington County. We passed out handbills to the employees at Gehl Manufacturing, who make farm machinery, and they all joined the union. There we had a strike right off the bat. This time the organizing was done by the UAW-CIO region. So many UAW unions were being formed that there weren't enough charters to go around. We were all put into one local union—Local 444. We organized at West Bend Woolen Mills, although we never won a contract there. We organized everybody, even the city employees, although they went into a different union. I was the first president of that local.

George Kiebler was the director of the region and Lawrence Carlstrom was the secretary-treasurer. They were full-time officers who directed the organizing and negotiations. Kiebler had been president of UAW Local 75 at Seaman Auto Body in Milwaukee, the plant that later became Nash and then AMC. Finally Kiebler and Carlstom worked out the jurisdictional problem and we were issued separate charters. Our local at Line Material became Local 533 and Gehl became Local 579.

Then came the split in the UAW. I went around to all the shops in Washington County and we all voted to stay with the AFL. That probably happened because Kiebler was such a strong AFL man and a supporter of Homer Martin, who was president of the UAW-AFL. After we became the UAW-AFL, we really went out and organized. I was still working in the plant full-time as a maintenance electrician at the time. We organized

'I got a job with Davidson and Thompson in West Allis in 1937 for 35 cents an hour with no fringe benefits. We worked ten hours a day and five hours on Saturdays. The company president vowed that the plant would close down if the workers formed a union.'

Local 849 at Regal Ware in Kewaskum. In fact, the workers there really organized themselves. In many cases, we could just give people a bundle of cards to sign and the next day they'd be back with everyone signed up.

From 1941 to 1943, I was representative of Region 9, working for George Keibler. In those days, we got $40 a week, plus $3 a day for food and 2 or 3 cents a mile for using our car. Union dues were $1 a month and the per capita tax was 35 cents a month. I was elected Regional Director in 1943 when George Kiebler declined to run so he could become educational director for the international union, which by then had moved its headquarters from Detroit to Milwaukee.

Looking back over those organizing efforts, I must say they were relatively easy. A lot of it had to do with the fact that most employers recognized in those days that the workers were going to organize, regardless of what the bosses did. So, they felt, why not agree to it and not get into a major fight that would wreck the company's public image and cause other long-lasting problems. In those days, you didn't have people walking the streets who would scab on their sister or brother workers. Today, laborers who want jobs are a dime a dozen and are almost forced into scabbing.

Also, our organizing efforts came after the great sit-down strikes of 1937. Workers were excited about unions and had strong solidarity. So the bosses didn't really want to challenge the workers if they wanted a union. They knew they couldn't break down worker solidarity.■

A founder of UAW Local 533 at Line Material in West Bend, Wisconsin, in 1937, Carl Griepentrog became a regional director for the UAW-AFL in 1943. He was the first regional director for Allied Industrial Workers union, which represents workers at Briggs and Stratton, Harley-Davidson, and many other plants.

State Historical Society of Wisconsin WHi (X3) 8641
A general lay-off of workers in Milwaukee.

Building the Union
at Ray-O-Vac in Madison

BY ROBERT H. ZIEGER

Proponents of unionism and collective bargaining often suggested that it would lead to a more balanced and mature relationship between labor and management. But even after a union had been established, establishing the mechanism for meaningful collective bargaining proved to be a difficult task. As Robert Zieger shows in his pathbreaking study of the union at the Ray-O-Vac battery plant in Madison, both unionists and managers had to learn to function in the new system of industrial relations.

DESPITE their dissatisfaction with the company, French Battery workers in the 1920s had displayed little interest in trade unionism. The weakness and lassitude of the labor movement in that decade discouraged even ardent laborites around the country. In addition, most Madison workers had roots directly in the countryside of the Midwest. Few battery workers had had earlier contact with unions, nor was there a substantial element in the plant with immigrant radical background. In some industries that unionized suddenly in the 1930s, men and women with family histories in the mine workers or in the Socialist party led the way, but French Battery workers reflected Wisconsin's sturdy progressivism.

As it turned out, the absence of a laborite background made little difference, for the battery workers brought important strengths to their efforts to create a union. They were a literate and articulate group, perhaps reflecting the value that Wisconsinites attached to education. Moreover, while few had grown up in a trade union environment, some were products of the La Follette progressive political tradition; if their social milieu had not included unions, their political backgrounds were squarely in the dissenting, progressive tradition. Ray-O-Vac employees were usually able to find energetic spokesmen and spokeswomen for their common grievances, for their individualism was one of protest and political activism, not simply a negative agrarian privatism.[1]

The birth of the union at Ray-O-Vac was intimately bound up with the emergence of mass unionism in Wisconsin. Following the passage of the National Industrial Recovery Act in June 1933, Henry Ohl, Jr., and J. J. Handley, president and secretary-treasurer respectively of the Wisconsin State Federation of Labor (WSFL), eagerly seized upon Section 7(a) to spur organization. Throughout the summer and fall of 1933, organizing campaigns achieved immediate success in laborite

Milwaukee, while around the state, even in cities previously immune to the union appeal, workers surged into the unions. "Labor chieftains," observed one state newspaper, "regard the current activity as the greatest single advance in [the state's] union history.[2]

Nor was the WSFL particularly concerned with traditional methods of organization or jurisdictional boundaries. In Kenosha, Racine, Milwaukee, Manitowoc, Two Rivers, Janesville, and other cities in the state's industrial belt there toiled tens of thousands of workers in metal fabrication, farm implements, autos and auto parts, furniture, aluminum, and other mass production industries, largely ignored by the crafts, but now ripe for unionism. The state federation and its organizers actively recruited these unskilled and semiskilled workers. Ohl addressed mass meetings in several cities and, in the absence of organizers from national unions, urged workers to take out federal charters directly from the AFL. At times, in a spirit reminiscent of the old mixed assemblies of the Knights of Labor and the One Big Union dream of the Wobblies, workers signed up helter-skelter, regardless of place of employment, under a common federal charter. Thus, from the beginning of the resurgence of organized labor in Wisconsin, federal labor unions, though often regarded as anomalous appendages or temporary holding bodies elsewhere, received the enthusiastic support of the state's labor establishment and assumed a significant role in the experience of the state's workers.[3]

It was natural, then, that as Ray-O-Vac's workers caught the union fever, they would apply for a federal charter. Apparently no single dramatic event triggered the establishment of the union. Veterans of its early days recall simply that in 1933 and 1934, in view of general difficulties with the company and because of a desire to improve their lot, a group of workers became interested in trade unionism. The decision to form a union seemed logical and appropriate, an extension rather than a negation of their stiff-backed individualism. William McCutchin, who had worked in the toolroom since 1923, was the leading spirit, visiting workers after hours and defying his supervisors warnings to stop stirring up trouble. In May 1934, "a few of us decided we should organize a Union," recorded one of the founders. "We met at the Labor Temple [one] evening and signed up for a charter with the A.F. of L." It was that simple.[4]

Although many of the federal unions established in the wake of the NIRA quickly collapsed, Federal Labor Union 19587 survived an early challenge from management and firmly established itself among the employees. David Saposs, a leading academic authority on industrial unionism, declared in 1934 that the fate of these newly formed FLUs would be "the crucial test of the ability of American unions to organize the basic industries and to exist as a vital movement." The attrition rate among FLUs was high between 1933 and 1935, however, as fledgling organizations succumbed to employer's coercion and blandishments, found the government weak in its support of the alleged guarantees of Section 7(a), or found the established labor movement unresponsive, contemptuous, and suspicious. The union at Ray-O Vac surmounted these obstacles and throughout the 1930s maintained a relatively high level of organization.[5]

Ray-O-Vac employees supported the union loyally during its crucial formative years. An AFL report for 1936 put the average monthly membership since the union's inception at 260, an impressive figure given the seasonal nature of the battery trade and the chronic difficulties that many new unions encountered in collecting dues. Although local leaders frequently complained of poor attendance at meetings and erratic dues payment, the minute books usually recorded over a hundred members present at meetings throughout the 1930s, suggesting that the officers' complaints owed more to their own fervor and expectations than to any unusual failings on the part of the membership. Of course, both membership and attendance increased during controversies with management, and in general the union was able to retain the active interest of at least some among the newly aroused. Because there was no automatic dues checkoff, the union had to rely on constant contact with the membership and the workers' sustained and active support to maintain itself in the 1930s. By 1937, union officials claimed 80 percent organization, a figure that seems too high as an indication of regular dues-paying support, although it is clear that by this time the union was accepted by most employees. Certainly, in contrast with many local unions formed in the ebullient days of 1933 and 1934, Federal Labor Union 19587 took root among the workers rapidly and firmly. In all, given the low-keyed and even cautious nature of the work force, which included many older women particularly fearful of work stoppages and susceptible to company threats to move operations elsewhere, the degree of attachment to the union is impressive.[6]

Of course, the willingness of Ray-O-Vac workers to embrace and support the union depended largely on its effectiveness in conducting collective bargaining. The union's struggle to pry concessions from a reluctant management, to improve working conditions and rates of pay, and to reduce some of the arbitrariness and insecurity characteristic of employment in the Madison factory posed the basic test of its ability to survive and grow. Throughout the 1930s, relations between 19587 and Ray-O-Vac veered sharply between easy accommodation and rancorous dispute. The pattern was not one of increasing maturity and stability through collective bargaining, but neither was it one of intransigent mutual antagonism. Periodically, the company executives behaved in such a way as to convince many workers of the company's determination to weaken or even break the union. This was not a systematic policy, however, and the company gradually displayed a willingness to bargain, at least in a de facto way, with union representatives. In 1937, the company signed a union shop agreement with 19587, but only after a particularly bitter dispute the previous year. The signing of this agreement did not signal harmony, however, for in November 1938 a union-management dispute led to a shutdown which lasted into February 1939. In short, while labor management relations at Ray-O-Vac lacked some of the drama of the Flint sit-down and the Little Steel strike, neither did they settle quickly into benign patterns of narrow, ritualized negotiations presumably common to mature industrial relations.

Trade unionism was as new to Ray-O-Vac's management as it was to the workers. The company president, W. W. Cargill, viewed the labor provisions of the NIRA suspiciously. Unschooled in the nature and functions of labor unions, he had to call on his father-in-law, a veteran of one of the railroad brotherhoods, to educate him.[7] At first the company limited its relationship with the union to the letter of the law, and not always even that. Although they had no carefully thought-out antilabor program, company executives apparently hoped that the union fever would die out and that Ray-O-Vac could soon return to its customary methods of employee relations.

Ray-O-Vac had no overt union-breakers on its staff, but the company did harass the union in a sporadic and haphazard way. For example, it failed to post the labor provisions of the code of fair competition for the battery industry, as required by the NRA for firms such as Ray-O-Vac that sought the advantages of doing business under the code. Company officials closely questioned early union supporters about their activities and in May 1934 laid off five of them, including William McCutchin, the leader in the organizing campaign, immediately after the local's initial meeting. This move nearly precipitated a work stoppage. Sol Reist, the Madison Federation of Labor organizer who was advising the new local, reported that a strike vote would be taken "as the men are desperate." With a nervous eye focused on the explosive middle western labor milieu of 1934, he added darkly that he feared "another Toledo affair in Madison." The aggrieved unionists eventually appealed to the Chicago Regional Labor Board, which functioned as the regional office of the National Labor Board, and won reinstatement. Even so, the company resisted the board's intrusion into its affairs, consistently denied any connection between the layoff of the workers and their participation in union affairs, and delayed returning them to work.[8] Thus despite this early victory, union representatives realized that the company could easily, within

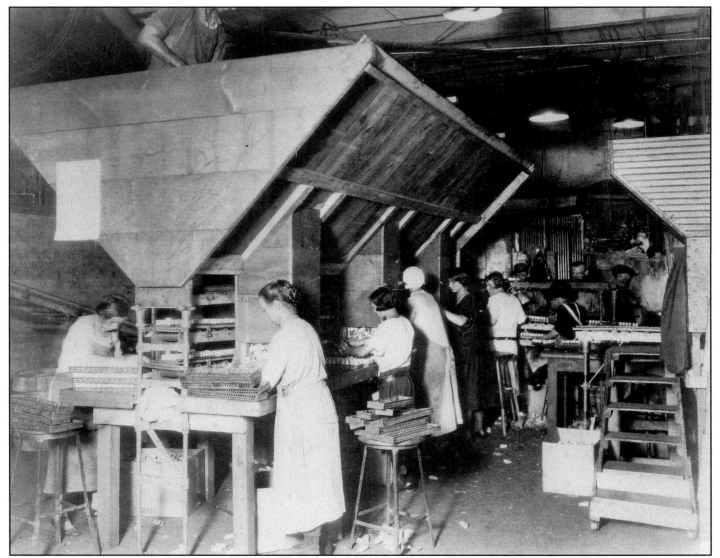

Workers at the French Battery Company (Ray-O-Vac) during the early 1920s.

State Historical Society of Wisconsin WHi (X3) 9336

the permissive boundaries of existing legislation, which provided little more than rhetorical endorsement of workers' rights, utilize delay and obfuscation to avoid real collective bargaining.

Neither the battery industry in general nor Ray-O-Vac in particular enjoyed a reputation among workers for generous treatment of employees or pleasant working conditions. Many of the operations in manufacturing dry cell batteries involved the handling of carbon, asphalt, and harsh chemicals. Most jobs required little skill or initiative but called for careful visual and tactile attention, thus combining routinization with tension. Low wages characterized the industry, partly because of the semi-skilled nature of the work and partly because battery factories, which were usually in rural and quasi-rural areas, were able to tap reservoirs of seasonal farm workers and females. Although Eveready had a major plant in Cleveland, much of the country's battery production took place in Lancaster, Ohio; Freeport, Illinois; Dubuque and Sioux City, Iowa;

Williamsport, Pennsylvania; Paducah, Kentucky; and Wausau, Fond du Lac, Wonewoc, and Madison, Wisconsin. Labor organizers and other unionists in Wisconsin viewed workers in the battery trade as unfortunate and disadvantaged, sympathizing with Ray-O Vac's employees especially because the company, although its wages compared favorably with those paid by competitors, was widely regarded as stingy, stubborn, and eccentric. Its contracts, declared one veteran federal unionist and AFL organizer, were often "weird," containing quirky clauses dealing with vacations, seniority, and other matters. Once the company's leadership grew accustomed to the notion that the union was there to stay, they were willing enough to grant the union shop, but they bargained hard for every nickel and showed little desire to join the union in seeking to change the battery trade's reputation for backwardness in labor relations and employee compensation.[9]

The union bargained with management through a grievance committee elected by the membership. The local called for and received help from the AFL Regional Office and from Wisconsin State Federation of Labor organizers operating

AFRICAN AMERICAN WORKERS AND THE LABOR MOVEMENT IN MILWAUKEE, 1930-1945

AFRICAN Americans had entered the city's industrial labor force in large numbers during World War I and its aftermath, but the onset of the Great Depression arrested, and even temporarily reversed, the process. Black unemployment rapidly exceeded that of whites and persisted at disproportionately high levels throughout the period. Yet, by the late 1930s and early 1940s, the emergence of the Congress of Industrial Organizations signaled the rise of a new relationship between blacks and organized labor. The era of separate all-black locals gave way to a new era of integrated unions, involving blacks and whites in an unprecedented pattern of class solidarity across racial lines. The emergence of interracialism in Milwaukee's labor movement was nonetheless a slow and arduous process.

During the early years of the depression, racial conflict within the labor movement intensified. In 1933, a new AFL local of bartenders, cooks, and waiters "steadfastly refused to accept" black applicants for membership. Because blacks were so numerous in these occupations, however, the local offered to assist African Americans in setting up a segregated local. In another instance, black workers took an AFL carpenters' union to court in order to break racial barriers to their participation in the trade. On the other hand, where companies retained a significant core of black workers despite hard times, race relations became especially abrasive. When the Wehr Steel Company continued to employ black workers during the depression years, for example, white workers launched a movement to remove them from their jobs. Utilizing its new found power to organize under Section 7(a) of the National Recovery Act, the AFL organized a union at the Wehr Steel Foundry and struck the plant by mid-July, 1934.

According to the Milwaukee Urban League (MUL), the AFL local called a walk-out "without the knowledge" of black workers. The chief aim of the strike, the MUL said, was "the dismissal of Negroes from the plant." The Wehr Steel strike soon escalated into the first clear-cut case of racial violence in the city's labor relations. Police joined strikers in attacks on black strikebreakers. Although the company had summoned police to "protect" black strikebreakers, the officers "joined with the strikers in overturning an automobile" filled with black workers. Despite white workers' resistance to black employment, the Wehr Company closed the plant and reopened as an "open shop," one of the few cases where a Milwaukee employer was able to do this.

As late as 1935, the AFL discouraged black membership in a local butchers' and meat cutters' union. After a local firm hired a black butcher, he was denied union membership, because "there were [white] union butchers yet to be supplied with work." Equally important for local conditions, the AFL continued to carry twenty-four national and international unions that barred blacks by constitutional fiat or ritual. Still, not all AFL locals were equally discriminatory. As early as 1934-35, blacks and whites belonged to Milwaukee's International Longshoremen's Association, Local 815. Black workers made up over one-third of the city's dock workers, and, in 1938 a black dock worker, Aaron Tolliver, became president of the Milwaukee local. Tolliver and six other dock workers were was soon expelled for attempting to transform the local into a CIO body, again highlighting the racial limitations of the AFL.

Only slowly did the CIO emerge and make inroads on racial barriers in the Milwaukee labor movement. By the late 1930s, however, in Milwaukee, as elsewhere, the CIO enlisted black organizers and established close contact with the black community. LeRoy Johnson, a black butcher and packinghouse worker, played a major role in the campaign of the United Packinghouse Union. Associates described Johnson as an "aggressive sort of a guy and quite articulate." Johnson helped to organize Milwaukee Local 681 (later Local 50). Under the leadership of men like LeRoy Johnson, blacks entered the CIO in growing numbers. They helped to displace the AFL's Amalgamated Meat Cutters local at the Plankinton Company. At the Allis Chalmers Corporation, blacks also joined United Automobile Workers Local 248. As early as October 1940, black committeeman Bill Wallace filed a grievance against the company's discriminatory layoff policies. The Wisconsin edition of the *CIO News* also played a positive role in creating interracial unionism. It consistently attacked racial discrimination by the railway brotherhoods, and the AFL unions like the boilermakers, plumbers, and machinists. Under the impetus of the Fair Employment Practices Committee (formed in 1941), the Milwaukee CIO expanded its efforts on behalf of black workers. UAW Local 248 established its own FEPC committee, and variously promoted the employment and upgrading of black workers. The union sent representatives to the national FEPC hearings and endorsed written affidavits of racial discrimination at the Allis Chalmers Company.

As important as the new interracial unionism had become by the end of World War II, it was nonetheless incomplete. Black workers repeatedly complained of racial discrimination within the rank and file of the CIO and the AFL. In the columns of the *CIO News*, black union steward Luther McBride emphasized "the need to build understanding among the workers themselves and break down old prejudices." In early 1944, at the Chicago regional conference of the FEPC, William V. Kelley, director of the Milwaukee Urban League, warned that it was not true that all racial discrimination in the Milwaukee labor movement emanated from the conservative AFL. In one plant the AFL had been very cooperative; in another case the greatest difficulty had been the CIO. More importantly, there is little evidence that

Blacks played on a baseball team sponsored by the Wehr Steel Foundry in 1935. The foundry became the scene of a major racial confrontation in 1934, when white workers walked out in an effort to remove black employees. Violence erupted when blacks served as strikebreakers. The company, however, soon reopened on an open-shop basis.

Black Heritage Project, University of Wisconsin-Milwaukee Extension

the Milwaukee CIO made any special effort (before 1941-1942) to promote the equal reemployment of blacks and whites. UAW Local 248 at Allis Chalmers emerged as the strongest CIO union in the city, but Allis Chalmers employed no more than two blacks between 1937 and 1942, even as thousands of whites returned to work. Only with the coming of World War II and the wartime labor demands would blacks recover their pre-depression foothold in the city's industrial economy.

Between 1870 and 1945, race relations in Milwaukee's labor movement were characterized by several overlapping phases of change. Each era was tightly interwoven with changes in the larger urban economy, black population growth, and most of all the complicated interplay of race and class in the development of the black industrial working class. During the pre-World War I years, African Americans faced exclusion from both the industrial labor force and the organized labor movement. They worked primarily in domestic, personal service, and common laborers' jobs, where they waged vigorous struggles to improve the terms of their labor. They also gained some industrial jobs as strike-

breakers, but they were unable to retain their industrial foothold, organize, and protect their position in the expanding industrial sector of the urban economy.

Only during World War I and its aftermath did black workers gain a substantial footing in the industrial labor force. Although they occupied the lowest rungs of the industrial ladder and continued to face exclusion from white unions. African American industrial workers were more successful than their prewar counterparts in developing separate all-black labor organizations. They used their new organizations to fight the discriminatory practices of employers and labor unions alike. Despite the difficulties that black labor organizations faced in the hostile class and racial climate of the 1920s, they helped to pave the way for interracial unionism during the New Deal and World War II. As federal legislation secured the right of workers to organize on their own behalf, and, as the Congress of Industrial Organizations broke ranks with the racial policies of the AFL, black workers joined predominantly white labor unions in growing numbers. Although the process of integrating blacks and whites into the city's labor movement remained incomplete by war's end, the events of the late depression and World War II had set in motion the rise of Wisconsin's modern civil rights movement.

—JOE W. TROTTER, JR.

From *Wisconsin Labor History Newsletter* (1989).

out of Milwaukee. The AFL representatives participated actively in the bargaining process and at times seem to have been the primary spokesmen for the union, although aggressive local leaders frequently followed their own counsel and opposed AFL recommendations. When the local committee reached an agreement with Ray-O-Vac, it submitted and explained its terms to the membership, which had the final voice. In addition, the negotiating team often came before the membership during negotiations to sample opinions about particular features of the contract before the agreement was written.

Union veterans regard Ray-O-Vac as having been a tough and difficult bargainer. Moderates in the union sympathized with the company's disadvantageous competitive position in the battery industry and were extremely sensitive to the company's threats to move operations out of Madison if the union pressed unreasonable demands. The presence of large numbers of "second income" female employees and the lack of alternative industrial employment in Madison reinforced the tendency toward a modest negotiating stance on the part of the union. On the other hand, 19587 had its share of militants who viewed Ray-O-Vac's threats as bluffs and who felt that the company was in a far better position to upgrade its wage scale than its officials admitted. Despite the tendencies toward moderation, the members of 19587 were entirely willing to reject settlements and to back negotiating demands with strike votes. Whatever their internal disagreements, the battery workers showed militancy and solidarity whenever the company seemed to be attacking the union. Between 1934 and 1948, the union passed strike votes on at least four occasions. Although 19587's members did not actually walk a picket line during this period, on more than one occasion they chose their picket captains and had their signs printed before last-minute settlements. Over the years, Ray-O Vac and Federal Labor Union 19587 were regular customers of the National Labor Relations Board, the War Labor Board, and the United States Conciliation Service.[10]

Spurts of tension and reconciliation characterized the first several years of the relationship between the company and the union. In August 1934, just three months after the company officials responded to the initial organization of 19587 by laying off the activists, the union issued an open letter to Ray-O-Vac's customers, declaring its moderate intentions and assuring the business world that relations between labor and management were stable and harmonious. In December, the membership "gave the Ray-O-Vac Co. a rising vote of thanks" for the year-end bonus and expressed the hope that labor-management relations in the new year would be as harmonious as those in 1934.[11]

Nevertheless, Ray-O-Vac was reluctant to enter into a contractual relationship with the union. Local 19587's secretary reported in August 1935, "Our employer has never refused to bargain with us," but the vague and elaborate series of conferences that company and union officials held throughout the spring and summer of 1935 fell far short of bona fide collective bargaining. For its part, the company demurred at the strict application of seniority in making seasonal work force adjust-

ments. Moreover, company officials felt uncomfortable about the union's reliance on Ed Hall, a militant Wisconsin auto worker and at the time a volunteer AFL organizer, for negotiating advice. Unionists criticized the company for the slowness with which it had implemented earlier agreements and for its generally dilatory and confusing response to the union's request for information and workplace adjustments. Unionists feared that the company hoped to erode rank-and-file support through a policy of delay and petty confusion. In view of the protracted nature of the negotiations and the company's unwillingness to enter into a specific collective bargaining contract, the union voted in April 1935 to withdraw its letter of assurance of uninterrupted production, earlier sent to major Ray-O-Vac customers. On August 12, after a lengthy period of ill-defined quasi-negotiations concerning wage rates, union recognition, grievance procedures, and other matters, the membership rejected a vague company offer of an informal working agreement. Eventually, at the suggestion of Hall, the union requested the efforts of a conciliator from the United States Conciliation Service (USCS).[12]

Robert Mythen of the USCS arrived in Madison on September 18. He reported that the union membership had rejected another vague Ray-O-Vac proposal. In addition, he found that Cargill refused to compromise and stood adamantly against entering into a collective bargaining arrangement with the union. After considerable consultation with both sides, Mythen secured an agreement. On October 1, the union membership voted approval of a document that granted concessions in such matters as seniority and grievances and specified that the company would bargain concerning wages, hours, and conditions of employment with a three-person committee representing unionized production workers. The document went on to assure nonunion employees that they could approach the management individually or through their own, separately chosen representatives. These provisions suggested a kind of de facto acceptance by the company of the fact of widespread union membership, but at the same time they revealed that Ray-O-Vac was reluctant to award 19587 official recognition.[13]

Mythen described this document as a collective bargaining agreement, but it was one only in the loosest sense. By withholding recognition and encouraging employees to deal with management on an individual basis, the company may have hoped that the union would lose influence. Certainly, the 1935 document imposed heavy restrictions, backed up by harsh penalties, against the solicitation of union membership or the discussion of union business on company premises. Although there is no evidence that Ray-O-Vac contemplated the creation of a company union, a device to which many other employers resorted in the 1930s in their efforts to undermine trade unionism, the terms of the 1935 agreement convinced many of the unionists of the company's hostility.

Then in the spring of 1936 a quarrel erupted resulting in Ray-O-Vac's dismissal of two union leaders. This action deepened unionists' suspicion and resentment. On one level the quarrel revealed the inexperience of both the company and the union. Both were unfamiliar with the practice of industrial relations and displayed impatience and lack of wisdom in the critical area of grievance handling. On another level, however, the month-long dispute represented a major challenge to the union and a significant effort on the part of the company to test 19587 and its membership. The difficulties that occurred, the negotiations that followed, and the resulting settlement were crucial events in 19587's struggle to survive.

The 1935 document allowed workers in production departments to choose stewards, who were to have direct access to the Ray-O-Vac personnel department in grievance matters. The document also assumed that the three men—William McCutchin, William Skaar, and Max Onsager—named to conduct collective bargaining with the company were to serve as a kind of overall grievance committee as well, at least insofar as union members were concerned. Although the 1935 document did not specify exclusive union responsibility for grievance handling, everyone in the plant knew that McCutchin, Skaar, and Onsager were prominent members of 19587 and that McCutchin and Skaar were, respectively, president and vice-president of the local.

The dispute began on April 7 when a foreman discharged Andy Christianson, a union production worker, for allegedly refusing to obey orders. The controversy concerned the foreman's demand that Christianson work a split shift, a practice common at Ray-O-Vac but one resented strongly by production workers. According to company officials, Christianson had been given a legitimate assignment in the normal way. He had consulted with Skaar and McCutchin as to whether he was obliged to accept the assignment. Without advising Christianson of the regular grievance procedures, the two union officials urged him to disobey his foreman's orders. Upon following this recommendation, Christianson was fired.

Christianson's dismissal created dismay among unionists, but open opposition erupted shortly after when Ray-O-Vac announced the firing of both McCutchin and Skaar. The company charged the two union leaders with arbitrary interference with its prerogatives and with sabotaging its authority. Cargill denied that his action signaled an attack on the union, declaring that it was in reality the two union leaders who had undermined the spirit of the 1935 agreement by their gratuitous encouragement of Christianson's insubordination. No union business was involved, the president argued; the matter was closed. He would gladly meet with a reconstituted grievance committee (Skaar and McCutchin being ineligible since they were no longer in the employ of Ray-O-Vac), but he blankly refused to reinstate any of the three men or agree to arbitration of the dispute.[14]

Throughout the controversy, company officials acted imperiously. Unionists responded with truculence and resentment. Shortly after the original incident took place, Cargill called each of the three principals separately into his office for interviews. He chided Christianson, an inarticulate production worker, and elicited from him the implication that Skaar and McCutchin had advised him to defy his foreman. McCutchin, then the union president, proved somewhat more obdurate. He insisted that his advice to Christianson was in the way of an informal comment and in no way violated the company's prerogatives or the rudimentary grievance procedures established in 1935. He bridled at what he considered "cross examination" by Cargill.

In the end, however, he succumbed to the persistent interrogation and gave verbal agreement to Cargill's carefully phrased interpretation of events.

With Skaar, Cargill met a dead end. The union vice-president challenged the legitimacy of the entire proceedings, arguing that the whole matter was union business and had to come before the Grievance Committee. He refused to discuss the situation on an individual basis. Realizing that Cargill could easily find discrepancies between statements made by the three unionists in the separate interviews, Skaar asked what McCutchin had said, whereupon Cargill snapped, "I'm asking *you* questions." Continuously rebuffing Cargill's demand that he speak as an individual, Skaar accused the official of trying to destroy the union. He eventually won the right to confer with McCutchin and Onsager before answering further questions. After a brief consultation among the three union leaders, Skaar returned to Cargill's office to inform him that they would answer no more questions and would wire the AFL and federal authorities for advice and conciliation help.[15]

Whether or not Ray-O-Vac consciously sought to destroy the union's influence through these dismissals, its officials could hardly have been surprised when the battery workers interpreted the firings as an assault on 19587. Skaar was convinced that the company was "taking picks on the union" through him. David Sigman, the AFL representative sent to Madison by William Green to investigate, agreed. He acknowledged the company's assertion that it was dealing with Skaar and McCutchin only "as individuals," but he was convinced that Ray-O-Vac's action was "an attempt to break the labor organization by discharging its most active and responsible members." On April 13, the members of Federal Labor Union 19587 voted overwhelmingly to authorize a work stoppage against the company as a means of securing reinstatement of their leaders. The next night they listened as Sigman "gave advice and answered questions of what to do in case of a strike."[16]

To the relief of almost everyone, no strike occurred. On May 1, Sigman endorsed the local's request for AFL strike sanction, declaring to Green that it was "necessary to the welfare of organized labor that the men discharged be re-instated." Green approved his recommendation, but both AFL officials hoped for a prestrike settlement. Soon after taking its strike vote on April 13, the union had sought the aid of Region 12 of the National Labor Relations Board, headquartered in Milwaukee. Skaar appeared before the board, and Nathaniel Clark, director of Region 12, tried unsuccessfully to induce Ray-O-Vac to agree to arbitrate the dispute. Eventually, 19587 brought charges of unfair labor practices against the company, charging it with discrimination against union members, under the provisions of the National Labor Relations Act. Meanwhile, Sigman contacted Dean Lloyd K. Garrison of the University of Wisconsin Law School, a personal friend and former chairman of the NLRB, for informal help. In addition, the United States Conciliation Service entered the picture on May 4 with the arrival of Commissioner Robert Mythen.

With the union, backed by the AFL, determined to strike in support of McCutchin and Skaar, and the company immune to the combined blandishments of Clark, Garrison, and Mythen, a strike seemed certain. At the last minute, however, the company—likely at the suggestion of Mythen, who conferred continually with Cargill during the second week in May—offered a compromise. It would reinstate the three unionists after ninety days, provided they publicly acknowledge responsibility for the dispute and pledge to recognize the company's sole right to make work assignments. On May 14, at the urging of Sigman, Garrison, Clark, and Mythen, the membership unanimously accepted the proposal and agreed to compensate McCutchin, Skaar, and Christianson for their lost time.[17]

Despite the ungenerous terms of the settlement, it was a milestone in the union's development. Sigman noted that the battery workers had rallied enthusiastically to the union in the face of Ray-O-Vac's challenge and that it had, "since the controversy began, increased its membership."[18] Although it must have been distasteful for a strong-willed man such as Skaar to have signed a public statement accepting the company's interpretation of events, he used his free time to work on union affairs and to broaden contacts with battery workers elsewhere. While Ray-O-Vac had the satisfaction of wringing verbal concessions from the two union leaders, it had succeeded in enhancing rather than in discrediting their influence among their follow workers. Upon reinstatement, Skaar returned to an active role in the union. While some of their cohorts may have resented the trouble and expense their actions caused, many more were heartened by the willingness of Skaar and McCutchin to stand up to the company. Had their dismissals stood uncontested, the union would have been crippled or destroyed. With the solidarity displayed by the membership and the eventual reinstatement of the two controversial men, it was strengthened.[19]

To Sigman, the lesson of the 1936 dispute was clear: both the union and the company had to face up to the realities of mature collective bargaining. The union had to be schooled in the handling of grievances and in the need for caution and tact in its approaches to the company. At the same time, he told Green, "I believe that some time in the near future it will have to be determined . . . whether or not the company intends . . . to come to [an] . . . understanding on working conditions, wages and hours through the form of a signed agreement."[20]

The 1936 controversy did indeed spur union and management into a more regular relationship. The May agreement, which led to the eventual reinstatement of Skaar, McCutchin, and Christianson, was followed in the fall by a signed contract governing wages, seniority, grievances, and working conditions. On March 4, 1937, the parties entered into a union shop agreement. Thus, beginning in 1936, annual negotiations provided a continuing contractual relationship between union and management, a relationship virtually unimaginable at Ray-O Vac before 1934 but one that rapidly supplanted ties of personal loyalty, sentiment, or individual employment arrangements with the company in the minds of most workers.[21]

The establishment of the union and the achievement of signed contracts had a palpable impact on the working lives of Ray-O-Vac production employees. Late in 1939, Gerald Lochner, at various times union president and chairman of the Grievance Committee, discussed the first five years of the union on a statewide radio broadcast—"Glances from a Worker's World." Lochner described the work performed at Ray-O-Vac, tracing the manufacture of a dry cell battery from the grinding of the carbon in the mill room through the mixing, core tamping, ripening, testing, and final assembly operations. He commented briefly on some of the social functions and political concerns of the union. Mainly, however, he sought to convey to his listeners on the Wisconsin State Broadcasting network some sense of the day-to-day impact of the union on the lives of the 600 battery workers at Ray-O-Vac. Wage rates, he noted, had risen from 23 cents and 32 cents per hour for women and men respectively in 1933 to 37-1/2 cents and 45 cents in 1939. He described the grievances that had festered before the establishment of the union, declaring that workers had feared to express complaints lest they be accused of dissidence and their jobs put in jeopardy. For Lochner, it was the establishment of a grievance committee, with the ability to give voice to workers' complaints, more than reductions in hours or wage increases, that was most important to the workers.[22]

Years later, another early activist, Evelyn Gotzion, recalled the start of her long involvement with the union in the late 1930s. At one point, the company instituted a new piece rate system, the operation of which mystified the workers. Some of the older women became frantic over their loss in income and their inability to keep pace with the new and complex formula. Gotzion seethed with anger over this disregard for hardworking people. After voicing her displeasure with this mistreatment, she found herself chosen departmental steward, despite her previous lack of interest in holding office. Once chosen, however, she shut down the line until the piece rates were explained and the most glaring inequities rectified. She recalls vividly the reaction of one older woman, a long-term employee, when a seniority system governing seasonal layoffs was negotiated by the union in 1937. For years this woman had felt sick with fear every spring, for it invariably appeared to her that the pretty girls who could joke and flirt with the foremen were kept on, while older women were laid off. To this woman, the freedom that the union represented was real and tangible, a matter as much of personal dignity as of economic security. It was in ways such as this that the union most directly entered into the lives of the battery workers.[23]

The battery workers' achievements were less spectacular than those of other American workers in the mid-1930s. Yet, they had shown courage and shrewdness in dealing with a recalcitrant employer. They had preserved and strengthened their union; despite later controversies, it would never again have its very existence challenged. A combination of militant leadership, rank-and-file steadfastness, and vigorous AFL support had proven effective. If 19587's achievement did not take on the stature of the events in rubber, steel, and autos in 1936 and 1937, it was nonetheless real and significant for Ray-O-Vac's workers. And it encouraged those who conceived of the union as a militant, activist instrument to press their program in the years ahead.■

From *Madison's Battery Workers, 1934–1952: A History of Federal Labor Union 19587* (Cornell University Press, Ithaca, 1974).

The Farmer-Labor
Progressive Federation

BY ROBERT W. OZANNE

The "personal union" between Wisconsin labor and the socialist movement took a new turn in the mid-1930s with the creation of the Farmer-Labor Progressive Federation. The new political coalition, with Philip La Follette running at the top of the state ticket as governor, won near-majorities in the Assembly and the Senate in 1936. Robert Ozanne describes the role played by labor leaders in forming the FLPF and the problems they faced in trying to hold it together.

N 1934 Henry Ohl judged that the time was again propitious for a farmer-labor party. The farm depression in Wisconsin had radicalized the farm organizations. By 1932 farm incomes had fallen to only 45 per cent of their 1929 level.[1] Farmer discontent even had reached the point of a milk strike which the governor had used the National Guard to break. This acute farm distress was a lever which Ohl might use to make farm organizations more receptive to cooperation with labor. Ohl was also aware that Thomas Amlie, a First District congressman, had established a political organization called the Progressive League which was agitating for a third party among both farm and labor groups.

By the spring of 1934 the sentiment for a farmer-labor party had become so compelling that Philip and Robert La Follette, Jr., quickly moved to head off this new party, which they would not control, by beginning a third party of their own. They issued a call for a conference to be held at Fond du Lac on May 19, 1934. This conference set up the Progressive party of Wisconsin which was completely under the control of the La Follette brothers and their political followers who had formerly run on the Republican ticket.

Ohl felt that the La Follettes had stolen the third party which labor had nursed and groomed. In addition, he was unhappy with the party itself. Labor, farm, and other liberal organizations were excluded from its leadership, and its platform omitted any significant modification of capitalism toward socialism, which Ohl believed was essential to create jobs for the millions of unemployed.[2]

The new Progressive party did win major offices in the November, 1934, elections. Philip La Follette was elected governor a second time and Robert retained his U.S. Senate seat. It did not win a majority in either house of the state legislature. Although the WSFL had not endorsed Governor La Follette, it worked closely with him in the legislative session as it had in the

School of Workers

Henry J. Ohl, Jr., President of the Wisconsin State Federation of Labor, 1917-1940.

1931-1932 session. In the 1935 session labor, with the governor's blessing, introduced a "Little Wagner Act" bill which would give Wisconsin workers not engaged in interstate commerce the protections which the national Wagner Act gave to workers engaged in such commerce. A second major bill which labor supported was a $209 million jobs bill that Governor La Follette proposed. But a coalition of Republicans and conservative Democrats in the state Senate killed both bills and all other legislation in which labor was interested. This same conservative Senate coalition also killed major farm legislation, primarily a bill to slow down farm foreclosures.

The 1934 election and the 1935 legislative session had made clear that when the liberal vote was split between Socialist and Progressive candidates, candidates with a name like "La Follette" could win statewide races, but conservative Democrats and Republicans would win enough legislative seats to defeat legislation wanted by labor, by farmers, and by the unemployed.

The WSFL therefore, in October and November of 1935, called a series of conferences to form its type of third party, the Farmer-Labor Progressive Federation. It included the following nine economic and political groups: the WSFL; the Wisconsin Workers Alliance (an organization of unemployed); three farm organizations—the Wisconsin Milk Pool, the Farm Holiday Association, and the Farmers Union; the Railway Brotherhoods; the Progressive League (a liberal organization headed by Tom Amlie, a left-of-center Progressive); the Socialist party of Wisconsin; and the Progressive party.[3] The CIO, which was not yet established in Wisconsin, joined the party a year later.

As the FLPF took shape, in preparation for the 1936 elections Ohl chaired every conference, knocking heads together to establish a unified program among these diverse groups, each of which wanted to push its own interests within the FLPF. For example, the Socialists, a large and crucial group, demanded that the platform contain a plank calling for "production for use" instead of for profit, that the FLPF make a pre-primary election endorsement of one candidate for each office, that it only endorse candidates who were members of the FLPF, and that some of the candidates endorsed by the FLPF run under the Socialist party label.

The Progressive party, in order to gain majorities in the Assembly and the Senate, desperately needed urban votes. They hoped they could get them by enlisting the support of the WSFL and the Milwaukee Socialists. At the same time the Progressives, who were strong in rural Wisconsin, did not not wish to share this rural influence with anyone else, and hoped that the FLPF would restrict its organizing to a few urban counties. They stood by the traditional La Follette view of an open primary. The Progressives also demanded that the FLPF support Philip La Follette for governor even though he refused to join the organization. The Progressive party did not want any class-conscious proposals, such as "production for use," in the FLPF platform. In fact, it felt that the use of "Farmer-Labor" in the name evoked too strong a sense of class consciousness.

The Progressive party appointed Governor La Follette's secretary, Thomas Duncan, as a board member of the FLPF. A former Socialist and former secretary to Socialist Mayor Daniel Hoan of Milwaukee, Duncan was well equipped to contribute leadership and promote Progressive party interests in the FLPF.

The farm organizations were interested chiefly in planks to help the farmers, such as one preventing foreclosures of farms which were in default on mortgage payments.[4]

Miraculously, Ohl succeeded in maintaining unity in the FLPF through the November, 1936, election and well into the 1937 legislative session. His success was due, in part, to the fact he was president of the WSFL, the largest organization in the FLPF with the exception of the amorphous Progressive party. Also, Ohl could draw on the labor movement for many of the experienced people needed by the FLPF. For instance, when the Federation needed an organizer to build up membership, Ohl produced an able candidate, Henry Rutz, who headed an eleven-state Workers' Education Program for the federal Works Progress Administration. Rutz, a union printer and member of the Socialist party, worked skillfully even though the Federation never provided his promised two-hundred-dollar monthly salary. Ohl had additional expertise in Jacob Friedrick, executive board member of the WSFL and an organizer for the Milwaukee FTC; the FLPF borrowed him full time. At FLPF conferences Friedrick served as chairman of the Federation's constitutional committee and as chairman of the resolutions committees, where his skill at drafting did much to maintain the unity of the diverse groups.

Although each of the groups within the FLPF pushed for its own particular interests, the important thing was the concessions which each group was willing to, or induced to, make for the sake of presenting one united, liberal slate to the voters. Heretofore the two main political groups within the FLPF, the Socialists and the Progressives, each had presented a full slate of candidates. The Socialists in 1936 agreed to no longer put Socialist party candidates on the ballot as they had been doing since 1898. This left the FLPF one slate, that of the Progressive party, upon which to concentrate its resources.

The Progressives, in turn, agreed that in some of the districts in which Socialist and Progressive party candidates had formerly fought each other, particularly in certain Milwaukee state Assembly and Senate districts, the Socialists would choose one of their own members to run for that seat, albeit under the Progressive party label. The Socialists agreed that in certain other districts no Socialist would run against the Progressive party's candidate in the primary election.

The Socialists also agreed to give up their "production for use" plank in the FLPF platform. These agreements and concessions by the Socialists were crucial to the success of the FLPF, because the Socialists had 50,000 votes in the Milwaukee area, without which the Progressives could not win control of the state legislature. Daniel Hoan, the mayor of Milwaukee, was a key figure in achieving these agreements. Also, the fact that the leaders of the FLPF, Ohl, Handley, Rutz, and Friedrick, were party members helped immensely in gaining this Socialist party action.

The three farm organization leaders, Kenneth Hones of the Farmers Union, Harry Jack of the Milk Pool, and Charles Goldamer of the Farm Holiday Association, stood with Ohl on all critical FLPF controversies.

Ohl was a hard-liner on excluding all Communist organizations and, for the first year, many individual Communists,

State Historical Society of Wisconsin WHi (X3) 25218

During the strike against the J.I. Case Company in Racine in 1936, food for striking workers was distributed at the headquarters of the Farmer-Labor Progressive Federation.

from the FLPF. Undoubtedly Ohl was well aware that the collapse of the farmer-labor political movement of 1920-1923, in which he was interested, was due, in part, to the Communist takeover of the movement at its Chicago convention in July, 1923.[5]

Excluding Communists was a difficult task. The Communist party of Milwaukee insisted on endorsing all of the FLPF candidates in Milwaukee. Its endorsement damaged the FLPF by alienating its rural membership and the more conservative Progressives. When the leadership of the Wisconsin Workers' Alliance, an organization of unemployed workers affiliated with the FLPF, fell to the Communists, and when the CIO joined the FLPF, it became impossible to screen membership to exclude Communists. Eugene Dennis, head of the Wisconsin Communist party, further embarrassed the FLPF on the eve of the 1936 election by publicly boasting that five of the FLPF's endorsed assembly and county office candidates were card-carrying Communists.[6]

Although the nine-group Farmer-Labor Progressive Federation was in many respects a creaky machine, the November, 1936, election justified all the effort which labor had put into it.

Labor at the summit: The "Little Wagner Act"

The state election of November, 1936, gave Wisconsin labor a degree of power it never had held before. Governor Philip La Follette was re-elected with a majority of 200,000 as compared to 13,000 two years earlier. The Progressive party gained control of both houses of the legislature, even though it had only 48 of the 100 seats in the Assembly and 16 of 33 in the Senate. Governor La Follette's persuasiveness (as well as patronage) convinced several conservative legislators to vote with the Progressives on organizing the two houses and on major bills.

The credit for the election victory of 1936 goes only partially to the FLPF. Franklin Roosevelt's landslide carried in liberal majorities nationally and in Wisconsin. But the FLPF deserves much credit for encouraging those liberal voters who favored the Democratic candidate for president to ignore the other Democratic contenders and vote instead for the Progressive party candidates.[7] In the Assembly, a Progressive and FLPF member, Paul R. Alfonsi, was elected speaker by a vote of 50 to 49. Andrew Biemiller, a Socialist and organizer for the WSFL, was elected majority leader. In the Senate, Walter Rush, who was a Progressive member of the FPLF, became the speaker. Labor's bills were at the top of the agenda, and a grateful governor gave complete support.■

From *The Labor Movement in Wisconsin: A History*
(State Historical Society of Wisconsin, Madison, 1984)

The Wisconsin Milk Strike of 1933

BY ROMAN PIECH

Wisconsin farmers got into the action with a strike of their own in 1933 to protest falling milk prices. In this lively account, written by Roman Piech when he attended a School for Workers training class in 1935, we see the milk strike from a unique vantage point: that of a young guardsman sent to restore law and order.

Farmers dump seven carloads of milk on the Soo Line tracks near Burlington, Racine County, 1934.

State Historical Society of Wisconsin WHi (X3) 27919

IN May, 1933, the farmers of Wisconsin went on strike. These farmers went out to fight against the capitalistic milk lords. But what did that mean to me? Simply nothing. At that time I was a member of the National Guards. Boy, here I thought is where I get some excitement. I was unemployed and here was a chance to earn some money. I held thumbs and hoped that the strike would reach such heights of violence that the guardsmen would be called. And they were called.

At the armory men were hastily packing, officers barking out orders. Some men would cuss to relieve their nervousness. Pistols oiled, extra pistols given to all men. At the railroad station, guardsmen were making last minute phone calls to their mothers, fathers and sweethearts before boarding the trains.

The train-ride was a mystery. Officers told no one our destination. We reached Green Bay. Orders to put out all train lights were given and all shades were drawn. The train passed through Green Bay speeding into the night, all lights out.

We rode through the night for five hours. The train slowed down, guardsmen looked into the night wondering where we

Milwaukee Journal WHi (X3) 45437

The "Battle of Durham Hill" during the milk strike in Waukesha County, May 18, 1933. Sheriff's deputies and National Guardsmen, sworn in as special deputies, charged farmers with bayonets.

were. The train stopped. Guardsmen picked up their packs ready to leave the train. They were quiet and tight-lipped, tense and nervous. The top-kick, a veteran of many wars, was right at home. It was two o'clock in the morning. We marched to the business of the town. We found out we were in Shawano, Wisconsin.

A breakfast, consisting of coffee and cookies was available. All guardsmen were sworn in as special deputies and clubs were issued. Little pieces of cloth were pinned on us to show that we were special deputies. Bullets and the clubs were issued. Many of them dropped to the ground as nervous hands tried to load their pistols. Last minute orders were given before we piled into trucks to tour the country. Our orders were, "don't shoot unless a striker shoots first and then don't shoot until your superior orders you to." Carloads of newspaper reporters and photographers joined the line of trucks. You could not see the end of the line. A couple of farmers in a Model T Ford were stopped and questioned. Two guardsmen, with pistols leveled, escorted the farmers back to the sheriff.

Few farmers were seen on the trip. At times the stream of trucks was broken. One-half would take one road and the other half another road only to meet at some prefixed point. The guardsmen were caked with the dust of dirt roads. But no trouble was encountered on the morning patrol.

We went back to town. It resembled a scene from some western thriller. Everyone carried pistols at their sides. Dime stores were filled with deputies buying small bats which were used as clubs. An officer came, barked out some orders, and once again a score of trucks filled with guardsmen left the town. We stayed behind wondering what the trouble was. We soon found out, for up the street came about 300 farmers, with guardsmen on all sides. They had been taken prisoners near town after a small skirmish.

The farmers were housed in a large county garage. We were detailed to watch them. The guardsmen were tense and nervous as they went to their posts. Flaps of holsters were opened and a tighter grip on the club was taken. Gas bombs and gas masks were issued. The farmers would group together and look men-

acingly in our direction. At times they would approach us in groups, only to go back as guardsmen put their hands on their pistols, and bring out gas bombs.

County workers removed every bit of machinery from the garage. More farmers were brought in. The garage was well filled now. County officials brought food for the farmers, milk and bread. This angered the farmers to such extent that the guard was doubled.

At night more guardsmen arrived. A machine gun company. Machine guns were placed on the roof of the garage. A machine gun on each end of the garage and next to it a searchlight. A barb-wire fence was strung up around the garage. Automobiles that the farmers were riding in were lined up as barricades. Army cooks now prepared food for the farmers. Much better food than the guardsmen had. This helped to keep the farmers pretty quiet.

The word sleep was forgotten. For rumors flew around thick and fast. We were always on the go. From one side of town to another, farmers' wives came to see them but were stopped at the fence and not allowed to see their husbands. Newspaper photographers were taking pictures right and left.

Ringleaders of the farmers were singled out and placed in solitary confinement. I was detailed to watch one of them through the night. It was night, but around the garage it was like day for the searchlights were on. At times I would doze off only to awake again. By now I didn't give a damn what happened. Once I dozed off only to be awakened by what sounded like pistol shots. It was a car on the highway backfiring.

By now the guardsmen and farmers dropped their hostile attitude to one another. We would sit with them for hours and talk farming and hunting. I got so that I admired these farmers who took two or three puffs on their pipes between words. We were out as special deputies for five days when the strike ended.

But now as I think back to those days I wonder if I was not a fool. I think I was. For why should the military forces of the country be called out against men who are fighting for their rights? I still have the little piece of cloth that showed everyone I was a deputy. And I'll probably have it forever. But I shall not be so proud of it anymore. For I believe the cause was not a just one.■

From "The Wisconsin Milk Strike of 1933"
(University of Wisconsin, School for Workers, 1935).

Sources of CIO Success:
The New Deal Years
in Milwaukee

BY DARRYL HOLTER

The Congress of Industrial Organizations or CIO enjoyed phenomenal growth in Milwaukee, expanding to nearly 50,000 members in less than two years. This section considers the reasons for the CIO's rapid growth, linking it to labor and political traditions and the inability of the national AFL leadership to develop a strategy for organizing industrial workers.

IN the summer of 1936 a handful of union activists from several shops in Milwaukee mapped out a strategy for organizing workers under the banners of the newly formed Congress of Industrial Organizations. One year later 300 delegates from fifty-eight labor groups met to found one of the first CIO central bodies in America. Other dual union movements had come and gone, but the fledgling CIO, in the space of several months, emerged to challenge the organizations affiliated with the American Federation of Labor. How do we explain the CIO's rapid success?[1]

Most studies of the CIO have approached this question from a national or industry-wide perspective.[2] Historians have focused their inquiries on key factors in the CIO's emergence: the decisive role played by John L. Lewis and other top CIO leaders, the dramatic break with AFL "craft unionism," and changes in Federal labor laws.[3] There is no question that these factors were vital to the new national labor organization. Nevertheless, a close examination of the CIO's emergence in Milwaukee, based on local archival materials and recent scholarly research, reveals a somewhat different formula for success. CIO insurgents castigated the AFL for its "craft unionism," but the new federation benefitted a great deal from industrial organizing undertaken by local AFL activists several years before the CIO's formation.

Across the nation the CIO provided a valuable focus for leftist groups and individuals who opposed the conservative AFL political strategies. In Milwaukee, however, AFL leaders committed themselves to a Socialist third-party strategy while the CIO was moving firmly into the camp of the Democratic party. The willingness of Lewis to leave the AFL and fund the new movement was critical for the CIO's emergence. Still, the new federation depended on active participation by local labor leaders and activist workers to challenge the AFL. Federal labor laws often shaped the parameters of industrial relations, but local and state labor laws also played an important role in widening or narrowing the tactics that could be used by organized labor. Moreover, the CIO challenge in Milwaukee sparked a vigorous AFL organizing counter-offensive that offset the large defections to the CIO in 1937. Ironically, the CIO's dramatic success resulted in stronger AFL affiliates.

The growth of the CIO in Milwaukee can be traced to four key factors. First, the CIO drew support from a local political climate that was relatively hospitable to labor and a progressive AFL tradition that was sympathetic to industrial unionism. Indeed, most of the CIO leaders were trained in the organizing drives and strikes led by AFL unions from 1933 to 1936. Federal labor unions established in 1934 and 1935 became launching pads for CIO organizing. Second, the policies of the national AFL did not allow the local labor movement to adjust its organizational structure to accommodate the new flood of unionization. As a result, the CIO often emerged victorious in workplaces where the AFL had failed to win a labor contract. Third, the CIO movement displayed a sense of elan and boldness that captured public attention. While the CIO became a catalyst for left-wing activists, shop floor militants, and young people who wanted change without delay, the AFL groups seemed more rooted in the past. The AFL's political strategy unraveled just as the CIO burst on the scene with new tactics and politics. Finally, state intervention helped the CIO by shielding its organizers from the blows that had repulsed previous attempts to unionize. The new federation emerged at an unusually propitious moment when heightened industrial conflict forced local, state and federal agencies to intervene in defense of the workers' right to bargain collectively.

Third anniversary of Local 174, International Laundry Workers Union, Milwaukee, 1937.

State Historical Society of Wisconsin WHi (X3) 40954

Historians have focused on the CIO's sharp break with the AFL with good reason. Yet many of the individuals who led the CIO began their careers as labor militants in the AFL unions in the days before the New Deal. The Milwaukee Federated Trades Council (FTC) and the Wisconsin State Federation of Labor (WSFL) had always been active in organizing.[4] They were "Milwaukee Socialists," trade unionists who criticized capitalism and favored independent political action. Skeptical of the two-party system, early AFL leaders built a surprisingly strong Socialist party as their political vehicle.[5] The call for "industrial unionism" runs through the speeches and convention resolutions in the years well before 1933. In 1922 WSFL president Frank J. Weber went to the national AFL convention and cast his vote for John L. Lewis and against Samuel Gompers because Lewis supported industrial unionism. Leading Milwaukee labor leaders did not view industrial unionism as a substitute for craft unionism. Rather, they saw the value of using both forms of organization to bring unionization to different sectors of the workforce.

In Milwaukee, organizing drives launched in the late 1920s met with only limited success. But in 1933 the FTC moved quickly to capture the enthusiasm of workers who sought to unionize under the National Industrial Recovery Act. The council's small group of officers and staff plunged into vigorous organizing drives in 1933. The Machinists and other unions launched a coordinated drive in the metals shops.[6] Leo Kryczki brought together four unions for a campaign in Milwaukee's sweat shops.[7] An effort in the needles trades was led by John Banachowicz.[8] The FTC activists furnished speakers, installed officers, distributed pamphlets, led strikes, drew up contracts. The FTC president, Herman Seide, led an organizing drive of laundry workers through a strike and to a contract. During 1933, in just a few weeks time, 5000 workers joined unions.[9] Industrial workers and others who did not fall under the jurisdiction of an existing AFL affiliate were placed into federal labor unions. Sixteen federal labor unions were established in Milwaukee in 1934.[10] The Milwaukee AFL council claimed fifteen new unions in the first ten months of 1934, a year that witnessed 107 strikes. Between 1932 and 1936, the number of workers brought into AFL unions in the area increased from 20,000 to 60,000.[11]

However, success in building unions on an industrial basis posed new problems. Carrying out the day to day work required of the new federal labor unions soon overwhelmed the small staff of the FTC. The established unions questioned how these new giant unions would be serviced. After a heated debate at an FTC meeting in June 1935, Jacob Friedrick—a young FTC organizer—was given the task of writing to William Green to request a full-time AFL organizer for Wisconsin. His letter

THE WISCONSIN PLAN FOR LABOR UNITY, 1936

The labor movement split into two parts at the national level when several unions, led by John L. Lewis of the Mine Workers, left the AFL to form the Committee of Industrial Organizations (CIO) in 1936. At the heart of the dispute was the unwillingness of the AFL craft unions to organize industrial workers. But unions in Wisconsin had a long history of industrial union organizing. In a last-ditch effort to prevent the splintering of the movement, the Wisconsin unionists proposed a plan to maintain labor unity. It is hard to say whether or not the plan might have succeeded. It was ruled out of order at the AFL convention in 1937.

State Historical Society of Wisconsin WHi (X3) 31203

John L. Lewis (third from right) meets with Wisconsin CIO leadership, Pittsburgh, 1938. From left to right: (unknown); Emil Costello, President Wisconsin State CIO; Harold Christoffel, President UAW Local 248; Meyer Adelman, director Steelworkers District 32; John L. Lewis, President CIO; Gunnar Mickelsen; James DeWitt.

THE only significant effort to avert the final break was a "Wisconsin Plan" for settling the differences between the craft and industrial unions. This had been adopted by a unanimous vote of the Wisconsin State Federation of Labor convention in July 1936 at Beaver Dam. A report formulated by the Wisconsin convention's committee on adjustments set forth the plan.

The report coordinated a section of the general executive board report headed "Industrial and Craft Unions" and nine resolutions. After extensive hearings, the committee report was written by Jacob F. Friedrick, the general organizer of the Milwaukee Federated Trades Council. It said:

> There are certain lines of work in which craft unions have been successful and in which lines the imposition of a new form of organization is on the face of it impractical.
>
> There are other industries in which a combination of semi-industrial and craft union organizations co-operating together have brought favorable results.
>
> There are, however, also large and important industries in which craft unions have not been able to reach the masses of the workers....
>
> In the discussions which have taken place on this subject there has been a great deal of confusion and misunderstanding because there usually is no clear definition of what is meant by the terms industrial unionism and craft unionism. As a matter of fact many of the so-called craft unions have broadened their organizations so that they are closer to a semi-industrial than a craft form. Indeed it would be difficult, if not impossible, to give a logical answer as to why some of the existing organizations

insist on being called craft unions while others no broader in their base insist that they are industrial unions.

The committee submitted in its report "a reasonable plan upon which it might be possible to re-establish harmony" which it recommended for adoption and transmittal to the executive council of the AFL and the committee for industrial organization. The main points of the plan were (1) that all charges against unions affiliated with the committee for industrial organization be dismissed and all plans for ouster of such unions from the AFL be dropped; (2) that the AFL join with the CIO in organizing the steel and rubber industries on an industrial union basis; and (3) that the CIO confine its organizing to the steel and rubber industries until further action was taken by the AFL. Then, the plan went on, the president of the AFL would appoint a special committee "to study all phases of organizational setup within the labor movement" and make a written report to the 1937 convention of the AFL.

Copies of the plan were sent to the officers and members of the executive council of the AFL and the presidents of the CIO unions and to all the affiliated international unions and state and city centrals of the AFL with the request that they endorse it. The Milwaukee Federated Trades Council endorsed it.

The Wisconsin unionists could have handled their own problems without a split if they had been left to themselves, many people believed; but Wisconsin was not an island, entire of itself, and the next year the Milwaukee labor movement was split, too.

—ELMER A. BECK

From *The Sewer Socialists*, Vol. II
(Westburg, Fennimore, Wisconsin, 1982).

identified the problem that confronted local AFL leaders as they sought to capture the new upsurge of unionism with the stopgap strategy of federal labor unions. Friedrick wrote

> During the last two years many federal labor unions have been established in Milwaukee. There are over 8,000 members in such unions who are now paying per capita tax directly to the AFL. These unions have a very large membership and practically all of these members are new in the organized labor movement. As a consequence, they need a great deal of help and attention in the conduct of their business affairs.

Friedrick noted that the FTC and WSFL had done a great deal to help organize these unions but that it had become impossible to do more because other unions affiliated with national unions also demanded service. Identifying a central flaw in the AFL's organizing strategy, he added

> Federal unions, some with very large memberships, have never seen or heard a direct representative of the AFL at their meetings. At the recent FTC meeting, the president of one of these large unions claimed, 'We have never had a representative of the AFL at our meetings nor have any of our officers ever seen one. As a result, many of our members think that the AFL is just a sort of myth.'[12]

Ironically, the CIO benefitted both from the local AFL's achievements and its failures. The formation of several large federal labor unions in 1933 and 1934 provided CIO organizers with key positions from which they could challenge the AFL. And as these new affiliates elected officers, struck their employers, and negotiated settlements, they taxed the resources of the local AFL and quickly exposed the inability or unwillingness of the national AFL to lead the new movement.

The CIO's most dramatic membership gains in Milwaukee came when entire AFL unions went over to the CIO in 1937 and 1938. These included stove workers at Lindemann-Hoverson, auto workers at Seaman Body, farm equipment workers at Allis-Chalmers, and small engine workers at Briggs. Other smaller AFL groups that left the Federation included filling station workers, gas workers, hosiery workers, the newspaper guild, and garment workers. A closer examination of several cases where AFL unions defected to the CIO reveals how AFL organizing helped in the formation of industrial unions but failed to hold the workers allegiance over the long haul.

The Lindemann-Hoverson stove works, a south side plant employing 700 workers, was a bastion of anti-unionism. Its owner, eighty-year-old A. J. Lindemann was described by a former company executive as "domineering, unreasonable, labor-hating and contentious."[13] Lindemann had defeated two previous organizing efforts by refusing to bargain with the union and forcing strikes that failed. Such had been the fate of the Molders Union in 1917 and the Metal Polishers Union in 1926. With the passage of the N.I.R.A. in 1933, unionists again tried to organize the plant. Management countered with a pay raise and support for a company union. The organizing drive stalled. But it soon became clear that the company union was not an effective vehicle for representing the employees and a group of workers approached the FTC and asked for help. Jacob Friedrick, FTC organizer, met with workers who were members of the Machinists, the Molders, Foundry Employees, and the Metal Polishers. The drive was then turned over to the Metal Trades

Council, led by the Machinists' veteran organizer Otto Jirikowic.[14]

New organizing efforts made headway. But in August 1935 management retaliated by laying off fifteen workers employed in the wick weaving department, a union stronghold. Two days later, 350 workers met and decided to strike the plant for union recognition. Soon nearly 700 workers had joined the strike, while a group of about forty crossed picket lines.

The strike at Lindemann-Hoverson quickly escalated. Management refused to negotiate with the union and initiated an aggressive campaign to convince workers to abandon the union and come back to work. The strikers turned to mass picketing and the picket lines were soon reinforced by relatives and friends. Other local unions led parades of workers to the plant in support of the strikers and some demonstrations involved as many as 5,000 picketers. The children of strikers also marched on the lines from 3:30 to 5:30 after school. As the strike dragged on the conflicts between picketing workers and scabs increased and police were called on a daily basis.

Federal mediators tried to resolve the conflict, but Lindemann would only meet with his own employees. Meanwhile the confrontations outside the plant spilled over into the surrounding neighborhoods. At this point Mayor Dan Hoan stepped in, claiming that the strike and demonstrations were destroying public order. He demanded that Lindemann either negotiate with the union or close down his plant until the situation cooled. Lindemann threatened to move the firm to another city. But when the Common Council passed a measure that would force the plant to close until a special commission of employers, employees, and clergy could hammer out a settlement, Lindemann decided to close the plant.

The strike continued for seventeen months until it became clear that the strikers' demand for union recognition could not be won. Many of the strikers had drifted off to other jobs and a few went back to work when the firm reopened. In January 1937, a group of 300 strikers met and voted 156 to 128 to return to work and the strike ended.[15] The strikers had received financial and other support from the Milwaukee AFL, but they may have been upset when A.O. Wharton, president of the International Association of Machinists, turned aside requests for financial assistance on the grounds that Jirikowic had not filed the proper type of form with the international.[16] Two months later at a meeting organized by workers sympathetic to the CIO, a large group of Lindemann-Hoverson employees voted to leave the Machinists and join the UAW.[17]

With more than 2,000 employees, the Seaman auto body manufacturer was a key target for unionization in the 1930s. Workers at Seaman Body produced auto bodies for General Motors. A Federal Labor Union, Local 19059, was established in 1934. Its rapid growth was reflected in the per capita tax paid to the state Federation of Labor: 348 members in 1934, and 1423 members in 1935. When the union became Local 75 of the AFL Auto Workers in 1936, union membership jumped considerably so that the local paid "per caps" to the state federation on nearly 2,000 members.

Workers at Seaman Body were enthusiastic about unionism but the new local created problems that the national AFL could not resolve. A jurisdictional dispute between the Machinists and the new Auto Workers union flared in 1934. When auto workers in Milwaukee, Racine, and Kenosha struck in March 1934, the machinists in Racine and Kenosha also struck. Machinist organizer Otto Jirikowic noted that six non-striking tool and die makers in the Seaman plant were members of the Machinists union. Crossing the picket line hardly endeared the Machinists to the 1,300 auto workers who were on strike. During the summer of 1934, Jirikowic complained that about 15 members of the Machinists union in Seaman were being pressured to join the auto workers union on the threat of losing their jobs.[18]

F. J. Dillon, President Green's organizer for the campaign in the auto industry, attended a December 1934 meeting between the union and management and was shocked by the way the new union was conducting its operations. Dillon reported that the company was willing to negotiate, but the bargaining committee was plagued by "a total lack of leadership." Worse, Dillon claimed, "the union is infested with communists who seem to be interested in making it impossible to accomplish anything."[19] Nor did Dillon like his first meeting of Local 75, when the members decided to vote on whether or not to hear his speech. In a compromise, they gave the AFL's top auto organizer five minutes.

Green dispatched Paul Smith, an AFL organizer, to Seaman Body. Smith found that communists and various left wingers were gaining leadership positions in the union. He also reported that the local was planning to send five delegates, including their newly elected president, to a communist-sponsored meeting of auto workers in Detroit. "Some destructive and evil influence is at work in the local organization," wrote William Green, adding that if the local did not conduct its affairs according to the rules and regulations of the AFL, its charter would have to be revoked.[20]

Yet the AFL strategy of combining craft unionism with federal labor unions did not produce success at the Seaman plant. Jirikowic wrote, "Our experiences with AFL organizers in this city amounts to zero. None of them have been in this community to do any kind of organizing."[21] An early member of the auto workers union, Gabe Jewell, who later became a leader in the UAW-AFL, reflected that the AFL seemed to be uninterested in organizing the auto workers in 1934.[22] True, the AFL's adoption of the federal union strategy had succeeded in enrolling many auto workers. But the AFL had failed to bring the bosses to the bargaining table. Nor had the AFL created mechanisms that channeled worker enthusiasm in ways that enhanced the local's chance to win a contract.

The crowning jewel in the CIO's new collection of local unions in the Milwaukee area was the huge Allis Chalmers plant located in the industrial area of West Allis. Some 8,000 employees toiled in the foundry, electrical workshops, and assembly areas, building tractors and other agricultural equipment. Organizing efforts undertaken by AFL unions never succeeded in bringing all the Allis Chalmers workers under the union banner. However, there was a union presence in the plant, especially among the skilled trades workers. Small groups of electricians, foundry workers, and machinists had

THE NATION'S FIRST UNEMPLOYMENT COMPENSATION LAW

JOHN R. Commons was the decisive influence in Wisconsin. He had written the state's workmen's compensation law, enacted in 1911, and his student, Arthur Altmeyer, was secretary of the administrative agency, the Wisconsin Industrial Commission. The statute's major feature was experience rating, the employer's contribution rate varying directly with the accident record in his plant. This was naturally an incentive to reduce the number of accidents. After World War I, Commons applied the same principle to unemployment. The goal, again, was prevention rather than relief, to induce the employer to stabilize employment by offering him a financial incentive by a flexible contribution rate. Hence Commons rejected the European precedent based on contributions by employee and state as well as by employer. The idea was both original and ingenious. It was also, as Commons wrote, "extraordinarily an individualistic and capitalistic scheme," adapted to the American mood of the twenties.

In 1921 Senator Henry Huber introduced the Commons bill into the Wisconsin legislature. That maverick within the AFL, the Wisconsin State Federation of Labor, was the main backer. Nevertheless, the bill met defeat in 1921 and in each succeeding session of the legislature during the decade. In 1931, Paul Raushenbush, a student of Commons' and an economist at the state university, redrafted the old measure. Major changes were individual company reserves rather than a state-wide fund and a limit on the employer's liability by linking his contribution to the length of time the employee had worked for him. Assemblyman Harold M. Groves, also a Commons student, introduced the bill. The Legislative Interim Committee on Unemployment held hearings all over the state during the summer and fall.

The support was impressive: the State Federation of Labor, organized farmers (who preferred that industry rather than property taxpayers support the unemployed), several religious denominations, and experts. Andrews, himself a former student of Commons', set up an effective publicity organization. The jobless insurance issue here, as in other states, produced strange bedfellows. The Communist Party and the Wisconsin Manufacturers Association joined to fight the Groves bill. When the employer representative testified before the Interim Committee, he referred jokingly to the Communist who preceded him as "my colleague in opposition." The Committee reported the bill favorably by a margin of 5 to 2. The Wisconsin Manufacturers Association then voted to engage an expert to draft a plan for voluntary unemployment compensation, thus admitting the soundness of the jobless reserve principle.

Governor Philip F. La Follette called the legislature into special session in November 1931 to enact the Groves bill,

State Historical Society of Wisconsin WHi (X3) 43008

Neils B. Ruud (at left) of Madison is shown receiving the first unemployment compensation check issued in Wisconsin from Voyta Wrabetz, chairman of the state industrial commission. Professor Edwin E. Witte (center) was a University of Wisconsin economist and author of the national social security act. To his right is Professor John R. Commons, also a University of Wisconsin economist, who had urged the legislature to pass the Unemployment Compensation Act in 1911.

which he called "the soundest and fairest plan yet suggested anywhere." The governor capitalized on the opening provided by the Manufacturers Association. Employers would receive the opportunity to set up voluntary plans. "If by July 1, 1933," the bill read, "the employers of not less than two hundred thousand employees have voluntarily established systems of unemployment reserves. . .then the compulsory system. . .shall not take effect; otherwise, it shall take effect July 1, 1933." This maneuver broke the back of the opposition. The only amendment in the legislature was to reduce the quota from 200,000 to 175,000 employees. The Assembly, dominated by Progressives, passed the Groves bill 63 to 15; the Senate, where a close contest had been anticipated, concurred 20 to 10. La Follette signed the law on January 28, 1932. Wisconsin was the pioneer in enacting the first unemployment reserve, if not insurance, statute in the United States.

If employers failed to set up voluntary plans, the Groves Act would establish a compulsory system of company reserves. At the outset the employer would contribute 2 per cent of his payroll to his fund; when the reserve per employee passed $55, his rate dropped to 1 per cent; at $75 he no longer needed to contribute. The worker's benefit was 50 per cent of the weekly wage with a $10 maximum and a $5 minimum. The duration fluctuated with his length of service with the individual employer but might not exceed ten weeks a year. The law did not cover workers with incomes of more than $1,500 a year, persons who had resided in the state less than two years or worked there less than forty weeks, farm laborers, domestic servants, relievers, teachers, government employees, part-time workers, employees in the railroad and logging industries, the physically handicapped, strikers, and workers in firms with fewer than ten employees. The Industrial Commission administered the system with funds provided by a separate contribution by employers of not over 0.2 per cent of their payrolls.

The sponsors of the Groves Act were overjoyed by its passage. Their exultation was soon dampened by the difficulties of putting the Act into operation and the storm of controversy it provoked. The law was scheduled to take effect a year and a half after passage, July 1, 1933. Since business conditions were bad at that time, the date was pushed forward another year. In 1934, because the federal social security law was under consideration, Wisconsin again delayed. The statute did not actually begin operation until July 1, 1936. Hence it afforded no relief in the unemployment crisis out of which it arose.

—IRVING BERNSTEIN

From *The Lean Years: A History of the American Worker, 1920-1933* (Houghton Mifflin, Boston, 1960).

joined unions along craft lines in the late 1920s and early 1930s. Even though they were not recognized by management, these weak organizations formed important pockets of unionism throughout the sprawling Allis-Chalmers plant. Frank Bolka attended the mass rallies held in 1934 by the Milwaukee Metals Trades Council and began to organize for the IAM in the tractor shop. Harold Christoffel, only twenty years old, organized in the electrical shops while his high school chum, Fred McStroul, organized in the foundries. The early AFL unions also provided a vital arena for political activists and union militants. Linked together by their common need to win a contract, rank and file leaders from different craft unions began to work more closely together.

Several attempts had been made to organize the large group of production workers, but these initiatives were too often blocked by management opposition and jurisdictional disputes. Then the union leaders were elected to positions in the newly formed company union Works Council. "As an official Works Council representative," wrote Christoffel, "I had the right to talk to workers during working hours. It was real handy for signing up members and collecting dues. I was able to roam around the entire plant talking with other workers." After a year of internal organizing the group received an AFL charter as a federal labor union.

Once the AFL charter was granted, however, key leaders of various craft unions began switching their cards and dues to the new federal union which grew from 30 to 2,000 in four months. After bitter complaints were registered by the craft unions with William Green, the AFL president ordered the Milwaukee Trades Council to refuse to seat the new federal union's representatives. At that point the Allis Chalmers unionists turned to the CIO and received a charter from the UAW. In the summer of 1936 activists from the various groups made plans to reorganize the union on a plant-wide basis, paving the way for a decision to leave the AFL for the CIO.[23]

When in 1934 union fever had swept Milwaukee, fifteen workers from Briggs and Stratton, Milwaukee's large manufacturer of small engines, met with organizers from the FTC. The next day, all but one was fired. Efforts to win their jobs back failed and interest in union activity apparently waned. But that changed in December 1936 when several workers went to the new UAW regional office in Milwaukee to find out how they could get organized. The UAW brought in Homer Martin, who met secretly with a small group of workers and later addressed several hundred workers with a dramatic preacher-style speech. Within a few days, nearly all of the 1,300 Briggs and Stratton workers had signed cards for the UAW. The company recognized the union without an election.[24]

Victories in these large plants anchored the CIO's operations in the Milwaukee area. In August 1937 the CIO in Wisconsin sent fourteen full-time men and women organizers into the field.[25] By 1938, the Milwaukee CIO routinely claimed 55,000 workers in the area. Several large UAW and United Electrical Workers (UE) locals had been formed, and a vigorous drive was launched by the Steel Workers Organizing Committee. The nation's first CIO state federation was established in Wisconsin. Its offices in Milwaukee served as the nerve center for the new movement.[26]

The CIO succeeded in Milwaukee in part because it intervened in politics at a time when the local AFL's political program was stalemated. The CIO demonstrated a boldness and elan that captured public attention and turned many nonunionized workers toward unionization. The CIO even had its own tactic, the sit-down strike. And most of the CIO unions were willing to work with anyone who wanted to help build the movement, no matter what their political convictions. Under these circumstances, the CIO became a catalyst for leftwing activists, union militants, and young workers who wanted change with little delay. By contrast, the AFL unions seemed to many to have failed to change with the times.

Since the turn of the century the labor movement in Milwaukee had pinned its political hopes on an organic link with the Socialist Party. By the mid-1930s, however, the "personal union" between labor and the Socialist party was unraveling in ways which offered the CIO new political space in Milwaukee.

The Socialist party in Milwaukee was faltering. Its members were active in progressive causes, but not necessarily in the various Socialist organizations. Others were attracted to FDR and the Democratic Party. Still others linked up with the resurgent Communist Party. Working-class leaders who in previous times had gained their organizational experience in the Socialist movement now staffed the emerging new unions or the various New Deal programs. The Socialist movement was split on the question of the CIO and this was clearly reflected in the *Milwaukee Leader,* the nation's only Socialist daily newspaper. Its editorialist backed the rights of workers to organize as they saw fit. Articles about the CIO unions appeared alongside those of the AFL. Several writers, including the columnist Heywood Broun, published sympathetic views of the CIO. In addition, the Socialist Party at the national level, caught up with the militant mood of the times and pushed forward by an influx of Trotskyists and left-wing activists, moved forward to support the CIO, at the expense of the AFL. In the spring of 1937 this issue led several labor leaders in Milwaukee to resign publicly from the Socialist Party.[27] The "personal union" between labor and Socialism was coming to an end, and the AFL leaders were occupied with trying to hold together an increasingly fragile coalition of labor, farmers, and progressives. Meanwhile the CIO, buoyed by dramatic success across the country and fueled by the energy of young activists, claimed to be the new wave in American politics.

Was the labor movement divided by a generation gap? Some evidence in Milwaukee suggests this possibility. Frank Weber, a living legend in the Wisconsin labor movement, was eighty-five when he turned over the reins of the FTC to Herman Seide in 1934. WSFL president Henry Ohl was sixty-four in 1937; Secretary-Treasurer Handley was sixty-one years old. By contrast, many of the CIO leaders were very young men. Harold Christoffel, president of the new UAW local at Allis-Chalmers, was twenty-five when he was elected president of the Milwaukee CIO council. The secretary-treasurer, Meyer Adelman, a former pastry cook who became the key leader in organizing the steel fabricating industry in Milwaukee, was

Worker parade in the early 1930s, Milwaukee.

The Milwaukee Journal

thirty-four in 1937. Emil Costello, a talented union organizer, was twenty-eight when he was elected president of the nation's first state CIO federation. In their publications, the CIO writers criticized the old FTC leaders whose organization "gets duller and smaller every week." AFL partisans attacked the CIO leaders as young opportunists and political adventurers.

It had always been easy for critics to criticize socialism as an outmoded and foreign ideology—something imported from the "old country." The Milwaukee Socialists' opposition to "capitalist wars," a radical posture during the First World War, appeared anachronistic to many in the face of international fascism. Partisan critics, including Communists and Democrats, attacked the Socialist Party as an organization that had outlived its usefulness. Local newspapers routinely charged that socialism was an idea whose time had passed.[28] While top state and local AFL leaders tried to hold together a third party coalition of farmers, labor groups, and progressives, the CIO backed FDR and the New Deal Democrats.

If the AFL appeared to be mired in the past, the CIO projected itself as a dynamic movement with a bright future. Young labor activists headed new CIO unions that dwarfed the older AFL groups. Aggressive young staff reps and organizers plunged into the fight for industrial unionism and, partly by their enthusiasm, swept along a good share of the rank and file. Young workers from Socialist backgrounds found themselves gravitating toward the new movement, often working closely with college-educated radicals and communists.[29] Sections of the Young Socialists and the Socialist-backed Workers Alliance began to align themselves with the Communists. The new CIO built ties with the black community, defended the Scottsboro Boys, and hired black organizers.[30] It also rallied single young people around the need for WPA jobs.[31]

Despite the AFL's emphasis on tradition and the CIO's self proclaimed role as the new labor movement, it is not fully accurate to view the AFL-CIO split as reflecting a generation gap. Many local AFL and Socialist activists were also in their teens and twenties. The back page of the *Leader* announced daily and weekly community activities for young people and several young Socialists, including Alice Holz, staffed the daily newspaper. Young Socialists like Frank Zeidler, elected mayor in 1948, and Kenneth D. Clark, later a legislative representative for the Wisconsin AFL-CIO, became active in politics and AFL organizing during the mid-1930s. Nevertheless, the upstart CIO leaders stressed the youthful nature of their movement for industrial unionism. And the CIO supported new tactics, such as the sit-down strike, that caught the attention of young workers.

The CIO introduced the most important new tactic in labor's arsenal during the 1930s—the sit-down strike. In the rubber industry, the tire builders had learned the value of sitting down on the job, in effect, taking control of the factory floor. Auto workers at Fisher Body used the sit-down successfully in November 1936. "Akron created a fashion," wrote Edward Levinson, "Flint popularized it." After nearly 50 years it is easy to underestimate the importance—both tactical and psychological—of the sit-down strikes which swept across industrial America in 1936 and 1937. The rapid success of the sit-down sparked a new wave of enthusiasm among workers and a sense of hysteria in the business community. The sit-down was quick, efficient, usually peaceful, and always illegal. In the six months between November 1936 and May 1937 nearly half a million workers in a wide variety of occupations were involved in sit-down strikes.[32]

The sit-down movement struck Milwaukee in the spring of 1937, part of a large strike movement that was sweeping the country. More than 50 strikes took place in Milwaukee in 1937 including more than 20 sit-downs, as indicated below:

SIT-DOWN STRIKES IN MILWAUKEE, 1937-1938[33]

DATE	FIRM	UNION
4-12-37	Seaman Auto Body	UAW CIO
4-15-37	Yahr Drugs	Retail Workers, CIO
4-16-37	Torres Cafe	Catering Workers, CIO
4-21-37	Schroeder Hotel	Hotel Workers Union, AFL
4-21-37	Louis Allis	UE CIO
4-26-37	Rhea Mfg.	ILGWU CIO
4-29-37	Rundle Mfg.	Foundry Employees, AFL
4-29-37	Pfister Hotel	Catering Workers CIO
4-29-37	Belin Garment	ILGWU CIO
5-05-37	Wisconsin Shoe	United Shoe Workers, CIO
5-06-37	Milw. Athl. Club	Catering Workers, CIO
5-06-37	Pfister Hotel	Catering Workers, CIO
5-06-37	Triangle Restaurant	Catering Workers, CIO
5-12-37	Harnischfeger Co.	Iron and Steel Workers, CIO
5-10-37	Holmes Motor Co.	UAW-CIO
5-15-37	Milw. Lace Paper	Machinists, AFL
5-17-37	Wrigley's	Catering Workers, CIO
5-21-37	Gas Specialty Co.	NA
6-05-37	Trostel Tannery	UAW, CIO
6-08-37	Yahr Drugs	Retail Clerks, AFL
7-26-37	Solar Corporation	UE, CIO
5-04-38	Allis Chalmers	UAW, CIO
5-05-38	Allen Bradley	UE, CIO
5-10-38	Allen Bradley	UE, CIO
5-12-38	Allen Bradley	UE, CIO
5-17-38	Mueller Furnace	Foundry Employees, AFL and UAW-CIO
5-20-38	Harnischfeger Co.	Iron and Steel Workers, CIO
5-24-38	Harnischfeger Co.	Iron and Steel Workers, CIO

As the table below indicates, auto workers at Seaman Body were the first to use the new tactic. A few days later, a group of retail clerks at a drug warehouse sat down to demand the ouster of the firm's general manager.[34] Restaurant workers at two chains of coffee shops also sat down briefly, led by a group of pro-CIO workers. The sit-down tactic, however, was not strictly limited to CIO unions. On April 21 an estimated 1,000 hotel workers from four AFL unions at 19 Milwaukee hotels struck. Many sat down on the job. After seven hours, the agreement was reached and the strike ended. Workers won a 5% to to 15% raise and union recognition.[35] That same day, 450 electrical workers at the Louis Allis plant sat down for fifteen minutes in order to bring management to the bargaining table. As negotiations resumed, the UE leaders counseled the members to return to the job.[36]

Garment workers at the large Rhea Manufacturing plant were the next to use the sit-down, this time in order to demand the resignation of the supervisor, a pay hike, better working conditions and a forty hour week. An estimated 900 workers, nearly all women, took part in this seventeen-hour sit-down. Four floors were occupied and connected with two-way radios. A dance contest took place and women on the fourth floor lowered ropes to the ground where friends and relatives attached boxes of food and blankets for the sit-downers. Children came to say goodnight to their mothers. A reporter from the *Milwaukee Leader* wrote "it is hard to know if the Rhea sit-down was a strike or a workers' holiday." Strict rules of conduct were maintained, however, and all boisterous activity ceased in the evening. The strikers won their demands even though the strike was not officially supported by the International Ladies Garment Workers Union. A few days later, sixty women at the Belin Garment Company, located on the same block as Rhea, sat down at 9 am. By 4:30 they had won a wage increase and an agreement on limiting overtime. In May seventy-two shoe workers took over the Wisconsin Shoe Company after bargaining broke down.[37] Twenty women workers occupied the fifth floor while men took over the third and fourth floors.[38]

Milwaukee's longest sit-down strike occurred at the Solar Battery Company. Led by the UE, 130 strikers sat down on July 26 demanding a closed shop and a pay raise. The sit-in continued for twenty-three days until an agreement was reached.[39]

The sit-down strike proved highly effective in 1937, but it was quickly mired in a web of legal obstruction and political opposition. Employers requested court injunctions to prohibit sit-downs. Where this proved impossible, they charged the unions with violations of the city's municipal zoning ordinances for sleeping in non-residential industrial zones. In the state legislature labor beat back two attempts to outlaw the sit-down, but a circuit court judge declared the tactic illegal in 1937. Dean Lloyd Garrison of the University of Wisconsin Law School, a former NRLB official, wrote critically of the sit-down and editorialists in the local press chimed in to condemn the sit-down strike. Prohibited at the national level, the tactic was abandoned.

In Milwaukee, the sit-down strikes of 1937 differed from those of 1938. During the turbulent spring months of 1937, diverse groups of workers used the sit-down to fight for recog-

State Historical Society of Wisconsin

United Auto Workers sit-down strikers leave the Chevrolet plant in Janesville, January, 1937.

nition, to demand a supervisor be fired, or to shock a weak union into action. Many sit-downs lasted for several days. By contrast, the sit-downs in 1938 were brief protests, undertaken by militant workers often without the official support of the union, but carried out under the new protection of a labor organization. The five sit-downs of 1938 occurred at Allen Bradley and Allis Chalmers, large plants where the union was new but powerful, and at Mueller Furnace, where an AFL union held sway among the foundry workers and the UAW had organized the production workers.[40] These sit-downs were not launched for union recognition, but rather to refine the features of an existing contract or in order to force movement at the bargaining table or because of a break down in communication between union leaders and rank and file militants.

Nearly half a million workers across the country challenged the sanctity of private property by sitting down on the job. Yet there is little to indicate that their goal was to end private enterprise or to challenge the government. Indeed, workers were willing to take this dramatic step in large part because they believed that the law, and the power of the state, had finally moved to their side. But while the "revolution in labor law" contributed a great deal to labor's ability to organize, the N.I.R.A. and the Wagner

Act were themselves products of the powerful working-class upsurge that swept across industrial America. Likewise, CIO success was not merely the result of the recently created National Labor Relations Board, even though the new organization benefitted from many of the early Board decisions. The workers themselves made the breakthrough by taking direct action at a moment when most employers chose to ignore the government's intervention.[41] The result was a significant reshuffling of relations between labor, business, and the state.

Historians have generally regarded state action in labor relations during this period as beneficial to the union movement and particularly to the CIO. More recently, however, several scholars have looked more critically at the state's role in labor relations and have concluded that the state intervened in large part to stem the tide of worker resistance, forcing the movement to undertake its initiatives through legitimate and safe channels. As David Montgomery has described it, "this governmental activity was simultaneously liberating and co-optive for the workers."[42] Another very recent study by Christopher Tomlins takes this criticism even farther by asserting that state intervention greatly weakened the movement by undermining long-standing union jurisdictional claims and supplanting the private relationship between employer and union.[43]

In Milwaukee both the "liberating" and "captive" elements of state intervention were involved in the CIO's emergence.

While several policies that developed in response to labor's upsurge made it easier for industrial unionism to grow, others were aimed at limiting union growth and curbing labor's power. On balance, the protective policies were more important than the restrictive actions, especially during the first years of the CIO. But an important shift from policies that benefitted labor to ones that limited its power took place in Wisconsin and pre-figured a similar pattern on the national level.

Section 7(a) of the National Industrial Recovery Act of 1933, viewed as labor's Magna Carta by the AFL leaders, set off a tidal wave of organizing, but failed to resolve industrial conflict. Although the act directed employers not to inhibit the workers' right to organize, it did not require them to bargain with the union representing the employees. This set the stage for the bitter strikes in 1934 and 1935 as workers, demanding their rights under the new law confronted employers who sought to circumvent the law by establishing company unions or simply refused to bargain in the hopes that the new law would be soon overturned. In the absence of federal laws compelling employers to bargain, state and local officials intervened in efforts to end strikes and to promote collective bargaining.

The CIO in Milwaukee benefitted from labor's power in the city's political arena. Together with progressive Republicans or Democrats, the Socialists usually held a majority in Milwaukee's Common Council during the 1930s. Mayor Dan Hoan actively supported the CIO and the new working-class upsurge. During strikes, Hoan appeared at picket line rallies in support of the union cause. In March 1934 Hoan addressed thousands of Seaman Auto Body strikers. When intransigent employers refused to bargain and strikes threatened to destroy public order, as during the Lindemann-Hoverson strike in 1935, Hoan pushed through legislation, authored by Alderman Frank Boncel, that would close down the plant until management came to the table. The business community loudly denounced Hoan's policy and the newspaper editorialist claimed that the new law could lead to legalized fascism.[44] Communist militants, active in the Lindemann-Hoverson strike, also criticized the ordinance, albeit for different reasons, arguing that state intervention was an attempt to end the mass picketing. Although the controversial Boncel Ordinance was later repealed, it succeeded in sending a message to the business community that the Mayor supported the workers' right to unionize and would not remain neutral in labor disputes.[45]

Hoan's appointments helped as well. On the Police and Fire Commission, for example, a majority of unionists, Socialists, and liberals held sway. During the big strike wave of 1937, the county sheriff, a Socialist, disputed the notion that police action was necessary during strikes. He pointed out that the unions had their own systems of discipline.[46] Critics charged that the police looked the other way when union pickets blocked entrances to struck workshops and abused those who crossed the picket lines. Labor's political clout on the local level helped create a climate that was relatively sympathetic to the spread of unionization.

The pattern of government intervention in labor relations at the state level in Wisconsin had begun in the 1890s. In 1895 Wisconsin created a state board of conciliation to mediate

MAUD McCREERY: UNIONIST AND SUFFRAGIST

This description of Maude McCreery, one of the most interesting figures in Wisconsin labor, appeared in the Milwaukee Leader *upon her death in 1937.*

MAUD McCreery, champion of the underdog, newspaper writer and editor, orator, labor organizer, fighting Socialist and Farmer-Labor Progressive, former suffragette, is dead.

Active to the end, Mrs. McCreery, 55 years old, had last been seen alive by hotel employees when she retired to her room following conferences Saturday night with leaders in the workers' educational movement and in the Farmer-Labor-Progressive Federation.

Maud McCreery devoted a lifetime to causes. At one time or another, Maud, as all who knew her and were attached to her called her, actively campaigned for most major causes or movements in America that had for their purposes the "achievement of justice, the defense of the oppressed or the restoration of rights to individuals or to groups." Tom Mooney, Sacco-Vanzetti, peace, all were of prime concern to her. But her dominant interest was the labor movement and there are few unions in the county and not many more out in the state that had not at one time or another heard Maud's voice at their meetings.

Battled for Suffrage

Mrs. McCreery, when still young, threw herself into the women's suffrage cause, traveled the country from one end to the other in her campaign.

After suffrage was won, Mrs. McCreery came to Milwaukee at the invitation of Victor L. Berger, founder of the *Milwaukee Leader* and took a post as editor of the women's page for workers' wives, and daily she wrote an original article in which she discussed the problems of the wife of a wage earner in her home, among neighbors, and in the movements which concerned her husband.

In editing her page, Mrs. McCreery was careful to keep everything within the bounds of the interest of the workers' wives and would permit no fancy recipes or fancy style designs to appear which she regarded as beyond the abilities of workers' wives to acquire.

"Covered" Labor Front

But the women's page was too confining for Mrs. McCreery and soon she was appointed labor editor where her reporting of labor news often became a parallel interest to whatever struggles labor was waging. Mrs. McCreery as reporter often appeared in picket lines and on soap boxes. She would then rush back to the office to write her stories. For a time she also "covered" the city hall for *The Leader*.

Mrs. McCreery was known as one of the best money-raisers in the liberal movements. She was a dynamic speaker

State Historical Society of Wisconsin WHi (X3) 33295

Maud McCreery, organizer for the Political Equality League, campaigning for woman's suffrage, Brown County, 1912.

with a penetrating voice that carried its message to the far corners of even large halls. And to her often were assigned the chores of raising the wherewithal not only with which to pay for the hall in which the meeting was being held, but also to finance the cause or movement in the interest of which the meeting had been called. There are few liberals hereabouts who had not heard Mrs. McCreery's voice on the platform. Many of them, however, did not know that voice had also been trained for music. But to that use Mrs. McCreery rarely put it.

Active in Sheboygan

Mrs. McCreery's last newspaper work was with *The Sheboygan New Deal*, now the *Sheboygan Times*, which she edited for two years. In Sheboygan, as in Milwaukee, she was soon identified with labor and civil causes and her weekly publication became the rallying point for the progressive forces of that city.

She was a member of the Socialist Party, the Farmer-Labor Progressive Federation, and the trade union move-ment here. She was in regular attendance at the meetings of the Federated Trades Council and organized for it the Milwaukee County Council of Women's Auxiliaries to Trade Unions. Her last work was with the School for Workers in Industry of the University of Wisconsin where four times a week she taught parliamentary law and public speaking.

Reared in Wauwatosa

Mrs. McCreery was 55 years old last February 26. She was the daughter of the late Dr. S.S. Leonard and lived in Wauwatosa until her marriage to Rex I. McCreery, an attorney in Green Bay. One son was born to the marriage but he died at an early age. She married again in 1926 to James Walker of California, but they were divorced. In Milwaukee, she made her home at the Republican Hotel.

But Mrs. McCreery's physique never measured up to her energies and her interests. Physical breakdown came with greater frequency and each one left her a little weaker. Nevertheless, her white hair, a whiteness which came to her very early in life, was still seen at any number of gatherings where workers, peace lovers, or progressives met.

From *Milwaukee Leader*, April 11, 1938.

industrial conflicts. This office was incorporated into the new Industrial Commission in 1911, but the legislature failed to appropriate funds for mediation until 1919 when a great wave of strikes forced the state to intervene. Once the strikes subsided, the board of conciliation fell into dormancy and it was abolished in 1931. The state's labor code was rewritten in 1931. The new laws encouraged collective bargaining, tightened the existing ban on "yellow dog" contracts, and widened the tactics labor could use without restrictions by court injunction.[47] This removed a key weapon from the employer's arsenal in Wisconsin. During the turbulent years from 1933 to 1941, employers won injunctive relief from state courts on only 16 occasions. Nevertheless, an increase in the number of violent strikes in 1934 convinced many lawmakers of the need for more state intervention in labor relations.

The CIO benefitted from policies adopted at the state level. In this case, the CIO was able to capitalize on the work of the state and local AFL leaders who, beginning in 1934, crafted a farmer-labor-progressive coalition that swept the state capitol in 1936. The compelling victory won by the Farmer-Labor Progressive Federation opened the way to a reformulation of the rules of industrial relations with the passage of the Wisconsin Labor Relations Act (WLRA), sometimes referred to as a "little Wagner act." The measure had passed the Assembly but failed in the Senate by two votes in 1935. It sailed through the state legislature during the big strike wave in the spring of 1937.

A key feature of the Wisconsin Act was the creation of a Wisconsin Labor Relations Board. The three-member labor board, appointed by Governor La Follette, intervened in nearly 800 labor disputes between April 1937 and December 1938. It was involved in almost every strike that occurred in 1937 and 1938, including about fifty in the Milwaukee area. The board also mediated 680 labor disputes and played key roles in resolving many others.[48] Modeled partly after the federal act, the WLRA was also based on experience with industrial relations in Wisconsin. It differed from the federal law by specifically directing the new labor board to mediate and arbitrate labor disputes. This provision proved quite advantageous to union organizing drives.

The labor board assumed another duty that proved critical to the success of the CIO: the listing of bona fide labor organizations. Under the WLRA, listing was not extended to company unions. The CIO benefitted a great deal when the labor board refused to list several of the strong employee associations in some of the larger steel mills and large auto supply plants. The provisions for listing bona fide unions was initially proposed by the business leaders who argued that the provision was needed to guard against racketeers and radicals. The Wisconsin State Federation of Labor resisted the measure, fearing a new state-run blacklist. But they later agreed to its inclusion after making certain that the bill's definition of a bona fide union would not extend to company unions, organizations that were funded or led in whole or in part by the employer or its agents. In the first four months of the Board's existence, 612 of the 616 unions listed as bona fide organizations were AFL or CIO unions.[49]

The Board's intervention also helped CIO organizing

Mayor Daniel W. Hoan of Milwaukee.

efforts in workshops with no history of AFL unionism. CIO activists in candy factories, retail services, gasoline stations, smaller metal fabricating plants, and automobile parts firms appealed for and received listings as bona fide unions by the new labor board. For decades, workers of all trades and industries had fought for a chance to sit, almost as equals, at the bargaining table with the bosses. But the CIO, after only a year in operation, was able to win rights that had long eluded earlier labor groups. In this way, the Board's intervention boosted the CIO's image and bestowed instant credibility on fledgling labor organizations.

While labor benefitted from the Board's actions, neither the AFL or the CIO was totally comfortable with its intervention. The state AFL's chief counsel, Joseph Padway, a Socialist and state senator from Milwaukee, was concerned that AFL craft jurisdictions would be undermined in majority rule elections. But the state Board upheld the role of craft unions and separate elections in various plants owned by the same firm. (Called to Washington to head the national AFL's legal staff, Padway argued successfully for the right of craft unions in the Allis Chalmers case.) But the CIO gained from several Board rulings, as when workers belonging to the AFL Glove Workers Union were locked out by the Fried-Ostermann company in Milwaukee because they refused to join the CIO Amalgamated Clothing Workers, which had a closed shop agreement.[50]

State intervention in support of unionization, however, was

short-lived. Employer groups and the press attacked the WLRA as one-sided legislation.[51] In 1939 business and farm groups, benefiting a great deal from the divisions in labor's legislative activities and the break-up of the labor-farmer alliance, pushed through legislation abolishing the Board and repealing the state's labor act. Anticipating the Taft-Hartley Act of 1947, Wisconsin's Employment Peace Act of 1939 compiled a list of unfair union practices and rewrote the state's labor laws to put new restrictions on union activity. Whereas the previous law had aimed to protect the right of workers to organize, the new labor law sought to protect the public, the employee, and the employer. Employers were not allowed to make union-shop agreements unless at least three-fourths of the employees in the bargaining unit approved in a secret ballot election. Dues check-off was prohibited unless the employee agreed to a payroll deduction in writing.

The new law extended unfair practices to the unions, prohibiting picketing or boycotts unless a majority in a unit voted by secret ballot to do so. Mass picketing and obstruction of public streets and highways was banned along with secondary boycotts and sit-down strikes. A ten day cooling off period was required for workers involved in processing agricultural products. Unions were required to present an annual financial report to each member. A new board named to administer the act consisted of a former district attorney, a sidewalk contractor, and a former representative of the Locomotive Engineers.[52] Both the AFL and CIO opposed the Employment Peace Act, but they could not prevent its passage. Despite the restrictive nature of the new revised labor law, the movement continued to grow in the Milwaukee area.

The CIO-AFL split at the national level brought words of caution from local AFL leaders. In their view, industrial unionism had become an established fact. They tended to see the split as a temporary rift that would end in a compromise that would allow industrial unions to be formed.[53] During the summer of 1936, as various CIO groups began to form in Milwaukee shops, the FTC at first admitted their delegates to the labor council meetings.[54] At the WSFL convention, in an effort to maintain unity, two CIO leaders were put on the "official" slate and elected to the executive board. FTC leaders also developed a unity proposal, endorsed at the July 1936 convention of the WSFL, to be offered at the national AFL convention. The "Wisconsin Plan" derived from the findings of a special WSFL committee which studied the issue and concluded that: "No hard and fast rule seeking to establish one uniform organization set-up can adequately or effectively meet all the varied needs of workers in every line of work . . . there are large and important industries in which craft unions have not been able to reach the masses of workers."[55] FTC organizer Jake Friedrick and other Wisconsin delegates took the unity plan to the national AFL convention, but it was killed on a procedural maneuver by the Carpenters' William Hutcheson.

After the ten national unions comprising the Committee on Industrial Organization were expelled by the AFL executive board in August 1936, the WSFL called a statewide leadership meeting, including many CIO supporters, in a desperate attempt to hold the movement together. In March 1937, however-

er, CIO proponents called a meeting to form a caucus to run an opposition slate aimed at winning the leadership of the FTC. That action, together with disputes over which union represented the Allis Chalmers workers, resulted in many of the pro-CIO delegates leaving the FTC after a heated meeting in March 1937. A similar split unfolded a few weeks later on the state level. John Banachowicz, the Clothing and Textile workers (CIO) organizer, resigned from the executive board of the WSFL, parting on good terms with unionists with whom he had worked for several years. The other CIO board member, young Emil Costello, refused to resign his position on the WSFL executive board, even though he was organizing full-time for the CIO. Eventually the WSFL executive board conducted a "trial" and expelled Costello.

With the departure of the CIO unions, the Wisconsin State Federation of Labor launched an ambitious organizing drive to counter the CIO threat. In April 1937 a large group of local union presidents and secretaries, together with organizers and central body officers met in Milwaukee to establish an organizing campaign which promised to work on an industrial basis where practical.[56] Meanwhile, CIO initiatives fell short in several areas. The CIO restaurant workers union, which had sparked a few sit-down strikes, dissolved in 1938 after its leadership left the CIO and returned to the AFL. The Machinists defeated the CIO in the formation of a city-wide local of automobile mechanics.

A CIO effort to organize construction workers never got off the ground and an attempt by pro-CIO activists to start a rival musicians union was abandoned on recommendation from the CIO's national office. The Garment Workers returned to the AFL in 1939. Several UAW locals declined to affiliate with the CIO's city central body. Some local UAW union presidents were critical of left-wing UAW leaders. The more conservative Homer Martin retained a following among some Milwaukee UAW leaders. The large UAW unions at Harley-Davidson and Briggs and Stratton soon left the CIO and affiliated with the UAW-AFL. Several campaigns by CIO unions failed to draw the 3,000-member federal labor union at A. O. Smith out of the AFL. It remained AFL 19806. As the following table shows, the AFL managed to retain most of the federal labor unions located in the Milwaukee area:

MEMBERSHIP IN FEDERAL LABOR UNIONS IN MILWAUKEE, 1934-1938[57]

(Includes locals paying per capita tax on more than 100 members)

Number	Firm/Occupation	1934	1935	1936	1937	1938
16456	(Office Workers)	42	138	140	106	210
17710	(City Laborers)	73	496	538	(CIO)	—
17992	(Sewerage Plant)	104	110	102	(CIO)	—
18499	(Steel Workers)	202	525	569	417	506
18546	(Coke and Gas)	163	435	315	306	319
19059	(Seaman Auto Body)	348	1423	(UAW)	(CIO)	—
19340	(Corrugated Metal)	—	144	229	338	246
19806	(A. O. Smith)	—	1031	2329	3290	2489
19829	(Fabricated Metal)	—	144	356	402	167
19926	(Square D)	—	—	115	181	173

Strikers at the Allis-Chalmers plant in West Allis in the 1940s.

Milwaukee County Historical Society

The split in the labor movement resulted in sometimes bitter competition, but the net effect on membership was to increase the number of workers enrolled in unions. The CIO consolidated its position in the large farm equipment, auto, and electrical firms and in a dozen large metal fabricating plants. The CIO also had strength among packinghouse workers, gas workers, and county and city employees. In Milwaukee the CIO claimed to represent 55,000 workers in 1938. While the CIO grew between 1937 and 1945, the AFL grew even more rapidly. The FTC claimed 80,000 members in 1939. With some justification, a writer in the *Wisconsin CIO News* commented, "Take a look at Wisconsin. If we hadn't had this 'tragic split' at least 125,000 men and women enrolled in CIO or AFL unions would still be unorganized."[58]

Despite the CIO-AFL split, formal discussions between the two organizations continued until the spring of 1938. A Labor Disputes Committee, established late in 1938, coordinated strike efforts between the rival federations in the years between the split and the merger in 1955.

The rise of the CIO in Milwaukee marked a new departure for the labor movement. Employers from firms that had never before been organized now came to the bargaining table. The anti-union strongholds in the auto industry, farm implements, and steel products were conquered by the CIO. The sit-downs

electrified the movement and added to the CIO's reputation as a tough fighter for workers' rights. Scrambling for effective organizers, the CIO offered jobs to left-wing activists, men *and* women. Soon the organization served as a catalyst for union activists and radicals, black workers and working-class youth.[59]

Meanwhile the local AFL's political strategy stalled. AFL leaders who had long supported organizing the industrial workers and working with the political forces on the Left, mainly Socialists, found themselves on the defensive following the defection of large unions to the CIO. More conservative labor leaders, strong in the building trades and the teamsters union, argued that Socialism and other "old-world ideologies" had to be scrapped in favor of a "nonpartisan" political program. New elections in 1940 began to extinguish the Socialist elements that had guided the leadership of the FTC and the WSFL for half a century. While the WSFL's political program floundered in transition from socialism to nonpartisan politics, the CIO unions increased their involvement in the Democratic party, paving the way for labor's first Political Action Committee.[60] The spectacular emergence of a popular movement for industrial unionism, the CIO's dramatic challenge, and the response of local AFL unions transformed the labor movement in Milwaukee during the New Deal years, marking a period of conflict and growth.■

From "Sources of CIO Success: The New Deal Years in Milwaukee," *Labor History*, v.29, n.2 (1988).

Unionism at Oscar Mayer
in Madison

BY ROBERT H. SCHULTZ, JR.

*Robert Schultz, an original member of the first union at the large
Oscar Mayer plant in Madison, recalls how the union was built.
Note the importance of secrecy and how radical students from
the University of Wisconsin helped the workers to organize.*

THE first packing plant on the present site of Oscar Mayer was constructed and run by the Farmer's Co-op. The Oscar Mayer Company bought the plant and started its operation on November 24, 1919.

I was hired by Bill Wagner, foreman of the trimming room, on June 13, 1927. Starting wage was $.40 an hour for men and $.35 an hour for women... Mr. Mayer welcomed all those experienced German and Polish men from Cudahy. For over fourteen years there was no union here. But Oscar Mayer employees had a short sit down strike in 1928 and two in the early 1930s, several years before the flood of sit down strikes in 1937 which were outlawed in 1939.

Bill Wagner was promoted to superintendent and the company hired Clifford Clark from Waterloo, Iowa, as foreman of the trim room. His first day as foreman he said, "I will not allow anyone to talk, whistle or sing in this department." If a man cut his finger he would not let him go to the first aid room. There was blood on the cutting bench and the meat, so all the departments walked off the job to the locker room. When Plant Manager Bolz and superintendent Wagner were told about what had happened Mr. Bolz asked, "What shall we do, Bill?" Bill Wagner answered, "Let him go." Twelve minutes later we were all back on the job and Cliff Clark was fired. Cliff was also a slave driver. I was walking down the hall as fast as I could to scale trimmings and he said to me, "you can run a little can't you?"

Then Fred Pape, a $.40 per hour man was appointed foreman of the trim room until he went out with us on the one day strike and he was fired by Mr. Bolz with the help of stoolpigeon Mr. Bast.

After the 1929 stock market crash there were many reports of wage cuts. In the early 1930s there was a wage cut notice on our bulletin board. All the employees walked to the locker room. Mr. Bolz promised no more wage cuts for a year if we went back to work. In three months there was another wage cut notice. We again walked off the job. Mike Lynch reminded Mr.

Bolz of his promise. He informed us that his orders came from Chicago. When we argued against the cut he told the department timekeeper to take the names of those who wanted to work. With high unemployment and with twenty-five to fifty people at the front entrance every morning looking for jobs, we all went back to work.

The company would hire several men when the fall and winter hog rush started, about November. We worked six long days a week, no overtime, no rest periods except the half hour for lunch at noon. When there was not room in the yards for all the hogs. The U.S. Inspectors would order the hogs unloaded, fed and reloaded on the railroad cars. Those days the company would give us a $.35 meal at 5:30 or 6:00 P.M. then we would kill hogs until 8:30 or 9:00 P.M., all straight time. It made us think and talk about starting a union.

In the summer of 1933 we posted a meeting notice on the bulletin board, to be held at the end of a hay field out old Packers Avenue. There were only two watchmen on twelve hour shifts. Mr. York on nights and Mr. Decker on days. Stoolpigeon Mr. Bast told Mr. Decker about the meeting. There were about twenty to twenty-five of us present. Two University of Wisconsin students spoke to us about how to start a union. Mr. Bolz got his report of the meeting from Mr. Decker. It was clear we had to start with small secret meetings. The first one was at Charlie Swope's house and the eight men present were: Charlie Swope, Ed Beaudette, Robert H. Schultz, L. Chapman, Ed Sechrest, Jack Sechrest, George Watson, and Lloyd Millette. There were only 350 production workers and very few had cars so the stoolpigeons knew who was at the meetings and where they were held. I had a 1926 Star.

We chipped in and called Frank Ellis at Austin, MN. for advice. He met with us the next night at Charlie Swope's house. He told us to get informational sheets out about the company's finances if possible and list the complaints. Then we were to call or write the Amalgamated Meat Cutters and Butcher Workmen at Chicago for application blanks. He said it would be easier to sign up members if you get the sheets out first. He said to do this before the stoolpigeons can start a company union, because two factions in a plant is worse than no union. After you have most of them signed up call the International Union to charter your local. Ed and Jack Sechrest contacted a University of Wisconsin student by the name of Johnson who owned an old typewriter and mimeograph machine. That night the seven men listed below (Ted Lee, Ed Beaudette, Robert H. Schultz, Jack Sechrest, Charles Swope, Ed Sechrest, and Lloyd Millette) met Johnson in his $2.00 a week third floor room on Webster Street.

We drew up an outline for the information sheet and chipped in to buy a ream of paper. The next night we met Johnson in his room. He told us he had gone to the I.R.S. office and told them he was writing a thesis on a large company in Madison. They gave him the records of the Gisholt Machine Company and Oscar Mayer Company. He looked them both over briefly and then selected Oscar Mayer's records. The following is a duplicate of the contents of the first informational sheet.

ATTENTION OSCAR MAYER EMPLOYEES

Oscar Mayer & Co., paid income tax on $327,000 for 1932 after buying a fleet of new Ice Trucks and paying all expenses including Oscar Mayer I salary of $50,000 and Oscar Mayer II salary of $25,000.

Layoffs are without regard to seniority.

The company uses a polite way to discharge an employee, they lay him off and never call him back.

Miss Silbaugh, the nurse, must think she is the superintendent as she threatens to fire anyone breaking a safety rule.

Get your Application Card and pay your dues.

Elect your officers.

Set up a Steward system.

Signed—The Committee

Then the question was how to get them into the plant? Johnson said "Tell me how to get in, they can't fire me." We told him Mr. Decker, the Watchman, is always on the front dock. Go in the back entrance, up the stairway to the second floor locker room at 11:30 A.M. There will be only four people eating lunch and they are all pro-union. Spread the sheets on the tables and leave the way you came in. The next night we met with Johnson again. He told us there was an older man wearing a white coat eating lunch in the locker room. That was superintendent Wagner. We had forgotten that he eats lunch early also. The next morning the superintendent came into the trimming room where most of our committee worked and said after reading the sheet he gave it to Miss Silbaugh to read. He then told her it looked like she was trying to get his job. She just smiled. He then took it to Mr. Bolz to read. Mr. Bolz, in an angry tone of voice said, "Get the name of the man who brought this sheet in here." Wagner told Mr. Bolz that the "little curly headed kid

don't work here and he had never seen him before." He told Bolz that this man had scattered a paper bag full of these sheets on the locker room tables and left before he had time to read it. Bolz remarked that the information on the sheets would have to come out of his office and the only person that obtained it would have to be Brigham, a former company employee in his office that had been fired by the company because he had been caught by the police robbing a restaurant on University Avenue in Madison.

Our last secret meeting was attended by thirteen men: Ed Beaudette, Stan Weisrock, Robert H. Schultz, Charles Swope, Thor Shakstad, Earl Shinneman, Rollie Conant, Jack Sechrest, Ed Sechrest, Art Sommers, George Watson, Bill Woertz, and E. Chapman. It was held on a very warm Sunday afternoon in Blooming Grove just off the Cottage Grove Rd. We stopped at Schillinglau's little grocery store and each had a cold $.15 twelve ounce bottle of home brew. It was legalized shortly after. Then we went to the back lot on a little grassy knoll in the shade of a large oak tree, which is still standing. We had used the advice of Frank Ellis to call Amalgamated International Office in Chicago for application blanks. Mike Pietrak, International Representative of the office brought the blanks and met us at the Labor Temple. We did not post a meeting notice so as to prevent the stoolpigeons from attending. We decided to each contact ten good pro-union men. Mike told us the initiation fee would be exonerated and to just sign the application and pay $2.00 per month dues. Wages at that time were $.28 per hour for men and $.25 per hour for women. Mr. Pietrak concluded with a short rousing pep talk.

The Labor Temple Association gave us the use of the meeting hall rent free during the period of our organizing and also their very valuable knowledge of their many years of experience. Mike Pietrak was again present at the meeting which resulted in a Charter for Local 538 by the Amalgamated Meat Cutters, dated August 7 1933....

Nine months after the charter for Local 538, at the end of May 1934, the company still refused to recognize our union to bargain for its members. We called a meeting at the Labor Temple for a strike vote. At that time there were only twelve paid up members. The strike was to start at 12:00 midnight, May 30, 1934. Only 51% voted for the strike. The International refused to sanction the strike, so a wildcat strike started on the above time and date.

Six men in the shipping department and all of the ice truck drivers went in to work a few hours before midnight. Most of the employees were at the three entrances by midnight. About 1:30 A.M. a Model-A Ford police car with a police officer and Chief McCormick came down Mayer Avenue at a high rate of speed, headed straight at the main entrance pickets. The pickets were angry at the chief's disregard for life. Tony Jeroma, who owned a dump truck and a few more P.W.A. men, hauled a load of logs and large rocks and dumped them, in the main entrance area. About 2:00 A.M. Mr. Bolz drove his Packard touring car in the main gate and around the pile of logs. No words were exchanged between them. About 2:30 A.M. the Chief's car came at us again at a very high rate of speed, but we stood in front of the pile of logs and stones as long as we dared. The first four-

Oscar Mayer workers, Madison, c.1930.

Jim Cavanaugh, Madison Federation of Labor

wheel brakes on a Ford prevented his car from hitting the pile. The Chief warned us of an injunction if we did not clear the entrance and have only one picket at a gate. We cleared the entrance, because with one picket at a gate we would lose the strike.

At 10:00 A.M. on May 31, 1934, Bolz came out and said "Let's bury the hatchet and all go back to work." Mike Lynch told him that not until the union was recognized would they go back to work. At noon Mr Bolz came out again and told us he had gotten a call from Chicago and that Oscar Mayer told him to get the men off the street. He told Mayer that we wouldn't move unless our union was recognized. Mr. Mayer said he didn't care what I give you because this strike will be a "black-eye that could never be erased." Mr Bolz agreed to meeting with our committee at 3:00 P.M.

The three sections of the first contract were: union recognition; no discrimination because of the strike or union activities; and seniority rights would prevail for all below the grade of foreman. The next morning, June 1, 1934, superintendent Wagner showed us a list of ten men from Mr. Bolz to be discharged. The discharge list was as follows: Earl Shinneman, Art Sommers, Ed

Sechrest, Jack Sechrest, Stan Weisrock, Robert H. Schultz, Karl Garbarski, Ed Beaudette, Fred Pape, and Charles Swope. Mr. Bolz called us in one at a time and asked the same questions, "Why did you want a union?" and "Why did your group urge a strike with only 51% voting in favor of it?" I told him that because a man with ten years rights is laid off and I'm still working and that someday I will be that old man. I also told Mr. Bolz that we did not urge this strike but that the 51% was the deciding factor in the strike. His reply to me was "You're still fired." Charlie Swope took a one week vacation when the one day strike was on, and for some unknown reason he was the only one of the ten on the list that was not fired. Karl Garbarski was discharged by Mr. Bolz with the help of stoolpigeons Mr. Decker and Mr. Linsaicum. Mr. Tompkins was department timekeeper, not eligible to join the union. Some members said, Tommy is for us or he would not have been at the strike vote meeting and on the picket line. Because he said to me and others, to H— with Oscar Mayer, don't worry about the S.O.B. he is not worrying about us. I and others knew he was a stoolpigeon so we did not answer him. He had bad luck, in the 1940s his young wife died while on vacation and he was discharged by Mr. Bolz.■

From *Wisconsin Labor History Newsletter* (1984).

Industrial Unionism:
A Communist Perspective

BY PEGGY DENNIS

Radicals of all stripes were involved in labor activities in the 1930s. Besides the socialists, there were anarchists (like Rose Pesotta) and anarcho-syndicalists (like the Industial Workers of the World or IWW). But the most significant radical group within the labor movement was the Communist Party. In Peggy Dennis' autobiographical account we see how Party activists viewed their work with unions during this dynamic period in the 1930s. Assigned to Wisconsin in 1935, the young couple found a rather unusual situation where Socialists were well represented in the unions and local and state politics. Note the complex way in which Dennis and her husband Gene confronted the existing Socialist "establishment" in their efforts to fashion an American form of communism.

IN Wisconsin the established labor movement had a unique local twist. The AFL leaders were closely inter-connected with the Progressive Party state administration and the Socialist Party city administration of Milwaukee. In this governing third party dominance, a radical aura served as facade for a cynical, pragmatic conservatism. In the factories of Falk, Harnischfeger, and Allis Chalmers the new union activists contended with employers' Pinkerton labor spies. In the labor movement they battled oldtime, sophisticated Red scare tactics of the A.F.L.-Socialist leaderships.

But the industrial union drive did not abate. In Racine, Janesville, Kenosha, Milwaukee, the workers organized their new unions, ignoring orders that they disband and individually join the proper craft union. The Wisconsin Committee for Industrial Organization was formed inside the A.F.L. in November, 1935, with sixty-two union affiliations. The young leadership was closely allied to the political and anti-fascist coalitions being formed throughout the state. Gene's manner of contact with all these diverse movements was individual, personal, casual, and varied. Over a beer in a tavern with workers off a strike picketline he helped plan new, independent, rank and file action. In the kitchen of a C.I.O. organizer he helped committees map a two-prong campaign to organize the factory over employer resistance and to wrest a charter from the A.F.L. Lounging around the living room of Left Socialist Meta Berger, he discussed with young militants how to force debate within the Socialist Party for united action with the Communists. In hotel rooms with staid A.F.L., Progressive, and Socialist Party leaders he argued, cajoled, smilingly threatened. He talked from the strength of a small but cohesive state Communist Party,

which despite its 600 members, had more than one hundred union officials, nearly three hundred of its members active in the C.I.O. and A.F.L., and a popularity and influence far beyond its numerical status. And these leaders with whom he met knew that members of their organizations were joining our party at the rate of some sixty each month . . . .

When the state A.F.L. leadership ordered the C.I.O. committee to disband or be suspended within eight months, Gene's office rang with fierce debate. In carloads the union activists, Party and non-Party militants, came from outlying towns. The mood was fighting mad and many urged a mass exodus from the A.F.L. "Screw the piecards, let's leave 'em cold," was the sentiment. Absorbed in his slow-burning pipe, concentrating on packing fresh tobacco into its bowl, Gene listened. He asked questions—How many workers in the factory would leave the security of the established and national A.F.L.? Who had the work contract, the individual new union or the A.F.L. charter? The questions turned the anger towards discussion of hard facts, to reports on the specific situation in each factory, in each department.

Consensus began to form. "Gene's right; we gotta fight inside as long as we can"; "we gotta give the workers a chance to see who are the real splitters of the labor movement"; "we gotta consolidate C.I.O. nationally, not act alone"; "Gene's right." But Gene had given no "line." He had made no opening speeches or summary analysis. Those who had come to get The Word from The Leader had, instead, probed their own views and, given the opportunity to collectively examine the facts, had come up with the decisions Gene had known they would.

The decision to stay in the A.F.L. and fight for both unity

May Day labor rally in Milwaukee in the 1930s.

and the right to industrial unions won the respect of the rank and file. So effective was this policy that the Federation of Labor's state convention at Beaver Dam that summer of 1936 was compelled to drop the September expulsion threat. The entire Wisconsin delegation to the A.F.L. national convention voted against the expulsion resolution. For the first time two C.I.O. leaders were elected to the state federation's executive board. Six months later, however, in line with national policy, the Wisconsin state federation began to expel C.I.O. delegates from the Central Labor Councils. Physical force was used when the militants refused to relinquish their elected seats. The onus for splitting the labor movement was now squarely upon the A.F.L. leadership.

Emil Costello, president of Federal Industrial Union No. 18456 in Kenosha, was also a newly elected member to the state legislature on the Farmer-Labor-Progressive Federation ticket. He was chairman of the C.I.O. committee and one of the two elected to the A.F.L.'s executive board at the Beaver Dam convention. The Board asked him to resign in compliance with the national A.F.L.'s actions to remove all C.I.O. people. Young Costello refused and was put on trial for "aligning himself with alleged Communists." He boycotted the trial, informing the Board that he was "too busy in union organization and helping to conduct the strikes at Bucyrus-Erie [one of the largest excavation machine building plants in the world] and at plants in steel and auto . . . ."

As a result of the expulsions, the C.I.O. formed a new, independent labor organization. In Wisconsin sixty-two local unions formed the independent C.I.O. state council, affiliated to national C.I.O. Emil Costello became its chairman and Harold Christoffel, the young president of the new industrial union at the giant Allis Chalmers machine building complex, became its state secretary.

The political realignments forming in other states appeared in characteristically different form in Wisconsin. Elsewhere around the country polarization was occurring inside both the Democratic and Republican parties. The single main issue was the social aspects of the Roosevelt New Deal programs. In Wisconsin the governing Progressive and Socialist third parties joined with the State Federation of Labor, the Worker's Alliance, Railway Brotherhoods, and the three state farm organizations to form the Farmer-Labor-Progressive Federation, an electoral alliance nominally to the left of and independent of the Democratic party.

To Governor La Follette and his Progressive Party contingent, and to Milwaukee Mayor Dan Hoan and his Socialist old guard, the Federation was a horse-trade deal to deliver votes to each other. It was intended to meet the rising demand of their rank and file for militant, independent, united, political action.

We Communists were aware of the leaders' motivation. However, we welcomed the new formation as a possible embryo of a people's coalition. We urged broadening its base beyond the original founding organizations. Our comrades and other militants inside the new Federation, and inside its affiliated

MADISON LABOR IN THE 1930s

THE Madison Labor movement changed dramatically during the 1930s. Although the explosive strikes that rocked Minneapolis, Toledo, and the Southern mill towns were not repeated in Madison, there was a dramatic shift in the size and composition of the city's union movement.

The Depression hit Madison hard. Between 1929 and 1933, the number of building permits shrank from nearly 5,000 to 312. Thousands were thrown out of work, and many of those with jobs saw their wages slashed by 30% to 50%. Lower wages did not mean more work, however, and the trades membership dropped by 50%. The unions helped their members as best they could. Building trades locals voted assessments on those with jobs, the Typographical Union blocked pay cuts at the profitable *Capital Times* and used assessments and jobsharing to aid its members.

For many workers, however, there was no alternative to public relief. In 1933, the Dane County Unemployed Workers League confronted the County Board over relief policies. Led by Boilmakers' activist and former Madison Federation of Labor officer William Forrest, more than 1,000 relief workers struck against the Board's policy of paying 80% of relief earnings in store orders. Strikers sought cash wages for relief work and an end to make-work jobs. They demanded that the county stop using them to replace regular county employees. Insisting that "we don't want charity, we want cash for our work," protesters stopped trucks, picketed supervisors' homes, and packed the courthouse to force a meeting with relief officials. But after three months, the supervisors broke the strike.

Industrial Unionism

The Thirties were a watershed for the Madison labor movement as the hard times of the Depression spurred some workers to act on longstanding grievances. By 1940, workers had shattered the open shop on the East Side by organizing the city's three largest factories—Gisholt, Oscar Mayer, and Ray-O-Vac. Other workers made breakthroughs in the service sector. Although legislators would not pass collective bargaining laws for public employees until the 1950s and 1960s, city, county, and state workers began organizing for better conditions. During 1931-32, public employees fought back against budget-cutters. In 1931, firefighters formed

Local 311. Two years later, a 15% to 30% pay cut spurred activity among other municipal workers. After three years, they won a public referendum restoring their wage rates.

Organizing began among state workers in 1932. At first, they formed an independent AFL local; and by 1934, the Wisconsin State Employees' Association was the largest local in the Madison Fed. In 1936, the WSEA joined with public employees elsewhere in the country to form AFSCME and became Local 1 of the new union. The WSEA's head Arnold Zander, became AFSCME's first president; and the union's national headquarters remained in Madison until 1957.

Oscar Mayer workers made the breakthrough at the city's industrial plants. In summer, 1933, a handful of workers held their first union meeting. During the Depression, management had slashed wages to 28 cents per hour for men and 25 cents for women. More importantly, workers objected to favoritism and arbitrary treatment by management.

Bob Schultz, one of Local 538's founders, recalled that "there were no set hours at all before the union. There was just whatever the boss wanted you to do, and you had nobody to complain to."

"After you had the union, why you got some protection. There was no protection before. The 'yes' men were protected pretty good but the other ones weren't."

Aided by local unionists and a campus supporter, the meatpackers formed Amalgamated Meatcutters Local 538. For nine months, the company refused to deal with the union. Membership dropped off as the union was unable to do anything for its members.

In May, 1934, the union took a strike vote. Because only 51% voted to walk out, national union officials told the Madison local to stay on the job. Fearing that inaction would kill the union, activists decided to risk a wildcat strike. "Some of us thought it was now or never," said Schultz. "We were afraid if we lost the chance, well nobody else would sign up again."

The gamble paid off. Once the union acted, the strike was nearly 100% effective. Within twenty-four hours, the company had come to terms, recognizing the union and agreeing to seniority rights. Management reneged on a non-reprisals pledge, firing Schultz and other activists; but the union's position was secure.

organizations, put substance into the form. Despite efforts of the Progressive and Socialist leaders to keep the Federation as an ad hoc electoral channel for themselves, our people organized active rank and file clubs in the neighborhoods.

The more the Hoan Socialists tied their party to the La Follette kite, the more they claimed Socialist victory in getting into the Federation's preamble the socialist-tinged commitment to a future society based upon production-for-use. We Communists, however, saw the Federation as a broad, anti-fascist alliance committed to militant economic and social pro-

grams for immediate action, not a revolutionary substitute for the Socialist or Communist parties. We publicly urged Communist and Socialist working-class unity outside the Federation while supporting the Federation for the broad coalition it should be. Rank and file Socialists supported our efforts, the officials turned us down cold every time.

We encouraged militant Left activists to become Federation candidates and we helped organize their campaigns. As a result, a core of young, first-time legislators, rooted in the new C.I.O. and anti-fascist mass organizations, were sent to the state capitol.

Convention of the Wisconsin State Employees Association, December 2, 1938.

State Historical Society of Wisconsin WHi (D487) 11419

Several weeks before the Oscar's strike, workers began organizing at Ray-O-Vac. One women activist explained that "few of us decided we should organize a union . . . we met at the Labor Temple . . . and signed a charter."

Like many industrial unions formed during the Thirties, Local 19587 was concerned about social and political issues. When other workers struck, they could count on donations and picketline support from the battery workers.

A second wave of union activity swept Madison during the late Thirties. CIO sympathizers at the Madison Federation of Labor helped Gisholt workers organize a Steel Workers local and helped establish the UAW at Burgess Battery.

At first, local unionists opposed the bitter rivalry between national AFL leaders and the CIO. This policy changed in 1937 when the MFL expelled its treasurer, Cedric Parker, for helping Gisholt and Burgess workers organize.

The CIO controversy involved jurisdictional jealousies as well as pressure from AFL officials in Milwaukee, but the dispute also reflected a split between some longtime Madison Federation of Labor members and the newer unions that favored more aggressive policies and a broader view of the labor movement that meant closer ties to unemployed groups and concern for issues like public housing.

This conflict had a high price. Competition made the AFL more active in organizing; and the AFL dominated the city's labor movement; but the split caused some AFL industrial unions to cut back their involvement in the Fed.

Still, the union movement made major advances during the Thirties. In 1930, approximately 1,500 workers belonged to unions—nearly all of them skilled craft workers employed on construction sites or in small workshops. Ten years later, six to seven thousand carried union cards, and workers had organized the city's three largest plants. Besides the building trades, Madison unions now represented thousands of factor and government employees as well as semi-skilled service workers.

—DEXTER ARNOLD

At the same time, we were candidly critical of the specific weaknesses of the Socialist, Progressive and Federation leaders . . . .

The strike of the newly organized Newspaper Guild against the Hearst-owned *Wisconsin News* and the *Milwaukee Sentinel* dramatically merged economic struggles with the anti-fascist movement. Union-busting Hearst was one of the nation's chief protagonists of U.S. fascism and an outspoken admirer of Adolf Hitler. The picketlines at the newspaper plants swelled to thousands—project workers from the Workers' Alliance and smartly dressed women of the American League Against War and Fascism marched together with strikers from Cudahy Packing and Harnischfeger's Metal, and all mingled with Wisconsin's best-known columnists and reporters. National Guild president Heywood Broun declared the six months' long demonstration of solidarity "the most remarkable seen yet in any newspaper strike in the history of the country."

Four years earlier millions had starved before gratefully going to work on New Deal projects. Now they militantly closed those projects down. They went on strike for a living union wage and protested the firing of their Worker's Alliance organizers. They refused to work outdoors in zero weather without proper clothing provided by the state. When federal and state appropriations for works projects and relief were cut back, Communist and militant non-Communist caucuses organized confrontation with the liberal La Follette administration.

From towns and rural areas across the state, project strikers and their families marched on the state capitol. They were joined by C.I.O. union members and led by the organization of the unemployed—the Worker's Alliance. They took over the state assembly charters. While their children played tag in the domed rotunda and the aroma of stew simmering in giant cauldrons on the capitol lawns penetrated the halls, men in overalls and women in calico "legislated" appropriations for the hungry. Governor La Follette refused to appear, but newly elected Federation legislators joined their constituents.

On the second day of deliberations police, sheriffs and state militia stormed the sedate halls. They dragged us out of the leather chairs we had expropriated and overturned the field kitchen where we had fed many hundreds for two days. My mind flashed-back to the scalding coffee tank deliberately overturned on children in that raid upon the I.W.W. headquarters in San Pedro some twelve years earlier in 1924, and I wondered, does nothing ever change? However, a few weeks later, the Wisconsin legislature voted a two million dollar emergency appropriation to increase wages on the projects and a 20% increase in cash relief payments to the totally unemployed.

Gene continued to stress the need for continued pressure upon the large bloc of newly elected Progressive-Socialist-Labor Federation state legislators. He insisted the mass movements intensify, not diminish, the consolidation of electoral victories.

After the project workers' effective take-over of the capitol, a people's conference on farm problems and proposed legislation was held in early March, 1937, encompassing the upper Wisconsin farm areas. A short time later a statewide People's Legislative Conference was held in the state capitol.

Leaders of the Socialist and Progressive parties and the A.F.L. urged a boycott of the conference as a "Red take-over." Still, some 200 organizations from all over the state sent large delegations—local Worker's Alliance councils, farm groups, A.F.L. and C.I.O. unions, ethnic federations, Black churches, anti-fascist committees. Some fifty newly elected Federation legislators actively participated. Out of sharp debate, a tenuous unity was achieved around the main features of a number of social legislative measures they would fight for together.

Not before nor since has our Party successfully carried through such a complex and valid policy and activity as it did in the years 1935, 1936, and 1937. Amazingly enough, for persons who had never done this before, we developed, not in articles and reports but in action, the broadest, most flexible coalition relations within the mainstream. At the same time we delineated clearly our own independent Communist identification.

While we had a national presidential ticket, the energies of all Party members were concentrated upon the local and state levels where, intimately involved in grass-root movements and organizations, we moved with people because we were of them.

Our effectiveness throughout the country was, of course, uneven. Our Wisconsin experiences became a "showcase"

example at Party conferences and Gene was called upon to make lengthy analyses at national committee meetings. He was sent to meet with our comrades in Minnesota and New York where the Farmer-Labor party and the newly-organized American Labor Party had complex relations with the Democratic Party and the Roosevelt New Deal similar to ours in Wisconsin with the Progressive, Socialist, and Democratic parties and the Farmer-Labor-Progressive Federation.

Locally our comrades built the Federation clubs into centers of community struggle. They worked tirelessly for the election of those young militants who ran on the Federation tickets. They helped organize rank and file pressures upon the leaderships of the unions and other organizations to force them in a progressive direction.

Meanwhile, independently and as known Communists, we distributed a half million pieces of Party literature at factory gates. We issued weekly a special Wisconsin edition of the Party's national newspaper. At a time when that media was little used in electoral campaigns, except for President Roosevelt's fireside chats, we raised money for forty-four local Communist Party radio broadcasts around the state. We held few party rallies. Instead, we officially participated in symposia around the state where I, among other comrades, debated spokesmen of other parties and organizations.

We were ruthless with the Republicans and conservative Democrats. We chided the vacillations of the Progressives and Socialists. We urged steps to strengthen the Federation. Appreciative laughter always greeted my quote of Earl Browder's headline-getting charge that "Roosevelt roars like a lion and acts like a rabbit." Yet we emphasized, at all times, our tenacious activity in defense of all those positive aspects of the New Deal which the unholy alliance of the reactionary Republicans and Dixiecrat Democrats were out to scuttle.

Our national slogan at the time, "Communism is 20th Century Americanism," was not entirely precise in its theoretical concept. However, it became a popular form of introducing our belief that socialism was the ultimate solution to the people's needs. It also served to undercut the rabid anti-Communism introduced as a main issue by the reactionary coalition. It was an over-simplified but effective response to the flag-waving, law-and-order Liberty League clique's attempts to label us as foreign, un-American, subversive . . . .

It was an exciting, engrossing, satisfying time. Not all was perfection, by any means. Our policy of coalition and independence was not always well balanced. Some comrades worked tirelessly in the New Deal and Federation campaigns and in the new unions and Worker's Alliance branches, but not as Communists. Some interpreted coalition as working agreements with Progressive, Socialist, and A.F.L. leaders instead of as struggle on issues which would sharpen rank and file pressures on these leaders. Oldtime Communists distrusted anyone not in the Party and could not adapt to the diversity of the movements we worked with. They were accustomed to having directives handed down among Party members and were inept at convincing non-Party people of the rightness of our views.∎

From *The Autobiography of an American Communist*
(Laurence Hill, Westport, Connecticut, 1977).

The Riot at Kohler, 1934

BY WALTER H. UPHOFF

In 1934 the attractive village of Kohler, Wisconsin, was rocked by a labor dispute that resulted in the deaths of two workers and the wounding of nearly fifty others. In this account, written as a master's thesis by Walter H. Uphoff, readers gain an inside view of the evolution of the strike, mass picketing, and violence that erupted between the striking members of Federal Local Union 18545 and men deputized by the Kohler company. The strike officially lasted until 1941. Another strike occurred at the Kohler plant from 1954 to 1960.

Sheboygan Press/State Historical Society of Wisconsin WHi (X3) 20070

Pickets lift rope for Walter J. Kohler, Sr., entering the plant on day one of the strike. In dark coat and overalls, behind and to the left, is Charles Heymanns, then a member of the bargaining and strike committees and later a regional director of the AFL-CIO, Milwaukee.

ACCORDING to Rudolf Renn, men from the payroll department went out through the picket lines to go to Sheboygan Falls and Sheboygan to induce men to become deputies or to work in the plant. The number of deputies had increased to such an extent that nearly every available non-striker in the village and some men from the surrounding territory had "jobs at $4 a day." They worked in eight-hour shifts and the total number was estimated to close to six hundred. Some of the squads were given black shirts and badge to wear. They all had badges which were made in the Kohler plant according to a deputy with whom I talked. According to this same deputy their "billies" were allegedly made in the chair factory in Sheboygan Falls with a hole drilled in and the lead was poured into this hole in the Kohler plant. The deputies were told to bring whatever guns they had at home to supplement the available guns and tear-gas sticks at the headquarters. Mr. Renn stated: "Sworn testimony at the inquest, held on September 11–13, given by Mr. McWilliams of Kohler, puts the number of special deputies up to over a thousand. Recruiting centers were the Kohler Village Hall and the Carpenter Shop on the west side of Kohler. Drilling of men took place at the rifle range of Kohler and on property belonging to Kohler in back of his "mansion." The fact that the deputies were taken from the immediate vicinity made it hard for them to command respect because they were known by the pickets and were called "yellow" in numerous instances. The deputies on the other hand were "swelled-up" with authority because it was the first time they had the law in their own hands and the "badge" helped them to become indignant about the language hurled at them by the pickets. It was said that many had never shot a gun and it was a real job for Captain E.R. Schuelke of Battery C at Kohler, who was put in charge of the special deputies, to whip them into shape.

To facilitate the rapid transportation of large groups of deputies, four special trucks were bought by the village of Kohler. These trucks had heavy-gauge metal sides and wire screens over the windshield and radiator for protection. The newspapers and strikers spoke of these trucks as "armored." These trucks sped up and down the streets and the lines were generally open for all who wanted to enter the plant because of the ultimatum that, "from now on law and order will be enforced in the village of Kohler."

Some misunderstanding had arisen relative to another car of coal. The strikers maintained that according to their agreement the car was not to go in until Saturday. Peter Horn and eleven other pickets stood on the railroad tracks and refused to let the coal pass. According to Mr. Horn's testimony the special deputies approached them with several squad cars and the four armored trucks. Captain Schuelke is supposed to have lined the deputies up twenty abreast and said, "Forward march, shoot to kill." Men on the roof of the plant hollered, "Go back to Russia where you came from." L.P. Chase, the company attorney, said that there were eighty deputies in the group while the pickets claim there were 150. At any rate the twelve pickets were so vastly outnumbered and the guns and billies were on the other side so they gave up without resistance. There was considerable shouting and epithets of "Yellow" etc.

As a result of the morning's activities the strike committee issued the following statement:

Since Mr. Kohler promised no production would be carried on in the plant, there is no necessity of 250 men coming to the scene in armored cars, with clubs and guns, and we feel that such actions are unwarranted at this time. The men in the lines are picketing legally and peacefully, and the trouble today was started by the Kohler company.

Because of the large deputy force, additional accommodations had to be provided and the American Club was turned over to them. The American Club can accommodate about 500

persons and the most consistent estimate was that 240 moved in. In the afternoon of July 27th the deputies took the trunks and belongings of Steve Graeber and Frank Tadler and put them out on the street. These men were living in the Club and had worked for the company for many years, and this action helped to tantalize the pickets. According to L.L. Smith the publicity man for the company, they were put out for, "getting too much information and using it unwisely." They had been informing some of the pickets about the supply of ammunitions in storage.

A young woman and her husband saw her own father on one of the deputy trucks and hollered: "Daddy, get down from there" because she was in the picket line. When he saw that his own family was on opposite sides, he tried to get out but the other deputies refused to let him do so. They did let him quit his job after they were away from the pickets.

The picket lines continued in motion, carrying their signs as usual. About 5 P.M. all the deputies and trucks withdrew from the streets. This was an unusual event and every one wondered what would happen next. The *Sheboygan Press* gave an account of the day's happenings and printed a notice, "not to come to Kohler" that night. This statement was just the thing for excitement seekers and between four and five thousand spectators went to the scene of activity. Numerous pickets told me that some of the men on the top of the factory roofs threw stones at them. Herbert Schutt, who worked at the cook shanty, that day, told me that he treated a man who had been hit on the nose by a rock thrown from the south foundry. It is hard to determine just how much stone throwing there was earlier in the afternoon and evening. Boys had been throwing stones at the men on the roofs and occasionally hit the windows in the factory. Chief of Police Case chased them off and blamed the pickets for it; so Rudolf Renn, the strike committee chairman, told him that he would station several of his men on the company property just to keep the boys away and to maintain order.

By 8 P.M. the village was crowded with spectators and there was much activity; it was impossible to keep such a heterogeneous mob under control. The atmosphere was tense and various theories were proposed to explain the absence of the deputies for the first time. The first indications that something was going to happen were noted at about 8 P.M. when the crowd appeared to be concentrating on High Street near the south foundry. The crowd was slowly moving along the industrial walk, everything still quiet.

Suddenly there was a jangling of crashing glass and the thud of a rock landing within the south foundry. Rocks started flying in every direction and the yelling and mob spirit of the people centered the attack on the windows in the factory and office. Men and women, young and old, joined in sailing missiles until most of the windows in the factory were broken. The mob moved north on High Street and smashed most of the windows in the office building and twenty-one plate glass windows in the Recreation Club. This attack lasted for ten to fifteen minutes and then shots fired from the American Club and the office building evidently served as signals for the deputies, for they popped up everywhere. They were apparently in hiding near the office building, and began shooting the tear gas bombs from

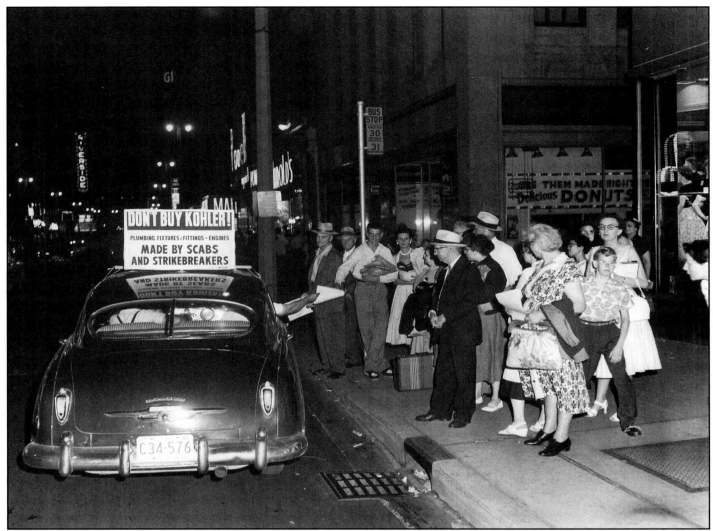

Kohler strikers distribute propaganda from the car window in downtown Milwaukee, during 1954 strike.

a distance of about 200 feet; the bombs landing everywhere.

Women and children screamed. They started running, at the same time covering their faces with handkerchiefs. Some escaped into the drug store and other buildings. Children were separated from their parents, wives from their husbands, and much confusion prevailed. The mob was infuriated and some of the men hollered, "let's blow up the place," and "tear down the office, brick by brick" and "let's go back and get those yellow rats" and similar epithets. These threats engendered more determination on the part of the deputies to drive the mob out of the village and keep them out.

Evidently some of the deputies ran out of gas and "started to use lead" shortly before 9 P.M. It is impossible to describe just how the events followed each other after that, because of the fury that prevailed, and the quickness of it all. Two men were killed and forty-seven were wounded. Most of the shooting occurred at the north end of High Street near Highway 23. After the shootings, the pickets and spectators still persisted in their howling and yelling and stone throwing from their gather-

ing place north of Highway 23. The armored trucks stood cold and specter-like at the end of High Street, and deputies in various platoon formations stood ready in the middle of the street, along the sidewalks, behind the trees and lamp posts and on the lawns north of the street. The clang of stones as they struck the iron sides of the huge armored trucks rent the air, and now and then a stone pounded its way past the trucks and rolled into the gutter ineffectively.

Every so often the strikers seemed to rally in their anger, and they pushed closer to where the police and trucks were waiting, but volleys of tear gas soon drove them back again to their stations across the road. Some had their cars parked on the south side of the road on Upper 23 but when they attempted to get to their cars the deputies evidently thought they were coming back into the village and repulsed them with gas or lead. The men who wanted to resume their picketing were also driven out.

The two persons who were killed were Lee Wakefield, 25, and Henry Engleman, 26, both of Sheboygan. The ambulances and available cars were kept busy transporting the injured to the Sheboygan hospitals and clinic. The crowd stopped the cars that happened to be coming by and forced them to take the

Kohler strikers, circa 1954.

injured to Sheboygan for treatment. The injured list included five women; the total number being forty-seven, most of whom had been wounded by buckshot or bullets.

Although the company lawyer told me that they could produce affidavits to prove that there was shooting from the side of the pickets, no deputy was shot and I found few spectators who would say that they saw any shooting from the mob. Of those who spoke about shooting from their side, the most persistent story I got was that, at about 10:30 P.M. a man on the side of the pickets stepped out ahead of the line and fired a pistol at the deputies. He stepped back to load it and again stepped out and fired but no one was hit. Mr. Wakefield, father of one of the victims, told me that he was right there and felt sure he could identify the man. Mr. Wakefield said he was convinced that this man was stationed there by someone to shoot blanks, because "he acted too brazen and no one shot at him" while others were being shot at.

It was truly a night of terror—ghastly terror, the like of

which the community had never seen and hopes never to see again. The menacing silences, broken by the shrieks of gas shells flying through the air, the cries of the wounded and injured, and the horrible threats will stand out vividly in the memories of those who witnessed the frightful happenings of the evening of Friday, July 27, 1934. . . . An order came to the deputies to clear the streets of all villagers and spectators. The deputies cleared the streets by force of their authority of their clubs and other weapons. When groups failed to comply with the orders, tear gas shells sent them scurrying.

Along High Street in the dark recesses of, and on the balcony above the Recreation building police armed with guns and wearing iron helmets hid in wait for any attempt of the pickets to storm the streets again. Word was sent out that any attempt to move across Highway 23 and into the village again would be met with machine gun fire. The pickets across the road continued to curse and yell and hurl stones down the street at the trucks and into the village.■

From *The Kohler Strike: Its Socio-Economic Causes and Effects* (master's thesis, University of Wisconsin, 1935).

Organizing Garment Workers

BY ROSE PESOTTA

Rose Pesotta, the dynamic young organizer from the International Ladies Garment Workers Union (ILGWU), offers this insightful account of her work with garment workers in Milwaukee. Note the creative tactics used by Pesotta, Martha Hart, and others in organizing. Pesotta's account also underscores the difficulty faced by union leaders as they tried to set up a new system of collective bargaining that went against the grain of tradition and employer rights.

SOMEWHERE in the Talmud there is an ancient Hebrew saying: *The soldiers fight, the kings are heroes.* It comes to mind as I review the rise of the International Ladies' Garment Workers' Union.

To write a truly comprehensive history of the ILGWU and get at the real source of our organization's phenomenal strength, the historian would have to visit many an odd corner of these United States in search of original data. Behind its growth in the face of political and economic vicissitudes there would be revealed a legion of men and women unheralded and unsung, rank-and-file people with natural ingenuity, strong working-class loyalty, readiness to sacrifice for an ideal, and all-around unselfishness.

The top leadership gets public recognition for the success of the International, but few outside the union know how much credit is due to members whose names rarely if ever see the light of print.

Martha Hart of Milwaukee was such a member . . . .

Early in 1934 some cotton dress workers in that city decided that they must organize the local shops in their industry for self-protection. They were working long hours, for less than a living wage. Martha, a girl with no knowledge of union technique, made the first contacts with potential members of the projected union. She began at the plant of the Rhea Manufacturing Company, one of the largest cotton dress houses in the Midwest, which normally employed from 1,000 to 1,200 women and girls.

To approach these workers was difficult because of their fear of being discharged. But Martha, who came of French

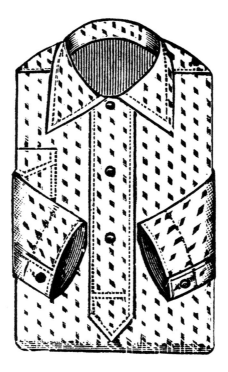

Style J.

Revolutionary stock, had determination and imagination.

A new brand of pudding advertised in the newspapers gave her a happy inspiration. She clipped out one of the ads, pasted it on a piece of cardboard, and bought a couple of packages of the pudding, bright-colored and eye-appealing. Walking into the Rhea factory at lunchtime, she spoke to an elderly woman who sat eating at one of the machines.

"I have a gift for you," Martha said. "I represent the Miracle Confection Company. To get new customers, we are giving away free samples of this new and delicious pudding. What flavor would you like? Strawberry, peach, pineapple, vanilla, chocolate, or what? Let me have your name and address and a package will be mailed to you."

Women and girls crowded around her. Before she left she had more than a hundred addresses. On succeeding days she got the rest, and repeated the trick at the other factories. Then a request to the ILGWU brought in a squad of organizers, headed by Abraham Plotkin, the International's general organizer in Chicago, and an intensive educational campaign was begun. One of our most competent men, Plotkin has a wholesome sense of humor and is eloquent both with his pen and on the platform.

Each of the workers was invited by letter to the union's first organizational meeting. When they caught sight of Martha Hart their faces first registered astonishment, then amusement.

"So this is our pudding?" one of them asked.

"Yes," Martha answered, "and the more you have of it the better you'll like it."

Under Plotkin's guidance, a new local, No. 188, was char-

Christmas party for children sponsored by the United Automobile Workers, CIO, Locals No. 95 and 121 and Auxiliary No. 8.

tered, and within a year it had more than 1,000 members, with Martha as secretary-treasurer.

As a labor organizer I have learned that one must be ready at all times to go any place, day or night, in bitter cold, snow, rain, or scorching sun. In the course of my work, I became geared to pick myself up at a moment's notice to take train or plane, or drive my car, to serve in an emergency, and invariably I got to the trouble scene on time.

More often than not, after speeding somewhere to save a bad situation, organizers are forgotten, while the local leadership reaps the laurels. But I have usually enjoyed pinch-hitting for fellow workers in the field, and felt that I was doing it for the welfare of the greater number involved.

In *Ecclesiastes* is the proverb: "Cast thy bread upon the waters: for thou shalt find it after many days." There is, however, another version which I seem to have known since early childhood: "Cast thy bread upon the waters, and after many days it will return to thee a hundredfold."

My father believed in that principle, gave of himself freely in service to friends and strangers alike, and found innate satis-

faction in the doing. Memory of his attitude toward humankind was a sustaining force for me in my years afield. And the proverb justified itself. Organization campaigns and strikes in one city or another took great toll of nervous energy, and frequently left me empty and shaken. Yet replenishment and reward came in appreciation shown by countless fellow-unionists, and in a host of enduring friendships across the land, and beyond its boundaries.

One of my emergency assignments was to Milwaukee. I was asked by our president to go there quickly soon after my return East from Seattle in the fall of 1935.

A sharp struggle involving the Rhea plant had taken place in the Wisconsin city in the previous September. After a twenty-four-day strike, Local 188 had won an agreement with that company, including most of the standard provisions and a seven-and-a-half percent wage increase. But the management had not thought it necessary to live up to this, and continued to violate several clauses. So our union submitted demands for an additional 10 per cent wage increase, and for arbitration of sixteen separate grievances, in line with the agreement.

With arbitration soon to begin, Salvatore Ninfo, jovial, gray-haired International vice-president, had suddenly become ill, and I was asked to take over in his place.

When I reached Milwaukee, Martha Hart and Kate Fadness, Rhea shop steward, took me to Ninfo's apartment. He was in bed with a three days' growth of beard, and looked haggard. I guessed correctly, however, that his illness was not physical; he simply was disheartened.

For weeks Ninfo had spent most of his time at the Rhea plant trying to adjust union complaints. The management's policy was to humiliate him at every turn. Repeatedly he was made to wait in the outer office, like a soliciting salesman, to demonstrate to the employees that a union representative was a nobody.

"It's important for you to shave," I told him. "I saw Abe Plotkin last night in Chicago, and he's coming to the meeting this afternoon. You'd better come, too . . . . I'll guarantee to bring you back alive."

A RADIO TALK BY JACOB F. FRIEDRICK

CONTRARY to the belief held by many people, the labor movement does not arise out of any preconceived planning or scheming of any individual or small group of individuals, and unions are not created by "labor agitators." Labor unions, like all other phases of social activities, grow out of the needs and desires of people. The basis for labor organization can be found in our system of industry and commerce in which we have employers and employees. That this is true, can readily be seen in the fact that labor unions are not confined to any locality or any nation, but that they have grown throughout the world in every place where modern civilization has created the employer and employee relationship.

The reason that labor unions are formed is because those who are employed on a wage or salary basis have certain common interests which they feel can best be protected and advanced by organization. This is true even though workers may have interests in common with employers and professional people along certain lines. The fact, however, remains that to a worker the interests centered around his job are his major interests.

In the years since 1934 many thousands of workers previously unorganized came into the organized labor movement in Milwaukee either by joining already existing unions or by organizing new unions. In the years of 1934 and 1935 particularly there was a heavy influx of new members. The vast majority of those who have come into our movement in these years were not sought out and contacted by union officials. Rather, when legislation under the N.I.R.A. and later the Wagner Act removed their fear of discrimination or discharge should they organize, they came to the union officials seeking organization. That is still going on and frequently workers come to our office and other union offices seeking to enter established unions or help in forming a new union.

—JACOB F. FRIEDRICK, 1940

By 6 P.M. Miller's Hall was packed with dressmakers. I studied their faces-the faces of hard-working people, German, Polish, Italian, French, and some of Scandinavian, Irish and English ancestry. They were unfailingly attentive and aware, I was sure, of events of social significance, the kind of folk one would expect to find in a city with a Socialist mayor and a long working-class tradition.

Under Mayor Daniel W. Hoan, Milwaukee's workers enjoyed the protection of the Bill of Rights. Police were prohibited from acting as strike breakers, the co-operative movement flourished, and municipal markets helped keep down living costs. But the administration lacked the power to make garment manufacturers pay adequate wages.

The meeting having been opened by the local president, a slim young girl with an olive complexion began reading the minutes. I was struck by the quality of her voice, a deep agreeable contralto. Where had I heard those tones before? I closed my eyes and searched my memory. The answer came like a flash across a movie screen: Eleanora Dusé! I had listened spellbound to the Italian dramatic actress at the time of her American tour in the early Twenties which ended abruptly with her death. The girl's voice sounded almost like hers; I must talk with her after the meeting.

While Plotkin was speaking Ninfo entered the hall, a salvo of applause greeting him. Touched almost to tears by this warm reception, he found it difficult to express his appreciation. The sympathetic attitude of the union membership made him well again.

The arbitration hearing was set for September 25, with Dr. Arthur Rubin of the University of Chicago as arbitrator. I had met him on the West Coast when he was there in the interests of the Cloak and Suit Code.

While Ninfo was busy preparing a brief of the union's case, we took steps to reinforce the Rhea workers. At my suggestion Mary Sortino, the girl whose voice so impressed me, was added to our office force. Mary and her sister Josephine were special machine operators in the Rhea plant. She was willing to take the job, but we had to reckon with her family. The mother, a deeply religious Italian, fearing something might happen to Mary if she stayed out late, objected vociferously. We gave her a solemn promise that only on meeting nights would she need to stay.

The educational department, directed by Modiree Compere, announced its fall program, including the publication of a monthly mimeographed periodical, *The Emancipator*, which was the special concern of Ninfo. We applied to the WPA Training School in Madison, of which Tom Tippett was head, for the services of teachers for ILGWU classes in both Milwaukee and Racine. The plea was granted and our educational work in both cities proceeded with vim.

On a visit to Racine, a city of 68,000, some thirty miles south of Milwaukee, I found that our rainwear local needed encouragement and stimulus. Its meetings were conducted in the manner of an old fashioned lodge, the members sitting silent around the walls, not participating. Called upon to speak, I asked them to come forward and occupy front seats.

"You're not wall flowers," I told them. "I know that, because I've heard a lot about the splendid courage and aggressiveness you displayed in your victorious strike against the Chicago Rubber Company."

I recalled the admiration and respect with which Morris Bialis told our GEB about the women in that strike, who lay down on a railroad track in front of a freight train at the factory gates and dared the union engineer to run over them.

The dramatic reminder pleased them and added warmth to the gathering. I had the audience join with me in the singing of some of our union songs and the evening ended pleasantly.

It was agreed that the recording secretary would supply material for *The Emancipator*, which would devote a full page to Racine news. We also arranged to have someone present at their meetings, to help them revitalize their local activities.

With the first issue of *The Emancipator* just off the mimeograph, still wet with ink, it was taken to the factories for distribution. Kate Fadness and I went to the Rhea plant at noon. Rashman, the company's production manager, asked Kate for a copy. She introduced me to him, and I asked whether he had time to talk with me.

He invited me into his office, but immediately went out again. After waiting ten minutes I left a note saying that I could be reached at our union office, and if he was interested, he could phone for an appointment. He needed that lesson, telephoned later, and then we talked at length. We, of course, could not settle the local grievances which were now in the hands of the arbitration board, but our conference smoothed out some differences.

Mr. Rashman explained that prior to this he had never been confronted with a labor problem. Marketing, styles, and production comprised his job. Evidently he realized that the union was there to stay, and was beginning to take cognizance of the fact that the labor problem also was an important factor in the production of cotton dresses, and I gently suggested that he pay a bit more attention to the well-being of his working force.

Departing, I said: "Mr. Rashman, I would advise you to take our union seriously. The President of the United States does."

When I visited the Rhea factory again, the newly appointed efficiency engineer explained to me the new "progressive system" to which the employees were being subjected. A battery of eight machines was given a task. Eight operators at those machines had to turn out at least twenty-five dozen garments per day - 300 cotton dresses! The price rates were based on the unit system, and figured out about 14 cents per worker per dozen, or a little more than a penny per garment.

The method was simple: A bundle of cut garments was given to a group of eight. One worker seamed together the shoulders, passing the material to the next, who made the collar; a third put in the sleeves—and so on until it reached the eighth operator. She finished the job, by blind-stitching the bottom of the garment, which then went to the presser, inspector, and shipping department. The speed of each worker had to be geared to the machine and to the next operation, which was regulated by the engineer's stop watch, and other gadgets, to make 3,400 to 4,000 revolutions per hour, which nettled the workers, keeping them at a constant high tension.

That system, the efficiency engineer explained to me, was in operation in about thirty plants, and had proved satisfactory to the managements. Human movements could be made to correspond with the operations of the machines, with no waste of machine capacity, so as to produce the exact amount of work required by the company.

"What about rest and relaxation?" I inquired.

"Oh yes, a worker is allowed 35 per cent of rest in each eight hours. Do you know what 35 per cent rest means?"

I confessed my ignorance, so he explained that it amounted to about two and a half hours' rest per day.

"Does that mean," I asked, with seeming ignorance, "that an operator has 15 minutes of rest every two hours, to walk through the factory and get a breath of fresh air?"

"No, no, not that," the expert hastened to explain. "Thirty-five per cent rest means, when a girl wants to stretch out during work hours near her machine, or relax when she gets tired—that is calculated as rest."

I was not satisfied with that system. As a machine operator myself, I contended it was better to work and take a rest when there was need for it. Moreover, as a human being, I refused to be geared to a machine like a robot; for the benefit of all concerned, I felt that the best way to make it easier for the workers to produce more was to determine the causes of industrial fatigue and eliminate them at the source, give the employees the kind of work they liked best, and pay adequately. This would give the worker an incentive to work with enthusiasm and produce more like a human being than a beast of burden.

After a two-day hearing the arbitration board made certain constructive recommendations for better relations between the union and the company. It also recommended to the company ways to eliminate any misunderstanding in the future by having a union representative present when timing for piece rates took place, and advised it to refrain from any attempts to form a company union.

At a final dinner in Ninfo's apartment we spoke about the manifold duties in which an out-of-town union representative becomes involved.

Ninfo, who had been manager of the Italian Cloak Local 48, and a vice-president of the ILGWU for many years, admitted to me that he never had such headaches as in Milwaukee, because in New York in most cases complaints were first handled by his business agents; when they failed, Ninfo himself would phone the firm, and if that, too, was unavailing the case went through the regular channels.

"What are the 'regular channels' in New York?" Martha Hart wanted to know.

The case would be referred to the general manager, who would invariably pass it on to the industry's impartial chairman.

But out of town he now learned one had to be all in one—business agent, general manager, organizer, lawyer, public relations director, family consultant, health adviser, with no limit to one's working hours or physical energies.

"In New York it is all so very simple," Ninfo sighed nostalgically. "Before I came here, when I used to read some of the reports in *Justice* telling about conditions the organizers found in the field I thought they were balmy. Now I know." ∎

From *Bread Upon the Waters*
(Cornell University Press, Ithaca, 1987).

Gerald Boileau and the Politics
of Unemployment

BY JAMES J. LORENCE

In the depth of the Depression, battered unions and unemployed worker groups like the Workers Alliance called for government action to establish a relief system and jobs program. They found a valuable ally in Gerald Boileau, Congressman from Wisconsin's Seventh District, a fiery orator who embraced the Alliance program and introduced it with vigor in the House of Representatives.

ONE of the crucial issues confronted by liberals in the wake of the Roosevelt landslide of 1936 was the problem of unemployment and relief. As leaders in the struggle for adequate federal relief expenditures, Wisconsin Progressives joined Minnesota Farmer-Laborites in pressuring the administration for a program that would provide the jobless with at least a minimum level of security against the ravages of depression. The central figure in the battle was Congressman Gerald J. Boileau of Wisconsin's sprawling Seventh Congressional District, by 1937 the militant floor leader for the Progressive-Farmer-Labor Group in the House of Representatives. Cooperating in the establishment of a united front on the relief issue, Boileau worked with both radicals and liberals to move Congress towards a major commitment to the dispossessed.

Any interpretation of the debate must not overlook the key role played in Wisconsin and elsewhere by the aggressive Workers Alliance of America, founded in 1935 under Socialist auspices as a "voluntary association of the unemployed" dedicated to "work for all at union wages." In Wisconsin, the organization was especially active in Milwaukee, Sheboygan, Superior, Racine, and Kenosha, all labor strongholds. While Alliance leadership was divided between Communists and Socialists, a merger with the Unemployment Councils in 1936 clearly strengthened the CP element. Because of WAA strength in Wisconsin, it was natural that the Progressive-Farmer-Labor coalition emerged at the forefront of efforts to aid the unemployed in 1937. As a result, increasingly pragmatic Communists embraced the Progressives and Farmer-Laborites as domestic allies in the Popular Front.[1]

Boileau was a willing partner in the new coalition. Joining WAA President David Lasser in January, 1973, at a mass meeting in Madison Square Garden, he dismissed Roosevelt's proposed appropriation for 1938 as inadequate. The Wisconsin firebrand argued that "so long as the government is slow in enacting social legislation, it is necessary to support the Workers Alliance program." Calling for a revamped economic order, Boileau warmly praised the Alliance for performing a "great public service" in dramatizing the plight of the jobless."[2]

When a Workers Alliance-trade union delegation pressed its case in Washington, it was the House liberal bloc, under Boileau's leadership, that provided a public forum by meeting with the body in the House Office Building. Responding to the demonstrators' demands after Roosevelt refused them an audience, Boileau gave assurances that the bloc was "solidly behind" the Alliance proposal for a $1,030,000,000 deficiency appropriation, but added that they "should put pressure on the Eastern Congressmen for increased relief for farmers." Moving to consolidate the new ties, Boileau collaborated with Lasser to testify on behalf of the Alliance proposal before the House Appropriations Committee. Endorsing the minimum wage and work-sharing, the Progresive floor leader argued that the government must be employer of last resort and insisted that it "has not yet assumed its full responsibility." When the Appropriations Committee rejected the Alliance program in favor of the administration's more modest proposal, he dismissed the committee plan as "totally inadequate" and promised that the liberals would "get the relief appropriation boosted to what we think it ought to be."[3]

Unsuccessful in committee, Boileau carried the Progressive Group's battle to the floor, where he attacked the relief bill as "entirely inadequate to meet the needs of the present conditions in the country." Endorsing the Workers Alliance program, the Progressive leader branded recent WPA payroll reductions as "unjustified" and existing wage levels as "cruelty." It was "wrong and inhuman" to remove workers from WPA employment" until we have found a place for them in our society."[4] Boileau was unsuccessful in an attempt to first amend the deficiency appropriation and then return the bill to committee.

The January struggle was merely a preview of the main event, which unfolded in March and April after Boileau's introduction of H.R. 5822, the comprehensive Public Works and Relief Standards Act, which called for a $3 billion relief appropriation for fiscal year 1938. No measure better revealed its sponsor's collaboration with the WAA and his shift to the left in 1937. The organization's executive secretary, Communist Party member Herbert Benjamin, reported that the bill was *written by the Alliance* and introduced on behalf of the unemployed by Congressman Boileau of Wisconsin, the leader of the Farmer-Labor-Progressive Bloc." Benjamin was exuberant over the Boileau Bill, which fully met WAA criteria for humane unemployment legislation; he welcomed the initiative as more than "a program for mere agitation," but rather as a plan "to rally for immediate action the millions of unemployed."[5]

Boileau's efforts did not go unnoticed. Administration spokesmen expressed confidence that the "budget busters" could be turned back, while in Wisconsin moderates and conservatives attacked the Boileau proposal, which the *Milwaukee Journal* viewed as an opportunity to "make a start of hauling expenditures down to budget limits, if the President wants to do it." Boileau's home town newspaper was even more blunt in attacking "Gerry Boileau's Three Millions" as an unwelcome addition to the "New Deal spending orgy." Counseling caution, the *Wausau Record-Herald* worried that "the time may come when there will not be anyone left off the government payroll to . . . keep all those Utopian ideas functioning."[6]

Of greater significance was the reaction on the left, where the Communist Party took an active interest in the relief fight. When Roosevelt announced his intention to ask for only $1.5 million, *The Daily Worker* featured Boileau's proposal in an article describing the campaign to resist reductions in relief appropriations. Boileau's prominence in this struggle later drew the attention of the F.B.I., which identified him as a "congressman in favor with the CP." Boileau understood that he was being linked with the Communists, but he proceeded with the effort because he felt the legislation was too important to drop due to the "fact that he might have the label 'communist' attached to him."[7]

Undaunted by allegations of Communist influence, Boileau proceeded to accept a key role in the controversial Wisconsin Peoples Conference on Labor and Social Legislation. This meeting, held April 3-4 at the State Capitol in Madison, resulted from the initiative of Assembly Speaker Paul Alfonsi and CIO Activist-Assemblyman Emil Costello and was endorsed by both the Wisconsin Workers Alliance and the State CIO. Supported by Communists working within the two organizations, the conference also had the active backing of respected figures on the non-communist left. Alfonsi later declared that if WAA goals were Communist, "then I must be a Communist." The moving force behind the call to conference was Harlan Fenske, State Chairman of the Workers Alliance; however, the meeting was legitimized by the sponsorship of legislators such as Alfonsi, Costello, and State Senator Walter Rush. Ostensibly intended to dramatize WAA legislative demands, the Peoples Conference became an embarrassment to the Wisconsin State Federation of Labor and a threat to its leadership of the Farmer-Labor Progressive Federation. Perceiving the work of CIO operatives and suspected Communists such as Costello and

Harold Christoffel, FLPF leader Henry Rutz quickly distanced himself from the meeting, described by Rutz as "another fast one" by the Communists. Supporting Rutz's charge, Mayor Dan Hoan wrote Socialist Party officials that both Costello and Communist State Organizer Gene Dennis "promoted this legislative conference."[8]

Although Rutz was accused of red-baiting because of his efforts to torpedo the conference, the Rutz-Hoan analysis of its ideological origins has considerable validity. Peggy Dennis later wrote that Gene "insisted that mass movements intensify . . . the consolidation of electoral victories" and therefore worked to bring about the Peoples Conference. Similarly, Party activist Sigmund Eisenscher recalled that the conference "originated in the recognized need of a vehicle that would develop and struggle for a comprehensive legislative program enveloping the multitude of unsolved problems within the New Deal." Eisenscher confirmed that the "foundation of the conference" was the "more progressive" element in the labor movement and that the meeting "was initiated with the help of the Wisconsin Communists."[9]

None of which made Boileau a Communist. Peggy Dennis noted that the CP did see WAA as an organization which could be a vehicle for making gains on the relief and unemployment issue; more important, however, was the fact that the Alliance membership contained people very likely to be attracted by the party's goals. Moreover, the CP worked with progressives of all parties who were willing to pursue common objectives. Eisenscher remembered Boileau as such a person, a Congressman who was "a steadfast progressive who worked with all elements of the progressive spectrum, including Communists." He regarded Boileau as an honest man motivated by a sense of "common decency and a social conscience," but not unaware of the fact that "there was a powerful movement to back him." On the latter point, Socialists concurred. Frank Zeidler, the youthful Secretary of the Milwaukee County Socialist Party Central Committee, thought of him as a willing cooperator, "closely involved with CP members and fronts at this time," who later managed to disentangle himself from his Communist connections. As soon as Rutz became aware of Boileau's deep involvement in the Peoples Conference, he wrote to inform the Congressman that FLPF had "ample proof" that the Communists engineered the conference "for the purpose of perfecting a united front with groups which usually excluded them."[10] He enclosed a copy of the FLPF letter warning its county units of the Communist move and denouncing the united front concept. Boileau was clearly conscious of the ideological company he kept in 1937.

Convinced that his position was sound and the cause just, Boileau ignored the FLPF Secretary and joined the united fronters for a love-fest in Madison on April 3. Exhilarated by top billing and an enthusiastic introduction as the leader of a forty-man liberal bloc, Boileau used the occasion to promote his unemployment proposal and to demand an end to both child labor and the forty-hour week. Encouraged by a receptive audience, he went on to shift responsibility for heightened labor militancy to a recalcitrant business community and dilatory tactics by the Supreme Court. Assailing the high court, Boileau

State Historical Society of Wisconsin WHi (X3) 14584

Distribution of rough fish to the poor at a relief station in Winnebago County, 1935.

accused the justices of staging their own "sit down" on the Wagner Act, which helped create the "conditions that aggravated labor to the point where they engage in sitdown strikes." In an unanticipated jab at both conference planners and FLPF boycotters, Boileau also decried disunity in the labor movement "because labor should be organized in such a way as to speak for all labor."[11]

Conservatives saw his call for a united labor movement as evidence that Boileau might be headed for a disagreement with AFL and CIO. One noted that an exhausted speaker, his shirt soaked with perspiration after an hour of oratory, was "further harassed" when "individual cranks" posed questions in the form of speeches; Boileau reportedly "sped back to his hotel" with "gasps of relief" to take the first train out of town. The stalwart *Wausau Record-Herald* cynically applauded "Mr. Boileau's Good Advice," which was to eschew state legislation on the thirty hour week for a more sensible national approach. The *Herald* added that he spoke "wisely in regretting the circumstances which have placed organized labor in two warring camps." While always a friend of labor, Boileau had stepped into a hornet's nest; accounts varied on the result. Some noted the pitfalls of his involvement, but a sympathetic audience responded with extended applause following an energetic and challenging address; later the body adopted a resolution com-

mending Boileau and Progressive Group Congressmen for their "active and persistent work on behalf of the program of the Farmer Labor Progressive Federation."[12]

The participants got what they wanted. The conference adopted a radical legislative program which exceeded the goals of FLPF. Communists were pleased with the outcome, which included the establishment of a legislative newsletter as "a guide to progressive legislation." Moreover, the meeting provided "a center around which progressives could rally that did not depend on being in the vest pocket of the La Follettes." Peggy Dennis later wrote that despite the official FLPF-AFL-Socialist boycott, over two hundred state organizations sent delegations and after sharp debate forged a "tenuous unity" around the legislative program, just as they appreciated Boileau's attack on the behavior of the Supreme Court. For his part, the Progressive Group leader secured a valued endorsement for several aspects of the liberal program, most significantly his own unemployment-relief proposal, which was before the House at the time.[13]

Given his close cooperation with WAA and willingness to form political liaisons without regard to ideology, Boileau's selection as featured speaker at the Alliance's national convention in Milwaukee was a foregone conclusion. Equally predictable was the warm welcome extended by his supporters, who regarded him as "the hero of America's jobless." At Milwaukee, Boileau "tore into reactionary senators and congressmen" with an exhortation to WAA to mobilize public opinion in favor of the unemployed. Contending that Roosevelt's reelection was a mandate to continue WPA at existing levels, Boileau demanded that those "who accumulate tremendous wealth" be forced to "pay for taxation . . . and pay the millions they have put out of work." Embracing unionism, he again urged workers to "encourage the consolidation of all American labor," since a united movement would "preserve democracy" and "raise the standards of the whole American people."[14]

Boileau's sharp class appeal drew a standing ovation from a cheering crowd whose spirits were ignited by their spokesman's fiery rhetoric. The Alliance's endorsement, though politically useful in the short run, created long-term image problems for a young politician on the make. And Boileau was not oblivious to the difficulties created by his shift to the left in 1937. In a frank letter written just before the Milwaukee convention, he told his brother not to "think I am a Communist or Socialist because of the gatherings I am addressing." Promising to address "Progressive philosophy," Boileau clearly articulated his personal legislative style, which was "advocating the liberal point of view" without rejecting support wherever coalitions could be built. He concluded simply that "as a consequence some of the organizations that are more to the left then we Progressives, are glad to support us as far as we go."[15] A tolerant approach helped cement political alliances and was consistent with advocacy of positions he believed just, but the long-term ramifications were potentially dangerous to his political future.

Accepting the challenge, Boileau assumed the offensive upon return to Washington. When he rose to defend his bill on April 29, he denied that the Alliance was a Communist organization and characterized Lasser as "a man of outstanding ability and courage." Turning to the legislation, he bitterly denounced the "laissez faire attitude we have adopted," arguing that failure to act was "encouraging Communism in this country." Boileau warned that Communism could "breed fast among people who look to their . . . Government" and find it "year after year becoming less sympathetic with their plight." The Boileau Bill provided relief to the needy and would demonstrate the House's "faith in democracy" by doing what was necessary in order to "preserve our democratic form of government."[16]

Relief measures, in Boileau's view, were necessary but not sufficient. The heart of the solution, he argued, lay in the regulation and reorganization of the national economy so that all would have the satisfaction and fruits of labor. He then advanced the Progressive Party concept of work-sharing through the elimination of child labor, the adoption of a mandatory thirty-hour week, and the institution of early retirement. Chiding the House for its unwillingness to endorse a sweeping solution, Boileau maintained that the only alternative was a humane relief program. If the body persisted in its failure to grapple with the underlying structural problem, the Progressive Group demanded that the House accept the relief method "in its entirety" and "meet the challenge by providing adequate incomes for those . . . unable to find employment."[17] The Boileau Bill, he asserted, was the solution.

The Alliance proceeded to mount a national campaign in support of the doomed effort, prompting expressions of support from disparate sources. The Minnesota Alliance endorsed Boileau's initiative while its Wisconsin counterpart rallied at the capital in Madison to underline solidarity with their brothers nationwide. Simultaneously, the Upper Wisconsin Alliance unit adopted a resolution which scored the "would be budget balancers" who sought to "deprive needy women, children, and willing working people" of even a "sub-standard living." Pressing the issue in Washington, the organization urged Roosevelt to endorse not only H.R. 5822 but also an immediate hike in WPA wages.

Finally, the national Alliance brought its "Women's Brigade" to Washington to make the case for the Boileau Bill. In a mass meeting in their honor, Boileau told the women's delegation that this visit marked the first time in his Congressional career that other House members had beaten a path to his office to assure him that they were solidly behind a bill he had introduced. When Boileau addressed the House as the women listened attentively, he denounced the "economy craze" which had infected so many House members. His voice rising with the intensity of his concentration, he appealed for humane action in the "best interests of the country," which required that the Congress "do something else before we balance the budget." In a rhetorical flourish, Boileau argued that if the Congress hoped to "preserve . . . American tradition, . . . and democracy," it was obligated to "make it possible for the lowliest citizen . . . to eke out an existence."[18] For the unemployed, he asserted, the depression was not over, and there was no democracy without opportunity.

Political pressure notwithstanding, time and circumstances worked against the proponents of heavy relief expenditures. WPA officals acknowledged the reality of unmet needs, but could only express a hope for job creation in the private sector. Worse yet, the administration's budget-cutting proposal encouraged Virginia conservative Clifton Woodrum to escalate the attack on WPA with a plan to slash an additional $500 million from the Relief Act. Although Boileau's $3 billion spending package failed, the liberal bloc was able to unite with administration supporters to defeat "reactionary" efforts to trim expenditures to $1 billion. While Progresives were disappointed with the result, most took comfort in their success in beating back the economy bloc initiative.[19]

For Boileau, however, the modest victory came at a price. Not only was his left-wing image solidified, but the entire struggle revealed a careless disregard for political reality that contributed to his eventual defeat in 1938. Boileau's activities on the labor front throughout 1937 marked him as more cooperative with CP organizations than any other member of the Wisconsin Progressive delegation on the eve of an election year. Staunch support of the Workers Alliance and the unemployed had produced minimal gains in Washington; for Boileau the result in Wisconsin was disaster at the polls, when he went down to defeat in the liberal electoral debacle of 1938. Class politics provided an insufficient base for a solid political movement as Wisconsin voters moved towards conservatism in the wake of the upheaval experienced when workers claimed their organizational rights.■

From *The Workers Alliance and the Unemployed: Progressivism and the Wisconsin Left* (University of Missouri, Columbia, 1994).

The United Auto Workers at Nash Motors in Kenosha

BY JOHN DREW

*Attempts to organize the large Nash automobile works in Kenosha
began in 1929, but only in 1933 did the union really get off the ground.
John Drew describes these events, shedding light on the work done by
Felix Olkives and showing how the local union, which started as a federal
labor union, played a part in the founding of the AFL-affiliated United
Auto Workers in 1935. He also notes the union's involvement in educational
and recreational activities in the Kenosha community.*

I N 1916 a rising young automobile executive named Charles Nash bought the T.B. Jeffery Company of Kenosha, Wisconsin. For the $15 million purchase price, Nash acquired the Jeffery plant with about 1,000 workers on the payroll and the facilities to produce 4 wheel drive trucks and automobiles.

The work force that Nash inherited was made up mostly of southern and eastern European immigrants who spoke as many as twenty-one different languages. Nash was an ambitious man who expanded his business quickly in the 1920's. By 1928 the Kenosha plant was turning out 138,000 cars a year and Nash was raking in profits. But in 1929 the Great Depression began and production at Kenosha dropped dramatically to less than 15,000 cars for the entire year. Thousands of Nash workers were laid off while those still working rarely got a full week in. It was in this desperate setting that Nash workers began to organize their union.

In fact, the conditions in the plant were such that the workers had little choice but to organize. The foreman held absolute power over each worker's job, having full authority to hire and fire. Seniority counted for nothing within the Nash plant, or in any other auto plant for that matter. If the foreman did not like you or was upset with your work, he could fire you on the spot for any reason or no reason at all. Once fired there was no union to file a grievance with, no seniority restoration committee to go before, no one who would even listen to your complaint. There was nowhere for the worker to turn for justice.

By the time a worker reached forty years of age he was often burned out by the pace of the work in the plant. After a model change older workers were simply not called back while the younger and quicker men were kept on. During those Depression years there was no shortage of young men desperate for a job. In fact, every day crowds of jobless workers would congregate outside of Nash's and other auto plants looking for work.

In order to keep their jobs many Nash workers had to resort to bribing the all-powerful foreman. It was quite common for workers to bring their foremen gifts such as baskets of fruit and vegetables or perhaps a bottle of bootleg whiskey during Prohibition.

For those able to keep their jobs the deck was totally stacked in favor of the company. Wages averaged from 40¢ to 48¢ an hour and could be as low as 35¢ an hour in the early 1930's. Wages on the assembly line were based on a group piecework system that only paid for cars that went past your work station. There was no pay for down time caused by any reason. There was also no such thing as paid vacation, paid holidays, health insurance or pensions.

In peak periods, such as just after model change, the work day was nine hours a day with a half-day on Saturday. There was no such thing as time and one-half after eight hours and it was not uncommon for a man to work eighteen hours a day at straight time. Of course overtime was not distributed equally. The foreman gave the overtime to his favorites and others got none at all.

In slack periods the work week could be cut to as little as eighteen hours. In those days there was no SUB or call-in pay, nor was there any unemployment compensation. The W-2 form of Lawrence Michel of Department 833, Final Assembly, showed total earnings of $282.31 for the year 1932.

In the Nash plant there were no sweepers to clean up. The production workers were supposed to get out their day's work and sweep up before they went home. Not only was there no paid up wash-up period at the end of the day, there was also nowhere to wash up. Old paint buckets filled with water were used by the workers to clean up.

The workers at Nash had no right to transfer to another department and there was no upgrade or job bidding proce-

**Machine operators at the Nash Motors shop
in Kenosha, circa 1918.**

dure. The foreman decided what job to put the worker on and if the employee was too old or slow for the job, the street was the next stop. It was this total lack of control over their jobs and their lives that drove workers at Nash to organize a union. To those pioneers who began to band together, the union was the only way they could obtain fair treatment and a living wage.

Early Organizing Attempts

As early as 1920 Nash workers attempted to act together to improve their lot. In that year trimmers in the body finishing department walked off their jobs demanding a 10% raise. When the assembly line stopped, a red light bulb lit up Charley Nash's office. He personally came out to the finishing department and responded to the workers' demands by telling the men that they were on piecework and the only way they would get a 10% raise was to work 10% harder. Again in the summer of 1928, just after model change, workers in the rubbing department walked out in protest four times in three weeks.

The first serious attempt to organize the workers at Nash

into a union started in 1929. Felix Olkives, the president of the Kenosha Trades and Labor Council, started a drive amongst Nash workers to sign up with the American Federation of Labor. According to a story on the drive in the *Kenosha Labor*:

> Progress was slow due to the need for secrecy. Felix went house to house talking to workers. He held small meetings. Key men were selected in each department to feel out the workers and to secure names and addresses of others to be contacted.

At the time of the stock market crash in the fall of 1929 Olkives had signed up about 100 workers with many of them paying all or part of the $2.00 initiation fee. After the market crashed the union drive died out as many of those interested in the union were laid off as production at Nash came almost to a standstill. Olkives refunded the initiation fees to the laid-off workers who needed every cent to make ends meet.

1933—The Birth of a Nation

In 1933 another drive began to organize the workers at Nash. This time the drive met with great enthusiasm amongst the workers at Nash, especially in the foundry and on the final assembly line. The drive started soon after the National Recovery Act was passed as part of Franklin Roosevelt's New

Deal legislation. Roosevelt's program was designed to bring America out of the Depression. Section 7(a) of the NRA gave labor the right to "organize and bargain collectively through representatives of their own choosing." Charles Nash denounced the New Deal as socialistic and un-American.

It was in this setting that Felix Olkives and his fellow unionists on the Kenosha Trades and Labor Council once again targeted the 3,000 workers at Nash for unionization in the summer of 1933. The summer and early fall of 1933 was an exciting time for workers in Kenosha. Felix Olkives and others gave soapbox speeches to workers at shift change and handed out leaflets and union authorization cards to those who crowded around to listen. Harold "Red" Newton, a former editor of the *Kenosha Labor* describes those organizing efforts this way:

> I recall vividly the union ferment in Kenosha in 1933 and 1934 and the hectic days that ensued. All of us officers of the Trades Council were on an exciting merry- go-round shuttling from the Nash plant to the Simmons plant, to the American Brass, to Vincent McCall, Frost, Specialty Brass, Snap-on Tools . . . .

As part of the drive a big labor march up 60th Street calling for unionization was attended by workers from many plants in Kenosha, including a contingent from Nash.

The union drive found tremendous support within the Nash plant. Workers in the foundry and in final assembly, along with those in other areas of the plant, signed union cards and began to pay their initiation fees. By September of 1933 enough workers had signed up with the union that the American Federation of Labor issued a charter to the Nash group which then became known as AFL-Federal Labor Union 19008. Temporary officers were appointed to head the new union with Eugene Stauder chosen the first president and Lawrence Michel appointed as vice-president.

Membership in the new union increased gradually until November of 1933 when two events started a chain reaction that led to the unionization of the entire Nash plant. Charles Nash and the rest of management were bitterly opposed to the union movement within the plant. Nash called union organizers such as Felix Olkives "communistic" and said he would never recognize a union in his plant. In an attempt to hold off the growing support for Local 19008, Nash management proceeded to set up a company union on November 7, 1933. GM, Ford, and Chrysler all had company unions at that time as the corporations tried to circumvent Section 7(a) of the NRA which gave workers the right to organize. The Nash company union or "department representation plan" as it was called, was to include both hourly and salaried workers in its ranks. Local 19008 publicly attacked the company union concept and there was little enthusiasm for it amongst the hourly work force.

Nash Workers Sitdown

At the same time that Nash was trying to organize the company union, management attempted to institute a new group piecework system in Department 833, Final Assembly. The average wage in 833 was about 35¢ an hour at that time. After a one-day trial of the new piecework system, workers found it no better than the old system. The following day, November 9, 1933, the 100 or so workers in 833 sat down in protest. This was one of

State Historical Society of Wisconsin

Homer Martin, president of the United Automobile Workers of America, addresses a Janesville labor rally in 1937.

the first, if not the first, use of the sitdown strike in the auto industry. It would be almost four years later that the sitdown would be used by workers at General Motors to gain union recognition.

The sitdown strike in Final Assembly brought Charles Nash himself out to the department. Nash promised the workers he would look at adjusting their rates if they would give the new system a longer trial period. The workers refused to give in to Nash and he responded by locking out all 3,000 workers at the plant.

When the sitdown strikers left the plant that afternoon, they were met in the parking lot by hundreds of Nash workers from other departments who had heard about the sitdown. Felix Olkives called a mass meeting of all Nash workers for that night. Over 1,500 jammed the Italian American hall to hear reports from the strike leaders and to sign membership cards in Local 19008. According to Paul Russo, a leader of the sitdown strikers, that day, November 9, 1933 was "the birth of Wisconsin's largest labor union, Local 72."

The members of the union elected a committee of three workers from the Final Assembly department to deal with management. The three elected in that first vote ever held were Paul Russo, George Nordstrom, and W.G. "Bill" Kult. The committee demanded that Nash recognize the union and grant a wage increase.

On the second day of the strike the very active pickets turned away two train carloads of sand destined for the foundry. According to the *Milwaukee Journal* of November 11, 1933:

> The trainmen, being union members, held the cars outside the factory gates for an hour at the request of the pickets and then returned them to the Northwestern yards.

After the plant was shut down for a week Charles Nash finally agreed to meet with the committee. Nash chose a plant storage room as the site for the first meeting between elected representatives of the workers and management. No chairs were provided for the committee so they presented their demands to Nash standing up. Nash responded to their demands by dangling the keys to the plant in front of them and threatening to close the plant and "throw the keys in Lake Michigan" before he would recognize a union.

But one week later, after the Chicago office of the Regional Labor Board had gotten involved, Nash relented and came to an agreement. He verbally agreed to recognize collective bargaining, bargain with the committee elected by the workers, and to not discriminate against any of the strikers. When the plant reopened, Local 19008 was much stronger than ever and the company union was never heard from again.

In the following months Local 19008 got down to the business of functioning as a union. Felix Olkives provided much assistance in setting up the new union. Members of Local 19008 who had been members of other unions in coal mining and railroading before coming to Nash were also a great help in getting the union started.

Elections of officers were held quickly, with Eugene Stauder becoming the first elected president on December 30, 1933. Less than one month later he resigned and John Milkent was elected president without opposition. Milkent was to hold that post for five consecutive terms until 1939.

As of January 1, 1934, the Local had a paid-up membership of 970 with about the same number partially paid up. There was, of course, no dues checkoff so it was up to the officers of the new union to collect the dues from the members. Local 19008 also began to set up other operating procedures, such as the requirement that all grievances submitted to the bargaining committee be in writing.

First Union-built Car in America

During this period the union tried to negotiate a fair seniority system with Nash, but the company still refused to honor plantwide seniority. In February of 1934, the workers at the Seaman Body plant in Milwaukee, which shipped bodies to Kenosha and also those at the Nash plant in Racine went on strike for increased wages and a seniority system. On March 1, 1934, the Kenosha local, with 1,866 paid-up members, joined the other two locals on strike.

In a show of solidarity the three locals agreed to remain on strike until an agreement acceptable to all three was reached. On March 9, the Grand Executive Council made up of repre-

sentatives from the three locals presented six demands to Nash management. The demands included a call for Nash and Seaman to recognize a plantwide bargaining committee in each plant, adhere to seniority in layoff and recall, and to increase wages.

For seven weeks the strikers held out for their demands. In Kenosha, local merchants, who were themselves just getting by in that Depression year, donated fuel and food to the strikers.

Once again the Regional Labor Board entered into the negotiations between the unions and Nash. Finally an agreement was reached and all three locals ratified it. The final settlement as proposed by the Regional Labor Board and approved by all parties was a great victory for the unions. Nash agreed to collective bargaining, the principle of seniority in layoff and recall and wages were raised. The agreement was formalized on April 11, 1934, when Nash president E.H. McCarty signed a one paragraph statement summarizing the settlement. That single paragraph represents the first written contract for auto workers in the Kenosha plant. Local 19008 members celebrated their victory with a huge party at the Eagles ballroom.

In June of 1934 the three locals at Kenosha, Racine, and Milwaukee could claim with justifiable pride that the 1934 Nash Lafayette was the first automobile built entirely with union labor in the United States.

After the successful 1934 strike the union became ever more powerful in the shop. President John Milkent reported that by the end of April, 1934, nearly 100% of the workers had joined Local 19008. The elected bargaining committee met each Monday with management to take up the workers' complaints. The union also created a post known as the Director of Employment. During periods of layoff and recall one of the Board Members would be appointed to that position. His job was to make sure that seniority was followed and no new men were hired while those with seniority were laid off.

Kenosha Local Calls for a National Union

Not only was the young Kenosha local active in the shop, but it was also a strong force in the efforts to form a national auto workers union. Workers at Nash knew from their own experience that industrial type unions covering all the workers in a plant were more effective than separate unions made up of many different crafts. For this reason they were very much in favor of a national auto workers' union made up of industrial unions like Local 19008. The leaders and members of the Kenosha local realized that there was only so much that could be obtained from Nash in wages and working conditions while the rest of the auto industry, including the giants like GM and Ford, were not organized.

Pursuing their goal of an auto workers union, representatives of Local 19008 went to Detroit in June of 1934 to participate in the first nationwide Auto Council. The meeting was made up of representatives of AFL Federal Labor Unions like Local 19008. Attending besides the Kenosha delegates were only six other locals: Milwaukee-Seaman, Racine-Nash, and one local each from Studebaker, Packard, Hudson and Willis-Overland of Toledo. These "independents," as they were called, were sharply critical of the AFL leadership for their inac-

The Nash Motors assembly line, 1935, Kenosha.

tivity in organizing the auto industry and they called on the AFL Executive Council to form a national auto workers' union.

UAW Formed

Again in 1935 Local 19008 sent delegates to Detroit, this time for the first national convention of auto workers called by the AFL. The twenty-one delegates from Kenosha joined representatives of sixty-five other local unions at the convention. Finally, at this convention, the AFL granted a charter for the new United Autoworkers Union. Delegates from Kenosha helped lead the fight on the convention floor for an elected leadership for the new union. Local 19008 submitted a farsighted eleven-point resolution to the Convention that called for a union that organized all workers in the auto industry "regardless of kind of work, race, creed or color." The Local 19008 resolution also asked that:

> . . . all officers be elected from actual workers in the industry by the delegates at the Convention, salaries to be comparable with auto workers' wages, but not to exceed $2,500 per year.

AFL president William Green ignored the desires of the majority of the delegates who agreed with Local 19008's posi-

tion on elected officers and he appointed the president and top officers of the new organization.

Disappointed in the AFL leadership as they were, Local 19008 leaders realized that the convention was a huge step forward for auto workers. Shortly after the convention, on November 8, 1935, Federal Labor Union 19008 was rechartered as AFL-UAW Local 72.

In the following year, 1936, Local 72 sent twenty-two delegates to South Bend, Indiana, for the second UAW Convention. It was at this convention that the AFL ended the probationary status of the UAW and delegates were allowed to elect their own officers with Homer Martin becoming the first president of the UAW.

Help for the Unemployed

The 1930's were difficult years for Local 72 members, even with their newly won union protection. Jack Beni, who was later to become a Local 72 president, recalled that he usually worked only three or four months per year and was laid off the rest of the time. The winter of 1937-38 was an especially rough one, with Nash running the plant on only an eighteen-hour week. At a membership meeting in February of 1938 it was pointed out that working an eighteen-hour week paid less than the weekly

A solid-cast iron runner manufactured at Allis-Chalmers for the Alabama Power Company's Mitchell Dam Project.

State Historical Society of Wisconsin WHi (X3) 49605

unemployment compensation rate. That winter Local 72 set up an Unemployment Committee that counseled unemployed members on "how to get prompt attention when applying for relief or unemployment compensation." The Unemployment Committee also worked with other unions in the city in trying to provide for adequate relief and other aid for the unemployed.

Local 72, a Center for Membership

During the difficult years of the 30's Local 72 began to establish itself as a center for the membership, both on and off their jobs at the Nash plant. The Friday night membership meetings held twice a month at the Moose Hall and later the Italian-American Hall or Union Club regularly drew 1,000 to 1,200 out of a membership of 3,000.

In 1936 Local 72 formed a baseball team to play other industrial teams such as Simmons and the Ke-Nash-a Club 9. The Local 72 team was consistently one of the top teams in the area and members flocked to the Nash Stadium which was located where Building 40 now sits, to see their team play. Local 72 also established a bowling team and began to hold the popular union picnics in the summer and the children's Christmas parties in the winter.

Local 72 members marched as a group in the big Labor Day parades in Kenosha. In 1938 the membership voted a $1.00 fine for anyone not marching in the parade. The *Kenosha Labor* reported that Local 72 members marched "7 abreast in a line stretching 1/2 mile long" in the 1938 parade.

The Local also put a strong emphasis on education holding frequent classes on such topics as effective speaking and parliamentary procedure. In 1937 the membership voted to send the first students to the University of Wisconsin-School for Workers summer school in Madison.

Solidarity Local 72 Style

In its early years Local 72 established its reputation for generosity and union solidarity that lives to this day. The recent Local 72 contributions to the MacWhyte strikers was just the latest example of this tradition which started almost as soon as the union was formed.

In a membership meeting at the Moose Hall on May 25, 1934, just a few weeks after coming off their own seven week strike, the membership approved a donation to the sitdown strikers at the Autolite plant in Toledo. In July of 1936 Local 72 members raised $2,200 to aid the UAW's national organizing campaign that had targeted GM. Within a period of a few months in early 1937 Local 72 donated $1,000 to strikers at J. I. Case in Racine and another $1,164 to the popular "dime store girls" who were striking Kenosha's 5¢ and 10¢ stores for union recognition. In May of 1938 the International Executive Board of the UAW presented a plaque to Local 72 to honor the 100% participation of the membership in a fund drive to assist the organizing drive at Ford.

Local 72 members knew that they could only advance so far in wages and working conditions while the rest of the auto industry was non-union. It was not uncommon for Nash management to respond to Local 72 demands by pointing out that Nash, with only 29% of the auto market, could not afford to raise wages or benefits while the industry giants, Ford and GM, did not even have unions. So it was welcome news to Local 72 members when the Kenosha Labor announced on February 12, 1937 that General Motors had agreed to recognize the UAW after a forty-four-day sitdown strike at Flint, Michigan.■

From *UAW Local 72: The First 50 Years* (UAW Local 72, 1985).

Student Summary (all assignments) for 'Quarter 2', 12/2/03   Page 1
Instructor: Anderson   File Name: Calculus Sem1 Hr10.cls
2nd Quarter progress report

Name: Kathryn Adams **ID:** 44673 **Grade:** A- (80.5%) **Class Rank:** 15

	Score	Grade	Date
Total Points (100%, 133)		**80.5% A-**	
Slope Fields Packet (3.8%, 5)	5.00	100.0% A+	11/10/03
Spot Check #1 (3.8%, 5)	5.00	100.0% A+	11/12/03
Related Rate Quiz (7.5%, 10)	5.00	50.0% D-	11/13/03
Spot Check #2 (3.8%, 5)	5.00	100.0% A+	11/18/03
Test 2.5 & 2.6 (47.4%, 63)	46.00	73.0% B	11/19/03
Quarter 2 Project (26.3%, 35)	32.00	91.4% A	11/25/03
Spot Check #3 (3.8%, 5)	5.00	100.0% A+	12/2/03
CQ#9 (3.8%, 5)	4.00	80.0% A-	12/2/03

THE FOUNDING OF AFSCME

The American Federation of State, County and Municipal Employees, one of the largest unions in the United States, was born in Madison in the 1930s

IN the depths of the Depression, on October 16, 1936, the American Federation of Labor chartered a new international union to represent and organize state and local government workers. The union was named the American Federation of State, County, and Municipal Employees, AFL.

The fledgling union got its start in Madison, Wisconsin, just four years earlier. At that time State Federation of Labor Pres. Henry Ohl, Jr. and state personnel director Col. A. E. Garey feared that a Democratic victory in 1932 might bring efforts to weaken Wisconsin's civil service system, the third oldest in the nation.

After Governor Phil La Follette gave his blessing, Garey began signing up members. His first recruit was state personnel examiner Arnold S. Zander. Thus was born the Wisconsin Administrative, Clerical, Fiscal and Technical Employees Association. Its organizational meeting began at 4:10 P.M. on May 10, 1932. Zander was elected financial secretary. Later that month, the AFL chartered the Wisconsin union as Federal Labor Union 18213. After the International union was formed, the union became the Wisconsin State Employees Association, AFSCME Local 1.

On January 17, 1933, with just fifty members of a 1,700 potential, the new union faced the crisis its founders had feared. The Democrats had swept into power on FDR's coattails, and they indeed did plan to scrap civil service so they could offer jobs to Depression-poor party faithful. The Wisconsin union organized, lobbied, and scrapped. And it won—convincing the new administration that state civil service should continue. By June that year, the union's membership had risen to 700—an accomplishment that attracted the AFL's attention.

Zander began seeing the potential for a national union representing workers at the state and local government level. Already there were AFL affiliates representing federal workers—the American Federation of Government Employees, the National Association of Letter Carriers, and the Post Office Clerks—but no national affiliate represented state and municipal workers. Zander took on the job of convincing the AFL of the need for this new union. Over the next three years, he developed contacts with other AFL-affiliated local unions representing state and local workers. He lobbied and cajoled and prodded until the AFL recognized the need for a new national union.

On September 17, 1936, delegates representing ninety local unions in nineteen states met at Detroit's Book-Cadillac Hotel. Their dream realized, they formed AFSCME, and they elected Zander president. Pennsylvanian

State Historical Society of Wisconsin WHi (N48) 123

Wisconsin personnel director Col. A.E. Garey (left) recruited Arnold Zander (right) to form the American Federation of State, County and Municipal Employees.

David Kanes was chosen secretary-treasurer. The delegates adopted a constitution that included in its preamble the words—advanced for their time—"barring none, without regard to race, color, or creed." Then they returned home to implement the new union's organizational priority—to grow.

It is doubtful that any of them imagined that fifty years later theirs would be the largest affiliate of the AFL-CIO.

Arnold Zander was born in Two Rivers, Wisconsin, on November 11, 1901. His father was an active socialist—naming his second son Eugene after hearing Eugene Victor Debs speak—and young Zander grew up with an appreciation of social issues. Although the Zander family was always in tight financial straits, the children were encouraged to pursue education. Arnold and Eugene took turns working and supporting each other at the University of Wisconsin.

Arnold studied city planning. He had almost finished his Ph.D. when he was offered the position of senior personnel examiner for the state. It was Depression time—and a good job—so Zander began working for the state while he finished work on his degree.

He and his wife Lola joined the Capital Club—a social club for state workers. He tried to focus some club activities on job-related issues. It was just at this time that Zander's supervisor, mentor, and life-long friend Col. A. E. Garey talked with him about forming a state workers' union. Zander was hooked; he was the first to sign up.

Four years later that local union served as the launching pad for the American Federation of State, County, and Municipal Employees, AFL—with Zander as its president.

For thirty-two years, Zander devoted his energy to organizing public employees—"public servants" they were called when he started. He led the union from "collective begging" to collective bargaining, from a membership of 9,700 in 1936 to a quarter of a million in 1964.

From AFSCME, *Public Employee*, v.51 no.5 (1986).

A lone picket walks the line during the strike against the J.I. Case Company of Racine in 1936 and 1937.

Organizing the Unemployed:
Case Strike of 1936

BY JOSEPH M. KELLY

*The union at the large J.I. Case plant in Racine was rebuilt in the
aftermath of a strike that began in 1935. Joseph Kelly reveals the important
role played by local leaders in pulling the different labor factions together.
The Case experience also shows the growing importance of government
intervention to resolve labor disputes, with sometimes dubious results.*

THE immediate occasion of the strike was the accidental
death of a nineteen-year-old worker who was crushed
between a loading truck and a tractor driven by a man
employed less than one month. The union stressed that both
the young man and the tractor driver had replaced more experienced workers for less money and that the incident demonstrated the necessity for seniority. On March 13, workers began a sit-
down strike which lasted for three days—until the sheriff
requested that the strikers leave, which they did, marching four
abreast out of the plant behind an American flag. This time, in
addition to receiving informal support from railwaymen and
truck drivers, the strikers received formal support from engineering employees, who had generally been uncooperative in
the previous strike in 1933. Other Racine strikes were often
mediated by outside arbitrators, but the Case Company had
consistently been cool to any such mediation, and this attitude
had prevented municipal officials and Fr. O'Boyle from arbitrating the Case dispute. Only reluctantly did the company allow
Harry Schecke, considered by labor to be one of the most conservative U.S. Department of Labor conciliators, to sit in on
labor-management discussions.[1]

During the strike a pattern emerged which recurred during
every Case strike through 1960. Basically, the union claimed an
informal agreement with the company to allow foremen and
office workers to pass the picket lines as long as they did no
production work or any work outside their fields, such as loading railway cars. When the union became convinced that the
company had broken the agreement it refused to allow railway
cars to leave the plant or foremen to enter. Once the Case management heard of this it became intransigent and refused to discuss anything until "law and order," including the freedom to
cross a picket line, were established.

In order to bring about law and order in the 1935 strike,
pro-company employees sought and won an injunction to prevent the union from interfering with strikebreakers. Tension

increased with the arrest of several picketers for assault when
they tried to stop foremen and engineers whom the union
claimed were walking closely behind a female strikebreaker in
order to pass the picketers. Strikers had also refused for forty-
eight hours to allow several foremen to leave the plant.[2]

Before the union could be penalized for contempt in ignoring the injunction, the Assistant Secretary of Labor was able to
effect a settlement based primarily on the company's proposal
of May 29. This offer stated that the company would bargain
"individually or collectively" with employees and would treat
"impartially" the representatives of the WIU or any other "duly
authorized [employee] representatives." The proposal emphasized that "there is only one Seniority rule, so-called, which will
work well in practice, and that is granting each man a square
deal." The union at first rejected the offer overwhelmingly but
later approved it, reportedly by a very close vote, upon the federal mediator's insistence that continuation of the strike could
result in more violent action by the foreman, "possibly backed
up by vigilante bands."[3]

One result of the strike was the emasculation of the WIU.
During the strike the company encouraged the creation of a
company union (the Independent Employees Council), whose
members they supposedly assured of preferential treatment in
case of layoffs and whose controlling board consisted of three
employees and three company representatives. The plant superintendent decided any tie. The company union played upon a
suspicion of immigrants and asked all potential members to
declare whether they were citizens. The company union president later illustrated this nativism in his attack on the national
leaders of the automobile workers union. He claimed they were
responsible for the labor turmoil at Case since they controlled
"scabs" (i.e., the new independent Local 180 members) who
had to "pay tribute [for their jobs] to a lot of Russian kikes."[4]

Had it not attempted to dominate the company union so
completely and had it not laid off so many members of that

**Police and strikebreakers clash with striking workers
at the J.I. Case plant, May, 1935.**

union in the massive layoffs of July, 1936, Case might have prevented the establishment of a viable independent union. At any rate, through the persistence of "Jap" Michel, one of the original UAW organizers, by September the machinists union at Case and the remnants of the WIU merged with the AFL-affiliated automobile workers union to form United Auto Workers Local 180. The local claimed 1,400 paid members, showed increasing strength, and asked the company to negotiate. Suddenly, starting in late September, the company laid off seventy-nine Local 180 employees, including all the union leaders. As a leading management expert explained:

> It can be seen that the company was then making every possible move to dislodge the union [Local 180] and was using every conceivable technicality and means to drive the union from the plant.

They refused to discuss grievances and fired most of the active union employees—then turned around and told them they could not discuss the matter.

The union leaders then met and certain members volunteered to take over the machines of the seventy-nine who were laid off. They did so and were immediately fired. The pattern continued until by mid-October the company had fired between seven hundred and eight hundred employees, and the Racine police had "escorted out" those who "sat down" and refused to leave.[5]

On October 23, Local 180 began a five-month strike. Union members carried out one non-striking worker bodily, and this time there were picketers at all plant entrances. Members of the company union, estimated at between one hundred and three hundred, began to run newspaper ads praising the company and claiming they had requested that the original seventy-nine be discharged because they "intimidated" employees. When Local 180 concluded that the company union was

utilizing Case offices for this type of propaganda, the local refused permission on November 12 for office workers to cross the picket lines. Consequently, the company moved all employee records to the home of the company union president.[6]

Relief payments at that time were granted by the County Board chairman during a strike only if he approved of the way the strike was conducted. The Board chairman felt that otherwise it would be unfair to the taxpayer, in effect, to assist the automobile workers in maintaining strikes. Furthermore, welfare workers told each striker that if he wanted relief, he must supply a statement of earnings from the company, which in turn told him that the records were at the company union president's house. Once there, the striker was strongly encouraged to join the company union; Local 180 even photocopied a note, signed by the company union president, stating that the recipient had been investigated and found "worthy of relief."[7]

As a result some members went to the company union

president's house and "forgot" to let go of his screen door or gate and were subsequently arrested. Other union members, acting on their own, picketed the house, but Local 180 disavowed their tactics.[8]

By winter Local 180's reserves had been depleted, and, of course, strikers received no union benefits from a national union organization as they do today. Union members depended on charity of groups, such as union barbers for haircuts. Their leaders had to buy cheap beans from farmers, and bone marrow from butchers—who often gratuitously threw in some meat-and would throw everything into a fifty-gallon tank for soup. When the company announced a seventy-dollar Christmas bonus to all who returned to work, the strike leaders concluded they would have to provide something as an alternative to the company offer. In desperation, Frank Sahorske, the real leader of Local 180 during the strike, asked Grocer Joe Dominick for chickens and other food for a Christmas celebration and told

A strikers' hut, pictured above, slapped together from scraps in the 1936–1937 strike against the J.I. Case Company of Racine.

State Historical Society of Wisconsin WHi (X3) 25219

him that the union would be able to pay him only if the strike proved successful. After reflection, the merchant agreed to pay the entire cost, and the union informed a jubilant membership that there would be Christmas baskets.

Next to William Sommers, Sahorske was probably the most important person in Racine unionism. He was born in Milwaukee and worked as a case maker in the Case foundry; early in his life he became completely dedicated to the industrial union movement. Sahorske was motivated by what he saw as terrible working conditions in industry and a complete lack of dignity for workers. If he was influenced by any ideology, it was that presented in the encyclicals of Pope Leo XIII and not by socialist or radical literature. As president of the WIU at Case, he more than anyone had supported the UAW as the only viable alternative for Case workers. Once the Case strike was over, Sahorske was discharged from the company on a technicality; he then joined the UAW national staff.[9]

By early 1937 the company was eager to settle the strike before the usual spring rush of orders. L.R. Clausen, Case president, demanded, however, that the picketers be removed from his office so he could negotiate from there. By the middle of February an agreement was reached whereby the company allowed the seventy-nine to return to work and recognized Local 180 as the only collective bargaining agency. Clausen required, however, that Local 180 representatives sign a letter,

dated February 6, 1937, which probably was responsible for more mischief than any other document in Racine labor history. Clausen insisted that the letter, drafted by a company attorney, was necessary in order to preserve the safety of members of the company union, and the government mediator supposedly assured the union representative that the signed letter would not be detrimental to their future position.

The controversial parts of the letter granted "full recognition of the unquestioned right of any employee to either join a union or similar association of his own choosing, or to refrain from joining" and stated that the union recognized fully "the right of any individual employee not a member of Local 180 to deal directly with the company." The legal validity of this agreement, of course, was questionable. The members of Local 180 never ratified the letter, the company never signed it, and neither the local nor the company ever set any time during which it would be in effect. Moreover, it had other serious deficiencies, in that the right of a union to collective bargaining could not be waived indefinitely—a right irreconcilable with the right of individual employees to deal directly with the company. Its effect at the time, however, was negligible. The workers ratified the contract and returned to work on February 15. The leader of the former company union cooperated actively in persuading his supporters to join Local 180, and "Jap" Michel, UAW regional director, asked Local 180 to forget all past hard feelings.[10] ■

From "Growth of Organized Labor," in Nicholas C. Burckel, *Racine: Growth and Change in a Wisconsin County* (Racine County, Racine, 1977).

SECTION

4

From World War to Cold War

Wisconsin Telephone workers' strike in Milwaukee, April 4, 1947.

Battery Workers
at War

BY ROBERT H. ZIEGER

*The advent of World War II had an important effect on labor unions.
In this section Robert Zieger discusses the war's impact on the federal labor union
at the Ray-O-Vac plant in Madison. Zieger focuses on the rise in employment,
the influx of women workers, and the bureaucratic machinery set up by
the federal government to regulate labor relations during the war years.*

WORLD War II posed new challenges and new opportunities for the American labor movement. The discipline imposed by wartime production helped to undermine the feisty activism of the 1930s. At the same time, unions grew in membership through extension of the organizing launched in the thirties and through a variety of union security schemes. Industrial relations moved away from the overt confrontations of the Depression years toward more bureaucratized forms during the war.

At the shop level, however, the extraordinary burdens and pressures of wartime production frequently triggered vigorous grass-roots activism. Although American workers loyally supported the war effort and achieved tremendous feats of productivity, they were not willing to abandon their traditions of protest and insouciance. Wildcat strikes, short work stoppages, informal sit-downs, and other forms of on-the-job protest punctuated the war years. Burdened by unsettled family circumstances, difficult working and living conditions, and lagging wage rates, American workers resorted in the war years to the same devices that they had always employed, often in the face of the objections of their union leaders.[1]

Ray-O-Vac battery workers followed this pattern of loyalty, productivity, and stubborn defense of their rights. As large numbers of war workers crowded into the Madison plant, conditions deteriorated. The union, by now firmly established, reaped the benefit of large numbers of additional members. Ray-O-Vac workers willingly toiled overtime and tolerated substandard conditions of employment. At the same time, they kept a careful eye on their contract and vigorously asserted their demands for wage and benefit adjustments. While duly impressed with the importance of their work for the war effort, they were entirely willing to voice their grievances and to authorize strike action.

Paralleling their dual course of cooperation and protest vis-a-vis the company was the workers' attitude toward the union. There was no question as to their basic commitment to trade unionism. Still, the war years were unusually turbulent ones, even chaotic, in the local's internal history. While the conflict between militants and moderates abated with the departure of Skaar and Lochner, personal animosities, differences over negotiation strategy, and jurisdictional problems combined with the pressures of wartime factory work and social life to make the period from 1941 to 1945 a bitterly divisive time for 19587.

During the war, Ray-O-Vac's Madison plant switched almost entirely to defense production. By 1943, over 90 percent of its output of batteries and related items went directly to the United States Army Signal Corps. Employment mushroomed, rising from around 500 production employees in 1939 to more than 1,500 by early 1943 and nearly 2,000 toward the end of the war. As Madison's young men went off to war, the labor force became increasingly female; by 1945 over 70 percent of production employees were women.[2]

Ray-O-Vac production workers during the war, as before, were largely unskilled or semiskilled. Battery production in Madison called for more than one hundred distinct operations. "There are employees engaged in mixing the ingredients that go into the core of the cells . . ., operators of core tamping machines, operators on the assembly line . . ., operators who seal cells . . ., operators who solder cross-connections and terminals, cell and battery testers . . ., operators who put the batteries into cartons and pack them into cases," noted a company job description form. "Most of the work," this report declared, "is not heavy work but is work that requires dexterity." Another survey of Ray-O-Vac's operations revealed in the workers' own words the nature of the tasks typically performed. Lucile Hubbard dipped papers in asphalt for placement on the tops of batteries. Thelma De Gregory soldered sockets and loose wires, while Esther Torteria inspected dry cells and used "a gas torch to flame them and an air hose to blow off all excess dust and dirt." Another operation entailed transferring approximately 24,000 cells a day from a punching operation to a capping machine. The influx of new workers and the urgent demands for increased production robbed the plant of some of the familiar camaraderie of earlier days and underscored the burdensome routinized character of much of the work performed in the battery plant.[3]

Fatter pay envelopes only partially compensated for the difficulties of wartime work. Throughout World War II industrial wages in general lagged behind price increases. The Little Steel formula of 1942 pegged wage increases to an assumption of modest inflation, but as early as 1943 workers around the nation had grown resentful over the deep inroads that the cost of living was in fact making on their relatively stable wages. The average industrial worker, if he or she did not achieve an upgraded job classification or considerable overtime work, lost ground in buying power during the war.[4]

Ray-O-Vac's workers followed these patterns. Wage rates recovered somewhat in 1940 and 1941 from the 1939 cutback, but basic structures changed little during the war. Many of the new war workers, of course, began employment at relatively low wage and skill levels. Moreover, the increasing percentages of female labor further depressed the wage structure, since the company typically observed at least a 20 percent wage differential between male and female labor, a situation that unionization had done little to change. Expansion of operations and the siphoning off of some experienced workers into the armed forces, of course, created opportunities for promotions and hence for higher pay through reclassification and upgraded skill levels. Moreover, the Madison plant's expanded work force could not meet Signal Corps needs in a normal work week and the battery workers eventually toiled a fifty-four-hour week, with time and a half for the overtime. Still, the economic benefits of World War II, insofar as the battery workers were concerned, derived largely from regularity of employment and these temporary opportunities for upgrading and extra income, not from intrinsic improvements in their basic circumstances.[5]

Even this relative prosperity exacted a toll. Facilities were crowded and inadequate. Accident rates soared. The large numbers of new workers created a degree of anonymity and impersonality hitherto not present. Even the company's efforts to brighten spirits evoked criticism at times. On one occasion some thirty-seven production employees signed a petition calling on the Grievance Committee to "ask the management to buy an entire new collection of records to replace the old ones, which everyone is tired of listening to." Some parts of the plant were plagued with alternating periods of overheating and frigid drafts of outside air. With annoying frequency the pitch pile caught fire and sent employees straggling from nearby work areas to escape the acrid, pervasive fumes. What with these inconveniences, pressures, and hazards, the incessant repetition of even the most popular tunes must indeed have tried the patience of the overworked battery makers.[6]

The war years had important consequences for the union also. The local became increasingly dependent upon the AFL for leadership and advice. Its members paid little attention to political and social issues as it underwent serious internal instability. While the existence of the union itself was never in question and while membership rolls reached record figures, a group of machinists moved toward the formation of an IAM lodge. This development, together with personal conflicts and other obscure quarrels related perhaps to the rapidly changing composition of the work force, led to a series of chaotic meetings, periodic exchanges of personal insults, and frequent and sweeping changes in the local's leadership.

The growing influence of state AFL functionaries in the affairs of 19587 predated the war. David Sigman and Andrew Biemiller had played decisive roles in settling the 1938-39 lockout and had closely monitored the pro-CIO tendencies that cropped up. During the war, collective bargaining became a tripartite labor-management-government matter as never before. Although local men and women sought changes in the contract and at times seriously contemplated strike action, the key importance of Ray-O-Vac's product in the military effort ensured that essential matters of controversy would be mediated among the three elements at the upper echelons and would not be fought out on the picket line. Sigman and later WSFL Representatives Charles Heymanns and Patrick Rogers assumed the major burden of negotiations and bargaining, for these men, with their national perspectives, access to AFL expertise, and contacts in government, were presumably better able than 19587's fluctuating local leadership to thread the way through the bureaucratic maze that characterized wartime labor relations. Of course, many members of the federal union continued to criticize the AFL servicing of these directly affiliated bodies, feeling that the federation's functionaries were too preoccupied with legislative matters and too solicitous of the strong national unions to fight aggressively for the small federal unions. Many, however, were satisfied with Sigman, Heymanns, and Rogers, and during the war, efforts to increase the autonomy and influence of the federal unions virtually stopped, with meetings of Wisconsin federal unions consisting of little more than good fellowship and routine resolution-passing.[7]

Turbulent conditions within the local also encouraged AFL officials to expand their role. The departure of Skaar and Lochner by no means ended the internal conflicts, although after they left the union's controversies appeared to have little ideological content. As early as 1939, elections of officers became closely contested and even disputed. Three ballots were required to determine the president in that year. Between December 1943 and December 1945, no fewer than four men held the presidency, with at least one resigning under fire. Membership on the Grievance Committee also shifted frequently. In January 1940, the members of the union adopted a motion "that the president appoint four or five sarg. at arms to help keep order at . . . meetings." Two years later they adopted a motion "to stop dissension and false propaganda in [the] union." For several days in February 1941, Biemiller met with 19587's executive board, seeking to restore order and "to straighten out internal dissension" arising from factional conflicts.

In 1945, charges circulated that some union members were criticizing the local's leaders in clandestine meetings with Ray

Electrical workers at the Louis Allis plant in Milwaukee during World War II.

Wisconsin State AFL-CIO

O-Vac officials, while other rumors held that the local's president was using union funds for beer parties. Sigman, Biemiller, Heymanns, and other AFL representatives repeatedly warned 19587 to stop its backbiting and quarreling. Finally, in December 1945, Frank Fenton, AFL director of organization, threatened the local with a disciplinary receivership. "The union," wrote its secretary in a paraphrase of Fenton's warning, "would be watched very close by the AFL regional office. Unless the discontentment stopped they would take this local over."[8]

Several factors contributed to this chronic internecine conflict. The great expansion of the labor force, the problems of civilian life in a scarcity-prone economy, the departure of some trusted leaders to military service, and the generally unsettled and trying working conditions no doubt played their parts. In addition, many workers found the practice of unionism unusually frustrating during the war, since so many matters formerly subject to legitimate dispute were now beyond the pale.[9] The breaking away of a group of skilled machinists to form Badger Lodge 1406, IAM, in 1945 concluded a long and bitter quarrel. Some machinists had felt thwarted by being in the same bargaining unit as unskilled production workers, while battery workers resented this display of disunity and elitism. Moreover, the AFL increasingly encouraged federal unions to accede to craft encroachments or to be taken over in toto by the appropriate national union. Still further unsettling matters for 19587 was the fact that between 1939 and 1943 its president and other officers were machinists, who later became charter members of Badger Lodge 1406.[10]

In addition to wartime tensions and jurisdictional problems, much of the conflict within the local was purely personal. In December 1943, Paul Hein was elected president, only to resign nine months later amid charges that he sought domination over the Grievance Committee. Some members suspected fellow workers of being too friendly with management and of making de facto collective bargaining arrangements with company officials outside the negotiating structure. In August 1945, a former president of 19587 active in the IAM Lodge accused the incumbent president of the federal union of personal use of union funds.[11]

Whatever the sources of discontent and antagonism, they had little to do with ideology or even militancy. Aside from the jurisdictional dispute over the machinists, 19587's members seemed to quarrel in part because the field for legitimate confrontation with management was so greatly narrowed by the contingencies of war and by the dominance of AFL officials. With membership growing—thanks to union security arrangements—the union was frustrated in its desires to do the things that unions were designed to do. The members of 19587, cut off from the heady combination of militant bargaining and trade union activism of the prewar years, fell to attacking each other over the shreds of prestige and limited emoluments available.[12]

This sense of frustration and powerlessness was revealed in the pattern of collective bargaining that developed during the war. Since output at the Madison factory consisted largely of high-priority items for the Signal Corps, neither the AFL officials nor government labor experts were content to leave matters to company management and the union, for both sides had proved stubborn and headstrong in the past. Ray-O-Vac's unionists were compelled to defer key demands and to watch as their fate was decided by government agencies and cumbersome bureaucratic processes.

For the union, collective bargaining became a kind of shadowboxing. Its position was frustrating in that the war years swelled membership rolls and created a demand for industrial labor in the area, a unique circumstance in Madison. With a strong union and a tight labor market, 19587 could normally have expected to redress the historically low wages at Ray-O-Vac. In 1940 and 1941, union contracts did gain wage concessions, but these did little more than balance the reductions forced in 1939. Throughout the war, local unionists sought to reopen the basic contract and make improvements in wages, vacation provisions, seniority, and other matters. Before American entry into the war, the company and the union engaged in a confusing round of disputes in which Ray-O-Vac unilaterally announced a wage increase, possibly after the urging of some moderate unionists who felt the company's generosity would help to mend the bitterness of 1938-39. Other unionists vigorously condemned Ray-O-Vac, however, arguing that the proffered increase was substantially lower than what company officials had verbally promised and that the method of granting it usurped the union's function. The affair culminated in a full-fledged dispute, with commissioners from the United States Conciliation Service entering the picture. In the end, union members received a small additional wage increase, but many emerged from the affair further convinced of the company's duplicity.[13]

Bargaining during the war years proper proved even more frustrating. By December 1942, with union ranks augmented by new war production employees and with wages lagging behind prices under the Little Steel formula, resentment against the company burst forth again. Unionists felt that the time had come to redress the reductions embodied in the 1939 contract and to achieve other improvements in their basic working agreement, including better provisions regarding down time, seniority, regularity of the workday, and vacations. Unionists also sought strong arbitration provisions, hoping that this device might pry from the company concessions that its normally stubborn bargaining posture would not otherwise permit.[14]

With the contract up for renewal as of February 25, 1943, the Grievance Committee informed Ray-O-Vac on December 22, 1942, of its desire to seek changes. Company officials interpreted this to mean that the union desired the termination of the contract upon expiration, in which case, under a Wisconsin statute passed in 1939, the union would be required to obtain recertification for union shop purposes. For the next four months the company bargained on specific issues only reluctantly, contending that until the legality of the union shop—to which it claimed it had no objection per se—was decided, it could not sign a binding contract. Unionists felt strongly that the union shop issue was a bogus one, designed to tie up the union in legalistic maneuvering and to erode the solidarity and enthusiasm displayed by the membership in its demands for contract improvements.[15]

Early in February, the two parties reached an impasse in their direct negotiations. Because of Ray-O-Vac's importance in war work, U.S. Conciliation Commissioner James B. Holmes was quickly dispatched to Madison. According to his report the battery workers were convinced that the company was using the union's adherence as an AFL affiliate to the no-strike pledge as a means of avoiding substantive collective bargaining. The union, Holmes was convinced, felt it "absolutely essential to change [the existing] contract."[16]

Company officials reiterated to Holmes their unwillingness to contemplate contract changes until the legal issue of the union shop was decided. Vice-president Leroy Berigan repeatedly stated that the company was entirely satisfied with the contract originally negotiated in 1939 and slightly amended in 1940 and 1941. He felt that the wartime emergency was no time to contemplate substantial revisions in the document, arguing that wage rates were entirely adequate and that existing rules governing down time, seniority, and hours of operation had to remain exclusively within the company's control because of the seasonal and sporadic demand for its products. Ray-O-Vac especially opposed any efforts to introduce permanent arbitration provisions, contending that over the years the union and management had settled all disputes and grievances amicably through direct discussions. The introduction of third parties, company spokesmen argued, would disrupt what had been a harmonious and efficacious pattern of labor relations.[17]

Faced with such obduracy and emboldened by its restive membership, the union stood poised to strike. Holmes worked to achieve an interim agreement while negotiations continued. On February 18, he thought he had reached a tentative settle-

Heavy machinery worker at the Falk Corporation, 1945.

State Historical Society of Wisconsin WHi (X3) 51166

ment, wherein the old contract would continue while both sides reviewed their bargaining positions. The company, however, took Holmes' effort to mean that the union had agreed to extend the contract for another year without change. At this point Holmes recommended certification of the case to the National War Labor Board.[18]

Company officials professed to dislike the interjection of federal agencies into the bargaining process, but they used the resultant bureaucratization of collective bargaining effectively. On the one hand, company officials felt that the union would have been content with the old contract and would not have made demands that Ray-O-Vac deemed extravagant "if there were no Board from which the union thought it might obtain something without having the responsibility of reaching an agreement." On the other hand, company officials repeatedly insisted on punctilious observance of bureaucratic details, often to the annoyance of the federal representatives assigned to the case. Thus, Harry Malcolm, NWLB special representative assigned to effect mediation, met with both parties in late March

1943. After the March 26 meeting, he was convinced that a basis for settlement of the union shop issue had been laid and that in the interim collective bargaining on substantive contract proposals would proceed. But at the next meeting on April 7, company representatives arrived with new proposals concerning the union shop problem and adamantly resisted every union bargaining demand. Thus, observed Malcolm, "The Company's action in reviving the all-union shop issue and their [negative] attitude towards arbitration" and other contract issues seemed to wipe out all previous progress. Furthermore, the company insisted that its own very narrow concessions on bargaining issues would have to be accepted by the union without change. All of this, Malcolm felt, substantiated statements made by company officials during previous negotiations "that the Company preferred to operate without a Labor Contract of any kind."[19]

Eventually, the National War Labor Board's Region VI headquarters in Chicago named a tripartite panel to hear arguments in the case. Union and management representatives filed briefs and on April 22 appeared at a hearing in Madison. The panel eventually agreed with the union's contention that the union shop issue should never have been allowed to interfere

'If the battery workers were a disputatious lot, prone to internal bickering, they had always rallied around the union when its existence was threatened.'

with the collective bargaining process and issued an order, under powers granted by presidential proclamation, to maintain union shop status. Meanwhile, the panel, according to its chairman Meyer Kastenbaum, "put considerable pressure on both parties to attempt to reach an agreement by negotiation."[20]

By now, the union found its bargaining position eroded. Eager for a showdown around the turn of the year, its energies had been dissipated in legal and bureaucratic maneuvering. The Grievance Committee had started out by demanding substantial changes in the contract but had had to devote much of its attention to the company's oblique attack on the union shop. Bound by the no-strike pledge and by the unwillingness of AFL representatives to encourage bold militancy, and under great pressure from federal authorities for patriotic reasons to reach a settlement, the Grievance Committee abandoned many of its demands. The contract eventually signed on May 3 and ratified by the membership shortly after represented little improvement over previous documents. The company's concessions were largely temporary. Improvements were made in seniority and down time arrangements, but the company insisted on a provision that reaffirmed its ultimate control over all work assignments, thus blunting the force of these gains. The union abandoned its demand for a 10 percent wage increase, while the company agreed to incorporate the current wage rates, which were in effect higher than those negotiated in 1941, in the contract. But even this modest concession was to prevail only during the war, with union and management to renegotiate wage rates upon the termination of the conflict. The Grievance Committee succeeded in having Ray-O-Vac agree to submit irresolvable differences to NWLB arbitration, but the contract pointedly specified that these third-party arrangements were wartime expedients only. In short, although its membership was large, its place in the labor market uncommonly favorable, and its product in great demand, Federal Labor Union 19587 was largely unable to take advantage of its position of temporary strength. As usual, the company bargained hard and skillfully, using the very bureaucratic processes it condemned to blunt the unions militant thrust and to ensure that changes in the contract and in the pattern of labor relations would be minimal.[21]

Throughout the war, neither party professed to like the regimentation and bureaucratization of collective bargaining that resort to the NWLB occasioned. Unionists felt frustrated, unable to use their unusually strong position to improve basic contractual provisions. Moreover, local officers were forced to rely on AFL representatives, because governmental processes involved briefs and other paperwork far beyond what the unpaid local officers were able to prepare in their spare time. For its part, Ray-O-Vac resented the intrusion of federal authorities, feeling that the presence of third parties constituted an undesirable precedent and finding them overly sympathetic to labor's point of view. In outrage over an NWLB hearing officer's

findings on a 1945 job classification case, Leroy Berigan accused the official of believing that "American labor needs to be coddled to the point where publicly appointed officials must call black white in order to make cases come out labor's way " Still, just as federal involvement in labor relations had been instrumental in the birth of Federal Labor Union 19587 and had been an important factor, through the efforts of the Conciliation Service, in establishing a pattern of regular bargaining, the National War Labor Board also served its purpose. Although unionists were frustrated and resentful and the company chafed at interference, Ray-O-Vac employees kept on the job, turning out batteries and related products uninterrupted throughout the conflict.[22]

Thus, during World War II Madison battery workers made significant contributions to the war effort. At the same time, they kept a sharp eye out for their own interests. Although the wildcat strikes and periodic slowdowns and job actions that affected other war factories did not occur on a large scale at Ray-O-Vac, the battery workers were keenly aware of the inconveniences and lagging wage rates that accompanied the war. Their militancy succumbed to the increasing dominance of AFL officials, eager to cooperate with governmental efforts to step up wartime production. They were frustrated by a company management that wanted to ensure the preservation of existing arrangements, and they were stymied by the bureaucratization of industrial relations to which the war gave birth. Partly because of these abnormalities, 19587's members turned upon each other and the union leadership in a series of nasty upheavals and internal conflicts.

Still, by the end of the war, the local's status was even more firmly assured. Whatever else had been accomplished, 19587 survived internal conflict as it had survived earlier company harassment. The National War Labor Board reaffirmed its union shop in 1943, and it seemed unlikely that the company, although disturbed over the problems that might arise in dealing with two distinct unions after the creation of the IAM lodge in 1945, would really want a confrontation. If the battery workers were a disputatious lot, prone to internal bickering, they had always rallied around the union when its existence was threatened. Now with the war over and the likelihood of government wage restrictions being eased, the union could turn away from its internal conflicts and begin to improve its members' standards. Thus, some thought it an augury of future progress when at its December 1945 meeting the membership overwhelmingly chose the sober, responsible, widely respected Max Onsager as president over the controversial incumbent, Frank Bidgood.[23] After the sacrifices of the war years, 19587's members hoped that they had put aside turbulence and contention and could resume the progress in a brighter postwar world.∎

The Madison Battery Workers
(Cornell University Press, Ithaca, 1974).

ROSELLA WARTNER: THE MAKING OF A WAUSAU UNIONIST

Rural women were also drawn into the war effort, especially in defense-related production. Rosella Wartner, interviewed by Joanne Ricca, describes her work at the Marathon Battery plant in Wausau during the war years and beyond. For Wartner, union activity was a vehicle for being involved. Serving as the union's financial secretary, she faced the daunting task of collecting monthly dues "by hand" from 700 members. In 1990, Rosella Wartner was the recipient of the first Catherine Conroy Award, given by the Women's Committee of the Wisconsin State AFL-CIO.

Courtesy Joanne Ricca

Jack B. Reihl, Helen Hensler, Rosella Wartner, and Ann Crump.

AT the recent Wisconsin State CIO Convention, Rosella Wartner was presented with the first Catherine Conroy Award. Named for the great leader of the Communications Workers of America and Executive Board Member of the Wisconsin State AFL-CIO, the Catherine Conroy Award is presented by the Wisconsin State AFL-CIO Women's Committee. Rosella Wartner is a veteran unionist who has certainly left her mark on the labor movement in the Wausau area. The following is an interview of Sister Wartner conducted by State AFL-CIO Staff Representative Joanne Ricca.

J.R.: Could you just tell me what year you were born and a little bit about your earliest days?

R.W.: I was born in 1914 in Minnesota. My folks moved to Wisconsin, bought a farm. We had a lot of sickness and had to help at home. We had to do farm work, go to school and come home, go out in the field and pull weeds, and work and hoe, do the cornfields in the fall of the year, dig potatoes, go out and husk the corn husks out of the stalks, do all that work, milk cows morning and night, feed chickens. I did most of the housework because my mother had to go out, my dad was sick and my mother had to be out with the boys. And we didn't have anything. We were absolutely down to rock bottom. We didn't have a thing so we just lived on a shoestring.

J.R.: Where was your farm?

R.W.: Out in Birnamwood (Shawano County), between Aniwa and Birnamwood. Then my dad passed away. He died of pneumonia and my mother and us kids just kept plugging away at it. The boys went in service, I went to work, just kept right on. There never was a dull moment.

J.R.: Rosella, how did you get involved with the Wisconsin labor movement?

R.W.: I joined the union in January, 1944. A federal labor union, 20690 at Marathon Battery in Wausau.

J.R.: What did you in the plant?

R.W.: Well, I was mostly sealing film bags and packing flashlight batteries. Of course, I started during the war in which they ran all these bazooka guns and stuff, and we had to keep the boys supplied on the front lines with those.

J.R: Were you the only woman working in the plant at that time?

R.W.: There were more women than men.

J.R.: Was that because of the war?

R.W.: Yes. That was when they went out from door to door and got the women to go to work. In 1943, when I started at Marathon Battery. And of course they had just had negotiations and the boss came around and he says to me,—I started at 38 cents an hour—he says you're lucky—starting tomorrow you're going to get 40 cents. So then we went penny by penny, and I got on all these lists, and the only thing that made me stay with all this stuff was my attendance at the meetings—that is important.

J.R.: Why did you feel at the time, as a woman, that it was important for you to go to those meetings?

R.W.: Well, for one thing I liked it and my theory has always been if you don't like it, don't do it. If you like it, do it. I liked it. It was something for me to do. I lived in a room. I didn't care about running around, so I would go to the meetings. That's how I got involved in everything. They found out I'm always there.

J.R.: How do you see that the union made a difference in your life?

R.W.: Well, it made me realize that there's more to working and more to living than just working and doing a job. There's more to think about, you've got other people to worry about, you're more alert to your fellow workers, you're thinking about how you can help those people, and who you can help over here.

J.R.: What message would you have for women in the workforce today?

R.W.: You can't wait to be asked, you have to go in and sit down and show them that you're going to attend and be a part of that organization in order to be involved. A bunch of women had a meeting and they wanted some advice, so I told them they had to go in, sit in, and get themselves involved. If they waited for anybody to come out, they'd have to wait till hell freezes over before they'd get called.

J.R.: And that's been your philosophy?

R.W.: You better believe it. Attendance is the biggest thing. If you're present, you don't have to say a whole lot, just be present. It's a big education. That's how I got involved. We had several union meetings and they needed delegates for the labor council, so one guy gets up and he says, we have somebody that likes to attend meetings and he says I think we should make her a delegate, so they made me the delegate to the labor council. In the labor council, I went from one committee to another. I was sergeant at arms for a few years, I was recording secretary for a few years, I was on every committee that walked and stood, I think, in that labor council at that time because I was present.

J.R.: And this was the Marathon Labor Council?

R.W.: Marathon County Labor Council. And then in 1955 when the AFL and CIO went together, I had the honor to be on that committee to draw up the constitution and by-laws, so I helped draw up the constitution and by-laws of the two combined labor movements. We had a CIO group and an AFL group in the City of Wausau at that time so we got the two groups together, we wrote a constitution and by-laws and made it one. Then I was on a committee from the labor council and the other labor councils in the northern area of Wisconsin. We would meet every so often and I was elected secretary of that group. While I was in the federal labor union, they started this federal labor union conference where they met quarterly. So I went to one, I went to two, I went to three—it didn't take very long I got elected as secretary to that and I was in there seventeen years. I was in every city in the State of Wisconsin that had a federal labor union. We had speakers and interesting programs. Then around 1950 they started sending delegates to School for Workers. The labor council sent me at least three or four years and at that time they had two week schools. You learned so much and I never missed a class when they came to the City of Wausau. I went to every one. I have enough certificates to paper a room.

J.R.: So the School for Workers was very important.

R.W.: It was because I only had an eighth grade education. I never went to high school. My mother couldn't afford to send us all to high school, somebody had to stay home and help with the farm work. She figured it was important for the boys to go to high school but it wasn't important for me to go to high school, so the boys went to high school. So

I never got to go any further than the eighth grade. But all my education I got through the School for Workers which I am very thankful for.

J.R.: Did you feel during your years working at Marathon Battery that you were ever treated differently because you were a woman, discriminated against?

R.W.: No, because there were more women than men because of the war. There were less men and more women.

J.R.: What happened after the war?

R.W.: After the war, they kind of laid off a little bit according to seniority and we still had more women and less men—it didn't make any difference how you looked at it.

J.R.: So, women continued to work at the plant.

R.W.: Till the plant shut down and went to Texas.

J.R.: Could you tell us a little bit about the mayor's commission on the status of women that was organized in Wausau?

R.W.: We used to have a meeting once a month and would meet in City Hall and once a year we'd have what you'd call a big meeting, and we'd invite everybody in. We'd get speakers and there were certain things that we did, like getting other people involved in some of these things that were in the city, and thought they should be involved and they weren't.

J.R.: What issues of particular concern to women did you deal with?

R.W.: I don't think we really dealt with what was plain, straight women. I think we dealt with issues of the day, issues that touched everybody.

J.R.: How did you get appointed to this commission?

R.W.: By the mayor.

J.R.: I know that you have been on the Wisconsin State AFL-CIO Women's committee from its founding. Could you tell us a little bit about the beginning of that committee?

R.W.: We first started that committee—there was a bunch of us—and we decided it was time that we had something to say and so we kind of got together and we decided that there should be a women's committee.

J.R.: Who were some of the people involved with that?

R.W.: Catherine Conroy, there were two gals from Eau Claire, and I was the only one out of northern Wisconsin, Helen Hensler. I can't remember all the names—anyway there were 10 or 12 of us that started. So then they right away took pictures of us after we got it started, and Johnny Schmitt says, well, there's another commission, so we got under his skin a little bit, and I've been on it ever since.

J.R.: I think the Wisconsin State AFL-CIO Women's Committee was the first AFL-CIO Women's Committee in the country.

R.W.: I think it was too.

J.R.: Where do you feel you got the confidence to speak up and participate? What inspired you?

R.W.: I used to battle it out when there was something that wasn't right. And you see, I was financial secretary of the union and there was a good bunch of officers and they would

Women workers at Moe Brothers, Fort Atkinson, 1946.

Photograph by Bob Boyd/State Historical Society of Wisconsin WHi (M56) 5412

audit the books. At that time, you collected dues by hand and I collected dues by hand for 700 people and worked on the line at the same time. They'd poke you on the shoulder—here's my dues—and I'd stick them in my pocket and write their names down. At lunch time, I'd spend my lunch periods finding their books, get the money and books together, go home at night and sit till eleven or twelve o'clock at night putting those stamps in those books to get them back into the office. We had a little office in the plant, get them back in the rack—their dues books—and that was the thing that kept the people together.

The people got separated when they started check-off and the officers didn't get a chance to see the people anymore because when you had dues check-off, it got taken off your checks. You didn't have to go meet anybody, you didn't have to talk to anybody. I would once a month get a chance to talk to almost every individual in that plant—either say hi or if they had a problem, they'd tell me about it. I got involved in everything. So then there were a couple of people that worked in the plant that had problems at home and they

were pouring hot stuff and running machines, and they just couldn't go on the job—just like that. So they'd ask me when I'd be in the office in the morning—I'd get there at 6:30—if you're in at 6:30, can we come in and talk to you? So they'd come in and tell me their whole life story of the night before. This one woman had a husband in a wheelchair, he had a leg off, and she was going through hell and I don't know what was wrong with this guy that run the machine, but he had problems at home with his wife and he says he just cannot run that machine unless I get this stuff off of my chest. So they would tell me their whole story from the night before and because I was a good listener and I would listen to them, there'd be a big sigh out of them and they'd say "now I can go to work." So I was a counselor and a listener as well as collecting dues.

J.R.: Rosella, I have one final question: what message do you have for our union brothers and sisters today?

R.W.: Get involved. That's the biggest thing you can do. Get involved!

—ROSELLA WARTNER

From *Wisconsin Labor History Newsletter*, v.9, n.1 (March 1991).

Organizing
Clerical Workers

BY ALICE HOLZ

*While industrial workers had joined unions by the tens of thousands,
very few office workers worked under the protection of a union contract.
Alice Holz was a pioneer in these efforts. In this account, she defines the
obstacles that made it hard to organize office workers. Alice Holz went on to
become an international vice-president of the Office and Professional
Employees International Union (OPEIU).*

WHEN I rummaged in my sagging memory for experiences to talk about, the images of friends' faces came to my mind—friends who shared these experiences with me; friends who were as zealous and dedicated as I; friends who worked as hard as I; friends who shared disappointment, anger and occasionally satisfaction. Were we successful? How can one equate success in the labor movement? The best we did was to scratch the surface and perhaps prepare a foundation for others to follow.

In order for me to relate to you some of our early organizing experiences, I must give you a time frame. I became a member of the Stenographers, Typewriters, Bookkeepers and Assistants Union Local No. 16456, a federal labor union, on August 15, 1935. This local was directly affiliated with the American Federation of Labor—it had no international union of office workers. A year later, according to its constitution and bylaws, I was eligible for an office. I can't recall if I became the financial secretary that year or the following year. At any rate, I held the position of secretary-treasurer for more than fifteen years.

Our local was made up of employees employed in a variety of offices. For example, we had employees of the *Milwaukee Leader*, the Co-operative Printery, the Socialist Party, Wisconsin State Federation of Labor, Federated Trades Council, either the Building Trades Council or Bricklayers' Union, the Commonwealth Bank, employees of the Padway legal firm, later known as the Padway, Goldberg, Previant offices; we had as a member the secretary to Mayor Daniel W. Hoan, the secretary to the city treasurer, a librarian, and the few unions which existed at that time. Of course when the State, County and Municipal Employees International Union was organized, the city employees left us to join their respective unions of their newly-created international. This took a sizable chunk out of our membership as well as humanpower.

Let me digress a moment to tell you about the make-up of

the possible potential of our membership. Remember in the 1930's the role of women was very narrow. We were slotted to relatively few occupations. Marriage was the uppermost goal with the role of wife and mother the accepted role of women. Those who had careers prior to marriage were in the fields of office workers, teachers, librarians, and in the nursing field. In the office field, the classifications were telephone operators, typists, stenographers, file clerks, maybe secretaries, some classifications in the bookkeeping areas. Supervisory jobs or office management jobs were usually held by men.

In 1935, the Wagner Act was passed, giving workers the right to organize. The economy was beginning to rise a bit with the start of war industries and unions were busy with organizing. This was great, of course, but presented problems for us. Our friends in the labor movement worked industriously to organize workers whatever particular craft they were engaged in, but when it came to hiring a union worker for their own office that was a different story altogether. Local 16456 had a so-called "hiring hall" and I was top on the list and available to be hired; however, the union which needed an employee wanted to hire a relative and ignore the Office Worker's Union. Local 16456 was adamant about its position and threatened a picket line in front of the office. So I was hired under these circumstances. I desperately needed a job and our union needed to make a stand if it were to survive the coming period of organization.

In reading some old newspaper clippings of the thirties, almost every article which appeared in the *Milwaukee Leader* or *Milwaukee Evening Post* about the Office Worker's Union carried a plug advertising our union and exerting pressure in a passive way to use the union's label on every letter sent out of an office. The label was diamond-shaped with the numbers in the center and was stamped with the typist's initials on the bottom of the page. Later on, when we were a local of an International Union, we typed "opeiu #9" on the letter. I recall that frequent-

Courtesy Joanne Ricca

Alice Holz was a pioneer in organizing office workers.

'In 1937 women pretty much adhered to the role prescribed for them as so-called "ladies." Rosie the Riveter had not as yet arrived on the scene!'

ly we could prevail upon our employers to put in a p.s. to this effect, "Please see that the Office Worker's label is used hereafter on correspondence." That was a broad hint that meant, "Is your office organized by Local 9?" Of course, we always followed through.

At this time, as I mentioned before, workers were being organized into their respective unions and unions were being established with officers and office help. Now it was our job to convince these union officers that their office employees should be organized into an office workers union. We heard the same old arguments we heard from employers—they were hiring relatives; they needed someone whom they could trust; the employee was only going to help out a short time, or they wanted them to belong to their craft union, they could not pay the wage scale we had established. One wondered to whom one was speaking—officers of the ABC Company or trade union people. If our arguments were not persuasive enough, there was always the final suggestion that we would take our dispute to the Trades Council and do a little public advertising.

Meanwhile we were bombarding William Green, president of the American Federation of Labor, with letters and resolutions petitioning for an International Union of Office Workers Unions. We needed some concentrated attention given to our organization. Our pleas were sloughed off with statements that "it is not the right time" to grant an International charter for Office Workers. These statements did not deter us.

Now that all labor was hell bent on organizing, we too wanted part of the action. Remember, please, we had an office, but no full-time person, either secretary or organizer, we had very little money, no training. We did have ambition, enthusiasm, intelligence, and a lot of nerve. We were young, resilient,

and blissfully naive. We believed in a cause. And so we set out to organize the office workers of Milwaukee.

Esther Baumann, the secretary to Herman Seide of the Federated Trades Council, and I teamed up to call upon the office employees of the Gridley Dairy Company. We had some indication that they were interested in organizing. We had to make house calls after work, of course. My father, who was a union barber and an ardent socialist, was always interested in his daughter's activities and listened to many a sad tale of woe from me. He was always supportive and cooperative. In order to get around the city to make these calls, dad lent the family car to me—a tan Ford model A, usually filled with gasoline. These were very lean times you must remember, and yet there always seemed to be some gas in the tank when I wanted the car. This particular night, I recall, I was going to be a big shot and buy gasoline. I had started to say, "Fill it up" when I recalled it was a few days before payday and the purse was slim. I called off the order until I could check my money. I had exactly 10 cents to spare! Gasoline was 20 cents a gallon. Without blinking an eye, the filling station attendant sold me a half gallon without a murmur. I suppose he thought a ten-cent sale on a dreary evening was better than nothing at all. Times have changed—now I check to see if I have a charge card with me.

When we got to the home of the Gridley Dairy worker, we were let in but not with a friendly attitude. Esther and I gave our sales pitch, the office worker sat glumly on the sofa listening. When we were finished, she turned to the *Milwaukee Journal* which lay on an end table, open to our view, with headlines screaming, "John L. Lewis threatens to pull unions out of AFL." She pointed to the headline and said, "How do you expect anyone to join a union when you can't get along with yourselves?" We made some excuses that we were like a big family—we quarreled among ourselves but when the issues were down, we really stuck together and helped each other. This upheaval in labor, which ultimately resulted in the split in 1935, did us no good, particularly when John L. was threatening a general strike.

The immediate years preceding World War II, and even the war years, were tough years for us. I recall two bitter situations where our organization just fell apart, despite all our best efforts. Why did this occur? Basically, because the men who were members of these units and who were active leaders in the units, and who encouraged the more timid women members, were drafted or enlisted. That left a weak unit and eventually it

WOMEN AND THE WAR EFFORT AT ALLIS-CHALMERS

The huge influx of women into war-related industries forced management and labor to change their attitudes toward women in the workplace.

WITH the expansion of Allis-Chalmers' industrial facilities and the departure of draft-age male workers for European and Pacific battlefields, women war workers entered the West Allis plant in ever-increasing numbers. In July 1937, women numbered only 144 in a total production work force of 4,727, or 3.0 percent of the total. They performed relatively light work in traditional women's jobs as core makers and coil winders. In December 1941, the expansion of defense production increased the number of women workers to 750 of the 11,250 Allis-Chalmers workers, or 6.7 percent of the total. By late 1942, approximately twenty-five hundred men were on military leave of absence from the West Allis plant. The 385 female workers in January 1942 increased to 2,770 in August 1944. At its peak, the wartime employment of women amounted to 25 percent of the West Allis works. These women worked in sixty-one different shop classifications, which included traditional women's jobs and many nontraditional ones, such as "crane operation, riveting, soldering, brazing, and gear cutting."

But this was only at the main West Allis plant. Allis-Chalmers opened two other Milwaukee-area industrial plants for the production of war materials. These were the Supercharger plant and the interconnected Hawley plant (which manufactured equipment for the Manhattan Project) and the Electrical Control plant (which manufactured electric control panels for navy ships). Both the Supercharger plant and the Electric Control plant employed large numbers of women. For example, the Supercharger plant, which manufactured turbo superchargers for the Army Air Force's "flying fortresses," first opened in early 1942. It expanded quite rapidly. In 1943, Christoffel reported: "This is the largest aviation plant in the area. It employs well over 80% women." In September 1944, the Supercharger plant employed 5,600 workers, of whom 3,000, or 53.6 percent, were women.

At the Supercharger works, plant managers and engineers simplified and redesigned tasks for the new, female work force. Traditionally, the electrical and metalworking shops were male-dominated. A craft tradition guided skilled male journeymen through their varied tasks and routines. But Supercharger work, the plant superintendent claimed, had to be "tailored" for women. He cited the example of gauges that "showed quite a swing of the needle to register a thousandth of an inch." Unfamiliar and unschooled in the use of shop equipment, women workers may have missed important "dimensional variations" without the redesigned gauges. In 1942, the Supercharger plant employed seventeen men to redesign the tools and to solve the "special problems" of women's tasks. Moreover, foremen were "especially trained by management to instruct women in the operation of big machines." For plant managers, the special job simplification and job redesign program so greatly improved worker productivity and product quality that one researcher reported that this plant "achieved the lowest unit cost among supercharger manufacturers."

In addition, Allis-Chalmers officials offered a full range of training programs, social activities, and welfare services for women and other workers. For training women workers, management "offered shop math, blueprint reading and precision measuring." In an effort to win worker loyalty, the firm sponsored welfare and recreational activities— bowling and softball teams, a rifle club, parties and picnics for shop groups, United Service Organization campaigns to donate cookies, cakes, pies, and money for servicemen, and campaigns for War Loan, Red Cross, and Community Chest drives. The Foremen's Club brought in guest speakers. The Welfare Department handled 7,773 cases of absenteeism and illness. In 1944, an employee counseling program conducted over one thousand interviews on myriad problems from evictions to citizenship papers. Sometimes, these Allis-Chalmers activities reflected gender-based stereotypes of women's roles and interests. For example, in a play on the corporate name, Allis-Chalmers officials adopted "Allie Charmer" as the firm's female image. Allie Charmer was a female cartoon figure and mascot for the firm's literature and activities for women workers. A gendered and weakened image, it replaced the more powerful and conventional wartime icon, Rosie the Riveter.

In 1942, the Allis-Chalmers Industrial Relations Department published a pamphlet, *Women: Safe at Work at Allis-Chalmers,* to acclimate women to the new world of the workplace. In its opening lines, the brochure praised the new role of women in industry:

> Every day, women's war efforts open up new and exciting fields. Working shoulder to shoulder with men in factories, women are being called to master the various crafts of the machine age . . . and master them quickly.
>
> In this and in every other critical period of our history, women are making a real job of it. Just as the pioneer women took up the musket to defend the home, so today women are taking up the wrench, the riveting gun, the micrometer.

On the surface, the pamphlet appeared to present a stirring appeal about the new role of women in American industry.

However, the pamphlet emphasized the traditional and gender stereotyped work skills of dexterous, fine handwork. In a section that described "fingers" as "fighters" in the war effort, the pamphlet advised: "Skillful, quick-moving fingers and keen eyes uniquely qualify you and millions of other women for home, shop and office work today. Precision work is at once your pride, your breadwinner, and your bit for victory." The patriotic rhetoric praised skill, but the reality stressed repetitive precision work.

The Allis-Chalmers pamphlet contained other gender-

LET'S "COME THRU" for OUR SOLDIERS — THEY'RE COMING THRU FOR US

EVERY MINUTE COUNTS — 10,000 SUITS MUST BE SHIPPED by Oct. 30

They're on their way to you, Men – ON TIME!

Oshkosh Public Museum No.2937

Oshkosh B'Gosh workers fulfill an order for US Army camouflage overalls during World War II.

based stereotypes about its female work force. It paternalistically cautioned women workers to avoid frantic or frenzied behavior. "Try to develop a calm and quiet way of working to promote safety." At the same time, it advised women to avoid feminine dress: "Experience, often tragic, brings quick agreement on WHAT NOT TO WEAR. Frills are out! Skirts, jewelry, cuffs, ties, loose belts, metal fastenings, long sleeves, outside jackets, outside pockets, flowing sleeves and thin-soled, high heeled, narrow-toed shoes are hazards in any job, especially around *moving* machinery." Instead of "glamorizing the jobs" with "tricky work outfits," the Allis-Chalmers approach emphasized a more serious attitude to the traditionally male world of the shop floor. "The girls," a corporate researcher related, "wore a rather unattractive, though practical, one-piece work outfit made of heavy grey and white striped denim." The "idea" was "to 'de-sex' the women's appearance."

A patriotic tone also saturated the Allis-Chalmers characterization of women war workers. The women were a "national strength" and "Uncle Sam's girls," working for "freedom's cause." Allis-Chalmers officials connected health to good citizenship and patriotism. "You, as a woman worker," the pamphlet observed, "will want to know best how you can best preserve your health as you serve in new capacities." In fact, illness was near treason. "These are days," the pamphlet warned, "in which lost minutes may mean a lost cause. Every sniffle of a cold is sabotage! Preventable aches and pains as well as accidents are definitely unpatriotic."

If Allis-Chalmers officials stereotyped, undervalued,

and demeaned women's role and contribution to the war effort, Local 248 leaders recognized the need to represent women workers, frequently voicing ideals and principles of the equality of men and women. Although some lapses existed, the Allis-Chalmers electrical and metal tradesmen asserted the principle of "equal pay for equal work." The union position stemmed from several considerations. Unionists may have simply taken the purely pragmatic position that lower wages for female workers undermined males' wages. They may have feared that avoiding women's issues could exacerbate the persistent factional struggles at West Allis. Or they may have actually taken their democratic rhetoric seriously. At any rate, they frequently defended female grievants and recruited women into the Allis-Chalmers union.

For example, shortly after the Supercharger plant opened, the union newspaper featured a story on seven of Local 248's leaders in the new factory. "They are women and each is a leader," the *CIO News* reported, "taking their place along the side of the men to build a better union, raise wages and improve the conditions in the shop." Since the UAW local began, Mary Roeder had served the local as a "committeewoman." Esther Zarling was an executive board member. "I'm not the veteran unionist that Mary is," she said, "but I've been here long enough to know that the union is the solution for both men and women. My dad and I are both a part of 248." Five others were either shop stewards or committeewomen. Another newspaper issue featured three black women, two filers and a drill press operator. All three expressed a hope for more skilled work and a chance to earn piece rates.

—STEPHEN MEYER

From "*Stalin Over Wisconsin*": *The Making and Unmaking of Militant Unionism, 1900-1950* (Rutgers University Press, New Brunswick, 1992).

fell apart. Also key women leaders in the unit left to join their husbands or boy friends at camp and their leaving left another hole in the organization. We did not have a union-shop agreement at that time. This happened at the Graf Beverage Company but fortunately our union was able to absorb the remaining employees and found good jobs for them. A similar situation occurred at the Blatz Brewing Company where we were negotiating our first contract and had run into some snags with management. We had a picket line and I remember that on my lunch hour I would run over to the brewery and take a turn on the line. I turned back a coal truck from Michigan. I remember the grin on the face of the truck driver. He was enjoying the situation while my knees were quaking—he was so much bigger than I and my sign was so flimsy. Coal was the source of power for the brewery and we were watching the supply very closely. That day I earned two brownies—one for Local 16456 and one for the Coal and Ice Drivers Local Union No. 257 for which I worked. This local had already halted delivery of coal. Those were the good old days when labor could support one another without breaking contract clauses. In this particular situation, we resolved our problems but with more and more male members being drafted, our unit fell apart. We had no union-shop agreement, of course.

Situations which were more successful, in my opinion, were those which involved plant office workers or shop office workers. These people worked very closely with organized factory or shop workers who were familiar with the labor movement. They, then, were aware of what a union could do for them too. They had no false pretenses—they considered themselves workers and as such deserved the considerations of a worker. At the Milwaukee Electric Rail and Light Company, the forerunner of our current transit system, the office employees were given great support by the shop workers. This I know particularly well, as Walter, or Pop as he was lovingly called, was a customer of my father's and we had a two-way communication system going. Pop was deeply respected by all the workers and respected by the company as well. He gave the needed courage and took time to explain what would happen—"Now, the government will arrange an election—you will have representation, etc." "Be patient, these things take time." He kept me informed of what was going on, usually stopping at the house on his way home. This was great as we could tackle any adverse situation immediately. We won the election and entered into contracts, with much thanks to the support of Pop who was proud as Punch. We experienced a similar situation with the Harvester Company where the plant office employees were given much consideration and support by the plant workers' union.

Let me digress a bit here to say that the makeup of the front office and the shop office was sharply different. First of all, there might have been more male office workers in the unit which gave the needed strength and support; shop women clericals knew what the production union was doing for its members; often they were older employees and were out to get a higher wage—they were not interested in the executive or sales types, nor were they eager to invest in a fashionable wardrobe that was usually called for in a front office.

At the Miller Brewing Company, it was the salespersons

and related classifications who were the ringleaders of the organization there. They were all men, of course, and were personable individuals with long years of employment. They were primarily concerned with job security. If I recall correctly, the company tried to defeat our efforts by saying there was not a proper unit. Well, we made it a proper unit by going after the clerical employees with the help of the salespersons and won the election. We still have contracts with this company.

Each organizing situation, of course, had to be played by ear. When we had a lead we would meet with the person or persons and work with his or her suggestions. If handbilling was called for, we handbilled. Handbilling announced to the company our interest in the company and triggered off promotions, often without pay increases or wage increases. This could be the end to our campaign. Sometimes we would get a telephone call asking when we were going to handbill the office. In response to our question, "Why?", we would be told that the office then got a wage increase. Needless to say, we did not handbill unless absolutely necessary.

We had joint organizing drives with the Retail Clerks, the Hotel and Restaurant Employees, and our Office Workers local, in an effort to organize the department stores, particularly Boston Store. We had a picket line at the Boston Store for months. Our day to picket was on a Thursday and the late Hannah Biemiller took her stint on this day with us.

In 1936 or 1937, we hired Maud McCreery as general organizer for our union. We had a hot campaign going on with the office employees of the Northwestern Mutual Life Insurance Company. On April 28, 1937, Maud held a meeting with 1,200 employees of the company. The big question was the AFL local or an independent union. Hiring of Maud for this venture, at this time, was pure disaster. Maud was a generation ahead of the times—she openly smoked, she had shingled white hair, she did not pussyfoot around but spoke in a vigorous voice and bluntly told the facts. Again, remember the background—this was 1937 and just a month previous, president Green had issued orders to his AFL unions to expel all delegates from suspended CIO unions. The whole of labor was in a turmoil. Remember also that in 1937 women pretty much adhered to the role prescribed for them as so-called "ladies." Rosie the Riveter had not as yet arrived on the scene! We lost the election to the independent union. Company unions, or independent unions, flourished at this time all over the U.S.A., in all industries. Later on, the independent unions in Milwaukee had the audacity to ask Local 16456 to join them in a council. Naturally we refused. Maud resigned and took on other assignments where she was better suited personality-wise.

Harold E. Beck was an employee of another insurance company and had worked very actively in our campaign and jeopardized his job through his bold activity. Here was our opportunity to hire a general organizer and so Hap was hired by our local. This was a big leap forward. When he took a leave of absence for military duty, the old relationship asserted itself—we again did the legwork and the Trades Council's organizers, chiefly Otto Jirikowic, and Henry Ohl of the State Federation helped us in negotiations or sticky situations we could not handle ourselves. During this time I had become an officer of the

Alexander Archer/State Historical Society of Wisconsin WHi (x3)8645/CF 66

AFL President William Green meets new leaders of the Wisconsin State Federation of Labor at the organization's convention in Milwaukee, 1943. Standing, left to right: George Hall, Leonard Pilerson, Frank Ranney, Ernest Terry, Arthur Olsen, seated, left to right: George Haberman, Mathew Woll, William Green, William Nagorsne.

new Council of Office Workers and in 1945, when we became the Office and Professional Employees International Union, our local became Local 9 and I was vice-president again. I spent more and more of my time out of the city, either with International problems or helping our locals in the state.

In reviewing a radio talk that Hap and I did, we talked about office workers' problems, particularly the psychology of the office worker, their hang-ups, etc. I would like to quote the following: *Question*: What can the office workers gain by joining an office workers' union? *Answer*: The same protection as persons in a plant: security, grievance procedure, wage and fringe benefits, etc. (Classifications were important, not only for wage scales but inclusion or exclusion in a voting unit.) "White collar," we said, "denotes an outward appearance of respectability and an inner attitude of smug complacency." Those are not flattering words, but, oh, so true.

To sum up our experiences, these are a few of the reasons given for not joining our office workers' union:

1. Going to be married—would not have to work anymore.
2. Unions were okay for factory or laboring people but not for office workers.
3. Office workers were able to take care of themselves, implying they were smarter.

4. The boss will give promotions, etc. as office workers merit them.
5. Unions are too radical—they are communist.
6. Unions are always fighting among themselves, referring to the split.

I would like to say that the women workers wanted to know precisely what their initiation fee and dues money would buy. Try and answer that! They were very much bread and butter persons, not interested in what the labor movement had done for humankind or could do.

What helped to defeat or make difficult organizing efforts:

1. Employers issued titles and increases, usually with the statement, "don't tell anyone."
2. Confidential employees—everybody became a confidential employee and therefore could be excluded from the unit.
3. Outside influence—economic situation, labor unrest.
4. Right to organize meant that independent unions sprang up quickly and were a constant threat to legitimate unions.
5. Lack of money, lack of trained personnel.

To wind up this long narration, I do want to say that it was an exciting time for me. It was a period of personal growth as my friends and I had to do everything ourselves—design attractive meeting notices, learn to conduct meetings, write contracts and newspaper articles, sort our classifications, argue and cajole. We spent our money as well and thought nothing of it. I met many wonderful persons who were sincerely dedicated to the labor movement and other important causes. They left their mark upon me. I have never regretted those early years.■

From *Wisconsin Labor History Newsletter*, v.6, n.3 (Sept., 1988).

NELLIE WILSON: A BLACK WOMAN MEETS THE UNION

Because of the labor shortage caused by the war, black women were able to enter industrial jobs for the first time. Nellie Wilson offers this account of how she got involved with the union movement after being hired by A.O. Smith. Wilson became a staff representative for the AFL-CIO's Human Resources Development Institute (HRDI). Her remarks were presented at the annual meeting of the Wisconsin Labor History Society in 1989.

■ HAVE been asked to tell you what is was like for me working in a unionized, industrial, defense factory during World War II—that is, what is was like for me working there while laboring under the dual handicaps of being black and female. The very words black and female introduce the elements of racism and sexism into the equation; and that is as it should be because racism and sexism are as inherent to the American Psyche as motherhood and apple pie. So I am supposed to talk about my personal relationship with the union—what impact the union had on me and what impact I had on the union, if any.

But before I get into that I need to say that Professor [Joe William] Trotter's book took me a long way back in time for although I was not a part of the heavy action, I was a part of the scenarios as it evolved. I remember how proud we sixth ward residents were of our respected lawyer Dorsey; I was reminded that the daughters of Carlos Del Ruy were my classmates; that the wife of Doctor Edgar Thomas taught me piano lessons; that my father was a strong supporter of the Marcus Garvey movement, the UNSA, and the FEPC; that the Reverend Cecil A. Fisher officiated at my wedding; and yes I shall always remember what a devastating blow it was for my father when he was finally laid off from the International Harvester Corporation following the stock market crash of 1929.

I was not yet a teenager in 1929, but by 1940 I had acquired the dubious distinction of shedding a husband, trying to function as a single parent, and competing in the job marketplace. It was a learning experience that began in high school with Career Counseling day for girls who were interested in becoming Registered Nurses. The speaker announced, up front, that if any Negro girls are present in this assembly, you may as well leave because there is no nurses training facility in the state of Wisconsin that will accept Negro girls as students. I learned about female occupational stereotyping where female traditional jobs paid less than comparable jobs for men, and I learned about the division of labor where white women worked in light factory jobs, or as typists, retail clerks, telephone operators etc., while black women worked at lower paid, undesirable, menial or domestic jobs. Of all the places I went, I never even once got a job

interview. Employment managers would tell me there were no jobs and then call the white girl who was standing in line behind me to come into the office for a job interview. My early job searches were exercises in futility.

AT the same time that I was learning the economic facts of life about America the beautiful, the land of the free and the home of the brave, with liberty and justice for all—A.Philip Randolph, president of the Brotherhood of Sleeping Car Porters, was having a running battle within the labor movement with William Green and the AFL about their overt racist exclusionary employment policies—and with President Roosevelt about the same policies in defense contracts. Now after Randolph had convinced Roosevelt that he was prepared to bring over 100,000 black demonstrators to the nation's capitol to protest employment discrimination, Roosevelt capitulated, signed Executive Order #8802 and created the Fair Employment Practices Committee.

Two years later, February 15, 1943, I was hired in a semi-skilled occupation in a unionized defense factory. I'm certain demographics had some bearing on my being hired since the demand for healthy white male employees was far greater than the supply, but the truth is I was hired because of the labor union activity and agitation of Philip Randolph period. So getting the job in the first place was my first labor union contact. The question now becomes what was it like working in that environment? Let me tell you that from beginning to end it was pure job utopia—beginning with the plant guard who gave us new hires our in-plant orientation. He told us not to take any crap from anybody, that we were just as good as anyone else, that we should holler loud if we even thought we were denied something of value because of our skin color, and that we should get our fair share of all handouts. I couldn't believe it. It was simply incredible. Here was this white man telling me about brotherhood, equality, and fraternity after I had suffered a lifetime of blatant overt discrimination. To this day I wonder what happened to that man and his ideals.

Now my first personal union contact was with the department steward. He told me about the value of union membership—and I had to agree with what he said because here I was working at a clean good paying job ($33.00 a week), getting periodic union negotiated wage increases and getting a $100 check for a Christmas bonus, and best of all I had job security. The steward assured me that nobody, but nobody would fire me unless they had a very, very good reason and even then they would have to come by the union first. So following the steward's suggestion, I joined the open shop union, went to several meetings and finally limited my union participation to my union dues. But life was good.

Then the United States dropped the atomic bomb on Nagasaki and Hiroshima, the war was over, I was out of a job—and right back where I started from. The job market

Courtesy Joanne Ricca

Nellie Wilson began her career as a defense worker at the A.O. Smith factory in Milwaukee.

was just as discriminatory as it had been before the war and I could not find a job. Rumors said that women would be recalled to work after industries had converted from defense to peacetime operations; but not too many companies recalled their women workers. Actually my company resisted the idea of having women work in peacetime operations, because they said the work was too strenuous for a woman to perform. But my union insisted that the company recall women workers because we were members of the union. So I went to work in metal fabrication, but because of the union, I did have a job. Pressure was brought to bear to fire women workers and replace us with returning ex-servicemen. The union resisted this effort and we kept our jobs. But it wasn't easy. The company did not want us there. Our male co-workers did not want us there. However lay-off and recall based on plant-wide seniority did prevail and we women kept our jobs.

Our union was also out front with the principle of equal pay for equal work. Our male co-workers made sure the women worked as hard or harder for our equal pay. If one job required more physical stamina than another, the men made sure a woman got the hardest job. But the union did protect that job. Before I take my seat I would like to tell you about two more incidents having racial and sexual overtones.

By the late 1950's I had learned my way around my department so well that I had an almost photostatic memory regarding incentive pay rates. When a rate posted for a particular job that was less than it should have been, it meant

the operator was forced to work harder for less money. And I was always arguing with management to get them to raise the rates back to what they should have been in the first place, especially if it was my rate and my money. This activity did not go unnoticed.

One day my co-workers, all high seniority white males, came to me to ask me to be their steward; they said we have been watching you and see that you are not afraid to tackle these foremen and rate setters when you see they are messing with our rates. It took some doing but I agreed to be the steward, especially after they told me they had elected good stewards before, but that every time they got a good steward the company either buys him off or makes him a temporary supervisor. We figure that with you being black and a woman we don't believe the company is going to do any of those good things for you—so we should have a good steward for a long time. Racism, sexism, and reverse discrimination.

The day before the steward's election Mary-Anna Kiefer, also a white co-worker, approached me and said, Nellie I see you are running to be department steward and I said yes, as a matter of fact I am and she said, well you go and take your name off that board right now, because the steward job is a job for a white man. Well! I felt that I was as capable as the next person to function as department steward. Anyway when the votes were counted I had beaten my opponent by a count of two to one. I not only won the race for that steward's job, I kept on running for office and I kept on winning. When I won election to the union's executive board I was the first black female to win in a plant-wide contested election. Finally I left the company to work for two AFL-CIO programs. There were people both in the company and the union who were happy to see me leave; and they wished me well wherever I went and whatever I was doing because of my union activity.

So what has been my relationship with the union? It has enabled me and mine to live comfortable lives and it provided me with a lifetime of challenges. But I hope that somewhere along the way I have helped motivate other women to continue the union struggle for better wages, hours and working conditions.

—NELLIE WILSON

From Wisconsin Labor History Society Conference, April 22, 1989, Milwaukee.

Labor Law: Wisconsin's 'Little Wagner Act' and the Road to Taft-Hartley

BY DARRYL HOLTER

The National Labor Relations Act (NLRA) or Wagner Act of 1935 was a landmark in American labor law. But opposition to the NLRA grew during the 1940s. In 1946, a new Republican majority took control of Congress and approved a set of amendments to the NLRA authored by Senator Taft and Representative Hartley. The Taft-Hartley law was enacted into law in 1947. One interesting sidelight is the story of Wisconsin's "Little Wagner Act" of 1937 and its relation to the Taft-Hartley Act. In the wake of the NLRA's passage, the legislatures of several states, including Wisconsin, enacted their own so-called "Little Wagner" acts. But in 1938 a much more conservative state legislature was elected in Wisconsin. The new legislature rewrote the Wisconsin Labor Relations Act with a set of amendments that put new limits on union activities and generally weakened labor's power. A few years later, many of these features were utilized at the federal level by Wagner Act opponents in the drafting of the Taft-Hartley amendments. In this way we see how the road to Taft-Hartley wound its way through the state of Wisconsin nearly a decade before the controversial amendment was enacted at the national level.

LABOR laws reflected shifts in political power at the national, state, and local levels. The Wisconsin law, like the Wagner Act, was important to labor because its purpose was to protect the rights of workers. In fact, the "Little Wagner Act" widened the scope of labor's power beyond that of the Wagner Act. Union activists were quick to use the rights granted under the act to win recognition, resolve labor disputes, and force employers to bargain in good faith.

But labor's success on the picket line and in the National Labor Relations Board's actions generated a powerful opposition movement to repeal the Wisconsin law. Business leaders and farm groups demanded new legislation to make the law "more balanced" by placing tough limitations on union activity. After nearly 300 strikes in 1937 and 1938, including twenty-nine sit-down strikes in Milwaukee alone, much of the public was receptive to lawmakers who sought to "do something about the strikes."[1] In addition, the collapse of the Farmer Labor Progressive Federation in 1938 left the legislative field open to a reaction against labor. The split in the labor movement contributed to the FLPF's demise, especially after labor activists affiliated with the CIO tried to organize agricultural coopera-

tives run by farm groups that were part of the coalition. Also, Governor La Follette's ill-fated national third party effort threw the new coalition into disarray. This combination of factors led to a Republican sweep of both legislative houses, the ousting of La Follette by a Republican industrialist, Julius Heil, and a radical reshaping of the state's labor law.

The new restrictive legislation, called the Wisconsin Employment Peace Act, substantially rewrote the Wisconsin labor relations law. Enacted in 1939, it prefigured the restrictive provisions of the Taft-Hartley act of 1947. This is clearly revealed by comparing provisions of the four laws: the Wagner Act of 1935, the "Little Wagner Act" of 1937, Wisconsin's Employment Peace Act of 1939, and the Taft-Hartley law of 1947.

Unit Determination and Labor Representation

The collective bargaining process began with the establishment of an appropriate bargaining unit.[2] Yet considerable debate erupted in the course of determining exactly which workers belonged in which unit. Under the Wagner Act, the NLRB determined appropriate bargaining units. Initially, the NLRB

State Historical Society of Wisconsin

A course for steelworkers teaching at the University of Wisconsin School for Workers, 1940.

favored large industrial units represented by one union. This approach, however, led to conflicts with smaller craft unions that existed within large industrial plants. The "Little Wagner Act" of 1937 was more sensitive to long-standing union jurisdictional claims. The Board decided whether the appropriate unit should be on the basis of employer, craft, plant, or other unit. However, it could also decline to make such a determination and leave the decision in the hands of the employees. When the situation was in doubt, employees, but not employers, could ask the Board to determine the appropriate unit. The NLRB required employers to take a "hands off" attitude toward unit determination, but allowed a closed shop agreement if a union was designated as a representative agent by a majority vote. Wisconsin labor leaders drafted the 1937 bill to allow employers to make a closed shop agreement with any specific classification of employees, with or without a vote.[3] As interpreted by the WSFL chief counsel, Joseph Padway (who became the national AFL's chief counsel in 1938), this meant that an employer could not enter into an agreement with bricklayers that required that the carpenters belong to the bricklayers union.[4] Clearly the rise of the CIO and its attempts to bring skilled tradesmen into "wall-to-wall" industrial units was part of the reason for this provision. In one of the first key decisions

regarding unit determination, Padway successfully argued for the AFL craft unions (against the CIO position) in the *Allis-Chalmers* case. This approach was also rooted in common law, past practices, and long-standing union claims for "exclusive jurisdiction" in certain occupations.

The 1939 law changed the process of unit determination in several ways. While the 1937 law had sought to balance the rights of employers and unions, the 1939 law purported to balance the rights of employers, individual workers, and the public—as if unions were no longer affected entities. The 1939 law departed from the Wagner Act and other state labor acts by limiting the Board's discretion in unit determination.[5] The 1939 Board was given no power to decide what the unit should be, but it could engage in "fact-finding" in order to determine what kind of unit or units actually existed. Under the 1939 act the Board supported "self determination" in which the smallest unit requested by an interested party must be placed on the ballot. Charles Killingsworth noted that this policy led to "virtually unlimited gerrymandering."[6] The 1939 act also departed from the original Wisconsin act by prohibiting closed shop agreements unless three-quarters of the workers in a single craft, department or plant voted affirmatively.

The 1939 law changed the way workers chose their bargaining agent. The 1937 law had allowed only employees to petition for a representation election. The 1939 law, however, allowed employers to order an election at any time. Labor organizers complained that many employers petitioned the Board for an election at the outset of a union drive. This led to premature elections and union defeats.

In thirty-one cases where employers requested elections, the union won seventeen and lost fourteen. In twenty-two cases where unions requested elections, the union won twenty and lost two.[7] Also, while the 1937 law refused to list company-dominated unions and the Wagner Act excluded company unions from appearing on an election ballot, the 1939 law provided that all claimants could appear on the ballot. In addition, under the 1939 law, the Board did not conduct run-off elections. If no union received a majority vote, even if the total vote for the unions was a majority indicating a desire for collective bargaining, the result was the same as if a majority had voted against bargaining.[8]

The Taft-Hartley law changed the Wagner Act in the area of unit determination and representation in somewhat similar ways.[9] Taft-Hartley provided that in deciding the unit appropriate for bargaining, the NLRB could not "decide that any craft unit is inappropriate . . . on the ground that a different unity has been established by a prior Board decision, unless a majority of the employees in the proposed craft unit vote against separate representation." In the mass production industries the unions that were organized "wall-to-wall" felt the impact immediately as craft unions began to carve out small units within the plant. Even when employers and recognized unions opposed such petitions, the Board overruled them and demanded elections for separate craft units. The other highly divisive element in Taft-Hartley, the anti-communist affidavit provision, did not appear in the 1939 law. However, a somewhat similar provision in the Wisconsin law deprived a union found guilty of an unfair labor practice from being included on the ballot for a representational election.

Union Security

Besides making it harder to form a closed shop, the 1939 law placed other obstacles in front of the union. A "union shop," in which an employee was required to join the union as a condition of continued employment, was permitted only if two-thirds of the workers in the unit voted to authorize it.[10] Dues check-off was prohibited unless each employee signed a statement agreeing to it. After 1939 the Board accepted petitions from individual employees who sought to oust the union. Also accepted were petitions from employers supposedly acting in the name of several employees who sought to remove the union.[11] Taft-Hartley outlawed the closed shop but permitted a union shop after an election. Taft-Hartley also amended the Wagner Act to provide a procedure for decertification. But unlike the 1939 Wisconsin law, Taft-Hartley did not allow employers to file for decertification elections.[12]

Unfair Labor Practices, Strikes and Boycotts

The drafters of Wisconsin's 1937 act and the Wagner Act began with the assumption that merely stating the rights of employees to organize and bargain was not sufficient to guarantee those rights when employers were determined to interfere. Thus, cer-

TABLE 1: Work Stoppages in Six States, 1934-1946: Percentage of Total National Work Stoppages						
Year	Wisc	Mass	Mich	NY	PA	MN
1934	4.1	6.0	3.4	15.1	15.9	1.2
1935	2.3	5.5	2.7	17.3	15.9	1.2
1936	2.3	5.5	2.1	18.1	16.8	2.5
1937	4.0	5.5	2.1	18.1	16.8	2.5
1938	3.2	5.8	6.5	18.9	13.7	1.6
1939	2.1	4.4	2.9	27.6	12.7	2.1
1940	2.0	4.1	2.9	22.0	12.0	1.0
1941	1.5	4.1	2.9	22.0	12.0	1.0
1942	1.5	4.1	5.9	17.8	12.7	1.1
1943	.8	3.4	8.8	12.5	13.8	.9
1944	1.8	4.0	11.3	5.3	16.6	.4
1945	2.0	5.0	10.1	7.6	15.6	.6
1946	1.8	5.3	6.2	13.7	12.8	1.1

tain types of conduct that hampered the employees' freedom of association were described as "unfair labor practices" (ULPs). In the 1937 act, these ULPs included the following: interference with employees in organizing or bargaining, creating or encouraging a company union, using power to hire, fire, and promote to discourage union membership, discrimination, refusal to bargain, spying on workers, and blacklisting. Only employers could be charged with committing ULPs. When a union filed a ULP, the Board could hold a hearing and order the employer to discontinue such conduct. Even without the filing of a charge, the Board could ask the court for an injunction to prevent and restrain an employer from committing a ULP. As noted above, unions filed 425 ULP charges against employers in 1937 and 1938.

The 1939 law commenced with a different assumption, namely that unions, as well as management, were guilty of ULPs. The 1939 Act put restrictions on union organizing tactics by allowing employers to charge employees or the union with a ULP and by penalizing unions and individual unionists charged with committing a ULP. Reflecting a desire to curb the strikes, the 1939 law narrowed the legal ground around strike tactics. Unions were required to provide 10 days' advance notice before striking firms involved with agricultural or dairy products. Workers were not allowed to "engage in any concerted effort to interfere with production except by leaving the premises in an orderly manner for the purpose of going on strike." Based on this provision, union leaders at Briggs and Stratton were found to have violated the law when they called a series of "quickie" union meetings during working time in order to get management to start bargaining. Slowdowns, mass picketing, sit-downs, and preventing entrance or exit from a struck plant were all considered violations. Unions were prohibited from enforcing production standards that might limit production. A ULP was committed if a union struck during the period of a contract if the contract contained a no-strike clause or when an impasse in bargaining led to a strike if the contract provided for arbitration. Picketing was prohibited except where a majority of employees in a bargaining unit had voted to strike. Another ULP occurred when a minority union picketed in

Members of the Ladies Auxiliary of UAW Local 248 prepared meals during the strike at Allis-Chalmers, 1946.

Wisconsin State AFL-CIO

THE 1939 law prohibited secondary boycotts, which were defined as any combination or conspiracy to injure one with whom no labor dispute exists. The law even prohibited primary boycotts in the absence of a strike vote. A "labor dispute" was narrowly defined while "secondary boycott" was broadly defined. The result, wrote Killingsworth, "outlaws even sympathetic strikes under many circumstances."[14] He added, "By putting uppermost the old common law right of an employer to do business without interference, they tip the balance of bargaining power in his favor."[15] The Taft-Hartley limits on secondary boycotts, he noted, were less sweeping than the Wisconsin Act of 1939.

The unions challenged the many restrictions on picketing as violations of free speech. But in 1942 the Wisconsin Supreme Court supported the Board's power to order the unions to cease and desist from picketing in four key cases.[16] In another case a union that had lost much of its membership was denied a second contract. The firm, Lakeside Bridge and Steel Co., which was engaged in construction work for the federal government, filed charges against the union when its pickets were honored by the members of various AFL construction unions. The state Board found all the union parties guilty of ULPs, including all workers who had refused to cross the picket line. When the CIO and AFL unions in Racine agreed to work together to organize the large retail stores, the Board found that the unions had committed ULPs when they set up picket lines telling Sears' customers that management had refused to recognize the union. The Supreme Court stood behind the Board's decision, arguing that picketing, while technically legal, was prohibited because it threatened to injure the economic interests of the firm and its employees.

Eva Schwartzman, in an early analysis of the issue of "free speech," picketing, and secondary boycotts under the Wisconsin act, concluded that the Board would allow peaceful picketing, unless it was successful for the union. "The Act," she wrote, "is designed to 'balance' the interests of the employer,

hopes of convincing an employer to recognize it as the bargaining agent. Other unlawful practices included picketing before a certification election, picketing following the union's defeat in an election, and continuously soliciting non-union employees to join the union. A union that announced in a labor newspaper that picketing would continue until the firm's employees joined the union was also guilty of a ULP.[13]

**TABLE 2: Unfair Labor Practice Cases:
WLRB and NLRB, 1939-1945**

	Unfair Labor Practices		% of ULPS
Years	NLRB	WLRB/WERB	filed in Wisc.
1937-1939	10,500	425	4.0
1939-1941	8,000	10	1.3
1941-1943	20,000	61	.3
1943-1945	19,000	56	.3

employee, and public, but the effect . . . is to achieve 'imbalance' in placing such restrictions upon employees and their representatives as to effectively throttle unionization and make the 'right to organize' an empty phrase."[17] Between 1939 and 1947 the WERB issued nearly forty cease and desist orders against unions. In many cases the Board ordered the cessation of all picketing and boycotting. In one case the board placed limits on picketing even though the employer had committed a ULP that caused the strike in the first place.[18]

The 1939 law required the Board to protect the rights of individual employees against the union and also permitted it to take action against individual employees who were active in the union. Any employee found guilty of a ULP was excluded from definition of "employee" and thus lost any "rights, privileges, and remedies" under the law. The Board found individuals guilty of ULPs for mass picketing, fist fights, interfering with deliveries, and threatening non-union employees. In one case a union president was barred from representing the members of his union for a year for calling a strike that was determined to be illegal. The union, already certified by the Board, was forbidden to act as the bargaining agent until it had replaced the offending officer.[19] Withdrawing the protection of the law from the union meant denying it access to the election process, a penalty that prefigured Taft-Hartley's power to keep certain unions off the election ballot. It also left the employer free to commit any and all ULPs against the union. Killingsworth's description seems understated when he noted the "somewhat one-sided" effect of this policy.[20]

The Taft-Hartley Act of 1947, like Wisconsin's 1939 law, placed restrictions upon unions while broadening management rights. Several of the restrictions were virtually identical in both acts. Unions could be found guilty of ULPs and subject to injunctions and penalties. New restrictions were put on strikes, boycotts, and picketing. Meanwhile the right of employers to fight unionization openly was broadly protected. In both laws, management was given the right to call for a union election. Both laws protected the rights of the individual employee against union officials.

Unionists charged that the 1939 law tipped the balance between labor and management back to management's side by limiting labor's ability to strike and redefining ULPs to favor management. Looking at strikes and ULP claims offers insight into this issue. When we compare work stoppages in several states (all with state labor laws) from the pre-Wagner years to the years preceding Taft-Hartley, we see that the percentage of strikes occurring in Wisconsin during the period from 1934

ERIK BJURMAN: KENOSHA UNIONIST

A NUMBER of local leaders in Socialist Party and union affairs in Wisconsin, when they slackened or stopped their party work, stepped up their union activity, many moving into the upper echelons of union organizations and into well-paid full-time positions. An outstanding example was Eric Bjurman of Kenosha. His career clearly reflected the evolution and devolution of the "personal union."

Bjurman was born in Sweden in 1899 and came to the United States at the age of ten. He came to Kenosha in 1916. He learned the machinist and tool-and-die maker trade at Nash Motors. He became a journeyman in 1922 and joined Lodge 34 of the International Association of Machinists early in 1923.

Machinists Lodge 34 in Kenosha was organized in 1897; its number tells that it was the thirty-fourth local union to be affiliated with the International. It was a Socialist union. From the beginning, the leaders and many of the members were Socialists and would continue to be. Lodge 34 used to hold its meeting in Socialist Hall, a landmark building located on the southeast corner of Sheridan Road and Prairie Avenue, now 60th Street. The Socialists had formed the Kenosha Unity Association to buy the building which had been the University School. In 1923 they sold the property to the Standard Oil Company of Indiana for the site of a service station.

Eric Bjurman learned the philosophy and economics of socialism from the journeymen who taught him the machinist trade, some of whom were Swedes. After he learned his trade, he worked at it in many places as far away as Berkeley and Seattle. Back in Kenosha with the

and 1937 averaged about 3.2 percent of the national total (Table 1). During the period of the Little Wagner Act, strikes in Wisconsin accounted for about 2.7 percent of the total strikes. After the enactment of the 1939 law, the percentage of strikes occurring in Wisconsin dropped to about 1.6 percent. Comparing the number of ULPs filed with the Wisconsin Board with the number of ULPs filed with the NLRB reveals that the Wisconsin Board abandoned the activism that had marked its first two years of existence (Table 2).

Wisconsin's Employment Relations Board After 1939

The 1939 law transformed the Wisconsin Labor Relations Board into the Wisconsin Employment Relations Board (WERB). The new Republican governor, industrialist Julius Heil, named a new Board: Henry Fuldner, a sidewalk contractor; Laurence Gooding, former district attorney of Fond du Lac County; and R. Floyd Green, formerly a representative for the Brotherhood of Locomotive Engineers and member of the

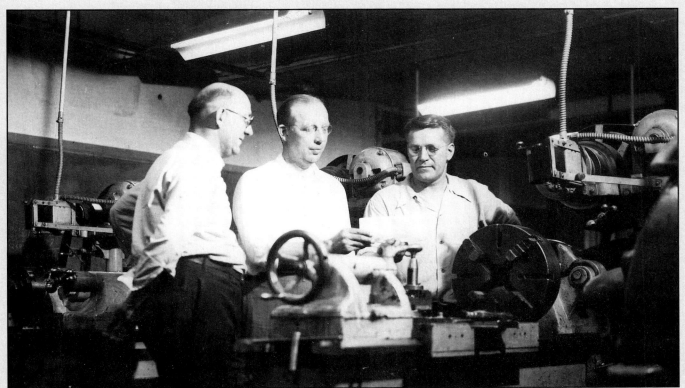

Courtesy Erik Bjurman

Erik Bjurman (center) and fellow machinists.

start of the Great Depression, he was active in union organizing, especially among the machinists and tool-and-die makers. He was elected at different times as treasurer and president of Lodge 34. At the same time he was active in the Socialist Party, being the Party spokesman at meetings of the city council and the school board. He was a persistent exponent of vocational education.

He was regularly a delegate or attendant at Socialist conferences and conventions. He became a grand lodge representative of the IAM in April 1941, headquartered in Kansas City. His Socialist activities came to an end, but he held on for the rest of his life to his beliefs in social democracy, as did so many other Socialists.

—ELMER A. BECK

From *The Sewer Socialists*, Vol. II
(Westburg, Fennimore, Wisconsin, 1982).

state's Public Service Commission.[21] The Board's role changed from being a facilitator of collective bargaining to an agency regulating labor activities. Its methods of recording information about labor disputes was also altered. The standard form used to gather information during the first two years was abandoned and different data were gathered, making it impossible to make a comparable analysis of the Board's actions before and after 1939.

With the enactment of the 1939 law, the labor movement launched an unofficial boycott of the WERB. The unions filed 381 claims in 1937 and 258 claims in 1939, or roughly thirty claims per month. But in the wake of the November 1938 elections, only one claim was filed by the unions for the remainder of that year. Between 1939 and 1945 the unions filed about thirty ULPs annually against employers. The number of ULPs filed by employers against unions fell from 1939 to 1945, from twenty-three to three. Unions also refrained from using the new Board for mediation after 1939. During the 1937-1938 period, unions went to mediation 680 times. After the enactment of the

Employment Peace Act in 1939 the number of cases brought to mediation fell from fifty-six in 1939-1940 to 0 in 1944-1945.

During the war years, the newly created War Labor Board intervened in many labor disputes. The WERB, however, remained active, especially in nullifying closed shop agreements made before 1939 and in calling for new elections requested by small units of craft workers.[22] CIO members at the Milwaukee Foundry Equipment company struck to protest a WERB ruling that a previous strike by the unions was a ULP.[23] Wisconsin labor consistently attacked the 1939 law and labor lawyers contended that several provisions would be struck down as unconstitutional.[24] But the new law continued in force. When Taft-Hartley was enacted in 1947, Wisconsin labor leaders were hardly surprised. They felt they had been operating under the same restrictive legislation for nearly a decade.■

From "Labor Law and the Road to Taft-Hartley: Wisconsin's 'Little Wagner Act,' 1935–1945," *Labor Studies Journal*, v.15, n.2 (1990).

Cold War Politics
at Allis-Chalmers

BY STEPHEN MEYER

The Cold War had important consequences for unions, especially those in which radical and communist labor leaders held sway. Such was the case for Local 248 of the United Auto Workers at the sprawling Allis-Chalmers plant in West Allis. In this section by Stephen Meyer, we pick up the story in the midst of a strike at Allis-Chalmers in 1946. Note the electoral tactics used by the CIO unions, the role of the "John Sentinel" editorials, and the eventual outcome of the 1946 elections.

FROM August through October 1946, the ongoing economic struggle merged with a bitter political struggle. At that time, Local 248 leaders entered the urban political arena and fielded Milwaukee CIO Political Action Committee (CIO-PAC) candidates in the August Democratic primary and in the November general election. Simultaneously, they engaged in an internal union battle against CIO and UAW conservatives who disliked the militant and leftward drift of Milwaukee unionism. From September through November, Allis-Chalmers officials and the Milwaukee press vigorously excoriated pro-Communist union leaders in the city and state labor movements. The bitterness of the economic struggle dramatically escalated. The Milwaukee strike commingled with several Cold War political battles. By November, Joseph McCarthy had become a U.S. senator from Wisconsin, and militant unionism in Milwaukee was in decline.

As the strike continued through the late spring and early summer, the politics of production meshed with urban and union politics. Milwaukee CIO leaders saw the upcoming election season as an opportunity to combat the advantage of a politically influential management. They embarked on an ambitious campaign to endorse or field pro-CIO candidates, to provide financial assistance and campaign support for them, and ultimately to remake the Milwaukee Democratic Party. Originally formed to support New Deal Democrats in 1943, the Milwaukee CIO-PAC became a vehicle for left union political involvement in 1946.[1]

In Wisconsin, a unique party structure facilitated labor's foray into politics. A much more vibrant left tradition existed in the state than on the national level. In addition to the Republican and Democratic parties, Wisconsin also had politically significant Progressive and Socialist parties that had dominated Wisconsin and Milwaukee politics since the early twentieth century. By the early 1940s, however, the national New Deal

coalition had contributed to the dissolution of these two Wisconsin parties. Under Roosevelt, the Democratic Party turned to the Left and allied with both Socialists and Progressives in Wisconsin. The Republicans, still the national party for many Wisconsin Progressives, moved to the Right.[2]

In the 1946 elections, Wisconsin electoral politics became a confusing bundle of social, economic, and political contradictions. In the spring, Progressive senator Robert La Follette Jr., personally faced the dilemma of whether to run for reelection in the Republican or Democratic primary. Faced with political extinction, his Progressive party had to re-form as a bloc in one of the two Wisconsin political parties. Although his heart was with the New Deal Democrats, he chose the Republican Party since it represented a stronger force in Wisconsin politics. As a result, he entered an electoral contest with Joseph McCarthy, the choice of a new, young generation of Republican conservatives.[3]

In Milwaukee, union activists confronted a somewhat similar dilemma. In line with national CIO-PAC tendencies, they decided to work with the Democratic party. Some other labor activists, particularly AFL craft unionists associated with the old Socialist urban political machine, remembered La Follette's prounion stand and followed him into the Republican primary. Other AFL unionists supported traditional Democratic candidates. Religious and ethnic politics further complicated labor's political allegiances. By summer, Milwaukee labor and its political leaders had split into several camps, each fielding different slates of candidates for the fall elections.[4]

As the largest single CIO union, the Allis-Chalmers local dominated the Milwaukee and Wisconsin CIO councils. In Milwaukee, the CIO-PAC endorsed a full slate of candidates for the August primary election. At a July legislative conference, which met in the Local 248 union hall, 150 delegates representing Milwaukee County CIO unions selected local candidates

Aerial view of the West Allis Works of Allis-Chalmers Manufacturing Company, Milwaukee.

State Historical Society of Wisconsin WHi (X3) 49570

who received CIO endorsement. The CIO slate included both representatives of the Democratic party establishment and CIO union favorites. For the fourth congressional district, the CIO delegates refused support for the incumbent, Thaddeus Wasielewski, and endorsed a young war veteran, Edmund Bobrowicz. They also endorsed a mixed slate of Democratic and Republican incumbents for the state senate. For the state assembly, the delegates endorsed a few traditional Democratic candidates and a large number of union candidates, including three Local 248 members and several others from UAW and CIO locals.[5]

THE Republican primary pitted Joseph McCarthy, a newcomer to statewide politics, against the well-known Progressive-turned-Republican, Robert La Follette. In the August primary, McCarthy unexpectedly defeated LaFollette, largely on the strength of a 10,000-vote majority in Milwaukee County. Milwaukee County, the *Milwaukee Journal* observed, "turned the trick for McCarthy—the same county that saved La Follette from defeat in 1940." The next day, the Milwaukee newspaper blamed labor for La Follette's defeat. The AFL, the CIO, and the railroad brotherhoods, the *Milwaukee Journal* charged, "did not lift a finger for La Follette."[6]

However, labor, particularly the CIO and the Left in the CIO, had been unable to help La Follette because they had directed their attention to the Democratic primary. In the Fourth Congressional District, Edmund Bobrowicz, an army veteran and former organizer for the Fur and Leather Workers Union, scored a major upset over Democratic incumbent Thaddeus Wasielewski. "The smashing primary victory," the *CIO News* proclaimed, "overcame the campaign of the present congressman, a campaign which was largely devoted to Redbaiting of both the CIO as a whole and its candidate." The other major Democratic victors were Howard McMurray, a University of Wisconsin political scientist, for senate, Daniel Hoan, Milwaukee's former Socialist mayor, for governor, and Andrew Biemiller, a former Socialist, for Fifth Congressional District. In addition, many other CIO-PAC candidates won Democratic primary victories for the Wisconsin State Assembly. Emil Mattson, a founder of UAW Local 248, defeated the Democratic incumbent in the third assembly district. In all, ten union candidates won the opportunity to run for Wisconsin assembly seats. For the most part, these were rank-and-file CIO union leaders, shop stewards, and bargaining committeemen.[7]

The Bobrowicz victory was extremely unsettling for the Milwaukee establishment. An electoral novice had defeated a two-term Democratic incumbent. The *Milwaukee Journal* correctly concluded that "Jimmy Higgins," the classic rank-and-file union member, provided the political "legwork" and contributed to Wasielewski's defeat. Indeed, over two hundred workers from CIO unions, Slavic organizations, and the American Polish Labor Council conducted a doorbell and phone campaign in the ethnic working-class neighborhoods of the fourth ward. Wasielewski agreed with the newspaper's "Jimmy Higgins" analysis. The defeated congressman blamed a CIO vendetta against him. He wrote his brother, "I am told they canvassed all of the wards in which I have been strong in the past from house to house and spread gossip to the effect that I was anti-labor and called the working man a loafer and a lot of other things. They followed up this personal contact with literature carrying the same message." Wasielewski mused, "[T]hat they licked me in my strong wards" was "paradoxical and ironical."[8]

The August primary activated the more conservative Milwaukee CIO leaders. Since early summer 1946, anti-Communist CIO "progressives" had held caucuses to plan a union campaign against the Milwaukee CIO's left leaders. Walter Reuther's recent winning of the UAW presidency inspired the conservative Milwaukee auto, steel, and textile union leaders. Within the UAW, "rank-and-file" caucuses emerged to fight pro-Communist union leaders. In the Milwaukee and Wisconsin CIO, Hugh Swofford, a *Milwaukee Sentinel* labor reporter, actually participated in meetings with several of these right-wing leaders. According to him, these CIO leaders "were holding secret caucuses with the purpose of ousting the alleged left wingers from power." Their hopes "rose and fell" as their fortunes waxed and waned in the struggle to oust militants from the Milwaukee "CIO Council. In a pessimistic mood, one leader, Walter Cappel, told Swofford, "if the right wingers weren't successful in removing the left wingers . . . the right wing locals, some 17 in number, including auto, steel, brewery and hosiery workers, would secede from the CIO council and set up their own Milwaukee County Association of CIO Unions."[9]

Given militant labor's successful foray into Milwaukee politics and the possibility of a conservative CIO opposition, the Milwaukee newspapers expressed more than the usual interest in American labor. In their Labor Day reports, they showed a keen interest in opponents to militant CIO unionism and in Communists in the labor movement. The *Milwaukee Sentinel* featured a story on the CIO dissidents in Milwaukee—"CIO Red Purge Due Here." Swofford and Ellis Jensen, the Allis-Chalmers researcher, worked together on their long series of press exposés of labor and Communists. "On Labor Day of 1946," Swofford claimed, "I wrote the first of a series of stories on the coming right-left battle which was to get under way at a CIO council meeting to be held shortly after Labor Day."[10]

In his first article, Swofford reported on a "twin offensive" among ten steelworker and eleven autoworker locals to unseat the left incumbents on the Milwaukee County CIO Council. Moreover, electrical worker, hosiery worker, and brewery worker locals were "sympathetic" to the possible CIO purge. Over the last five months, Swofford added, "the militant locals have held 'progressive caucuses' where ways and means have been discussed of eliminating Communists from the ranks of CIO circles." Apparently, the impending struggle would revolve around CIO council resolutions that would remove Communists from the council and prevent left CIO leaders from running for office. "Reports have been rife lately," Swofford continued, "that various CIO locals in this area are dissatisfied with PAC endorsed candidates."[11]

A few days later, the *Milwaukee Journal* reported the defeat of the conservative CIO dissidents. "Opposition to the allegedly left-wing leadership of the county CIO council," the newspaper related, "got mangled Wednesday night when it tried to tangle with the incumbent administration." After votes on the two resolutions, "the score remained decidedly in favor of the incumbents."[12]

Two weeks after their defeat, the CIO dissidents returned to the Milwaukee CIO council to renew their struggle against the CIO Left. Their challenge took the form of four constitutional amendments—to ban Ku Klux Klan, Bund, and Communist Party members; to equalize participation of new locals on the council; to restrict the number of delegates from a single local to ten; and to limit the number of delegates from one local to the CIO Council Executive Board. For the most part, these changes were an effort to reduce Local 248's control over the CIO council. However, the crucial vote came on an early resolution attacking the rightist Franco government in Spain. A member of the National Maritime Union favored the disavowal of Franco. Walter Cappel, a business representative for twenty small UAW locals, argued that the council should leave international matters to the international unions. Since the large UAW Local 248 controlled 85 votes, the 101-77 vote total favored the left incumbents. Still, the ballot demonstrated a respectable showing for the right caucus. The *Milwaukee Journal* concluded that the result was "indecisive . . . for the comparative strength of the anti-left-wing bloc."[13]

The CIO-PAC political victory and the vigorous CIO right caucuses also inspired more aggressive press coverage of Communists in the Wisconsin labor movement. The two principal Milwaukee newspapers consistently pounded away at the theme of labor and Communism in the Milwaukee CIO. In late September, the *Milwaukee Journal* reported that, although the Wisconsin Communist Party was small, with only 1,200-1,300 members, its "influence is widespread and increasing." Despite its small size, the Communist Party "controls the Milwaukee county and state CIO councils through leadership and hence the destiny of 75,000 CIO workers in the state." In addition to "playing an increasing part in strikes," as among the Allis-Chalmers workers and Milwaukee public employees, it was also "increasingly active in politics." The Communist Party, the newspaper charged, "now is engaged in a membership campaign among factory workers, war veterans, and nationality groups." UAW Local 248, the "pride" of the Wisconsin Communist Party, exerted "strong influence" in labor circles. The Milwaukee newspaper then identified the principal Communists in the Milwaukee area, including Harold Christoffel, who "recently returned here a few days ago from army service."[14]

The next day, the *Milwaukee Journal* further detailed the pervasive Communist influence on the Wisconsin labor movement. "The Communists of Wisconsin," the newspaper reported, "plan unceasingly to gain control of the labor unions. Such control on a mass scale would greatly help them in their avowed aim to impose the Communist system on the United States." Citing the Allis-Chalmers UAW local as a prime example of a Communist-dominated union, it noted that Owen Lambert, a

Street action during the Allis-Chalmers strike in West Allis, 1940–1941.

Milwaukee Journal/State Historical Society of Wisconsin WHi (X3) 21974

Local 248 committeeman and Communist Party member, actively recruited Party members from among the Allis Chalmers strikers. The chief union leaders, Robert Buse, Harold Christoffel, and Joseph Dombek, it charged, were Communists. At union meetings, the Local 248 education director, "showed movies glorifying Russia and the Communist system." A subsequent article described the activities of the various Communist front groups in Wisconsin.[15]

Almost simultaneously with the *Milwaukee Journal* revelations about the Communist Party in Wisconsin, the *Milwaukee Sentinel,* with its masthead proclaiming "Dedicated to Truth, Justice, and Public Service," inaugurated its own series on the role of Communists in Milwaukee and Wisconsin. Each day from September 23 through November 21, 1946, a front-page story appeared. Written by a fictitious correspondent, "John Sentinel," the stories relied on information derived from Allis-Chalmers researchers. Hugh Swofford, the newspaper's labor reporter, identified the real John Sentinel as Allis-Chalmers

researcher and speech writer Ellis Jensen. The son of a Wisconsin quarry owner and a former minister, Jensen wrote speeches for Harold Story, another son of a quarry owner, and Walter Geist, the Allis-Chalmers president. "In short daily articles," the newspaper explained, "the *Sentinel* will focus the light of publicity on each detail of the Communist menace here at home so that the thinking power of intelligent reader audience will be brought to bear on the situation every day." Although couched in informational and intellectual terms, the conservative newspaper clearly intended to arouse Milwaukee citizens and especially labor leaders against the "Red Fascist" menace.[16]

The initial John Sentinel article featured a political cartoon with the Stalin-headed spider and bore the title, "Stalin Over Wisconsin: Reds Aim for Control of Our State." Elaborating on the new theme of "Red-Fascism," it denounced the "Red" leaders of UAW Local 248 and the Communist infiltration of the Milwaukee and Wisconsin labor movement. The second article featured a photograph of Joseph Stalin with quotations from speeches to American Communist leaders. After describing Wisconsin's industrial importance, John Sentinel moved to the Communist failure to capture the AFL and the subsequent

Communist role in the formation of the Milwaukee and Wisconsin CIO. The key figure was Eugene Dennis, then the successor to Earl Browder as secretary of the American Communist Party, who brought together Milwaukee labor leaders "to discuss forming a big union at Allis-Chalmers, for the purpose of getting control of that plant."[17]

Subsequent articles targeted the practices and programs of UAW Local 248 and the Communist connections of its leaders. One John Sentinel article, for example, discussed the Allis-Chalmers strike: "It doesn't make sense to take 11,000 people out on a five or six months' strike at Allis-Chalmers over a few comparatively minor contract issues. We have to look for bigger causes for such a big event." The bigger cause—the "Communist policy" that opposed "American prosperity." In the analysis of the Communist plan, John Sentinel concluded: "Hence, if American reconversion is hamstrung with strikes and slowdowns, America will be unable to carry through its 'imperialist' program." In the mind of John Sentinel, the Allis-Chalmers strike obviously demonstrated that a small minority of Communist union leaders had duped eleven thousand workers into a long strike for "a few relatively minor contract issues." Later articles savagely attacked Local 248 officers, bargaining committee members, and shop stewards. For the most part, they proved guilt by simple association, vague allusions, and sometimes huge leaps of logic.[18]

About the same time, Allis-Chalmers officials obtained the nomination papers for Sigmund Eisenscher, the Communist candidate for governor. They published a glossy pamphlet, *Principle Represented: Communist,* and mailed it to all Allis-Chalmers workers and to the Milwaukee press. The pamphlet contained photographically duplicated pages of the nomination papers with red lines that identified the signatures and provided the titles of Local 248 officers, bargaining committeemen, shop stewards, and shop committeemen. According to the Allis-Chalmers pamphlet, "a majority of the top-ranking officers, "[a]bout 40% of the Stewards," and many other local union members and associates signed the Eisenscher nomination papers. "And finally," it charged, "of the 227 sets of the nomination papers circulated in Milwaukee County, 84, or 37% were circulated by members or officials of Local 248."[19]

When congressional investigators later questioned him about the Eisenscher nomination papers, Robert Buse replied, "These petitions are circulated around in taverns and [on] picket lines. Everybody's nomination papers are." Eisenscher claimed that he needed 5,000 signatures and received "800 of these signatures from the Allis Chalmers picket line." Although he admitted signing the Communist candidate's papers, Buse claimed that he voted for the CIO-endorsed candidate for governor, a Democrat, and also emphasized that his signature indicated "support so far as the right to run for office is concerned."[20]

The anti-Communist campaign played an extremely divisive role within the Milwaukee labor movement. In October, Joseph Mattson, the UAW regional director, wrote to Walter Reuther about the influence of the newspaper reports on the Milwaukee labor scene. In the midst of the bitter Allis-Chalmers and J. I. Case strikes, Mattson told the UAW president: "the forces of reactionary newspapers and employers are mobilizing everything that they have in an all-out drive to break our strikes, if possible, this fall."[21]

Mattson also emphasized the interconnection between the coming Milwaukee elections and internal CIO politics. "At the same time," Mattson continued, "they are using the strikes for all they are able in connection with the fall elections." For two weeks, he added, the *Milwaukee Sentinel* "carried a systematic attack that consists of the most vicious type of 'red-baiting' that we have ever witnessed in this region. They have named almost everyone, in the hope of dividing the forces within the UAW so that they may break the strike." The UAW regional director went on to suggest that the union should "consider the possibility of challenging this newspaper" or should "issue a statement to the effect that the forces within the UAW will not be divided by these kind of attacks."[22]

Milwaukee press reports on labor Communists also inspired a new opposition movement within UAW Local 248. In early October, Leon Venne, a founding member of UAW Local 248 and long-time union activist, announced the formation of the Rank and File Membership Committee (RFMC) to remove the Communist leaders from UAW Local 248. A union member since 1937, Venne had been a shop steward in the tractor shop. His experience demonstrated the process of a CIO unionist's gradual disaffection with the militant UAW local's leadership.

The UAW dissident first became disenchanted with the Local 248 leadership in the fall of 1938 amid Martin's charges about the Communist affiliations of the Local 248 leaders. He told a congressional committee, "I thought it was plain Red baiting." But he gradually became convinced that the charges were true. In his mind, the 1946 strike vote was fraudulent. At the strike vote, Venne recalled, Local 248 leaders were "agitating strike, and so forth, and the strike vote was called for." The security was loose, Venne believed, "anybody could have walked in there." At the union meeting, he remembered, Robert Buse chaired: "All in favor of holding a strike will vote aye. There was a scattering of ayes. A couple of the members rose on the floor and shook their hands trying to get the floor to speak on the issue, but Robert Buse couldn't hear any of that. 'All in favor say "Aye".' 'So ordered.'" As a result of such union methods, Venne grew more and more dissatisfied with the Local 248 leadership.[23]

In October, Venne organized the Rank and File Membership Committee, an apparent outgrowth of the right CIO caucuses, with seventy Allis-Chalmers workers on its original organizing committee. Three other Allis-Chalmers worker caucuses, which numbered around 155 workers, also offered to join with Venne's group. The new RFMC caucus issued a press release: "We of Allis-Chalmers know that we must have a union. A union to us is as important as foremen are to the management. We of Allis-Chalmers are going to have a union. We are going to have local 248." The caucus then criticized left unionism:

> We do not believe in communism or fascism. Our belief lies with Americanism. We live under a democracy, we believe in a democracy, and our union is going to be run under the democratic system.

Ed Eisenscher/Wisconsin State AFL-CIO

Hundreds of police were involved when thousands of strikers demonstrated in November, 1946, on the picket lines at the Allis-Chalmers plant. On this day, sixteen arrests were made.

This is a warning to the Communists in local 248—get the hell out of our union and stay out. From now on it is open season on Communists in local 248.... You have taken us out on three strikes at great loss to us. You have had three strikes and you are out!

At the same time, the RFMC distanced itself from Allis-Chalmers management: "This is not an appeal for a back-to-work movement, but an appeal to a back-to-unionism movement." It appealed for conservative trade unionism that stressed "harmonious relations" among workers and with management.[24]

After the news stories about the RFMC's formation, Venne began to receive angry telephone calls from Local 248 loyalists. He recalled the threats: "'Venne, you rat.' 'Venne, you stooge, we are coming to get you tonight.'" He also received some commendations:

"Venne, keep up the good work. Don't let them scare you. Don't let them scare you." "Don't let them do this." "We are a hundred percent for you." I received hundreds of letters and postcards.

Some people were so afraid that they didn't sign their names. The anti-Communist dissident received personal threats, obscene calls to his wife, threats to his family and children, and unsolicited tradesmen and merchants who were sent to paint his house, to move his family, and to sell his house. "I was getting the 'nerve' treatment," he recalled.[25]

Shortly after he announced the formation of the new Allis-Chalmers workers organization, Venne sent telegrams to Walter Reuther and Philip Murray. "The long drawn out strike of Local 248," Venne wired Reuther, "will result in the destruction of our union at [the] Allis-Chalmers West Allis works unless you and Philip Murray give your support to the majority of the members who are sincerely interested in removing the leaders who are communistic." Venne charged that the Allis-Chalmers union was "completely under communist domination" and that the long strike was "a Communist strategic work stoppage." After claiming that many of the almost two thousand strikebreakers would hit the streets again under a new UAW leadership, Venne concluded: "There is a fast growing rank and file movement to overthrow the Communist leaders of our local."[26]

In mid October, the RFMC tried to hold an evening meeting to expand its membership base. According to the *Milwaukee Sentinel,* the anti-Communist caucus attempted "a quiet little meeting at the Marine Memorial Building." Soon after the meeting began, "a squad of four appeared and cased the situation." One of the men made a phone call. About ten minutes later, John Kaslow, a Local 248 bargaining committee member, "appeared with a handful of companions." After another ten minutes, Arne Hansen, another bargaining committee member, appeared with around thirty other union members. The Local 248 "flying squad" took the floor and denounced Venne for his connections to Allis-Chalmers attorney Harold Story. A short while later, "the whole meeting filed down the stairs and into the night."[27]

After the Local 248 flying squad broke up the RFMC meeting, Venne pressed his attack on the Allis-Chalmers union's leaders at the next union membership meeting. He called for the suspension of the Local 248 bargaining committee, a UAW administratorship for Local 248, and a special committee to negotiate a strike settlement. The rank and file responded with "boos and catcalls" and the leadership charged Venne with "conduct unbecoming a union member," requested his suspension from the union, and called for a union trial to look into Venne's meetings outside the union with foremen in attendance and his public statements to the newspapers. Eventually, the UAW local tried and expelled Venne. When he did return to work, he joined the ranks of Allis-Chalmers strikebreakers.[28]

Also in October, CIO conservatives, pressured by press revelations from without and the anti-Left factions from within, finally ousted the militant CIO leaders from the Milwaukee CIO Council. The anti-Left strategy centered on the admission of several new unions to the council. Especially important was the large brewery workers local, which had recently affiliated with the CIO. If this union, entitled to fifty-two delegates on the council, could be seated at a special meeting before elections were held, then the insurgents might gain control of the CIO organization. In combination with conservative steel- and autoworker delegates, the fifty-two brewery worker delegates would give the anti-leftists a majority on the Milwaukee CIO Council.[29]

The anti-Communists called for a special meeting for the admission of the brewery workers and other conservative locals to the CIO council. Over strong leftist opposition, the conservatives managed to schedule the special meeting for 9 A.M. Sunday, an hour which fortuitously conflicted with a Local 248 membership meeting. At the Sunday meeting, the anti-Communist group unanimously voted to seat the large brewery worker delegation and an additional twenty-five delegates from packinghouse, steel, auto, and hosiery locals. Although the brewery worker delegates were "cautious" in their statements to the Milwaukee press, one new delegate said "the brewery workers will be down there pitching to keep the labor movement American." The brewery workers' business agent facetiously lamented the "little bit of dissension," but he said the new delegates "were proud, happy, and confident of the future of your great labor organization." The following day, the CIO Right caucus sent CIO President Philip Murray an explanation of their meeting along with a copy of the meeting's minutes.[30]

At the next regular meeting, both the Left and the Right were prepared for rancorous confrontation for control of the Milwaukee CIO. In the annual election for CIO officers, the central issue, the *Milwaukee Journal* noted, was "control of the council and possibly the entire state CIO." If the incumbents attempted to "override the action of the special meeting," the rightist insurgents were already prepared with court restraining orders.[31]

The CIO Council meeting began with Left and Right struggling over the legality of the special meeting and the seating of the brewery worker delegation. The left group vigorously criticized the previous "rump meeting" that had admitted the new CIO delegates. One leftist leader charged, "This action is in concert with the Allis-Chalmers Company to break the strike and to defeat the PAC endorsed candidates in the November election." Nonetheless, the right-wing group prevailed, and the new delegates cast their ballots in the CIO council election. In the "hotly contested election," the final tally indicated that the Right won thirteen of the fifteen CIO council elective offices. In fact, they swept the election. The Left won only two uncontested seats. Most of the Milwaukee CIO Council seats now went to members of dissident steel- and autoworker locals.[32]

Milwaukee's press cheered the results. "The defeat of the left wing group," the *Milwaukee Journal* reported, "marked the first major break in the nation in the revolt which has been smoldering against so called Communist domination of the CIO. Milwaukee and Wisconsin represented a major stronghold for the left wingers." Milwaukee's "defeat" of the Left, the newspaper continued, "struck at the heart of the state." The Milwaukee CIO elections well might have "repercussions" in the Wisconsin state CIO organization.[33]

The right CIO leaders soon set their eyes on the forthcoming December Wausau convention of the Wisconsin State CIO. Charles Newman, the rightist secretary of the Milwaukee CIO, said that the "first order of business" would be the preparation of state CIO slates against Communists and Communist sympathizers. He also estimated that the state CIO organization would probably split evenly between the left and right factions. With inauguration ceremonies scheduled for the next regular Milwaukee CIO Council meeting, newly elected Milwaukee CIO president Arthur Conn stated, "The new administration wishes to call on the entire council affiliation to close ranks and stand solidly in this rededication of the council as a genuine American institution, devoted above all to the interests of the American working people."[34]

A *Milwaukee Journal* editorial lauded recent developments in the local labor movement. The defeat of the left leaders, it proclaimed, was "a healthy thing for the CIO movement and for organized labor in the city and the state." The Left used the unions as a "tool of the Communist party and a weapon of Russian foreign policy." Praising the hard work of conservative union leaders, the newspaper added: "The internal fight against the left wingers has been going on for months. It took courage and it took persistence." Nonetheless, more work needed to be done. An important item still remained on the *Milwaukee Journal's* agenda—the role of the Left in the upcoming general

Ed Eisenscher/Wisconsin State AFL-CIO

On December 7, 1946, five years after the bombing of Pearl Harbor, UAW Local 248 sponsored a march during the strike at Allis-Chalmers.

election. "The new leaders of the CIO," the editorial advised, "will also turn their attention to the activities of the CIO-PAC in the state. The PAC, too, hereabouts, has been dominated and directed by left wingers."[35]

The fall general election campaign mirrored the growing Cold War consensus against militant CIO unionism. Despite his defeat in the Democratic primary, Thaddeus Wasielewski did not intend to give up his Democratic congressional seat without a fight and decided to run as an independent candidate against Edmund Bobrowicz. In the South Side Milwaukee Polish and Slavic communities and the Democratic ward halls, the two congressional candidates waged an intense struggle for Milwaukee's ethnic voters. At one South Side election rally, attended by four hundred supporters, Wasielewski emphasized an anti-Communist theme: "Our fight is for God, country, home, and family. I never was anti-Russian, but I am against communism."[36]

The conservative Polish press quickly reacted to Wasielewski's charges of Communism, expressing dismay with Bobrowicz's victory. According to one Polish newspaper, Polish voters "departed from the American and Polish flag and stood

under the hammer and sickle and do not even know that they committed a betrayal." In a similar vein, another declared: "The democratic candidate, even though he has a Polish name, is a man of clearly declared pro-Soviet sympathies, for whom everything that is against the politics of Moscow is 'fascistic.'"[37]

In the midst of the campaign, a *Milwaukee Journal* editorial decried the CIO's political strength. The CIO-PAC "has developed into a husky youngster." The Milwaukee newspaper feared two possible outcomes of labor's foray into politics. A labor group could capture or take control of a major political party. The result would be a labor party with "class divisions and class strife." And this "might bring an American fascism." Or a "conspiratorial minority" could gain control of the labor movement. If successful, they could "stir up strife, foment strikes, create discord." Through their control of the CIO-PAC, the Communists would "worm their members or sympathizers into positions of power." In order to survive, the CIO-PAC "must remain an American labor movement with the purpose of *improving America for Americans*."[38]

In mid-September, the *Milwaukee Journal* pulled out all of the stops in its campaign against the "Communist" Democratic candidate. In a front-page story, it proclaimed: "Deep Red is Background of Candidate Bobrowicz." The newspaper boldly stated, "Edmund V. Bobrowicz . . . is a communist." It then cited "the pattern on Bobrowicz," which included his position as international representative for the Fur and Leather Workers Union, his friendships and associations with known Communists, his engagement in Communist political activities, his "ploddingly" following the Communist Party line, and his nomination papers, which shared circulators and signers with Communist Party candidates. A classic formulation of guilt by association and innuendo, the long newspaper article detailed Bobrowicz's associations and activities in recent years. Despite the Democratic candidate's recent denials, the newspaper proclaimed: "In thought and action, he has shown himself to be a communist, spelled with a small 'c.'"[39]

The next day, the newspaper published an editorial "To the Democrats of Wisconsin." After again painting Bobrowicz with a Red brush, the editor proclaimed: "This man is an impostor in the Democratic ranks. The organized Democrats owe him neither allegiance nor support." It concluded: "The Democratic organization owes it to the people of this city and this state to repudiate this man as its candidate."[40]

Democratic leaders quickly responded. From mid-September to early October, the Democratic party attempted to solve the problem of the "Red" Democrat. Initially, critics claimed that Bobrowicz did not even hold a Democratic party membership card, but he produced it as proof of his party credentials. Robert Tehan, the Wisconsin member of the National Democratic Committee, promised Democratic action against him, publicly stating that he was "violently opposed to communism and communists." At one point, Tehan even personally interviewed Bobrowicz to assess his loyalty to the Democratic party's ideals.[41]

In such a climate, the Republican candidates had a field day with charges against "Red" Democrats. At one election forum, Charles Kersten, the Republican candidate in the Fifth Congressional District, attacked his opponent, Andrew Biemiller, a former Milwaukee Socialist. Biemiller's "record," he charged, "stamps him as an extreme left winger." After a reference to Bobrowicz, Kersten also quipped: "the Democratic party is in the position of 'a bear on roller skates.'"[42]

Confronted with Red charges against its candidates, the Democratic party soon decided to take action against Bobrowicz. According to the *Milwaukee Journal,* the congressional candidate was the Democrats' "No. 1 headache in the November 5 election campaign." But the CIO-PAC problem extended beyond the boundaries of Wisconsin. The National Democratic Committee, the newspaper reasoned, was "wary about repudiating Bobrowicz for fear it will offend the CIO Political Action Committee." Since the Wisconsin CIO-PAC endorsed and supported other Democratic candidates, including McMurray for senate, Hoan for governor, and Biemiller for Congress, the political situation required extreme delicacy.[43]

After intense behind-the-scenes maneuvering within the state and national Democratic parties and the national CIO-PAC, Tehan finally decided to drop Bobrowicz from the Democratic ticket and to denounce him as a Communist. He announced that he would "actively oppose Bobrowicz in the Nov. 5 election." He also urged similar action from "every loyal Democrat and every other citizen devoted to liberal principles of government." The next day, Charles P. Greene, the

Wisconsin and Milwaukee Democratic chairman, added: "the entire state Democratic organization is now on record as being in favor of ditching Bobrowicz." While McMurray, the senatorial candidate, did not immediately disavow Bobrowicz, Hoan, the gubernatorial candidate, and Biemiller and William G. Rice, two other congressional candidates, fell into line. And, after praising Tehan for his "political integrity," a *Milwaukee Journal* editorial proclaimed: "The slyly laid plan of the Communists to invade the Democratic party and to build up their power in the American congress could not go unchallenged." Eventually, McMurray also joined his fellow Democrats in the general denunciation of Bobrowicz.[44]

Once the Democratic Party regulars had repudiated the congressional candidate, they targeted other leftist CIO-PAC candidates. For example, Milwaukee Democratic leader Greene reported that his executive committee "urged Democratic voters to withdraw their support of Emil Mattson," a Local 248 member who had won a Democratic nomination for the state assembly. During a four-hour closed session, the Milwaukee Democratic leaders also investigated the charges against Bobrowicz and Mattson and interrogated three other CIO-PAC assembly candidates. The Milwaukee Democratic committee then formally "voted to revoke the membership cards of Edmund V. Bobrowicz . . . and Emil E. Mattson." The three CIO-PAC candidates "signed statements addressed to the county Democratic leadership attesting that they were not Communists." The Democratic leaders exonerated two but decided that the third needed further investigation.[45]

Two weeks before the general election, a *Milwaukee Sentinel* editorial repudiated the CIO-PAC candidates as "Moscow's Candidates." The Hearst newspaper declared: "Once again, Soviet Russia is intervening in an American election, campaigning actively on behalf of its candidates." Moscow supported the CIO-PAC in three ways—through Communist Party rallies and radio speakers, through financial assistance to states and congressional districts, and through direct appeals on Soviet radio. In an English-language broadcast, it charged, "The Russian speaker especially commended the candidates in this country WHO HAVE THE ENDORSEMENT OF THE CIO POLITICAL ACTION COMMITTEE." The long Red arm from Moscow constituted an "intolerable interference in American political affairs by a foreign government."[46]

The "average citizen," the editorial concluded, "has the right and the duty—as well as the power—to repudiate at the polls in November the CANDIDATES OF SOVIET RUSSIA for the CONGRESS OF THE UNITED STATES." And the American voter could "identify" the Communist candidates, "For, on the declaration of Moscow, the candidates of Soviet Russia are THE CANDIDATES OF PAC."[47]

Ironically, once the mainstream Democrats opened the Pandora's box of Red-baiting, the specter of Communism remained to haunt their more moderate candidates. After the Communist charges eliminated or silenced the Democratic party's Left, similar charges reappeared against the Democratic party's centrist candidates. Joseph McCarthy, the Republican candidate for the Senate, used this tactic against his liberal Democratic opponent McMurray. At a forum attended by both

Ed Eisenscher/Wisconsin State AFL-CIO

The Relief Committee of Local 248 assists Allis-Chalmers strikers to obtain strike relief and old age benefits. Assisting applicants are (left to right) Ben Cizewski, Lulu Belle McBride, Casey Walker, William Ostovich, Luther McBride, and Arnold Vogel.

candidates, McCarthy "flung the charge of 'communism' at his rival." After McMurray criticized the Republican's association with American Action, Inc., a conservative political action group, McCarthy vehemently responded: "If it is organized to fight communism as they say, I welcome their help in defeating communists and those who are communistically inclined like McMurray. "In his campaign literature for the fifth congressional district race, Charles Kersten successfully contrasted his Americanism with Biemiller's Communism. Thus was "Mc Carthyism" born, in the fire of Milwaukee labor politics.[48]

As the November general election approached, the Communist issue attracted the attention of a growing number of voters, swelling Milwaukee voter registration lists. Further, the state ballot contained a referendum on state aid for busing to private schools. Sponsored by conservative Republicans, the referendum proposed the use of public funds to transport parochial and private school children. This, too, increased voter interest in the election, especially among Catholics, who often played a conservative role in Milwaukee labor politics. By the end of October, more than 300,000 Milwaukee voters were registered to vote in the general election.[49]

Although Wisconsin Democrats later charged that Communist labor leaders were responsible for the eventual

Republican victory, Milwaukee labor went in several different directions in the election campaign. The more conservative AFL leaders refused to endorse Bobrowicz and supported his Republican opponent. Thus, Frank Ranney, the Federated Trades Council leader, announced his support for John Brophy, the Republican candidate in the Fourth Congressional District. The Milwaukee AFL leader condemned Bobrowicz as a Communist and also repudiated Wasielewski for his support of the antilabor Smith-Connally Bill. Moreover, some conservative labor leaders even supported McCarthy, because his opponent had the CIO-PAC endorsement. However, the United Labor Committee, a new coalition of Democratic conservatives in the AFL, CIO, and Railroad Brotherhoods, although refusing to endorse Bobrowicz nevertheless endorsed Hoan, McMurray, and Biemiller, the other Democratic candidates.[50]

In late October, the struggle again shifted to the West Allis plant gates. Earlier, the recently discharged Harold Christoffel had returned from eighteen months of army service to help lead the Allis-Chalmers strikers. At a plant gate rally, around two thousand Local 248 members had welcomed their former union president. Repeating Buse's call for arbitration of the unresolved strike issues, he declared: "That is our basic answer to those who say that the company can't negotiate with this union and these Communists over here," referring to the platform group of UAW leaders. "The cheers which greeted Christoffel," the *Milwaukee Sentinel* reported, "were more enthusiastic than for the other speakers. There is apparently hope among the workers that Christoffel can do what the incumbent union leadership has failed to do—bring the costliest Allis strike in history to an early end." Despite hopes for accommodation and settlement, Christoffel and the other speakers "loosed bitter words against the Sentinel's campaign to expose the Communist dominated leadership of many CIO locals here, including Local 248." Christoffel's reappearance on the Milwaukee labor scene, however, stiffened management resistance to all union demands.[51]

One week before the general election, Allis-Chalmers officials inaugurated a back-to-work movement. In response to such corporate appeals, Local 248 president Robert Buse addressed a Sunday morning strike rally of about one thousand union members. The militant union, he announced, had reached "the turning point of the strike." The Local 248 bargaining committee, he told strikers, had offered to return to work and to submit "all disputed issues to the binding decision of an impartial arbitrator." Management had refused the offer to arbitrate. He then urged strikers to return to the streets to prevent strikebreakers from entering the West Allis plant. "The only way," Buse declared, "that the company can be forced to negotiate or arbitrate is to have a show of solidarity on the picket lines." One shop steward also urged the union members to demonstrate their solidarity on the picket lines and even suggested "enlist[ing] the scabs to get on the picket lines and atone for their sins."[52]

Union attorney Dan Sobel offered advice to union pickets. He "instructed the strikers to obey the Wisconsin employment relations board rulings defining picketing at the plant." In order to avoid company charges of violating Wisconsin labor law, he recommended compliance with the earlier WERB rulings on mass picketing. "Just remember," he added, "that order does not prevent you from picketing. That is a constitutional right. Keep your hands in your pockets on the picket line and try to persuade everybody not to pass through the line." Then he reminded the workers, "But if anybody endangers your life, you have a right to protect yourself." Sobel's advice resulted in massed "belly-to-back" picketing, where striking workers formed a tight wall at Allis-Chalmers gates.[53]

The next day, five hundred to eight hundred strikers blocked the seventeen Allis-Chalmers plant gates. Three violent incidents occurred at the main gate near Greenfield Avenue and South 70th Street. The *Milwaukee Journal* reported: "Several score strikers and workers were severely mauled Monday morning in three bloody skirmishes on the Allis-Chalmers picket lines." In three instances, "the fighting started when groups of 10 to 20 non-strikers attempted to fight their way through closely massed pickets." In "each melee," the strikers and non-strikers overpowered the two West Allis policemen on duty. "The gate," the newspaper related, "is about eight feet wide and about 35 pickets kept their tight line moving so closely that no one could shove through. A number of workers who attempted to squeeze through were bumped away and urged to go home." In the first incident, "a big worker in a white shirt," who had been denied entry, "stood back on the street, shouted to the crowd of workers outside to join him, and, then, with about 20 of them, hit the massed pickets with a flying wedge." The result

was a general melee: "Strikers, nonstrikers and police were piled three deep in a furious slugging and kicking fight that lasted about five minutes." After about twenty minutes, two other incidents followed, "when other groups of workers decided to force their way through in the same manner."[54]

Over the next week, angry Allis-Chalmers strikers fiercely fought supervisors, strikebreakers, and police. For the most part, after calm mornings, violence occurred with the afternoon change of shifts. As strikebreakers exited and entered the plant, scuffles often developed into fights. Often sympathizers from the surrounding community supported the union strikers. According to one account, "From 3,000 to 5,000 spectators, including children and housewives, were gathered in the park near the plant known as Allis-Chalmers grove." The "surging mass of humanity" called the nonstriking workers "scabs," "rats," and "yellowbellies." The pickets and spectators also threw oranges, tomatoes, and paint bombs at the strikebreakers and their automobiles. Small groups of strikebreakers formed "flying squadrons" to charge through picket lines. In several instances, furious strikers damaged automobiles, overturned some, and set some on fire. Sometimes police officers escorted nonstriking workers through the picket lines. Sometimes strikers fought off police and strikebreakers. In several instances, strikers freed arrested picketers from the police.[55]

Two incidents revealed the savage intensity of the struggle to keep the West Allis plant closed. At one gate, the *Milwaukee Journal* noted, "About 80 to 100 workers massed across the street from the gate, shouted to the deputies, 'Open up a path for us; we're coming through!'" The police attempted to assist the strikebreakers. "The workers," the newspaper continued, "hit the picket line on the run, and in a moment there was a wild scuffle of workers, strikers, and officers. About 40 of the workers had gone through when pickets managed to close ranks again." At another gate, "a group of about 25 workers gathered their forces in the middle of the street and attempted to smash their way through the middle of the picket line. Fists flew briefly until the workers and pickets were disentangled by the police." At this gate, the deputies sometimes opened pathways for strikebreakers and their automobiles. The angry pickets broke the windows of two cars. "The deputies," the newspaper related, "attempted to seize one picket suspected as a window breaker but the officers were surrounded by a swarm of pickets who took the man away from them."[56]

The worst "riotous flareups" appeared on Halloween. According to the head of the Milwaukee police detail, "most of the trouble so far has occurred when large groups of thrill seeking teen-agers and spectators would shout and boo at police, egging on the pickets, and then would swarm in among the pickets whenever there was any jostling or other disturbance on the picket lines. Then a full sized fight would develop." The trouble began in the evening when an automobile drove through one of the plant gates. "At that time," the *Milwaukee Journal* reported, "there were more than 6,000 spectators milling around on S. 70th St. and fewer than 1,000 pickets. Many of the spectators were youngsters." As the automobile attempted to leave, the police and deputies sought to clear a path through the pickets. "When the car reached the pave-

Ed Eisenscher/Wisconsin State AFL-CIO

**Counting the votes during the Allis-Chalmers strike.
The Wisconsin Employment Relations Board conducted this vote
following an attempt to decertify Local 248 as the bargaining
representative for Allis-Chalmers workers. Local 248 retained
its role as bargaining agent by a narrow margin.**

ment," the newspaper continued, "some of the pickets started to
close around it again. This was the signal for the crowd, and
hundreds of spectators rushed in. A riotous scene developed
with fists flying and rocks being thrown for around five minutes." Later, the crowd grew to around eight thousand, including about two thousand teenagers. The Halloween crowd
stoned strikebreakers and police. Describing two arrested
teenagers, the Milwaukee police chief said: "These youngsters
deliberately threw rocks at a patrolman and a deputy sheriff."[57]

The real trouble began when "guest" pickets from other
CIO unions, around two hundred fifty from the Pressed Steel
Tank Company and fifty from the National Maritime Union,
appeared on the scene to express solidarity with the forty Allis-
Chalmers picketers. The authorities, who now had achieved a
strict separation of picketers and spectators, prevented the sympathetic picketers from joining their union brothers. When the
union sound truck complained about the denial of the constitutional rights of the other spectators who could want to picket,
the maritime union members, the *Milwaukee Journal* noted,
"broke away from the picket line for about 10 minutes and
marched through the crowd that was being held back by the
police. When it returned to the picket line, it had picked up
about 200 additional marchers." A Milwaukee police captain
decided to prevent a march to another gate and created a police
line to hold back the picketers. The union supporters at the rear
pushed the others into the police line. "In an instant," the newspaper continued, "what had been a shoving match became a
twisting melee and, as tempers flared, fists flew and the swirling

mass moved down 70th st. *[sic]* to in front of the Allis-Chalmers
clubhouse." The union sound truck ordered the marchers to
return to their line, and the police arrested several of the
ringleaders.[58]

In the midst of the turmoil, the boundary line between
pickets and spectators broke down and "several thousand spectators, including many teen age boys and girls, . . . swarmed to
the west side of 70th st." The swelled ranks of the picketers
started another shoving match. A final incident occurred after
police arrested a spectator. As they marched away with their
prisoner, "they were surrounded and pulled by about 150 to
200 other spectators who were trying to rescue the prisoner
from the police." This time, however, the police held their captive. After an hour and a half, the pickets and spectators left the
streets outside the West Allis plant.[59]

The breakdown of social order brought renewed calls for a
return to the bargaining table, and the union again offered to
have all unsettled strike issues arbitrated. Management again
declined the prospect of a mediated settlement. At a Local 248
membership meeting, UAW secretary-treasurer George Addes
reaffirmed the national UAW's pledge of its "unqualified" support for the embattled local. For Addes, the Allis-Chalmers and
J. I. Case strikes were a part of a National Association of
Manufacturers strategy for "breaking unionization in every other basic industry." The Allis-Chalmers strike, he asserted, was
"a life and death struggle against one of the most arrogant, stubborn and irresponsible employers in Wisconsin." Given the
strike's national significance, he promised that the UAW would
continue its $25,000 strike support payments. And responding
to the repeated charges of Communism, he concluded: "If fighting for a decent level of living for our families is communistic,
then there are 140,000,000 Communists in America."[60]

The mood was tense on the eve of the November election.

In response to a union charge that an Allis-Chalmers memorandum invited "foreman and scabs to break picket lines by force," W. C. Van Cleaf replied, "If these reports are correct, the plan has been worked out independently by employees. This is undoubtedly a protective measure against picket line violence engineered by the Communistic leadership of Local 248." At the Sunday Local 248 membership meeting, Buse appealed to one thousand union members for "a heavy picket turnout" on Monday morning. But both company and union appeals had little effect, since only seventy persons appeared for the Monday's "mass march," and the normal contingent of about 220 pickets were at the plant gates. The next day, after a full week of front-page newspaper headlines about the widespread violence on the Allis Chalmers picket lines, Milwaukee voters went to the polls.[61]

Just before the general election, the *Milwaukee Journal* offered an analysis of Milwaukee labor's important role in the coming vote. The McCarthy-McMurray, Biemiller-Kersten, and Bobrowicz-Wasielewski contests offered exciting races between Democratic and Republican candidates. McMurray, the newspaper reasoned, "is banking on strong support from organized labor in Milwaukee, Racine, and Kenosha counties to overcome whatever lead McCarthy might pile up in rural areas." In an editorial, the influential newspaper endorsed Republican Walter Goodland for governor and Democrat Andrew Biemiller and Independent Thaddeus Wasielewski for Congress. It failed to endorse either McMurray or McCarthy in the Senate race. It also supported the school busing referendum. On Bobrowicz, the newspaper asserted, "His deceit should bring his defeat on Tuesday."[62]

The November general election was a rout for the Left, for liberals, and for the Democrats. Nationwide, the Cold War, domestic social upheaval, and labor and Communism pushed conservative Republicans into national and state offices. In Milwaukee, the long Allis-Chalmers strike, the press exposes of Communist leaders, the struggle for control of the CIO council, and strike violence produced a victory for Republicans. Although the busing referendum lost statewide, it won in Milwaukee and brought out large numbers of conservative Catholic voters who voiced their dissatisfaction with militant labor at the polling booth.

For Wisconsin and Milwaukee Democrats, the general election was a major disappointment. By a margin of over two hundred thousand votes, the *Milwaukee Journal* reported, Republican Joseph McCarthy soundly defeated Howard McMurray for the La Follette Senate seat, "thus ending the La Follette 'dynasty,' which had endured in the state for so many years." McCarthy won in all Wisconsin counties except Dane County, a traditional La Follette stronghold. Moreover, the Republicans swept all major state offices. The conservative *Milwaukee Sentinel* gloated over the massive Republican victories:

WISCONSIN'S ADMINISTRATION IS 100 PER CENT REPUBLICAN. WISCONSIN'S CONGRESSIONAL DELEGATION—TWO SENATORS AND 10 REPRESENTATIVES—IS 100 PER CENT REPUBLICAN.

Indeed, a fundamental shift had occurred in Milwaukee politics. "Chief surprise of the election," the Hearst newspaper continued, "was the fact that Milwaukee County, historically the home of Socialism, Dan Hoan, New Dealism, and labor-liberalism, followed the rest of the state into the Republican column. Both [Walter] Goodland and McCarthy carried the county."[63]

The *Milwaukee Journal,* the liberal voice of the Milwaukee establishment, reported: "McCarthy's strength—and McMurray's weakness— in Milwaukee county, was the surprise of the election to Democratic leaders." Problems from both the Left and the Right had bedeviled the Democratic candidate. "The hapless McMurray," the newspaper concluded, "was caught 'in the middle' on the 'Communist' issue. He lost strength, not only with the anti-Communist element which had been voting with the New Deal since 1932, but with the 'radicals' who backed Edmund Bobrowicz on the Democratic ticket in the fourth district." In effect, a divided and embattled labor movement had undermined the Democratic campaigns for all Wisconsin offices.[64]

By nearly as large a margin, the eighty-four-year-old Republican Walter Goodland handily defeated Democrat Daniel Hoan, the former Socialist mayor of Milwaukee, in the gubernatorial race. The *Milwaukee Journal* came to the "inescapable" conclusion that "the Progressives followed their leadership and voted for Republicans, including McCarthy." In the Fifth Congressional District, Charles Kersten, the Republican, soundly defeated Biemiller, the AFL candidate. The Republican victories dramatically symbolized the end of the Wisconsin Socialist and Progressive traditions.[65]

In the Fourth Congressional District, the Republican Brophy defeated the upstart CIO-PAC candidate Bobrowicz in a relatively close race. Brophy received 47,935 votes; Bobrowicz, 43,268. Wasielewski, the three-term incumbent, was a distant third with only 36,780 votes. The *Milwaukee Journal* characterized the Fourth District campaign as "one of the hottest and most unusual campaigns" in Milwaukee. It dramatically symbolized the tortuous process of Wisconsin's political realignment. "The campaign," the newspaper observed, "cast Wasielewski, the Democratic incumbent, as an Independent, against Brophy, a former Socialist and Progressive who became a Republican last spring in the merger of the Republicans and Progressives, and Bobrowicz, a Communist running under the banner of the Democrats without the party leaders' blessing." It brought out over 130,000 voters, a record number for a Milwaukee off-year election. Brophy's strength was in West Allis and West Milwaukee, two areas affected by the picket line violence, and Wauwatosa, a Republican residential suburb. Bobrowicz's strength was in Cudahy and South Milwaukee, two ethnic and working-class suburbs. He also carried five of the district's "strongly Polish" wards. According to William G. Rice, the Democratic congressional candidate for Madison, "Bobrowicz came closer to election than any other Democratic Congressional candidate in Wisconsin." Milwaukee voters, he added, considered the Communist charges "either untrue or irrelevant."[66]

In the Wisconsin senate, Milwaukee voters returned all of the incumbents, three Democrats and one Republican, to office. Robert Tehan, who had figured prominently in the Bobrowicz

Wisconsin State AFL-CIO

Thaddeus Wasielewski, Democratic Congressmen from the Fourth Congressional District, speaks at a campaign rally in 1946. Upset by a CIO-backed candidate, Edmund Bobrowicz, in the Democratic primary, Wasielewski ran for re-election in the general election as an Independent. Note the strategic tear in the campaign sign.

affair, won by the narrowest margin. In the Wisconsin assembly contests, the Democrats also suffered some significant defeats. Charles Greene, the Milwaukee and Wisconsin Democratic leader, lost a close race to his Republican opponent. Five CIO-PAC-endorsed union candidates won assembly seats and five lost. Three CIO-PAC assembly candidates who the press identified as Communists (including Local 248 members Emil Mattson and Charles Fisher) lost. A fourth loser, John Killian, publicly had supported Bobrowicz's campaign. All in all, the Milwaukee Republicans took two seats from incumbents, Fisher and Green, and gained three more seats in other uncontested races.[67]

In an election postmortem, a *Milwaukee Journal* editorial analyzed the role of labor in the national and local elections. "All over the nation," it observed, "the people vented their wrath at Labor's spokesmen. Moderates as well as radicals went

down." The formerly "strident and boastful" robust CIO-PAC, the editorial added, "flattened out completely this time. Its 'Jimmy Higgins' house to house campaign, its pamphlets, its radio broadcasts availed nothing. It neither 'purged' its opponents nor elected its friends. Many of its bitterest enemies won reelection by tremendous margins." In sum, the political mood of the nation and Milwaukee took a decisive turn toward social and political conservatism.[68]

In the 1946 election, conservative AFL leaders and militant CIO leaders shifted labor's political loyalties and altered the alignment of political forces. Progressives went into the Republican party. Old-guard Socialists went into either the Democratic or the Republican parties. In effect, fear of the Left in the Democratic Party drove conservative AFL and CIO labor leaders toward the Republicans. Moreover, in the campaign, the specter of Communism loomed large and resulted in considerable Red-baiting of left and liberal candidates. The result was a stunning victory for Joseph McCarthy and other Republicans.■

From Stephen Meyer, *"Stalin Over Wisconsin":*
The Making and Unmaking of Miltant Unionism, 1900–1950
(Rutgers University Press, New Brunswick, 1992).

Anatomy of a Strike
in Marinette

BY BERNARD KARSH

*Bernard Karsh's unique study of a strike by garment workers in
Marinette offers an inside look at labor conflict and resolution in the 1950s.
Because of the controversial nature of the sometimes violent strike, Karsh did
not use the real names of the company (Marinette Knitting Mills) or the union
(International Ladies Garment Workers Union Local 480) when the book
was first published in 1958.*

SHORTLY before 6 o'clock on the morning of July 12, [1951] a picket line formed at the main entrance of the Saylor Company. Although more than a hundred employees had voted to strike the previous night, the line consisted of exactly two persons—Phil and Helen. Small groups of union members gathered across the street from the mill entrance, awaiting directions from their leaders. Only a handful had any notion of what a picket was supposed to do. The rest had never before acted on a strike stage.

Because the strike had been called in a hurry, there had been no time to organize picket teams, appoint picket captains, secure necessary placards, or assign pickets to the different mill entrances, driveways, and loading dock. Yet the organizers anticipated that any sort of a picket line would serve as a deterrent if the employer should attempt to continue production and employees who were not union members should attempt to enter the plant.

The mill itself stretched over almost half a city block with one side facing an alley and the other three facing city streets. The alley separated the mill from a parking lot which occupied the remainder of the block. About sixty of the workers standing across the street volunteered for picket duty, but Phil had to know precisely where the company property was located before he could assign them. Three city policemen who appeared on the scene told him that the entire block was Miller property. Phil decided that his small force could not possibly cover the whole area and that the immediate need was to place pickets at the four mill entrances, the loading dock, and the rear entrance facing the alley. However, he could see no way to block attempts to enter the mill from the alley.

It quickly became evident, as the organizers had anticipated, that at least some employees did want to work. The pickets had been hastily instructed to stop such attempts, but at this point they did not consider physical resistance as proper. As small groups of non-members approached the plant entrances, the strikers confronted them and tried to talk them out of going in. Sometimes simple conversation was enough. When discussion failed, the pickets would shout for Phil or Helen or one of the few experienced pickets to come and help. Sometimes they succeeded, but most often they failed. Phil was kept extremely busy rushing from one plant entrance to another, trying to keep people away from their jobs and, at the same time, trying to organize an orderly picket line and to assign specific people to definite picketing tasks.

Many other arrangements had to be made. The force of professional organizers had to be augmented. Arrangements had to be made with the union's Midwest officials for financing the strike. Strike benefits had to be paid. A union kitchen had to be set up and staffed for serving three meals a day to the strikers and their families. A strike headquarters near the plant had to be rented. Arrangements had to be made with the union's international headquarters for bail bond in case any of the union people were arrested. News releases and pickets' placards had to be prepared. All of these matters required Phil's immediate attention.

Phil spent much of the first morning of the strike away from the picket line making these arrangements by telephone and telegraph. One time when he returned to the strike scene he saw a police officer across the street talking to four women workers who were not union members. The officer escorted the women to the picket line in front of the mill's main entrance and told Phil that he was going to take them through and into the plant.

He told me that he has orders that I'm supposed to open up, and I told him his job was to see that everything was run peacefully but not to take scabs through the picket line and that we wouldn't permit it. Then he pushed his weight around a little bit, but it didn't do any good.

Shortly after this, the Mayor of Saylor, the Chief of Police,

Labor Day celebration in Wausau in 1945.

and twelve or thirteen of the city's seventeen-man force appeared on the scene. Phil attempted to explain privately to the Mayor the union's position with regard to the picket line and the non-strikers. He was unsuccessful. Instead, the Mayor addressed some general remarks to the crowd, saying that it was his "duty to enforce the law and preserve order." What happened next is related by Phil:

> The Mayor decided that he wasn't going to listen to anyone, and he and the Chief with the other coppers back of them formed a wedge. They tried to get the people to disperse, and at my suggestion, they didn't. And then they formed a flying wedge and tried going through with the scabs in the center of the wedge. They kicked and pushed their way through the picket line. At this time we had about twenty-five or thirty girls on the line, and I think there were maybe four or five men including myself. It was nothing serious, but there were a number of bruises that turned up a week later on the arms and legs of the women. At first the people on the line didn't know what to do, but when they saw what happened, they became very determined that the Mayor and the cops weren't going to break through. And so they held the line, and then the cops pushed them aside and they went back and formed a new line in back so they were about four or five deep and all across the entrance. And then there was a skirmish—I don't know how long it lasted, but I imagine it didn't last more than a minute, and they held the line and they were screaming at the cops and the Mayor, and Helen was leading the way and screaming at the cops, and then the cops must have realized that they couldn't break through unless they wanted to cause some real physical damage. Even though they

seemed determined enough to get the scabs in and bust up the line, they stopped and went away because they didn't have the courage to cause real physical harm to those women.

The Mayor confirmed in substance this account of the incident. A police officer had telephoned him to say that pickets were stopping workers from entering the mill. During the phone conversation, Tom Miller got on the line and confirmed the policeman's report. The Mayor continued his account:

> After this telephone call, I went out there with some of the police force, and I told those people who were picketing that anybody who wanted to work had a right, under the law, to do so. It was my duty as Mayor to see that law and order were kept. It was incumbent upon me as Mayor to get the police out there and to see that those who wanted to work were permitted to do so. The maintenance of law and order and the preservation of the peace is my responsibility under local and state statutes. I saw one striker grab a woman by the arm as she tried to go into the place and hold her back. That was enough for me. Four of the women wanted to go in, and I told the pickets that they better open up and let them in or there would be trouble. But that Draper kept running up and down the picket line yelling, "Hold the line—don't let them in!" He got those women out there all excited and I thought what the hell was the use of trying to take those four women in—it would only stir them up more.

At this point the two accounts depart slightly. The Mayor related that the pickets permitted him to enter the plant to discuss the situation with the employer.

> They opened the line and let me through. I told Tom Miller that he should close the place up tight—don't try to run it until the strike was settled. I told him that he and his family were living in

the horse and buggy days. Labor is here to stay, and they might as well realize that. I told him that if General Motors and the Ford Company gave in to unions, who the hell did he think they were that they could break a union with a little dinky company like that. Especially this union. But those Millers are proud and stubborn people.

Later that morning he spoke in private with the union's chief organizer.

I told that Draper that if he would stop getting those people so riled up and keep them quiet, I'd take the police out of there. But he wouldn't do it. He just kept running around getting people more and more excited. I could have picked him up and that woman organizer he had down there and thrown them in jail for a spell. But that would have only added fuel to the fire and then what would I have on my hands?

Phil was a bit disappointed at the Mayor's refusal to arrest him.

I was trying to get myself picked up. I wanted either one of the organizers or myself to be arrested. You know the old story—the martyr gag. We knew that nothing would happen, but our people didn't. We wanted them to see that in a strike it was possible to get arrested and that it doesn't hurt and not to be afraid. But they wouldn't pick us up. I did everything I could to get them to arrest me, anything that wasn't completely illegal.

Although Phil's desire remained frustrated, he assessed the incident as extremely valuable to the union:

From that moment on, the people knew that a picket sometimes has to fight—they just don't always simply walk a line. And the Mayor did us a tremendous favor. From then on the people were all ready. The feeling was that if they could stop the Mayor, then they could stop anybody from coming in. That educated them as much or more than anything else.

The Mayor was indeed stopped and did not attempt to cross the picket line again. But others were not stopped.

Throughout the remainder of the first day, Phil took care of the many necessary details. The national headquarters of the union arranged with a Saylor insurance firm to provide up to $10,000 bail bond in cases of arrest. The international's regional vice-president approved strike benefits of $10.00 a week for women and $16.00 for men, the difference based on the assumption that women had working husbands. Further, both men and women were given an additional $2.00 for each dependent. Strike duty was to begin at 6 o'clock in the morning, Monday through Friday, and all members who spent at least four hours a day on strike duty were eligible for benefits.

An empty store about two blocks from the mill was rented as a combination strike headquarters and kitchen-dining room. Cooking facilities, tables, and chairs were hastily installed. All workers were asked to picket, but those who felt they could not were assigned to help in the kitchen. A few fence-sitters did daily turns on the picket line, but most of them elected to work in the kitchen. Two additional organizers were sent in from the Chicago regional office, and Chuck, who had been sent out from the state office on a temporary basis, was now assigned to Saylor for the duration of the strike. A local sign painter prepared appropriate picket signs. The "inside" committee was transformed into a strike committee.

Harassment and Violence

During the second day of the strike, the city police made the first of a series of arrests. A picket was charged with assault when she attempted to stop a non-striker from entering the plant. The local newspaper reported the incident on its front page:

A woman picket was accused of assault and battery today in the two-day old strike at the Saylor Company. Mrs. Helen Dobbs was accused of scuffling with Mrs. Esther Blaine who was trying to enter the strike-bound plant earlier today. Philip Draper, . . . International Representative for the union, posted $100 bond for Mrs. Dobbs in Police Judge Dan Cowen's court this morning.

Draper pleaded not guilty on behalf of Mrs. Dobbs, who was taken to Saylor General Hospital shortly before she was to appear in Judge Cowen's court. Trial was set for July 23 at 10:00 A.M.

The report went on to say that Draper criticized the conduct of the police, blaming them for causing Mrs. Dobbs to become hysterical, which necessitated the trip to the hospital. Tom Miller was quoted as saying that about twenty-five or thirty workers were inside the plant, which was operating, and the story stated that eight of the city's seventeen police, almost the entire day force, were on duty at the plant.

From the outset of the strike, Phil maintained a rigid schedule to set an example for the strikers:

One simple rule that I set down for myself and organizers was that the picket lines form at 6 o'clock and that we were to be the first ones there. We would have a short meeting every morning, and every damn one of them was there, including myself. And when it rained or poured, the organizers walked the line and I walked the line, and the wetter it got, the more we were out there. And then the people could see that we weren't just a bunch of outsiders who were in there fattening ourselves at their expense. We were in there fighting—not just by word of mouth but by actual deeds. They saw that if there was anything dangerous to do, I did it or one of the other organizers did it. We never asked them to do anything that we didn't do first or that we didn't do more of. And that must have given them a feeling of confidence. They learned by example. You can't make a good picket by telling him, "You be a good picket—a good picket does so and so." You get out there and you pitch with them, that's all.

Subsequent events demonstrated that the organizers' lead had an important impact.

As the non-strikers made daily efforts to enter the plant, the strikers added a new word to their vocabularies—"scab." It was shouted and screamed at the non-strikers from the moment they appeared on the scene until they left. Scuffles became routine, even with half of the town's police force present. Several more arrests on charges of assault or disorderly conduct were made—of both organizers and rank-and-file members. Almost a hundred workers were on the picket line. When the union learned that the alley separating the loading dock at the rear of the plant from the parking lot was city and not company property, it was able to shorten the picket line and concentrate its forces at the main entrances of the mill.

Phil appealed to the officials of the Trades and Labor Council for cooperation in carrying on the strike. Through the Labor Council, union members in Saylor were urged to ask

Women making fur coats at the Simpson's Garment Company, 1936.

State Historical Society of Wisconsin WHi (D487) 9679

their friends or relatives who worked in the mill to participate in the picketing or, at minimum, not to cross the lines. The Labor Council leaders offered to raise funds in support of the strikers, but the offer was turned down by the union leaders on the grounds that it simply was not needed. They were asked, instead, for their moral support and, if need be, their physical support. "And I got it," Phil said. "I got it with an open hand. I got it so wonderfully that I can't imagine a better response, especially in a small community." Many members of other unions in town began showing up for picket duty either before or after going to their regular jobs. The leaders of the Trades and Labor Council were convinced that the strike of the mill workers would have an important effect upon their own union-management relationships. They were more than willing to cooperate in every way.

On the fourth day of the strike, the city attorney called a meeting in an effort to deal with picket line violence. Present were the union's attorney, the employer and his attorneys, and the city attorney. Mr. Miller and his lawyers demanded that the union agree in writing to restrain the pickets from interfering in any way with those who wanted to work in the plant. After much discussion, both sides signed a memorandum of agreement providing that the picketing strictly conform to what was permissible under the law and that all pickets desist from the following practices:

1. Going into the premises and property of the employer.

2. Blocking access from the street into the plant by means of standing pickets across the main entrance into the plant; blocking any other entrances to the plant whether by means of the alley or any other means; blocking automobiles seeking to enter into the parking lot of the employer.

3. Using vile and abusive language and threats.

4. Assaulting the person of any employee when entering or leaving the plant.

5. Molesting any employee in any manner when entering or leaving the plant.

The document was in the form of a "gentlemen's agreement," and the organizers informed the pickets of its content and asked them to conduct themselves in accordance with it.

Yet, violence occurred again the following day as non-strikers sought to enter the plant in automobiles by way of the alley and parking lot. Several of the strikers blocked the path of at least one car and, led by sympathizing union members from other plants, tried to upset it. Police intervention prevented any injuries but resulted in new arrests. No production workers crossed the picket lines for the next three days.

When the strike was a little more than a week old, the union officials again contacted the Federal Mediation and Conciliation Service in an effort to bring about a meeting with the employer. The government agency denied the union request for intervention on the ground that

the present strained relationship between the parties concerned does not provide the proper atmosphere for our service to attempt conciliation at this time. Another week or ten days, if tempers have cooled, the Commissioner will again attempt to bring the parties together in a joint conference, conducive to reaching settlement of the existing dispute.

However, ten days later tempers were even more strained.

The Injunction

Four days after the "gentlemen's agreement" was negotiated, the company, on behalf of a group of non-striking employees, made formal application to the Circuit Court for an order restraining the union's leaders and pickets. Phil Draper, Helen Crowne, and three members of the bargaining committee were named as defendants. The company charged that the union "had wholly and completely prevented and hindered" persons from entering the plant and that persons congregating on the picket line had adopted the device of building a "solid wall of human flesh" in the approaches to the plant.

The petition asked that the pickets be restrained from maintaining a picket line in excess of twelve persons or from having a picket line of more than four persons at any one time at any of the plant entrances. Further, the petition asked that the pickets be enjoined from mass picketing, threatening employees, or "engaging in use of abusive, oppobrious or obscene language." The complaint charged that "upwards of thirty or more employees" had attempted to enter the plant on several occasions, but that they were prevented or hindered by "large numbers of pickets who ripped clothing and struck persons with picket signs." Failure to halt such activities, the company charged, would result in "substantial and irreparable injuries to the plaintiff's property and the right to earn a livelihood." The union was ordered by the Court to show cause why the injunction should not be issued. The hearing was scheduled for the following Monday.

On the same day that the company petitioned the Court, the union increased efforts to mobilize community support on its behalf. Phil offered publicly, in a half-page advertisement in the town's only newspaper, to submit the entire dispute to impartial arbitration.

WE ARE ON STRIKE AGAINST SAYLOR COMPANY

Last October we voted in a National Labor Relations Board election to have the Union represent us. We know, as does all of labor in this community, that only through a union would we be able to obtain adequate and decent wages and working conditions. The owners of other factories in this area have learned to work with their employees through the union chosen by those employees. But the owners of the Saylor Company have not learned by the experience of others in Saylor nor do they seem to wish to learn.

They did not accept the decision of their employees in the National Labor Relations Election. They refused to deal with our union and fought that decision for five months through three delaying appeals, until required to negotiate by the National Labor Relations Board.

Nor have the last three and a half months of negotiations shown any greater desire on the part of the Saylor Company to deal fairly with us. We made certain fair demands of the Company. We asked for a general wage increase. We asked for shift differentials, paid holidays, for improvements in the vacation and insurance plans,

and we asked for union security. These are the conditions which exist generally in organized industries in the United States—including our own Saylor. The Saylor Company met with us to discuss these demands, but made no effort to arrive at a fair compromise. We waited patiently for almost nine months while the Company stalled us by means of its appeals through the National Labor Relations Board and months of fruitless negotiations. When it appeared that we would not be able to reach an agreement with the Saylor Company, we notified the Federal Mediation and Conciliation Service of the United States and requested that a Federal Conciliator be assigned. We hoped that he might be helpful in bringing both sides together and settling the dispute. That, too, failed.

When the Federal Conciliator realized that no agreement would be reached, he suggested to the Company and to the Union that they arbitrate their differences—that they jointly choose a fair-minded person and let him make a decision. *The Union agreed to arbitrate and to abide by the decisions of the arbitrator but the Saylor Company refused to arbitrate.*

Apparently the Company thought they can break up our Union by refusing to grant fair terms and by refusing to arbitrate. The Company thought that we would not want to strike nor would we be strong enough to strike. The Company was right about one thing—we did not want to strike. We did show, however, that we were strong enough to strike and determined enough to strike and carry on that strike to a successful conclusion.

Although we did not seek it, our strike is a good one and will be a successful one. Our primary interest, however, is not merely a victorious strike. It is rather a decent contract and amicable relations with the Company under the terms of such a contract. It is the thought of the Federal Conciliator and of leading citizens in this community that having failed to reach an agreement through negotiations, the parties should solve their differences amicably through arbitration. Therefore, we are still willing to arbitrate all of the issues involved.

IF THE COMPANY AGREES TO ARBITRATE, AN ARBITRATOR IS CHOSEN AND AN AGREEMENT SIGNED THAT IT WILL ACCEPT THE DECISION OF THE ARBITRATOR, WE ARE WILLING TO WITHDRAW OUR PICKET LINES, RETURN TO WORK, AND ACCEPT THE DECISION OF THE ARBITRATOR.

THE STRIKING WORKERS
At the Saylor Company

The company did not accept the union's offer to arbitrate. Indeed, the employer made no mention of the arbitration offer in a letter sent out to all employees the next day. Instead he recounted the history of the negotiations, stating the union's demands and the company's counteroffer. The letter ended by encouraging members to withdraw from the union by writing to the union's state office. It notified all workers that the plant would continue operations and that anyone wishing to work should report. However, unlike Tom Miller's previous appeal, this one produced no further defections from the union's ranks.

At the hearing on the restraining order, Phil was examined by the Court and flatly denied all allegations concerning his own participation in the violence. A number of photographs showing skirmishes between pickets and non-strikers were introduced,

Strike at Chain Belt, Milwaukee, by United Steelworkers of America, Local 1527, 1946.

including one which allegedly was a picture of Phil physically restraining workers from entering the mill. The face on the picture was not clear and Phil denied that it was a picture of him.

The company's attorney questioned him at length on the number of professional organizers involved in the strike.

The Company thought we had a lot of male organizers to help us. During the injunction proceedings, I was on the witness stand, and their attorney kept lambasting me with "... whom else did you have as an organizer?" And again I enumerated our organizers over and over again, and he would ask again and again: "Are you sure that you didn't have others?" until I thought he was nuts. It was only later that I realized that the Company thought that we had prepared all sorts of goon squads and what have you. But it was just these other union guys from around town that they must have meant—these guys who would come to the line and help out. Throughout the whole strike whenever there was something to do that took a little pushing, we had plenty of local people from various other unions who volunteered.

The employer was certain that Phil had committed perjury before the Court on this point. Mr. Miller later accused the union of planning the strike while it was still meeting with the Federal Conciliator and of not bargaining in good faith. The proof, he said, was in the augmented staff of organizers in Saylor the first day of the strike.

At 6 o'clock of the morning the strike began, they had pickets out including six outside organizers, people who had not been there before. How could they have come in so soon if the strike had not been agreed upon much earlier? They must have been on the way while our meetings were going on because the only train that came into town before 6 in the morning was on its way while we were meeting. But he denied this at the hearing.

Tom Miller was amazed at Phil's conduct and greatly disappointed at the apparent willingness of his employees to follow the union's leadership.

When we had our hearings in the courtroom on the injunction, the organizer was called on to testify. He had come on our property seventy-five feet to our door and kept a girl from entering the plant. When he was asked whether he had been on our property, he denied it, and everybody in the courtroom gasped because they had seen him and they knew he was lying. When the girl he kept from entering was pointed out to him, he said he had never laid eyes on her before. We had taken pictures of him keeping her from entering, and when he was shown the pictures, he denied that he was the person. Yet, soon after, on the picket line, the people were singing that he was their leader. They were proud of him.

The employer reported that he was most impressed by the way people "can be so easily taken in by complete strangers."

Prior to the certification election, I talked to the employees four or five times, refuting things that had been told them in union bulletins. But they would believe the union organizer, not me. If I said that the wall was green and the union official said it was black, they would believe him though they could see that it was green. And these were people that I've known all my life.

Judge Murray enjoined the union and its members from committing any acts of violence on the picket line. The Court ordered that a maximum of forty-eight pickets could be at the plant at any one time, that not more than twelve pickets could be placed before any one entrance, and that the pickets must walk at least six feet apart.

While the injunction proceedings were under way, the force of city police was augmented by the County Sheriff and several of his deputies. It was the Mayor who insisted that the Sheriff assume the policing function. At first Sheriff Spencer refused on the grounds that the Mayor was specifically charged with this responsibility. When violence became a daily occurrence, the Sheriff agreed to supplement the city's police but still refused to assume principal responsibility. The Mayor was bitter about the refusal.

He runs for office and he didn't want to get the union people around here against him. He ducked his responsibility, and that made me the goat because I had to keep the city police out there. He didn't give a damn about me. His jurisdiction superseded mine because as County Sheriff he is the principal peace officer in the county. He should have come in right from the beginning when he saw there was violence out there, but he didn't. And then when he did bring in some deputies, he played politics all the way through. The deputies weren't doing their job right. They weren't neutral—they sympathized with the union people, so that got everybody in town down on the police and me.

As the strike continued, the question of which governmental agency, city or county, should pay for the policing became an important one in the town council because the cost was becoming a burden on the limited city treasury. Approximately fifteen law enforcement officers were now stationed daily at the mill—ten of them deputies assigned by the County Sheriff. The City Attorney argued that the ten should be paid $10.00 per day each, $4.00 from county funds and $6.00 from the mill owner. The city would provide two squad cars manned by three policemen. The county authorities argued that it would be difficult to justify expenditure of taxpayers' money for the protection of Miller property, but the city asserted that it was the Sheriff's duty to maintain order in the county and that the city was not excluded. The motion in the council meeting to require the mill owner to pay part of the cost of policing was defeated on the ground that this would greatly aggravate the entire situation. Finally it was decided that salaries for deputies should come from the county treasury. The issue was settled, but not without straining the relationship between the city and county law enforcement agencies. . . .

The United Labor Committee

After the injunction was issued, Phil increased his efforts to mobilize the support of the townspeople on behalf of the union. He had been in almost daily contact with officials of the Trades and Labor Council and kept them fully informed of the union's activity. He addressed numerous meetings of various local unions in Saylor and neighboring towns. During these meetings and discussions he constantly urged the trade unionists to use whatever influence they had with mill workers to support the union's cause. He did not directly attack the Miller family or their power in the community. When he referred to the employer or his family, it was in general terms—the company. Yet he constantly sought to point out that the strike and all later events need not have happened if "the company" had wanted it otherwise.

He suggested to the leadership of the Labor Council and to officials of the several local unions affiliated with the CIO that a United Labor Committee might be useful. The suggestion quickly bore fruit, and a committee composed of representatives of twenty-three local unions in Saylor and two neighboring towns was organized. Its sole purpose at the time was to aid the strikers, and union leaders were invited to speak both on the picket line and during meal hours in strike headquarters.

More than a thousand people gathered in the City Park to hear Phil speak at a mass meeting arranged by the committee. He reviewed the many delays which preceded the contract negotiations and charged the company with responsibility for the delays and with lack of good faith in its negotiations. He claimed that the strike was forced upon the union by the company's refusal to compromise and its failure to agree to fair terms which would have made a contract possible. He further emphasized the company's refusal to arbitrate. He insisted that the court injunction in no way had affected the conduct of the strike. If anything, he said, the strikers now were more determined than ever to continue their fight to a successful conclusion.

Several members of the United Labor Committee also spoke and the invocation was given by a leading Catholic priest of the area. The meeting was a huge success from the union's point of view; nothing like it had ever happened before in Saylor. Indeed, this was the first time both AFL- and CIO-affiliated unions had ever engaged in a joint enterprise.

The various unions in Saylor cooperated with the mill strikers in even more important ways. The Teamsters Union respected the strikers' picket lines, and all deliveries to the mill were cut off. This left only the mill's small pickup truck to bring in or ship out mill materials, and the non-union truck driver was followed and harassed whenever he left the mill. Shipments of materials to the struck plant began coming in by Railway Express.

After the strike had been going on for about three months, Phil learned that business had fallen off about 20 per cent at the Miller Brothers Department Store, the largest retail merchandising establishment in an area of about 2,500 square miles.

Picketing at the Plankinton Packing Company, Milwaukee, in the early 1950s.

The union found that at least some of the townspeople were boycotting the store, although neither the United Labor Committee nor the strikers had made an attempt to initiate or urge it. Both groups encouraged the boycott, however, once it was under way.

Leaders of the committee, under Phil's prodding and direction, sought ways to increase the pressure on the employer through the department store. However, they needed to be extremely cautious since the store had no direct or legal connection with the mill. Sustained activity directed against the store in an effort to increase pressure upon the mill's management would have been a clear-cut violation of the secondary boycott bans in the Taft-Hartley Act.

Phil used an indirect method; he told the regional officials of the AFL Retail Clerks' Union about the unorganized department store which employed several hundred persons in Saylor. The Retail Clerks agreed to attempt an organizational drive and sent a representative to Saylor to seek union recognition from the store's management. Of course the employer refused. The Clerks' Union posted pickets in front of the store entrances and delivery docks, proclaiming that the Miller Brothers Department Store did not employ union labor. The Teamsters

Union respected the picket line, and the store was forced to hire additional non-union drivers to get merchandise into and out of the store. It was reported that business at the store fell off by almost 60 per cent.

Friday evening is the traditional shopping time for residents of the Saylor area. The town takes on a holiday atmosphere as crowds converge in its main shopping district and the Miller Brothers' store. The farm people of the area come to town on Friday evenings to shop and perhaps to attend a movie. On two Friday evenings, the United Labor Committee, again prodded by Phil, organized demonstrations in support of the AFL Retail Clerks' Union. Approximately a thousand pickets formed a continuous line around the entire city block occupied by the store. They carried signs urging shoppers not to buy at the store. Phil specifically instructed the mill strikers to stay out of the demonstration so that if the secondary boycott question should be raised subsequently, the union would be able to point out that it had no connection whatever with the demonstrations. Business at the store practically came to a standstill each Friday evening. Other merchants in the downtown area complained that business in general declined sharply while the demonstrators were parading and the citizenry gathered to watch the spectacle. The town's newspaper estimated that several thousand shoppers gathered in the square to watch. Automobile traffic through the downtown area was completely tangled.

JACOB F. FRIEDRICK IN 1954

The rapid growth of unions in the 1930s and 1940s allowed them to play a more important role in American society. As unions became stable institutions, and as the labor movement began to increase its political power, many policymakers came to believe that unions, like businesses and other institutions, should be represented in public policy bodies at the local level. This job was usually assumed by local labor leaders, especially those who led large labor federations in major cities. This sidebar is a profile of Jacob F. Friedrick.

A FEW weeks ago at a school board meeting a man was making a speech against what he considered "frills" in modern school buildings.

Slumped in a seat in the spectators' section was another man whose face clearly showed impatience mixed with anger. When the opponent of "frills" finished, the impatient man brushed a lank lock of brown hair off his forehead, rose, hooked his thumbs into his vest pockets and unburdened himself of sentiments he had expressed many times.

Jacob F. Friedrick's text was this: Education is vital because the future well-being of this community's children and through them, eventually, of the community itself, depends on it. Because of that, you shouldn't try to save money at the expense of children.

Friedrick's voice was a familiar one to school board members, as it is at the meetings of other public bodies where he often speaks for 75,000 Milwaukee county AFL members. Friedrick is the general secretary and top officer of the AFL Milwaukee Federated Trades Council, the county's central AFL body.

Mild and unassuming in appearance, the very antithesis of the familiar portrait of the tough union "boss," Friedrick has become known here as labor's most lucid spokesman. While some persons doubt that there is presently a "Mr. AFL" in Milwaukee County, Friedrick is the undisputed leader of what, for want of a better term, is sometimes called the "idealistic wing" of the AFL in Wisconsin.

Even Friedrick's opponents criticize him only for minor defects. Here is what a local CIO leader said: "Friedrick has a wide range of knowledge, stability and he doesn't shoot his mouth off half cocked. He's honest, outspoken, and frank. I've yet to hear a word against him in the CIO."

A state official with whom Friedrick has worked: "He does not fail to push his people's point of view, but he does it as a reasonable man."

A management man: "We don't square with his views completely, of course. But he is a perfectly fine gentleman.

State Historical Society of Wisconsin

Jacob F. Friedrick was an early Socialist Party member and a leader of the Machinists Union. He also served as general secretary to the Milwaukee Federated Trades Council.

Once his word is given, you can trust him."

Now sixty-two, Friedrick is still a student. He has read widely, particularly in the field of economics. His formal nonvocational education ended with the eighth grade....

Young "Jake" came to this country in 1904, when he was thirteen, an immigrant Hungarian of German ancestry, unable to speak English. His father, the late Frank Friedrick, had earlier abandoned his job as a government woodsman in the forests dotting the flat plains around Perjamos, Hungary (now Periam, Rumania), for a job as a Milwaukee tannery worker.

Young "Jake" finished the eighth grade at what is now the Maryland Avenue School, then spent a year and a half learning the machinist's trade at what is now Boys' Technical high school.

The year 1913 was eventful. He returned here, got married, and joined his first labor union—Lodge 66 of the International Association of Machinists (AFL).

Motivated by the poor conditions under which he and other workers labored Friedrick almost immediately became an active unionist. He participated in Lodge 66's successful organizing drive of 1915. In 1917 and again in 1918 he was elected president of the union. In 1919 he became a full-time union business agent.

Those early years were not all clear sailing for the young labor leader. He was fired twice within two years for union activity. The first time was the day after World War I ended. The cause was participation in a one-day wartime walkout in a successful effort to make an employer abide by the overtime rules of the World War I version of the War Labor Board.

The next year Friedrick was fired because his name was published in a list of union delegates to a Chicago protest meeting in behalf of Tom Mooney, militant unionist, who was then in jail for alleged participation in a 1916 San Francisco bombing. Mooney, after more than twenty years of protesting his innocence, was pardoned in 1939.

In 1929 he quit his business agent's job to become a reporter of labor and city hall news for the *Milwaukee Post.* In 1935 he was elected general organizer of the Federated Trades Council, a post he held until 1945, when he was made AFL regional director here. In 1951 he returned to the council as general secretary.

Friedrick's full-time jobs give no hint at his activities in several areas. For example, he is a mainstay on both the city and metropolitan sewerage commissions.

A catalogue of Friedrick's other current civic endeavors includes membership on the policy committee of the county's five major taxing units, Governor Kohler's education advisory committee to handle state participation in the GI bill of rights for Korean veterans, the board of directors of the Community Welfare Council and the United Hospital Fund drive, and the common council's special committee to study health insurance plans for city employees.

Although he did not play any role in the enactment of the nation's first workmen's compensation law in Wisconsin in 1911, he has been a labor member of the state industrial commission's advisory committee on workmen's compensation for the last fifteen years and off and on before that.

Friedrick's biggest legislative contribution is in the field of unemployment compensation. He worked with the late Professor John R. Commons of the University of Wisconsin to prepare the first unemployment compensation bill introduced into the 1921 legislature. Given impetus by the depression, such a bill was finally passed by the 1931 special session of the legislature and became law in 1932—again the first of its kind in the nation. Friedrick was appointed to the first industrial commission advisory committee on unemployment compensation in 1932 and has served on it since.

Early in his union career, Friedrick felt that it was vital to provide workers with an opportunity to learn something about economics and the trade union movement. Thus, with others of the same persuasion, he helped establish in 1920 the Milwaukee Labor College, a night school for workers sponsored by the Federated Trades Council. The school went out of existence in the 1940's. In 1925 Friedrick was one of the group instrumental in setting up the School for Workers at the University of Wisconsin at Madison. Friedrick was a member of the original board of directors of the labor college, later became its secretary and finally did some of the teaching. He has been a member of the advisory committee of the school for workers since its inception.

Friedrick's thinking was influenced early by the Socialists. He became a member of the Socialist party in 1918, and left it in 1935 at the time of the exodus of Socialists into the Farmer-Labor-Progressive Federation. When the Federation folded, Friedrick abandoned political party activity. He has not been a member of a party since about 1940.

—JOHN D. POMFRET

Milwaukee Journal, November 18, 1954.

The annual Trades and Labor Council picnic was held on Labor Day in the City Park. The city band, a group of acrobats, students from a local dancing school, and several amateur boxers provided entertainment. Soft drinks, hot dogs, and the usual picnic fare were served. The crowd was estimated to number well over a thousand. Phil was the chief speaker. He again outlined the issues in the strike and said that an amicable outcome was as important to the community as it was to the strikers since wages and working conditions in the mill inevitably affected wages and conditions in all other local firms. Although Labor Day celebrations had been held before in Saylor, this was the largest and most successful. It indicated to the strikers that a large section of the community supported their cause. The enthusiasm developed at the picnic carried over to the following meeting of the Trades and Labor Council when a resolution was passed calling for a city-wide half-day holiday of all union labor in support of the strikers. The pressure was mounting.

The Turning Point

It was now late September. The cold weather of fall and winter was approaching and the coal supply at the mill was running short. One Saturday afternoon, while pickets were absent from the scene, a truckload of coal was delivered by a firm which employed non-union drivers. All truck markings were covered. The coal was dumped behind the mill, and the driver, in a hurry to leave before being discovered, made no arrangements to deposit his cargo in the basement of the factory.

A passing striker soon discovered the delivery and called Phil, who arrived at the mill in time to see the truck drive off after dumping a second load. He and the striker followed the truck to a neighboring city where the driver headed for a police station after discovering that he was being followed. Phil went into the station behind the driver and asked him for the name of the coal company which employed him. When the driver refused to answer, Phil went outside to the truck and ripped off the paper covering the firm's name. His next step was to notify the Teamsters' local leaders. As a result, union drivers employed by other dealers agreed to refuse to deliver coal to the Miller Brothers Department Store, and Teamster officials urged their members to stop dealing with the non-union company. Four loads of coal had been ordered by the mill, but only two were delivered. From this time until the end of the strike, the mill was picketed around the clock every day.

Non-strikers rigged a number of large tarpaulins around the coal pile behind the mill. The following night someone threw two large bags of dry cement over the coal, making it useless until several days later when it was thoroughly washed several times and carted inside the mill by wheelbarrow. The tarpaulin curtain shielded the non-strikers from the glares and jibes of the pickets.

Since the company could no longer buy coal in Saylor, it looked for supplies from outlying communities. A supervisor arranged with a Saylor resident, who had no connection with the strike, to buy coal from a dealer some thirty miles away. One truckload was delivered and dumped in the intermediary's back yard. From this point, the mill's supervisors and some of the non-strikers packaged the coal in thirty-pound boxes, carried it by car to the Saylor Post Office, and mailed it to the mill. The company believed that this method of delivery could not be stopped since the coal was mail in custody of an agency of the federal government. Some of the pickets suspected that coal had somehow been delivered to the mill since there was evidence of dust on the receiving dock. Phil laughed at their suspicions, saying that nobody could get coal delivered by mail. But a picket captain insisted that coal must be coming in by mail since all other avenues had been blocked. A friend who worked in the Post Office confirmed his suspicions.

Phil immediately protested to the local postmaster, charging that the Post Office was directly aiding one side in a labor dispute. The local postmaster checked with the Chicago postmaster and was told that under Post Office regulations, unusual items of mail not ordinarily delivered to a firm could not be handled during a strike. The coal deliveries were stopped.

In the meantime the company continued to purchase coal from the same out-of-town firm and box it in the same way. While negotiations were proceeding with the Post Office, several tons of packaged coal were delivered to the freight platform of the North Western Railroad in Saylor. Miller Brothers Department Store trucks, escorted by some Sheriff's deputies, picked up the packages and deposited them in the mill's coal chute. Phil discovered what was happening only when a railroad employee, who was a member of the Railway Clerks Union, phoned him the details.

When Phil arrived at the railroad freight office, he found several score packages of coal on the freight platform. He told the freight master that the railroad was permitting the mill to use it to break a strike because the coal was not regular freight consigned to the railroad. He asked the freight-master to reject it. When the freight-master refused, Phil called the railroad's Chicago district office and insisted that orders be given to the Saylor agent to stop accepting the coal parcels. If the railroad would not do this, he said, the union would consider it a direct party to the mill dispute and would picket the Saylor freight and passenger stations.

An exchange of telephone calls between Phil, the Saylor freight office, and the district office went on through the day. In the meantime the department store trucks continued to pick up the packages at the freight platform. Phil recruited two carloads of pickets who took up positions nearby. He and two other organizers stopped a truck from backing into the freight platform by standing in its path. The driver left without coal when he realized that he would run down the organizers if he attempted to back his truck in to the platform. There were no police present at the time, but shortly afterward a contingent from the Sheriff's force arrived and parked some distance away. However, the police refused to interfere with the pickets blocking the pickup trucks.

Higher officials of the railroad came to Saylor later that day. After several hours of discussion with Phil, who continually threatened to picket the station, the officials agreed to put the coal aside and declare it impounded. It was not to be released until the strike was over or until the union okayed the movement. (Indeed, it was not released until the strike ended with a signed contract. Then it was brought directly into the plant so

that steam pressure could be brought up and the plant reopened.)

The coal impasse was one of the major turning points in the strike. With winter rapidly approaching, the mill could not be operated without coal, and the strikers knew it. They also knew that the company was heating workplaces with portable electric heaters and that non-strikers had to wear sweaters and coats as they worked. They felt that there might be some hope of bringing the employer to terms if the coal supply were not replenished.

Devising strategies to block the coal became a welcome diversion for the strikers and a source of renewed morale in a strike which had dragged on for more than three months with no apparent progress. The direct issues in the conflict became submerged, and coal became a new symbol for the entire struggle. The critical situation with regard to coal at the mill and the mounting pressure on the Miller store combined to compel the employer to renew negotiations with the union.

Negotiations Resumed

Phil's position from the very beginning was that constant efforts had to be made to negotiate with the employer. He considered this fundamental strategy: "The people had to believe and had to know that the union was trying to settle the strike." Phil continually pressed for negotiations through the Federal Mediation and Conciliation Service. On two occasions formal meetings were held in another city, and on several other occasions mediators talked to Phil and Tom Miller separately in Saylor. "We kept after the Federal Mediator to keep his finger in the pie so the people would see that we were trying to settle it."

During the seventh week of the strike a meeting was arranged at which Mr. Miller and his attorneys sat down with an international vice-president, Phil, and the local strike committee. A company attorney spoke on the subject of strike violence for about ten minutes. When he finished, the vice-president spoke, saying, in effect, that the Miller family was very rich and powerful in Saylor but that the union could buy and sell all the Millers in the state. For every dollar the Millers had to spend, he continued, the union had at least ten, and if the company wanted to continue the strike on this basis, the union was more than prepared. And as for the picket-line violence, he added, "What else could you expect in a war which is what a strike is? What do you expect the pickets to do—walk on the line with flowers for the scabs?" The local strike committee was much impressed and found renewed hope for the success of the strike and renewed faith in the union leadership.

But no progress was made toward settling the conflict. Another effort to resume negotiations was made a few weeks later when emissaries of the employer approached the Sheriff to arrange a meeting between the company and the union. Phil notified the Sheriff that he would be happy to meet with the company any time and any place. But the company now stated a condition for the meeting: they were ready to meet with the strikers provided that Phil was not present.

Phil raised the question with the strike committee: "You can do what you want, but you see what they're trying to do. They're trying to break you and me apart." He left the commit-

Members of the Executive Board of the Wisconsin State Industrial Union Council in 1946.

tee to discuss the matter. The committee members unanimously agreed that they would meet with the employer only if Phil was present and the Sheriff was so notified. This condition was unacceptable to the employer and the brief contact was broken off for the time being.

Meanwhile Phil thought it was wise to bolster the morale of the strikers again, particularly since he was sure that the employer would continue efforts to split the strikers from their leadership and negotiate a "private" settlement. Accordingly, he invited one of the union vice-presidents and the Midwest general organizer to Saylor to address the strikers at a meeting in strike headquarters. The general organizer, a very effective speaker, told the audience that all of the resources of their union of over 400,000 workers were at the disposal of the 125 mill strikers. The union vice-president added that the international would never withdraw from the Saylor conflict and was prepared to finance the strike until the union's demands were won. They sought to leave the impression that a relatively small operator such as the mill owner had little chance against the combined resources of the powerful union. Only grit and determination were needed on the part of people directly involved.

The employer's effort to split the union ranks from its leadership failed completely. However, the attempt indicated to the union's leadership that the company was being pressed to the wall and was seeking ways to end the strike. Other developments confirmed this feeling.

The firm's Chicago and New York sales offices were picketed by union people, and the company's salesmen were becoming increasingly dissatisfied. Phil reported it this way:

In a strike, especially when it runs as long as this one did, you're always letting out feelers. You don't let out the feelers in your own name, but you get some guy, maybe a lawyer or another manufacturer who knows somebody who knows somebody else to say, "Why can't we do something? I think I know these union guys and maybe we can do something." The company was doing this too through their salesmen and people who their salesmen knew in the industry in Chicago and New York. Those of us who were directly

involved in the strike weren't directly involved in these feelers—we kept ourselves out at this stage. This is a very diplomatic sort of procedure, something like international relations with neutrals during a war. But through this kind of thing both sides maintained some kind of contact with each other. All the feelers we let out in the beginning were chopped off, and we stopped sending them out for a while. But when the coal situation got so rough and the community support became so evident, it seemed to us that the company realized they were either going to have to settle it or go out of business. We heard from Chicago and New York that their salesmen were getting fed up—getting ready to quit because no products were getting through. We were hoping that this would occur.

As a result of these "feelers," a meeting was arranged in Chicago between Chicago officials of the union and the mill's attorneys. No immediate progress was made, but negotiations were not broken off entirely this time.

In mid-October, when the strike was entering its fourth month, a new development occurred. The Mayor appointed a Citizens Committee to meet with representatives of both sides to try to end the struggle. Phil initiated the move by dropping hints to the Trades and Labor Council officials, to clergymen with whom he had good contact, and to others. He did not anticipate that a citizens group could really be instrumental in settling the strike, but it was part of his strategy to keep the situation in constant motion.

The president of the Saylor Chamber of Commerce also thought that the committee idea was good, but his feelings were mixed.

Draper has got the people all stirred up. I don't know what it is—if it is the people who worked at the mill for twenty-five years suddenly got up and found that their wages are very low, conditions bad, or that Draper has a spell over them or what. You know how emotional women can get, and that place has mostly women working there. Draper is an outsider who came here just to stir things up. He doesn't have any stake in this community, and what the hell does he care what he does to this town. He doesn't care a thing about Saylor. That's his profession and he knows all the tricks in the trade about how to stir people up. He came in here driving a big Cadillac and started to tear the place apart. If it lasted much longer, there would have been a committee of fifteen men in town that would have run him out and told him to stay out.

But still, he felt, the situation had gotten out of hand and it should not have been permitted to continue. Though his private sympathies were with Tom Miller, he recognized that every effort had to be made to end the strike. Yet he was reluctant to involve the Chamber as an organization.

> The Chamber of Commerce can't mix in politics, and this had become a political issue because of the relationship of the Millers and the store to the Chamber and the community as a whole. It would have created dissension amongst ourselves.

He called the manager of the store, one of Tom Miller's brothers, to ask if there was anything he could do as a private individual.

> He asked me what I had in mind. I told him that it was my idea to get a group of reputable businessmen in the town, unbiased people, who spoke for the community as a whole and see what we could do. We didn't know what we could do, but I wanted to experiment and find out. He asked me who I had in mind for such a committee, and I named a few and he named a few. We wanted to show both sides that the community had a stake in this and that it wasn't their private war. We wanted to talk to one side and then the other separately and see what we could do to get them together.

The Mayor agreed to sponsor the effort. He appointed five of the town's leading citizens, all businessmen but one, to attempt mediation. The pastor of the Methodist church was selected as chairman. The Mayor issued the following statement to the press:

> The strike at the Saylor Company is now going into its 13th week and should give the people of this community more than passing concern. It affects not only the economy of a city of our size, but has disrupted the harmony which should prevail between some of our citizens. I have waited hopefully for several weeks for an adjustment of the dispute between the parties through a compromise settlement. This failed to materialize and it is quite evident that negotiations between the parties are now at a standstill and such a condition will exist unless some attempt is made by an intervening third party. It must be an effort to bring the parties involved together in an attempt to effectuate an amicable settlement. With this in mind, I have appointed a Citizens' Committee to meet with representatives of both employees and employer immediately and assist them in negotiations toward bringing about an early settlement of their differences. The members of the committee have agreed to serve at my request as a public service to Saylor. I have confidence that my selection will meet with the approval of the parties as they are leaders in various professions and businesses, and have no direct or in direct interest in the matters in the dispute.

The chairman of the committee told Phil about the new development and asked his cooperation. Phil replied that the union would be very happy to have such a group intervene.

> The pastor forced me into the position where I had to open up with him. I figured that I'm better off talking to a minister than I was to a businessman—that I could trust him more. And I told him that I was speaking to him off the record, but the situation was such that there was the possibility of a settlement and, off the record, I would appreciate it if the entire committee would stand back until they were needed, if they were needed. And he understood, and

promised to keep out of it until we had a chance to settle it ourselves.

The committee never met. As a result of a rapidly moving series of events in Chicago the following day, the company moved to negotiate directly with the strikers and their representatives.

The manager of the company's Chicago sales office and the union's Midwest general organizer met on a Chicago streetcar. The sales manager told the union official that the company wanted to settle and that it had retained a new attorney with considerable experience in the industry and close ties with one of the unions in the industry. The new attorney also knew the union's lawyer, who had been involved from the beginning in the Saylor strike.

A meeting was arranged for October 24th in Chicago with top union officials, Phil, and their attorney representing the union, and Tom Miller and his new attorney representing the company. They reached agreement quickly, and after the local union strike committee was flown from Saylor to Chicago to sit in on the discussion, the parties arrived at a general settlement on all issues except the union shop. The company wanted two years from the time the contract was signed before the union shop was to become effective; the union insisted on six months. After the question was discussed for some time, the union vice-president met privately with Tom Miller. Ten minutes later they emerged arm-in-arm from the former's office. At Mr. Miller's request, the vice-president had given his word that the demonstrations at the Miller Department Store would be stopped immediately if the company conceded on the union shop question. The parties finally agreed on a compromise—installation of the union shop in ten months.

Under the terms of the agreement, the company recognized the functions of the shop chairman and the piecework price adjustment committee. The new grievance procedure included an arbitration step, and a plant-wide seniority system was installed. Provisions were made to adjust the pay of workers who were shifted from one job to another so that they would not lose any income. A minimum of four hours' call-in pay was stipulated. The company agreed to develop an equitable piece-rate system by consulting with an engineer from the union's staff as well as one chosen by management. Piece rates in all departments would be increased while the piecework system was being studied. Adjustments were made in vacation benefits, and a 10 per cent across-the-board wage increase for all workers was granted.

Phil called Helen in Saylor to ask her to announce and publicize a settlement ratification meeting for the following evening. Phil and the local union bargaining committee took the first available transportation to Saylor and came before about 125 union members to describe the terms of the agreement. After a very short discussion, a motion was made to accept the contract as proposed. The vote was enthusiastically affirmative. The union and the strikers viewed the settlement as a clean victory. After almost a year and a half of continuous effort, including a bitter fourteen-week strike, the union had a contract.■

From Bernard Karsh, *Diary of a Strike* (Illinois University Press, Urbana, 1958).

SECTION

5

Labor and Contemporary Society

Harvey Goldberg speaks to striking teaching assistants at the University of Wisconsin-Madison in 1976. A popular professor of history and legendary orator, Goldberg served as an intellectual and political mentor to students and many others in the Madison area.

Madison Labor in the 1960s and 1970s

BY DEXTER ARNOLD

The Sixties and Seventies brought new directions and new challenges to Madison's labor movement. New groups of workers became the focal point for renewed organizing. Increased unionization among service-sector and public employees reflected the importance of these workers to the local economy.

IN 1916, a small group of public school teachers had formed American Federation of Teachers Local 35. Although its members were active in the Madison Federation of Labor (MFL) and the union won some benefits for teachers, Local 35 never held bargaining rights. In 1964, the Madison Teachers Association (now Madison Teachers Inc.) won a union representation election and began to build a solid, majority union.

Collective bargaining legislation passed during the 1950s provided a tool for public-sector workers, but teachers, firefighters, and other municipal employees still had to force improvements from reluctant public officials through strikes and sick-outs.

Unionization also reached new groups of state workers. In 1966, Teaching Assistants at the UW began organizing for job rights and educational quality. Four years later, after a month-long strike, they won a union contract. During the 1970s and early 1980s, the TAA would play a leading role in local labor solidarity efforts.

During the Seventies, state clerical workers, attorneys, and education, science, and science professionals organized. Student workers and limited term employees at the UW's Memorial Union also forced university managers to recognize their union—the Memorial Union Labor Organization. More than twenty years later, they remain the only state LTEs with union protection.

Most private-sector organizing during the early Seventies occurred in small workplaces where workers faced bitter opposition. The Madison Independent Workers Union waged hard-fought campaigns at local restaurants—at times, facing owners who preferred to close rather than concede that their employees had rights.

Aggressive Teamster campaigns helped cannery and warehouse workers and cab drivers organize. A grueling seventeen-week strike by General Beverage workers demonstrated that solidarity and forceful community support could win union rights despite employer resistance and attacks by the local press. Like the campaigns of the 1930s, this victory gave confidence to other workers and spurred more union drives.

Despite these victories, events during the Seventies made it clear that the sense of security enjoyed by many workers had been the result of postwar economic expansion and union strength. Gisholt and Red Dot workers faced traumatic plant closings. In 1966, Giddings and Lewis bought Gisholt. Five years later, 800 workers lost their jobs when the company closed the East Washington Avenue machine shop. In 1984, the remaining workers were thrown out of work when Giddings and Lewis closed its foundry.

More than 1,000 workers lost their jobs as Oscar Mayer cut back local operations. Despite extremely profitable operations, the firm's new owner, General Foods, joined other meatpacking companies in pressing for concessions.

Since the late 1970s, uncertain economic conditions, management decisions about how to use new technology, the growth of conglomerates, and the increasing use of unionbusting consultants have posed threats to even the most well-established unions.

The 1976 strike by Madison Teachers Inc. and the state employees' strike the following year were among the last major walkouts in which unionists tried to break new ground. Since then, most strikes have become defensive battles in which workers struggled to hold on to what they had.

MNI Strike

The key confrontation came at Madison Newspapers Incorporated. During the 1970s, newspapers across the country shifted from hot metal to computerized typesetting. In most cities, managers bargained in good faith with the International Typographical Union over this changeover and avoided confrontations. But at MNI, managers used the shift in technology as a weapon against their employees.

Management tried to keep its plans secret even after it had ordered the new equipment. "They didn't know this, they did-

Workers out on strike picket Madison Newspapers, Inc., 1977.

Lisa Genesen/Daily Cardinal Photo

n't know that, and the damn stuff was ordered," recalled one union leader. "You're put in a spot where you have to wait and see. And while you're waiting to see, they're doing everything. They have got all the ducks in a row. They've got their attorneys lined up and you don't know for sure what's happening.... It was like we'll see when we get there. We don't know yet. You can't bargain impact on that...."

In spring, 1977, MNI moved against the union, forcing seventeen printers to give up their jobs in violation of their seniority rights and unilaterally cutting the wages of the remaining printers by one third.

These actions—combined with MNI's pressure on the other newspaper unions—led to unprecedented cooperation among the five locals at the plant. In October, the five unions struck. One spinoff of the struggle was the creation of the *Madison Press Connection*. Begun as a strike paper, it survived for a year and a half as an independent publication.

The strikers received widespread community backing. But neither unions nor community groups were able to mobilize the strength required to help the strikers beat back management's efforts to drive unions from MNI, the *Capital Times*, and the *Wisconsin State Journal*.■

From "Building a City, Building a Movement: Madison Labor, 1941-1993," *Union Labor News* (May, 1993).

An Isolated Survivor:
Racine Labor

BY RICHARD W. OLSON

If the Milwaukee Leader *held up the banner for independent labor journalism in the 1920s and 1930s,* Racine Labor *has continued that tradition into the last decade of the twentieth century. In this selection Richard Olson, a former editor of* Racine Labor, *discusses the unique role played by the weekly newspaper and the reasons for its success.*

A FEW years ago, a contest judge for the UAW Local Union Press Association commented that "every community should have a community-based labor paper like the Racine Labor."

But few do. Today, in the United States, the local labor press has virtually disappeared. Yet the *Racine Labor,* after fifty years of publication, is still going strong. How has the *Racine Labor* survived financially and thrived as a strong advocate for social justice? The answer is worth exploring.

Racine is an industrial city of some eighty-five thousand people about thirty-five miles south of Milwaukee. It's a city where the social justice tradition runs deep. In the city's early labor days, nationally famous Milwaukee socialists such as Victor Berger exerted a strong influence on the Wisconsin labor movement.

When Loren Norman was hired in 1941 as the first editor of the *Racine Labor,* the head of the trades council was a socialist. And thirty years later, when I was hired to edit the *Racine Labor,* the president of the paper's board was an IBEW electrician named Earle Poulsen, a friend and backer of Frank Zeidler, the longtime socialist mayor of Milwaukee.

Milwaukee socialism, often disparaged by left critics as "sewer socialism," never tried to turn Milwaukee into a utopia, but it delivered progressive, honest government, and social services for half a century. In spirit, this socialism was the social democracy that has created a comprehensive welfare state in Sweden and other countries: a mixture of private ownership, strong trade union involvement in government, and elaborate social benefits "from cradle to grave."

Racine workers, perhaps animated by this spirit, have long seen the need for a voice of their own. In the late nineteenth century, the town's printers published a daily labor paper after a lockout of union typographers. The paper, the *Racine Daily News,* gave labor extensive coverage in its early years, including a motion-by-motion account of the 1896 convention of the

Wisconsin Federation of Labor, which was held in Racine. But the newspaper folded after several years.

From 1915 to 1927, a paper called the *Labor Advocate* offered Racine trade unionists a heavy dose of news from the national and international levels. But the paper lacked a real local focus and, without much public support, had to suspend publication.

The Depression brought renewed interest in unionism in Racine, and it was only natural that a paper would emerge to reflect the growing labor activity. In rapid succession, the Racine labor community supported weeklies called the *New Day,* the *Racine Day,* and, finally, the *Racine Labor.*

The *New Day,* radical in tone, lasted only a few years. The *Racine Day* and its successor, the *Racine Labor,* found a more successful formula. Clearly, for Depression Racine, a daily labor paper was too ambitious. A paper that just reprinted national and international news was too dull and irrelevant, and the tone of the *New Day* was too strident. By the time *Racine Labor* had survived its first year, Racine trade unionists had the paper they wanted: an activist weekly paper that would be community-oriented. Its politics would be left of center, but not too radical either for the times or the area.

Loren Norman, the first editor of the *Racine Labor,* got his start in labor journalism when Oscar Ameringer, editor of the *Illinois Miner,* offered him ten bucks for a story about the indignities of living off the welfare system. The topic was near to Norman's heart and close to his belly. He had worked off and on in the coal mines of central Illinois for four years.

Norman wrote for the *Illinois Miner,* then ended up studying at Brookwood Labor College in Katonah, New York, where he met his wife, Bette, in 1932. Norman eventually headed back to Illinois, where he helped edit a paper for a miners union challenging the United Mineworkers. He lost that job in a factional fight, then moved on to help organize unemployed workers' committees and the DuQuoin Miners Defense Committee, which sought a pardon for a group of young men charged with killing a young girl during the wars between the UMW and its rival, the Progressive Miners.

It was about this time that Norman learned that a weekly labor paper called the *Racine Day* was in trouble. So Norman headed to Racine to see Francis Wendt, an attorney who was the receiver for the paper and later the mayor of Racine. Wendt asked Norman if he was a communist. Norman replied that he was a socialist. Fine, Wendt replied, Racine was used to socialists, but "we don't want communists around."

Against the advice of a leading local trade unionist who feared that the paper could not survive, Norman accepted Wendt's offer to edit the *Racine Day*. The day he arrived in Racine to begin work, the printer cut off credit.

The *Racine Day* soon folded, and Norman emerged as the editor of the new *Racine Labor*. He quickly found himself under attack first from the left and then from the right.

The first conflict began after three local union presidents brought Norman a press release asserting that "the Yanks aren't coming," from a movement that opposed U.S. entry into World War II. Norman considered the group a communist front and refused to run the release. He had to defend that position before the autoworkers council, but his opponents didn't get any support for their position, and that challenge quickly faded.

The next challenge came from the right and was more serious. The president of the board of the paper and the manager for the paper claimed the Racine police department had a dossier that labeled Norman a subversive.

The two had Norman fired. At the next meeting of the autoworkers council, one of the leaders of the largest UAW locals in Racine, and a socialist, got up to defend Norman. "Is he guilty of horse thievery?" the union leader asked, then announced that if Norman was fired, his local would pull its subscribers from the paper. With that threat in mind, the paper's board of directors asked Norman to return to work and paid him for the week he had lost.

In Norman's opinion, the paper's business manager and the president of the paper wanted a gossipy, friendly sort of paper— a pap sheet in Norman's view. But Racine unionists were after something very different, an active, socially conscious paper.

In some ways my history as editor of *Racine Labor* mirrors Norman's. Like Norman, I was an activist before I became editor of the *Racine Labor,* first in the movement that opposed the Vietnam War and then as a member of an alliance that wanted to pull together farmers, workers, and students in Wisconsin into a third party.

I was hired in 1972 and became the paper's second editor. I quickly learned that the *Racine Labor* is set up as a cooperative. Every local union that buys subscriptions gets proportional voting strength at the annual meeting at which a board of directors is elected. Most Racine unions subscribe for all their members.

The *Racine Labor* is not—and has never been—the official publication of any local central labor council. The absence of formal links between the paper and the council has clearly helped the paper weather the various splits and mergers within the labor movement. The *Racine Labor* has always worked to keep local unions united, no matter what their national affilia-

tions. In the days before the AFL-CIO merger, for instance, editor Loren Norman convinced the paper's board of directors to adopt a policy that when disputes split the AFL and the CIO, he would either print both sides or none.

In 1970, when the UAW left the AFL-CIO, the *Racine Labor* would likely have disappeared if it had been an official AFL-CIO central labor body publication. The UAW has a strong presence in Racine, and the paper couldn't have survived if it had to publish without that support.

On the whole, the Racine labor movement has done a good job resisting pressures to split the labor movement. During the 1970s, for instance, when both the UAW and the Teamsters were outside the AFL-CIO, Racine unions formed an umbrella organization known as the Alliance for Labor, which included the AFL-CIO unions, the Teamsters, the UAW, and the Racine Education Association.

When I left the *Racine Labor* in 1979, about half the subscribers were UAW members and a third belonged to AFL-CIO unions. The Racine Education Association, the local affiliate of the National Education Association, which isn't affiliated with the AFL-CIO, started subscribing for its members in the mid-1970s, after a bitter strike, and continued that support until 1991.

During that hard-fought teacher walkout in the 1970s, the Racine daily, the *Journal Times*, lashed out stridently against the striking teachers right from the start. The *Journal Times* editor ran a front-page box every day to remind Racine exactly how many days the "illegal" strike had lasted. In response, the *Racine Labor* became the teachers' champion. When the teachers sat in at the school administration building, the *Racine Labor* was there. We were partisans, but we figured the daily paper was plenty partisan as well.

Outside of our dedicated subscribing unions, the *Racine Labor* has always had several hundred individual subscribers: people in the community, union retirees, and a few readers whom I suspect have been attracted by the paper's want ad policy. The paper offers free want ads to all subscribers, one per issue for many decades, but now once every other issue.

This policy has made the want ads a gold mine for bargain hunters. People who can't find anything else good to say about the paper always remark that they sure enjoy the want ads.

Paid subscriptions, either by unions or individuals, accounted for about half of the paper's income during my tenure as editor. The rest came from paid display ads. In the early years, the paper was packed with ads from local merchants. But by the time I became editor, the local merchants had been largely displaced by discount chains like K Mart that would only advertise in the local daily. We received some advertising from the local banks and savings and loans, but gradually the banks became appendages to Milwaukee banks, and they had trouble finding Racine on the map.

Increasingly, the *Racine Labor* has had to turn to its local unions. In the 1970s, bulk subscription rates for local unions rose to $6 a year per member. Today the rates stand at $14.50. Even these higher rates aren't enough, alone, to keep the paper going. The paper has had to hold numerous fund-raisers. The ever-increasing postal rates, meanwhile, aren't helping any.

Members of UAW Local 180 on strike against J. I. Case Company, Racine, 1960.

State Historical Society of Wisconsin WHi (X3) 28135

Still, the paper survives. The community needs it. The *Racine Labor* serves the community—in many ways.

Politically, for instance, the *Racine Labor* plays a role that goes beyond standard election endorsements and editorials. *Racine Labor's* investigative journalism has sometimes exposed damaging information that other media have failed to uncover.

When I first came to town, Steve Olsen, a local union president who had served as an alderman for many years, was run-

ning for mayor. Racine had never elected a labor mayor, and many business leaders were worried.

Olsen (no relation to me) finished second in the primary. With the encouragement of local union leaders, I began digging into the financing of the front-runner, an insurance salesman who was running as the champion of the average citizen. Racine's big shots, it turned out, were financing the insurance salesman's campaign in a big way, and we had a good time exposing the salesman's campaign financing. On election day, Racine chose a union president as mayor. How big a role we played is hard to say. But Olsen's opponent gave us a good share of the blame for the turnaround between the primary and general election.

A few years after I left the *Racine Labor,* the paper took out after Terry Kohler, the Republican candidate for governor who was running on a program to bring "jobs, jobs, jobs" to Wisconsin. Kohler also happened to be president of the Vollrath Corporation, which was moving jobs out of Wisconsin to southern states and Mexico. *Racine Labor* editor Roger Bybee, my successor, interviewed workers at Vollrath's plant and checked out sources in the South who talked about the region's low wages. Tax records revealed that Vollrath had moved jobs out of Wisconsin despite considerable tax breaks from Wisconsin taxpayers.

The *Racine Labor* stories on Kohler were eventually picked up by a reporter for a Milwaukee daily. Later, an aide to Tony Earl, who went on to defeat Kohler, said the expose in the *Racine Labor* marked a turning point in the gubernatorial campaign.

The *Racine Labor* keeps a constant eye out for stories that would never interest the commercial dailies. One example: A local barber, who had been elected alderman with labor support, pulled out of the barbers' union. The barbers' union brought the news to the labor paper, and we published it. Our story angered Racine's union community, and the alderman got the message. Not long after the article appeared, he dropped out of his reelection race, paving the way for the unopposed election of a progressive candidate.

Not every controversy is as clear-cut. In the mid-1970s, when local public employees and the mayor began to go at each other over the cost-of-living issue, the *Racine Labor* found itself in the middle of conflicting forces. The journalistic highlight of that conflict was our picture of the mayor, the former union president, driving a snowplow during the strike. Somehow, everything ended well. The workers got their cost-of-living increase, and the mayor was reelected with labor's endorsement.

The *Racine Labor* considers itself both a labor paper and a community paper, not just a labor paper for unionists or a community paper citizens, but both.

During the 1970s, the *Racine Labor* took on an early savings and loan (S&L) crisis. In Racine, local S&Ls had been selling mortgages with an escalator clause that gave them the right to raise interest rates on already existing loans. People signed these loans never dreaming these clauses could be implemented, but in the mid-1970s, the S&Ls began giving their mortgage holders the bad news. Irate homeowners started picketing the S&Ls, talking to politicians, and complaining to the Racine daily newspaper. But despite the good visuals, the newspaper wasn't interested. Finally, some union members who were watching in horror as their mortgage rates were jacked up came to the *Racine Labor* to get coverage.

Their protests made front-page news in the *Racine Labor* for several weeks running. I wondered, at the time, what the effect would be on our advertising, since some of these same S&Ls took ads with us. We did lose some advertising from the S&Ls that were directly involved. But, ironically, the S&Ls that

were more conservatively run and didn't need to escalate their mortgages started increasing their ads. I figured we broke even.

In 1990, the *Racine Labor's* crusading helped restart bus service at a large mall. The mall's owner had banned the buses from the mall, and that ban was working real hardship on many elderly people, who had to wait outside the mall area to catch buses home. Editor Roger Bybee interviewed the bus patrons and generally kept hitting on this injustice issue after issue. Finally, Racine mayor Owen Davies ordered the restoration of the bus service.

Racine's daily did cover this story, but it never gave any editorial support to the suffering bus riders. The alliances between commercial dailies and their advertisers are very strong indeed. *Racine Labor's* contributions have gone far beyond Racine's city limits. The widely admired labor cartoonist Gary Huck first began drawing for a union audience in the late 1970s for the *Racine Labor.* The *Racine Labor's* role in providing a forum for Huck has helped labor editors across the country encapsulate the day's issues in wit.

So how is it that Racine has supported a paper like the *Racine Labor* for fifty years when so many other community-wide labor papers have folded?

I credit, first, the Racine labor community, the Racine trade unionists who every year give their support to the paper. When rough times set in during the 1980s, Racine trade unionists dug into their pockets at several fund-raisers to bail the paper out of its printing bills.

The survival of the *Racine Labor* also demonstrates the importance of having a strong editorial hand. If an editor is subordinate to the business manager, you'll get the "pap" that Loren Norman worried about in the early days of *Racine Labor.* A labor editor needs to have a strong commitment to the labor movement, an interest in labor history, the skill to stay in touch with the thinking of labor leaders and members, and the desire to put out a lively paper that the readers will want to read. The editor needs a gut-level interest in issues like minimum wage and trade and the future of the labor movement. Editing a labor paper can't be just a job.

But an editor can't simply regard a labor paper as his or her personal vehicle, because it's not. The editor of the *Racine Labor* has the same relationship to the paper's board of directors that the editor of a daily has to the publisher. A publisher who tries to call every shot will soon lose the editor. On the other hand, the publisher has the ultimate power to hire and fire.

The editor of the *Racine Labor* has traditionally had considerable latitude, but I once ran into trouble—and put my job as editor at risk—when I decided to get arrested with the public employees who were picketing outside the mayor's house to protest an ordinance banning residential picketing. And the current editor, Roger Bybee, once took an unscheduled "vacation" from writing his column for several weeks after writing a critical piece about Congressman Les Aspin.

Despite these episodes, over the course of fifty years, the Racine unions have never permanently tossed out an editor. That's a tribute to a relationship of trust on the part of the publisher-unions and good judgment on the part of the editors.

Down through the years, the *Racine Labor* has taken

United Auto Workers Local 180 on strike against the J.I. Case
Company, Racine, 1960. Strikers are posed in front of a list
of eighteen negotiating points.

Courtesy Harvey Kitzman, State Historical Society of Wisconsin WHi (X3) 25221

stands on international issues that ranged from supporting U.S.
entry into World War II to opposing our involvement in
Vietnam. Currently, the paper is opposing the proposed free
trade agreement with Mexico. Loren Norman once said that the
Racine Labor is a voice of sanity in a mad world. And, hopefully, it was and is.

But the editors have built support for the *Racine Labor* by
covering the issues that hit closest to home: jobs and workplace
issues. Over the years, the *Racine Labor* has helped the building trades in their fight against nonunion construction, the public employees in their battle for cost-of-living protection, the
postal workers in their struggle for political rights, and the
industrial unions in their campaign to keep good-paying jobs in
the United States.

The *Racine Labor* has also reached out into the community with photos of ethnic festivals, features on canoeists reenact-
ing historic explorations, reviews of Bruce Springsteen albums,

interviews with religious leaders such as Archbishop Rembert
Weakland, and a popular column by local writer Bette Norman
that mixed gardening, grandkids, and sharp-witted political
commentary. All in all, the *Racine Labor* has offered an eclectic
mix. Today, only a handful of cities have competing daily papers
with differing editorial views. Racine once supported several
dailies, today only one, the *Journal Times,* which belongs to
Lee Enterprises, a small out-of-state newspaper chain.

For good reason, most labor leaders don't like the coverage
their unions get in the daily press. But a community labor paper
gives average workers a forum. The only catch is that it's not
free. If the labor movement really wants its voice heard in the
public debate, it has to be willing to pay the price. The Racine
labor movement thinks the *Racine Labor* is worth the effort and
the $14.50 per member per year. And that's why the *Racine
Labor,* after fifty years, is still around, still advocating the cause
of social justice.■

—RICHARD W. OLSON

From "An Isolated Survivor: Racine Labor," Sam Pizzigati
and Fred J. Solowey, eds., *The New Labor Press: Journalism for
a Changing Union Movement* (Cornell, Ithaca, 1992).

JOHN W. SCHMITT: A PROFILE

John W. Schmitt served as president of the Wisconsin State AFL-CIO from 1966 to 1986. This profile, written in the middle of Schmitt's tenure as president, offers a summary of his activities. Schmitt's most important contribution was probably his role in building labor's political action apparatus across the state in the 1960s.

Milwaukee Journal

John Schmitt, president of the Wisconsin State AFL-CIO, 1960–1984.

JOHN W. Schmitt was born in Milwaukee on February 3, 1920. He became active in the union movement in 1946 soon after joining Milwaukee Brewery Workers Local 9. He served this local as steward, committeeman, Executive Board member and was named recording secretary in 1952, a position he held until 1960.

Becoming active on a state union level, he served first as a member of the Executive Board of the Wisconsin State Industrial Union Council (CIO) (1951-1958). When the AFL and CIO merger was consummated in 1958 he was elected to the Executive Board of the merged organization, the Wisconsin State AFL-CIO and held this post until elected to the Presidency in 1966. He has been reelected at every convention since then.

A major interest of Schmitt during most of his union career has been labor political action. He learned early that what workers could gain at the bargaining table could also be taken away in the legislative halls of government. Labor, he knew, had to get into politics for its own protection and advancement. In his role as Executive Vice President of the State AFL-CIO and as Director of COPE (the political arm of labor) he journeyed back and forth across the state, carrying the message of the need for labor political action and seeking to activate local and district COPE committees.

Under his guidance the political action program of labor has paid off in big gains on election day and many victories in the Legislature. This success in Wisconsin has won the admiration and respect of organized labor elsewhere in the country, including National AFL-CIO in Washington, D.C.

While the primary function of the State AFL-CIO is to serve Wisconsin labor unions and their members in legislative activities, organization, collective bargaining, education programs and public relations, it also promotes and coordinates the participation of labor in a large number of public activities. These include voter registration and educational programs, service by labor on state and city governmental bodies and in civic programs, and cooperation with other groups in seeking legislation on matters of public concern.

As a result Wisconsin labor has played an increasingly important role in elections and in the development of public policies and programs to meet challenges in such fields as race relations, equal rights, housing, education, welfare, pollution control, consumer protection, health, and numerous others.

Schmitt, himself is a member of more than thirty state and city boards and commissions in the fields of unemployment compensation, worker's compensation, industrial development, education, vocational education, apprenticeship, etc.

At fifty-six Schmitt is a hard-hitting advocate of organized labor—its policies and programs. Because of his blunt, no-nonsense approach he has inevitably aroused the ire of some people in the business, governmental, and professional fields. He shrugs off the attacks of his enemies and of the "so-called friends of the labor movement." He is labor's elected advocate and "come hell or high water" will continue to serve in that capacity.

—HAROLD "RED" NEWTON

From *Labor History and Stories* (Wisconsin State AFL-CIO, 1976).

Wisconsin: Teaching Assistants' Strike Ends in Contract Signing

BY ANDREW HAMILTON

In the 1970s new groups of employees looked to unions to improve their working conditions and wages. In Madison, graduate students employed as teaching assistants at the University of Wisconsin blazed a new trail in labor history by waging a strike that eventually resulted in a new contract. Too often the university administrators and top labor officials dismissed the graduate students as "middle-class radicals" who had little in common with ordinary working people. But the TAs had important grievances and they used unionism to advance their cause. They benefited from strong internal organizing techniques and from old-time solidarity provide by the local Teamsters union, whose members frequently honored the TAA picket lines and refused to deliver food and supplies to the university. Today the TAA continues to represent teaching assistants at the University of Wisconsin-Madison.

A WHOLLY new chapter in the annals of American university politics was formally inscribed on the University of Wisconsin campus in Madison on April 9-10, 1970. After a year of negotiations and a twenty-four-day strike, the University of Wisconsin signed a labor contract with the Teaching Assistants Association (TAA), a local labor union of graduate students who are paid for part-time teaching and research assistance at the university. The contract not only covered various "bread and butter" issues traditional in labor-management bargaining but also granted, in a fuzzy fashion, the right of students and teaching assistants to participate in planning the educational courses in which they are involved.

While the University of Michigan was settling a successful strike by black students earlier the same month, its sister Big Ten school was in the grip of a highly organized, disciplined, and nonviolent student strike called by the TAA. The strike was particularly effective against the faculty of letters and sciences, where course attendance averaged less than 30 per cent until the last four days, when a settlement appeared near.

The Wisconsin strike was fundamentally different from other student manifestations of recent years. The organizers, as teaching assistants, were not only students but workers as well, with an economic weapon. By staying out of the classroom they were able to prevent instruction in many courses.

As workers, they availed themselves of the traditional collective bargaining process to present their demands to the university. But their demands went beyond the traditional economic aims of American trade unionism to embrace policy and power issues that have motivated other student strikes across the country. The strike leaders claimed, in effect, the right to speak for undergraduate students as well as for their own constituency in bargaining on such issues.

Although neither side could claim a smashing victory in the settlement, the contract clearly altered the university's power structure by acknowledging the TAA as a force to be reckoned with in the formulation of educational policy at Wisconsin. And the potential exists for a similar movement at every university across the country that relies on graduate students to help teach courses and grade papers. One of the TAA's leaders in bargaining with the university, James Marketti (a graduate student in industrial relations), said shortly before settlement that his union had been contacted by teaching assistant organizations or by individuals from "fifty or sixty" campuses during the course of the strike.

The story of the TAA's negotiations with the University of Wisconsin is one of a challenge to the school's class structure and power relationships, which are probably not very different at other major public universities. A visitor who wants to get a sense of the physical layout of the university quarter here may seek out three high spots. One is Van Hise tower, the skyscraper where the university regents have their offices; a second, a short distance from the campus, is the Wisconsin state capitol. In between is the third vantage point, Bascom Hall, where Chancellor Edwin Young has his offices atop a hill occupied by the major classroom buildings of the faculty of Letters and Sciences (L&S). The men who sit in these high places govern, in collaboration with the faculty, one of the nation's largest centers of higher education. The Madison campus has 35,549 students (fall semester, 1969-70), of whom 22,000, including graduate students, are in L&S. It had an annual operating budget of $169 million in 1968-69, of which $58 million went to research. Last year the Madison campus produced 745 doctorates and 2,350 M.A.'s.

With its liberal, open reputation, the Madison campus draws a large number of out-of-state students, particularly for advanced studies. Last fall 26 per cent of the undergraduates and 66 per cent of the graduate students, in all some 12,600 students, came from outside Wisconsin. In recent years, Madison students haven't needed a weatherman to tell which way the political winds are blowing. From the Dow riots of 1967 to recent disturbances in connection with the conspiracy conviction of the Chicago 7, student clashes with police have been regular occurrences. Last year, violence attended a week-long strike by black students, which led the university to institute a new black studies program and caused authorities to call out the National Guard. Along two main streets that lead from the campus toward the state capitol, a few businesses have given up replacing their plate glass windows and now present bricked-up or boarded facades. The latest to follow the trend is the university branch of the First National Bank of Madison, whose windows were "trashed" several weeks ago during a brief demonstration that had no connection with the TAA strike.

"Outside Agitators"?

The state legislature and the university regents, both conservative bodies, appear to equate student activism with nonresidents, although Wisconsin has its own populist-radical political tradition—Marketti is a Wisconsin resident—and although campus violence recently erupted at Whitewater, one of the campuses in the state university system where there are a few "outsiders." Even Chancellor Young seems, after two fairly troubled years in office, to share the xenophobia, although he himself hails from Maine and first came to Madison as an out-of-state graduate student. (Young returned to Madison as chancellor in the fall of 1968, after a brief stint away from Wisconsin as president of the University of Maine.) "This university," he said recently, "has the greatest collection of radical students in the country—they flock here. . . . Of course, some of them go on to become insurance agents, and I don't worry about them. . . . But we've had a lot of trouble here. It seems that the farther people are from home, the less restrained their behavior is." Young is considered a member of the liberal establishment in Wisconsin. But he has been under pressure from the legislature and the regents to curb the radicals. The regents, for instance, recently banned the use of outdoor amplifying equipment except at meetings which have administration sanction, such as football rallies. The regents also have decided to reduce the number of out-of-state undergraduate students by limiting them to 15 per cent of the student body by the academic year 1971-72. The economy-minded legislature manifested its disapproval of the university, at least indirectly, when it refused last year to raise faculty salaries enough to keep step with other major Midwestern schools. As a result, the Wisconsin faculty is, on average, according to the administration, the lowest paid of the Big Ten universities.

A threat by the state legislature in January 1969 to reduce the nonresident tuition remission for graduate assistants from out of state-in effect reducing their take-home pay-led to the first serious talk of a strike and gave strong impetus to the TAA's effort to organize itself as a labor union. By mid-March 1969, TAA president Robert L. Muehlenkamp was able to report to Chancellor Young that a majority of the teaching assistants (TA's) on the Madison campus had signed cards designating the TAA as their exclusive agent for collective bargaining with the university, and to request the start of the negotiations which finally ended last week.

Teaching assistants play an important role in the large modern university. At Wisconsin, they teach the great bulk of lecture sections and low-level required courses. The TAA estimates that, at Madison, 56 per cent of undergraduate courses and 68 per cent of freshman and sophomore courses are taught by TA's. The university administration prefers another measure, which it calls "contact hours," each involving one student before one teacher for one hour. By this measure, a professor giving a lecture before 250 students would chalk up 250 contact hours, while an assistant meeting with a class of twenty-five students would score only twenty-five contact hours. By the administration standard, TA's teach 31 per cent of the contact hours, campus-wide. But the concentration in certain departments is notably higher. These include English, history, chemistry, mathematics, and various foreign languages.

The TA's Plight

At Wisconsin as elsewhere, teaching assistants hold half-time or lesser appointments, the rest of their time being devoted, in theory, to pursuit of an advanced degree. But TA's complain that their jobs consume a disproportionate share of their working hours. The Madison TAA, citing university studies, claims that a half-time appointment, twenty working hours in theory, actually demands about twenty-eight hours of work a week. At Wisconsin, according to the TAA, the average TA earns $2,800 a year. (At half-time he would earn $3,555 or more, depending on his experience. But there are few half-time appointments.) In addition, graduate students with teaching assistantships pay only the tuition charged Wisconsin residents, $526 this year, instead of the out-of-state tuition for graduate students of $2126. The university counts this tuition arrangement additional compensation. Thus, it claims, a half-time teaching assistant actually earns $5100 of more. In terms of take-home pay, however, the TA earns far less money. About half of Wisconsin's TA's are married and in their middle twenties; perhaps one-quarter have children. Their graduate studies are stretched out by the need to take a part-time job; thus the time when they can begin earning full-time professional salaries is delayed. "Since graduate course credits cannot be transferred to another university, once a TA is here he must remain to complete his degree," declared a recent TAA broadside. "During that time he or she may arbitrarily lose the TA position or find his or her teaching time and salary reduced. A TA has no power over the terms of his employment, no job security, no voice in course assign-

Daniel Czitrom

Teaching Assistants' Association work stoppage at the University of Wisconsin, Madison, 1976.

ments. In real terms, we are a captive labor force."

The TAA's complaints have been echoed at other schools. The *Wall Street Journal*, on 8 January 1969, recorded the plight of teaching assistants at the University of Colorado in an article on what it called "Academia's serfs." Teaching Assistant associations are nothing new in the student political movements of the past decade. The first TAA, at Berkeley, went on strike in 1964 in support of the Free Speech Movement. Two years ago an association of teaching and research assistants at the University of Minnesota unsuccessfully sought to bargain with the university for better working conditions.

Besides low pay and long hours at present, teaching assistants in the humanities and hard sciences face a highly congested job market for full-time teachers and researchers. This puts them in double bind, because to get ahead they need the recommendation of the faculty members who, many TA's feel, are "exploiting" them. At Madison, many TA's turned to unionism to combat the resulting feelings of powerlessness and alienation.

The Madison TAA was founded in the spring of 1966, according to present members, by TA's concerned about the possibility that the grades they gave would affect the draft status of students. The organization did not become broadly representative, however, until the Wisconsin legislature's threat to increase tuition for TA's in 1969 gave it a "bread and butter" issue around which to organize as a labor union. TAA's leaders sent cards to all 1,900 Wisconsin TA's proposing that their organization be authorized to act as the exclusive bargaining

agent for teaching assistants. They got approximately 1,100 affirmative returns.

At first, Chancellor Young rejected collective bargaining with the TAA. He suggested that the TAA seek an amendment to state law that would give them that right. But the TAA held firm, insisting that state law presented no obstacle to a grant of representative status to the TAA by the university. Under the implied threat of a strike, with the possibility that the university might become vulnerable to attack by the Wisconsin labor movement for ignoring documented TAA claims, Young agreed to recognize the TAA as an agent for bargaining with the university and its departments, provided its claim to representative status was confirmed by a Wisconsin Employment Relations Commission (WERC) election. The tentative recognition was signed on 26 April 1969, as part of a "structure agreement" defining broad areas for negotiation. Shortly thereafter, the TAA won 77 per cent of a campus-wide vote supervised by the WERC. A majority of teaching assistants in fifty-two of eighty-one faculty departments picked the TAA as their exclusive bargaining agent.

Clearly, recognition was the critical hurdle for the TAA in its effort to establish itself as a power on the Madison campus. It was, also, a historic event because it marked the first time, so far as can be ascertained, that a union has been recognized as a collective bargaining agent for university teachers, let alone teaching assistants. Young has often stressed the fact that his grant of recognition was voluntary: the TAA responds that it was voluntary only in the sense that he was not *legally* required to deal with them. Morally and politically, they believe, he had little choice.

CATHERINE CONROY: UNIONIST AND FEMINIST

While women unionists like Maude McCreery and Alice Holz broke new ground in the 1930s and 1940s, Catherine Conroy rose to prominence in the 1960s and 1970s. The following article, written in 1978, describes how Conroy combined feminism and unionism in creative new ways. Apart from her many achievements, including her service as a member of University of Wisconsin Board of Regents in the 1980s, Conroy served as a role model for women unionists who moved into positions of leadership in the last two decades.

SEVEN years ago—that'd be 1971—Catherine Conroy, staff representative for the Communications Workers of America (CWA), ran for district vice-presidency of the union.

She was the first women ever to run competitively for the job and had she won, she would have become only the second woman ever to serve on the executive board of a union that is more than 50% female.

Early in the running, Kay Clarenbach of Madison, a close friend, offered her help. She seemed a strong ally—a distinguished scholar, president of the Interstate Association of Commissions on the Status of Women, a founder and the first chairperson of the National Organization for Women (NOW), chairman of the Board of Trustees of Alverno College, et cetera.

"I said, 'What can I do to help your campaign?'" recalled Ms. Clarenbach. "And Catherine said, 'The most useful thing you can do is just to keep still and not let anyone know that I know you.'"

Ms. Conroy's reasoning probably had something to do with the fact that even though she was a twenty-four year veteran of the union—one of its charter members—she was, above all, a woman.

Ms. Conroy also realized that her status as a nationally recognized feminist, her involvement with NOW—she, too, was a founder—her membership on the Governor's Commission on the Status of Women and her general image as a "liberated" woman were traits not worth stressing in the election. Ms. Conroy knew that her two life concerns—the labor movement and the women's movement—sometimes mixed about as well as ice cream and artichokes. . . .

She has been in the labor movement since 1947 and in the women's movement since its "second wave" beginnings in 1963 (the "first wave" being the struggle for the vote in the early 1900s). In her years with the labor movement, she has amassed a reputation as first-rate organizer, negotiator, loyal advocate of the union cause and lately, the feminist cause.

She has been a staff representative of the union since 1960, a job in which she negotiates contracts, represents union employees in grievance matters and monitors the activities of ten locals in the southeastern corner of Wisconsin.

She is the first woman to serve on the state's sixteen-member AFL-CIO board, to which she was elected in 1974 and is one of only a dozen women in Wisconsin who hold full time positions in labor unions. In the women's movement, Ms. Conroy is sometimes referred to as St. Catherine; there she is a matriarch, professor emeritus of Experience 101.

Ms. Conroy's involvement in the women's movement began in 1963 when she was appointed to the governor's Task Force on the Status of Women. That eventually took her and other Wisconsin women to a gathering of similar groups in Washington. There, activists desiring more concrete purpose—of which Ms. Conroy was one—formed the National Organization for Women (NOW)

While working for the CWA in Chicago from 1965-71, Ms. Conroy founded the Chicago Chapter of NOW and served as its first president. The chapter came close to folding after she left office and active involvement, so Ms. Conroy got reinvolved and stabilized the group. The Chicago chapter is now the second largest in the country, with 500 members.

Ms. Conroy returned to Milwaukee in 1971, and soon after became the first president of the newly formed Coalition of Labor Union Women, a group dedicated to raising the consciousness of women in labor unions. . . .

Ms. Conroy was adopted as an infant and grew up on Milwaukee's west side. Her father, one of 11 children, was an art dealer until the economy crashed in 1929. He lost his job and was forced to take odd jobs wherever he could, while Ms. Conroy's mother earned what little she could by taking care of children in Shorewood.

The family moved from apartment to apartment, each time to one with lower rent, until at one point the family was living in housekeeping rooms. Catherine attend seven different grade schools and two high schools while she was growing up. . . .

Because of the hard time, when Catherine finished high school she went to work at kitchen and housekeeping jobs for Milwaukee County for about three years. In 1942, she took a job as a telephone operator with Wisconsin Telephone.

Like many young people in their 20s, Catherine hadn't though much about her future; her parents hadn't pushed her to marry and she had no serious thoughts of it. Five years after she joined the telephone company, its workers went on strike in the first nationwide walkout against Ma Bell, and Catherine became a picket line captain. She was twenty-eight.

She suddenly became more involved in the union (then called the National Federation of Telephone Workers—NFTW), first as a local steward, later as state business manager and then as a division officer.

At the time, the union was still in its formative stages; in

Catherine Conroy, 1983.

Courtesy Wisconsin State AFL-CIO

1951 it reorganized into the Communication Workers of America. Even though NFTW division officers were offered local staff positions in the new organization, Catherine decided to learn about unions from the rank and file up, so she ran for president of her local—a position in which she'd have more contact with all union members, not just union officials. She won and subsequently was re-elected to three more two-year terms. . . .

Things began to change within Ms. Conroy in the early '60s. She became involved in the Governor's Commission on the Status of Women and then went to Washington with a number of soon-to-be national leaders in the feminist movement—Ms. Clarenbach; Jean Boyer of Beaver Dam and Sisters Joel Reed and Austin Doherty, both of Alverno (Sister Reed is now president). There she and others joined to form NOW.

Catherine made her first mark on the organization at a luncheon meeting on the last day of the Washington meetings when she tossed $5 on the table and uttered the semi-immortal words: "Well, if we're going to form an organization, we'd better put our money where our mouth is." Whereupon a treasury for the newly founded organization was created.

Ms. Conroy returned from those and other meetings with a different perspective.

"When Catherine was a feminist back in the early '60s," recalls Ms. Fryman, back in the Washington union offices, "we all looked at her with a jaundiced eye. Many of us felt that she was sticking her neck out too far by being part of this radical group, the National Organization for Women, vocally supporting women's rights, asking questions about why women weren't getting certain jobs, equal pay for equal work.

"Nobody was asking these questions but Catherine. She was one of the first women in this country to start this—she was way ahead of her time. It turned out that she was completely right and now we're all feminists.". . .

—Tony Carideo

Milwaukee Journal, July 9, 1978.

Contract Demands:

For the long-run success of the TAA on the Madison campus, however, recognition had to be followed by negotiation of a contract spelling out significant concessions to the TAA. The union asked for an end to year-to-year TA appointments in each department with arbitrary dismissal, or layoffs due to reduced workloads; instead it demanded appointment for the duration of an individual's graduate career, up to ten years; limits on the number of students in TA courses; sick leave and fringe health benefits. It also asked the university to set up, in each department, a committee for review of each TA's performance in class, to consist of one-third faculty. Some TA's see this procedure as a prototype for eventual evaluation of faculty performance as well.

In general, the TAA won on these economic and work-performance issues, except that TA appointments for the duration of graduate studies will last only up to 4 years. But it yielded in the end to the university's demand for a no-strike clause for the life of the contract, to September 1971.

The union also sought two policy-related clauses in the contract, which drove to the heart of the power and ideological differences between the faculty and administration, on one side, and the activist core of the TAA and undergraduate students on the other. The lesser of these dealt with "human rights," and included a statement recognizing "that much of the structure and content of University education reflects and perpetuates an inequitable society through forms of explicit and de facto discrimination." It stipulated that the university and the union must work to develop programs to end discrimination "through hiring, admission and education policies." The university held out for a statement of nondiscrimination in hiring, admission, and education policies, withholding any pledge to bargain with the union on such questions. Its objective was to prevent the TAA from filing grievances on issues like open admissions.

The second and more important policy issue dealt with "educational planning." In essence the union demanded that each department engage in collective bargaining with the TAA to establish "decision-making" mechanisms that give student and TA's a share of power over educational planning of courses in which teaching assistants are involved.

The TAA's drive for collective bargaining with departmental faculty over mechanisms for codetermination ran head on into the faculty's professional ego and sense of autonomy. At Wisconsin, explains a member of the research staff, "The faculty controls almost all issues that deal with education. Nominally this preserves academic freedom; actually it means power to compete for students, research funds, and departmental budgets. This university does not have a pyramidal power structure, it's a hydra." Moreover, he said, "the faculty is on the defensive," sensing a threat to their autonomy from the regents and the legislature as part of the reaction to student activism.

At one point, shortly after the TAA strike began in March, the university offered the union an educational planning clause which conceded that the union could bargain with each department. But the university rapidly withdrew the offer, apparently under faculty pressure. Both Young and the TAA reported that several prominent faculty members had threatened to resign if the bargaining clause went in.

A two-day faculty meeting on 7-8 April made clear how far the majority of the university establishment was willing to go toward meeting the TAA demands. A resolution proposing department-by-department negotiations between faculty, students, and teaching assistants was rejected by a 2-to-1 margin. So was a resolution repudiating the entire TAA-university bargaining effort of the past twelve months. The position which won faculty support, and was embodied in the contract signed next day by the TAA, was that "collaboration" between students, teaching assistants, and faculty in course planning is desirable, but the statement avoided all mention of collective bargaining and stipulated that the faculty must bear ultimate responsibility. "If we give the slightest inch on academic matters, then everything will be settled by power," warned one of the speakers at the tightly packed meeting. Collective bargaining would make education decisions "subject to the haggling of the marketplace," complained another. Although the clause does not appear to be binding on any department, the TAA accepted the provision as an opening wedge for future negotiations. As the strike entered its final week, the TAA found its bargaining position eroded by several pressures. A state court declared the strike illegal and enjoined teaching assistants to return to the classroom. Although the union voted to ignore the injunction, leaders were aware that support was fading. Another pressure came from students who began returning to classes to catch up on missed work. Yet another pressure, on both the TAA and Young, was a regents' meeting scheduled for 10 April.

Some campus liberals thought the union should have settled early in the strike, when it seemed to have obtained a major concession on educational planning. But union leaders reply that they still had, overall, an unfavorable contract at that time. Besides, one said, the union had succeeded by flouting the rules of "conventional liberal wisdom."

Teaching Assistants Association
Not for Bread Alone

The decision to make policy and ideological issues a part of the negotiations is cited. The university and leaders of the state AFL-CIO tried to talk TAA out of insisting on an educational planning clause because, they said, it "wasn't a union issue."

"We're a different kind of union," Muehlenkamp and Marketti reply. "Policy-making power over the nature of production and the administration of . . . resources is hardly extraneous to worker interests," declared a TAA newsletter in discussing why the TAA is both a "bread-and-butter" and an ideological union. "Ultimately, our union exists because in our community of the knowledge-industry, like in all other aspects of the American economy, wealth and power are concentrated in the hands of a few nonworkers. The Administration is a management which has manipulated the University not for the well being of teaching assistants, or students, or secretaries, or janitors, but rather for the commercial interests of a capitalistic state . . . If America is to be changed, it should be obvious that our generation is going to have to do the changing . . . We do right by opposing through our contract demands, union education, and direct action the racism and imperialism which drain our natural resources as they divide our working class. What parody

David Newby, a leader in the TAA, was elected President of the Dane County Labor Council in 1982 and President of the Wisconsin State AFL-CIO in 1994.

of progress it would be for us to march backward eating bread and dusty butter as we drag the polluted and competitive present into a lost socialist and democratic future."

"They can't be both management and workers," retorted Young recently. "The labor unions," he said, "are on our side except some Teamsters." The Madison Teamsters local supported the TAA strike by permitting its drivers to refuse to cross student picket lines, and by taking campus bus drivers off the job for a time. But Local 171 of the Wisconsin State Employees Association, representing blue-collar workers on the campus, did not back the strike. Neither did the state AFL-CIO.

The TAA has "a transitory membership," Young commented. "We were worried about that until the strike," commented a TAA spokesman. The TAA called the strike because, it said, the university had refused to engage in satisfactory negotiations over the preceding nine months. But a major purpose was organizational—to consolidate the union's strength and develop leaders for a continued campaign of pressure on the university and its departments. What long-term success the union achieved toward this goal remains to be seen.

A "student-worker alliance" has long been a romantic dream of certain campus radicals from Berkeley to Nanterre. Having in their way realized the dream on a small scale, despite a lack of support from the AFL-CIO, the Madison TAA leaders now talk of organizing teaching assistants, junior faculty, and campus workers across the nation into an international, industrial-style union.∎

From *Science*, vol. 168, no. 3929 (April 17, 1970).

A Female Machinist
in Milwaukee

BY SUE DORO AND KAREN MATTHEWS

*Sue Doro, a machinist-turned-poet, offers this
personal account of what it was like for a woman to
break into a male-dominated occupation.*

WAS born in 1937 into a working-class Milwaukee family. My father worked in a factory and sometimes as a child I'd go with him to his job. Milwaukee used to be the machine tool center of the country, which meant that there were more machine shops and heavy-equipment metal-cutting jobs there than there are now. When I was growing up a lot of people I knew were machinists or were working where machining was done. They were mostly men, though I knew some women who did assembly-line work. But not until the last three years I was working as a machinist did I come across another woman machinist apprentice who was working at another factory. We weren't very common.

I went to school to become a machinist under the Manpower Training Development Act, MTDA. This was before they had CETA, which was the predecessor to the one they have now, JTPA—they keep changing the names. The good thing about the MTDA program was that you got paid for going to school. This was in 1972-73. They gave you six months of training, and your schooling, books, and transportation were paid for. You received wages for the entire six months. Then there were two weeks of job development. This was a joke because all you did was go to a job counselor, who handed you the morning paper. You looked at the paper to decide if there were any jobs for you.

I was the first woman in the machine shop training class, so the teacher didn't like me. The men in the class were very helpful. The one guy I had trouble with was the teacher. He was a horrible person with an alcohol problem. I mean, he just drank while he was talking to us. It was amazing how he could get away with that. He wouldn't let me train on the turret lathe or on the automatic screw machine. Both of those machines are high money-makers if you know how to run them, because they are high production-rate machines. An automatic screw machine makes thousands of parts in a very short time, so companies love people who know how to run them. But I wasn't trained on one. The only reason I learned how to operate a turret lathe was because the teacher would go to sleep for a couple

of hours at a time and then the guys would show me. Most of the guys there knew how to run the machines because they learned in high school shop classes or the military. They all knew what they were doing much more than I did. Because of them I feel I got a good, solid training from the class in spite of the teacher!

After that, I got a job at Hellwig Corp., a small carbon brush factory, in the engine lathe department—where I was the first woman they'd ever hired. There were other women working in that factory, mostly doing bench assembly work. They sat at long tables putting little tiny parts together, going crazy. It was a non-union shop and I stayed there for a year and a half. Several of us tried to organize a union, and lo and behold, I got laid off. The point was that nobody had ever been laid off there. They prided themselves on never having layoffs. They cut people's hours, but they would never lay you off. So everyone just assumed it was because of the union activity. But I also wanted to move on because I wasn't making much money, and the reason I had become a machinist was to have enough money to raise the five kids I had to care for when my ex-husband took off. Being a machinist was one of the highest paying jobs in Milwaukee at that time because it was a skilled trade.

After Hellwig, I heard they were hiring at Allis Chalmers, a large tractor plant. It had 10,000 workers in it, as opposed to a couple of hundred in the carbon brush factory. They had no female machinists and no women working in the maintenance department where I ended up. This was a union shop. UAW. I had heard that they were hiring so I went down to apply and they told me they didn't have any work. I figured that something was screwy. I knew people that worked there, so I had them report to me about who they were hiring, and what jobs they were hiring for. It turned out they were hiring all men and they were hiring them for everything from sweeping the floor to working as a machinist. Certainly, I knew how to sweep a floor. I went back and told them that I knew they were hiring and I wanted a job, but they still wouldn't give me one.

At that point, one of the people at the shop told me to call his union representative, who was a woman. I called her and she said, yes indeed, they're hiring and she sent me the hiring list which told me who was hired and for what jobs. I marched myself down to the EEO (Equal Employment Opportunity) office and told them what had happened, and I filed a complaint. Within a week's time, I was called in for an interview at Allis Chalmers. At the end of the interview, the guy said, "Well, we'll probably hire you, you have enough experience. We want to put you in the maintenance department. And, by the way, we have this paper from the EEO." He brought out a letter that I was supposed to sign saying that I was hired and therefore was signing away the suit. I said I'd have to think about it.

The next thing was the physical, which, I was told later, was unlike any physical that anybody had ever had. They took so many X-rays of my back and my front that I felt like I was going to glow. They were trying to find something wrong with me so that I wouldn't pass the physical—then they could say that they were going to hire me, only I didn't pass the physical. But I did pass the physical! I didn't have anything wrong. Their next tactic was to put me in a department where not only had a woman never worked before, but where all the guys were older, very conservative white men who didn't want a woman there. They wanted to just go to work and smoke their cigars and every once in a while do a little work. At the maintenance department, our job was to fix a part that had something wrong with it—for example, maybe a transmission part had a hole that was drilled too big or too small. Besides being very highly skilled work, it was very complicated for me to learn after going to school for only six months and spending only a year and a half on the engine lathe. But I learned how to do it and slowly won over all the guys except one, whose name (appropriately) was Dick.

Dick had a thing for pornographic literature. When he realized that I really was staying, he always harassed me by leaving dirty pictures wherever I was going to be working. He also tried to sabotage my work. He was on first shift and I was on second shift, on the same machine. When you're working in a specialized place and you set up a machine with a certain part in it, nobody messes with it; they just leave it for you to come in the next day and finish what you have to finish. Well, I had to start checking all the parts on my machine because Dick would loosen stuff on it, which could kill you. Like, he would loosen a big drill, a huge part. If it's not tight, and it hits, it will shatter in your face. Safety glasses wouldn't help; you'd be real cut up. He did stuff like that.

Eventually I went to my union and made a complaint. They said they'd talk to him, but they didn't. So I went back and said, either you talk to him or I'm going to file a suit against you, against the union because this is dangerous, it's harassment. I just threatened them, I never did file anything. Now the union president and vice-president in a big factory like that didn't work in the shop, they are in an office someplace else. They wear suits. So the next morning I see five or six guys in suits come down the aisle and go over to Dick with this piece of paper—I don't know what the heck it is—and they were yelling and shaking their fingers at him. He looked real scared. After that he stopped doing everything. But I had to really fight to get him to stop.

BLUE-COLLAR ARISTOCRATS: THE VIEW FROM A WORKING-CLASS TAVERN

For four years, E. E. LeMasters, a professor of social work at the University of Wisconsin-Madison, was a "regular" at a working-class tavern. Interacting with the patrons, LeMasters became a participant-observer of the lifestyles and attitudes of the blue-collar, mostly male patrons of the bar. After a few hours with the plumbers, sheet-metal workers, electricians and other construction workers, LeMasters would record his observations regarding the attitudes and problems of blue-collar workers.

OVER 90 per cent of the blue-collar workers who frequent The Oasis are members of trade unions. The men tend to be realistic about the need for labor unions: they realize that they would be at the mercy of their employers if they were not organized. One bricklayer said: "We would get a good screwing from those bastards if we didn't have a union." He was, of course, referring to the employers.

There is no idealism or social reform content in the talk of these men about their unions: they see them as a means of improving wages, fringe benefits, and working conditions. They do not think of the union as an instrument for social change or social reform. This same view of the union was found in the English studies of affluent blue-collar workers by the Goldthorpe research group.

One of the most negative aspects of trade unionism in the construction industry as observed at The Oasis is the attitude of the men toward their union officers and leaders. The attitude is one of complete cynicism. "The bastards are in it for what they can get out of it," a truck driver said. "And that's the same reason why I'm in the union."

One factor in the attitude of these men toward union officials is that the union officers have become white-collar workers—people who earn their living "shuffling papers" or "with their mouth." This places the union leaders in the same category as politicians in the eyes of these blue-collar workers.

Historically, of course, craft unions in the United States, unlike industrial unions such as the Automobile Workers, have been conservative (if not reactionary) for a long time. If the men at The Oasis are at all representative it is difficult to see how any social reform could emanate from craft unions.

Some of the older workers at The Oasis can see that the

Card and billiard players at a Milwaukee Municipal Social Center, 1965.

Robert L. Miller/State Historical Society of Wisconsin WHi (X3) 43552

construction industry is not what it once was—the emphasis today is on production and volume, not craftmanship. A skilled carpenter put it this way:

"You take those apartments we're working on now. There's 120 units, almost exactly alike. The kitchen cabinets come completely finished. All we do is hang 'em on the wall. The goddamn foreman doesn't care how well we do the job—he wants volume. He has orders to complete so many units this week and by God that's what he does, whether the work is done right or not."

He paused to order another beer. "The younger men don't mind it—that's the way they were trained. But my old man taught me how to be a carpenter and by God when you cut a piece of wood for the old man it either fit or else. He was particular as hell." After a few moments of reflection he

added: "I don't enjoy the work any more."

For the blue-collar aristocrats in this study the job is still the center of their world. Unlike factory assembly line workers, most of the men at The Oasis still seem to enjoy their work.

In a society that is becoming increasingly white-collar these blue-collar workers distrust the middle-class white collarites and are antagonistic toward them. This attitude influences the feeling of these men toward their union leaders and also toward public officials.

As America becomes more and more computerized and mechanized and as jobs become more routine, these men emerge as a sort of remnant of a world that is fast disappearing. Some of the men realize this but others would prefer not to think about it.■

—E. E. LeMasters

From *Blue-Collar Aristocrats: Life-Styles at a Working-Class Tavern* (University of Wisconsin, Madison, 1975).

I was at the tractor plant nearly four years and was even elected steward. Then came the massive layoffs. I got hired at the Milwaukee Road railroad, where I worked for eight and a half years. I was hired on as a machinist there, the first woman machinist ever hired. The railroad was under a federal order to hire women and minorities, so after I got hired, they hired some more women in the welding department and a couple of women machinist's helpers. They kind of came and went. They were harassed a lot and didn't feel like putting up with it.

It was pretty good work at the railroad. We would make train wheels. You'd get a raw casting from the foundry, that sort of looked like the shape of a train wheel. Then you'd have to bore out the middle of it, where the axle's going to fit in, to the right dimension, using a boring mill machine. I also ran a fifteen-foot engine lathe. You'd lift both wheels and the axle with a crane and put that in the machine. All this work had to be very precise, like plus or minus one-thousandth of an inch. I also worked in the bearing room, rebuilding the bearings that go on the ends of the axles. When you see a train moving along, that great big round thing on the end of the wheel, that's a bearing; that's what keeps the wheel rolling. It's got grease inside of it so it doesn't freeze up and cause a train wreck.

For awhile I worked in the diesel house, which was not a good job. Nobody really wanted it because it meant crawling underneath the trains. They'd park the train over a big pit and then you'd go inside the pit and work under the bottom part of the diesel engine, regreasing. It was really dirty work; you had to scrape off all kinds of filth before you could even get to the part that you had to work on. I didn't like it at all. But after awhile, when a lot of layoffs began happening there too, your seniority didn't keep you in the job that you liked. If you were low on the seniority, you'd get bumped. Bump, bump, bump. And you'd end up with stuff like the diesel house.

Machining is a process that has a lot of stages to it. It's very dialectical. If you do the wrong thing in the beginning, the end product isn't going to be right. So every step of the way, you have to analyze what you're doing. And when you do everything the right way, it's going to be perfect. That's a very powerful, good feeling. The work requires brains to figure out what you can use besides physical strength. So in other words, if you had to tighten up something, there'd be ways of putting a hollow bar on the end of your tool for leverage. You'd learn how to get little wooden pallets to stand on so you'd be taller, so you could get more leverage. You usually had cranes to pick up the heavy stuff, but you still needed upper body strength—I didn't have enough, which is why I got hurt a couple of times. When I counsel women now, I encourage them to do exercises and train with weights, under proper guidance, to develop their strength. I didn't have that kind of training; I developed my strength on the job, which is not a good way to do it.

The railroad was eventually sold. There's nothing there now except rubble from the buildings, and apparently one or two buildings that they don't know what to do with. All the machine tooling inside has been sold or destroyed. I could list you twenty-five big companies that are no longer in Milwaukee. I have been writing a lot of poetry recently about plant closures. Milwaukee is probably going to end up like Minneapolis, with

Sue Doro, machinist and poet.

Courtesy Sue Doro

insurance companies and stuff like that replacing heavier industries. It's hit me in the face that heavy industry is shifting to robotics, with one person in the shop pressing buttons, and no other people around, just a bunch of shiny robots. I could see that the people I was working with were the end of their kind, and we should be celebrating what they know how to do. But the fact is, women who want to be machinists now had better learn how to work with computerized machinery.

I miss the work a lot. I miss the machining itself—that feeling of creating a part out of a piece of raw steel. When you're done with it, you've got this really pretty, shiny part. You put in your eight hours of work and you have something to show for it. I liked that. And I miss the people. We had a real comradely bonding because we were working in a dangerous job. At the railroad we all watched out for each other, because there were axles going over our heads on conveyor belts—anything could go wrong. People got killed doing their jobs while I was there. I almost got hit in the head with an axle. It missed me by about two inches. I was real shook up; I sat down on the floor for awhile and didn't move.

Another thing that I found out in all my jobs was that the

When I look back on it, I have to be very careful, because sometimes I gloss over a lot of the hard stuff now, I just like to talk about the good stuff . . . I had these wonderful friends and it was good work. The truth is that it was also very, very hard work and very, very dirty and very, very dangerous.

people who would be the friendliest and the people that I could bond with right away were mostly Third World men. I mean, Third World women, too, but I'm talking about the men in this situation, because it was mostly men I was working with. They knew. They could see what I was going through. They had gone through the same thing themselves. Earl was the first black machinist, and Doc, another friend, was the first black laborer ever hired, back in 1943. These were people who knew what was going on. They didn't have a feminist consciousness, but they were fair. And they could tell unfairness.

When I look back on it, I have to be very careful, because Larry, my second husband, says that sometimes I gloss over a lot of the hard stuff now, I just like to talk about the good stuff. You know, you look back and think oh, I had these wonderful friends and it was good work. The truth is that it was also very, very hard work and very, very dirty and very, very dangerous. I'd be extremely tired when I'd come home. I mean, now I can stay up until eleven o'clock at night, just like the big kids! But when I was working, I would go to bed some time between eight and nine o'clock. I was so tired I couldn't keep awake any later than that.

My menopause began the last two years of my machinist life. I didn't realize what was happening. I'd had a partial hysterectomy years before and didn't even have the menstrual cycle changes to signal that menopause was ensuing. I thought I was just getting really hot because the shop windows were being nailed shut with plastic sheeting. (Being Wisconsin, it was extremely cold in the winter and they put plastic over the windows to keep the wind out.) Of course, this didn't explain why I was hot walking through the snow drifts in the morning, before I even got to the shop!

When I went to work in this trade, my youngest child was five and the oldest was thirteen. It was very hard on the kids and it was very hard on me. Not just the physical stuff, but the emotional stuff—feeling guilty that you weren't home. Because the mother, in my mind, was supposed to be home taking care of the kids. The main reason I decided to become a machinist was that I could make enough money to support my family. I never got any child support from my ex-husband. None. So the big thing was the money—I didn't have a "pioneer" idea about the job until after I got into it more.

I didn't identify with feminist politics at that time. I thought that the feminist movement was a really good thing, but that I didn't necessarily need it. Because I could take care of myself. I always had this survival thing—I don't need anybody to take care of me. After my husband left, and the divorce was so terrible, I quickly changed my mind. The feminist movement did have something to do with me. And even though I didn't know many women from my class, from the working class, that were active in feminist politics, we talked about it a little bit, and eventually I got involved myself.

Being in the trades taught me to be stronger. I think it taught me to stick up for myself. That and the feminist politics helped to tell me that I was an important person and that I wasn't just a housewife—and that even if I were to be a housewife someday, that was important, too. So it gave me a sense of self-worth. Working with machinery also gave me a feeling of power that I had never experienced before.

Ninety-nine percent of my co-workers were men, so I had to join women's organizations to find the support I needed. I was a member of the Feminist Writers' Guild in Milwaukee for maybe nine years, right from the first year it started. I also joined Tradeswomen, Inc., when I was back in Milwaukee, and Women of the Americas, which was a women's support group for anti-intervention in Central America. So at least once or twice a week I would get together with all women. I really needed that—especially having four sons and one daughter, there was a lot of maleness in my life! And I'm glad that I discovered that being with women was good for me. Another really important aspect of getting involved in the Feminist Writers' Guild was that it helped me develop my poetry.

I write a lot of poetry today, mostly about the lives of working people. I'm now the executive director of Tradeswomen, Inc., which is a national non-profit membership organization for peer support, advocacy and networking for women in non-traditional, blue-collar jobs. I've been in this position since 1986. I help women who come to the office for job counseling and other advice and information, such as how to deal with sexual harassment. We try to act as a resource for women, to keep the women in the trades from leaving when they feel discouraged. If a woman doesn't have any support at her job, if she's working with a bunch of guys who are all just assholes, and there's nobody she can relate to, then at least she can come to a Tradeswomen potluck or support group and find other women to talk to. It feels good to be doing this work, and I'm proud to be part of it. Woman power can change the world!■

From "Sue Doro, Machinist," interview by Karen Matthews, *Hard-hatted Women*, Molly Martin, ed. (Seal, Seattle, 1988).

The Hortonville
Teachers' Strike of 1974

WISCONSIN EDUCATION
ASSOCIATION COUNCIL

One of the most bitter strikes in Wisconsin history took place in Hortonville in 1974 when public school teachers walked off the job, frustrated by a stubborn school board that refused to bargain in good faith. The conflict left its mark on Wisconsin labor legislation when lawmakers subsequently enacted a new law providing for a system of mediation and arbitration in order to resolve labor disputes in the public sector.

N 1961, the Wisconsin legislature passed a public employee bargaining bill, which was revised in 1971. The 1971 law, 111.70, mandated good faith bargaining. However, there was nothing in the law that forced school boards to comply. Teachers were frustrated by the fact that they had no effective recourse in the face of regressive bargaining by school boards, except to resort to striking illegally. In August of 1972, over 200 associations were still without settled contracts for the 1972-73 school year, with seventy-nine still unsettled in September. At that time, this lack of settlements was unprecedented. The same pattern continued the following school year, with over 80 contracts still unsettled in September.

Although the 1971 Wisconsin public employee bargaining law maintained the illegality of public employee strikes, at least thirty local teacher associations, frustrated by the inability to reach settlement, undertook illegal strikes in 1972-73 and 1973-74. These strikes involved locals of from thirty-five to 700 teachers, lasted from three to thriteen days, and focused on such issues as just cause for non-renewal (the main issue in most of these strikes), salary, health insurance, retirement, class size, the length of the school day, and/or teacher-pupil contact time.

Once a strike occurred, settlement was reached within no more than two weeks, with the associations achieving many of their goals, especially the addition of a just cause for non-renew-al clause and improvements on salary and insurance issues. While few local associations suffered any serious repercussions from their illegal strikes, some were threatened. Attempts to open Wausau schools with replacement teachers failed in 1970. And while thirty-five Wild Rose teachers who struck in February 1973 were threatened with firing, the school board did not follow through. The Kenosha Education Association, on strike in October 1973, was fined $37,000, which was subsequently significantly reduced.

What happened in Hortonville? In 1973, the Hortonville Education Association (HEA) and the Hortonville school board began bargaining the 1973-74 contract. By January 1974, after ten months, negotiations were at a stalemate. Teachers had then been teaching for nearly five months without a contract, a situation that was unusual in those years.

The sequence of events in Hortonville was as follows:

January 24-30, 1974
HEA engages in informational picketing.
January through March
Further job actions, continuing negotiations.
March 18
Teachers strike.
March 23
Second invitation sent; teachers disregard this invitation also.
April 1
HEA teachers, with counsel, appear en masse, refusing individual hearings.
April 2
Special school board hearing terminates employment of striking teachers and withdraws offered 1974-75 contracts.

School was closed in Hortonville from the first day of the strike until April 8, except for two days. Classes had operated on March 26 and 27 with substitutes, but the school was closed during the rest of this period. Following the firing of the striking staff, the school board began hiring "replacement teachers" and school reopened on April 8.

Approximately 500 teachers spent portions of their spring vacation supporting the HEA on the picket line. In response to the influx of out-of-town teachers and other labor supporters, a Hortonville Vigilante Association formed to counter the pickets and escort the "replacement teachers" across the picket line. As hostilities between the strikers and their supporters and the

Local police drag striking teachers on picket lines at Hortonville.

Wisconsin Education Association Council

Hortonville community became more heated, an army of deputy sheriffs from at least five neighboring counties joined the Outagamie County Sheriff Department in trying to maintain order on the picket line. At one point the sheriff requested that Governor Lucey call out the National Guard to relieve his tired men, a request he later withdrew. Though school remained open during this time, over 240 persons were used to replace the eighty-four still-striking teachers, many of those persons quitting after one day.

In August 1974 the HEA brought a class action suit in the Outagamie County Circuit Court against the Hortonville Joint School District on several grounds, including violation of due process and violation of the open meeting law. Judge Allan J. Deehr ruled against the HEA. On appeal, by the HEA, the Wisconsin State Supreme Court upheld the illegality of the strike and the rejection of the open meeting law contention. However, it found that the HEA's rights of due process had been violated because the Hortonville school board was not an "impartial observer" when it fired the teachers. The Hortonville school board appealed this decision to the U.S. Supreme court, which reversed the Wisconsin decision, finding in favor of the School board.

Many of the 240 replacements spent only one day in the Hortonville classrooms. Some classes had an almost constant turnover of teachers. Parents withdrew forty-nine students from school to attend an alternative school begun by striking teachers

Donations to striking teachers arrived from around the state.

in April 1974. A Parent's Action Committee attempted to address concerns through letters and through legal recourse but were unsuccessful. Students' reports of their experience were mixed, but an editorial in Hortonville's school newspaper that year indicated negative impact upon students' learning and motivation.

According to Wisconsin Statute 121.02: Every teacher, supervisor, administrator and professional staff member shall hold a certificate, license, or permit to teach, issued by the Department of Public Instruction before entering on duty for such position. However, investigation by the HEA revealed that not all strikebreakers were certified, or even certifiable. Several of these "teachers" were still undergraduates; others were parents or community members. Two had been convicted of crimes. The HEA listed twenty-four strikebreakers, employed at Hortonville as of June 11, 1974, who did not hold teaching licenses. Seven had substitute licenses, twelve had applications for a license pending (all dated 5/17/74), four others had no license. One was not offered a contract for the following year: he was not certified nor certifiable. Several others were non-renewed, also, for the next year since they could not be certified.

In cases of classes being taught by unlicensed persons, which violated the statute, the state DPI was expected to cut off state aids for every day that such unlicensed persons were employed. Although State Superintendent Barbara Thompson reiterated the working of the statute in several letters to parents and to HEA president Mike Wisnoski, she did not enforce the statute. Even after Supt. Thompson had been provided with the HEA's list of unlicensed strikebreakers, Hortonville continued to receive state aids.

From January-March 1974, during the crucial period of negotiations, the HEA received support from two WEAC staff persons and from their UniServ (WUU-N) director. Hortonville teachers made the decision to strike after other job actions failed to achieve settlement. Once it became clear that this was no "ordinary" strike, WEAC brought nearly a dozen staff to the area in April and began a statewide campaign to settle the contract and get the school board to rehire the eighty-four fired strikers.

In April, hundreds of UniServ and WEAC local affiliate leaders met in Appleton to consider actions aimed at reaching a settlement in Hortonville. One of the recommendations was that a statewide teacher strike be called on Friday, April 26. Within ten days a vote on whether to support the April 26 walkout was taken by teachers in every WEAC affiliate. Public and media interest was at a near fever pitch. When the voting was completed, WEAC locals, by a 4 to 1 margin, had voted not to participate in the protest walkout.

At a press conference WEAC President Lauri Wynn said: "The rank and file members, whom we support and whom we represent, have indicated that a statewide strike is too drastic at this time. They have volunteered and offered their bodies and their money to the Hortonville teachers. It has been a tumultuous decision that they have made. We would hope that the public would understand that our concern for the Hortonville teachers has not died, but rather has turned in another direction. We have been in the courts and we will remain in the

Wisconsin Education Association Council

In response to the influx of out-of-town labor supporters, a Hortonville Vigilante Association was formed to counter the pickets and escort "replacement teachers" across the picket line.

courts. We will be at the Legislature so that they can understand that the law under which we find ourselves working is a deformed law and needs to be changed."

Although a statewide strike was not called, many individual WEAC members became very actively involved in Hortonville: donating a substantial amount of money and traveling to Hortonville to participate in strike activities. More than 70 HEA supporters were arrested during picketing. In addition to staff support and member involvement, WEAC also provided counsel and funding for HEA's legal suits, from the circuit court to the U.S. Supreme Court.

Why Was Hortonville Different From Other Strikes?

Previous teacher strikes in Wisconsin, all illegal, had resulted in settlements in 1972-74; why not in Hortonville? In one of their legal briefs, the HEA argued that the Hortonville school board had gone beyond the usual methods employed at that time to resolve strikes: instead of mass firings, as in Hortonville, most schools boards used injunctions against the strike and immediately resumed bargaining. Settlement of the disputed contracts occurred soon after in this typical scenario.

Why did the Hortonville school board take atypical, stronger action? The following are some possible factors:
• The school board hired the Madison law firm of Melli, Walker and Pease, which built its reputation on aggressive union-busting. Certainly, that contributed to the board's intransigence.

• The community, in general, did not seem to have a positive attitude toward education, nor a strong commitment to it.
• There was, in fact, very little core "community" in Hortonville; most of the area consisted of farms, though a new subdivision was growing on the edge of town. There was also division between these two elements of the Hortonville community.
• Hortonville had a strong, long-term undercurrent of anti-union sentiment.
• Most of the teaching staff (three-fourths) lived outside of the community and were considered outsiders, regardless of how long they had been teaching. The average length of teaching career in Hortonville, judging by the HEA scrapbook, was only ten years.
• Teachers had been overheard dismissing the school board as "those farmers"—intensifying the adversarial atmosphere.

The outcomes of the Hortonville strike were as follows: Eighty-four teachers lost their jobs; the Hortonville strike itself has never been settled; and there is presently a group of teachers in Hortonville not affiliated with WEAC. But, although unsuccessful in achieving settlement of the contract or in rehiring the fired teachers, the Hortonville strike is considered to have been instrumental in securing the current collective bargaining law. By providing a mediation-arbitration process, that law remedied the situation that brought about the Hortonville strike. At that time, though good-faith bargaining was part of the law, there was no way to enforce it; no way to take action against an intransigent school board except—as 30+ locals did—through illegal strikes.■

From Wisconsin Education Association Council,
"The Hortonville Teachers' Strike, 1974."

The Union Comes to Wisconsin Physicians Service

BY CYNTHIA B. COSTELLO

Just as "scientific management" and time-motion studies revolutionized American industry and changed the nature of work in heavy industry, similar patterns emerged in offices and non-industrial workplaces. Clerical workers increasingly faced the stop watch as managment efforts to increase productivity were backed up by tighter monitoring and discipline. In many cases, like the industrial workers before them, clerical workers looked to union organization to improve their situation. But clerical workers, especially those employed in the private sector, often found it difficult to organize and win a contract. Even where the union effort succeeded in its early phases, as in the following case at Wisconsin Physicians Services in Madison, the road to subsequent contracts proved to be lined with obstacles.

ACROSS town from the Trust [the firm that manages the pension fund for the Wisconsin Education Association Council] a second group of office workers confronted equally problematic conditions at the Wisconsin Physicians Services Insurance Corporation (WPS). When working conditions at this medium-sized insurance company took a turn for the worse in the mid-seventies, the employees voted to affiliate with a labor union. The company responded by harassing union supporters and instituting a rigid and authoritarian set of policies throughout the firm. Conflict between management and union employees at WPS peaked in 1979 when the union threatened a strike but later backed off after the company offered a union shop. Subsequently, management's decision to hire hundreds of nonunion, part-time office workers including more than one hundred clerical homeworkers weakened the office workers' capacity to challenge the company.

The unionization drive at WPS was sparked by many of the same factors that catalyzed the strike at the Trust. A move to a new building brought with it a deterioration in working conditions that crystallized the office workers' grievances while opportunities to communicate shared grievances increased. The two companies differed in one important respect, however. The ties between the Trust and a labor union constrained Trust management during the strike and led to improvements following the strike. WPS management faced no comparable institutional pressures and, if anything, conditions worsened following unionization. Continued harassment provoked employee dissatisfaction but it also created a climate of fear that impeded clerical activism.[1]

Work and Conflict at WPS

WPS was founded in 1946 by the State Medical Society (SMS), a professional association of Wisconsin doctors. In the mid-seventies, approximately four hundred office workers processed health claims at WPS. Like the Trust, WPS responded to growth by expanding to several office buildings, by streamlining the work process, and by introducing computers. The larger size of WPS allowed for greater specialization of the claims process. An entire floor of one building, for example, was devoted to processing Medicare claims.

Despite its greater size, WPS was only slightly more automated than the Trust by the mid-seventies. The Medicare department used video-display terminals for on-line adjusting, but many departments processed claims through a combination of manual and keypunch systems: after confirming the fee for service, claims adjustors coded the appropriate information on code sheets and keypunch operators entered the coded information into the computer. WPS had not automated more of its work process because adjustors specializing in the processing of one type of claim could achieve great speed in a short period of time. As a manager explained, "People were almost as fast as the computer."

WPS was an authoritarian company. The president maintained a tight monopoly of control over all policies, employing a small cadre of loyal managers to carry out his directives. "The president had the attitude," explained one manager, "that you will do this and I am deciding as the president what the priorities will be." Excluded from input into company policies, some middle managers were uneasy with the arrangement. "We

Pickets marching in front of Northwest Airlines ticket-sales office, Milwaukee, 1970.

Milwaukee Journal/State Historical Society of Wisconsin WHi (X3) 49286

were told to get subordinates to do things or else," stated one manager. "Managers were dissatisfied with the decision-making process and how we were instructed to treat our subordinates. It was difficult to get loyalty and have humanitarian arrangements."

Arbitrary decisions were commonplace at WPS. Management granted new employees higher wages than long-term employees performing the same job and decided on promotions and raises arbitrarily. "It was all in who you knew," emphasized one office worker. Some long-term office workers had never received a raise or promotion. Others found that a promotion did not necessarily bring a raise since the company sometimes downgraded the new position to the salary level associated with the old one. Management was unsympathetic to employee objections to these practices.

In 1974, several developments heightened employee dissatisfaction with working conditions at WPS. The state insur-

ance commissioner filed an antitrust suit against WPS, charging that the institutional relationship between the company and the SMS represented a conflict of interest (because SMS doctors could influence insurance rates to their advantage). The impending separation of WPS from SMS threatened the employees' insurance benefits—the one compensation for the low wages and negligible promotional opportunities at WPS.

Then, WPS moved all its employees to a new building. The top executives received plush new offices, but small cubicles awaited the office workers. "[The top managers] had gold plated faucets and knee-deep carpets," recalled one woman. "[It] looked like a set from a movie. [I thought,] why do you have to show us this.... Do you want us to feel worse than we already do?" For WPS employees, the contrast between management's extravagant offices and the "sweatshop conditions" of the clerical staff symbolized the gender hierarchy at the company. Declared one office worker, "At WPS, all the top brass were men and they had the power."

The move to the new building brought with it productivity standards and layoffs. The company hired consultants to streamline the claims adjustors' work. As a result, management eliminated some jobs and announced that layoffs would follow. "Lots of women ended up crying in the bathroom," reported one woman. "It was a bad decision on the part of the company. The company should have consulted the employees about improvements in efficiency. They treated the employees like they were a notch below intelligent. It was grossly unfair." For those employees who remained, the productivity expectancies, or "reasonable expectancies" (REs) as they were called at WPS, became the basis for more rigid and standardized jobs, as well as speedups.

Motivated by the heightened dissatisfaction that followed the move to the new building, the imposition of productivity standards, and the threatened loss of benefits, a small group of office workers contacted Local 1401 of the Retail Clerks in the spring of 1975. An organizing committee targeted potential sympathizers and visited them at home to promote unionization. Once a majority of WPS workers had signed union cards, a representational election was scheduled for December of 1976.

WPS executives launched a campaign to undermine the unionization effort. Middle managers and supervisors were instructed to prevent union representatives from entering the premises and to reprimand employees for distributing union materials. Office workers received memos describing the negative aspects of unions, and the president of the company called meetings to discourage office workers from voting for the union. And management singled out union activists for harassment. "Management increased its pressure on the employees, picking at us for how we did our work," reported one union supporter. "They had the attitude that we were just underlings and don't we dare think otherwise."

The work force was divided about unionization. Afraid of jeopardizing future wage and promotional opportunities, some office workers avoided union organizers. But among other employees, management's behavior and patronizing attitudes reinforced their need for a union. On the morning of the certification election, the company distributed a leaflet stating that the women were "insufficiently educated" to make an informed decision about unionization. The memo backfired: it pushed many of the undecided to vote for the union. As a result, Local 1401 won the election by a slight margin.[2] Union supporters celebrated their victory, but the narrowness of the vote put the union in a weak position.

WPS hired a law firm well known for aggressively challenging unionization—Seafarth, Shaw, Fairweather, and Geraldson—and appealed the election results to the National Labor Relations Board (NLRB).[3] The NLRB eventually decided in favor of the union but the appeal stretched out for almost a year, preventing Local 1401 from entering into contract negotiations with WPS until the fall of 1977.

The negotiations for the first contract were protracted and difficult. The outcome was a weak contract that gave the union workers a grievance procedure and salary schedule, but entry-level wages remained low—between $2.65 and $4.78 an hour for most positions. In addition, vacation and sick-leave benefits were reduced, and a strong management-rights clause guaranteed the company exclusive control over job restructuring, work rules, and discipline procedures. Most important, the contract granted management an open shop: new employees were not required to pay union dues.

WPS Tightens Its Control

Over the next several years, WPS tightened its control over the union work force.[4] Scientific management provided the rationale for the establishment of REs throughout the firm. Explained one supervisor:

> Time-motion experts came in with stopwatches. [They] analyzed each procedure—dictating a letter, opening envelopes and determining where the contents should go—[to get] a consistent step-by-step procedure. They would time individuals who had been doing it for a while, those who had just started, etc. Then they would take the average.... They had a system that was supposed to be foolproof: For every person, no matter what tasks they were doing, it was made up of so many small components. So they would add up the components and voila here is a task and a reasonable expectancy figure based on those tasks.

Productivity determined promotions and raises. Management closely monitored new employees and often fired those who fell short on their REs during probation. "It was pretty common to dismiss people on probation," reported one supervisor. "An example was trying to be set for other employees that WPS was a hard-line company and would not put up with a lot of goofing around or not focusing on the job or not taking responsibility."

The REs provoked extensive dissatisfaction among office workers at WPS. The "scientific method" for arriving at the expectancies was unclear. "When management tries to explain how they arrived at the numbers," one woman stated, "they throw so many numbers at you that you [can't] figure out what they did." At bottom, workers perceived the expectancies as "unreasonable."

The REs imposed a rigid standard on a work process with unpredictable elements. The system failed to take into account the time required to process claims. "They might expect seventeen claims an hour for hospital claims," explained one woman, "but if you get a difficult claim, it might take you fifteen to thirty minutes to do it. Then you have to make up the time. You can't say you had a difficult claim and that is why your RE was low." In addition, no adjustments were made for computer malfunctions. " Sometimes the computer is slow and this isn't recorded in your RE," stated a second woman.

The REs created considerable stress among the office workers at WPS. "We know we are expected to do more and more work for the same pay," emphasized one office worker. "Hence, the stress level keeps going up." Office workers also saw the REs as dehumanizing. "If you could just answer the phone and close everything off and not have to deal with the REs which are degrading. REs tell you that you are dishonest and they need to monitor your work."

Along with the REs came a tightening of managerial control in other areas. The absenteeism policy was particularly harsh. If a supervisor suspected an employee of lying, she called the employee's home to verify her illness. Employees were

> **Under budgetary pressures from upper management to cut costs, supervisors used demotions, productivity expectancies, and reprimands to pressure older, more highly paid employees to quit.**

harassed when they returned to work, and absenteeism was the one "transgression" that alone could result in dismissal. Supervisors also reprimanded employees for leaving their department and talking with co-workers. Management told new employees that they could be fired for leaving their work area. Supervisors closely monitored their employees' interactions and reprimanded those found conversing with their co-workers: "One woman was looking up a code and the supervisor came up in back of her and in front of everybody said, 'What are you talking about, don't you know you should be sitting at your desk? You've talked all day and hardly done any claims.' The women [responded that] their conversation was work-related. The supervisor said she didn't care, that they were supposed to be at their desks and if they had any questions, to come to her."

Managers and supervisors were erratic in their treatment of union workers. "Some girls get harassed for sneezing or looking up from their desk," one woman explained. "Others can [get away with talking] for an hour or two." Supervisors treated their subordinates like children, degrading them in front of their peers to assert their authority. "The attitude—the way they treat their employees—I've never been treated this way in all my adult life as a working person," exclaimed one woman with thirty-six years of work experience in factories and offices. A co-worker agreed: "[We] are treated very bad[ly]. One supervisor refers to all the women as 'kids.' She is in her early thirties and there are some women in her department who are sixty years old. This is degrading."

Older women were especially vulnerable to management harassment. Under budgetary pressures from upper management to cut costs, supervisors used demotions, productivity expectancies, and reprimands to pressure older, more highly paid employees to quit. "The longer you work at WPS," stated one woman, "the less job security you have. They can get rid of old employees and get new ones for cheaper." Echoed another woman: "The older women are afraid. They don't understand women's rights or union rights. All they know is they have to have a job and that is all they can handle."

The company's tactics created a climate of fear at WPS.

One response was to "break down." "If you intimidate them long enough," stated one union employee, "the only escape they have is to burst into tears. Not that that will get them out of it. But it is their way of dealing with all the tension they have within them because they can't let it out for fear of being charged with insubordination." Another response was to quit. "Anybody who could get out did," declared a second office worker. "And those who were left behind told them to come back and get them as soon as they could."

Resistance to Managerial Policies

Those women who were "left behind" resisted managerial policies in a variety of ways. Some women ignored the company policy that they remain at their desks. "People do take long walks to get a drink in order to get a break," one woman reported. "You will find women in the bathroom touching their toes to relieve the monotony." Others challenged the company rule against talking. "Once a week we sit there on company time and have a gab session," explained one office worker.

> We start out discussing work and then go into other topics. The supervisors eye us but we eye them back as if to say, "Come on and say something to us." The supervisors know they can't intimidate us. You have to cut loose occasionally.... [They] can't expect someone to sit at their desk eight hours a day and work constantly. You just can't. We play on the status differences between ourselves and the supervisors who are lucky to have a high school education.

A second woman told a similar story: "You are supposed to get permission to go to another department. People don't mostly. Regardless of what the supervisor says, people talk to each other anyway. It varies.... The more work there is, the less talking.... You can talk and open mail without any problems; people would probably open it faster if they talked to keep their mind off the boredom of the work. People talked mostly about their personal lives. If they are complaining, they are talking about work."

Collective challenges to "tyrannical" managers were more sporadic, but they did occur. Women in one department reported to upper management that their supervisor abused her phone privileges and consistently returned late from lunch. The result: "This supervisor got her hand slapped." In a second department, women waited to turn in their time cards until one minute before the end of the workday, forcing the supervisor to stay an additional half hour. And, in response to an arbitrary policy regarding phone calls; the women in a third department initiated a slowdown: "We aren't supposed to get phone calls but occasionally someone is allowed to and this is done to create friction between employees. The supervisor was purposely trying to make the union employees angry under the assumption that when angry, employees work harder. However, sometimes it backfires and we work twice as slowly . . . but then they get us with the REs."

The REs provoked various reactions. In a few instances, women's strategies were collective. When the company suspended an older woman for reportedly "cheating on her RE" the entire department refused to speak to the supervisor, an action that helped to win a successful grievance settlement. More common were individual strategies to overstate or regu-

THE FORMATION OF THE STATE AFL-CIO WOMEN'S COMMITTEE

Women in the Wisconsin labor movement take pride in their role in establishing the first State AFL-CIO Women's Committee in the country. Helen Hensler recounts the story in this piece which Ms. Hensler prepared in 1981 for an upcoming Wisconsin State AFL-CIO Women's Conference.

THE Wisconsin State AFL-CIO Civil Rights Conference held November 22, 1969, in Milwaukee, laid the groundwork for the formation of the State AFL-CIO's Standing Committee on Women. Clara Obrenovich and Helen Hensler who attended the conference can be called the "instigators" that brought about the formation of the State AFL-CIO's Women's Committee. How did it happen? President Schmitt was naming the numerous conferences sponsored by the State AFL-CIO, e.g. Community Services, Building Trades, Educational, Civil Rights, Legislative, Apprenticeship, Industrial Union Department conferences, etc. when Sister Hensler poked Sister Obrenovich who was sitting next to her urging her to ask President Schmitt why the State AFL-CIO did not sponsor a Women's Conference. Sister Obrenovich replied, "Oh no, I couldn't do that." To which Sister Hensler replied, "Well I guess I will have to ask the question" which she promptly did.

President Schmitt promptly replied by asking the question, "Well, what do you 'girls' want?" We informed him that we wanted the State AFL-CIO to sponsor a Women's Conference. After all there were 50,000 women in the state who belonged to unions affiliated with the State AFL-CIO and we felt that it was time that the problems and special concerns of union working women were heard. Nothing more was said.

Late in December 1969 President Schmitt called Sister Hensler and told her that he had set a date for the first Wisconsin State AFL-CIO Women's Conference—March 7, 1970 in Wisconsin Rapids and that he was appointing Lenore Hahlbeck and Helen Hensler as co-chairmen. He instructed Sisters Hahlbeck and Hensler to set up a program and make all necessary arrangements—and we were off and running!

Committee members were appointed: Rose Marie Baron, State, County & Municipal Employees #1954—Milwaukee; Marcella Dougherty, State, County and Municipal Employees #1280—Oshkosh; Sharon Kobza, Service Employees #292—Wisconsin Rapids; Irene Henderson, Communication Workers #5500- Milwaukee; June Michelfelder, State, County and Municipal Employees #1—Milwaukee; Connie Miller, Meat Cutters #538—Madison; Bernice Reck, Kenosha City Labor Council—Kenosha; Florence Simons, Allied Industrial Workers #322—Milwaukee; Ann Stockman, Allied Industrial Workers #232— Milwaukee; Anita Thom, Printing Pressmen #662— Eau Claire; Rosella Wartner, Marathon County Labor Council—Wausau; Nellie Wilson, State AFL-CIO Staff Representative—Milwaukee and co-chairs Lenore Hahlbeck, Bakery and Confectionery Workers #205—Milwaukee; and Helen Hensler, Office and Professional Employees Union #9—Milwaukee.

March 7th in Wisconsin Rapids—mid-winter—cold and snowing—who would come? One hundred and fifty-four women and a few men representing forty-one local unions, seventeen Internationals, twelve Central Labor Councils and seven Auxiliaries attended the conference. There were delegates form the Allied Industrial Workers, Bakery and Confectionery Workers, Building Service, Boot & Shoe Workers, Brewery Workers, Communication Workers, Garment Workers, Directly Affiliated Local Union, Electrical Workers, Machinists, Office Workers, Paper Workers, Postal Clerks, Retail Clerks, Steelworkers, Woodworkers, State, County and Municipal Employees and Textile Workers.

Co-chair Helen Hensler called the conference to order at 9:10 A.M. on a cold blustery March 7, 1970, in Wisconsin Rapids, Wisconsin, and history was made.

President Schmitt welcomed the delegates and stressed the importance of women becoming active in their unions. He urged women to become active in their union's legislative committee, pointing out that bad laws and legislation could wipe out all the gains made through collective bargaining.

The keynote speaker was Dr. Kathryn Clarenbach, specialist in the field of Education for Women at the University of Wisconsin—Madison. She spoke of the need and importance of instilling in girls the value in preparing for better jobs, for it is estimated that nine out of ten girls who are in school today will be working sometime in their lives and

late an office worker's output. In departments where work was performed manually, office workers kept their own production records. This provided the women with an opportunity to inflate their productivity scores. "If they only knew that what they are doing is cultivating dishonesty," stated one woman. "The very honest don't mark everything they should; the dishonest mark things they shouldn't. If I have questions about whether I should mark or not, I go ahead and do it."

Where work was automated, the computer tabulated the productivity scores. In that case, the only option for the office workers was to regulate their own output. "I tell new employees who are performing at 100-150 percent of the RE that if they keep it up," one woman explained, "management will expect them to maintain that level." The RE system also fostered competition among union employees at WPS. Supervisors rewarded workers who met or surpassed the standards and reprimanded those who fell short. To enhance their performance, some women overreported their output, hoping to get special recog-

Courtesy Joanne Ricca

Helen Hensler, 1989.

Council AFL-CIO; "Consumer Problems," chaired by Rita Collins, State Treasurer of the Wisconsin Consumer League and "Women's Participation in Politics and Legislation," chaired by Ruth Colombo the Director of the Eastern Division of the Women's Activity Department of the AFL-CIO.

The luncheon speaker was Nellie Wilson, Staff Representative of the Wisconsin State AFL-CIO OEO Leadership Trainee Project and a member of the Women's Committee. Sister Nelson is the second woman to hold a staff job in the history of the Wisconsin State AFL and now merged State AFL-CIO. Sister Wilson described her duties and what the program is trying to accomplish.

The delegates at the general session passed several resolutions—one being especially noteworthy—the resolution reads as follows:

> That the delegates to the first Women's Annual Conference of the Wisconsin AFL-CIO assembled in Wisconsin Rapids, Wisconsin March 7, 1970 go on record as favoring the passage of the Equal Rights Amendment to the Constitution of the United States.

The Wisconsin State AFL-CIO Executive Board at its meeting April 10 and 11, 1970, concurred in the resolution and was the first State AFL-CIO to go on record favoring the passage of the ERA. The National AFL-CIO did not go on record in favor of the ERA amendment until October 1973.

A resolution was also passed to hold a State AFL-CIO Women's Conference annually and another resolution that women be appointed to the Wisconsin State AFL-CIO Legislative Committee.

The delegates, after considerable discussion, passed a motion to support an abortion law stating that women should have the right to determine whether or not to have children, to use contraceptives, and to demand an abortion if so desired.

The questionnaires revealed that a very small number of women serve their union in any capacity—be it an officer, steward or committee member. Some of the comments on the questionnaire were; "Enlightened of problems confronting women today"; "Challenge to become more involved"; "Women finally being recognized."

At 12:30 P.M., March 8, 1970 the first Wisconsin State AFL-CIO Women's Conference was adjourned. No longer will it be necessary to use the slogan "The Forgotten Trade Unionists—Women in Wisconsin Labor."

—HELEN HENSLER

most of them for twenty-five years or more. Dr. Clarenbach pointed out that today there are over thirty million women in the labor force in the United States or approximately 40% of the entire work force. 75% of the thirty million working women are in low paying occupations. She deplored the fact that so few women are active in politics and the pathetically small number appointed to committees.

The Women's Committee and the delegates to the State AFL-CIO Women's Conference owe a special thanks to Dr. Clarenbach who filled in at the very last minute after our keynote speaker called late Friday March 6th and said she would not be able to speak at the conference.

There were three workshops at the conference: "Women's Rights in Collective Bargaining," chaired by Robert Durkin, Vice President of the Milwaukee County Labor

nition. This brought promotions to some individuals, but it increased the pressure on the rest of the women in the department.

For those employees with low REs, office workers sometimes responded with their own sanctions. Since low productivity could lead to department reprimands, resentment surfaced toward those who, as one woman put it, "screwed around": "People get upset because they are working and this other person isn't. They will put up with the other person not working

for a while if there has been a trauma in that person's family but then there is a point where they think that is enough."

The Union Response

Local 1401 faced major obstacles to building a strong membership at WPS. The open shop required union representatives to "sell" the union to new employees. This was made especially difficult by management's practice of emphasizing to new employees that they didn't need to pay union dues to receive union benefits. High turnover contributed to the union's difficulties: approximately fifty employees left the company each month. No sooner would the business agent sign up one group of office workers for union membership than another group of union employees would quit. Other problems stemmed from the perception that the union was responsible for the loss of benefits in the first contract.

The union had fought hard to win favorable language during the first contract negotiations, but many office workers blamed the union for the "poor contract." The union's legitimacy was therefore in question.

The geographical separation of the office workers across several office buildings posed a further challenge. With growth in business, the company moved several of its departments to a second building in 1978. This made communication among union employees particularly difficult and fragmented the union's support. But management's recalcitrance confronted the union with the greatest obstacles. The company refused to settle union grievances. During the term of the first contract, the union filed almost two hundred grievances but, confronted with a management unwilling to negotiate, it dropped or lost most of them.

Six months before the second contract negotiations were scheduled to begin, the Retail Clerks merged with a much larger union—Local 1444 of the United Food and Commercial Workers (UFCW). As the union entered its second contract negotiations with WPS in the fall of 1979, a central priority was to gain a union shop. Without it, the union at WPS would forever be weak.

The second contract negotiations at WPS were especially difficult. The company harassed union employees, monitoring their phone calls, bathroom use, and conversations. Management's proposal for reduced benefits and a minimal raise was not received favorably. "When people found out [about the company's proposal], this made them madder than anything," one woman recalled. "They were looking for more, not less." In addition, the patronizing attitudes of the company bargaining team fueled the office workers' grievances. "Management would not deal with the women," reported one member of the bargaining team. "We felt so degraded listening to their attorney and representatives who would deal only with [the male union representatives].... They would act as if there weren't a woman in the room and make remarks. They made derogatory remarks about the divorced women and treated you as if you were an absolute imbecile and not worthy of consideration."

The union called a meeting to recommend that WPS office workers reject management's contract offer. Approximately 400 out of the 550 union employees were in attendance at a meeting negotiating stewards described as highly charged: "It was a feeling that I had never experienced before. There wasn't even standing room. The women on the negotiating team had been telling jokes. [The president of the local] said, 'Okay ladies, everybody is in consensus that we're not going to accept the contract.' As we walked in, the members gave us a standing ovation and clapped and cheered.... When [the president] said that the negotiating team had suggested they reject the proposal, the

place went wild." The vote was split. Two-thirds of the membership in attendance voted to strike if WPS failed to offer a better contract within ten days. One-third voted to accept management's offer.

Over the next week, some union workers prepared for the possibility of a strike. They removed job-related materials—manuals and coding notes—from their offices and made picket signs. "We had our picket signs ready," one woman reported, "and [we] were prepared to strike." But several factors undermined the momentum for a strike. The strike benefits of $40 a week seemed inadequate. "A lot [of employees] were worried because their husbands were laid off or they were divorced mothers," one woman explained. "They wouldn't have had anything to live on.... Strike benefits wouldn't have been enough." In addition, the membership was divided in its support for a strike. One hundred fifty workers were absent from the meeting on the night of the strike vote, and an additional 130 had voted against a strike. Finally, management's threats weakened the women's resolve. As rumors circulated that the company intended to hire nonunion replacements, the outcome of a strike became more uncertain. One strong union supporter thought to herself, "Oh great, in six months I'll be out of a job. I'm not going to strike."

Just before the contract expired, WPS proposed a union shop that would require all new employees to pay union dues. The company had met the union's central demand. Management also offered a better wage and benefit package. The negotiating stewards were hoping for a better contract, but they lacked the support to reject management's offer. "A lot of stewards were sitting back not very happy with the contract," one steward explained, "but the [union leaders] were the experts and people went along with their recommendations because they knew a lot of people who would vote strike would not picket." A majority of the union members voted to accept the contract.

WPS Hires Nonunion, Part-time Employees

Following the 1979 contract negotiations, WPS stepped up its assault on the union workforce. The cornerstone of the company's campaign was the recruitment of nonunion, part-time workers. The bargaining unit covered full-time employees, as well as part-time employees who worked more than twenty hours a week. A handful of nonunion, part-time employees had worked at WPS for several years. Because of their small numbers, Local 1444 did not see the nonunion, part-time workers as a threat. By early 1981, the company had hired hundreds of part-time workers who worked fewer than twenty hours a week and hence did not qualify for union membership.

WPS hired three types of part-time workers. The first group was hired through a WPS-owned subsidiary—Administrative Technical Services (Ad Tech)—to work as data-entry operators and mailing-service clerks. These part-time workers did not receive benefits, and their wages were lower than the union workers at WPS. Many of these part-timers, who were primarily women, worked the night shift. The erratic scheduling of work—some nights too much, other nights too lit-

Shoe workers at the Allen-Edmonds Shoe Company, Belgium, Wisconsin.

State Historical Society of Wisconsin WHi (X3) 51167

tle—made it difficult to meet the productivity standards. And without any grievance procedures, the part-time workers had no protection from arbitrary management decisions regarding raises and promotions. "Management said that all of the night employees would get a raise," reported one part-time worker. "But then only three to five people got them and others were mad. Management said that the others weren't making their quotas. People were told to call personnel if they were dissatisfied. One woman who had worked there for three years and was very dependable did call. And [the manager] said that he didn't care how long she had worked there. She was lucky to have a job and if she didn't like it, she could quit."

Local 1444 tried to organize the Ad Tech workers, but its efforts were unsuccessful.[5] The high turnover rate among the nighttimers—many of whom were students, homemakers, or workers with other full-time jobs—posed one obstacle to organizing. Not surprisingly, the company aggressively opposed the union's initiatives. Management isolated union sympathizers and distributed memos describing "facts and fictions about the union." The company also warned employees that if they signed unions cards they could be fired. Once the futility of the organizing drive became evident, the union abandoned the effort.

WPS hired a second group of nonunion, part-time employees to work as keypunch operators in its remote work center in South Beloit, Wisconsin. The working conditions for the mostly young, black women hired to work at WPS's remote center were especially harsh. Paid minimum wage and no benefits, few of the women received raises during their employment with WPS. Their productivity standards were high and their work schedule erratic. Many keypunch operators commuted long distances to work to be sent home after only two hours; others were laid off for days or weeks at a time with little notice.

In the fall of 1982, the union initiated an organizing drive at the remote work center. Initially, support for unionization was strong: a majority of the keypunch operators signed union cards and an election was scheduled. Two factors turned the tables, however. First, the Teamsters Union decided to try to organize these workers as well, thus dividing union support. And sec-

AN AGENDA FOR WORKING FAMILIES

The AFL-CIO, recognizing the dramatic changes in the composition of the workforce, began to broaden its legislative program in the late 1980s to include a new broad-based agenda for working families. The aim was twofold. On the one hand, labor began to promote a legislative program that directly addressed changes caused by the growing numbers of women who had entered the labor market. On the other hand, the AFL-CIO sought to deflate the political power of the Far Right, which had used its "traditional family values" agenda as a barrier against any type of progressive reform. In 1988 the Wisconsin State AFL-CIO staged an "American Family Celebration" rally at the state capitol in Madison. The following excerpts are from a speech by Jack Reihl, president of the Wisconsin State AFL-CIO from 1986 to 1994.

ON behalf of the 300,000 members of the Wisconsin State AFL-CIO, I want to welcome all of you. We've come together today from all corners of the state. As I look over this wonderful crowd I can see a cross-section of the working families of Wisconsin: mothers and fathers, children and teenagers, grandparents and friends.

We are the working families of Wisconsin. We are the people who produce the goods and provide the services that make out state prosper and grow. We are the auto workers from Janesville and Kenosha. We are the office workers and

Wisconsin State AFL-CIO

Jack B. Reihl was elected Secretary-Treasurer of the Wisconsin State AFL-CIO in 1970 and served as President from 1986 to 1994.

teachers from Madison. We are the machinists and nurses from Milwaukee. We are the firefighters and daycare workers from Green Bay. We are the service employees and paper workers from the Fox River Valley.

---

ond, WPS aggressively challenged the unionization effort. The company distributed memos warning employees about the costs of a strike. One memo stated: "Employees go on strike and lose their jobs should the employer hire permanent replacements during an economic strike." The union lost the certification election by a wide margin.

The third and most controversial group of nonunion, part-time employees hired by WPS were the homeworkers. Before the 1979 contract negotiations, the company employed five home typists, but by 1981, over one hundred women were working for WPS as homeworkers. Among union employees, the homeworkers provoked considerable controversy. Some union workers expressed concern that the homeworkers were exploited. "My concern is . . . with how the homeworkers are treated regarding pay, benefits, etc.," stated one union worker, a divorced woman with two children: "I have dealt with crummy situations at work but it isn't as bad as some woman in her home with three crying kids and really needing the money and

nowhere to go and no one to talk with.... You clean up the homeworker act and then maybe I'll talk to you about how beneficial it is to someone who needs it but right now, it is a rip-off, they are just using people."

Other union workers resented the homeworkers. One office worker described the homeworkers as a "privileged group": "I talked to one homeworker with grown children who just wanted something to do.... Must be nice not to need the money.... I find it hard to feel sorry for someone who needs pin money." A second union worker was more emphatic: "I absolutely have to have a job because I support myself.... If I had to chose between my having a job and a woman who has a husband with kids, I would chose myself.... If I don't have a job, I have nothing. I am against the homeworkers and definitely think there should be a ban [on homework]."

Local 1444 explored the possibility of organizing the homeworkers, but the company beat them to it. Supervisors warned homeworkers that union employees resented them for

With us today are all members of the working families of Wisconsin. The children of carpenters and clerical workers, the brothers of bakery workers, the sisters of steelworkers, and the parents of paperworkers. And today our family also includes the retired workers, the students, the unemployed and underemployed. Our family extends to the strikers and to those that are locked-out of their jobs. Also included in our family are the dislocated workers, the displaced home-makers, and the part-time and limited term workers.

No, we're not the big bosses of multinational corporations. We're not the Wall Street speculators or the masters of merger mania. When we speak alone, as individuals, our voices are difficult to hear.

But when we gather together, as we have today, then we become a power to be reckoned with. When we put down our pencils and hammers; when we shut down out our word processors and cover our typewriters; when we close our toolboxes and join together in a spirit of solidarity, then the Ronald Reagans and George Bushes of this world had better sit up and take notice. We're the American family—and we're here!

Gone forever is the old Norman Rockwell image of the "typical" American family. Gone is the "Leave it to Beaver" family where upper middle-class Dad returns from work to Mom's home-cooked meal and two little kids. Today only 4% of our families fit the old pattern of Ozzie and Harriet Nelson. Our families are changing and our policies must change to fit the new reality.

Our economy is changing too. We can see the steady transformation of our economy from a manufacturing base to the service sector. The Reagan years have produced a record 20 million new jobs in the decade of the 80s. But seven out of ten of those jobs are in low-wage categories. Nearly half the new jobs created between 1979 and 1984 paid under $7,000 a year. Who can raise a family on $7,000 a year? That's why a real pro-family policy in 1988 means a big boost in the minimum wage.

Our workplaces and home situations are changing as more and more women enter the workforce. In 1990 65% of the workers entering the workforce will be women. In the old days, our mothers cared for our children during the day. But now they're on the job bringing home a pay check so we can keep up with the cost of living. Therefore, a true pro-family policy today means searching for quality child care.

In the old days, when our children grew up they took care of grandma and grandpa when they were too old or sick to care for themselves. But now everyone must work in order to make ends meet. No one can stay at home to care for our senior citizens. Thus, a pro-family policy must also include expanded services for senior citizens.

Ten years ago, when our children grew up and got full-time jobs, they received health care through their employers. Now many of our children are working part-time or as limited term employees. Most of their employers do not offer them health care insurance. In today's America, 37 million people are without health insurance. That's why a pro-family policy today means a comprehensive system of health care.

These are some of the issues the labor movement is taking into the halls of Congress in Washington D.C. and into the State Capitol here in Madison. For too long the Far Right Wing conservatives have claimed a monopoly on "family issues." Meanwhile, these same politicians are the architects of policies that are making it impossible for working families to survive in the changing economy.

Our new program is an agenda for working families in the 1990s. It can be the rallying cry for a new majority of Americans who want to fight for their children, their parents, and their grandparents. The Reagan era will soon be over and that's good news for working families in America. But our fight has just begun.

—JACK B. REIHL
American Family Celebration Rally, Madison, May 14, 1988

---

taking their work away and underscored the negative repercussions that could follow from unionization. The company's tactics, together with the high turnover and relative isolation of homeworkers, undercut the union's efforts. Few homeworkers were open to discussing the possibility of joining a union.

Union Strategies, 1979-82

The union emerged from the 1979 contract negotiations in a weak position. The union shop required all new WPS employees to join the union, but many of the office workers were estranged from the union. Once again they blamed the union for what they perceived as a poor contract. Union stewards thought that a female business agent might encourage the office workers to identify with the union. In early 1980, Local 1444 hired one to represent the office workers at WPS and to strengthen the bargaining unit at WPS. She scheduled training workshops for stewards and informal meetings to advise union members on procedures for filing grievances. In addition, the business agent brought in union engineers to retime the REs.

These initiatives did not go unnoticed by the company. Managers interrogated union activists, pressuring them to reveal information about union meetings. They instituted management-controlled "Employee Communication Committees" to circumvent the union and harassed the new business agent, escorting her around the building, from the cafeteria to the restroom, whenever she visited on union business.

This last strategy backfired. To some union workers, management's behavior represented a form of psychological warfare meant to warn union employees, "If we can do this to your business rep, just look what we can do to you." The union women, however, saw the business agent as a role model. One office worker commented on the satisfaction gained from watching the union representative "hold her ground": "[The new business rep] has had to deal with . . . harassment. . . . Management is scared of her because she has stood up more and shows up

These members of the Carpenters Union donated wages to a community fund in Madison.

there all the time . . . to meet the stewards. It shakes them up to see her inside the doors. They get fidgety and stutter. She makes a point of being there for every little thing. It is funny to see a very cool manager stutter because she is in the lobby. I have seen this and I have to keep myself from laughing." A second woman agreed: "Since sex is around, it tickles the women that the new business rep got the best of one of the managers. He made a lot of mistakes in dealing with the union and she was quick to point them out; this led to the manager's losing points with the company. It tickles the people that the new rep has brains and guts."

Throughout 1981 and 1982, the pattern of management harassment continued. A dress code was imposed that prevented employees from wearing blue jeans, tennis shoes, T-shirts, tops with low necklines, and "extreme" hemlines. To some union workers, the dress code had one purpose: to reinforce managerial authority. Stated one woman: "The company imposed the code because they're interested in power, in imposing their

rights." A second woman resented dress requirements that workers couldn't afford: "If management wants to pay us the wages where we could buy three-piece outfits, then I would willingly oblige."[6] A few women ignored the dress code and continued to wear blue jeans and long skirts. Management reprimanded the women and they responded by filing grievances.[7]

Grievances were also filed over production standards, absenteeism, and job requirements. When the company refused to settle the grievances, the union turned to the NLRB. The NLRB did direct the company to provide information to the union on production standards and nonunion, part-time employees, but on the most important issue the board sided with the company: The NLRB ruled that WPS had not hired part-time, nonunion workers to undermine the bargaining unit.[8]

During the 1982 contract negotiations, the company proposed substantial reductions in union benefits, most important the imposition of a 25 percent employee contribution to insurance premiums, the institution of a twelve-month waiting period in the vacation policy, and a wage freeze. The average wage at WPS in 1982 was $4.74. Union workers were very dissatisfied with the company's offer, but the economic recession made a strike unlikely. Stated one woman: "With the financial situation of most people, with layoffs in other industries, and because many [employees] are self-supporting, people will think a lot harder about striking."

In addition, the presence of nonunion workers at WPS had seriously diminished the union's leverage. Between 1979 and 1982, the size of the bargaining unit had shrunk by over one hundred employees, while the combined number of part-time workers had increased to more than four hundred. "The union didn't have any power," one woman emphasized. "Management had three years to cover themselves for the eventuality of a strike . . . to where management could tell the union to 'go to hell.'"

The union held its own in the 1982 contract negotiations. Most important, the union was able to protect the union workers' health-insurance benefits. It also gained stronger language granting workers the right to union representation during meetings with management and a wage increase of 2 percent to 6 percent, depending on the grade level. The most significant loss was the institution of a twelve-month waiting period in the vacation policy. The business agent felt that the negotiations turned out "as best as could be expected."

After 1982

By the mid-eighties—ten years after the beginning of the initial unionization drive at WPS—management-labor relations had stabilized somewhat. The company had accepted the union, albeit grudgingly, as evidenced by the willingness of a new labor-relations manager to inform Local 1444 of relevant changes in company policy. Perhaps WPS management no longer perceived the union as any threat.

The worst fear of the union—that the company would steadily erode the bargaining unit with nonunion, part-time workers—had not come true. In response to increased business, WPS had expanded both its nonunion and union work forces. The increase in their own numbers made union employees less anxious about their jobs, but the persistence of the part-time, nonunion workers undermined the union workers' morale.

The basic managerial approach at WPS remained unchanged. Close monitoring and negative reprimands characterized managerial treatment of union employees. Stewards continued to encourage union members to file grievances; those who did were sometimes empowered by the experience. But the attitude of the company stood as a powerful deterrent to the office workers' initiatives. WPS employees didn't have to look very far for examples of women who had paid the price for challenging the company. As one steward stated, "There [are] very few who aren't intimidated by the power structure at the company." Each month, forty to fifty office workers left their jobs. For the women at WPS, quitting represented a strategy of last resort.

This analysis of authoritarian management and conflict at WPS demonstrates the contradictory impact of coercive managerial practices on clerical activism. WPS was a classic authoritarian workplace, reminiscent of nineteenth-century despotic employers.[9] At this company, Taylorism and negative sanctions reinforced management's ultimate authority. Company policies consistently generated widespread dissatisfaction and initially

provoked a successful unionization drive, but in the long run, the very managerial practices that alienated the clerical workers eroded their capacity for collective action.

A deterioration in working conditions catalyzed the initial unionization drive at WPS. Managerial harassment intimidated some office workers, but these efforts failed to overpower the momentum for unionization. Following the certification election, the aggressive campaign undertaken by WPS had mixed consequences for the union work force. On the one hand, the tightening of managerial controls created pervasive dissatisfaction with working conditions at WPS. Complaints about the company were widespread, as were employee initiatives designed to circumvent managerial policies.

On the other hand, managerial harassment created a vulnerable work force, many of whom were afraid to challenge the company. Not only did coercive working conditions weaken the women's confidence in their individual ability to confront management but managerial policies also undermined collective solidarity. Within departments, close supervisory surveillance and productivity pressures constrained the office workers' interactions. The forging of ties across departments was that much more difficult.

The 1979 contract negotiations marked a turning point in management-labor relations at WPS. As the linchpin of management's strategy, the hiring of nonunion, part-time workers weakened the union by providing potential replacements in the event of a strike. In subsequent negotiations, there was no evidence of a lessening of workers' grievances at WPS, but the capacity of the clerical workers to mount a collective challenge did diminish.

The office workers at WPS faced several barriers to collective action. First, the separation of employees across several buildings impeded the development of social ties, requiring the union to build support in several locations. Second, the threat of replacement by nonunion workers undermined collective solidarity among the union workers. Third, weak support for the union diminished possibilities for creating ties of solidarity outside of work. Finally, and most important, management repression intimidated the WPS office workers, led to high turnover rates, and stood as a constant reminder of the likely consequences of collective action.

A comparison of the Trust and WPS underscores that objectionable working conditions are a necessary but not sufficient condition for clerical activism. At both companies, dissatisfaction with managerial practices was high, but a crucial difference distinguished the two settings. At the Trust, the office workers were able to exploit the ties between Trust management and its parent union to gain improvements in working conditions. The absence of any constraints on WPS management left WPS office workers vulnerable to management retaliation. That WPS office workers successfully unionized and held onto their union in the face of management assaults was a tremendous accomplishment. Still, this case stands as a sobering testimony to the challenges faced by office workers in authoritarian work settings.■

From *We're Worth It: Women and Collective Action in the Insurance Workplace* (University of Illinois Press, Urbana, 1991).

Labor Cartoons:
Drawing on Work Culture

BY MIKE KONOPACKI
AND GARY HUCK

Mike Konopacki and Gary Huck are two of the leading labor cartoonists in the United States. Mike began drawing labor cartoons in 1978, between shifts as a school bus driver in Madison, for the Madison Press Connection, *the daily newspaper initiated by strikers during the newspaper strike in 1975. Gary Huck began his labor cartooning with* Racine Labor *and went on to become the cartoonist for the United Electrical workers union.*

WORKERS need cartoons, announced the *Industrial Worker*, the newspaper of the Industrial Workers of the World union, in 1918. The Wobbly paper wanted "cartoons on industrial union or revolutionary subjects."

That a workers' paper would call for cartoons on union issues is no surprise. That a workers' paper would seek cartoons on "revolutionary subjects" should be no surprise either. Cartoons on revolutionary topics ought to be running in every labor publication.

Revolutionary subjects, after all, have been the stuff of American political cartooning ever since Benjamin Franklin drew his famous severed snake representing eight disjointed colonies above the caption, "JOIN or DIE" (still wise advice for today's workers). A century later, Thomas Nast's indignant and persistent political cartoons helped topple one of America's most powerful politicians, New York City's William M. ("Boss") Tweed, and Frederick Burr Opper's hilarious antitrust satires burst inflated robber baron egos.

America's labor press was, at the start, slow to feature cartooning on such revolutionary subjects. The printing technology of the 1800s required painstakingly difficult wood engrav-

The Masses, a popular leftwing magazine from the period 1911-1917, had a great impact on cartooning.

ings and expensive machinery to print them, machinery too expensive for common workers. As a result, the elaborate woodcuts of the most popular cartoonists of the 1870s and 1880s—Nast, Opper, Frank Bellew, and Joseph Keppler— were found in the establishment publications of the day and not in labor papers.

"Illustrations of any kind were rare in the early American labor press," notes labor humor historian Franklin Rosemont. Other than "the famous arm-and-hammer emblem, first used by the New York General Society of Mechanics and Tradesmen, organized in 1786," early labor papers published little original art. Organized labor didn't develop its own graphic artists "until long after the Civil War," and it wasn't "until the second decade of our own century that labor cartooning really came into its own."

Labor cartooning blossomed, ironically, at the very time new printing processes were undermining the importance of art in the commercial press. In the early 1890s, nearly every large newspaper had a stable of artists to illustrate everything from advertisements to news stories. But with the advent of the photomechanical process and the more widespread use of the photo-halftone, newspaper illustrators

The problem facing labor unions when they collaborate closely with management is depicted in this cartoon by Art Young (1866–1943) who grew up in Monroe, Wisconsin, and became a renowned political cartoonist and social commentator with *The Masses*.

Art Young

and artist-reporters were soon replaced by photographers.

"The political cartoon was driven off the feature pages," Richard Fitzgerald notes in *Art and Politics,* "because photographs were easier and cheaper to produce, and could be supplied in great quantity." This switch from cartoons to photographs carried important consequences. Political cartoons, Fitzgerald points out, are by their very nature "subversive." Photographs mirror life's daily structure. Political cartoons disrupt it, making "jokes and stage whispers and asides at the process of everyday life."

The new printing technologies created more unemployed daily newspaper cartoonists. But they also enabled any worker with a pen and a bottle of ink, or a graphite pencil and sheet of coarse paper, to draw cartoons that were reproducible. As a result, political magazines like *The Masses* (1911-17) attracted numerous cartoonists eager to denounce their plight and the system that created it.

The Masses, one of the leading left magazines of the time, had a great impact on cartooning. Cartoonist John Sloan, famous for his *Masses* cover that depicted the Ludlow Massacre, came up with the idea of featuring full-page cartoons with one-line captions. He also chose to reproduce cartoons using linecut instead of halftone. The result was a sharper and more graphic reproduction, simply created by using graphite on pebbled paper. This style, perfected by Sloan and fellow *Masses* cartoonists Art Young, Maurice Becker, and Robert Minor, influenced

both labor and establishment cartoonists for decades.

The door was now open. The new technology made newspapers and magazines cheaper to produce, and labor cartoons flourished. Cartoonists such as Ryan Walker, William Gropper, K. R. Chamberlain, and Boardman Robinson appeared regularly in labor and socialist publications. The Industrial Workers of the World (IWW), for its part, developed a cartoon culture that was uniquely its own. The famous Ralph Chaplin, author of our labor anthem "Solidarity Forever," was also an accomplished cartoonist who, along with "Dust" Wallin, C. E. Setzer, and Ernest Riebe, created some of the best work of the 1910s and 1920s. Riebe created what is probably the earliest known labor comic strip, "Mr. Block," which first appeared in the *Industrial Worker* on November 7, 1912.

"Mr. Block is legion," IWW editor Walker C. Smith wrote in 1913. "He is the representative of that host of slaves who think in terms of their masters. Mr. Block owns nothing, yet he speaks from the stand point of the millionaire; he is patriotic

Mike Konopacki

Above, Mike Konopacki mocks the disingenuous concern of corporations for the American worker, and below, Konopacki skewers the media for its inadequate representation of unions.

Mike Konopacki

without patrimony; he is a law-abiding outlaw; he boasts of 'our tremendous wheat exports,' yet has no bread on his table; he licks the hand that smites him and kisses the boot that kicks him; he is the personification of all that a worker should not be."

What a worker *should* be is a creator of political art. What the labor press should be is the garden that nurtures the budding worker-artist.

Labor art in today's labor press falls into two categories, the story illustration (often appearing on the cover or within the body of a story) and the cartoon, be it the angry or satirical political cartoon or the occasional comic strip. Given the gradual decline of the labor movement—unions now represent only a small percentage of American workers—and the resulting shrinkage of the labor press, labor art is finding fewer and fewer gardens in which to grow, which means that America's existing labor media have a greater responsibility than ever to cultivate and protect this fragile crop.

Let us fantasize a bit. Let us envision a labor movement rebuilding itself, its media encouraging the best in political cartooning, satire, and art. The pages of the labor press now run political cartoons that are unafraid to skewer and lampoon both

THE RACE...

FINISH   FINISH   FINISH

NLRB

Gary Huck

In these two cartoons, Gary Huck captures the feelings many unionists felt regarding the activities of the National Labor Relations Board during the Reagan and Bush years. Long delays by the NLRB are satirized by showing the agency as even slower than a tortoise and a snail. In another cartoon the "labor" in NLRB has been turned upside down and, worse, is accompanied by a noose.

our oppressors and ourselves. We see comic strips that challenge the best in the daily papers. Labor video productions feature the finest animated political cartoons around (at this point, they would be the *only* animated political cartoons around). Labor humor and satire magazines that rival pop culture journals like *MAD*, the *National Lampoon,* and *Spy* appear everywhere.

This is the future we need to create. Labor's media must become outlets for the creative genius of American workers, breeding grounds for the satirists and artists who now toil unknown within the ranks. Labor's voice must be heard in *all* its incarnations, including the snicker, the laugh, and the guffaw.

Cartoon Power
Besides supplying ample doses of snickers, laughs, and guffaws, of course, cartoons play a vital role in the communication of political ideas. People don't just look at cartoons, they interact with them. They cut them out and stick them on refrigerators,

Gary Huck

WHAT DID YOU TELL THAT MAN JUST NOW?

I TOLD HIM TO WORK FASTER!

HOW MUCH DO YOU PAY HIM?

$25⁰⁰ A DAY...

WHERE DO YOU GET THE MONEY TO PAY HIM?

I SELL PRODUCTS

WHO MAKES THE PRODUCTS?

HE DOES...

HOW MANY PRODUCTS DOES HE MAKE IN ONE DAY?

$100⁰⁰ WORTH

THEN INSTEAD OF YOU PAYING HIM···HE IS PAYING YOU $75⁰⁰ A DAY TO TELL HIM TO WORK FASTER!

HUH?

BUT THE MACHINES BELONG TO ME—

HOW DID YOU GET THE MACHINES?

I SOLD PRODUCTS AND BOUGHT THEM

···AND WHO MADE THOSE PRODUCTS?

SHUT UP··· HE MIGHT HEAR YOU!

FRED WRIGHT
UE NEWS SERVICE

Fred Wright/United Electrical, Radio and Machine Workers of America

Fred Wright probably produced the best labor cartoons during the period from 1930 until his death in 1984. In this widely reproduced cartoon, Wright is able to convey an important but complicated point about the relationship between labor and capital in a simple and humorous way.

Political cartoons are a subjective means of *expression,* not an objective means of *information.* Political cartoons reside in the sovereign state of mind of the cartoonist known as the imagine nation.

In the imagine nation politicians are drawn, then quartered. In the imagine nation, like Pinocchio, lying politicians are apt to find their noses growing. Often accused of cynicism, political cartoonists are in truth rabid idealists who speak in negatives but think in positives, criticizing inept leadership because they believe that the ept are out there... somewhere.

If there is a science to political cartooning, it is that for every reaction there is an action. The cartoonist would rather reform than inform: "Did you know this? Can you believe this? What are you going to do?!"

As readers, we often have opinions on issues, but we may not know how we *feel* about an issue until we see a political cartoon on it. There is an emotional truth to cartoons that touches people in a way no other form of journalism does.

No one touched the labor press the way labor cartoonist Fred Wright did. For five decades, until his death in 1984, Fred Wright worked in his small office at the headquarters of the United Electrical, Radio and Machine Workers of America. There he almost single-handedly supplied the labor press with the best political cartoons of his era. The thousands of cartoons he drew on contract negotiations, health and safety issues, organizing the unorganized, civil rights, women's rights, shop floor humor, and other aspects of union life were published in the labor press around the world. One could easily compile a history of the labor movement from the 1930s to the 1980s from Fred Wright cartoons. The ultimate tribute to the significance of Fred Wright's work is that his cartoons are as much in demand today as ever.

Fred Wright could not have produced the body of work he did from outside the labor movement. He was a worker-artist, drawing on worker culture to draw worker culture.

Fred Wright drew more than a living history of the struggles of and in the labor movement. He also drew a road map for other cartoonists to follow. But of the cartoonists who attempt to follow Fred's map, almost all have to pull off the road to work for gas money. Of all the affiliated unions of the AFL-CIO, not one has a full-time political cartoonist.

Want to revitalize the labor press, want to move the labor movement? Educate, Agitate, Animate!■

From "Labor Cartoons: Drawing on Worker Culture," Sam Pizzigati and Fred J. Solowey, eds., *The New Labor Press: Journalism for a Changing Union Movement* (Cornell, Ithaca, 1992).

bulletin boards, office doors, machines at work. They wear them on T-shirts and carry them on picket signs.

Cartoons communicate with people the way people communicate with each other. They draw upon a full range of emotion, much like an impassioned political discussion. When the cartoon hits upon the right combination of intellect and humor, fact and fantasy, irony and anger, it is recognized in an instant with a "That's it! That's exactly the point!" Of course, the reverse is also true; anger over cartoons generates some of the best reading on the letters-to-the-editor page. But this range of emotion only underscores the effectiveness of cartoons.

Political cartoons rage and engage, criticize and idealize, employ and destroy. They are a language spoken at a shout.

New Union Strategies:
Electrical Workers in Wausau

BY DALE KURSCHNER

In the recession-wracked 1980s, most unions found they could no longer rely on the old "on-strike" tactic to hold their own against wage cuts, lay-offs, and job-shifting to low-wage venues. One interesting innovation of this period was the use of "in-plant" strategies and "work-to-rule" tactics that brought new pressures to bear on management and sometimes, as was the case at Marathon Electric in Wisconsin Rapids, led to new contracts.

BY the mid-1980's, allegations of union busting had become as common in the upper Midwest's labor environment as management claims that competition was forcing it to seek concessions.

Regardless of management's true intent, local unions from Milwaukee to Minneapolis often lost ground, either in contract talks or in keeping their members interested and supportive. They lost because they continued to fight the old way, while management was using a barrage of new weapons from corporate restructurings and plant modernizations to clever legal maneuvers. But a battle fought in central Wisconsin turned the tables on management there in 1987, when 590 members of Local 1791 of the International Brotherhood of Electrical Workers (IBEW) mastered the use of previously unheard of workplace strategies.

The new labor tactic saved Local 1791 and its members' jobs. It eventually led management to reverse its stand from harsh concessions to a healthy pay and benefit increase, and it sent a significant sign to management that labor had learned to fight back the modern way.

Demands for Concessions

To most of the 590 shop workers at the Marathon Electric Manufacturing Corp. headquarters plant in Wausau, Wisconsin, a request by management for concessions in September 1987 almost seemed justifiable. Growing competition from the global marketplace had given this manufacturer of generators and small electric motors little choice but to seek a 20%, $3-an-hour cut in labor costs, management told the workers. And they were told there was a real threat of their jobs moving to the South, where the company could get cheaper labor.

In justifying their request, Marathon Electric executives pointed to the loss of one of their largest customers a year earlier. They also pointed to a wage study the company participated

in with 13 of its competitors. The results indicated Marathon Electric employees were overpaid compared with national averages.

Both points, some employees thought, were reasons why they should help the management they had been good "team members" with only a few months earlier.

But leaders of IBEW Local 1791 saw the contract offer as the first distinct sign that the company's ultimate goal was to bust the union. Things had been looking that way for awhile, and the local had been preparing to counter if need be with a new weapon - inside strategies.

A three-year internal public relations campaign by Marathon Electric's management had significantly weakened the strength of Local 1791 by early 1987. Almost daily, shop supervisors had given union members briefings on and explanations for Marathon Electric's status. Their words focused on "team work" between management and individual workers, not through their union. And workers were told they were "the best in the industry."

At the same time, work had gradually been moved from Wausau to Marathon Electric plants in Lima and Bowling Green, Ohio, and in West Plains and Lebanon, Missouri. Shop employment levels had dropped from more than 1,000 seven years earlier.

Dave Wadinski, Local 1791's president from 1983 to 1988, said he wasn't sure of management's intentions before negotiations started on a new three-year contract in July 1987. All he was sure of was that membership interest was waning and management was definitely after something.

"I didn't really see signs that they were going to bust the union, but I used that concern as a foundation to get support back from the members," Wadinski later admitted. But his theory quickly became reality once formal bargaining sessions began. "The first real sign was when we met in bargaining and they offered us a $3-an-hour cut in wages," he said.

"We didn't think the first contract offer was really serious," said Randy Olmsted, an officer with Local 1791 who became president in 1988. "When we got into August, they wouldn't move and that's when we started getting nervous."

From that point forward, the local's leadership told its members that they should focus on one thing: saving their union. "We thought they would not bargain fairly, [that they'd] force us out on the street or on strike, fill the place with scabs and then we would be out for good," Wadinski said.

Convincing the local's membership was another story, however. Marathon Electric's management had done a good job of convincing many union members to trust it. And getting full unity among the local's members was necessary before workplace strategies could work.

"That was the hard part," Wadinski said. "Some of the workers believed what management was telling them. We could see interest in the union was fading."

Organizing the Membership

Local 1791's way of countering that was through a well managed, aggressive group of twenty-two union stewards and officers who spent time each day going over information with individual or small groups of shop workers. The goal was to clarify what Local 1791 considered to be misleading information, and to show management for what it was.

"The employer started a program that if you didn't miss a day of work in a year, you'd get something for it," Wadinski said. "People were thinking that was great, but for people who hadn't missed work for seven years, they'd get a calculator."

"We turned it around and said to the employer and to the workers that it was an insult, and instead, they should give those workers a $500 bonus," he said. "People started giving back the calculators."

While the issue may seem small, it was significant for Local 1791 in that it helped the local's leaders gain back ties to its members. There were other initial skirmishes that were fought before war broke out between labor and management.

Ingrained in the minds of Marathon Electric's employees was the very probable scenario of their jobs being eliminated. Management had voiced the possibility of moving the Wausau plant's work South, where Marathon Electric had done all of its expanding during the 1980's.

But Wadinski and fellow union officers saw the idea as a trap for Local 1791's members. If the workers believed saving their jobs was the most important goal, they could lean toward concessions more easily. Local 1791 instead worked at convincing the workers that if Marathon Electric would move down South, "we at least wouldn't go broke on them moving," Wadinski said.

Having spent weeks preparing members of Local 1791 for potential union-busting tactics by management, the shop workers were ready for the battle that started with the expiration of their three-year contract on September 1, 1987.

The union's leaders were also ready, according to Randy Olmsted. "The biggest key was our enthusiasm," he said. "We had an eight-man negotiating committee and we were really wrapped up in what we were doing."

Local 1791's negotiating team brought three contract offers to the membership in September. The first two were voted down by more than 90 per cent of the workers, and the third was the version management would later implement after declaring an impasse.

"We made copies of every proposal and had every steward take it out to the people and tell them about it. That way, we found out how they felt about it [before the union voted]," Wadinski said.

Between August and mid-November, Local 1791 had made four proposals, the last two of which would have given Marathon Electric $1.2 million and $3.2 million in concessions over three years. The last union proposal also called for converting the shop's piece work jobs to day work jobs, doing away with the incentive pay that 70 per cent of the shop workers were used to getting.

Marathon Electric's management refused to even discuss the proposals. It also refused to open its books to the union so that the negotiating committee could justify Marathon Electric's concession requests to Local 1791's members.

Four months after negotiations over a new three-year contract had begun, Marathon Electric declared an impasse and implemented its last contract offer on November 12, 1987. The move cut wages by 14 percent, or an average of $1.14 an hour. Cuts in benefits reduced average pay by about $3 an hour.

Management's actions had unfolded as the union leadership had predicted, and Local 1791's members were visibly frustrated and disappointed. It became even more evident that union busting was the goal.

The Fightback

Informational pickets began as soon as the last contract offer was implemented. So did the effort by a group of eight union stewards to contact 156 local businesses in Wausau to have them display "We Support Local 1791" posters. About 100 businesses chose to display the signs.

"We kept track of who supported us and who didn't," Wadinski said. "People who supported us, we would shop there or buy gas there in a group on weekends. Those who didn't support us didn't get our business and we let everyone know who they were."

Local 1791 also printed up a form letter and gave it to every shop worker. The letter was to inform the employees' banks and creditors that they might have to file for protection from creditors under a chapter of the Federal Bankruptcy Act because of Marathon Electric's pay cuts. The letters helped to increase negative public opinion toward the company.

Counter measures began inside Marathon Electric as well, as workers implemented several workplace strategies. They included:
• Asking for a written job description and working only as much as required—no more, no less. There was no more helping supervisors or pitching in to improve production or quality.
• Reporting all illnesses and injuries, no matter how slight.
• Documenting and dating every conversation or statement that was made to a supervisor.

Cab drivers and supporters rally against
the Yellow Cab Company in Madison.

Daily Cardinal Photo/Courtesy South Central Federation of Labor

• Asking to see one's personnel file at least twice a year.

• Wearing blaze orange clothing as a sign of solidarity (it was widely believed that company president Russ Hale hated blaze orange).

• Leaving work during breaks to march in protest around Marathon Electric's plant.

• Taking 15-minute bathroom breaks in mass, effectively shutting down the plant at various times during each shift.

• Holding sick days, where a large group of workers would call in sick.

Local 1791 leaders also were successful in working a connection to get one of the toughest inspectors from the Occupational Safety and Health Administration to inspect Marathon Electric.

"He spent three days, and only came up with $15,000 to $20,000 in fines," Olmsted said. "But the company had to change a lot of machinery to comply."

On the work-to-rule side, Wadinski figured about 70 per cent of the shop workers actually worked to rule. "On one job a guy operated, they had to move two parts of his job to two different stations." This resulted in a substantial loss of incentive pay. "He sacrificed a great deal."

Working at 100 per cent of incentive, rather than the 140 per cent to 150 per cent they had worked at prior to the work-to-rule campaign, meant additional wage cuts for those who participated.

Local 1791 leaders encouraged the other 30 per cent of the

shop workers to do what they could. "We didn't want to make them feel like outcasts," Wadinski said. "Some people truly couldn't afford to lose the money."

The stewards, Wadinski and Olmsted said, were the catalysts that kept the workers organized and fired up. Each steward stayed in near-daily contact with union officers and with a group of employees, keeping the lines of communications open for answering members' questions and for organizing members into pickets or marches.

By March 1988, however, workers had grown tired of the battle. A few, it was reported, were trying to negotiate behind the union's back and were trying to recruit other members.

The inside strategies had succeeded in pulling Marathon Electric's production rate down by nearly 40 per cent, making the company's tough financial condition almost unbearable. Both sides realized things had gone nearly to the point of no return, as was reflected in a newspaper article at the time.

"Loyalty toward Wausau as a manufacturing facility is diminishing with every day that goes by and, quite frankly, if our employees in Wausau are no longer interested in our jobs, we know plenty of other people who are," the company's vice president of administration told the press.

Wadinski was just as pessimistic: "Marathon Electric will never have a contract with its employees in Wausau because they want one dictated to the workers and shoved down their throats. We'll do whatever we have to do. If they ruin our lives, we'll ruin their corporation. It won't stop here."

Looking back today, Olmsted said the situation was tough to manage for Local 1791's leaders. "We were looking at the possibility of losing. Marathon Electric, I believe, was going to make a big move in Wausau because we were really killing their business. We were turning out terrible products and the long-term repercussions were going to be devastating to them."

For that reason, Local 1791 called a two-week truce in March 1988, and workers went back to working as hard as they could. Within weeks, negotiations had resumed and a settlement was reached. Shop workers were given job security, a profit-sharing plan, a signing bonus of $750, and one holiday that otherwise would have been cut. But management kept its wage cuts as prescribed in its implemented offer.

Once More, With Feeling

"That was probably one of the biggest mistakes we made," Olmsted said. "There was a lot of bitterness after the contract was accepted and people went back to work with a contract nobody wanted."

That bitterness continued to fuel the workplace strategy of working only to one's job description—with or without the direction of Local 1791's leadership. Morale continued to drop in the shop, and the cost of saving the union started to wear on everyone.

"After the 1988 settlement was the toughest time," Olmsted said. "Grievances started piling in and a lot of hostilities between the union and the company were formed." During Olmsted's three years as Local 1791's president, there were 383 grievances filed. The normal rate had been about 15 a year before the end of the three-year contract in September 1987. "It

was an every day battle and you didn't know what you were going to run into," he said. Marathon Electric's management, however, began a process that Local 1791 would later describe as its biggest mistake: it began building up its order base as soon as the March settlement was reached, anticipating that work would return to normal in the plant by late 1988. But production didn't improve, Olmsted said, because workers remained bitter.

Company president Hale, meanwhile, suddenly left his post and was replaced in December 1988 by long-time Marathon Electric veteran and previous vice president John Slayton. Olmsted said that about four months after the change in command, he received a phone call at home from someone he believes was Hale. "The guy on the phone asked me 'What are you going to do about Marathon Electric?' and it sounded just like Russ Hale," he said. "He told me how they had screwed us over, that they didn't need the money, and after that, things started eating at me."

Olmsted then decided that members of Local 1791 needed to encourage Marathon Electric in its pursuit of higher order volume because, he said, "We knew damn well that if they got their customers back and we went to war again, they would never get them back again."

By mid-summer of 1989, Olmsted had sent Marathon Electric's executives a letter saying that because the overall economy nationwide had improved, and because the company's hardships had faded, the shop workers deserved a pay increase. "We went in and told them flat out that they were going to have to give these people something back, and if they didn't, it would get terrible again in the shop," Olmsted said.

By September, both sides had negotiated a new contract that gave the 590 shop workers a 16 per cent increase in wages, all of their holidays back, significant increases in pension benefits, and increase in accident benefits, and a $250 signing bonus.

"Surprisingly enough, the new package was passed 260 to 218, and we had 100 members who didn't even vote on it," Olmsted said.

Since the first of this year, productivity is back to 1987 levels at Marathon Electric, Olmsted said. Marathon Electric has finished investing $10 million into capital improvements at the facility and is planning to stick another $10 million into it fairly soon.

"It's just getting better out there now," he said. "But some of those people will never be the same again. Some started to realize that they were there to make a living," not support the company with extra effort.

Wadinski, Olmsted, negotiating committee member Tom Bittner and others also ended up paying a price for their efforts. Besides pay cuts, some of them became targets of managers who were unhappy with their use of the workplace strategies. And public support, though strong throughout most of the three-year battle, was often taxing to try and maintain.

"It was one thing to read about these things, and to listen to people talk about them," Olmsted said about the need for, and use of, workplace strategies. "It was another to live it." ∎

From "An Inside Game in Wisconsin: IBEW 1791 vs. Marathon Electric," *Labor Research Review* (Spring 1991).

Labor Meets History

BY ROBERT W. OZANNE, DARRYL HOLTER, AND DAVID NEWBY

*In celebration of the 150 year anniversary of the founding of
the State Historical Society of Wisconsin, a large group of "alumni"
were asked to recall their days or years within the circle of the Society.
The first two selections recall the ways in which labor "met" history through
the Society's auspices; the third is a final word from the current
president of the Wisconsin State AFL-CIO.*

ONE day in the late 1950's, the chairman of the University of Wisconsin economics department, Ed Young, said, "Bob, the Department has some Ford research money. Would you like to forgo teaching next semester and work full time on research?" I have never known a professor who would turn down such an offer.

My research concern was one that was popular among economists then and perhaps even today: "Do unions affect wages and income distribution? If so, how?" I had entered this debate in 1959 with an article comparing wage movements in the 1920's with those in the more unionized 1950's. I wanted to expand my study backwards, with wage data going back even into the nineteenth-century.

As a research assistant I hired not a Wisconsin economics graduate student, but a Wisconsin history graduate student who was more familiar than I with the broad resources of the State Historical Society Library. He described to me the Library's newly acquired McCormick Collection, from which several Wisconsin history professors already had written books about the charities of this pioneer manufacturing family. We wondered, might there also be data on the business and labor relations of the McCormick Harvester Company?

After a week's exploration, my assistant brought me a copy of one page from a wage book he had found in the McCormick Collection. He chuckled in anticipation of my excitement as he watched me read that page, which contained the names of twenty molders, mostly Irishmen, and for each of them their daily

State Historical Society of Wisconsin WHi (X3) 1565

Madison, 1950. Dr. Clifford L. Lord (right), State Historical Society director, plans the State Federation of Labor's share in the Labor History Project with SFL President George Haberman, Lester Schmidt, a labor historian, SFL research director George Hampel, Jr. (standing); and late SFL Secretary William Nagorsne.

and weekly hours of work and their weekly wage. The year was 1871.

The two of us charged over to the Historical Society Library. There, in the room set aside for the McCormick Collection, was not only the company's wage book for all of 1871, but *entire shelves* of wage books covering the hours and wages of all McCormick factory workers from 1848 through 1902.

But before beginning work on this hoard, I asked myself whether this collection was unique, or would other libraries such as the celebrated Harvard Business School Library have similar, perhaps even more extensive wage records from other companies? I spent a week in Cambridge searching in the business school library, and I did find interesting wage data: from an early steel mill, the x's each worker marked on the receipt as he received this weekly wage, revealing his illiteracy; the wages of workers in an early nineteenth-century textile mill. However, neither of these sets of wage records covered more than a dozen years.

So, even more impressed with the McCormick Collection, I went back to the long job of analyzing its half-century of wage data. There I found an unexpected but vital bonus. Accompanying the wage data was McCormick corporate and family correspondence, which vividly stated the motives for cutting or raising wages, the pros and cons of recognizing or breaking unions, and even detailed family views and reactions, such as a letter from the mother of the McCormick Company president bemoaning an 1884-1885 wage cut and the resulting strike. Extremely valuable in understanding the McCormick Company's wage policies were the Society's microfilms of the *Chicago Tribune's* detailed coverage of this strike and the labor radicalism of the subsequent Haymarket Riot of 1886.

By now, this wealth of material had made me greedy, insatiable. Why did these wage records end in 1902? What about the years beyond? The curator of the Collection, Lucile Kellar, explained: at the end of 1902, the McCormick Harvesting Company merged with two other companies to form the International Harvester Company. Consequently, wage data after 1902 was beyond the control of the McCormick family. But I determined it should not be beyond the scope of my study, so I enlisted Mrs. Kellar's assistance. She agreed to make some calls to the International Harvester Company in Chicago. Two weeks later, a special truck arrived with McCormick plant wage data from 1903 through 1960. The boxes of data completely filled a basement room in the Historical Society, where they were piled on the floor waist high!

Now I had the data to complete the study, but the volume of material had become overwhelming. I received funds for additional research assistants, and what I had envisioned as one book eventually became two books: *A Century of Labor Management Relations at McCormick and International Harvester*, and *Wages in Practice and Theory*, which won the Newcomen Society's award for the best books on business history for the years 1967-1969.

—ROBERT W. OZANNE

THE Society has earned an international reputation as a lodestone for professional historians and genealogists. Less well known is the important role the Society plays in non-academic areas of public policy. My memories of the Society reflect that imbalance in perception. When I was a graduate student in history at the University of Wisconsin, I knew very little about the State Historical Society. As a student of European social history, my use of the Society was limited to a few brief explorations. I was, however, quite envious of my colleagues in American history who could work in the beautiful reading room on the second floor while we Europeanists rummaged about in the dimly lit "Cutter" stacks in the basement of Memorial Library.

It was only later, after I had finished my Ph.D. and gone to work as a legislative representative for the Wisconsin State AFL-CIO, that I began to utilize the Society. It was then that I realized the Society's valuable role in helping to shape public policy. In the recession-wracked years of 1982 and 1983, Wisconsin's venerable unemployment compensation system faced a major crisis, setting off a bitter legislative battle that raised questions about the origins and structure of the program. Faced with the need to find information to answer several lawmakers' questions, I found myself heading down State Street in search of the historical record. In the Society's rich collections I found the documents and materials I needed. For the next nine years, until I left Wisconsin for UCLA, I was a regular at the Society, using the library, the microfilm room, the government documents section, and the manuscripts and special collections. Unknown to the public, the Society, in its own unique way, yielded information that was utilized in the crafting of a large body of legislation, including plant-closing laws, tax reform, workers' compensation, unemployment insurance, utility deregulation, employees' rights, and dispute resolution.

In an era when the locus of political power and legislative decision-making devolves to the level of the state, the value of the Society should not go unnoticed. The historical record, organized and preserved safely in the beautiful building on State Street, is a vital resource for producing good public policy.

—DARRYL HOLTER

Epilogue

A hundred years ago, the mill workers and factory hands of Wisconsin risked their livelihoods—and their lives—for the principle of the eight-hour day. Thirty years later, in the depths of the Great Depression, workers on a massive scale organized themselves into unions so that they could get a fair shake from the rich and powerful and gain a fair share of the wealth they created. As during the Great Depression, it is just as true today that men and women of organized labor—black and white, Asian and Hispanic, blue-collar and white-collar, craft, industrial, service, and public sector alike—must unite and continue the long struggle for social and economic justice.

Today's unions must intensify their organizing efforts, and indeed organizing is the top priority of the labor movement. But we must also educate the public—and especially the school-age public—about the long history of past generations of workers, their struggles and sacrifices, their successes and failures, in good times and bad. Wisconsin has been at the center of the labor movement since the 1850s, and Wisconsin's workers and unions have played a significant role nationally. Their stories, some of which are told in this labor anthology, are an important part of Wisconsin history. They are worthy of being retold and passed on to the next generation, as examples of the need for a powerful movement to promote the rights of all working people.

—DAVID NEWBY

Notes

INTRODUCTION

Darryl Holter.

1. William F. Raney, "The Building of Wisconsin Railroads,"*Wisconsin Magazine of History,* 19:4 (June 1936), 387-403.
2. The complete list of scholarly articles on the new labor history is too long to include here, but they include J. Carroll Moody's introduction in Moody and Alice Kessler-Harris, eds., *Perspectives on American Labor History: The Problems of Synthesis* (DeKalb, 1989); Robert Zieger, "Workers and Scholars: Recent Trends in American Labor Historiography," in *Labor History,* 13 (1972), 245-66; David Brody, "The Old Labor History and the New," in *Labor History* 20 (1979), 111-26; and David Montgomery, "To Study the People: The American Working Class," in *Labor History,* 21 (1980), 485-512.

SECTION 1

Thomas Gavett, "Early Unions in Milwaukee, 1840-1884." From Gavett,
***Development of the Labor Movement in Milwaukee* (Madison, 1965).**

1. Milwaukee *Sentinel*, Aug. 24, 1847; Theodore Mueller, "Milwaukee Workers," in *History of Milwaukee County* (Typescript, 1940, Milwaukee County Historical Society, Milwaukee, Wisconsin), 205; Bayrd Still, *Milwaukee: The History of a City* (Madison, 1948), 65; James S. Buck, *Pioneer History of Milwaukee* (Milwaukee, 1881), 50. Reports on many of the early strikes are fragmentary.
2. Mueller, "Milwaukee Workers," 205-6; Milwaukee *Sentinel*, Aug. 1, 1848.
3. Milwaukee *Sentinel*, Aug. 30, Sept. 1, 1851.
4. Mueller, "Milwaukee Workers," 206; Walter Osten [Theodore Mueller], "The Annekes," *Milwaukee Turner*, 3 (June 1942), 5.
5. Frederick Merk, *Economic History of Wisconsin During the Civil War Decade* (Madison, 1916), 162-63.
6. James S. Buck, *Milwaukee Under the Charter* (Milwaukee, 1886), 439-41; Milwaukee *Sentinel*, July 12, 13, 1853.
7. Milwaukee *Sentinel*, Aug. 18, 31, Sept. 7, 8, 10, 12, 1853.
8. *Ibid.*, Jan. 18, 22, 1855.
9. Mueller, "Milwaukee Workers," 206; Merk, *Economic History*, 162-63.
10. Milwaukee Writers Project, "History of Milwaukee County," 310. Typescript, Milwaukee Public Library.
11. Merk, *Economic History*, 160-61; Mueller, "Milwaukee Workers," 207-8.
12. Milwaukee *Sentinel*, Jan. 13, July 27, 30, 1860, Oct. 28, 1862, Jan. 15, 16, 17, 19, 21 24, 1863, April 12, 1864; Wisconsin Bureau of Labor Statistics, *Second Biennial Report, 1885-1886* (Madison, 1886), 204-5.
13. Wisconsin Bureau of Labor Statistics, *Second Biennial Report*, 206-7; Mueller, "Milwaukee Workers," 208; Merk, *Economic History*, 175-76.
14. Merk, *Economic History*, 166; Milwaukee *Sentinel*, Oct. 2, Dec. 7, 8, 1866.
15. Milwaukee *Sentinel*, Feb. 11, March 13, 1861, Aug. 4, 1870.
16. Milwaukee *Sentinel*, July 2, 4, 18, Aug. 8, 1878; June 12, July 19, 21, 1879.
17. *Ibid.*, Jan. 7, 8, 1880; Dec. 19, 1881, June 2, July 8, 1882; Wisconsin Bureau of Labor Statistics, *First Biennial Report, 1883-1884* (Madison, 1884), 123.
18. Milwaukee *Sentinel*, Jan. 2, April 21, Aug. 31, 1880, April 23, May 6, Aug. 30, 1881.
19. Wisconsin Bureau Labor Statistics, *First Biennial Report*, 132; *Printers Daily Bulletin*, May 5, 1881.
20. Milwaukee *Sentinel*, July 27, Aug. 26, 27, 28, 30, 31, Sept. 1, 3, 4, 9, 10, 1880.
21. *Ibid.*, April 29, May 2, 5, 6, 7, 10, 11, 16, 1881; *Printers Daily Bulletin*, May 5, 7, 1881.
22. Typographical Union Local 23, "Milwaukee Constitution, June 1881," U.S. MSS 113A, State Historical Society of Wisconsin, Madison, Wisconsin.
23. *Printers Daily Bulletin*, April 29, 30, May 2, 7, Aug. 2, 6, 20, Sept. 3, 1881, Feb. 28, March 6, 13, 1884; Milwaukee *Sentinel*, April 26, 1881, May 24, June 9, 1882; Wisconsin Bureau of Labor Statistics, *First Biennial Report*, 149-51, and *Second Biennial Report*, 267-68, 372-74; Milwaukee *Labor Review*, April 24, 1886.

Robert W. Ozanne, "Lumber Industry Strikes: Eau Claire, Marinette, Ashland, La Crosse." From Ozanne, *The Labor Movement in Wisconsin: A History* (Madison, 1984).

1. Eau Claire *Free Press*, July 19, 1881.

2. Vernon Jensen, *Lumber and Labor* (New York, 1945), 51.
3. Wisconsin Bureau of Labor Statistics, *First Biennial Report, 1883-1884* (Madison, 1884), 151.
4. Eau Claire *News*, July 30, 1881.
5. Oshkosh *Northwestern*, July 30, 1881.
6. Madison *Daily Democrat*, July 29, 1881.
7. Wisconsin Bureau of Labor Statistics, *First Biennial Report*, 152-53.
8. Reported in Madison *Daily Democrat*, July 30, 1881.
9. Marinette *Eagle*, September 23, 26, 1885.
10. Wisconsin Bureau of Labor and Industrial Statistics, *Second Biennial Report, 1885-1886*, 246.
11. Rhinelander *Vindicator*, August 3, 1892.
12. *Lincoln County Advocate*, issues of July 26 through August 2, 1892.
13. Oshkosh *Northwestern*, August 2-6, 1892; Wausau *Pilot Review*, August 9, 1892; Wausau *Torch of Liberty*, August 4, 1892; Rhinelander *Vindicator*, August 31–September 21, 1892.
14. La Crosse *Morning Chronicle*, April 26, 1892.
15. *Ibid.*, April 26–May10, 1892; Oshkosh *Daily Northwestern*, May 9, 1892; Wisconsin Bureau of Labor and Industrial Statistics, *Fifth Biennial Report, 1891-1892*, 122-3.

Leon Fink, "The Knights of Labor in Milwaukee." From Fink, *Workingmen's Democracy: The Knights of Labor* (Urbana, 1985).

1. Socialist mayors included Emil Seidel, 1910–1912, Daniel Hoan, 1916–1940, and Frank P. Zeidler, 1948–1960. Mayor Zeidler's tenure occurred through a Socialist-Democratic coalition, rather than an independent Socialist organization. As such it is not treated in this chapter, although reasons for Socialist absorption into the party of the New Deal may be inferred from the last section; Bayrd Still, *Milwaukee: The History of a City* (Madison, 1965), 258, 265-66; U.S. Eleventh Census, 1890, *Compendium of the Eleventh Census*, Pt. 2 (Washington, D.C., 1897), 680-82.
2. Still, *Milwaukee*, 323-27.
3. Still, *Milwaukee*, 257, 325; U.S. Tenth Census, 1880, *Report on the Social Statistics of Cities*, Pt. 2 (Washington, D.C., 1887), 676-77.
4. Still, *Milwaukee*, 335-39; Wisconsin State Department, *Tabular Statement of the Census Enumeration*, 1855 (Madison, 1906), 702-3; U.S. Eleventh Census, 1890, *Report of Manufacturing Industries in the United States*, Pt. 2 (Washington, D.C., 1895), 334-43.
5. Thomas C. Cochran, *The Pabst Brewing Company: The History of an American Business* (New York, 1948), 271-72.
6. Kathleen Neils Conzen, *Immigrant Milwaukee, 1836-1860: Accommodation and Community in a Frontier City* (Cambridge, 1976), 124-25; Milwaukee *Journal*, March 31, 1886; Gerd Korman, *Industrialization, Immigrants, and Americanizers: The View from Milwaukee, 1866–1921* (Madison, 1967), 16, 27, 36. When John Jarrett, president of the Amalgamated, delivered a protariff speech in the city in 1888, his remarks included the comment that he was ashamed of being born an Englishman. The Acorn Lodge of the Sons of St. George, composed largely of English-born workingmen, expressed outrage at the slur on their heritage. Besides the Germans and Poles, foreign-born groups in Milwaukee according to the 1890 census included the Irish (3,436), the English (2,409), and the Norwegians (1,821). John A. Hawgood, *The Tragedy of German America* (New York, 1970), 202-6; Robert C. Nesbit, *Wisconsin: A History* (Madison, 1973), 155-56, 242-43; Still, *Milwaukee*, 115-25; Wilhelm Hense-Jensen and Ernst Bruncken, "Wisconsin's German-Americans until the End of the Nineteenth Centry," esp. 5-6, 11, manuscript at the State Historical Society, Madison; Gavett, *Development of the Labor Movement in Milwaukee* , 33, 40-46, 51-53.
7. Still, *Milwaukee*, 151-63; Richard Jensen, *The Winning of the Midwest: Social and Political Conflict 1888–1896* (Chicago, 1971), esp. 55-88, 122; Wisconsin, *Blue Book, 1879–1883*; Milwaukee *Volksblatt*, April 8, 1883; Milwaukee *Trades Assembly Bulletin*, April 1, 1882.
8. Still, *Milwaukee*, 268-69; Paul Fox, *The Poles in America* (New York, 1970), 58-59; interview by telephone with Mrs. Celia Orzelska Wong, Aug. 11, 1975. The Orzelska family moved to Milwaukee from Kujany, Poland, in 1904 when Celia was still an infant. Mrs. Wong remembers her father trying to get his Polish neighbors to register as Poles, not Germans, during the census count of 1920. Milwaukee

Journal, March 30, 1886; U.S. Eleventh Census, 1890, *Compendium of the Eleventh Census*, Pt. 2, 604-11. The state census count of 659 Poles in Milwaukee in 1895 was ridiculously low. *Wisconsin State Census*, 1895 (Madison, 1895–96), 88-89; Still, *Milwaukee*, 273.

10. Milwaukee *Journal*, May 17, 1886.

11. Jerzy Jedlicki, "Land of Hope, Land of Despair: Polish Scholarship and American Immigration," *Reviews in American History*, 3 (March 1975), 87-94; reference to Detroit in Rutland (Vt.) *Herald*, March 21, 1887; for Cleveland see Henry B. Leonard, "Ethnic Cleavage and Industrial Conflict in Late 19th Century America: The Cleveland Rolling Mill Company Strikes of 1882 and 1885," *Labor History*, 20 (Fall 1979), 524-48; knowledge of Saginaw Valley drawn from Saginaw *Courier* and Bay City *Evening Press*, 1885.

12. Fox, *The Poles*, 78-79; Korman, *Industrialization, Immigrants, and Americanizers*, 51-52; Still, Milwaukee, 269-72; Francis Bolek, ed., *Who's Who in Polish America* (New York, 1943); *Kuryer Polski*, July 14, 1888; *Volksblatt*, April 8, 1883.

13. Jonathan Garlock and N. C. Builder, "Knights of Labor Data Bank: Users Manual and Index to Local Assemblies" (1973), manuscript at the University of Rochester. Two other early Knights' assemblies, including one of telegraphers, collapsed before the period of sustained growth; see Gavett, *Development of the Labor Movement*, 50-53. The order probably possessed 12,000-15,000 members at its peak in May 1886. Gavett's figure is corroborated by Henry Smith's recollection: "Reminiscences of My Political Life" (1912), 15, Henry Smith Papers, SHSW; D. L. Galehey to Powderly, May 22, 1886, Terence V. Powderly Papers, Catholic University, Washington, D.C.; Milwaukee *Journal*, March 19, 1886.

14. *John Swinton's Papers* (hereafter JSP), Oct. 1, 8, 1885, Dec. 20, 1885; the reference to "Schwarze Liste" is in Milwaukee *Boycott-Post*, March 6, 1886; Milwaukee *Journal*, Feb. 18, 20, 23, 26, March 3, 16, 19, April 4, 7, 1886.

15. Gary M. Fink, ed., *Biographical Dictionary of American Labor Leaders* (Westport, Conn., 1974), 319; Norman Ware, *The Labor Movement in the United States, 1860–1895* (New York, 1929), 11-18; Milton Small, "Robert Schilling and the Origins of Populism in Wisconsin" (1950), 3, manuscript at SHSW; *Volksblatt*, April 8, 1883.

16. Charles R. Smith, "Outline of the Life of Henry Smith, Public Servant, 1838–1916" (1916), 1-3, Henry Smith Papers.

17. Henry Smith, My Official Life" (1912), 7, 9, 14-31, Henry Smith Papers.

18. Henry Smith, "Why I Became a Greenbacker in Politics" (n.d.), 8, 10, 12-13, Henry Smith Papers, and "Reminiscences of My Political Life," 14; Conzen, *Immigrant Milwaukee*, 227.

19. Milwaukee *Journal*, July 6, 1885; Gavett, *Development of the Labor Movement*, 58; Garlock and Builder, "Knights of Labor Data Bank." Given the overlap of Poles and ironworkers and the large memberships of both the all-Polish and ironworkers assemblies, it seems possible that some Poles belonged to two assemblies, one for their trade and one for their nationality.

20. Victor Greene, *For God and Country: The Rise of Polish and Lithuanian Ethnic Consciousness in America* (Madison, 1975), 66-69, quotation, 67; Polish Academy of Learning, *Polski Slownik Biograficzny*, 15 (Poland, 1970), as translated by Mrs. Celia Wong. Michael Kruszka's younger brother, Waclaw, who did not arrive in the United States until 1893, became a prominent advocate for the recognition of ethnic pluralism and Polish rights within the Roman Catholic church. A generally liberal and reform-minded priest, the Reverent Kruszka was the first to install a playground in a Milwaukee parish school. Some parishioners were "shocked to see him ice-skating with children in the yard." Greene, *For God and Country*, 132-34; interview with Mrs. Wong, Sept. 12, 1975. See also the Reverend Alexander Syski, "The Nestor of Polish Historians in America: Reverend Waclaw Kruzska," *Bulletin of the Polish Institute of Arts and Sciences of America*, 3 (Oct. 1944), 102-11; Milwaukee *Journal*, Oct. 15, 1886; Henry Smith to Powderly, March 2, 1887, M. S. Cyborowski to Powderly, Jan. 24, 1887, Michael Kruzska to Powderly, Jan. 31, 1887, Michael Kruzska to Powderly, Jan. 31, 1887, Powderly Papers.

Robert Nesbit, "The Bay View Tragedy." From Nesbit, *The History of Wisconsin: Urbanization and Industrialization, 1873–1893, Vol . 3* (State Historical Society of Wisconsin, 1985).

1. Henry Casson, *"Uncle Jerry": Life of General Jeremiah M. Rusk, Stage Driver, Farmer, Soldier, Legislator, Governor, Cabinet Officer* (Madison, 1895), 167-173.

2. Casson, *"Uncle Jerry"*, 192; Jerry M. Cooper, "The Wisconsin National Guard in the Milwaukee Riots of 1886," *Wisconsin Magazine of History*, 55 (Autumn 1971), 42-43.

3. Gibson G. Glasier, ed., *Autobiography of Roujet D. Marshall, Justice of the Supreme Court of the State of Wisconsin, 1895–1918* (2 vols., Madison, 1923 and 1931), 1:62-63; Ruth M. Elson, *Guardians of Tradition: American Schoolbooks of the Nineteenth Century* (Lincoln, 1964), 251; Milton D. Small, "The Biography of Robert Schilling" (master's thesis, University of Wisconsin, 1953), 188-189; Wisconsin Bureau of Labor and Industrial Statistics, *Biennial Report*, 1885-1886, p. 317. Membership figures for the Knights of Labor are certainly suspect in the

light of the rapid rise and fall of the order, but it was probably close to 30 percent of the state's industrial labor force.

4. Gerd Korman, *Industrialization, Immigrants and Americanizers: The View From Milwaukee, 1866–1921* (Madison, 1967), 21-36; Milwaukee *Sentinel*, January 13, June 3, September 12, 1882.

5. Korman, *Industrialization, Immigrants and Americanizers*, 43-44, 51-53; Gavett, *Development of the Labor Movement in Milwaukee*, 25-26, 47.

6. Milwaukee *Sentinel*, February 16, 1882. See also January 18, 20, February 7, 1882; U.S. Senate Committee on Education and Labor, *Report Upon the Relations Between Labor and Capital, and Testimony Taken by the Committee* , 4 vols. (Washington, 1885), 1:279-280.

7. John Gurda, *Bay View, Wis.* (Milwaukee, 1979), 13-14; David Brody, *Steelworkers in America: The Nonunion Era* (Cambridge, 1960), 7-10; Bernhard C. Korn, *The Story of Bay View* (Milwaukee, 1980), 54-56. Both the Sons of Vulcan and the Milwaukee Iron Works went through name changes in the 1870's and 1880's. The Sons of Vulcan was an English transplant which became part of the National Amalgamated Association of Iron and Steel Workers in 1875. The name "Sons of Vulcan" remained in common parlance, as did "Milwaukee Iron Works" or "Bay View Works," although the plant became a part of the North Chicago Rolling Mill Company in 1878 and part of the Illinois Steel Company at the end of the 1880's.

8. *Dictionary of Wisconsin Biography* (Madison, 1960); Gavett, *Development of the Labor Movement*, 90-95.

9. Small, "Robert Schilling," 64-65, 273, 337; *DWB*; Milwaukee *Sentinel*, May 30, 1886.

10. Small, "Robert Schilling," 5-14, 22-28, 32-34, 49-58; Milwaukee *Sentinel*, May 30, 1886; Albert S. Bolles, *Industrial History of the United States . . .* (Norwich, Connecticut, 1881), 510; John R. Commons et al., *History of Labour in the United States* (4 vols., New York, 1918–1935), 2:74-76; Norman J. Ware, *The Labor Movement in the United States, 1860–1895: A Study in Democracy* (New York, 1929; Vintage paperback edition, 1964), 11-18.

11. Ware, *Labor Movement in the United States*, 26-42. The Knights of Labor "were the first to organize the unskilled of America . . . bringing these in large masses into the ranks of organized labor." Herman Schluter, *The Brewing Industry and the Brewery Workers' Movement in America* (Cincinnati, 1910), 113-114.

12. Small, "Robert Schilling," 152-156, 161-165; Ellis B. Usher, *The Greenback Movement of 1875–1884 and Wisconsin's Part in It* (Milwaukee, 1911), 57-61.

13. Usher, *Greenback Movement*, *passim*; Small, "Robert Schilling," 164-176. The resumption of paper-gold convertibility in 1879, combined with the Bland-Allison silver purchase act, gave the National Greenback party its deathblow. See Irwin Unger, *The Greenback Era: A Social and Political History of American Finance, 1865–1879* (Princeton, 1964), chap. 11. After the 1884 presidential campaign, in which Schilling was active as a popular speaker beyond Wisconsin's borders for the National Greenback Labor ticket, he closed down the *Reformer* and concentrated on the *Volksblatt*, which he had initially edited in the interest of the Milwaukee Trades Assembly.

14. Gavett, *Development of the Labor Movement*, 41-50.

15. Ware, *Labor Movement in the United States*, 123-125, 139-145. The national membership of the Knights grew from 111,395 to 729,677 between July, 1885, and July, 1886. The decline was less rapid, but membership fell to 259,518 two years later. *Ibid.*, 66. "By May, 1886, there were forty-two local assemblies with over 12,000 members in Milwaukee and 25,000 members in the state," according to Gavett, *Development of the Labor Movement*, 50. See also Small, "Robert Schilling," 191-195; Carl E. Krog, "Marinette: Biography of a Nineteenth Century Lumbering Town" (doctoral dissertation, University of Wisconsin, 1971), 222-226; Wisconsin Bureau of Labor and Industrial Statistics, *Second Biennial Report, 1885-1886*, 238-246.

16. Small, "Robert Schilling," 195, 197-200.

17. *Ibid.*, 197, 200-201; Ware, *Labor Movement in the United States*, chap. 13.

18. Gavett, *Development of the Labor Movement*, 56-57; Small, "Robert Schilling," 200-205; Morris Hillquit, *History of Socialism in the United States* , 5th ed. (New York, 1910), 209-220; Henry David, *The History of the Haymarket Affair: A Study in the American Social-Revolutionary and Labor Movements* (New York, 1936; revised paperback edition, 1963), chaps. 1-5; Howard H. Quint, *The Forging of American Socialism: Origins of the Modern Movement* (Columbia, South Carolina, 1953), 15-36; Milwaukee *Journal*, May 5, 6, 11, 15, 1886; Cooper, "Wisconsin National Guard in the Milwaukee Riots of 1886," 36-37.

19. Small, "Robert Schilling," 190-191, 202; Milwaukee *Herald*, March 1, 1886. Gavett, *Development of the Labor Movement*, 56-57, says that there were about 140 members of the German socialists who were followers of Grottkau and about forty members of the Hirth group.

20. Wisconsin Bureau of Labor and Industrial Statistics, *Second Biennial Report, 1885–1886*, 318-319; Cooper "Wisconsin National Guard in the Milwaukee Riots of 1886," 37; Milwaukee *Sentinel*, February 10, 11, 16, 27, March 19, 1886; Small, "Robert Schilling," 197.

21. Small, "Robert Schilling," 199-205.

22. Wisconsin Bureau of Labor and Industrial Statistics, *Second Biennial Report, 1885–1886*, 238-246, 249-251, 256-267, 282-296, 319-320, notes the shift from individual shop actions to industry to industry-wide disputes.

23. Small, "Robert Schilling," 203; Wisconsin Bureau of Labor and Industrial Statistics, *Second Biennial Report*, 256-267, 341-342, 372-382; Lawrence M. Friedman, *A History of American Law* (New York, 1973), 488-489; Gavett, *Development of the Labor Movement*, 67; Milwaukee *Journal*, May 12, 1886.

24. Thomas C. Cochran, *The Pabst Brewing Company: The History of an American Business* (New York, 1948), 271-283; Milwaukee *Journal*, May 1, 1886.

25. Wisconsin Bureau of Labor and Industrial Statistics, *Second Biennial Report*, 321-325.

26. *Ibid.*, 323-326; Milwaukee *Journal*, May 1, 1886.

27. Small, "Robert Schilling," 205-207; Milwaukee *Journal*, May 4, 5, 1886.

28. Milwaukee *Journal*, May 1, 3, 1886. May 1, 1886, was a national urban happening. There were an estimated 80,000 workers out in Chicago, 45,000 New York, 32,000 in Cincinnati, and 9,000 in Baltimore. See Commons, et al., *History of Labour*, 2:385.

29. Milwaukee *Journal*, May 3, 4, 5, 1886.

30. *Ibid.*, May 3, 1886.

31. Cooper, "Wisconsin National Guard in the Milwaukee Riots of 1886," 31-34, 39; Jerome A. Watrous, ed., *Memoirs of Milwaukee County: From the Earliest Historical Times Down to the Present, Including a Genealogical and Biographical Record of Representative Families in Milwaukee County* (Madison, 1909), 598-600; Casson, *Jeremiah M. Rusk*, 106-108, 223-225. Rusk's immediate predecessor, Governor William E. Smith, had been an enthusiastic advocate of a revived militia: "We cannot hope always to escape disorders and tumults similar to those which have arisen in other states and nations." *Wisconsin Public Documents*, 1880, Governor's Message, vol. 1, p. 22. In the summer of 1881, Smith had called out the militia to break the Eau Claire lumber strike, known popularly as the "Sawdust War."

32. DWB; Cooper, "Wisconsin National Guard in the Milwaukee Riots of 1886."

33. King, "Memories of a Busy Life," *WMH*, 5:374-375; Cooper, "Wisconsin National Guard in the Milwaukee Riots of 1886," 38-39; Milwaukee *Journal*, May 4, 1886.

34. Small, "Robert Schilling," 206-208; Milwaukee *Sentinel*, May 5, 1886; Milwaukee *Journal*, April 28, May 4, 1886.

35. Milwaukee *Sentinel*, May 5, 1886; Korn, *Story of Bay View*, 56.

36. Milwaukee *Journal*, May 4, 1886; Small, "Robert Schilling," 208-209. Bay View was organized as a village, not part of Milwaukee, and therefore the county sheriff had full jurisdiction. Also see the Milwaukee *Evening Wisconsin*, May 3, 1886. Sheriff Paschen gave his version of the affair some months later; see the Milwaukee *Sentinel*, December 28, 1886; and David, *History of the Haymarket Affair*, 168-177.

37. Cooper, "Wisconsin National Guard in the Milwaukee Riots of 1886," 40-41; Milwaukee *Journal*, May 4, 1886; Milwaukee *Sentinel*, May 5, December 28, 1886.

38. Cooper, "Wisconsin National Guard in the Milwaukee Riots of 1886," 41-42; Milwaukee *Journal*, May 4, 5, 6, 1886; Milwaukee *Sentinel*, May 5, 1886; C. N. Caspar and H. H. Zahn, *Maps of the City of Milwaukee and of Bay View, Wis., 1886* (Milwaukee, 1886). Wisconsin Adjutant General, *Biennial Report*, 1886, pp. 13-26, indicates that Company I of the Second Regiment from Watertown was also ordered to Milwaukee. Korn, *Story of Bay View*, 84-86, has a useful account from the perspective of the village.

39. Schilling's Monday evening meeting was apparently lost in the Monday and Tuesday press accounts of more interesting events occurring in Chicago and Milwaukee. On Tuesday, May 4, he was in Madison for a scheduled appearance. See the Milwaukee *Journal*, May 4, 5, 1886; Milwaukee *Sentinel*, May 5, 6, 1886; Milwaukee *Evening Wisconsin*, May 4, 5, 1886; Small, "Robert Schilling," 206-208; and Cooper, "Wisconsin National Guard in the Milwaukee Riots of 1886," 40-41.

40. Cooper, "Wisconsin National Guard in the Milwaukee Riots of 1886," 42-43; Milwaukee *Journal*, May 5, 7, 1886; Wisconsin Adjutant General, *Biennial Report*, 1885-1886, 18-19; Milwaukee *Evening Wisconsin*, May 5, 1886; Korn, *Story of Bay View*, 86-90. There is no way to reconcile the various newspaper accounts or official testimony about the distances involved or some other matters relating to the two occasions when the militia fired.

41. Cooper, "Wisconsin National Guard in the Milwaukee Riots of 1886, 43-44; Milwaukee *Journal*, May 5, 6, 1886. The firing at Bay View was confirmed by the *Journal* as occurring at 9:00 A.M. It therefore was known by the crowd at the Milwaukee Garden soon thereafter, and certainly at 3:15 P.M. when King asked permission to clear the streets. The Allis Works were opened that morning, with about 200 men reporting. They heard the firing at Bay View and made preparations. The militia was there with a Gatling gun to sweep the streets should a crowd appear.

42. The Milwaukee *Journal*, May 8, 1886, carried comment from the press around the state. See also Milwaukee *Germania*, May 12, 1886.

43. Milwaukee *Journal*, May 6, 8, 1886.

44. *Ibid.*, May 7, 8, 1886.

45. Cooper, "Wisconsin National Guard in the Milwaukee Riots of 1886," 34-35; King, "Memories of a Busy Life," *WMH*, 5:376.

46. Cooper, "Wisconsin National Guard in the Milwaukee Riots of 1886," 33-35, 42-43; King, "Memories of a Busy Life," *WMH*, 5:374-375.

47. Milwaukee *Journal*, May 8, 13, 1886. The paper suggested that the militia and businessmen making the gifts might well contribute to the widow of Mr. Kunkel, the man killed in his own yard.

48. Wisconsin Bureau of Labor and Industrial Statistics, *Second Biennial Report*, 343-344.

49. Milwaukee *Sentinel*, May 20, July 9, 1886; Wisconsin Bureau of Labor and Industrial Statistics, *Second Biennial Report, 1885–1886*, 345.

John W. Bailey, "Unions in Kenosha." From Bailey, "Labor's Fight for Security and Dignity," in John A. Neuenschwander, ed., *Kenosha County in the Twentieth Century* (Kenosha, 1976).

1. Carrie Cropley, *Kenosha: From Pioneer Village to Modern City, 1835–1935* (Kenosha, 1958), 56-59.

2. *Kenosha Evening News*, June 15, 1935; Cropley, *Kenosha*, 78-79.

3. *Kenosha Telegraph-Courier*, January 15, 1903.

4. *Ibid.*, April 23, 1903.

5. *Ibid.*, August 30, 1900; September 4, 1902; August 20, 1909.

6. *Ibid.*, September 8, 1904.

7. *Ibid.*, May 23, 1901; May 30, 1901; July 25, 1901.

8. *Ibid.*, August 14, 1902; January 15, 1903; January 7, 1915; January 4, 1917; January 17, 1918.

9. *Ibid.*, July 29, 1909; July 13, 1917.

10. *Ibid.*, November 28, 1907; June 25, 1908.

11. *Ibid.*, April 26, 1906.

12. *Ibid.*, May 16, 1906; May 23, 1907.

13. *Ibid.*, July 29, 1909.

14. *Ibid.*, November 7, 1907.

15. *Ibid.*, July 29, 1909.

Joseph M. Kelly, "Labor in Racine," from Kelly, "Growth of Organized Labor," in Nicholas C. Burckel, ed. *Racine: Growth and Change in a Wisconsin County* (Racine, 1977).

1. "1899 Minutes," p. 85, and "1903 Minutes," 28 December 1903, in Records of Local 118, United Association of Journeymen and Apprentices of the Plumbing and Pipe Fitting Industry, Parkside Mss 17, Archives and Area Research Center, University of Wisconsin-Parkside, Kenosha.

2. I wish to extend my appreciation to the late Tony Trentadue for permission to examine the records at Union Hall; see *Racine News*, 23 November 1899, 7 December 1899, 13 December 1899, concerning an early J.I. Case strike. Much of the early information about Racine trade unions comes from "History of the Racine Trades and Labor Council," dated 27 October 1912, placed in the cornerstone of the Union Hall, courtesy of *Racine Labor*; other documents, such as brief histories of existing unions were also placed there. I wish to thank the Racine AFL-CIO for permission to examine "Minutes," Racine Trades and Labor Council (RTLC), 26 May 1910, 14 September 1911, 8 August 1912, 23 January 1913, 14 March 1913, 14 April 1913, 22 December 1913, 12 August 1915, 11 May 1916; *Labor Advocate*, 23 May 1925.

3. "Minutes," RTLC, 26 March 1914, 24 April 1914, 28 January 1915, 22 July 1915, 4 October 1915. Liquor dealers were admitted to the RTLC as "fraternal" delegates; see "Minutes," 12 August 1915.

4. "History of the RTLC," in *Racine Labor* Files, 27 October 1912; "Minutes," RTLC, 12 January 1911, 11 June 1914, 12 November 1914, 11 March 1915, 12 August 1915, 13 February 1919, 10 September 1919; concerning the RTLC and World War I, see letter from RTLC to Sen. Paul Husting, 28 April 1916 in "Minutes," RTLC, p. 398.

5. "Minutes," RTLC, 9 January 1913, 28 August 1913.

6. "Minutes," RTLC, 28 October 1915.

7. "Minutes," RTLC, 9 October 1913 (e.g. stage employees and tailors), 22 June 1911, 14 December 1911; see "Financial Record Books," RTLC, for 1920 and 1921; "Minutes," RTLC, 27 August 1914, 25 May 1916. For Woodworkers and Novelty Workers and Engineers, etc., see "Account Book," RTLC, 1902-1911.

8. *Racine Times-Call*, 7 August 1919; interviews with Francis Wendt (attorney), 12 July 1976, Frank Sahorske, Local 180 leader, 7 July 1976, and Loretta Christensen, secretary of the RTLC during the 1930s and early organizer at Western Printing and Lithographing Company, 15 July 1976.

9. "Minutes," RTLC, 10 April 1919; *Racine Labor*, 14 June 1946; interview with Wendt, who recalls how Sommers would often be able to repay legal advice with only a shot of whiskey from the Union Hall bar. Sommers was not unique in being blackballed. John Brown, who was district attorney for Racine County during part of the 1930s, recalls how his father would explain to him that many men sitting on porches would never again work as moulders because of their strike participation.

Interview, John Brown, 6 July 1976.

10. "Minutes," RTLC, 24 October 1912, 23 January 1913, 27 March 1913, 12 August 1915, 26 August 1915, 23 September 1915.

SECTION 2

Leon Applebaum, "A Lock-out: The Hosiery Workers in Kenosha, 1928–1929."
From Applebaum, "Turmoil in Kenosha: The Allen-A Hosiery Dispute of
1928–1929," *Wisconsin Magazine of History*, 70:4 (Summer 1987), 281-303.

1. *The Hosiery Worker*, April 7, 1927; May 2, 1927; August 15, 1929.

2. Lawrence Rogin, *Making History in Hosiery: The Story of the American Federation of Hosiery Workers* (Philadelphia, 1938), 8-9.

3. *Ibid.*, 19.

4. *Ibid.*, 19.

5. The term gauge was used to measure the fineness of a knitted fabric in loops per one and one-half inches. The higher the gauge number, the finer the hosiery.

6. *Milwaukee Journal*, June 25, 28, 1929.

7. *The Hosiery Worker*, August 15, 1929.

8. Edward Thiers, "History of the N.R. Allen's Sons Company," in *Our Views and News* (New York, 1920); Frances H. Lyman, *The City of Kenosha and Kenosha County, Wisconsin* (Chicago, 1916), 29; Victor S. Clark, *History of Manufacturers in the United States, Volume III, 1893–1928* (Washington, D.C., 1929), 228; Richard H. Keehn, "Industry and Business," in John A. Neuenschwander, ed., *Kenosha County in the Twentieth Century: A Topical History* (Kenosha, 1976), 183.

9. *Ibid.*, 180.

10. *Chicago Tribune*, August 3, 1928; *Milwaukee Journal*, February 16, 1928; *The Hosiery Worker*, April 15, 1927.

11. *Kenosha Evening News*, September 23, 27, 1927; Interview with Mrs. John Kueny, September 23, 1985 (Mrs. Kueny was the late Maceo Kueny's sister-in-law); interview with Elva Mitchell, September 5, 1985.

12. "The True Facts About the Allen-A Dispute," Allen-A Files, Archives and Area Research Center, University of Wisconsin-Parkside, Kenosha.

13. *Fourteenth Census of the United States*, 1920; *Fifteenth Census of the United States*, 1930; John D. Buenker, "Immigration and Ethnic Groups," in Neuenschwander, ed., *Kenosha County*, 1, 4.

14. *Ibid.*, 8.

15. Keehn, "Industry and Business," 180.

16. *Chicago Tribune*, August 3, 1928; "The True Facts About the Allen-A Dispute."

17. *Kenosha Evening News*, February 15, 1928.

18. *Ibid.*

19. *Milwaukee Journal*, February 16, 1928; interview with Dorothy Stella, October 20, 1982. Ms. Stella, a striking topper, was married to one of the strike leaders, "Butch" Johnson, at the time of the dispute.

20. *Kenosha Evening News*, February 16, 1928.

21. *Ibid.*

22. *Ibid.*, February 20, 1928.

23. *Ibid.*, February 27, 1928; *Seventh Annual Report for the City of Kenosha, Wisconsin, for the Year Ending December 31, 1928* (Kenosha, 1929), 22.

24. Interview with Dorothy Stella; interview with Elva Mitchell.

25. *The Hosiery Worker*, August 2, March 1, 1928.

26. *Ibid.*

27. *Kenosha Evening News*, March 5, 1928.

28. *Ibid.*, March 8, 1928.

29. *Milwaukee Journal*, March 9, 1928.

30. *Ibid.*

31. *Kenosha Evening News*, March 16, 19, 29, 1928; *The Hosiery Worker*, April 2, 1928.

32. *Kenosha Evening News*, April 24, 1928; *Telegraph Courier*, April 26, 1928; *Milwaukee Journal*, April 24, 1928.

33. *Kenosha Evening News*, October 11, 1928.

Darryl Holter, "Labor Spies and Union-Busting." From Holter, "Labor Spies
and Union-Busting in Wisconsin, 1890–1940," *Wisconsin Magazine of History*, 68
(Summer 1985).

1. This is an expanded version of a paper presented at the North American Labor History Conference at Wayne State University in Detroit, Michigan, in October 1983. I would like to thank Gary Fink and Patrick Maney for their comments on an earlier version of this article.

2. Harold Newton, "The First Convention of the Wisconsin State Federation of Labor (WSFL)," in Wisconsin State AFL-CIO, *Labor History and Stories*, Book 2 (mimeograph, 1975).

3. *Wisconsin Laws* of 1895, Chapter 163. In the aftermath of Homestead, two congressional committees investigated the use of industrial detectives. See U.S. Congress, Senate, Committee on Labor and Education, *Investigation in relation to*

the employment for private purposes of armed bodies of men, or detectives, in connection with differences between workers and employers (52nd Congress, 2 session, Senate Report 1280, Washington, 1893) and U.S. Congress, House, Judiciary Committee, *The Employment of Pinkerton Detectives* (52 Congress, 2 session, House Report 2447, Washington, 1893).

4. Thomas Gavett, *Development of the Labor Movement in Milwaukee* (Madison, 1965), 88-89.

5. *Social-Democratic Herald* (Milwaukee), January 2, 1904, cited in Gavett, *Development of the Labor Movement*, 119.

6. Morris Friedman, *The Pinkerton's Labor Spy* (New York, 1907).

7. Edward Levinson, *I Break Strikes: The Technique of Pearl L. Bergoff* (New York, 1935), 231-233.

8. Wisconsin State Federation of Labor, *Proceedings of the Annual Convention* (Milwaukee, 1922), 113.

9. Jean Spielman, *The Stool Pidgeon and the Open Shop Movement* (Minneapolis, 1923); Frank L. Palmer, *Spies in Steel: An Expose of Industrial War* (Denver, 1928); and Sidney Howard, *The Labor Spy* (New York, 1924).

10. Leo Huberman, *The Labor Spy Racket* (New York, 1937).

11. Edward Levinson, "The Right to Break Strikes," in *Current History*, 77-82 (February, 1937). See also Clinch Calkins, *Spy Overhead: The Story of Industrial Espionage* (New York, 1938).

12. J. Bernard Hogg, "Public Reaction to Pinkertonism and the Labor Question," in *Pennsylvania History*, 171-199 (January–October, 1944). The same rationale, that detectives preserved order when the *posse comitatus* could not, was stated by Pinkerton representatives when questioned by a federal investigator around 1914. See Frieda Fligelman, "Violence: Notes on Pinkerton's National Detective Agency" (mimeographed, no date), Commission on Industrial Relations, SHSW. Other studies on the Pinkertons reveal very little about the firm's labor activities. See James Horan and Howard Swiggert, *The Pinkerton Story* (New York, 1951); James Horan, *The Pinkertons: The Detective Dynasty that Made History* (New York, 1968); and George O'Toole, *The Private Sector: Private Spies, Rent-a-cops, and the Police-Industrial Complex* (New York, 1978).

13. R. Jeffreys-Jones, "Profit Over Class: A Study of Industrial Espionage," in *Journal of American Studies* (December 1972), 233-248.

14. Thomas Beet [pseud.], "Methods of American Private Detective Agencies," in *Appleton's Magazine* (October, 1906).

15. GT-99 [pseud.], *Labor Spy* (New York, 1937).

16. Wisconsin Department of Regulation and Licensing, "Applications for Private Detectives and Agency Licenses, 1919–1939," Series 1881, Box 1, SHSW.

17. Stephen Meyer has shown how plant managers, industrial detectives, local police, and in-shop informants worked together during the "Red Scare" to weed out militants and union activists. "Red Scare in the Factory: Shop Militants and Factory Spies at Ford, 1917–1920," in *Detroit in Perspective*, 6:21-46 (Fall, 1982).

18. Gertrude Schmidt, "History of Labor Legislation in Wisconsin" (doctoral dissertation, University of Wisconsin, 1930), 314.

19. Gavett, *Development of the Labor Movement*, 117.

20. Federated Trades Council of Milwaukee, March 18, 1903, from Gavett, *Development of the Labor Movement*, 119.

21. Gavett, *ibid.*, 123.

22. Gavett, *ibid.*, 123.

23. Wisconsin State Federation of Labor, *Proceedings of the Annual Convention* (Milwaukee, 1907), 20.

24. *Ibid.*, 29-30.

25. Harold Newton, "Carl Sandburg," in *Labor History and Stories*, Book 1.

26. *Social-Democratic Herald* (Milwaukee), July 22, 1911.

27. Schmidt, "History of Labor Legislation," 310.

28. U.S. Commission on Industrial Relations, *First Annual Report*, October 23, 1914 (Washington, 1914); Graham Adams, Jr., *The Age of Industrial Violence, 1910–1915* (New York, 1966); and Anonymous, "List of Detectives" (1914) in unpublished reports of the Research Division of the Commission on Industrial Relations, Reel P71-1693, SHSW.

29. Elmer A. Beck, *The Sewer Socialists: A History of the Socialist Party of Wisconsin, 1897–1940* (Fennimore, Wisconsin, 1982), 37.

30. Schmidt, "History of Labor Legislation," 314.

31. Wisconsin State Federation of Labor, *Proceedings of the Annual Convention*, (Milwaukee, 1919), 106.

32. *Wisconsin Laws of 1919*, Chapter 444.

33. Gavett, *Development of the Labor Movement*, 126.

34. *Ibid.*, 133.

35. *Ibid.*, 135.

36. *Ibid.*, 139.

37. Wisconsin State Federation of Labor, *Proceedings of the Annual Convention* (Milwaukee, 1920), 50-51.

38. Schmidt, "History of Labor Legislation," 313-314.

39. Wisconsin State Federation of Labor, *Proceedings of the Annual Convention* (Milwaukee, 1921), 90.

40. Wisconsin State Federation of Labor, *Proceedings of the Annual Convention* (Milwaukee, 1923), 89.
41. Wisconsin State Federation of Labor, *Proceedings of the Annual Convention* (Milwaukee, 1925). 70-71.
42. *Ibid.*, 95-96.
43. Schmidt, "History of Labor Legislation," 316.
44. *Wisconsin Laws of 1925*, Chapter 289.
45. Wisconsin State Federation of Labor, *Proceedings of the Annual Convention* (Milwaukee, 1926), 79.
46. August Scherr, "Results of the 1925 Law Regulating Detective Agencies in Wisconsin" (mimeographed, 1926), Legislative Reference Bureau, Madison, Wisconsin.
47. Beck, *Sewer Socialists,* 107.
48. U.S. Senate, Subcommittee of the Committee on Education and Labor, *Senate Investigation of Violations of Free Speech and Rights of Labor,* Part 2, p. 507, quoted in a letter from subcommittee counsel Daniel F. Margolies to Paul Bau of Milwaukee, in the Edwin E. Witte Papers, Box 175, SHSW.
49. *Milwaukee Leader*, June 25, 1927.
50. Milwaukee Employers' Council, "Freedom and Employment: Members Supplement," August 1927 and May 1928 (Milwaukee).

Frederick I. Olson, "Organized Labor and Socialism: Two Views." From Olson, "The Socialist Party and the Union in Milwaukee, 1900-1912," *Wisconsin Magazine of History* (Winter 1960-1961), 110-116.

1. Marvin Wachman, *History of the Social-Democratic Party of Wisconsin, 1897-1910* (Urbana, 1945), 39-40; Milwaukee Federated Trades Council, "Minutebook," October 15, 1902; *Social Democratic Herald*, October 31, 1902, March 5, 1904, and March 23, 1907.
2. Wachman, *History of the Social Democratic Party*, 11, 39.
3. Herbert F. Margulies, *The Decline of the Progressive Movement in Wisconsin* (Madison, 1968), 153.
4. Robert C. Nesbit, *Wisconsin: A History* (Madison, 1973), 522.
5. Victor Berger, *Voice and Pen of Victor Berger: Congressional Speeches and Editorials* (Milwaukee, 1929), 699.

Robert Ozanne, "The Paperworkers' Fight for Saturday Night." From Ozanne, *The Labor Movement in Wisconsin* (Madison, 1984).

1. Charles N. Glaab and Lawrence H. Larsen, *Factories in the Valley: Neenah-Menasha, 1870-1915* (Madison, 1969), 225.
2. James I. Clark, "The Wisconsin Pulp and Paper Industry,"*Chronicles of Wisconsin*, Vol. 15 (Madison, 1955-1956), 6-8.
3. Glaab and Larsen, *Factories in the Valley*, p. 225.
4. Kaukauna *Times*, May 20, 1892.
5. Matthew Burns Papers, manuscript entitled "History of the International Brotherhood of Paper Makers," (1966), p. 2. Matthew Burns Papers, SHSW.
6. Glaab and Larsen, *Factories in the Valley*, 245.
7. Appleton *Weekly Post*, November 21, 1901.
8. *Ibid.*, November 21, 1901.
9. *Ibid.*, December 5, 1901.
10. *Ibid.*
11. Glaab and Larsen, *Factories in the Valley*, 248; Appleton *Evening Crescent*, December 10, 1901.
12. Appleton *Weekly Post*, December 12, 1901.
13. Oshkosh *Northwestern*, January 13, 1902. The full names of these mills are: John Strange Paper Company, George A. Whiting Company, Menasha Paper Company, and Winnebago Paper Company.
14. *Ibid*., January 16, 1902; Menasha *Evening Breeze*, January 13, 1902.
15. Neenah *Daily Times*, January 17, 1902.
16. Oshkosh *Northwestern*, January 21, 22, 1902; *Paper Makers' Journal*, 1 (June 1902), 5.
17. Oshkosh *Northwestern*, April 16, 1902; Burns, "History of the International Brotherhood of Paper Makers."
18. Neenah *Daily Times*, January 6, 1902; Oshkosh *Northwestern*, January 20, 1902.
19. Appleton *Weekly Post*, March 27, 1902.
20. *Ibid.*
21. Kaukauna *Times*, April 11, 18, 23, 1902.
22. Neenah *Times*, April 29, 1902.
23. Stevens Point *Daily Journal*, January 14, 1902; *Wood County Reporter*, February 6, 13, 1902; *Paper Makers' Journal*, 1 (December 1901), 22.
24. *Paper Makers' Journal*, 1 (May 1902), 4.
25. Stevens Point *Daily Journal*, February 7, 1902.
26. Appleton *Crescent*, April 5, 1902; *Wood County Reporter*, April 10, 1902.
27. *Wood County Reporter*, February 27, 1902; *Paper Makers' Journal*, 1 (February 1902), 22; 1 (March 1902), 6; 1 (April 1902), 22.

28. *Wood County Reporter*, February 27, 1902; Stevens Point *Daily Journal*, February 25, 1902.
29. Stevens Point *Daily Journal*, February 25, 1902.
30. *Wood County Reporter*, April 19, 1902.
31. Stevens Point *Daily Journal*, March 3, 1902.
32. *Ibid.*, March 15, 17, 1902.
33. *Wood County Reporter*, April, 1902.
34. Wausau *Pilot*, April 8, 1902; Stevens Point *Daily Journal*, April 3, 7, 1902.
35. *Wood County Reporter*, April 17, 1902; *Paper Makers' Journal*, 2 (December 1902), 21; 2 (January 1903), 21; 2 (February 1903), 22; 2 (March 1903), 21.
36. Eau Claire *Leader*, April 24, 1902.
37. *Paper Makers' Journal*, 1 (June 1902), 18.
38. *Ibid.*, 1 (November 1902) 20; Eau Clair *Telegram*, May 2, 1902.
39. Menasha *Evening Breeze*, September 8, 1902.
40. *Paper Makers' Journal*, 2 (March 1903), 1.
41. Menasha *Evening Breeze*, April 18, 1903.
42. Kaukauna *Times*, February 13, 1903.
43. Menasha *Evening Breeze*, April 17, 1903.
44. Wisconsin State Board of Arbitration, *Seventh Biennial Report, 1904–1906* (typescript, 1908), 14.
45. Kaukauna *Times*, April 24, 1903.
46. Wisconsin State Board of Arbitration, *Seventh Biennial Report,* 15.
47. *Paper Makers' Journal*, 2 (September 1903), 7; 3 (June 1904), 46.
48. *Ibid.*, 3 (June 1904), 46.
49. *Ibid.*, 3 (June 1904), 46; 2 (November 1903), 22; 3 (September 1904), 29.
50. Oshkosh *Northwestern*, May 3, 1904.
51. *Ibid.*, May 31, 1904.
52. *Ibid.*, June 1, 2, 1904.
53. *Ibid.*, June 4, 1904.
54. *Ibid.*, June 6, 1904; Kaukauna *Times*, June 10, 1904.
55. Wisconsin State Board of Arbitration, *Seventh Biennial Report,* 30; Oshkosh *Northwestern*, June 4, 11, 1904.
56. Oshkosh *Northwestern*, June 15, 1904; Menasha *Citizen*, June 20, 1904.
57. Oshkosh *Northwestern*, June 21, 24, 1904.
58. Appleton *Evening Crescent*, August 15, 1904.
59. Oshkosh *Northwestern*, July 7, 8, 1904.
60. Menasha *Citizen*, July 5, 20, August 23, 1904; Neenah *Daily Times*, June 29, July 8, 1904.
61. Menasha *Citizen*, August 1, 1904.
62. Appleton *Evening Crescent*, August 1, 6, 15, 1904.
63. *Ibid.*, August 15, 1904.
64. *Paper Makers' Journal*, 4 (June 1905), 11.
65. *Ibid.*, 4 (June 1905), 53.
66. *Ibid.*, 4 (May 1905), 25.
67. *Ibid.*, 5 (April 1906), 16, 18.
68. *Ibid.*, 6 (February 1907), 32.

SECTION 3

Darryl Holter, "Industrial Unionism in Milwaukee." From Holter, "Sources of CIO Success: The New Deal Years in Milwaukee," *Labor History* v.29, n.2 (1988).

1. A brief summary of this article was presented at the North American Labor History Conference in Detroit in October 1985. My thanks to Daniel Nelson for comments.
2. The best article on the historical literature is Robert H. Zieger, "Toward the History of the CIO: A Bibliographical Report," *Labor History*, 26 (1985). One of the best recent interpretive essays on the history of the CIO is David Brody, "The CIO after 50 Years: A Historical Reckoning," *Dissent* (Fall 1985). Some of the best industry-wide studies of the impact of the CIO include Daniel Nelson, "Origins of the Sit-Down Era: Worker Militancy and Innovation in the Rubber Industry, 1924–1938," *Labor History*, 23 (1982), Sidney Fine, *Sit-Down: The General Motors Strike of 1936–1937* (Ann Arbor, 1969); Raymond Boryczka, "Militancy and Factionalism in the United Auto Workers Union, 1937–1941," *Maryland Historian*, 8 (1977); Daniel Leab, *A Union of Individuals: The Formation of the American Newspaper Guild, 1933–1936* (New York, 1970); Ronald Schatz, *The Electrical Workers: A History of Labor at General Electric and Westinghouse, 1923–1960* (Urbana, 1983); John N. Schacht, "Toward Industrial Unionism: Bell Telephone Workers and Company Unions, 1919–1937," *Labor History*, 16 (1975); James Baughman, "Classes and Company Towns: Legends of the 1937 Little Steel Strike," *Ohio History*, 87 (1978); Joshua Freeman, "Catholics, Communists and Republicans: Irish Workers and the Organization of the Transport Workers Union," in Michael Frisch and Daniel Walkowitz, eds., *Working Class America: Essays on Labor, Community, and American Society* (Urbana, 1983); Jerry Lembcke, *One Union in Wood* (Urbana, 1984). On the CIO during the war years see Nelson Lichtenstein, *Labor's War at Home: The CIO in World War II* (Urbana, 1982).

3. Melvin Dubofsky and Warren Van Tine, *John L. Lewis: A Biography* (Chicago, 1977); John Barnard, *Walter Reuther and the Rise of the Auto Workers* (Boston, 1983); Walter Galenson, *The CIO Challenge to the AFL: A History of the American Labor Movement, 1935–1941* (Cambridge, MA, 1961); Edward Levinson, *Labor on the March* (New York, 1938); Irving Bernstein, *Turbulent Years: A History of the American Workers, 1933–1941* (Los Angeles, 1969); David Brody, *Workers in Industrial America* (New York, 1980); and James Green, *World of the Worker: Labor in Twentieth Century America* (New York, 1980); Christopher Tomlins, *The State and the Unions: Labor Relations, Law, and the Organized Labor Movement in America, 1880–1960* (New York, 1985); Theda Skocpol, "Political Response to Capitalist Crisis: Neo-Marxist Theories of the State and the Case of the New Deal," *Politics and Society*, 2 (1980); Frances Piven and Richard Cloward, *Poor People's Movements* (New York, 1979).

4. The most useful overview on labor in Milwaukee is Thomas W. Gavett, *Development of the Labor Movement in Milwaukee* (Madison, 1965).

5. In 1899 they gained a majority on the executive Board of the FTC and began to shape the movement in new directions. They disagreed with national AFL policies on several issues including unemployment compensation, third parties, and the value of organizing on an industrial basis. On the Milwaukee Socialists, see Elmer A. Beck, *The Sewer Socialists: A History of the Socialist Party in Wisconsin* (Fennimore, Wisconsin, 1982) and Frederick I. Olson, *The Milwaukee Socialists, 1897–1941* (doctoral dissertation, Harvard University, 1952).

6. *Milwaukee Leader*, June 26, 1933.

7. *Ibid.*, June 8, 1933.

8. *Ibid.*, June 17, 1933.

9. *Milwaukee Sentinel*, Aug. 18, 1933.

10. Wisconsin State Federation of Labor, *Officers Reports* (Milwaukee, 1934–1936). Clerical workers formed an Office Workers union and received a directly-affiliated AFL charter. See Alice Holz, "The Early Years: Office Employees International Union" (unpublished paper, Dec. 1987).

11. Gavett, *Development of the Labor Movement*, 166. Herman Seide reported that an FTC membership drive launched in July 1933 had signed up 15,000 new members by the end of the year, bringing the total membership to 35,000 by the end of 1933. *Wisconsin Labor, 1939*, 41.

12. Letter from Jacob Friedrick to William Green, June 15, 1935, Milwaukee Federated Trades Council Papers, Box 5, Area Research Center, Milwaukee.

13. *Milwaukee Sentinel*, Jan. 15, 1937.

14. Herman Seide, "The Lindemann and Hoverson Strike at Milwaukee, Wisconsin," report to William Green, Jan. 31, 1936, International Association of Machinists, District 10, Papers, Box 3, Lindemann-Hoverson file, State Historical Society of Wisconsin.

15. "O.J. Jirikowic, "Special Meeting of the Lindemann and Hoverson Strikers," Jan. 19, 1937, *ibid.*

16. A.O. Wharton to O.A. Jirikowic, March 13, 1934, *ibid.*

17. Gavett, *Development of the Labor Movement*, 157; *Milwaukee Leader*, April 5, 1937.

18. Letter from Otto Jirikowic to A.O. Wharton, March 13, 1934, International Association of Machinists, District 10, Papers, Box 4, SHSW.

19. CP members and supporters were active in Seaman Body. An effective young CP organizer, Eugene Dennis, arrived in April 1935 to lead a well-organized effort by radical workers to gain a foothold in Milwaukee area unions. The federal labor unions, noted Dennis, were particularly ripe targets for organizing (Gene Dennis, "Strike Wave Rises in Wisconsin," *Wisconsin Voice of Labor*, May 1, 1935). See also Peggy Dennis, *The Autobiography of an American Communist* (Berkeley 1977), 92-95; and Bert Cochran, *Labor and Communism* (Princeton, 1977), 67.

20. American Federation of Labor, Records, 1881–1953, Series 7, Box 19, folder 1B, SHSW; Theodore Mueller, "Milwaukee Workers," 30; Gavett, *Development of the Labor Movement*, 162.

21. Letter from Otto Jirikowic to H. W. Brown, September 20, 1934, IAM District 10, Papers, Box 4.

22. Irving Brotslaw, "The Other UAW: Cabe Jewell and the UAW-AFL" (unpublished manuscript, 1975), 24-25.

23. Stephen Meyer, "The State and the Workplace: New Deal Labor Policy, the UAW and Allis Chalmers in the 1930s and 1940s" (unpublished paper, 1984) and "Technology and the Workplace: Skilled and Production Workers at Allis-Chalmers, 1900–1941" (unpublished paper, 1984). Harold Christoffel, letter to the author, March 1, 1988.

24. Robert Ozanne, *The Labor Movement in Wisconsin* (Madison, 1984), 83. Joe Broderick, "History of Allied Industrial Workers Local 232: Briggs and Stratton, 1930–1950" (unpublished paper, May 1987).

25. *CIO News* (Wisconsin Edition), Sept. 3, 1937.

26. *Ibid.* June 5, 1937.

27. *Milwaukee Leader*, April 5, 7, 1937.

28. "Several local labor leaders, such as Friedrick, were born in Europe. Children of subscribers to the *Milwaukee Leader* were known to complain that the newspaper did not have the same comics as the capitalist newspapers." Alice Holz, "An

Insider's View of the *Milwaukee Leader*," presentation at the 4th annual conference of the Wisconsin Labor History Society, Milwaukee, April 1985.

29. Several CIO leaders, including Harold Christoffel, had been active in the Young Socialists. Two seminar papers by a young activist, Robert Repas, reflect a pro-Socialist, anti-Communist interpretation of the CIO's success: "The Socialist Party of Milwaukee, 1932–1938" (unpublished paper, University of Wisconsin–Milwaukee, May, 1943) and "Analysis of a Strike" (unpublished paper, University of Wisconsin–Milwaukee, June 1944).

30. Joe Trotter, Jr., *Black Milwaukee: The Making of an Industrial Proletariat, 1915–1945* (Urbana, 1985), 163-4.

31. "Single People Demand WPA Jobs," (Aug., 1938), Milwaukee County Industrial Union Council Minutes, Box 1, Area Research Center, Milwaukee.

32. On the sit-downs, see Nelson, "Origins of the Sit-Down Era," 169-186.

33. On the sit-down movement in Milwaukee, see Darryl Holter, "Sit-down Strikes in Milwaukee, 1937–1938," *Milwaukee History* (Summer 1986), 58-64. The list of sit-down strikes in the Milwaukee area was compiled from the records of the Wisconsin Labor Relations Board, 1937–1939 (Wisconsin Employment Relations Commission, *Closed Labor Dispute Files*, 1937–1939, Series 827, 40 boxes, SHSW), Mueller, and the three daily newspapers.

34. *Milwaukee Leader*, May 2, 1937.

35. *Ibid.* April 15, 1937.

36. *Ibid.* April 22, 23, 1937.

37. *Ibid.* April 27, 28, 1937.

38. *Milwaukee Journal*, May 6, 1937.

39. Wisconsin Employment Relations Commission, Case 348; *CIO News*, Sept. 10, 1937. A second sit-down strike erupted a few weeks later against an attempt to launch a company union.

40. *Ibid.*, Cases 672, 692 and 716.

41. David Brody, *Workers in Industrial America*, 103-4 and Green 158-9.

42. David Montgomery, *Workers Control in America* (New York, 1979), 165 and Frances Fox Piven and Richard Cloward, *Poor People's Movements* (New York, 1979), 153-161. For a survey of various theories regarding New Deal policy and the state, see Skocpol.

43. Christopher Tomlins, *The State and the Unions Labor Relations, Law, and the Organized Labor Movement in America, 1880–1960* (Cambridge, 1985).

44. Milwaukee Association of Commerce, "Boncel Ordinance to Close Industry," Sept. 27, 1935, IAM District 10 Papers, Box 3.

45. Charles W. Ogg, "The Boncel Ordinance: An Unusual Solution to Labor Strife," unpublished seminar paper, University of Wisconsin–Milwaukee, Dec. 1983.

46. *Milwaukee Leader*, April 23, 1937.

47. Gordon Haferbecker, *Wisconsin Labor Laws* (Madison, 1958), 161.

48. Wisconsin Labor Relations Board, *Report Covering the Period April 28, 1937 to November 30 1938* (Legislative Reference Bureau, Madison, 1938), 1-15.

49. Paul Krakowski, "Press Treatment of Wisconsin in Labor Issues" (master's thesis, University of Wisconsin, Madison, 1947), 87.

50. *Kenosha Labor*, Jan. 15, 1937.

51. *The Milwaukee Journal* warned against "the combination of Progressive politics and labor politics," adding that "labor will suffer further in public opinion if, just because it has the power, it puts a one-sided statute on the books" (Feb. 10, 1937). After failing in the 1935 session, the bill passed in April 1937, but only after a marathon debate and the defeat of 60 crippling amendments.

52. Haferbecker, *Wisconsin Labor Laws*, 162-167.

53. "The present dissension in the ranks of labor is a temporary condition," wrote WSFL president Henry Ohl, Jr. "It is inevitable that it will be dissipated by the driving force of sense and reason." *Wisconsin Labor, 1937*, 9.

54. Gavett, *Development of the Labor Movement*, 160-161.

55. WSFL, *Proceedings* (Milwaukee, 1936), 76 and Krakowski, 15-16.

56. *Milwaukee Leader*, April 22, 30, 1937.

57. Membership figures are based on per capita tax paid to the WSFL. WSFL, *Officers Reports 1934–1938*.

58. *CIO News*, March 26, 1938.

59. Three Veteran CIO leaders, Kenneth Clark (SWOC organizer, 1938), Carl Greipentrog (UAW organizer, 1937), and Victor Cooks (Wisconsin Industrial Union Local 1 Organizer, 1932) recently emphasized the CIO's role as a catalyst for progressive political activists and militant workers of many political persuasions ("Industrial Unionism in Wisconsin," Wisconsin Labor History Society Conference, Racine, May 1985).

60. James C. Foster, *The Union Politic: The CIO Political Action Committee* (Detroit, 1975). Frank Zeidler summed up the situation in the following terms: "The AFL was not prepared to take over organizing industrial unions because of trade union bureaucracy, the CIO was hindered from fully displacing the AFL across the board by the early Communist leadership, and the Socialists were ineffective in the face of the popularity of FDR, the movement of members into the Democratic party, and their relatively small numbers in the CIO." Letter to the author, December 1, 1985.

Joseph M. Kelly, "Organizing the Unemployed: Case Strike of 1936." From Kelly, "Growth of Organized Labor," in Nicholas C. Burckel, ed., *Racine: Growth and Change in a Wisconsin County* (Racine, 1977).

1. *Racine Day*, 15 March 1935, 29 March 1935, 5 April 1935, 12 April 1935, 3 May 1935, 24 May 1935; interview with Frank Sahorske, Local 180 leader, 7 July 1976.
2. *Racine Day*, 19 April 1935, 26 April 1935, 3 May 1935, 17 May 1935, 24 May 1935, 31 May 1935.
3. J.I. Case offer to the bargaining committee, 29 May 1935; *Racine Day*, 31 May 1935, 7 June 1935.
4. W. A. Wormet, "Report on Labor-Management Relationships at the J. I. Case Co.," SC 52, Area Research Center, University of Wisconsin-Parkside, 5-6; *Racine Day*; 4 December 1936, 1 January 1937; the company union president specifically mentioned David Dubinsky, who had nothing to do with the UAW but was connected with the International Ladies Garment Workers Union.
5. *Racine Day*, 11 September 1936, 18 September 1936, 25 September 1936, 2 October 1936, 9 October 1936, 16 October 1936; Wormet, 6-7; interview with Sahorske; Wormet, p. 7; Racine Day, 23 October through 4 December 1936.
6. *Racine Day*, 23 October through 4 December 1936; interview with Sahorske.
7. Report of T. Lucas, 30 December 1936, in D.P.W. D.P.A., Co. Admin. file, 1932-45, Racine, Box 108, 42/5/3; *Racine Day*, 6 November 1936, 13 November 1936; 20 November 1936.
8. Interview with Sahorske; *Racine Day*, 20 November 1936.
9. Racine Day, 18 December 1936, 24 December 1936; interview with Sahorske; interview with Wendt; *Racine Day*, 12 February 1937.
10. Clausen had the letter published frequently in the *Racine Journal Times* during the 1945–47 strike; see, for example, J.I. Case ad, 17 January 1946; for information concerning the validity of the letter, see "Matter of J.I. Case Company," 71, NLRB 1145 (1946) and *UAW Local 180 v. J.I. Case Company*, Wisconsin Supreme Court, 1947 (Wis. 26, N. W. [(2d)] 305); *Racine Day*, 19 February 1937.

Robert W. Ozanne, "The Farmer-Labor Progressive Federation." From Ozanne, *The Labor Movement in Wisconsin: A History* (Madison, 1984).

1. Lester M. Schmidt, "The Farmer–Labor Progressive Federation: The Study of a 'United Front' Among Wisconsin Liberals, 1934–1941" (Ph.D. dissertation, University of Wisconsin, 1954), 2.
2. *Ibid.*, 17-18.
3. *Ibid.*, 89.
4. *Ibid.*, 50-62.
5. Taft, *Organized Labor*, 384.
6. Schmidt, "The Farmer–Labor Progressive Federation," 84, 176.
7. *Ibid.*, 177-188, 211.

James J. Lorence, "The Politics of Fighting Unemployment." From Lorence, *Gerald Boileau, The Workers Alliance, and the Unemployed: Progressivism and the Wisconsin Left, 1937-1938* (University of Missouri, Columbia, 1994).

1. Harvey Klehr, *The Heyday of American Communism: The Depression Decade* (New York, 1984), 289-90. The most complete studies of WAA are Wilma Liebman, "The Workers Alliance of America: The Organization of Relief Recipients" (senior thesis, Barnard College, 1971) and James E. Sargent, "Roosevelt, Lasser, and the Workers' Alliance," paper presented at the Annual Meeting of the Organization of American Historians, Philadelphia, April, 1982. The Communist role in the Workers Alliance is briefly discussed in Peggy Dennis, *The Autobiography of an American Communist: A Personal View of a Political Life, 1925-1975* (Westport, Connecticut, 1977), 106, and Thomas R. Amlie, *Let's Look at the Record* (Madison, 1950), 332; additional evidence may be found in Sigmund Eisenscher to James J. Lorence, July 7, 1984; Frank P. Ziedler to Lorence, July 23, 1984; Walter Uphoff to Lorence, August 9, 1984; Alice H. Holz to James Lorence, August 14, 1984; interview (telephone), Emil Luchterhand, Unity, July 14, 1984; David Lasser, "Why I Quit the Workers Alliance," *New York Post*, August 7, 1940; Gavett, *Development of the Labor Movement in Milwaukee*, 178. The Communist Party's perspective on the importance of organizational work within the Workers Alliance is detailed in *Party Organizer* (January, 1937), 25-8. For a full statement of the Alliance program and its efforts to influence Roosevelt in 1936, see "Program of the Workers Alliance" and "Convention Demands Real Program for the Unemployed," Envelope 1, Workers Alliance of America Papers, SHSW. WAA support for a farmer-labor party is detailed in David Lasser, "Report to the National Executive Board of WAA," September 12, 1936, pp. 26-9, 1936 File, in Herbert Benjamin Papers, in possession of Ernest Benjamin, Bethesda, Maryland.
2. *New York Times*, January 10, 1937; *Capital Times*, January 10, 1937; *Project Councilor*, January 14, 1937; *Daily Worker*, January 14, 1937.
3. *New York Times*, January 24, 1937; U.S. Congress, House, Subcommittee of the Committee on Appropriations, "Hearings, on Emergency Relief Appropriation Act of 1937," 75th Cong., 1st Sess., 1937, pp. 430-31; FBI Records, File #61-7559; *Project Councilor*, January 27, 1937; *New York Times*, January 18, 1937; Amlie

Newsletter, *Waupaca County Post*, January 21, 1937; Boileau and Charles G. Binderup to Colleague, January 14, 1937, Box 41, Thomas Amlie Papers, SHSW; *Minnesota Leader*, January 23, 1937; Sargent, "Roosevelt, Lasser, and the Workers' Alliance," 9. The specific demands prepared for the unsuccessful Workers Alliance attempt to see Roosevelt are detailed in Lasser to Roosevelt, January 15, 1937, President's Official File #391, Franklin D. Roosevelt Papers.
4. *Congressional Record*, 75th Cong., 1st Sess., January 26, 1937, pp. 439, 453, 455, 469; *Wausau Record-Herald*, January 30, 1937.
5. Italics added for emphasis. Herbert Benjamin, "Long Range Program and Long Range Prospects for the Unemployed Movement," March-April, 1937, Benjamin Papers, 1938 File; "Report of the Secretary-Treasurer of WAA of New York," p. 17; *Project Councilor*, April 8, 1937.
6. *Wausau Record-Herald*, April 3, 1937; *Milwaukee Journal*, April 25, 1937, Scrapbook #4, Box 4K145, Maury Maverick Papers, Barker Texas History Center, Austin, Texas.
7. Interview with Maurice Pasch, October 19, 1984, Madison; Federal Bureau of Investigation, Reference File, Gerald J. Boileau, Report, December 14, 1940; Benjamin, "Long Range Program"; *Daily Worker*, April 6, 20, 1937.
8. Daniel W. Hoan to Frank N. Trager, March 22, 1937, Box 12, Daniel W. Hoan Papers, Milwaukee County Historical Society (hereafter MCHS); Henry Rutz to Amlie, March 2, 1937, Box 42, Amlie Papers; Interview, Paul Alfonsi, Minocqua, Wisconsin; Gavett, *Development of the Labor Movement in Milwaukee*, 162-5; Lester F. Schmidt, "The Farmer-Labor Progressive Federation: The Study of a 'United Front' Movement Among Wisconsin Liberals, 1934–1941" (doctoral dissertation, University of Wisconsin, 1954), 195-6; for discussion of CIO initiative in Wisconsin, see Darryl Holter, "Sources of CIO Success: the New Deal Years in Milwaukee." Labor History, 29 (Spring 1988), esp. 211-15.
9. Sigmund Eisenscher to James J. Lorence, July 20, 1984; Peggy Dennis, *The Autobiography of an American Communist*, 104; note card, March 20, 1937, Box 7, Eugene and Peggy Dennis Papers, SHSW; Russell Rattel to Harlan Fenske, March 10, 1937, Box 3, Farmer-Labor Progressive Federation Papers, MCHS.
10. Rutz to Boileau, March 12, 1937; Rutz to Secretaries of County Units, March 3, 1937, Box 42, Amlie Papers; Frank P. Zeidler to Lorence, July 23, 1984; Eisenscher to Lorence, July 20, 1984; Interview, Peggy Dennis, July 6, 1984, Milwaukee. The FBI later became interested in Boileau's role in the Peoples' Conference, which it treated as a subversive gathering. "Internal Security Report," Washington, D.C. FBI Records, "See" Reference File, Gerald J. Boileau, Report #100-1198.
11. "Proceedings of the Wisconsin Conference on Farm and Labor Legislation," April 3-4, 1937, Box 301, Ernest Lundeen Papers, Hoover Institution on War, Revolution and Peace, Palo Alto, California; *Capital Times*, April 9, 1937; *Wausau Record–Herald*, April 5, 1937.
12. "Proceedings of the Wisconsin Conference on Farm and Labor Legislation"; Wausau *Record–Herald*, April 5, 1937.
13. "Proceedings of the Wisconsin Conference on Farm and Labor Legislation"; *Daily Worker*, April 8, 1937; Dennis, *The Autobiography of an American Communist*, 104; Eisenscher to Lorence, July 20, 1984.
14. *Milwaukee Leader*, June 25, 1937; *Daily Worker*, June 26, 1937.
15. Boileau to Ernest Boileau, June 14, 1937, Correspondence File, 1937, Gerald J. Boileau Papers, SHSW; *Daily Worker*, June 26, 1937.
16. *Congressional Record*, 75th Cong., 1st Sess., 1937, April 29, 1937, p. 3983.
17. *Ibid.*, pp. 3981-3; *Wausau Record–Herald*, April 30, 1937; *New York Times*, April 30, 1937; *Labor*, May 11, 1937.
18. *Congressional Digest*, June, 1937, pp. 190-91; *Peoples' Press*, May 22, 1937; May 15, 1937; *Daily Worker*, May 21, 24 1937; *Capital Times*, May 23, 1937; Stanley A. Golden to Franklin D. Roosevelt, File 190, Box 274, WPA Central Files, Record Group 69, National Archives; Wilbur Fulks to Henry G. Teigan, May 20, 1937, and Teigan to Fulks, May 21, 1937, both in Box 16, Henry G. Teigan Papers, Box 16, Minnesota Historical Society, St. Paul; E.A. Scheffler to Lundeen, April 28, 1937, Mrs. Tom Robinson to Lundeen, May 12, 1937, and Dwayne W. Wolfe to Lundeen, May 1, 1937, all in Box 112, Lundeen Papers; Ray Cooke to Amlie, May 14, 1937, Box 45, Amlie Papers. For evidence of the economy bloc's opposition to relief appropriations during the relief battle see James E. Sargent, "Woodrum's Economy Bloc: The Attack on the WPA, 1937–1939," *Virginia Magazine* 93 (April 1985), 180; James T. Patterson, *Congressional Conservatism and the New Deal: the Growth of the Conservative Coalition in Congress, 1933–1939* (Lexington, 1967), 171-3. The Roosevelt administration's resistance to WAA pleas is discussed in Sargent, "Roosevelt, Lasser and the Unemployed," 9-10.
19. *Minnesota Leader*, May 29, 1937, p. 3; *Congressional Record*, 75th Cong., 1st Sess., 1937, June 1, 1937, pp. 5226-7; Sargent, "Woodrum's Economy Bloc," 180; Corrington Gill to New York Artists' Union, May 19, 1937, File 190, Box 274, RG 69WPA Central Files, National Archives.

Robert H. Zieger, "Building the Union at Ray-O-Vac in Madison." From Zieger, *Madison's Battery Workers, 1934-1952: A History of Federal Labor Union 19587* (Ithaca, 1977).

1. These impressions of the ethnic and social background of Ray-O-Vac workers were gleaned from interviews conducted in January 1975. Surnames in the records of the union are almost without exception German, Scandinavian, and English. See also James Paul Collins, "Real Property and Low Income Area Survey of Madison, Wisconsin" (masters thesis, University of Wisconsin, 1941), 17, and Daniel Herschel Kruger, "A Study of Collective Bargaining in Wisconsin" (doctoral dissertation, University of Wisconsin, 1954), 45-46, 179. In 1930, for example, Madison's foreign born constituted only 9.1 percent of the population, compared, for example, with Racine's 21.2 percent.

2. Interview by the author with David Sigman, June 13, 1976; clippings in Wisconsin State Federation of Labor Papers, Box 1, SHSW. (Hereinafter cited as WSFL Papers.)

3. Sigman interview; interview by the author with Gregory Wallig, June 13, 1976; Harold J. Newton, "Profiles of Past and Present Labor Leaders–Henry Ohl, Jr. (1917–1940)," *Wisconsin Labor–Bicentennial Edition* (Milwaukee, 1975–1976), 39; clippings, WSFL Papers, Box 1.

4. Marion Shaw particularly noted McCutchin's tireless efforts. *Ray-O-Lite News*, April 1925, carries a brief biography of him in recognition of his promotion to foreman. McCutchin's role and company harassment of him is revealed in a series of complaints, reports, letters, and rulings in Docket no. 241, National Labor Relations Board Records (RG 25), NLB 1933–34 and NLRB 1934–35 Regional Records, Region X (Chicago), National Archives, Federal Records Center, Suitland, Maryland. The words quoted in this paragraph appear in Myrna Auringer to Joseph Vejlupek, January 17, 1935, Box 1, FLU 19587 Papers, SHSW.

5. The best source for an explanation of the difficulties and high attrition rate of the federal labor unions is AFL Papers, Series 7, Strikes and Agreements File, American Federation of Labor Records, SHSW. (Hereinafter cited as AFL-Series 7.) For commentary, see Harry A. Millis and Royal Montgomery, *Organized Labor* (New York, 1945), 203-9, and James O. Morris, *Conflict within the AFL: A Study of Craft versus Industrial Unionism, 1901–1938* (Ithaca, 1958), 59-63, 146-47, 151-59. The words quoted in this paragraph are contained in David Saposs to Evans Clark, April 6, 1934, Box 3, David J. Saposs Papers, SHSW.

6. Most union veterans interviewed mentioned work force characteristics noted in this paragraph. Membership figures are contained in AFL report, May 4, 1936, AFL-Series 7, Box 27. Skepticism regarding the 80 percent figure is based on the fact that in 1935 there were about 700 production workers. Although no doubt organization grew between 1935 and 1937, there is no documented proof that the local had achieved such a high percentage, especially since the AFL based its calculations on monthly averages, always a lower figure than the most recent monthly report in a growing union. For some suggestive observations on the reasons for successful organization among rank-and-file workers, see E. Wight Bakke, "To Join or Not to Join," in Bakke, Clark Kerr, and Charles Anrod, eds., *Unions, Management, and the Public: Readings and Text*, 3d ed. (New York, 1967), 85-92.

7. Interview with Max Onsager by the author, Jan. 7, 1975.

8. Sol Reist to Carl Steffensen, acting secretary, Chicago Regional Labor Board, May 24, 1934, Docket 241, NLRB Records. Docket 241 contains the correspondence and rulings on this case, which resulted in William McCutchin's reinstatement without back pay.

9. H.E. Page to W. C. Holden, August 26, 1935, Box 36, American Federation of Labor Papers, Series 4, Industry Reference Files, SHSW. Interviews by the author with William Skaar (Jan. 15, 1975), Evelyn Gotzion (June 13, 1976), Byron Buchholz (Jan. 7, 1975), David Sigman, and Gregory Wallig.

10. The pattern of caution and militancy became clear in conversations with almost all of the veteran unionists interviewed.

11. William McCutchin and Myrna Auringer to Whom It May Concern, August 31, 1934; same authors to W. W. Cargill, December 12, 1934; Auringer to Joseph F. Vejlupek, January 17, 1935, Box 1, FLU 19587 Papers.

12. Myrna Auringer to Donal Weber, August 14, 1935, *ibid.*; FLU 19587 Minute Books (hereinafter cited as MB), April 16–August 12, 1935; correspondence between L. G. Berigan and William McCutchin, March 22, April 1, April 17, and May 2, 1935, FLU 19587 Papers, Box 1; Auringer to William Green, May 28, 1935, Green to Auringer, June 4, 1935, Green to Sol Reist, June 4, 1935, Auringer to Green, June 16, 1935, Reist to Green, June 18, 1935, Green to Auringer, June 21, 1935, and Green to AFL Representative Paul Smith, June 21, 1935, AFL-Series 7.

13. Robert E. Mythen to Hugh Kerwin, October 2, 1935, Robert E. Mythen "Preliminary Report," September 18, 1935, and "Agreement with Production Employees," dated October 1, 1935, all in United States Conciliation Service Records (RG 280), Federal Records Center, Suitland, Maryland, File 182-716 (hereinafter cited as USCS Records); MB, May 14–October 1, 1935, passim.

14. William McCutchin to William Green, April 8, 1936; W. W. Cargill to McCutchin and to William Skaar, April 9, 1936; W. W. Cargill to McCutchin and to William Skaar, April 9, 1936; Cargill to Employees of Ray-O-Vac, April 13, 1936, all in AFL-Series 7; statement of Cargill, ca. April 15, 1936, and letter from Robert E. Mythen to Hugh Kerwin, April 21, 1936, USCS Records, File 182-1388; MB, April 9–May 14, 1936, passim.

15. Transcripts of these meetings of April 8, 1936—made without the approval of the workers involved—are in USCS Records, File 182-1388.

16. MB, April 13, 14, 1936; transcript of Skaar-Cargill conversation, April 8, 1936, USCS Records, File 182-1388; David Sigman to William Green, April 14, 1936, AFL-Series 7.

17. David Sigman to William Green, April 20, May 1, 5, 15, 1936, AFL-Series 7; MB, April 8–May 15, 1936; Robert E. Mythen to Hugh Kerwin, May 21, 1936, USCS Records, File 182-1388.

18. David Sigman to William Green, May 15, 1936, AFL-Series 7.

19. In view of its subsequent success and militancy over the next several years, there is no reason to doubt Sigman's judgments on the strengthening effect of the 1936 controversy, contained in *ibid.*

20. Sigman to Green, May 15, 1936.

21. Unfortunately, FLU 19587's records, while unusually copious for a local union, do not contain a file of contracts. There is a model contract in *ibid.*, but it contained suggested benefits far beyond those the company was willing to comtemplate in 1936. Contracts for 1937, 1939, and the war years can be seen among the materials in Case No. 111-581-D, Selected Documents from Region VI Case Files, Records of the National War Labor Board (World War II) (Record Group 202), National Archives, Federal Records Center, Suitland, Maryland. The union's minute books, beginning with the entries for the ssummer of 1936, reflect the growing importance of the contract in the mines of union members. By 1938, it was the dominant feature of most meetings, as the membership sought improvements in the original union shop agreement of March 4, 1938. See MB, November 10, 1936; July 23, 1937; May 31, June 24, 1938. Also, interview with Evelyn Gotzion.

22. Lochner radio transcript, November 17, 1939, FLU 19587 Papers, Box 3.

23. Interview with Evelyn Gotzion.

SECTION 4

Robert H. Zieger, "Battery Workers at War." From Zieger, *Madison's Battery Workers, 1934–1952: A History of Federal Labor Union 19587* (Ithaca, 1977).

1. The standard account is Joel Seidman, *American Labor from Defense to Reconversion* (Chicago, 1953). See also Nelson Nauen Lichtenstein, "Industrial Unionism under the No-strike Pledge: A Study of the CIO during the Second World War" (Ph.D. dissertation, University of California, Berkeley, 1974); Joseph C. Goulden, *Meany* (New York, 1972), ch. 5; Jeremy Brecher, *Strike!* (San Francisco, 1972), 221-31.

2. John W. Alexander, *An Economic Base Study of Madison, Wisconsin* (Madison, 1953), 16, 35, 70; Situation summary, August 14, 1941, File 196-6124; James B. Holmes, USCS Commissioner, Preliminary Report, February 19, 1943, *ibid.*, File 300-2594; Holmes, Final Report, March 2, 1945, *ibid.*, File 455-0601, all in the records of the Federal Mediation and Conciliation Service, Record Group 280, National Archives, Suitland, Maryland.

3. A number of employees' handwritten job descriptions appear in FLU 19587 Papers, Box 6, Folder for December 1945–January 1946; company brief, n.d., but ca. April 1943, Case No. 111-581-D, Selected Documents from Region VI Case Files, Records of the National War Labor Board (World War II) Record Group 202), National Archives, Suitland, Maryland; Buchholz interview, Jan. 7, 1975.

4. For wartime wage trends nationally, see Seidman, *American Labor*, ch. 7, and Lichtenstein, "Industrial Unionism," esp. chs. 4-6.

5. A copy of the 1940 settlement, dated December 27, 1940, is in AFL-Series 7. Also, MB, November 29 and December 27, 1940. Negotiations and results of the 1941 settlement are revealed in USCS Records, File 196-6124, esp. B.M. Marshman, USCS Commissioner. Final Report, August 16, 1941. On overtime: MB, January 2, 1945.

6. On factory conditions: interviews with William Skaar and Byron Buchholz and letter from Skaar to the author, August 1, 1975. See also Haferbecker, *Wisconsin Labor Laws*, 30. There are many grievances filed on union forms in FLU 19587 Papers, Box 6.

7. The strengthening of centralized leadership was a national phenomenon during the war. See Seidman, *American Labor*, and Lichtenstein, "Industrial Unionism." Direct evidence of this pattern in 19587's affairs is fragmentary but appears, e.g., in USCS Records, Files 196-6124 and 300-2594, and in NWLB Records, Case No. 111-581-D and Case No. 111-15754-HD, as well as MB, esp. February 11, 1944, and January 2, 1945, and in interviews with Byron Buchholz, Max Onsager, and Evelyn Gotzion. Also conference of Federal Labor Unions of Wisconsin, *Proceedings* (meeting held in Madison, March 14–15, 1942; pamphlet, SHSW).

8. Election of 1939: MB, December 1, 1939, January 8, 1940. Biemiller's activities: Biemiller reports, February 20, 24, 1941, organizers' reports, WSFL Papers, Box 5. Turnover in leadership: MB, 1941–45, passim, esp. September 9, 27, December 9, 1944, January 10, February 10, 1945. Sergeants-at-Arms: MB, January 30, 1940. Motion against propaganda, etc.: MB, January 16, 1942. Rumors of 1945 and charges: MB, August 2, 1945. Receivership: MB, December 8, 1945. Also, interviews with Evelyn Gotzion, Pat Lowe, John Stromski.

9. See Lichtenstein, "Industrial Unionism," esp. ch. 11.

10. On the controversy, interviews with Evelyn Gotzion, Max Onsager, Pat Lowe, and John Stromski. Also MB, January 13, March 10, 27, April 21, 1945.

11. MB, late 1944–early 1945, passim.

12. This paragraph is somewhat speculative. These tendencies conform to national patterns. Interviews and MB references make it clear that internal conflict was intense and often personal and that, aside from the IAM matter, it invoked little in the way of ideology or even bargaining strategy differences.

13. Onsager interview; USCS Records, File 196-6124. esp. B. M. Marshman, Final Report, August 4, 1941.

14. Bertha Sime, Recording Secretary, to Leroy Berigan, December 22, 1942; union contract proposals in report by NWLB Tri-partite Panel, June 3, 1943, NWLB Records, Case No. 111-581-D.

15. Statement and brief of Ray-O-Vac Company, ca. March 20, 1943; David Sigman to Leroy Berigan, February 19, 1943; Berigan to FLU 19587 Grievance committee, February 18, 1943; Harry Malcolm. NWLB Special Representative, memo, ca. April 12, 1943; Patrick Rogers, AFL Representative, brief, April 15, 1943, all in *ibid.*

16. James B. Holmes, Preliminary Report and Progress Report, both dated February 19, 1943, USCS Records, File 300-2594.

17. Synopsis, ca. February 22, 1943, transferring case from USCS to NWLB; statement and brief of Ray-O-Vac Company, ca. March 20, 1943; Leroy Berigan to Grievance Committee, February 18, 1943, and to David Sigman, February 22, 1943, all in NWLB Records, Case No. 111-581-D.

18. James B. Holmes to Leroy Berigan, February 18, 1943, and February 23, 1943, *ibid.*

19. On the activities of the National War Labor Board during World War II, see Seidman, *American Labor from Defense to Reconversion*, esp. pp. 81-86, 91, 109-30, 145-49. Company perceptions that the board functioned to embolden the union are found in company brief, n.d., but ca. April 1943, NWLB Records, Case No. 111-581-D. Malcolm's observations are contained in his memo ca. April 12, 1943, *ibid.*

20. Tri-partite Panel report, June 3, 1943; Meyer Kastenbaum, chairman of tri-partite panel, to Henrietta Shaw, April 30, 1943; John O. Levinson, NWLB Assistant Director of Disputes, to members of Region VI Regional Labor Board, July 23, 1943, in *ibid.*

21. Leroy Berigan to Meyer Kastenbaum, May 4, 1943; Patrick Rogers telegram to Kastenbaum, May 10; Ralph E. Axley, attorney for Ray-O-Vac, to Kastenbaum, May 13, *ibid.*

22. Ray-O-Vac brief, ca. June 1945; Ray-O-Vac petition for reconsideration, ca. November 20 1945, in NWLB Records, Case No. 111-15754-HO. The acerbic comments, by Vice-president Leroy Berigan, appear in his comment on report by Hearing Officer, ca. July 1, 1945, *ibid.* The frustrations of unionists are seen in Al Breitzke, president of FLU 19587, to Harry Malcolm, April 8, 1943, *ibid.*, Case No. 111-581-D, and in the communications by NWLB Special Representative Malcolm and USCS Commissioner Holmes previously cited.

23. Interviews with Max Onsager and Byron Buchholz; MB, December 8, 1945.

Darryl Holter, "Labor Law: From 'Little Wagner' to Taft-Hartley." From Holter, "Labor Law and the Road to Taft-Hartley: Wisconsin's 'Little Wagner Act,' 1935-1945," *Labor Studies Journal* 15:2 (Summer 1990), 20-47.

1. Darryl Holter, "Sit-Down Strikes in Milwaukee, 1937–1938," *Milwaukee History* (Summer 1986), 58-64.

2. Both labor and management understood that unit determination could be the single most important factor in union success.

3. William Gorham Rice Jr., "The Wisconsin Labor Relations Act in 1937," *Wisconsin Law Review* (1938), 257.

4. Joseph Padway, "Handbook on the Wisconsin Labor Relations Act" (Wisconsin State Federation of Labor, 1937). On Padway's role in conjunction with the issue of unit determination and the NLRB, see James A. Gross, *The Reshaping of the National Labor Relations Board: National Labor Policy in Transition, 1937-1947* (Albany, 1981), 44-46.

5. Hugh J. Hafer, "A Study of the Wisconsin Employment Peace Act—Selection of Collective Bargaining Representatives," *Wisconsin Law Review* (March 1956), 287.

6. Charles C. Killingsworth, *State Labor Relations Acts* (Chicago, 1948), 194.

7. *Ibid.*, 155.

8. Eva Jacobs Schwartzman, "Collective Bargaining—Designation of Unit and Representative—Comparison of National and Wisconsin Acts," *Wisconsin Law Review* (March 1942), 251.

9. On Taft-Hartley, see American Federation of Labor, *History, Encyclopedia, Reference Book* (Washington, D.C., 1955), 2202-2220, R.W. Fleming, "Taft-Hartley Law to Date," *Wisconsin Law Review* (January 1949); Sumner H. Slichter, "The Taft-Hartley Act," *Quarterly Journal of Economics* (February 1949); *Congressional Digest* (April, 1949); and National Association of Manufacturers, *Employers Rights and Obligations* (New York, 1956).

10. Hafer, "A Study of the Wisconsin Employment Peace Act—Selection," 481.

11. Killingsworth, *State Labor Relations Acts*, 160.

12. Fleming, "Taft-Hartley Law to Date," 79.

13. Hugh J. Hafer, "A Study of the Wisconsin Employment Peace Act—Unfair Labor Practices," *Wisconsin Law Review* (January 1957), 138-143.

14. Killingsworth, *State Labor Relations Acts*, 68.

15. *Ibid.*, 74.

16. Eva J. Schwartzman, "Free Speech and the Wisconsin Employment Relations Act," *Wisconsin Law Review* (March 1943), 260-262.

17. *Ibid.*, 274-275.

18. Killingsworth, *State Labor Relations Acts*, 43, 47.

19. *Ibid.*, 48-49.

20. *Ibid.*, 51.

21. Haferbecker, *Wisconsin Labor Laws* (Madison, 1958).

22. Richard Pifer, "A Social History of the Home Front: Milwaukee Labor During World War II" (doctoral dissertation, University of Wisconsin, Madison, 1983), 423-425.

23. *Ibid.*, 442.

24. Wisconsin State Federation of Labor, *Report of Convention Proceedings* (Milwaukee, 1940), 51-55; J.J. Handley, "Labor's Legislative Program," *Wisconsin Labor* (Milwaukee, 1937), 37-41; and Joseph A. Padway, "Anti-Picketing Legislation," *Wisconsin Labor* (Milwaukee, 1939), 73-75.

Stephen Meyer, "Cold War Politics at Allis-Chalmers." From Meyer, "*Stalin Over Wisconsin*": *The Making and Unmaking of Militant Unionism* (New Brunswick, 1992).

1. Brody, Workers in Industrial America, 217-226; and James C. Foster, *The Union Politic: The CIO Political Action Committee* (Columbia, Missouri, 1975), 66-94.

2. Thomas C. Reeves, *The Life and Times of Joseph McCarthy: A Biography* (New York, 1982), 69-108; David M. Oshinsky, *Senator Joseph McCarthy and the Labor Movement* (Kansas City, 1976), 1-33; and William F. Thompson, *The History of Wisconsin*, vol. 6 (Madison, 1988), 449-466.

3. Reeves, *McCarthy*, passim; Oshinsky, *McCarthy*, passim; and Thompson, *Wisconsin*, passim.

4. Reeves, *McCarthy*, passim; Oshinsky *McCarthy*, passim; and Thompson, *Wisconsin*, passim.

5. *CIO News*, August 2, 1946.

6. *Milwaukee Journal*, August 14 and 15, 1946; and *Daily Picket*, August 9, 15, 22, and 24, 1946.

7. *Milwaukee Journal*, August 14, 1946; and *CIO News*, August 16, 1946.

8. *Milwaukee Journal*, August 16, 1946; and Thaddeus Wasiliewski to Regina and Gene Wasielewski, August 16, 1946, F. Correspondence, 1946, Box 1, Thaddeus F. B. Wasielewski Papers, Milwaukee Area Research Center, University of Wisconsin–Milwaukee (hereinafter MARC).

9. Hugh Swofford, Affidavit, Jan 23, 1950, pp. 7-8, File 15, Box 7, Nat Ganley Papers, Archives of Labor History and Urban Affairs (hereinafter ALHUA), Walter P. Reuther Papers, Walter P. Reuther Library (hereinafter WPRL), Wayne State University, Detroit, Michigan; Pat Greathouse to Walter Reuther, June 14, 1946, and c. August 3, 1946; and "Policy Statement of UAW-CIO Progressive Caucus of Region #4," F. 1, Box 212, WPRP.

10. Swofford Affidavit, 8.

11. *Milwaukee Sentinel*, September 2, 1946.

12. *Milwaukee Journal*, September 5, 1946.

13. *Milwaukee Sentinel*, September 19, 1946.

14. *Milwaukee Journal*, September 22, 1946.

15. *Ibid.*, September 23 and 24, 1946.

16. See front-page articles in *Milwaukee Sentinel*, September 23–November 21, 1946; and Swofford Affidavit, 7-10.

17. *Milwaukee Sentinel*, September 23 and 24, 1946.

18. *Ibid.*, September 25, 1946.

19. Allis-Chalmers Manufacturing Company, *Principle Represented: Communist* [West Allis, 1946].

20. Robert Buse, HELC, *Hearings before the Committee on Education and Labor. . . Bills to Amend and Repeal the National Labor Relations Act, and for Other Purposes* (Washington, D.C., 1947), 1986; and Dale Treleven, interview with Sigmund Eisenscher, Jan. 16, 1982, Wisconsin Labor Oral History Project.

21. Joseph Mattson to Walter Reuther, October 9, 1946, F. 8, Box 36, WPRP.

22. *Ibid.*

23. Leon Venne, in HUAC, *Hearings before the Committee on Un-American Activities, Feb. 27, 1947* (Washington, D.C., 1947), 33, 37, 40-41.

24. *Ibid.*, 45.

25. *Ibid.*, 45; and *Milwaukee Journal*, October 7, 1946.

26. Telegrams, Leon Venne to Walter Reuther and Philip Murray, October 8, 1946, Folder 8, Box 36, WPRP.

27. *Milwaukee Sentinel*, October 12, 1946.

28. *Milwaukee Journal*, October 14, 1946; Venne to Reuther, November 8, 1946; and Venne to Local 248 UAWA, CIO, November 4, 1946, Folder 9, Box 36, WPRP.

29. *Milwaukee Journal*, October 9 and 10, 1946; and Gavett, *Development of the Labor Movement*, 185-189.
30. *Milwaukee Journal*, October 9, 10, 1946, 11, and 14, 1946; and *Milwaukee Sentinel*, October 14, 1946.
31. *Milwaukee Journal*, October 16, 1946.
32. *Ibid.*, October 17, 1946.
33. *Ibid.*
34. *Ibid.*
35. *Ibid.*, October 18, 1946.
36. Thaddeus Wasielewski to Regina and Gene Wasielewski, April 16, 1946; *Milwaukee Journal*, August 21 and 23, 1946; and *Labor Views* (August 1946).
37. *Milwaukee Journal*, August 16, 1946.
38. *Ibid.*, August 25, 1946.
39. *Ibid.*, August 25, 1946.
40. *Ibid.*, September 14, 1946.
41. *Ibid.*, September 14, 1946.
42. *Ibid.*, September 25, 1946.
43. *Ibid.*, September 29 and 30, 1946.
44. *Ibid.*, October 2, 3, 5, and 6, 1946.
45. *Ibid.*, October 6, 15, and 16, 1946.
46. *Ibid.*, October 6, 15, and 16, 1946.
47. *Ibid.*, October 24, 1946.
48. *Milwaukee Journal*, October 17, 1946; and Kersten Campaign Literature, Box 1 Series 4, Charles J. Kersten Papers, Marquette University.
49. *Milwaukee Journal*, October 18, 23, and 25, and November 3, 1946.
50. *Ibid.*, October 25, 1946.
51. *Milwaukee Sentinel*, October 7, 1946.
52. *Milwaukee Journal*, October 28, 1946.
53. *Ibid.*
54. *Ibid.*
55. *Ibid.*, October 29, 30, and 31, 1946.
56. *Ibid.*, October 29, 1946.
57. *Ibid.*, October 31, 1946.
58. *Ibid.*, November 1, 1946.
59. *Ibid.*
60. *Ibid.*, November 1, and 4, 1946.
61. *Ibid.*, November 4, 1946.
62. *Ibid.*, November 1 and 3, 1946.
63. *Milwaukee Sentinel*, November 11, 1946; and *Milwaukee Journal*, November 6, 1946.
64. *Milwaukee Sentinel*, November 11, 1946; and *Milwaukee Journal*, November 6, 1946.
65. *Milwaukee Journal*, November 6, 1946.
66. *Ibid.*, November 6, 1946; and William G. Rice to Lewis B. Schwellenbach, March 17, 1947, Box 183, RG 174.
67. *Milwaukee Journal*, November 6, 1946.
68. *Ibid.*, November 13, 1946.

Bernard Karsh, "Anatomy of a Strike in Marinette." From Karsh, *Diary of a Strike*, 2nd ed. (Urbana, 1982).

1. This verse refers to an incident which occurred toward the end of the strike. Members of the Teamsters Union refused to cross the union picket line, and the mill's only pickup truck could not carry all of the materials moving in and out of the plant. One mid-morning, the company's purchasing agent attempted to drive his car out of the plant area. He was stopped by a wall of strikers who demanded that he open the trunk of his car for inspection. While he was arguing with the pickets, one of the strikers removed the keys from the ignition. No one would admit to the police on duty that he had the keys. Meanwhile the argument about opening the trunk continued. The keys were produced when the supervisor finally agreed to let the strikers inspect the contents of the trunk. The trunk was found to contain several large boxes of finished products. The pickets refused to permit the supervisor to leave the plant until the "contraband" was removed. The police were reluctant to insist that the supervisor be allowed to take the finished products out since that action almost certainly would have provoked considerable violence. When the bundles were removed, the purchasing agent was allowed to drive his car away.
2. At the time of these events Phil drove a two-year-old Dodge.

SECTION 5

Cynthia B. Costello, "The Union Comes to W.P.S." From Costello, *"We're Worth It": Women and Collective Action in the Insurance Workplace* (Urbana, 1991).

1. The data for this article were derived from fifteen semistructured interviews with office workers at WPS, six semistructured interviews with former managers at WPS, and several semistructured interviews with the business agents for Local 1444 of the United Food and Commercial Workers. The interviews with office workers covered work history, union background, family status, work experiences at WPS, and union participation. The interviews with former managers included questions on managerial policies, decisions, and attitudes, as well as questions on the relationship between the company and the union. Interviews with the business agents covered the history of unionization at WPS, management union relations, grievances, and contract negotiations. The interviews have been slightly edited for grammar and punctuation. Additional materials for this chapter—union contracts, newspaper articles, and union leaflets—were provided by Local 1444 of the United Food and Commercial Workers.
2. A second union, the Office and Professional Employees International Union (OPEIU), was also on the ballot and received nine votes in the election.
3. Seyfarth, Shaw, Fairweather, and Geraldson is one of the largest and most successful anti-union law firms. Among other cases, the firm was linked to the events that surrounded the elimination of the union at the *Washington Post,* as well as to the events that undermined the Steelworkers' Union in Newport, Rhode Island. (See "The Heat Is on at WPS," *Free for All,* Nov. 5–8.) More recently, this law firm was hired to advise Yale University regarding the union organizing drive by its clerical workforce (see "Yale Strike on Hold," *In These Times,* Apr.4–10, 1984). The most direct evidence that Seyfarth, Shaw, Fairweather, and Geraldson advised WPS management comes from the company's 1982 annual report to the state insurance commissioner listing payments of $177,676 to the law firm (WPS Annual Financial Statement, Wisconsin State Insurance Commission, 1982) . Former supervisors, the business agents for the union, and union employees reported the presence of lawyers from the firm at bargaining sessions and arbitration negotiations.
4. Several of the union employees suspected that the tightening of managerial authority, together with the erratic supervisory behavior, reflected a managerial strategy forged in consultation with the law firm of Seyfarth, Shaw, Fairweather, and Geraldson. They based this assessment on memos found on supervisors' desks and on informal comments made by managers. The evidence indicates that the consulting firm was at least indirectly involved in supervisory training through consultations with upper-level managers regarding supervisory practices.
5. Initially, not all the night-shift workers were non-union employees. After 1979, WPS management replaced union workers with non-union workers as the former quit or transferred to day-shift work.
6. Not all the union employees shared this opposition to the dress code. One older woman expressed strong disapproval at the way the younger women dressed and complained that discussions about the dress code absorbed a disproportionate amount of time at union meetings. She stated that several of her friends had stopped attending union meetings over this issue.
7. See Janice Czyson, "Long Skirts Prompt Legal Battle," *The Feminist Connection,* Dec. 1982.
8. *UFCW Monitor,* Jan. 1982, June 1982, Dec. 1982.
9. See Michael Burawoy, *Manufacturing Consent: Changes in the Labor Process under Monopoly Capitalism* (Chicago, 1979).

Credits

Thomas W. Gavett's "Early Unions in Milwaukee, 1850-1884" as well as other selections are extracted from his book *Development of the Labor Movement in Milwaukee* (University of Wisconsin, Madison, 1965). Reprinted with permission from the University of Wisconsin Press.

Daniel M. Parkinson's "Lead Mining In La Fayette County" is extracted from *Wisconsin Historical Collections, II* (Madison, 1856). Reprinted with permission from the State Historical Society of Wisconsin.

John Muir's "Work on a Farm, 1848" is extracted from his book *The Story of My Boyhood and Youth* (Houghton Mifflin, New York, 1913). Reprinted with permission from Houghton Mifflin Press.

Robert W. Ozanne's "Lumber Industry Strikes: Eau Claire, Marinette, Ashland, La Crosse," as well as several other selections are extracted from his book *The Labor Movement in Wisconsin: A History* (State Historical Society of Wisconsin, Madison, 1984). Reprinted with permission from the SHSW.

Leon Fink's "The Knights of Labor in Milwaukee" is extracted from his book *Workingmen's Democracy: The Knights of Labor* (University of Illinois, Urbana, 1985). Reprinted with permission from the University of Illinois Press.

Gordon Haferbecker's "Early Labor Legislation" as well as several other excerpts are extracted from his book *Wisconsin Labor Laws* (University of Wisconsin, 1958). Reprinted with permission from the University of Wisconsin Press.

Robert Nesbit's "Unemployment: 'The Tramp Problem' in Beloit" as well as several other selections are extracted from his book *The History of Wisconsin Volume III: Industrialization and Urbanization, 1873-1993* (SHSW, Madison, 1985). Reprinted with permission of the SHSW.

Lee Baxandall's "Women and the Oshkosh Woodworkers Strike, 1898" is extracted from an article that appeared in the *Green Mountain Quarterly* (1976). Reprinted with permission from *Green Mountain Quarterly*.

John W. Bailey's "Unions in Kenosha" is extracted from his article "Labor's Fight for Security and Dignity," in John A. Neuenschwander, *Kenosha County in the Twentieth Century* (Kenosha County, Kenosha, 1976). Reprinted with permission.

Joseph M. Kelly's "Labor in Racine" and other selections are extracted from his article "Growth of Organized Labor" in Nicholas C. Burckel, *Racine: Growth and Change in a Wisconsin County* (Racine County, Racine, 1977). Reprinted with permission.

John D. Steven's "War Hysteria and the Wobblies" is an excerpt from the author's "Wobblies in Milwaukee, " *Historical Messenger*, v. 24, n. 1 (March, 1968), reprinted in Barbara and Justus Paul, eds., *The Badger State: A Documentary History* (Eerdmans, Grand Rapids, 1979). Reprinted with permission.

Paul W. Glad's "Vocational Education" is extracted from his book *The History of Wisconsin Volume V: War, a New Era, and Depression, 1914-1940* (SHSW, Madison, 1990). Reprinted with permission from the SHSW.

Elmer Axel Beck's "Labor's Daily Newspaper" and other selections are extracted from his book *The Sewer Socialists: A History of the Socialist Party of Wisconsin, 1897-1940* (Westburg, Fennimore, Wisconsin, 1982). Reprinted with author's permission.

Darryl Holter's "Labor Spies and Union-Busting" is extracted from his article that appeared in the *Wisconsin Magazine of History* (Summer, 1985). Reprinted with permission from the SHSW.

Darryl Holter's "Organizing the Unorganized in Milwaukee, 1900-1903" is extracted from an article that appeared in the *Milwaukee Labor Press* (April 25, 1985). Reprinted with permission of the Milwaukee County Labor Council, AFL-CIO.

Frederick I. Olson's "Organized Labor and Socialism" is extracted from his article "The Socialist Party and the Union in Milwaukee, 1900-1912," *Wisconsin Magazine of History* (Winter, 1960-1961). Reprinted with permission from the SHSW.

Leon Applebaum's "A Lock-Out" is extracted from his article "Turmoil in Kenosha: The Allen-A Dispute of 1928-1929," *Wisconsin Magazine of History* (Summer, 1987). Reprinted with permission from the SHSW.

Barbara Wertheimer's "The Wisconsin School for Workers" is extracted from her book *Labor Education for Women Workers* (Temple University Press, Philadelphia, 1981). Reprinted with permission of author's family.

Joe W. Trotter Jr.'s "African American Workers and the Labor Movement in Milwaukee" and other selections are printed with the author's permission.

Debra E. Bernhardt's "'Fighting Bob' La Follette" is reprinted with permission from the New York State Labor History Association.

Robert Zieger's "Building the Union at Ray-O-Vac in Madison" and other selections are excerpted from his book *Madison's Battery Workers, 1934-1952: A History of Federal Labor Union 19587* (Cornell University Press, Ithaca, 1974). Reprinted with permission of Cornell University Press.

Darryl Holter's "Sources of CIO Success" is extracted from his article which appeared in *Labor History* v. 29 n. 2 in 1988. Reprinted with author's permission.

Irving Bernstein's "The Nation's First Unemployment Compensation Law" is extracted from his book *The Lean Years: A History of the American Worker, 1920-1933* (Houghton Mifflin, Boston, 1960). Reprinted with author's permission.

Peggy Dennis' "Industrial Unionism: A Communist Perspective" is extracted from her book *The Autobiography of an American Communist* (Laurence Hill, Westport, Conn., 1977). Reprinted with permission from Eugene (Dennis) Vrana .

Rose Pesotta's "Organizing Garment Workers" is extracted from her book *Bread Upon the Waters* (Cornell University Press, Ithaca, 1987). Reprinted with permission from Cornell University Press.

James Lorence's "Gerald Boileau and the Politics of Unemployment" is extracted from his book *Gerald Boileau and the Progressive-Farmer-Labor Alliance: Politics of the New Deal* (University of Missouri Press, Columbia, 1994). Reprinted with permission from the University of Missouri Press.

Stephen Meyer's "Women and the War Effort at Allis-Chalmers" and other selections are extracted from his book *"Stalin Over Wisconsin": The Making and Unmaking of Militant Unionism, 1900-1950* (Rutgers University Press, New Brunswick, 1992). Reprinted with author's permission.

Darryl Holter's "Wisconsin's 'Little Wagner Act' and the Road to Taft-Hartley" is extracted from an article that appeared in *Labor Studies Journal*, v. 15, n. 2 (1990). Reprinted with author's permission.

Bernard Karsh's "Anatomy of a Strike in Marinette" is extracted from his book *Diary of a Strike* (University of Illinois Press, Urbana, 1958). Reprinted with permission from the University of Illinois Press.

Richard W. Olson's "An Isolated Surviver: Racine Labor" and Mike Konopacki and Gary Huck's "Labor Cartoons: Drawing on Work Culture" are excerpted from their articles in Sam Pizzigati and Fred J. Solloway, eds., *The New Labor Press: Journalism for a Changing Union Movement* (Cornell University Press, Ithaca, 1992). Reprinted with permission from Cornell University Press.

Andrew Hamilton's "Teaching Assistants' Strike Ends in Contract Signing" is extracted from an article that appeared in *Science* on April 17, 1970. Reprinted with permission of *Science*.

Sue Doro's and Karen Matthews' "A Female Machinist in Milwaukee" is extracted from an article that appeared in Molly Martin, ed., *Hard-hatted Women* (Seal, Seattle, 1988). Reprinted with Sue Doro's permission.

E. E. LeMasters' "Blue-Collar Aristocrats" is excerpted from his book *Blue-Collar Aristocrats: Life-Styles at a Working-Class Tavern* (University of Wisconsin Press, Madison, 1975). Reprinted with permission from the University of Wisconsin Press.

Wisconsin Education Association Council's "The Hortonville Teachers' Strike" is extracted from a booklet of the same title published by the Council. Reprinted with permission from the Wisconsin Education Association Council.

Cynthia Costello's "The Union Comes to United Physicians Service" is extracted from her book *We're Worth It: Women and Collective Action in the Insurance Workplace* (University of Illinois Press, Urbana, 1991). Reprinted with permission from the University of Illinois Press.

Dale Kurschner's "New Union Strategies: Electrical Workers in Wausau" is extracted from an article that appeared in *Labor Research Review* (Spring, 1991). Reprinted with permission.

Index

A

Adamson Act, 96
Addes, George, 203
Adelman, Meyer. 104–105, 126
Administrative Technical Services, 250–251
Advocate, 94
Ady, Mr., 46
AFL-CIO, 224. *See also* Wisconsin State AFL-CIO
African Americans: and CIO, 127; in Milwaukee, 93–95, 110–111; and University of Michigan, 229; women and unions, 184–185
Agricultural Adjustment Administration (AAA), 89–90, 91
Ahearn, William, 45
Air Line Railroad. 34
Akron (Ohio), 128
Alabama, 94
Alfonsi, Paul R., 117, 152
Allen, Charles W.. 49, 51, 83
Allen, Nathan R., Jr., 83
Allen, Nathan R., Sr., 83
Allen, Robert W., 83
Allen-A Hosiery Company: demographics, 84; established, 82–83; labor disputes, 48, 85–87
Allen-Bradley, 91, 128, 129
Allen Tannery, 47. 49–51, 83
Alliance for Labor, 224
Allied Industrial Workers, 106, 248
Allis, E. P., Company, 19, 79
Allis, Edward, 27, 32, 36, 37, 38
Allis, Louis, Plant, 128
Allis-Chalmers: and AFL craft unions, 187; African Americans and, 94, 110–111; Christoffel and, 139, 180; CIO and, 123, 124–126, 133, 192; Clark and, 104; and cold war politics, 192–205; and communism, 194–196; and defense production, 180–181; and 1946 elections, 192–193; Industrial Relations Department, 180; Jensen and, 194; and molders strike, 74; Padway and, 132; and Pinkerton spies, 138; and Rank and File Membership Committee, 196–197; and sit-down strikes, 128, 129; and UAW strike, 192, 196, 198; Venne and, 196–197; women and, 180–181, 235–238
Allis Reliance Works, 38–39, 40
Allouez, 61
Althen, Fred, 45
Altmeyer, Arthur, 124
Alverno College, 232, 233
Amalgamated Clothing Workers, 91, 132
Amalgamated Meat Cutters and Butchers, 88, 95, 110, 135, 140
American Action, Inc., 201
American Brass, 85, 157
American Club (Kohler), 144
American Federation of Government Employees, 161
American Federation of Labor (AFL): African Americans and, 110–111, 184–185; and AFSCME, 103, 161; and Allis-Chalmers, 124–126; Boileau and, 153; and CIO, 120, 123–124, 126–128; and communism, 138–139, 142, 195; and Consolidated Water Power and Paper Company, 100; and Democratic party, 201; and 1946 elections, 192, 205; Friedrick and, 214–215; Hogan and, 50; and International Association of Machinists, 79; and J. I. Case Company, 104, 164–166; La Follettes and, 96, 192–193; in Madison, 140–141; and Mueller Furnace, 129; and Nash Motor Company, 156–158; and North Wisconsin Millmen's Union, 25; organizing drives, 121–123; Padway and, 76, 187; papermaking industry and, 58; and Racine Labor, 224; and Racine unions, 52; Rasmussen on, 91; and Ray-O-Vac, 108–114, 170–174; and Retail Clerks' Union, 213; roots, 37, 43; and state intervention, 130–133; and Stenographers, Typewriters, Bookkeepers and Assistants Union, 178–182; and Trades and Labor Council, 47; and UAW, 159; and

unemployment legislation, 124; and unfair labor practices, 189; in Washington County, 105; Weber and, 75; and "Wisconsin Plan," 122, 133; during World War I, 61; WSFL and, 41
American Federation of State, County, and Municipal Employees (AFSCME), 103, 140, 161, 178, 234, 248
American Federation of Teachers, 221
American Labor party, 142
American League against War and Fascism, 141
American Negro Labor Congress (ANLC), 95
American Polish Labor Council, 193–194
American Writing Paper Company, 63, 64
Ameringer, Oscar, 223
Amlie, Thomas, 115–116
Anchor Line, 18
Anderson, Nels, 75
Andrews, T. S., 69
Andrsezewski, Mr., 46
Anneke, Madame Mathilde Franziska, 14
Applebaum, Leon: "A Lock-Out: The Hosiery Workers in Kenosha, 1928–1929," 82–87
Appleton: C. P. R. Richmond Brothers and, 57; Hammel and, 63; IBPM and, 68; Kimberly-Clark and, 58–60, 64; strikes in, 59–60, 66–67; and WEAC, 242
Arbeiter (newspaper), 15, 37, 69
Aristotle, 37
Army, U.S., Signal Corps, 169–170, 172
Arnold, Dexter: "Madison Labor in the 1930s," 140–141; "Madison Labor in the 1960s and 1970s," 221–222
Art and Politics, 257
Ashland, 25, 40
Ashland Daily News, 25
Asphalt Workers Union, 95
Aspin, Les, 226
Assembly, Wisconsin, 193. *See also* Legislature, Wisconsin
Association of Tailors, 15
Atlas Company, 66, 67
Auto Council, 158
Autolite Plant, 160
Auto Truck Drivers and Teamsters Union, 88

B

Badger Brass, 48–49, 51
Badger Mill, 64, 66–67
Bailey, John W.: "Unions in Kenosha," 47–51
Bakers and Confectionery Workers Union, 47, 248
Banachowicz, John, 121, 133
Banner und Volksfreund (newspaper), 27
Barber, George, Company, 13
Barbers Union, 53, 54
Barkeepers, 47, 53
Baron, Rose Marie, 248
Barton, 105
Bascom Hall (UW), 229
Bast, Mr., 135
Battery industry: Burgess Battery, 141; Eveready, 109; and health and safety, 109; Marathon Battery, 175–177; Solar Battery, 128; and World War II, 169–174; and WSFL, 170. *See also* Ray-O-Vac
Bauer, Mr., 44
Baumann, Esther, 179
Baxandall, Lee: "'The Most Disorderly Elements': Women and the Oshkosh Woodworkers Strike, 1898," 46
Bay View: African Americans in, 94; and Eight Hour League, 34–36, 39, 42–44, 46; and iron and steel industry, 18, 27, 29; and strikes, 33
Bay View Iron Works. *See* Milwaukee Iron Works
Beaudette, Ed, 135–137
Beaver Dam, 122, 139
Beck, Elmer A., 77, 105: "Erik Bjurman: Kenosha Unionist," 190–191; "Labor's Daily Newspaper: *The Milwaukee Leader*," 69–70; "Organized Labor

and Socialism: Two Views," 80–81; "The Wisconsin Plan for Labor Unity, 1936," 122
Beck, Harold E., 182–183
Becker, Maurice, 257
Beet, Thomas, 72
Belin Garment Company, 128
Bellew, Frank, 256
Beloit, 32, 42, 50–51
Beloit Employers' Association, 51
Beloit Free Press, 23
Beloit Labor Journal, 51
Beni, Jack, 159
Benjamin, Herbert, 152
Bennington (Vt.), 84
Berger, Meta, 138
Berger, Victor, 69–70, 80–81, 94, 130, 223
Bergoff, "Pearl," 72
Berigan, Leroy, 172, 174
Berkeley (California), 190, 231
Berlin Machine Works, 50
Bernhardt, Debra E.: "'Fighting Bob' La Follette," 96
Bernstein, Irving: "The Nation's First Unemployment Compensation Law," 124–125
Best, Geoffrey, 27
Bialis, Morris, 150
Bidgood, Frank, 174
Biemiller, Andrew: and AFL, 170–171; and 1946 elections, 193, 201, 204; and Kersten, 200, 201; and Wisconsin Senate, 117
Biemiller, Hannah, 182
Biron, 62
Bismarck, Otto von, 29
Bittner, Tom, 264
Bjurman, Erik, 190–191
Black Cat Textiles. *See* Allen-A Hosiery Company
Blacksmiths and Machinists Union, 21
Blaine, Esther, 208
Blaine, John, 77
Blatz Brewing, 27, 182
Blitzstein, Marc, 266
Blue Mounds, 16
Bobrowicz, Edmund, 193, 199–201, 204, 205
Boehringer, William, 45
Bohemians, 40
Boileau, Gerald, 151–154
Boilermakers Union, 21
Bolka, Frank, 126
Bolz, Mr., 135–137
Boncel, Frank, 130
Boncel, Mr., 46
Book-Cadillac Hotel (Detroit), 161
Boot and Shoe Workers Union, 248
Borchardt, Francis, 30, 42
Boston (Massachusetts), 13
Boston Store, 69, 182
Bosworth, Benjamin, 13
Bowling Green (Ohio), 261
Boyer, Jean, 233
Bradley and Metcalf's, 15
Brand and Company, 42
Brewery Workers Union, 53, 248
Brewing industry: and CIO, 194, 198; in Milwaukee, 27; Powderly and, 46; and RTLC, 53; in St. Louis, 36; and Wisconsin State AFL-CIO Women's Conference, 248; and working hours, 38, 40; and WSFL convention, 1893, 50
Bricklayers and Masons Union, 21, 53, 54
Bricklayers' Union, 178
Briggs and Stratton, 106, 123, 126, 133, 188
Brigham, D. M., 18
Brightman, Horace, 15, 17
Brine, John H., 83, 86
Brisbane Hall (Milwaukee), 69
Brockhausen, Frederick, 41, 74, 92
Brokaw, 60, 62
Brookwood Labor College (Katonah, N.Y.), 223

Broommakers Union, 21
Brophy, John, 201, 204
Brotherhood of Locomotive Engineers, 190, 193, 201
Brotherhood of Sleeping Car Porters, 184
Broun, Heywood, 126, 141
Browder, Earl, 142, 196
Browning, Pfeiffer and Smith, 79
Bryn Mawr, 89
Buchanan, Thomas, 94
Buckmaster, A. E., 50
Bucyrus-Erie, 139
Bucyrus Steam Shovel and Dredge Company, 79
Budenz, Louis F., 85, 87
Buenger, Martin H., 86
Buffalo (New York) *Courier*, 21
Building Laborers Union, 52
Building Project, 90
Building Service Union, 248
Building Trades Council, 178
Burgess Battery, 141
Burke, John P., 98
Burns Agency, 74, 77
Burr-Herr Detective Agency, 74
Buse, Robert, 195, 196, 201, 204
Bush, George, 253
Butler, Ben, 32
Bybee, Roger, 226

C

Cabinetmakers and Joiners Union, 13–14, 47
Cady, George R., 86
California, University of, at Berkeley, 231
Capital Club (Madison), 161
Cappel, Walter, 194
Cargill, W. W., 108, 112–114
Carideo, Tony: "Catherine Conroy: Unionist and Feminist," 232–233
Carlstrom, Lawrence, 105
Carnegie Steel, 71
Carpenters Union, 28, 47, 54
Case, J. I., Company: company union established, 104, 163–164; and molders strike, 53; Sahorske and, 165–166; Sommers and, 54; and UAW, 160; workers strike, 163, 165–166, 196
Catholic Church: and Democratic party, 93; Germans and, 27; in Milwaukee, 201, 204; and non-union labor, 53; Poles and, 33
Centralia, 60
Central Labor Union, 37–38
Central Leather Company, 49, 83
Chamberlain, K. R., 257
Chaplin, Ralph, 91, 257
Chapman, Chandler P., 23, 40
Chapman, E., 136
Chapman, L., 135
Chase, L. P., 144
Chautauqua movement, 96
Chicago: anarchists in, 49; ANLC in, 95; Berger and, 70; Conroy and, 232; FEPC conference in, 110; and Haymarket Riot, 34, 37, 42, 44, 266; and ice handlers, 48; and iron and steel industry, 88; and railway industry, 19; RTLC and, 54; and tanning industry, 18
Chicago 7, 230
Chicago and Northwestern Railroad, 19–21, 32, 62, 158
Chicago Employers' Association, 51
Chicago-Kenosha Hosiery. *See* Allen-A Hosiery Company
Chicago, Milwaukee and St. Paul Railroad, 18–21, 39–40, 94
Chicago Post, 16
Chicago Regional Labor Board, 108, 158
Chicago-Rockford Hosiery Company. *See* Allen-A Hosiery Company
Chicago Rubber Clothing Company, 54

Chicago Rubber Company, 149–150
Chicago Seaman's Union, 18, 21
Chicago Tribune, 16, 266
Chicago, University of, 64
Chippewa Falls, 25
Christianson, Andy, 113–114
Christoffel, Harold: and Allis-Chalmers, 126, 180, 201–202; and Communist party, 152, 194–195; and State CIO, 139
Chrysler, 157
Cigar Makers Union, 15, 21, 47, 53
Cigler, Paul J., Jr.: "A Strike for Cash Pay in Two Rivers, 1895," 45
CIO Council Executive Board, 194
CIO News, 110, 134, 181, 193
CIO Political Action Committee (CIO-PAC): and conservative dissidents, 198–199; and 1946 elections, 192–194, 198, 204–205; La Follette and, 193; McMurray and, 201; National Democratic Committee and, 200
Citizens' Alliance, 51
Civilian Conservation Corps (CCC), 90
Civil War, 15–16, 18, 40
Clarenbach, Kathryn, 232, 233, 248–249
Clark, Clifford, 135
Clark, Kenneth, 127; "Industrial Unions: The Organizers' View," 103–106
Clark, Nathaniel, 113–114
Clausen, L. R., 166
Cleveland (Ohio), 30, 31, 36
Clothing and Textile Workers Union, 133
Coal and Ice Drivers Union, 182
Coalition of Labor Union Women, 232
Cochrane and Hubbard Brick Company, 14
Coleman, William, 88
Collins, Mr., 25
Collins, Rita, 249
Colorado, University of, 231
Colored Workingmen's Liberty Club, 95
Columbo, Ruth, 249
Combined Locks, 59, 64, 66
Combined Locks Paper Company, 59, 64, 66
Commission on Industrial Relations, 74, 132
"Committee of 18," 14–15
Committee on Industrial Insurance, 92
Committee on Political Education (COPE), 228
Commons, John R., 26, 92, 124, 215
Commonwealth Bank, 178
Communications Workers of America (CWA), 175, 232, 248
Communist party: and Allis-Chalmers, 192–205; and Boncel Ordinance, 130; CIO and, 127, 194–198, 200, 204; Dennis and, 138, 142; and 1946 elections, 192, 194; and FLPF, 116–117; and Groves Act, 124; and People's Conference, 152; and RFMC, 196–198; socialists and, 127; and Taft-Hartley Act, 188; and union activity, 138–142; and WAA, 151–154; and works projects, 142
Community Chest, 180
Community Welfare Council, 215
Comperre, Modiree, 149
Conant, Rollie, 136
Congress Hall (Kenosha), 49, 50
Congress of Industrial Organizations (CIO): African Americans and, 110–111, 127; and Allis-Chalmers, 124–126; Boileau and, 153; and Catherine Conroy Award, 175; and communism, 138–140, 194–197, 205; and conservative dissidents, 194, 196–199; Costello and, 152; and craft unions, 187; and Democratic party, 208; and 1946 elections, 192–194, 205; and FLPF, 116–117, 186; Friedrick and, 214; Heymanns on, 103; and labor espionage, 71; in Madison, 141; and Marinette Knitting Mills, 212; in Milwaukee, 120, 123–124, 134; and PAC, 192–194, 198–201, 204–205; and Racine County Workers Council, 104; and *Racine Labor*, 224; Ranney and, 201; and sit-down strikes, 128–129; Socialists and, 81; and state intervention, 129–133; and unfair labor practices, 189; in Washington County, 105; and WERB, 191; and "Wisconsin Plan," 122, 133; WSFL and, 41; youth in, 127
Conn, Arthur, 198
Conroy, Catherine, 175, 176, 232–233
Consolidated Water Power and Paper Company, 97–100
Conzen, Kathleen Neils, 27, 32
Cooks, Victor: "Industrial Unions: The Organizers' View," 103–106
Coon Branch, 16
Cooper, Peter, 32

Cooper, William John, 65
Co-operative Printery, 178
Coopers, 13, 31, 36, 38
Coopers' (International) Union, 31, 36
Corporations Auxiliary, 71, 74, 77–78
Costello, Cynthia B.: "The Union Comes to Wisconsin Physicians Service," 244–255
Costello, Emil, 126–127, 133, 139, 152
County Central Committee, 88
Cowen, Dan, 208
Cream City Typographical Union, 21
Crowne, Helen, 206, 210
Cruise, Timothy, 33
Cudahy, 79, 88, 135, 204
Cudahy Packing, 141
Cudahy Vocational School, 90
Cutler Hammer Manufacturing Company, 71

D

Daily Sentinel: on labor, 14; on labor shortage during Civil War, 15; and 1863 printers strike, 15–17
Daily Union, 17
Daily Worker, 152
Dampf, Mr., 44
Dane County, 96, 204
Dane County Labor Council, 266
Dane County Labor History Project, 266
Dane County Unemployed Workers League, 140
Darlington, 42
Darrow, Clarence, 46
Datara, Mr., 46
Datka, Mr., 46
David Smart (ship), 14
Davidson and Thompson, 105
Davies, Owen, 226
Debs, Eugene, 161
Decker, Mr., 135–137
Deehr, Allan J., 241
De Gregory, Thelma, 169
Delavan, 42
Dells Paper and Pulp Company, 62–63
Del Ruy, Carlos, 184
Democratic party: and AFSCME, 161; Bobrowicz and, 193, 199–200; Catholics and, 93; and CIO, 120, 127, 134, 196; and 1946 elections, 192–193, 204–205; and FLPF, 117; German-Americans and, 29; and labor legislation, 116; and McCarthyism, 201; and Milwaukee Trades Assembly, 28; and New Deal programs, 139, 142; and Progressives, 192; Smith and, 32; Socialists and, 127, 192
Dennis, Eugene, 117, 138, 142, 152, 196
Dennis, Peggy, 152, 153: "Industrial Unionism: A Communist Perspective," 138–142
Department of Labor, U.S., 163
Department of Public Instruction, Wisconsin, 242
De Pere, 63, 64, 68
Detroit (Michigan), 30, 158
Dillon, F. J., 124
Dobbs, Helen, 208
Dock workers, 18
Dodge, Henry, 17
Dodgeville, 16
Doherty, Austin, 233
Dolnig, Mr., 46
Dombek, Joseph, 195
Dominick, Joe, 165–166
Doro, Sue: "A Female Machinist in Milwaukee," 235–239
Dorse, Mr., 184
Dougherty, Marcella, 248
Draper, Phil, 206–208, 210
Drew, John: "The United Auto Workers at Nash Motors in Kenosha," 155–160
Dubuque (Iowa), 109
Duncan, Thomas, 116
DuQuoin Miners Defense Committee, 223–224
Durkin, Robert, 249
Dusé, Eleanora, 149

E

Eagle River, 25
Earl, Tony, 226
Eau Claire: lumber industry, 22–23, 25; papermaking, 60, 62–63; and "Sawdust War" of 1881, 35; and United Rubber Workers Union, 103
Eau Claire Daily Leader, 23
Eau Claire Free Press, 23
Eau Claire House, 63

Eau Claire Lumber Company, 22
Eau Claire River, 57, 62–63
Ecclesiastes, 148
Education: Hortonville teachers' strike, 240–243; TAA and, 229–234; vocational, 64–65, 90; Wisconsin School for Workers, 65, 89–91, 131, 176, 215; WPA Training School, 149; WSFL and, 41
Educational Project, 90
Eight Hour League, 37–42
Eisenscher, Sigmund, 152, 196
Electrical Workers Union, 51, 194
Eliot, Charles, 51
Ellis, Frank, 135–136
The Emancipator, 149–150
Enders, Peter, 16
Engleman, Henry, 145
Engleman, Nathan, 14
Equal Employment Opportunity (EEO), 236
Equal Rights Amendment (ERA), 249
Espionage Act of 1817, 70
Evening Wisconsin, 15, 18, 21
Eveready, 109

F

Fadness, Kate, 149, 150
Fairbanks-Morse Company, 50
Fair Employment Practices Commission (FEPC), 110, 184
Fair Employment Practices Committee, 184
Fair Play, 16
Falk, Otto, 40
Falk Brewery, 40
Falk Manufactory, 94, 105, 138
Farmer-Labor Progressive Federation (FLPF): Boileau and, 151–153; collapse of, 186; and communism, 139–142, 152–153; Costello and, 139; and 1936 elections, 132; Friedrick and, 215; McCreery and, 130–131; Ohl and, 115–117
Farmer's Co-op, 135
Farmers Union, 91, 116
Farm Holiday Association, 116
Farming: and AAA, 89–90, 91; Farmer's Co-op and, 135; Farmers Union and, 91, 116; Farm Holiday Association and, 116; and FLPF, 115–117; and Milk Pool, 116; and 1933 milk strike, 118–119; Muir and, 20; and People's Progressive party, 91
Federal Arts Project, 90
Federal Bureau of Investigation (FBI), 152
Federal Labor Union, 51, 108, 112, 113, 123
Federal Mediation and Reconciliation Service, 209–210, 216
Federal Theater Project, 90
Federation of Organized Trades and Labor Unions, 37
Feminist Writers' Guild, 239
Fenske, Harlan, 152
Fenton, Frank, 171
Ferris, James, 47
Filer and Stowell, 79
Fink, Leon: "The Knights of Labor in Milwaukee," 26–33
Finley, William, 94
First Congregational Church (Kenosha), 86
First Methodist Church (Kenosha), 86
First Regiment, 42
Fisher, Cecil A., 184
Fisher, Charles, 205
Fisher Body, 128
Fitzgerald, Richard, 257
Fitzgibbons, J. H., 24
Flambeau–Park Falls Lodge, 65
Flambeau River, 57, 65
Flanner, 25
Flat Janitors Union, 88
Flint (Michigan), 128, 160
Flower, Frank A., 23, 46
Fond du Lac, 109, 115
Foran, Martin, 36
Ford Motor Company, 157, 158, 160
Forest County, 91
Forrest, William, 140
Fox River Paper Company, 58, 60, 66
Fox River Valley, 57–60, 62–66, 68
Franklin, Benjamin, 256
Franklin, S. H., 86
Fraternity Hall (Milwaukee), 40, 71
Fratney, Frederick, 14
Die Frauen Zeitung, 14
Freedom in Employment, 76

Freeport (Ill.), 109
Freethinkers, 15
French Battery Company. *See* Ray-O-Vac
Friedman, Morris, 72, 74
Fried-Ostermann Company, 132
Friedrick, Frank, 214
Friedrick, Jacob F.: in 1954, 214–215; and FLPF, 116, 215; and Green, 121–123; at Kohler plant rally, 103; radio talk by, 149; and "Wisconsin Plan," 122, 133
Frost Company, 157
Fryman, Ms., 233
Fuldner, Henry, 190
Full Fashioned Hosiery Workers Union, 82–83, 84–87
Fur and Leatherworkers Union, 193, 200
Furriers Union, 88

G

Gabrielski, Mr., 44
Garbarski, Karl, 137
Garey, A. E., 161
Garment industry: Amalgamated Clothing Workers and, 91, 132; Association of Tailors, 15; Belin Garment Company and, 128; Chicago Rubber Clothing Company and, 54, 149–150; Clothing and Textile Workers Union and, 133; Garment Workers Union and, 51, 54; German Custom Tailors Union and, 15; ILGWU and, 90, 128, 147–150
Garment Workers Union, 51, 54
Garrison, Lloyd K., 113–114, 128
Garvey, Marcus, movement, 184
Gas Specialty Company, 128
Gastell, Mr., 46
Gaston Sons', N. B., Scale Works, 50
Gavett, Thomas W., 73; "Early Unions in Milwaukee, 1840–1884," 13–21; "The Labor Forward Movement," 88
Gehl Manufacturing, 105
Geiger, Ferdinand A., 87
Geiges, Gustav, 85
Geist, Walter, 195
General Beverage, 221
General Foods, 221
General Motors, 123, 157, 158, 160
George, Henry, 32
Georgia, 94
German Custom Tailors Union, 15
Germania (newspaper), 44
German Partition, 29
Germans, 27–28, 27–29, 135
German Society, 29
Gertz, Mr., 46
Giddings and Lewis, 221
Gilbert, George, 64
Gilbert Paper Company, 58, 60, 64, 66
Gilkey-Anson Company, 25
Gimbel's Department Store, 69
Gisholt Machine Company, 136, 140–141, 221
Glad, Paul W.: "Vocational Education," 64–65
Globe Mill, 57, 64
Glove Workers Union, 132
Goldamer, Charles, 116
Goldman, Emma, 48
Goldthorpe Research Group, 236
Gompers, Samuel, 62, 121
Gondek, Mr., 46
Gooding, Laurence, 190
Goodland, Walter, 204
Gordon and Ferris Agency, 74, 77
Gorman, James, 49–51
Gotzion, Evelyn, 114
Gould, Jay, 37
Graeber, Steve, 144
Graf Beverage Company, 182
Grand Army of the Republic, 40
Grand Rapids. *See* Wisconsin Rapids
Grand Rapids Pulp and Paper Company, 62
Grant, Ulysses S., 37
Grede Foundry, 105
Green, Louis J., 88
Green, Mr., 205
Green, R. Floyd, 190
Green, William: and African Americans, 184; and CIO, 126, 182; and Dillon, 124; and Friedrick, 121–123; and International Union of Office Workers, 179; and Ray-O-Vac, 113, 114
Greenback-Labor party, 28, 31, 36–37
Green Bay, 59, 118, 131
Green Bay Gazette, 23

Greene, Charles, 200
Greipentrog, Carl: "Industrial Unions: The Organizers' View," 103–106
Gridley Dairy Company, 179
Gropper, William, 257
Grottkau, Paul, 37–38, 39, 42, 46
Groves, Harold M., 124–125
Groves Act, 124–125
GT-99, 72, 73

H

Haferbecker, Gordon M.: "Early Labor Legislation," 30; "The Law to Limit Injunctions," 76; "The Wisconsin Labor Code of 1931," 90
Hahlbeck, Lenore, 248
Hale, Russ, 264
Hall, Ed, 112
Hamilton, Andrew: "Wisconsin: Teaching Assistants' Strike Ends in Contract Signing," 229–234
Hamilton, William, 58–63
Hamilton Lodge (Neenah-Menasha), 58, 60, 64, 68
Hammel, David, 63
Hampel, George, 88
Handley, Jack, 74–75, 77, 107, 116, 126
Hando, Mrs., 46
Hansen, Arne, 198
Harding, Warren, 96
Hard Scrabble, 16
Harley-Davidson, 106, 133
Harnischfeger Company, 128, 138, 141
Hart, Martha, 147, 149, 150
Harvard University, 51, 265
Haymarket Riot (Chicago), 34, 37, 42, 44, 266
Health and safety: in battery industry, 109; in factories, 43; at Nash Motor Company, 155–156; OSHA and, 43; in paper mills, 57; WSFL and, 41
Hearst, William Randolph, 141, 200
Heiber, Mr., 46
Heil, Julius, 186, 190
Hein, Paul, 172
Hellwig Corporation, 235
Henderson, Irene, 248
Hensler, Helen, 176; "The Formation of the State AFL-CIO Women's Committee," 248–249
Herold (newspaper), 31
Heymanns, Charles, 170–171; "Industrial Unions: The Organizers' View," 103–106
Hiroshima (Japan), 184
Hirth, Frank, 37, 46
Hitler, Adolf, 141
Hoan, Daniel: and African Americans, 94–95; and Allen-A Hosiery Company, 86; elected mayor, 70; and 1946 elections, 193, 200, 201; and Nash Motor Company, 155–156; and labor rights, 149; and Lindemann-Hoverson, 123; and Milwaukee County, 204; and People's Conference, 152; and Stenographers, Typewriters, Bookkeepers and Assistants Union, 178
Hoberg Toilet Paper Company, 59
Hofer, Mr., 46
Hogan, Robert, 50, 51
Hogg, J. Bernard, 72
Holmes, B. H., 67
Holmes, James B., 172–173
Holmes Motor Company, 128
Holter, Darryl: "The Founding of the Wisconsin State Federation of Labor, 1893," 40–41; "Labor Law: Wisconsin's 'Little Wagner Act' and the Road to Taft-Hartley," 186–191; "Labor Meets History," 265–266; "Labor Spies and Union-Busting," 71–78; "Organizing the Unorganized in Milwaukee, 1900–1903," 75; "Sources of CIO Success: The New Deal Years in Milwaukee," 120–134
Holyoke (Massachusetts), 57
Holz, Alice, 127, 232; "Organizing Clerical Workers," 178–183
Homestead (Pennsylvania), 71, 72
Hones, Kenneth, 116
Horn, Peter, 144
Hortonville, 240–243
Hortonville Education Association (HEA), 240–243
Hortonville Vigilante Association, 240
Hosiery industry: Allen-A Hosiery Company, 48, 84–87; Allen family and, 83; CIO and, 123, 194, 198; Full Fashioned Hosiery Workers Union, 82–83
Hotel and Restaurant Employees Union, 182
House, Dwight, 47
House of Representatives, U.S., 70, 151, 154
Howard, C. W., Paper Company, 66–67

Howard, Charles W., 66, 67
Hubbard, Lucile, 169
Huber, Henry, 124
Huberman, Leo, 72
Huck, Gary, 226; "Labor Cartoons: Drawing on Work Culture," 256–260
Hudson, 158
Human Resources Development Institute (AFL-CIO), 184
Hurlytown, 65
Hussfeldt, Mr., 44
Hutchinson, William, 133

I

Illinois Miner, 223
Illinois Steel Corporation, 88, 93, 94
Immanuel Methodist Church (Kenosha), 86
Industrial Brotherhood, 31
Industrial Worker, 256, 257–258
Industrial Workers of the World (IWW), 61, 91, 142, 256, 257–258
Ingalls, Wallace, 92
Inspection Bureau, 76
International Association of Machinists: and Berlin Machine Works, 50; Bjurman and, 190–191; Friedrich and, 214; and Lindemann-Hoverson, 123–124; and Ray-O-Vac, 170–172, 174; workers strike, 79
International Brotherhood of Electrical Workers (IBEW), 98, 223, 261–264
International Brotherhood of Papermakers (IBPM), 63–68, 98
International Brotherhood of Pulp, Sulphite, and Paper Mill Workers, 98
International Cigar Makers, 38
International Harvester, 105, 182, 184, 266. *See also* Milwaukee Harvester
International Ladies Garment Workers Union (ILGWU), 90, 128, 147, 148–150, 206–218
International Machine Wood Workers of America, 45
International Paper Machine Tenders, 63
International Typographical Union (ITU): and *Capital Times*, 140; and IBPM, 63; and Kenosha Trades and Labor Council, 47, 53; and Milwaukee, 14; and MNI, 221–222; and printers strikes, 15–18, 21
Interstate Association of Commissions on the Status of Women, 232–233
Iron and steel industry: African Americans in, 94; CIO and, 194, 198; Gisholt Machine Company, 136, 140–141; in Milwaukee, 27, 103–104; National Committee for the Organization of the Iron and Steel Industry, 88; Sons of Vulcan and, 35; and strikes, 18
Iron Molders Union, 42, 50, 51, 52–53
Italian Cloak Local 48, 150

J

Jack, Harry, 116
Janesville, 42, 107, 138
Jefferies Company, 48
Jefferson, Thomas, 37
Jefferson Banner, 23
Jeffery, T. B., Company. *See* Nash Motor Company
Jeffreys-Jones, R., 72, 73
Jensen, Ellis, 194, 195
Jermain, T. P., 15, 17
Jeroma, Tony, 136
Jewell, Gabe, 124
Jirikowic, Otto, 123–124, 182
Johnson, LeRoy, 77
"John Paul Lumber Company, 25
"John W. Schmitt: A Profile" (Harold "Red" Newton), 228
Judd, Charles H., 64–65
Justice, 150

K

Kaiser, Michael, 21
Kanes, David, 161
Karsh, Bernard: "Anatomy of a Strike in Marinette," 206–218
Kaslow, John, 198
Kastenbaum, Meyer, 174
Kaufman, William, 51
Kaukauna, 57, 58, 60, 64, 68
Kaukauna Times, 57

Kearney and Trecker, 79
Kellar, Lucile, 266
Kelley, William V., 110
Kelly, Joseph M.: "Labor in Racine," 52–54; "Organizing the Unemployed: Case Strike of 1936," 163–166
Kempsmiths, 79
Kenosha: auto workers in, 123; Bjurman and, 190–191; and hosiery industry, 82–87; International Association of Machinists and, 190; and Nash Motor Company, 155–158, 160; strikes in, 71; and unions, 47–51, 107, 138–139; WAA and, 151
Kenosha City Labor Council, 248
Kenosha County, 84, 204
Kenosha Education Association, 240
Kenosha Gas and Electric Company, 83
Kenosha Labor, 77, 156, 157, 160
Kenosha Trades and Labor Council, 47, 51, 86, 156–157
Kenosha Unity Association, 190
Keppler, Joseph, 256
Kersten, Charles, 200, 201, 204
Kewaskum, 106
Kiebler, George, 105–106
Kiefer, Mary-Anna, 185
Killian, John, 205
Killingsworth, Charles, 187, 189–190
Kimball, Roger N., 83
Kimberly, 58
Kimberly, James, 67
Kimberly, John A., 58, 59–60
Kimberly-Clark Paper Company, 57, 58–60, 63–64, 66–68
King, Charles, 40, 42, 44
King, Rufus, 40
K Mart, 259
Knickerbocker Company, 48
Knights' Agitation Fund, 31
Knights' Milwaukee Central Committee, 38
Knights of Labor: African Americans and, 94; and Bay View Tragedy, 43; and Eight Hour League, 36–39, 42; impact of, 34; and lumber industry, 24, 25; in Milwaukee, 26–33; Powderly and, 37; in Racine, 52; Schilling and, 31–33, 36–38, 42, 46; Weber and, 28
Knit Goods Weekly, 83
Kobza, Sharon, 248
Kohler, 42, 143–146
Kohler, Hayssen & Stehn Manufacturing Company, 42
Kohler, Terry, 226
Kohler, Walter J., Jr., 144
Kohler, Walter J., Sr., 103, 215
Kohler Company, 91, 103–104, 143–146
Kohler Workers Association, 103
Konopacki, Mike: "Labor Cartoons: Drawing on Work Culture," 256–260
Kosciusko Guards, 30, 42, 44
Kowalski, Casimir, 88
Kroeger, Mr., 46
Kruszka, Michael, 33
Kryczki, Leo, 121
Krytyka (newspaper), 33
Ku Klux Klan, 194
Kult, W. G., 158
Kulturkampf, 29
Kurschner, Dale: "New Union Strategies: Electrical Workers in Wausau," 261–264
Kyle, Mr., 105

L

L. W. and V. S. Lumber Company, 24
Labor Age, 85
Labor Disputes Committee, 134
Labor Forward Movement, 76, 88
Labor Spy, 72
The Labor Spy Racket, 72
La Crosse, 25, 103
La Crosse and Milwaukee Railroad, 14
La Crosse Chronicle, 23
Lafayette County, 16–17
La Follette, Philip: and AFSCME, 161; and communism, 142; and FLPF, 139–140; and Groves bill, 124–125; loses to Heil, 186; and Progressive party, 115–116, 117; and WLRB, 132
La Follette, Robert M., Jr., 71, 77–78, 96, 115–116, 192–193, 194
La Follette, Robert M., Sr., 34, 96
Lakeside Bridge and Steel Company, 189
Lambert, Owen, 194–195

Lampel, Mr., 46
Lancaster (Ohio), 109
Landis, Kenesaw M., 70
Lassalleans, 28
Lasser, David, 151, 154
Lead mining. *See* Mining
Leavenworth, 70
Lebanon (Missouri), 261
Lee, Ted, 136
Lee Enterprises, 227
Legislation: early labor laws, 30, 71; and injunctions, 76, 79, 90; and labor espionage, 74–75, 77; National Banking Act, 32; and sit-down strikes, 128; and unemployment, 124–125; Wisconsin labor code of 1931, 90; workers' compensation, 92
Legislative Interim Committee on Unemployment, 124
Legislature, Wisconsin: and good faith bargaining, 240; and UW, 230–231. *See also* Assembly, Wisconsin; Senate, Wisconsin
LeMasters, E. E.: "Blue-Collar Aristocrats: The View from a Working-Class Tavern," 236–237
Leo XIII, Pope, 166
Leonard, S. S., 131
Levine's Picklery, 94
Levinson, Edward, 72
Lewis, John L., 120–121, 179
Lima (Ohio), 261
Lincoln, Abraham, 37
Lindemann, A. J., 123
Lindemann-Hoverson, 104, 123, 130
Line Material Company, 105
Linsaicum, Mr., 137
Little Chute, 64
"Little Wagner Act," 115–116, 132, 186, 187–188
Lochner, Gerald, 114, 169
Lorence, James J.: "Gerald Boileau and the Politics of Unemployment," 151–154
Lucey, Patrick J., 241
Ludlow Massacre, 257
Lumber industry, 22–25, 43, 45, 57, 61
Lumbermen's Exchange, 25
Luppnow, Mr., 46
Lutter and Giess, 79
Lutheran Synod, 27
Lynch, Mike, 135, 137

M

Machinery and Stove Molders Union, 21
Machinists Union: and Beloit, 51; and International Association of Machinists, 79; Kenosha strike, 48; organizing drives, 121; and socialism, 190–191; and Trades and Labor Council, 47; and UAW, 123–126; women and, 235–238
Mackey, George W., 66, 67
Macrorie, Andrew C., 21
MacWhyte Company, 160
Mad (magazine), 259
Madison: and American Family Celebration, 252–253; First Regiment and, 42; Heymanns and, 103; and labor legislation, 77; and MNI strike, 221–222; and Oscar Mayer, 135–137; and People's Conference, 142, 152; and Ray-O-Vac, 107–114, 169–174; union activity in 1930s, 140–141; and UW, 229–234; and Wisconsin School for Workers, 89–91; Wolfe and, 61; and WPA Training School, 149; and 1893 WSFL convention, 40; and SHSW, 265–266
Madison Capital Times, 140, 222
Madison Daily Democrat, 23
Madison Federation of Labor, 141, 221
Madison Independent Workers Union, 221
Madison Newspapers Incorporated (MNI), 221–222
Madison Press Connection, 222
Madison Square Garden (New York), 151
Madison Teachers Association, 221
Maine, University of, 230
Maintenance of Way Employees Union, 88
Malcolm, Harry, 173
Malin, John, 64–65
Mallory, James A., 35
Manawa, 25
Manhattan Project, 180
Manitowoc, 103, 107
Mann, Henry, 45
Mann Brothers, 45
Manpower Training Development Act (MTDA), 235
Marathon Battery, 175–177

Marathon County Labor Council, 176, 248
Marathon Electric Manufacturing Corporation, 261–264
Margulies, Herbert, 81
Marine Memorial Building (Milwaukee), 198
Marinette: and lumber industry, 24–25; and papermaking, 60; strike in, 206–218; and ten-hour day, 37; Weber and, 28; and WSFL convention, 1893, 40
Marinette Eagle, 24
Marinette Knitting Mills: coal shipments blocked, 215–216; and Marinette Trades and Labor Council, 208–209, 212, 215, 217; strike against, 206–208, 210–212, 218; and United Labor Committee, 212–213
Marinette-Menominee Lodge, 65
Marinette Trades and Labor Council, 208–209, 212, 215, 217
Marketti, James, 229, 230, 234
Martin, E. Burns, 86
Martin, Homer, 105, 126
Martin, Kenneth D., 86
Martin, Mr., 196
Marx, Karl, 32
Marxists, 28
Masons, 13
The Masses, 257
Matthews, Karen: "A Female Machinist in Milwaukee," 235–239
Mattson, Emil, 193, 200–201, 205
Mattson, Joseph, 196
Mauston, 104
Mayer, Oscar, Company, 135–137, 140, 221
McBride, Luther, 110
McCall, Vincent, Company, 157
McCarthy, Charles, 65, 74, 92
McCarthy, Joseph, 192–193, 200–201, 204, 205
McCarty, E. H., 158
McCormick, Chief, 136–137
McCormick Harvester Company, 265–266. *See also* International Harvester
McCreery, Maud, 88, 130–131, 182, 232
McCreery, Rex I., 131
McCutchin, William, 108, 113–114
McElroy, Kathleen, 266
McMillan, 46
McMurray, Howard, 193, 200, 201, 204
McNaughton, John, 59
McStroul, Fred, 126
McWilliams, Mr., 144
Mead, George W.: "'Why I Unionized My Plant,'" 97–100
Mechanic (ship), 14
Mechanical Engineers Union, 19
Medicare, 244
Meiselbach, A. D., Company, 48
Melli, Walker and Pease, 243
Memorial Union Labor Organization, 221
Menasha, 58–59, 63–64, 65, 66–67, 68
Menasha Paper Company, 58, 60
Mendota, Lake, 91
Menominee, 60
Menominee (Mich.), 24–25
Menominee River, 57, 65
Menominee River Laborer, 24
Menominee River Laboring Men's Protective and Benevolent Union, 24
Menomonee Valley, 19, 21, 24–25, 40
Merrill, 25
Merrill, Sherburns, 8
Metal Polishers and Buffers Union, 47, 54, 123
Metal Trades and Founders' Bureau, 73–74
Metal Trades Council, 123, 126
Mexico, 227
Meyer, Stephen: "Cold War Politics at Allis-Chalmers," 192–205; "Women and the War Effort at Allis-Chalmers," 180–181
Michel, Lawrence, "Jap," 155, 157, 164, 166
Michelas, I., 49
Michelfelder, June, 248
Michigan, 24, 30, 37
Michigan, University of, 229
Militia. *See* Wisconsin National Guard
Milkent, John, 158
Miller Brewing, 182
Miller, Connie, 248
Miller, Tom, 207, 209, 211–212, 216, 218
Millette, Lloyd, 135–136
Milling industry, 18, 32, 57, 94
Milwaukee: African Americans in, 93–95, 110–111; and Chicago Seaman's Union, 18, 21; CIO and,

120, 123–124, 134, 192–194, 198, 204–205; and CIO-PAC, 192–194; Clark and, 103–104; clerical workers and, 178–183; and communism, 194–198, 201, 205; Conroy and, 232; crime in, 29–30; and Eight Hour League, 35–36, 38–40, 42–44; and 1946 elections, 192–194, 198, 204–205; Germans in, 27–29; and hosiery industry, 86–87; industrial plant closings, 238; and IWW, 61; and Knights of Labor, 26–33; and labor espionage, 72–74, 76–78; and Labor Forward Movement, 88; and machine tooling industry, 235–238; machinists in, 79, 123–124; and McCarthyism, 201, 205; McCreery and, 130–131; organizing drives in, 121–123; Poles in, 29–30; and Progressive party, 138; and "red-baiting," 194–196; and Rhea Manufacturing Company, 148–150; Schilling and, 31–32, 36–38; Schmitt and, 228; sit-down strikes in, 128–129; and socialism, 69–70, 74, 80–81, 116, 138, 223; South Side, 29, 35, 44, 199; and state intervention in labor issues, 129–130, 133; strikebreakers from, 50; UAW and, 124, 126; unions in, 13–21, 75, 107, 138, 147–149; Wisconsin Labor Relations Board and, 132; Wisconsin Workers Alliance and, 151, 153–154; and WSFL convention, 1893, 40, 71
Milwaukee Athletic Club, 128
Milwaukee Brewery Workers, 228
Milwaukee Coke and Gas Company, 94
Milwaukee County, 70, 192–193, 204
Milwaukee County CIO Council, 194, 198
Milwaukee County Council of Women's Auxiliaries to Trade Unions, 131
Milwaukee County Socialist Party, 152
Milwaukee Dock Laborers Union, 18
Milwaukee Electric, 79
Milwaukee Electric Rail and Light Company, 182
Milwaukee Electric Railway and Transport, 104
Milwaukee Employers' Council, 76, 78, 95
Milwaukee Evening Post, 178
Milwaukee Federated Trades Council (FTC): Berger and, 80; Friedrick and, 103, 116, 121–123, 214–215; and Labor Forward Movement, 75–76, 88; McCreery and, 131; membership, 73; and racial discrimination, 93–95; Ranney and, 201; on Rhea sit-down strike, 128; and Stenographers, Typewriters, Bookkeepers and Assistants Union, 178–179, 182; Weber and, 28, 40, 74, 75, 126; and "Wisconsin Plan," 122, 133
Milwaukee Foundry Equipment, 191
Milwaukee Garden, 39, 42, 44
Milwaukee Gas Company, 83
Milwaukee Harvester, 79. *See also* International Harvester
Milwaukee International Longshoremen's Association, 110
Milwaukee Iron Works, 27, 34, 35, 94
Milwaukee Joint Board of the Amalgamated Clothing Workers, 91
Milwaukee Journal: on Allis-Chalmers picket lines, 202–203; on Bay View tragedy, 43–44; on Bobrowicz, 199–200; on Boileau, 152; on CIO dissidents, 194; on Eight Hour League, 39, 40; on 1946 elections, 193, 204, 205; on Lewis, 179; on Milwaukee County CIO Council elections, 198; and *Milwaukee Leader*, 70; on Nash Motor Company strike, 158; on Wisconsin Communist party, 194–195
Milwaukee Knights Assembly, 37
Milwaukee Labor College, 215
Milwaukee Lace Paper, 128
Milwaukee Leader: on CIO, 126; funding, 80; as labor's daily newspaper, 69–70; on McCreery, 130–131; and Stenographers, Typewriters, Bookkeepers and Assistants Union, 178; Weber and, 65; and young people, 127
Milwaukee Light Horse Squadron, 42, 44
Milwaukee Merchants and Manufacturers Association, 76, 92
Milwaukee Post, 215
Milwaukee Road, 238
Milwaukee Sentinel: Bosworth quoted in, 13; on Christoffel, 201–202; on CIO dissidents, 194; Clark and, 104; on 1946 elections, 204; and Hearst, 141, 200; and Milwaukee Communist party, 195; on Oshkosh woodworkers strike, 46; and "red-baiting," 194–196, 200; on RFMC, 198; on Schilling, 36; and socialism, 70; and Swofford, 194, 195
Milwaukee Trades Assembly, 21
Milwaukee Trades Council, 126
Milwaukee Urban League (MUL), 110
Milwaukee Workers' College, 89
Mineral Point, 16

Mining, 16–17, 223–224
Minneapolis (Minnesota), 140
Minnesota, University of, 231
Minnesota Workers Alliance, 154
Minor, Robert, 257
Miracle Confection Company, 147
Mississippi, 94
Mitchell, Alexander, 32, 42
Moessinger, Albert, 46
Molders Union, 88, 123
Monroe, 57
Montgomery, David, 129
Monthly Labor Review, 77
Moody, C. E., 19
Mooney, Tom, 130, 214–215
Morgan, Tommy, 46
Morgan plant, 46
Moser, Karlos, 266
"Mr. Block" (comic strip), 257–258
Muehlenkamp, Robert L., 230, 234
Muelder, E. M., 86
Mueller Furnace, 128, 129
Muir, John: "Work on a Farm, 1848," 20
Mulberry, George, 50
Murray, Judge, 212
Murray, Philip, 197–198
Murray Hill Agreement, 79
Musicians Union, 47, 54, 95
Mythen, Robert, 112, 113–114

N

Nagasaki (Japan), 184
Nash, Charles, 155–158
Nash Motor Company (Kenosha), 85, 155–156, 157–158, 190
Nast, Thomas, 256
National Association of Letter Carriers, 161
National Association of Manufacturers, 203
National Banking Act, 32
National Committee for the Organization of the Iron and Steel Industry, 88
National Democratic Committee, 200
National Education Association, 224
National Federation of Telephone Workers (NFTW). *See* Communications Workers of America
National Industrial Recovery Act: causes, 129; FTC and, 121; Lindemann-Hoverson and, 123; Ray-O-Vac and, 107, 108; Section 7(a), 103, 107, 110, 130, 157; and union membership, 129
National Labor Relations Board (NLRB): and bargaining units, 186–187; and CIO, 129; and International Harvester, 105; and Marinette Knitting Mills, 210; and Ray-O-Vac, 112, 113; and Wisconsin's Employment Peace Act, 188–190; and WPS, 246, 254
National Labor Union, 31
National Lampoon, 259
National Maritime Union, 194, 203
National Metal Trades Association, 79
National Organization for Women (NOW), 232
National Recovery Administration (NRA), 89
National War Labor Board (NWLB), 173–174, 191
Neenah, 57–60, 63–64, 66–67, 68
Neenah Daily Times, 59, 60
Neenah-Menasha Trades and Labor Council, 68
Neenah Paper Company, 58, 64, 66
Negroes. *See* African Americans
Nekoosa, 28, 60–62
Nekoosa Paper Company, 62
Nelson, Ozzie and Harriet, 253
Nesbit, Robert C., 81; "The Bay View Tragedy," 34–46; "Employer Rights," 38; "Problems in Workplace Health and Safety," 43; "Unemployment: The 'Tramp Problem' in Beloit," 32
Newby, David, 266
Newcomb, Paul, 87
New Day (Racine), 223
New Deal: AFL and, 134; Boileau and, 152; Democrats and, 127; People's Conference and, 121; programs, 139, 141; Socialists and, 126
New Diggings, 16
New London, 103
Newman, Charles, 198
Newspaper Guild, 141
Newton, Harold, 157; "John W. Schmitt: A Profile," 228
New York General Society of Mechanics and Tradesmen, 256
New York Herald, 23

New York Sun, 23
Niagra, 58, 60, 67, 68
Niagra Lodge No. 43, 60
Nicolet Lodge, 63, 68
Ninfo, Salvatore, 148–150
Nordberg Manufacturing Company, 79
Nordstrom, George, 158
Norman, Bette, 223, 227
Norman, Loren, 223–224, 226, 227
Norris–La Guardia Anti-Injunction Act, 90
North Carolina, 93
North Chicago Rolling Mills, 18, 27
Northern Tissue Company, 59
Northwestern Manufacturers Association, 60–62
Northwestern Mutual Life Insurance Company, 182
North Western Railroad, 216
North Wisconsin Millmen's Union, 25

O

Oasis (Madison), 236–237
O'Boyle, Fr., 163
Obrenovich, Clara, 248
O'Brien, Mr., 63
Occupational Safety and Health Act (OSHA), 43, 263
Oconto Falls, 65
Oconto River, 57, 65
Office and Professional Employees (International) Union, 105, 183, 248
Office Workers Union. *See* Stenographers, Typewriters, Bookkeepers and Assistants (Office Workers) Union
Ohio, 109
Ohl, Henry J., Jr.: and AFSCME, 161; and detective agency licensing, 74–75, 77; and FLPF, 115–117; and NIRA, 107; and Stenographers, Typewriters, Bookkeepers and Assistants Union, 182; and WSFL, 28, 126
O'Keefe, William, 25
Olkives, Felix, 156–158
Olmsted, Randy, 262–264
Olsen, Steve, 225
Olson, Frederick I.: "Organized Labor and Socialism: Two Views," 80–81
Olson, Richard W.: "An Isolated Survivor: Racine Labor," 223–227
Omaha (Nebraska), 36
Onsager, Max, 113, 174
Opper, Frederick Burr, 256
Oshkosh, 28, 36, 40, 46, 67
Oshkosh Daily Northwestern, 46
Oshkosh Northwestern, 22–23, 59
Oshkosh Standard, 36
Outagamie County, 241
Ozanne, Robert W.: "The Farmer-Labor Progressive Federation," 115–117; "Frank Weber: Labor's 'General Organizer,'" 28; "From Union Town to Open Shop: Beloit 1903–1904," 50–51; "Labor Meets History," 265–266; "Lumber Industry Strikes: Eau Claire, Marinette, Ashland, La Crosse," 22–25; "The Machinists Battle the Injunction," 79; "The Paperworkers' Fight for Saturday Night," 57–68; "Workers' Compensation," 92

P

Pabst Brewing, 27
Pabst, Fred, 27
Pabst Theater (Milwaukee), 90
Packard, 158
Paducah (Kentucky), 109
Padway, Goldberg, Previant, 178
Padway, Joseph: and Allen-A Hosiery Company, 87; and Labor Forward Movement, 76; and labor spies, 77; and "Little Wagner Act," 187; and Strikers Aid Committee, 88; and WLRB, 132
Paine, Mr., 46
Painters and Decorators Union, 51
Palm, Anton, 46
Pape, Fred, 135, 137
Paper Makers' Journal, 68
Papermaking industry: Consolidated Water Power and Paper Company, 97–100; on Eau Claire River, 62–63; labor espionage and, 71; and unions, 57–60, 63–68; in Wisconsin River Valley, 60–62
Parker, Cedric, 49
Parkes, John C., 42
Park Falls, 65
Parkinson, Daniel M.: "Lead Mining in La Fayette

County," 16–17
Parysso, Anton, 33
Paschen, George, 40, 42
Patten Company, 59
Pawling and Harnischfeger, 79
People's Conference. *See* Wisconsin People's Conference on Labor and Social Legislation
People's (Populist) party, 36, 45
People's Progressive party, 91. *See also* Progressive party
Peshtigo, 24–25
Peshtigo River, 57
Pesotta, Rose, 138; "Organizing Garment Workers," 147–150
Pfister Hotel (Milwaukee), 128
Pfister-Vogel Tannery, 94
Philadelphia (Pennsylvania), 36, 82
Piech, Roman: "The Wisconsin Milk Strike of 1933," 118–119
Piepenberg, Mr., 46
Pietrak, Mike, 136
Pinkerton Agency, 41, 67, 71–74, 77
The Pinkerton's Labor Spy, 72, 74
"Pins and Needles" (play), 90
Plankinton House, 42
Plankinton Packing, 94, 110
Plasterers Union, 21
Plotkin, Abraham, 147–149
Plover, 62
Polakowski, Walter, 77
Poles: and Eight Hour League, 40, 42; in Milwaukee, 29–30, 33, 199, 204; at Oscar Mayer, 135
Political Action Committee, 134
Polonia, 33, 42
Pomfret, John D.: "Jacob F. Friedrick in 1954," 214–215
Pommeraning, Mrs., 46
Portage, 61
Port Edwards, 64–65
Porterville, 25
Post Office Clerks, 161
Potter, Fred, 67
Poulsen, Earle, 223
Powderly, Terence, 25, 31, 37–38, 44
Powers Lake, 48
Pressed Steel Tank Company, 203
Primrose Township, 96
Principle Represented: Communist (pamphlet), 196
Printers, 14, 15–18, 21, 30
Printers Bulletin, 21
Printers Protective Association, 21
Progressive Cigarmakers' Union, 30
Progressive League, 115–116
Progressive Miners, 224
Progressive party: and communism, 138–142; and 1946 elections, 192, 204–205; and FLPF, 116–117, 139; and Groves bill, 125; and labor legislation, 151–154; La Follettes and, 96, 115
Protzmann, Mr., 46
Public Service Commission, 191
Public Works and Relief Standards Act, 152

Q

Quarles, Joseph V., 51
Quiet House, 21

R

Racine: auto workers in, 123; Cooks and, 104; First Regiment and, 42; and ILGWU, 149–150; and J. I. Case Company, 163–166; labor in, 52–54; and Nash Motor Company, 158; and *Racine Labor*, 223–227; retail stores, 189; unions in, 107, 138; Wisconsin Workers Alliance and, 151; workers support Kenosha hosiery strikes, 86
Racine County, 204
Racine County Workers Council, 104
Racine Daily News, 223
Racine Day, 223
Racine Education Association, 224
Racine Journal, 15
Racine Journal Times, 224, 227
Racine Labor, 223–227
Racine Labor Advocate, 223
Racine Trade and Labor Council (RTLC), 52–54
Railroads, 14, 18–20. 37, 94, 96
Railway Brotherhood, 116, 139
Railway Clerks Union, 216
Rainfair. *See* Chicago Rubber Clothing Company

Randolph, A. Philip, 184
Rank and File Membership Committee (RFMC), 196–198
Ranney, Frank, 201
Rappaport, Julius, 86
Rashman, Mr., 150
Rasmussen, Darina: "The Wisconsin School for Workers: Two Views," 89–91
Raushenbush, Paul, 124
Ray-O-Vac: and defense production, 169–170; and NLRB, 112, 113; and NWLB, 173–174; and unions, 107–109, 109–112, 113–114, 140–141, 170–172; working conditions, 109
Reagan, Ronald, 253
Reck, Bernice, 248
Red Cross, 180
Red Dot Company, 221
Red Granite, 61
Reed, Joel, 233
Der Reformer (newspaper), 32, 36, 37
Regal Ware, 106
Reihl, Jack B.: "An Agenda for Working Families," 252–253
Reist, Sol, 108
Reliance Iron Works, 27, 33
Renn, Rudolf, 143–144
Republican and News, 21
Republican Hotel (Milwaukee), 131
Republican party: and 1946 elections, 192–193, 204–205; German-Americans and, 93; and labor legislation, 116; La Follette and, 96; and McCarthyism, 200–201; in Milwaukee, 29; and New Deal programs, 139; Smith and, 32; Socialists and, 70
Republican-Sentinel, 21
Retail Clerks Union: in Beloit, 50–51; and department stores, 182; and Kenosha Trades and Labor Council, 47; and Marinette Knitting Mills strike, 213; merges with UFCW, 250; and WPS, 246
Reuther, Walter, 194, 196–197
Rhea Manufacturing Company, 128, 147, 148–149, 150
Rhinelander, 25, 60
Rhode Opera House (Kenosha), 51
Ricca, Joanne: "Rosella Wartner: The Making of a Wausau Unionist," 175–177
Rice, William G., 200, 204
Richmond Brothers, C. P. R., Mill, 57
Riebe, Ernest, 257
Riverside Fibre and Paper Company, 66
Robinson, Boardman, 257
Rockwell, Norman, 253
Roeder, Mary, 181
Rogers, Patrick, 170
Roosevelt, Franklin: and anti-Depression legislation, 89; and Democratic party, 192; and discrimination, 184; 1936 election, 117; and New Deal spending, 152; and WPA, 154
Rosemont, Franklin, 256
Rossetter, Asher, 77
Roth, Adam, 21
Rozga, Mr., 46
Rubin, Arthur, 149
Rudzinski, August, 30
Rudzinski, Theodore, 30
Rudzinski's Hall (Milwaukee), 30
Rundle Manufacturing, 128
Runge, Mr., 46
Rush, Walter, 117, 152
Rusk, Jeremiah, 34, 39–40, 42–44
Russell Agency, 72–73, 76, 77
Russell House (Neenah), 66, 67
Russo, Paul, 157–158
Rutz, Henry, 116, 152
Ryan, Chief Justice, 32
Ryan, Hugh, 79

S

Sacco, Nicola, 130
Saginaw Valley (Michigan), 30
Sahorske, Frank, 165–166
Saint James Church (Kenosha), 86
St. Croix land grant, 34
St. Louis (Mo.), 36
St. Mathews Episcopal Church (Kenosha), 86
St. Stanislaus Church (Milwaukee), 42, 43
Sandburg, Carl, 69, 74
San Pedro (California), 142
Saposs, David, 108

Saunders, Stanley, 47
Saylor Company. *See* Marinette Knitting Mills
Schaick, A. G. von, 24
Schecke, Harry, 163
Scherer, Peter, 45
Schilling, Robert: and Bay View tragedy, 42–43; and Eight Hour League, 37–39, 42; and Knights of Labor, 31–33, 36–38, 42, 46; and lumber industry, 24–25
Schlitz Brewing, 27
Schmidt, Gertrude, 77
Schmitt, John, 176, 228, 248
Schoeffler, Moritz, 14
Schofield, 25
Schroeder Hotel (Milwaukee), 128
Schuelke, E. R., 144
Schultz, Charles, 67
Schultz, Robert H., Jr., 140; "Unionism at Oscar Mayer in Madison," 135–137
Schuster's Department Store (Milwaukee), 69
Schutt, Herbert, 144
Schwartzman, Eva, 189–190
Scrip, 22, 24, 25, 45
Seafarth, Shaw, Fairweather, and Geraldson, 246
Seaman Auto Body: and AFL, 124; and Auto Council, 158; and CIO, 123; Hoan and, 130; Kiebler and, 105; and Milwaukee, 133; sit-down strike, 128
Seamen's Act, 96
Sears (Racine), 189
Seattle (Washington), 190
Sechrest, Ed, 135–137
Sechrest, Jack, 135–137
Seebote (newspaper), 29
Seide, Herman, 121, 126, 179
Seidel, Emil, 88
Senate, U.S., 115
Senate, Wisconsin, 115–116, 117. *See also* Legislature, Wisconsin
Senate Bill 79, 77
Senate Committee on Education and Labor, 77
Senn v. Tile Layers' Protective Union, 90
Sensenbrenner, Frank J., 67
Sentinel: King and, 40; on Parkes, 42; and printers' strikes, 21; and railway industry, 18
Setzer, C. E., 257
Shakstad, Thor, 136
Shattuck and Babcock, 64
Shawano, 119
Sheboygan: and Allen-A Hosiery Company, 84; and Kohler Company, 143, 145–146; and lumber industry, 25, 143, 145–146; McCreery and, 131; union rally in, 103; Wisconsin Workers Alliance and, 151
Sheboygan Falls, 143, 144
Sheboygan Herald, 42
Sheboygan New Deal. See Sheboygan Times
Sheboygan Press, 144
Sheboygan Times, 131
Sheridan Guard, 43
Shillinglau's Grocery (Madison), 136
Shinneman, Earl, 136–137
Ship Carpenters and Caulkers Association, 13
Ship Carpenters Union, 88
Shipping industry, 13, 14, 18, 88
Shoe Artists Association, 94
Shoemaker, Alice, 89, 91
Shoemakers, 13, 14, 51, 94
Shoe Workers Union, 51
Shurr, Ferdinand, 16–17
Sigman, David, 113–114, 170–171
Sillbaugh, Miss, 136
Simmons Manufacturing Company: and AFL, 103; and Kenosha, 85; and Kenosha Trades and Labor Council, 157; and Metal Polishers Union, 47; and strikes, 48, 51
Simon, Carl, 46
Simons, Florence, 248
Sioux City (Iowa), 109
Skaar, William, 113–114, 169
Skrezipenzinski, Mr., 46
Slayton, John, 264
Sloan, John, 257
Smith, A. O., Company, 133, 184–185
Smith, Henry, 31, 32–33
Smith, L. L., 144
Smith, Paul, 124
Smith, Walker C., 257–258
Smith, William E., 22–23
Smith Brothers, Millwrights, 32
Smith-Connally bill, 201

Smith-Hughes Act, 64
Smithsonian Institution, 266
Snap-on Tools, 157
Sobel, Dan, 202
Social Democratic Herald, 80
Social Democratic party, 32, 46
Social-Democratischer Herald, 69
Social-Democratischer Verein. See Social Democratic party
Socialism: AFL and, 121, 134; Berger and, 69–70, 80–81; FLPF and, 116–117; FTC and, 75, 80–81; Hoan and, 70, 116, 139–140; and labor espionage, 72, 74, 77; Machinist Lodge 34 and, 190–191; McCreery and, 130–131; Milwaukee Germans and, 27–28; Milwaukee Common Council and, 130; Weber and, 28. *See also* Socialist party
Socialist Hall (Kenosha), 190
Socialist party: and AFL, 46, 120–121, 126, 134; Bjurman and, 190–191; and communism, 138–142; and 1946 elections, 192, 204–205; and FLPF, 116, 139; Friedrick and, 215; and FTC, 76; McMurray and, 131; and Racine County Workers Council, 104; and Stenographers, Typewriters, Bookkeepers and Assistants Union, 178; and Strikers Aid Committee, 88; and WAA, 151. *See also* Socialism
Solar Battery Company, 128
Sommers, Art, 136–137
Sommers, Mr., 166
Sommers, William, 54
Sons of Vulcan, 35, 42, 44
Sortino, Josephine, 149
Sortino, Mary, 149
South Beloit, 251
South Bend (Indiana), 30, 159
South Milwaukee, 204
Southport. *See* Kenosha
Sparta Herald, 15–16
Specialty Brass, 157
Spencer, Sheriff, 212
Springsteen, Bruce, 227
Spy (magazine), 259
Stafford, William H., 70
Stalin, Joseph, 195
Standard Oil Company, 36, 190
State Historical Society of Wisconsin, 81, 265–266
State Medical Society (SMS), 244
Stauder, Eugene, 157, 158
Steel. *See* Iron and steel industry
Steele, Harold E., 85, 87
Steel Workers Organizing Committee, 105, 126
Stemsen, Andrew, 47
Stenographers, Typewriters, Bookkeepers and Assistants (Office Workers) Union, 133, 178–183
Stevens, John D.: "War Hysteria and the Wobblies," 61
Stevens Point, 25, 60–62, 64, 66
Stockman, Ann, 248
Story, Harold, 195, 198
Strange, John, 59
Strange, John, Paper Company, 58, 64, 66–67
Street Railway Employees Union, 88
Strehlow, Mr., 46
Strikers Aid Committee, 88
Strikes: at Allis-Chalmers, 202–203; in Bay View, 33; and boycotts, 21, 189, 213; carpenters and, 13–14; dock workers and, 18; farmers and, 118–119; hosiery workers and, 86–87; iron and steel workers and, 18; ITU and, 222; at J. I. Case Company, 53, 163–166, 196; at Kohler Company, 42, 143–146; machinists and, 79; in Marinette, 206–218; millers and, 18; MNI and, 221–222; at Nash Motor Company, 158; in Oshkosh, 46; papermakers and, 59–63, 66–68; printers and, 14, 15–17, 18, 21, 30; railway workers and, 18–20; sawmill workers and, 22–25; shipping industry and, 14, 18; shoemakers and, 15; sit-down, 128–129; tailors and, 14–15; tanners and, 18; teachers and, 240–243; teaching assistants and, 229–234; in Two Rivers, 45; Wisconsin Employment Peace Act and, 188–189; women and, 46; woodworkers and, 46, 79
Stronach and Company, 14
Studebaker, 158
Stump's Planing Mill, 94
Suffrage, 41, 130
Sullivan, David, 63
Sullivan, Jerry, 22
Superior, 61, 103, 151
Supreme Court (U.S.) 77, 90, 152–153, 241, 243
Supreme Court (Wisconsin) 90, 189, 241
Switchmen's Mutual Aid Association, 21
Swofford, Hugh, 194–195

Swope, Charles, 135–137

T

Tadler, Frank, 144
Taft-Hartley Act, 133, 186, 188–190, 213
Tailors, 14–15
Talmud, 147
Tanners, 18, 38, 40, 94
Tannery Workers Union, 88
Teaching Assistants Association (TAA), 221, 229–234
Teal, H. L., 21
Teamsters Union: in Beloit, 51; in Madison, 221; and Marinette Knitting Mills strike, 212, 213, 215; and *Racine Labor*, 224; and TAA, 234; and WPS, 251–252
Teapot Dome scandal, 96
Tehan, Robert, 200, 204–205
Telulah Company, 66
Temple Beth Hillel (Kenosha), 86
Tennessee, 93
Textile Workers Union, 194, 248
Thilmany, Oscar, 60
Thilmany Pulp and Paper Company, 57, 60, 64
Thom, Anita, 248
Thomas, Edgar, 184
Thompson, Barbara, 242
Tioga Company, 66, 67
Tippett, Tom, 149
Tolan, James, 68
Toledo (Ohio), 140, 160
Tolliver, Aaron, 110
Tomlins, Christopher, 129
Tompkins, Mr., 137
Torres Cafe (Milwaukee), 128
Torteria, Esther, 169–170
Trades assemblies, 28–29, 30, 31
Tradeswomen, Inc., 239
Traeumer, George, 40, 43–44
Trane Company, 103
Triangle Restaurant (Milwaukee), 128
Trostel Tannery, 94, 128
Trotter, Joe W., Jr., 184; "African American Workers and the Labor Movement in Milwaukee, 1870–1930," 93–95; "African American Workers and the Labor Movement in Milwaukee, 1930–1945," 110–111
Turner Hall (Milwaukee), 24, 37, 39, 43
Turnvereins (Bunds), 15, 29, 194
Tuskegee Institute, 266
Tweed, William M., 256
Twin Lakes, 48
Two Rivers, 45, 107
Two Rivers Manufacturing Company, 45
Typographical Union. *See* International Typographical Union

U

"Unemployment: The 'Tramp Problem' in Beloit" (Robert C. Nesbit), 32
Unemployment Councils, 151
Unemployment insurance, 41, 104, 124–125
Unfair labor practices, 188–191
Union Bag and Paper Company, 64
Union Hall (Racine), 53, 54
Union Press Association, 223
UniServ, 242
United Automobile Workers (UAW): African Americans and, 110–111; and Allis-Chalmers, 126, 192, 196, 198, 201–204, 225–236; and Burgess Battery, 141; CIO and AFL affiliation, 133; and CIO-PAC, 192; and communism, 194–196; and 1946 elections, 192–193; founded, 159; and J. I. Case, 164–166; and Local 72, 159–160; and Local 248, 193–196; machinists and, 123–124; and Mueller Furnace, 129; and Racine County Workers Council, 104; and *Racine Labor*, 224; Reuther and, 194; and RFMC, 196–198; and Union Press Association, 223; in Washington County, 105
United Brotherhood of Paper Makers (UBPM), 58–60, 60–62, 62–63
United Carpenters and Joiners, 85
United Electrical Workers (UE), 126
United Electrical, Radio and Machine Workers of America, 91, 260
United Food and Commercial Workers (UFCW), 250
United Hospital Fund, 215
United Labor Committee, 201, 212

United Mine Workers, 223–224
United Press, 69
United Rubber Workers Union, 103
United Service Organization, 180
United States Conciliation Service (USCS), 110, 113, 172, 174
United States Steel Corporation, 93
University of California at Berkeley, 231
University of Chicago, 64
University of Colorado, 231
University of Maine, 230
University of Michigan, 229
University of Minnesota, 231
University of Wisconsin. *See* Wisconsin, University of
UNSA, 184
Uphoff, Walter H.: "The Riot at Kohler, 1934," 143–146; "The Very First Kohler Strike, 1897," 42
Upholsterers Union, 21

V

Van Cleaf, W. C., 204
Van Hise building (UW), 229
Van Horne, William C., 19
Vanzetti, Bartolomeo, 130
Venne, Leon, 196–198
Vietnam, 227
Vigilance Committee (Milwaukee), 80
Vilter Manufacturing Company, 79
Virginia, 93
Volksblatt (newspaper), 32
Volksfreund (newspaper), 14
Vollrath Corporation, 226
Vulcan Company, 66, 67

W

Wachman, Marvin, 81
Wadinski, Dave, 261–264
Wages in Practice and Theory (Robert W. Ozanne), 266
Wagner, Bill, 135–137
Wagner Act: Boileau and, 153; Kohler Company and, 103; and "Little Wagner Act," 115–116; passed, 178; popular support, 129; revised, 186–187; and rising union membership, 149
Wakefield, Lee, 145
Wakefield, Mr., 146
Walker, James, 131
Walker, Mayor, 14
Walker, Ryan, 257
Wallace, Bill, 110
Wallace, Henry Agard, 91
Wallber, Emil: and Bay View Tragedy, 44; and German-Americans, 29; and Knights of Labor, 31; and Rusk, 40; and Schilling, 38, 42
Wallin, "Dust," 257
Wall Street Journal, 231
Walworth, Justice, 14
War Labor Board, 112
Wartner, Rosella, 248; "Rosella Wartner: The Making of a Wausau Unionist," 175–177
Washburn, 25
Wasielewski, Thaddeus, 193–194, 199, 201, 204
Watson, George, 135, 136
Waukesha Motors, 105
Wausau: and battery industry, 109, 175–177; and lumber industry, 25; and Marathon Electric Manufacturing Corporation, 261–264; papermaking in, 60, 62; and teachers' strike, 240; Wisconsin State CIO Convention in, 198
Wausau Paper Mill Company, 60, 62
Wausau Record-Herald, 152, 153
Wauwatosa, 131, 204
Weakland, Rembert, 227
Weaver, James, 32
Weber, Frank J.: and AFL, 121; and African Americans, 94; and Commons, 92; and education, 65; and FTC, 28, 36, 75–76, 88, 126; and labor espionage, 72, 74; and papermaking industry, 62; and Two Rivers strike, 45; and WSFL, 40–41
Webster, Noah, 37
Wehr Steel Company, 110
Weisrock, Stan, 136–137
Welch's grape juice, 53
Wendt, Francis, 224
Wertheimer, Barbara: "The Wisconsin School for Workers: Two Views," 89–91
Wertheimer, Monroe A., 60
West Allis, 124, 197, 201–204

West Bend, 105
West Bend Heating and Lighting Company, 105
West Bend Woolen Mills, 105
Western Printing and Lithographing Company, 53, 54
West Plains (Mo.), 261
West Point, 40
West Superior, 40
West Virginia, 40
Wharton, A. O., 123
Whitefish Bay, 61, 77
Whitewater, 42, 230
Whiting, George, 59, 60–62
Whiting, George A., Paper Company, 58–60, 62
Wild Rose, 240
Wilkes, John, 45
Williamsport (Pennsylvania), 109
Wilson, Nellie, 248, 249; "Nellie Wilson: A Black Woman Meets the Union," 184–185
Winnebago County Courthouse, 67
Winnebago Paper Company, 58–59, 60, 64
Wisconsin, University of: African Americans and, 230; and Commons, 92, 215; Conroy and, 232; Education for Women, 248; Garrison and, 113, 128; La Follette and, 96; LeMasters and, 236; McMurray and, 193; and Oscar Mayer, 135–136; and School for Workers, 65, 89–91, 131, 176, 215; TAA and, 221, 229–234; and WSHS, 265–266; Zander and, 161
Wisconsin Administrative, Clerical, Fiscal and Technical Employees Association. *See* American Federation of State, County, and Municipal Employees
Wisconsin Arts Board, 266
Wisconsin Banner, 14
Wisconsin Bureau of Labor Statistics, 22, 24–25
Wisconsin Center for Theater Research, 266
Wisconsin Commissioner of Labor, 30
Wisconsin Committee for Industrial Organization, 138
Wisconsin Council of Defense, 61
Wisconsin Education Association Council (WEAC): "The Hortonville Teachers' Strike of 1974," 240–243
Wisconsin Employment Relations Board (WERB), 190–191, 202
Wisconsin Employment Relations Commission (WERC), 231
Wisconsin Humanities Council, 266
Wisconsin Industrial Commission, 77, 124–125
Wisconsin Industrial Union, 104, 163–164, 166
Wisconsin Labor History Society, 93, 184, 266
Wisconsin Labor Relations Act (WLRA). *See* "Little Wagner Act"
Wisconsin Labor Relations Board, 132. *See also* Wisconsin Labor Relations Board
Wisconsin Legislative Reference Library, 74, 92
Wisconsin Manufacturers Association, 92, 124–125
Wisconsin Milk Pool, 116
Wisconsin Motor Company, 88
Wisconsin National Guard: and Bay View Tragedy, 35, 42–44; and Hortonville teachers' strike, 241; IWW and, 61; King and, 40; Kosciusko Guards and, 30, 42, 44; and lumber strikes, 22–23; and 1933 milk strike, 118–119; and UW, 230
Wisconsin News, 141
Wisconsin People's Conference on Labor and Social Legislation (Madison), 142, 152–153
Wisconsin Physicians Services Insurance Corporation (WPS), 244–255
"Wisconsin Plan," 122, 133
Wisconsin Rapids, 60, 62, 97, 98, 248–249
Wisconsin River, 25, 57
Wisconsin River Valley, 60–62, 64–65
Wisconsin School for Women Workers in Industry, 89
Wisconsin School for Workers, 65, 89–91, 131, 176, 215
Wisconsin's Employment Peace Act, 133, 186, 187–188, 188–190, 190–191
Wisconsin Shoe Company, 128
Wisconsin State AFL-CIO: and "American Family Celebration," 252–253; Conroy and, 232; Holter and, 266; and Images of Labor from American Musical Theater, 266; Schmitt and, 228; and TAA, 234; Women's Conference, 175–177, 248–249. *See also* AFL-CIO
Wisconsin State Board of Arbitration, 50, 57, 58, 64, 66
Wisconsin State Board of Vocational Education, 64

Wisconsin State Broadcasting, 114
Wisconsin State Employees' Association. *See* American Federation of State, County, and Municipal Employees
Wisconsin State Federation of Labor (WSFL): and AFL, 121, 123, 133; African Americans and, 95; and battery industry, 170; Berger and, 80; 1893 convention, 40–41, 71; 1896 convention, 223; and FLPF, 116, 139; Friedrick and, 103; Heymanns and, 103–104; and Kenosha Trades and Labor Council, 51; and labor espionage, 72, 74, 76–77; and labor legislation, 76; La Follette and, 115; and mass unionism, 107; Padway and, 187; and papermaking industry, 62; and People's Conference, 152; and Ray-O-Vac, 109–112; Sommers and, 54; and Stenographers, Typewriters, Bookkeepers and Assistants Union, 178, 182; and unemployment legislation, 124; and vocational education, 65; Weber and, 28, 36, 40–41; and "Wisconsin Plan," 122, 133; and Wisconsin School for Workers, 89–91, 159; and WLRA, 132; and workers' compensation, 92
Wisconsin State Industrial Union Council, 228
Wisconsin State Journal, 222
Wisconsin Telephone, 232
Wisconsin Tissue Paper Company, 59
Wisconsin Vorwaerts (newspaper), 40, 69, 80
Wisconsin Workers Alliance of America (WAA): Boileau and, 151–154; and communism, 117; and FLPF, 116, 139, 141–142; and People's Conference, 152; and strikes, 141–142
Wisnoski, Mike, 242
Woertz, Bill, 136
Woicechowski, Mr., 44
Wolfe, Albert, 61
Wolf River, 57
Women: African American, 184–185; at Allis-Chalmers, 180–181; and ERA, 249; labor force increases during WWII, 169–170, 180, 184–185; machinists, 235–239; and NOW, 232; and Oshkosh woodworkers strike, 46; in printing industry, 14, 15–16, 21; and suffrage, 41, 130–131; unionism and feminism, 232–233; wages, 18, 170, 184–185; and Wisconsin School for Workers, 89–91; and Wisconsin State AFL-CIO Women's Conference, 175–176, 248–249
Women of the Americas, 239
Wonewoc, 109
Woodboro, 25
Wood County Reporter, 62
Woodmount Country Club, 104
Woodrum, Clifton, 154
Woodworkers, 46, 248
Workers' compensation, 41, 92, 96, 124
Workers' Education Program, 116
Workingman (newspaper), 15
Workingman's Advocate (newspaper), 15
Working Men's League, 95
Workmen's Compensation Act, 92
Works Progress Administration (WPA): and CIO, 127; established, 90; jobs reduced, 151; Rutz and, 116; training school, 149; and WAA, 153–154
World War I, 53, 61, 94
World War II, 169–170, 171–174, 179–180, 180–181
Wright, Fred, 260
Wrigley's, 128
Writers Project, 90
Wynn, Lauri, 242–243

Y

Yahr Drugs (Milwaukee), 128
Yellow dog contracts, 41, 90, 132
York, Mr., 135
Young, Art, 257
Young, Edwin, 229–231, 234, 265
Young Socialists, 127
YWCA, 89

Z

Zander, Arnold S., 140, 161
Zander, Eugene, 161
Zander, Lola, 161
Zarling, Esther, 181
Zeidler, Frank, 127, 152, 223
Zibulker, Matt, 51
Zieger, Robert H.: "Battery Workers at War," 169–174; "Building the Union at Ray-O-Vac in Madison," 107–114